(2.50

KUNZ

2500
99BB

EXPERIENTIA SUPPLEMENTUM 17

The Challenge of Life

Biomedical Progress and Human Values

Roche Anniversary Symposium

Chairman: The Lord Todd, F. R. S.

Basel, Switzerland,
31 August to 3 September 1971

Editors: Robert M. Kunz and Hans Fehr

1972 Birkhäuser Verlag, Basel and Stuttgart

Editorial Committee: Renée Baumgartner
Helga Gerster
Colette Kapp-Schwoerer
Walter K. Lindenmann
Hans R. Roth

Photographers: Urs Schachenmann
Hans Sigg

The Challenge of Life

Roche Anniversary Symposium

Chairman: The Lord TODD

Moderators: PHILIP HANDLER, RENÉ KÖNIG and JAN WALDENSTRÖM

Preface

In the autumn of 1971 F. Hoffmann-La Roche & Co. Ltd in Basel celebrated their 75th anniversary. The company was one of the first in the chemical industry to concentrate from the beginning on pharmaceuticals. Step by step new activities were taken up, but all within the frontiers of biology.

During the 75 years of Roche the research division has become by far the largest department in the company, with basic research assuming an increasingly important part in it. For this reason Roche cannot but feel a share of responsibility towards the many problems raised by biomedical progress. Hence, the idea of celebrating the anniversary along conventional lines could not be seriously entertained. The occasion was to show Roche at work. A special kind of work certainly, breaking away from the daily routine into the sphere of free communication with thinking people outside the purview of the company's usual tasks.

Thus was born the idea of a multidisciplinary symposium with a subject which would throw open to discussion the scientific endeavours of the company in their relation to society—the human problems of biomedical progress. The Symposium was intended to provide a forum of encounter between preeminent representatives of various cultures and fields of knowledge. The dialogue promised to point the way to fresh insights and new methodology. Besides this, Roche hoped to gain guidelines for future research. The anniversary came at a time of striking changes in established structures and functions. Particularly in the field of health, we are faced with tasks of unprecedented import.

As the idea took shape, the initiators gradually withdrew into the role of hosts. Roche deliberately limited its contribution to a general outline of the scope of the Symposium. The choice of the individual topics for discussion and the selection of discussion leaders and speakers were left to the active participants, who were all invited to a preparatory meeting near Geneva in November 1970, almost a year before the projected event.

The Geneva presymposium will remain alive in the memory of all participants. The close personal contact which soon developed paved the way for a free and fruitful exchange of views. Three main lines of thought and three discussion groups emerged spontaneously to form the three sessions of the principal meeting. The final programme kept closely to the concept worked out at the presymposium.

The manuscripts prepared by the authors for presentation in Basel were distributed to all active participants in good time. They therefore had the opportunity to become familiar with the way of thinking and particular concern of their partners in the coming discussion. For the guests and interested members of the Roche organization these papers were available in the form of a preprint. The stage was thus set for a constructive dialogue.

Yet the Symposium was an experiment. The general theme was wide, and the individual topics overlapped. This overlapping was intentional. It permitted to analyse the complex matter from various angles and to consider the different points of view in a final synopsis. Naturally this endeavour could not be expected to provide generally valid directives for disentangling the problems of our day. The Symposium in fact revealed once again the difficulties of interdisciplinary communication, and many contradictions remained. But these very difficulties in understanding having been brought into the open, the need and the desire to intensify cooperation across all boundaries have increasingly been felt by each participant. In the above sense the Anniversary Symposium was a beginning.

All who took an active part contributed to the success of the meeting. Particular recognition is due to the Chairman, Lord Todd, and to the Moderators, Professor Philip Handler, Professor René König and Professor Jan Waldenström. The intensive preparatory work carried out by the speakers furnished the basis for a creative encounter. The cooperative spirit of all these personalities not only facilitated the task of the organizers; without it the whole experiment would not have been possible. This spirit gives us confidence for future experiments.

A fish-eye view of the conference hall during the Symposium.

Contents

* In these talks the authors review in condensed form their papers appearing in full in the
Second Part of this volume. The papers served as a working basis and were circulated before
the Symposium.

*See page 9.

SECOND PART:
PAPERS AND CURRICULA OF THE ACTIVE PARTICIPANTS

Papers

FIRST PART: PROCEEDINGS

Contributors to the Symposium

Active participants

KENNETH J. ARROW, Ph.D., Professor of Economics,
Harvard University, Cambridge, Mass., USA.

BERNARD BARBER, Ph.D., Professor of Sociology,
Barnard College, Columbia University, New York City, N.Y., USA.

CHARLES A. BERRY, M.D., Director of Medical Research and Operations,
NASA, Houston, Texas, USA.

FRANZ BÖCKLE, Dr. theol., Professor für Moraltheologie,
Katholisch-Theologische Fakultät der Universität Bonn, Deutschland.

ERNEST BOESIGER, D^r phil., D^r ès sc., Directeur de recherche,
Centre national de la recherche scientifique, Gif-sur-Yvette, France.

ARNOLD BURGEN, M.D., Professor of Pharmacology,
Director, Institute for Medical Research, Mill Hill, London, England.

FRANK CLARKE FRASER, Ph.D., M.D., Professor of Medical Genetics,
Department of Biology, McGill University, Montreal, Canada.

COUNT D. GIBSON, Jr., M.D., Professor of Community and Preventive Medicine,
Stanford University School of Medicine, Stanford, Cal., USA.

ALFRED GILMAN, Ph.D., Professor of Pharmacology,
Albert Einstein College of Medicine, New York City, N.Y., USA.

AVRAM GOLDSTEIN, M.D., Professor of Pharmacology,
Stanford University School of Medicine, Stanford, Cal., USA.

PHILIP HANDLER, Ph.D., Professor of Biochemistry and Nutrition,
President of the National Academy of Sciences, Washington, D.C., USA.

JEANNE HERSCH, D^r phil., Professeur de philosophie,
Faculté des lettres, Université de Genève, Suisse.
Membre du Conseil exécutif de l'Unesco.

NIELS KAJ JERNE, Dr. med., Professor for Experimental Therapy,
Director, Basel Institute for Immunology, Basel, Switzerland.

SEYMOUR S. KETY, M.D., Professor of Psychiatry, Director of Psychiatric Research Laboratories, Harvard Medical School, Massachusetts General Hospital, Boston, Mass., USA.

RENÉ KÖNIG, Dr. phil., Professor für Soziologie,
Universität Köln, Deutschland.

JOSHUA LEDERBERG, Ph.D. (Microbiology), Professor of Genetics,
Stanford University School of Medicine, Stanford, Cal., USA.

SALVADOR E. LURIA, M.D., Professor of Biology,
Massachusetts Institute of Technology, Cambridge, Mass., USA.

MICHAEL F.J. MARLET, Dr. phil., lic. theol., Professor für neuzeitliche Philosophie, Katholisch-Theologische Fakultät der Universität Innsbruck, Österreich, und Freie Universität Amsterdam, Holland.

MARGARET MEAD, Ph.D., D.Sc., LL.D., Professor of Anthropology,
American Museum of Natural History, New York City, N.Y., USA.

JÜRGEN MOLTMANN, Dr. theol., Professor für systematische Theologie und Sozialethik, Evangelisch-Theologische Fakultät der Universität Tübingen, Deutschland.

Sir ROGER ORMROD, B.M., LL.D., Member of the Royal High Court of Justice, London, England.
Chairman of the London Marriage Guidance Council.

TALCOTT PARSONS, Dr. phil., Professor of Sociology,
Harvard University, Cambridge, Mass., USA.

PIERRE PICHOT, D^r méd., Professeur de psychologie médicale,
Centre psychiatrique Sainte-Anne de la Faculté de médecine, Université de Paris, France.

ALFRED PLETSCHER, Dr. med. et phil., Professor für Pathophysiologie, Universität Basel.
Leiter des Forschungsdepartements, F. Hoffmann-La Roche & Co. A.G., Basel, Schweiz.

ROBERT REICHARDT, Dr. phil., Professor für Soziologie,
Universität Wien, Österreich.

Lord ROSENHEIM, K.B.E., M.D., F.R.C.P., Professor of Medicine,
University College Hospital Medical School, University of London, England.
President of the Royal College of Physicians.

JOAQUÍN RUIZ-GIMÉNEZ CORTÉS, D^r en droit, Professeur d'éthique sociale et de sociologie et philosophie du droit, Université de Madrid, Espagne.

ALFRED SAUVY, D^r phil., Professeur honoraire de démographie sociale, Collège de France.
Ancien Directeur de l'Institut national d'études démographiques, Paris, France.

AXEL STRØM, M.D., Professor of Social Medicine,
University of Oslo, Norway.

Lord TODD, D.Sc., Dr. phil. nat., D.Ph., F.R.S., F.R.I.C., Master of Christ's College, Professor of Chemistry, University of Cambridge, England.
Former Chairman of the Royal Commission on Medical Education.

JAN WALDENSTRÖM, Dr. med., Professor der inneren Medizin, Universität Lund.
Direktor der Medizinischen Klinik, Allmänna Sjukhus, Malmö, Schweden.

ERNST ULRICH VON WEIZSÄCKER, Dr. rer. nat., Forschungsstätte der Evangelischen Studiengemeinschaft (FEST), Heidelberg, Deutschland.

Lord ZUCKERMAN, O.M., K.C.B., M.D., D.Sc., F.R.C.S., F.R.C.P., F.R.S., Professor of Anatomy. Chief Scientific Adviser to H.M. Government, London, England.

Further contributors

JEAN BERGIER, D^r méd., Président de la Fédération des médecins suisses, Le Mont-sur-Lausanne, Suisse.

DOUGLAS G. CAMERON, M.D., Professor of Medicine, McGill University, Physician-in-Chief, Montreal General Hospital, Montreal, Canada.

KARL GROEGER, Maschinenzeichner, Ingenieurabteilung, F. Hoffmann-La Roche & Co. A.G., Basel, Schweiz.

MARIE-PIERRE HERZOG, Directeur de la Division de la philosophie, Unesco, Paris, France.

ROBERT JUNGK, Dr. phil., Professor für Zukunftsforschung an der Technischen Universität Berlin, Salzburg, Österreich.

CYRILLE KOUPERNIK, D^r méd., Directeur général de la Rédaction scientifique du *Concours Médical*, Paris, France.

KARL LÄMMLI, Dr. med., Spezialarzt FMH für innere Krankheiten, Schaffhausen, Schweiz.

ALBERT F. PRINZ, Medizinischer Co-Editor, *Ärztliche Praxis* und *Euromed*, München-Gräfelfing, Deutschland.

RUDOLF SCHENKEL, Dr. phil., Professor für Zoologie, Universität Basel, Schweiz.

Preparation and Organization

HANS FEHR, Dr. oec. publ., Abteilung für Volkswirtschaft, F. Hoffmann-La
    Roche & Co. A.G., Basel.

ROBERT M. KUNZ, Dr. phil., Forschungsdepartement, F. Hoffmann-La Roche
    & Co. A.G., Basel.

Symposium Secretary

CHARLOTTE PFENNINGER, Forschungsdepartement, F. Hoffmann-La Roche &
    Co. A.G., Basel.

Close inspection of the facilities before the conference. Chairman and Moderators get
acquainted with the electronic equipment. From left to right: Lord Todd, H.D.Schmidt
(electronic engineer), Ernst Sorkin (an adviser in the preparation of the Symposium), Hans
Fehr, Romano Anselmetti (building overseer), Robert M.Kunz and Philip Handler.

Opening Session

Welcoming address

by ADOLF WALTER JANN

Mr Chairman, Ladies and Gentlemen,

It gives me very great pleasure to welcome you all to Basel on behalf of the Board and General Management of Hoffmann-La Roche. We are very honoured that you have consented to come to this Symposium – whether to participate actively or as guests.

The Challenge of Life – Historically, this is perhaps the most pertinent point in time to address ourselves to this subject, and it is a rare occasion indeed when so many distinguished scientists, medical specialists and men of letters from both sides of the Atlantic gather under one roof to do so. I have every confidence that, under the able chairmanship of Lord Todd, this meeting will be most fruitful. His eminence in his field has been acknowledged throughout the world, his interest in the training of young scientists has been an extension of his devotion to the application of knowledge and the projection of the role of science into the future. In his own country and in Switzerland he has also won recognition for his insistence that a partnership between the state and private enterprise in the field of scientific and technical research is not only a practical proposition, but a very necessary one if man is to reap the benefit of the discoveries to which so many of you here today have contributed so much.

Lord Todd will be supported in his task by those of you who have agreed to chair individual sessions and act as discussion leaders. I realize that these arrangements have involved all active participants in much preparatory work. My colleagues and I are grateful that so much effort has gone into ensuring that the proceedings will run smoothly, although, I am sure, not without controversy! Progress must be the end result of discussions, differences of opinion and exchanges of ideas among men of competence and good will.

It is my sincere hope that these deliberations will give fresh impetus to all of us in the pursuit of the common objective of improving the lot of man. We could think of no more worthy theme to mark the celebration of the 75th anniversary of Hoffmann-La Roche, which has been deeply committed to this objective for three quarters of a century. We will continue to be so committed. One need but glance briefly at our history and those who made it, to see how our tradition alone compels us to go forward with the same dedication towards our common goal.

The founder of our company, Fritz Hoffmann-La Roche, was no scientist,

Adolf Walter Jann, Chairman of the Board of Hoffmann-La Roche, in his opening address:
'...improving the lot of man. We could think of no more worthy theme to mark the celebration
of the 75th anniversary of Hoffmann-La Roche, which has been deeply committed to this
objective for three quarters of a century. We will continue to be so committed.'

but as an administrator of vision he was quick to realize that the mass production and distribution of pharmaceutical specialities would have to be soundly
based on, and supported by, scientific and medical research. He therefore built
up a team of keen young chemists and kept in closest touch with the important
clinics and medical centres of his day. At the end of his life, all his efforts seemed
to have come to naught, and he was near to ruin because of severe losses as a direct result of the First World War. But the path he had chosen was the right one.

He was succeeded by Emil Christoph Barell, one of the young chemists who
had joined our organization in its earliest days. His period of high office extended right through and well beyond the Second World War. The successful development of our company in those decades did not derive solely from its scientific
and technical progress, but also from the fact that Emil Barell was a first-class
executive with a rare talent for leadership and mastering the business problems
of his day. When the company reached its 50th anniversary, he was still in the
saddle and able at the same time to celebrate his own 50th year with the company.

His successor, Albert Caflisch, came from the legal profession and made the
long-range problems of an international organization his personal concern. In
accordance with our earliest tradition, he gave the highest priority to the research departments. During his period of office he lavished funds on the expansion of our laboratories and gave our scientists the highest degree of intellectual
freedom in their work.

Since then, the problems of society and of our organization have become
more complex. Research tends to spread out into fresh fields and make new

themes the object of its observation and analysis. Each of us, scientist or executive, physician or philosopher, is finally forced to the conclusion that all developments are interdependent, and this fact impinges on and influences action in all spheres; to go it alone is no longer possible. We live in a multi-faceted world, one in which science is multi-disciplinary with complex, reciprocal interrelationships.

This evolution has its repercussions on the management of a research-minded institution such as ours. The problem is not so much the advance of scientific research itself, but the constantly accelerating pace at which such advance is taking place. This means exposure to, study and assimilation of, an enormous mass of information. Its proper evaluation requires the most intensive effort if we are not to take the wrong decisions.

That is why all of us at Roche, non-scientists as well as scientists, look towards the forthcoming discussions, debate and interchanges for new perspectives. We hope that the record of these proceedings will provide a continuing guide and stimulus.

It may please you to learn that we are inaugurating this building with our meeting tonight. My own office is located just above, and I listened to the construction work for the best part of two years. It is therefore a great relief for me to know that however heated the arguments may become during this Symposium they will not achieve the decibel level of the bulldozers, pneumatic drills and concrete mixers which were my daily companions for so many months.

You might also be interested to know that this meeting will be followed by another international event, assembling Roche executives from all over the world. They too come here to bring our perspectives in line with current needs and coming challenges – and in so doing help chart our future course.

It is our hope that you will enjoy yourselves while you are in Basel. We shall have failed in our duty if we do not succeed in making you feel at home here. I wish you every success.

Roche and the human problems of biomedical progress

by ALFRED PLETSCHER

It may seem strange, at first sight, that a research-based pharmaceutical organization celebrates its 75th anniversary with a symposium on The Challenge of Life, focusing primarily on human problems resulting from biomedical progress. Roche has decided to do this since we view our company as a responsible social unit in a society undergoing rapid change. We are therefore sensitive to the effects of biomedical progress on societal structure. We are at the same time an active sector of the scientific community and, being involved in the explosion of scientific knowledge, are concerned about its impact on the future of man.

Biomedical research has brought about lasting changes in the structure of our society. In the past decades, it has indeed accomplished magnificent achievements, but these have, in part, led to results other than those hoped for. Everybody has now become aware of the problematic nature of biomedical advance. The pleasure of achievement is thus accompanied by concern about the uncertain issue of further developments engendered by this progress. It must be conceded that society has not considered soon and systematically enough the outcome and final consequences of biomedical advances. This omission must be remedied. The aim of the Symposium should therefore be to outline more clearly the problems created by biomedical progress and to find, if possible, essential facts or clues for their solution. The problems extend beyond the biomedical sphere, in which we feel competent. This is the reason for the interdisciplinary character of our Symposium.

In the following, various aspects of biomedical progress, the role of the pharmaceutical industry in this progress and a few illustrative examples of possibilities which may affect our future existence will be briefly sketched.

1. The ambivalence of biomedical progress

Biomedical progress has been ambivalent in its effect on the individual on the one hand and society on the other. This has been true for other phenomena. But because of the accelerating rate of biomedical change, the resultant conflict we experience has rarely been exposed so soon or so clearly. As scientists and doctors, we must constantly weigh our achievements, appraise those that favour the individual and evaluate the extent to which they may be injurious to society. As members of society, on the other hand, we must also evaluate those influences that can benefit society but may be harmful to the individual. Some may offer seeming benefits at short range but may react in the long run against individual or social interests. There are many examples in the classic spheres of medicine from which we may select a few for examination of this ambivalence.

How can benefits for the individual have potential unfavourable consequences for the community, particularly when such measures save and prolong life? How has the interposition of science affected the historic process of natural selection? The preservation of endangered life can and does contribute to the increase in total world population with consequent strains and pressures on its existing fabric and resources. The population explosion has been supported by chemotherapeutics, by synthetic vitamins and by antibiotics. Cardiovascular preparations prolong life, increasing the numbers in the aging sector of our population and increasing the relevant human, social and medical problems inherent in this effect. It must also be remembered that with successes of health services, the expenditures for the aged, the needs of those no longer working, the drain on physical and social facilities may increase. Antidiabetic agents such as insulin enable more young diabetics to live, increasing the numbers of individuals requiring life-long treatment; it not only enables them to reach the age of fertility, but encourages them to marry and to reproduce, raising the level of the diabetic factor in our total genetic pool. Advances in antenatal care and pediatric treatment maintain alive individuals who will presumably never be able to adapt or contribute to society under existing conditions. Similar factors are at play in regard to mental diseases. Thanks to psychopharmacology, schizophrenics, now so often treated as outpatients and not confined to institutions, have greater potential for reproduction. And, recently, the dramatic success of certain organ transplants, which may be miraculously life-saving for the individual, are beginning to raise not only economic but very serious ethical problems for society.

Even in the area of minor ailments various problems arise. The use of hypnotics, tranquillizers or mild analgesics to remedy agitation, anxiety, strain, aggression or transitory pain can, on the one hand, alleviate or prevent in many individuals the psychical and physical symptoms of emotional strain, increase efficiency and improve personal relationships. On the other hand, as with many consumer goods, there is the potential danger of abuse of some of these drugs and consequent harmful effects on the individual and society. It should, however, be remembered that the pharmaceuticals mentioned may protect against the use of more conventional, but no less problematic substances, such as alcohol and nicotine. Furthermore, neurobiology has benefited by research in the area of modern psychotropic drugs. With this help, new insights into the processes of the central nervous system have been gained. In time, therefore, remedies for 'minor ailments' may lead to pharmaceutical preparations with vital indications. Some are already being used successfully in certain forms of epilepsy.

Such considerations could be extended almost at will. Brief reference will, however, be made to one much discussed problem: the changed environmental influences and their potential effects on human inheritance. One thinks primarily, in this connection, of pollution of the atmosphere, the soil and water that we endure passively. Protection is available only to a limited extent, especially as the potentially toxic agents are not all defined. Hidden dangers are also inherent in biomedical progress, although proof of the occurrence of genetic changes in the population as a direct result of this progress has not yet been provided. Such changes would be particularly serious because a mutation, due to the disturbance of the process of natural selection – partly also a result of biomedical progress – could bring in its train negative rather than positive effect. In this connection the dangers of damage to the foetus in the womb (teratogenesis) and possible carcinogenic effects may be mentioned.

2. The role of the pharmaceutical industry in biomedical advance

Progress in the biomedical sphere has received a powerful impetus from industrial research. In his Harveian Oration in 1967 Lord Platt said, 'The phenomenal success of modern medical treatment seems to have depended almost wholly on non-clinical, often non-medical scientists, frequently working in, or in close collaboration with, the pharmaceutical industry'. As fundamental developments of industrial origin, Lord Platt referred to the vitamins, sex hormones, antimalarials and antihistamines.

Roche has from the outset played a leading role in like developments. It may be mentioned that the first industrial synthesis of vitamins was realized in our laboratories. Roche researchers developed the first effective drug, ‹Prostigmin › (neostigmine), able to demonstrate that the formerly almost fatal disease of myasthenia gravis could yield to chemotherapy. In regard to the scourge of tuberculosis, the first reliable and well-tolerated remedy, ‹ Rimifon › (isoniazid), was produced in the Roche laboratories. In respect to depression, the first pharmacological breakthrough, the monoamine oxidase inhibitor ‹Marsilid › (iproniazid), was synthesized by Roche scientists. More recently, as you know, Roche has pioneered the development of non-barbiturate narcotics and new types of psychotropic agents.

These contributions are not mentioned for the sake of creating impression. I wish expressly to emphasize that our successes would not have been achieved without the close collaboration with our academic and clinical research colleagues, and to acknowledge that the medicinal chemists and industrial biologists are ultimately largely dependent for the fulfilment of their efforts on the knowledge and experience of the doctor at the bedside. It is the practising physician who finally decides in respect to the sick individual as to the acceptance or rejection of a new drug. On the other hand, not only private enterprises, but also teaching and research departments at universities benefit from such partnership. Thus, the study of new drugs and their modes of action has contributed significantly to the building up and expansion of fundamental biological disciplines and clinical specialities at the universities.

The great influence exerted by modern medicaments on the structure of the population is based mainly on two factors. First, the substances concerned are often of high biological activity so that functional systems of the human organism may be markedly changed. Modern drugs can influence, for example, brain function, the cardiovascular system, the reproductive cycle of women or the interaction between man and microorganisms. But no drug has an absolutely specific action. Side effects, often unexpected, may occur, some of which may be a serious threat to human health or interfere with embryonic development. On the other hand, valuable drugs have been developed from the study of side effects, for example the oral antidiabetics and the first antidepressants.

A second reason for the great impact of modern drugs is their wide distribution and application. The pharmaceutical industry has not only contributed to the development of new possibilities of treatment, but, by developing large-scale production processes, has also made the products of research available, through doctors, to practically everybody throughout the world. The industrial production of therapeutic preparations and the improved living conditions in most industrial countries, which have advanced the need for better health services – in some countries even with public funds – first made possible the increased consumption of medicinal products.

3. Future problems

In many areas it may be said that some of the problems of the future are already here.

First, what can we do to avoid the potential harmful effects of research on mankind? There are those who speak of the possible necessity of setting limits to research. Should research be restricted in areas in which incalculable potential dangers to the human race could arise, as for example in the manipulation of the human genetic code or in the breeding of certain viruses? Can science tolerate restrictions in the dissemination of research findings or inhibitions on the publication of new discoveries? Do men of such stature exist that they could accept the responsibility of sitting as 'judges' evaluating the potentials for good or bad of a particular discovery? Can such prohibitions be effective in a species whose outstanding members have been characterized by a probing intelligence and a never-ending search for knowledge? I believe it has never yet been possible to prevent thinking man from ultimately doing those things that he is capable of conceiving. Paradoxically, we must acknowledge that the greatest dangers in this area are inherent in fundamental research. Can we accept inhibitions in this area, which would mean tying the hands of scientists when so many urgent human problems remain?

Secondly, what priorities should we set for biomedical progress? Which should take precedence, major diseases of rare frequency but with serious effects or minor ills of high frequency, reducing optimal function and impairing the quality of life? Considering the inherent danger of abuse, is it justifiable to use non-life-saving drugs, such as mild analgesics, hypnotics, tranquillizers? Should we avoid them and put up with slight disorders? Or can society in present cir-

Alfred Pletscher: 'Everybody has now become aware of the problematic nature of biomedical advance. The pleasure of achievement is thus accompanied by concern about the uncertain issue of further developments engendered by this progress.'

cumstances no longer manage without such preparations because of the unprecedented demands on modern man under stimuli of every kind, and of the resulting adaptation difficulties? Must society learn 'to live with these drugs'?

Associated with the problem of suppressing minor disorders is that of self-medication. The present growing importance of this problem is the consequence, *inter alia*, of freer communication and better information. It is to be expected that such information is not merely demanded but also used. In a world confronting an acute crisis in health manpower, what priority should we give to the development of preparations used as self-medications as compared with therapeutic agents requiring professional skills which are in short supply? What should the priority of our concerns be when medications essential for the many are abused by the few? Is it at all politically feasible to restrict self-medication in a society demanding ever-increasing freedom for itself?

Thirdly, how will we confront the moral and economic dilemma posed by our most dramatic successes in the biomedical sciences? In a world in which hunger is rampant, in which treatable diseases remain untreated, in which the simplest of health care is lacking for millions, what are our justifications for those therapeutic measures that are so costly both in manpower and money? I mention only organ transplants and haemodialysis. These are impressive achievements to which the pharmaceutical industry has contributed, e. g. with the development of antibacterial, cardiovascular and immunosuppressive agents. Perfection of these methods of treatment will continue, and it can be anticipated that the cost could assume such proportions as to be insupportable for most national economies. A French political economist has calculated, for example, that the present cost of treating all those waiting for haemodialysis would already equal that of all other health services put together in his country.

Who will decide which patients can receive and which go without the life-saving treatment? On what criteria will those 'worthy of treatment' be selected? Is the Hippocratic Oath outdated by the fact that the consequent practice of ethical principles conflicts with other requirements of human society, e.g. of economic nature? Should the cost of treating the less serious illnesses of the many be limited in favour of such large-scale funds for the treatment of the life-endangering illnesses of fewer people? How will we set social priorities and face the economic alternatives? Finally, the problem leads to the political question of how much each society is prepared to sacrifice for health at the expense of either more material benefits or other national considerations.

Each one of us is aware that biomedical progress demands new criteria for the evaluation of human health and life, for an appraisal of its qualities, for a better ultimate understanding of its goals. As a result, not only the doctor at the sick-bed, not only the pharmaceutical researcher, but scientists in every area of biomedical investigation are faced with critical decisions. The problems are too numerous to be dealt with exhaustively during a three-day symposium. In my view, however, the Symposium will have succeeded, if, in the course of the discussions, some of the questions now lacking clarity could be formulated more precisely, for even in so doing their solution might be brought closer to the realm of possibility.

Introduction to the Symposium – an outline of its scope and limitations

by Lord TODD

There is an old English rhyming proverb which runs

Early to bed and early to rise,
Makes a man healthy, wealthy and wise.

Whether or not the sequence of words in the second line was determined by the unknown author's need for a rhyme, it has always seemed to me that the word order has a deeper significance. The common aspiration of man is now, and I suspect always has been, to be healthy, wealthy and wise – and usually in that order of priority. It is certainly a matter for debate whether wealth deserves to occupy such an important place, but surely no one would question the need for health and wisdom if the pursuit of human happiness is ever to succeed. And how do we stand today in that pursuit? A look at our troubled world is hardly reassuring.

After several millennia during which progress, although not always steady, was in general slow, the industrial revolution in the latter part of the eighteenth century set in train tremendous and rapid advances in all the material aspects of our Western civilization. These advances had social and economic repercussions which in due course spread over and affected every quarter of the globe. The rate of advance accelerated even more markedly with the appearance of the new science-based technology around the middle of the nineteenth century. It is this new kind of technology, fed by and itself feeding the forward march of science, that has revolutionized the material aspects of our lives during this century and which has made Western man wealthy beyond his earlier dreams in the sense of living standards, social security and relief from the drudgery of back-breaking labour. Health has also improved in the same period beyond all recognition. This improvement has occurred for a variety of reasons, most of them associated with, or derived from, the drive to wealth through science-based technology. For one thing, of course, the rise of scientific medicine, by which I mean the application of the methods and more especially the results of scientific research to medical problems, was, essentially, part of the general development of science-based technology. Moreover, progress in medicine was further accelerated by

The Chairman, Lord Todd, in the Opening Session of the Symposium: 'Although it was probably the shock of the ethical and emotional problems raised by organ transplantation that really triggered off the widespread public discussion of such matters as the control of medical practice and research, I believe myself that this public reaction grew out of an increasing unease inspired primarily by the staggering advances made in molecular biology and the looming threat of genetic engineering which they seemed to imply.'

the stimulus to the pursuit of biomedical, as indeed of all natural science as a result of increasing affluence in society. There was, too, another and more direct impact of industrial technology on medicine through the development of the pharmaceutical industry in response to man's increasing demand for freedom from disease. It is indeed remarkable that the virtual conquest of most communicable diseases due to microorganisms and most progress in the control or cure of other ailments which we have seen during the past century have come, not from medical research as such, but from the chemical industry. That industry, too, has been a major factor in the enormous strides which have been made in such matters as public health and nutrition during the same period. Be that as it may, we certainly seem to have made fantastic progress in health and wealth; but in terms of human happiness our record in using this progress is not too impressive, and indeed in certain respects the progress seems to have served us ill. Can we harmonize biomedical science and human values – in brief, can we now be wise?

This is the challenge to meet which we are gathered here – clinicians, scientists, philosophers, theologians, lawyers, sociologists and industrialists – under the aegis of Hoffmann-La Roche & Co., one of the world's greatest pharmaceutical houses on this the 75th anniversary of its foundation. Throughout its history Hoffmann-La Roche & Co. has not only been in the forefront of the pharmaceutical industry, but has kept close to the advancing frontier of biomedical science. Its choice of subject for this Symposium is in line with the concern for human welfare which has marked its activities in the past and indicates that this concern will continue to characterize it in the future. And this is important, for human society is currently in a crisis, and biomedical science and the chemical industry which together have played no small part in its genesis will have to play at least as great a part in its resolution.

Although it was probably the shock of the ethical and emotional problems raised by organ transplantation that really triggered off the widespread public discussion of such matters as the control of medical practice and research, I believe myself that this public reaction grew out of an increasing unease inspired primarily by the staggering advances made in molecular biology and the looming threat of genetic engineering which they seemed to imply. Genetic engineering, if realizable in practice, could have profound effects not only on human society, but on the species itself, and it is appropriate therefore that we should begin our Symposium by examining the present situation in genetics, neurobiology and immunobiology and seek to assess its significance for the future of medicine, in the light of the scientific and ethical questions which it poses. The discussion of these matters under the guidance of Dr Philip Handler and his panel should lead us smoothly to our second session in which we shall look at the impact of biomedical progress on society and on the individual with Dr René König and his group of speakers. In this session we come to grips with some of the most intractable problems of our day. The dramatic increase which has occurred in world population doubtless rests on a complex of reasons. Among them medical progress is largely responsible for the changing age structure of society with all that this implies in changing life patterns of its individual members. Associated with population structure and changing morbidity patterns we have seen a great multiplication of psychotropic and other drugs which have, or could have, profound social effects. The power of the drugs produced by industry and the great advances which have been made in surgery have brought to the fore the question of man's right to live and his right to die in situations where biomedical progress seems to clash with human values and the dignity of man. How can we resolve such clashes, fraught as they are with real dangers to our society?

It is a characteristic of modern society that, as affluence increases, so too does the demand for medical care; ailments which were stoically borne in one generation always call for medical attention in the next. Moreover, every new advance in biomedical research and every new drug creates a new demand for treatment where none previously existed. In face of a demand which thus appears infinite it is evident that medical care must, in practice, be rationed, either by the state or by cost to the patient. A variety of questions at once arise. To what extent has the individual a 'right' to health and how can such a 'right' be defined? How should the provision of medical care be organized? What should be the targets for biomedical research, what part should human experimentation play and what, if anything, does space research contribute to biomedical science? Finally, and perhaps most importantly, how should the doctor determine his priorities – an age-old problem perhaps, but one which grows daily more acute? To these issues we shall devote a whole day of our discussions under the guidance of Dr Jan Waldenström. We shall then wind up our programme in a session where, with the help of Drs Franz Böckle, Salvador E. Luria, Talcott Parsons and Lord Rosenheim we shall endeavour to pick up and highlight the main themes and conclusions which have emerged in our discussions.

Such then will be the scope of our Symposium, and it is indeed wide. Even as it is, however, we have deliberately accepted certain limitations. For one thing, our discussions relate primarily to what are commonly described as the Western countries. In the Communist states and in many parts of Asia political and social systems differing from those in the West will alter the emphasis of various factors and their relative importance although the problems are probably basically the same; however, they have been excluded partly to keep the Symposium within reasonable bounds and partly because we lack the expertise to discuss them. Again we will, save perhaps in passing reference, omit detailed discussion of the rather special problems of the developing countries. Subject to these general limitations it is my hope that we will have a full and frank discussion and, hopefully, reach some consensus of opinion which may, even if in a small way, help to point the way ahead and show that man can indeed be at once healthy, wealthy and wise and thereby meet successfully the challenge of life.

Session I

Biomedical Frontiers

Introduction

PHILIP HANDLER: Let me begin by thanking the authors of our papers. I confess my surprise at the fact that they are all written in a rather neutral tone. Each has avoided any sense of radical advocacy, while each has also avoided the other extreme of utter complacency.

As Lord Todd mentioned in his introduction, the matters before us were set in train by the industrial revolution. Problems which now concern us may be recognized as the inevitable consequences of events that have been rolling along for almost two centuries. Now, rather suddenly, we find it necessary to take stock of human affairs, of the consequences of maximum industrialization to the developed countries and, worldwide, to a human society of assistance to the developing nations in their early industrialization.

The drives which once we took as given, which gave direction to human affairs, whose success we accepted without any other consideration, now appear to be held somewhat in question. Economic growth, sanitation, personal health, longer human lives, greater and more nutritious food supply, tacit assumption of a limitless supply of critical materials in the thin skin of this planet – all have been called into question, and in a remarkably short time. Strangely though, the calling into question of these previously given 'goods' occurs at a time when life would seem to be 'better' for more human beings than at any time in the history of our species; at least in a material sense – the opportunity to live human lives in what is considered human dignity.

Speaking specifically about drug abuse in his paper, Dr Goldstein seems to me to express well what we are trying to do. What he said was that we had a duty to devise humane and effective ways of preventing, controlling and mitigating both harm to the health of the individual and harm to the health of society caused by drug abuse. But one can use precisely the same statement about every other aspect of the consequences of industrialization and of the utilization of the tools provided by biomedical research. Presumably, that is our collective goal, to seek at least minimal guidance concerning what may lie ahead in man's future. A small school of system analysts has been attempting to model human societies on computers, using those parameters which they think they can quantitate and which, somehow, may influence the shape of human affairs. I do not know how reliable their models are, probably each has missed something critically important. But the one thing that they all agree upon is that, here at the end of this century, we have arrived at 'a hinge of history' (that felicitous phrase was coined by someone else, I know not whom) in the sense that decisions which mankind must take within the next few decades most certainly will give shape to human history for millennia to come.

That is an enormous responsibility. One cannot be certain of the extent to which it may be true, but it is an assumption with which we must now live. It may well be the real reason for calling this meeting. Most of those who have thought about such matters have been convinced that the most critical problem before us is probably the number of human beings on the face of the earth. The consequences of population growth in the industrialized nations are quite different from those in the developing nations. In both cases they are seriously damaging. In the industrialized nations each of us, by birth apparently, is entitled to a school desk, a hospital bed, drugs when they are required, eighteen feet of steel on the highway and all the gasoline it will burn, three meals a day of high protein and high vitamin content. This form of civilization makes enormous demands on the resources of the planet. In the developing nations, the very process of population growth itself serves as a brake on development, the overall consequence being failure to 'develop', because their populations grow more rapidly than the incremental resources of the system can manage.

Our troubles are generated principally by the fact that it now appears that Malthus was wrong. He thought – and most scholars have so agreed for the century and a half since – that the food supply would always remain a brake on the size of human populations. That statement remains true in some sense, but it has now become clear that we could surely feed a greater number of human bodies than are tolerable on earth by any other criterion.

This raises another problem, namely the evolution of man. From time to time, many of us must wonder whether the human species is a blind-alley in evolution, whether current homo sapiens is the end of the evolutionary process. Man, as we know him, is little different from his Cro-Magnon ancestor. His brain pan was as large as ours, the brain itself was presumably biologically and physically as well developed as ours. Nothing much has happened in the era since. Is nothing more to happen? Can we give direction to further human evolution? Have we a responsibility to do so?

We are well aware of the variety of potentially deleterious influences that may be affecting human beings, well aware of the fact that every clinic in the world seems to detect a new deleterious mutation about every six months. The list of hereditary diseases of man has grown so long that no one bothers to count them any longer, but it includes hundreds of defined diseases. Quite clearly, absolutely every metabolic aberration compatible with the existence of life itself has occurred and will occur again.

But this has little bearing on the total course of human evolution. It is very facile to state that perhaps we have already evolved in the sense that our population distribution is no longer determined by the classical forces of natural selection based upon the nature of the total environment, since we now fashion our environment ourselves, and therefore these forces are inoperable. Yet, in a different sense, by extending our senses with the cameras and amplifiers that are being used in this room, by extending our brains with powerful computers, by extending our hands with the impressive variety of mechanical tools man has fashioned, we really have evolved. Were we considering any species but man, taxonomists might well designate modern man as a new species. But such evolution consists of extensions of ourselves, rather than genetically transmitted alterations of ourselves. This fact itself may mean that, biologically, there is no place further to go. It seems conceivable that we may be the end of this particular branch of the evolutionary tree. Or isn't that true?

If we do have a responsibility in this area, I hope that our speakers will spend some time discussing it. Meanwhile there are problems which certainly are much more immediate. These have been exposed in some degree by our speakers in the printed papers they offered to us. I am now going to ask each of them to take about ten minutes to tell us what he has been thinking about since he wrote that paper and to emphasize whatever he would like to emphasize for us this morning.

Presentation of topics

SALVADOR E. LURIA: I begin by apologizing to our Chairman for the lack of radicalism in my written presentation. It is not that some of the problems that were on my mind when I wrote my paper and that we discussed in a preparatory meeting for this Symposium may not require radical solutions, but I thought it would be more useful in this environment to prospect the need for solutions rather than to advocate one or the other solution. I believe that we are likely to come up with suggestions that may turn out to be more radical than any that I as a professed radical would have thought of myself.

As it was said by Lord Todd and also by Dr Pletscher in their introductory speeches, the problems that we face in the area of biomedical research are problems of choice, of decisions on what to develop and how to apply what we develop. We have basic science which develops a certain knowledge on the basis of which we can formulate and devise technologies. Once these technologies have been developed, society has the alternative of using or not using them. If it uses them, it must choose how it uses them. There are many points in this chain of events that require decisions. There is the decision of whether or not to do problem-oriented research. There is the decision of whether or not to develop a technology once the basic knowledge is available. There is also the problem that very often gets ignored in gatherings of scientists and scholars, namely who decides and for whose benefit. One often thinks, in connection with the uses of technology, of society as a monolithic whole, but society within each group of nations and on the surface of the earth as a whole is anything but a monolithic whole, and decisions that are made by one group or by one nation or, in some cases, by one individual are sometimes made for the benefit of that group or nation or individual and sometimes for the benefit of humanity as a whole.

This brings me to what I have tried to make the main topic of my written paper, and here I have to apologize to the professionals in this field. I'm only a microbiologist and I was writing about values. But I had the feeling that this was something important to consider. Not only the well-known fact that values, which are the basis for decisions on developing technologies and applying technologies, change from time to time and from area to area, from group to group in society, but also that values have a very peculiar cybernetic type of interaction in society because they represent the embodiment of certain beliefs and influence what is done. Therefore they create new situations which in turn may make these values stronger, more valid, more adaptive or, on the other hand, they may make them obsolete. I think, one of the reasons we are gathered today is that our opportunities, our technologies and our choices and uses of technologies, not only today but in the foreseeable future, are subject to decisions that depend on more than one set of values, and we are not certain whether the values on which we are basing our major pattern of decision are adaptive and are going to remain so. I have tried to give a number of examples of that kind.

The reason for feeling that we are at 'the hinge of history' is not only that certain new specific techniques provided by science have become available, but that the rate at which these techniques are becoming available and the rate of change that they bring about within society throughout the world does not give time for testing our values by the results. Within the course of one human life like my own, just reaching the threshold of the 60th year, one has seen so many changes in the kind of things one can do technically, the diseases one can treat, the epidemics one can avoid, the nutritional deficiencies one can correct, that one has somehow the feeling of a breathless race with technology.

Therefore a number of people, especially among the young, are asking, 'should science continue to progress at the rate it has progressed, should technology be allowed to develop unfettered, or should science itself and the technology based on science be regulated?' And, of course, there remains the main question, who decides how and for what purpose the products of all these efforts are going to be used.

One of the reasons why my written presentation sounded so tame is that the more I thought about it and the more I drafted it, the more it dawned on me that one of the most essential things in a situation like ours is neither optimism, nor pessimism, but caution. Caution in the sense of avoiding irreversibility. I will just take a very simple example from outside the medical field. Between 1900 and, let's say, 1940 practically the whole economy of the United States became irreversibly committed to the technology of the automobile for a variety of reasons. Not because this technology was in itself superior in any way, but partly because it satisfied the desire of a large number of people and partly also because the whole structure of society could be geared to producing, advertising and selling automobiles in a way that it could not be geared to producing, advertising and selling railroad tickets. After spending three days travelling around Switzerland by railroad before this Symposium, I felt great nostalgia for the pre-automobile time and that's what made me think of this analogy. The important thing is to use caution in making decisions that are likely to be irreversible.

Now let me take the lead from what our Chairman said about population. Our attitude to the population problem was dominated for a long time by fear of the Malthusian law and the idea that the scarcity of food would restrict the size of the population, causing a great amount of suffering. Instead, we now realize that the limiting factor will be not food but matters relating to the desirability of life, the quality of life in a crowded society. And that, of course, has already brought a variety of changes in values. For example, there has been a deep change in our attitude since birth control became available in some acceptable form. More recently and much more important there has been a deep change in our attitude towards abortion, to the point where some states in the United States have legalized abortion at the will of the expectant mother. There has apparently been very little materialization of the fear that the legalization of abortion might lead to a widespread decrease in the respect for human life. Abortion has been with us in one form or another in the medical world, legally or illegally, for a long time, and it doesn't seem to have made any great change. But there has been a change in values.

There is a third problem area, that of genetic intervention. We are going to hear much more about that from Dr Lederberg. The only point I wanted to make is this: It is clearly not yet possible to change the genes in man, the heredity that man transmits to his descendants. It may become possible in not too distant a future to carry out what is called 'cloning', that is, by implantation of a nucleus from an individual into an egg, and then by the reimplantation of the egg into the womb of a woman an identical person is produced, or large numbers of identical persons.

We are inclined to believe that such things cannot have any great influence, considering the masses of people on the surface of the earth. But here is where the matter of caution becomes very important. Are we sure that we want to have the idea accepted in the world of deciding who will be born? It is a very different matter to think in terms of cloning and to think in terms of abortion. Abortion is a personal decision by a mother as to whether she wants or does not want that particular child. It is not a social decision. Once cloning becomes feasible the possibility arises that society, government or some other form of leadership will have the ability and the means of shaping people according to certain patterns; for work, for genius, for military purposes, for courage or for some other quality. The reason for being somewhat worried about this future prospect is not that cloning violates any intrinsic human right to be unique, but that – given the kind of society we have today and are likely to continue to have for a long time – the availability of such a power might make acceptable all sorts of other manipulations as well; manipulations of the human mind, the personality structure and of society, which we are certainly unwilling today to consider acceptable.

JOSHUA LEDERBERG: I will refer you to my written paper for any discussion about the technicalities of genetic modification. It would take a drastic act of genetic and psychological engineering to make me stop at the end of ten minutes. The one way I can make myself stop is by leaving out what are in effect really very fascinating but rather unimportant technicalities. They are unimportant from the point of view of a discussion based on *values* because the particular type of progress that can be anticipated from a technical standpoint is in a certain sense fungible, that is to say one kind is as good or as bad as any other. Very similar sets of problems are raised by a wide variety of advances, and one can make interesting case studies by looking at cloning, at genetic surgery or at the modification of development by various means; the basic underlying remains very similar. The basic issue is that, on the one hand, we have an ever-increasing capacity to alleviate the distress of disease and in the particular context of my discussion of genetic disease as it occurs in individuals and in their families – you all know the heartache that is involved when there is manifest genetic defect in being or in prospect. On the other hand, these are modifications of a kind that are bound to attract a considerable degree of social interest because they do have a bearing on the kinds of units of which a society is made up. They bear on the manpower pool for the army, on the requirements for planning the educational system, on the docility of the population with respect to remaining within the political system and so on.

I feel it is just hard luck that as a geneticist I have to answer questions of this kind rather more often than do some of my other biological colleagues. It is not necessarily that genetic modifications or the prospects of genetic therapy are any more alarming or any more exciting or offer any more important opportunities than other areas of medicine, but they make very good metaphors and provide a good basis for a poetic level of discussion that can be understood by the layman. They bring home very sharply questions of manipulation, questions of decisions that are everywhere present in every social interaction but do not have the same concentration of focus as is carried, at least to the popular mind, by the notion of making genes. For example Dr Luria made a remark that was just a metaphor. He talked about producing identical persons by means of renucleation cloning. I know he would not insist on that characterization if we were to pursue it further. Two twins, who are genetically identical, are not identical persons. They differ in many ways. Their personalities perhaps resemble one another more than those of ordinary siblings and even more than those of randomly selected members of the population, but they are in no sense of the term identical persons. Yet the ease with which a knowledgible scientist can lapse into that kind of terminology illustrates what I mean by the metaphorical attractiveness of genetic therapy for these kinds of discussion.

Underlying all these concerns is a controversy about the nature of man from both a political and ultimately a religious standpoint, which will never be resolved, which not even two genetically identical persons are likely ever to agree upon. In fact very rarely does any single individual have a simple single consistent point of view on this kind of question. We all harbor a great deal of schizophrenia in our views about this question. If it is not reflected in our speech and in our profession, it certainly is in our actions. No one of us behaves consistently as if he had a single and uniform philosophy about the nature of man. Most of us do not even know what our philosophy is. We know what we say, but we must judge this question more by our actions than by what we profess. Consider the unlimited diversity of actions that have been undertaken in the name of the Christian religion throughout the last 2,000 years of history and we can see that ideology is as often as not a rationalization for some implicit set of beliefs, often not well understood even by the person using them as a reliable basis for deciding the way in which he will live.

Genetics is at the focus then of discussions of what we might call 'biological axiology', the value systems reflected in biology, because it insists on the confrontation of questions that are morally very difficult and basically undecided in most people's ideology about the nature of man. Dr Handler's question of 'the responsibility for human evolution' is one that bears a very elaborate semantic analysis. There is hardly a single term in that phrase that would not require many hours of discussions merely to understand what was intended by the speaker when he made a statement of that kind, and I am sure that it was perceived by each one of you in a completely different fashion. We glide over such matters. The question was raised a moment ago: 'who shall decide who shall be born?' Exactly what is meant by that 'who'? Whenever a given pair of parents have made an affirmative decision to be parents, or have merely been a little careless, they have decided that someone will be born, and there is a long train of events they did themselves only dimly understand concerning the nature of that new individual. They surely bear some responsibility for that act of parenthood, for having decided that they among all others are worthy of being parents or that they may ignore their own obvious limitations as potential parents for the sake of their own selfish or unperceived motives. The question that is raised by genetic manipulation simply brings to a much sharper focus an issue that is with us in every phase of our lives.

Of course the new findings in genetics do open up specific technical options that will have to be answered. If there should be available a technology for cloning, for example, this certainly will be regulated. These are not events that will occur at random. The mere existence of this information does not oblige any pair of parents to use or not to use such a technology for the production of their offspring. But the exact nature of that regulation is very much open to question. Will we require a formal law and the power of the police to enforce the set of social standards with respect to inhibiting the use of such a technology, or would it be sufficient to rely on the common folk sense as to what is right and what is wrong? Do we really need to be concerned about what may be an occasional aberration, no more important than the aberration that some people will decide to be parents when everyone else strongly believes they should not?

In general, medicine and science certainly face a tempestuous period ahead where their autonomy and their objectivity will be increasingly threatened. They represent tools that are too powerful for policy to be ignored either by politicians or by the authorities in general. For the time being the approach that I have advocated in the article I prepared is one of evasion, that we might try to side-step some of the controversial questions by putting aside any utopian aspiration for the uses of genetics. Such an aspiration would inevitably require a specific decision on fundamental values for mankind, about which no two individuals will agree.

There are still services for the relief of misery that medicine can offer and that science can support, concentrating on the traditions of the relationship between the physician and his individual patient in the uses of genetic therapy. This is one approach in which many of us can to a certain degree feel somewhat comfortable; it is a long-respected tradition that goes back to Hippocrates at least. Nevertheless, it is necessary to remind oneself that even this has many implicit ideological assumptions. It requires a certain complacency with the status quo to feel that one is discharging one's responsibility in a major way by dealing with the sufferings of particular individuals. There are others who will place a much lower value on the relief of individual misery as compared with the pursuit of other approaches – of which each of us has some vision – to benefit mankind as a whole. This too is a question that deserves very detailed semantic analysis. It is not at all certain that we have criteria that would be acceptable to any of us as scientists in judging whether a particular policy is or is not of benefit to mankind as a whole. It is not merely mendacity or viciousness or fundamental evil that underlies the fact that there are very diverse policies being advocated by different people, which have a bearing on the welfare of mankind as a whole.

In the face of these challenges to scientific inquiry and to its fundamental traditions I commend the course that Dr Luria has advocated and has exemplified: a course of calmness, of attempting to understand where we are and of caution. It is very easy to be defensive, to be polemical, to refuse to see what is going on in the world around us. From my view of what is of benefit for mankind as a whole, I believe that there are very important values which distinguish the truth-oriented professions such as science from the value-oriented professions such as politics. We shall lose a great deal if we sacrifice the one under pressure from the other. But we are not likely to maintain the integrity of scientific work unless we understand much better than we do now the nature of the relationship between our culture and the pursuit of our scientific work. We hear many rather emotional and polemical remarks based on the way in which our own scientific work has been perceived by others, of the kind of impact that it has as interpreted by others. But these statements would hardly pass muster by the standards of scientific investigation that we would insist upon in our own professional sphere.

A symposium of this kind can have great value in motivating further inquiry into this aspect of the culture of, around and in science, but it can hardly be taken seriously as a significant scientific contribution to such an inquiry. It is obvious from my own words that those of us who work at the laboratory bench, where we may perhaps have something to offer in the analysis of this relationship, are not expert in this. We have some data, we have some feelings, we have both a passion for solutions and a dispassion in our respect for an objective analysis. I am not at all sure who has the appropriate methodology at this point for a deeper insight and a clear understanding of the maelstrom that rages around us.

NIELS K.JERNE: I intend first to make a few remarks about immunology and its interaction with medicine and, secondly, to give some comments on human values.

Immunology deals mainly with the function of the lymphatic system, which is essentially identical with the total population of lymphocytes in an individual. Lymphocytes have the characteristic property of being able to recognize molecules and structures on cells that are foreign to the body. After such a recognition the lymph cell will multiply and some of the progeny cells will produce antibody molecules, protein molecules, which can recognize this foreign substance, whereas other progeny cells will be able to attack and kill target cells that carry this foreign structure. The immune system is thus continuously surveying our body in order to remove substances and cells that it will not accept.

The hitherto most effective medical manipulation of this system is smallpox vaccination. This was already practised long before immunology came into being, more than a century before antibodies were even discovered. Vaccinations have saved many millions of human lives and have obviously made a considerable contribution to the increase in world population. It was the empirical success of vaccination that led scientists to study the biological mechanisms involved, and our understanding of immunology has since then repeatedly been advanced through medical observations and medical innovations. For example, one basic principle, that the immune system responds only to foreign substances, had to be revised when an ever increasing number of so-called autoimmune diseases were discovered, in which the system in fact acts against the cells of the individual himself. Another example is transplantation. As two individuals, except for identical twins, always differ, immunologists predicted that transplantation of organs could not succeed. But empirical surgical practice proved that they were wrong. This again led to a reconsideration of basic immunological concepts. In reverse, knowledge obtained from immunological research has frequently found medical applications. It is this close and rapid interaction between immunology and medicine that is one of the fascinating and attractive aspects of this area of biology.

Finally, I have to make some remarks about human values. I am hesitant because I find this subject much more difficult than immunology. First, it is my opinion that an increase in understanding of biology, and in this case immunol-

Niels Kaj Jerne: 'It is my opinion that an increase in understanding biology, and in this case immunology, is itself a human value and that therefore the pursuit of this science needs no further justification.'

ogy, is itself a human value and that therefore the pursuit of this science needs no further justification.

Secondly, the application of immunology in medicine gives rise to certain ethical problems. A simple example is again vaccination. Vaccination causes harm to a very small fraction of the persons vaccinated. Very rarely it can even be fatal. But this is also true for most other generally harmless medical and surgical interventions. The problem has always been with us in some form. There are many other examples of ethical problems. There are the dramatic ones like those that become apparent when one discusses donors and recipients in organ transplantation or similar, but less spectacular problems as, for example, blood transfusion. Medical practice has always had to face such problems, and I do not think the advance in immunology has aggravated them.

Thirdly, there are social problems. The most obvious example is again vaccination, which has been a considerable factor in population increase. But I cannot see that anybody in his right mind would advocate stopping vaccination in order to decrease the population by the death of children.

Fourthly, there have been speculations on the possibility of misusing biology, including immunology. I find it not easy to construct a far-reaching drastic science-fiction example of the misuse of immunology. Practically all knowledge can be misused. These questions relate to problems of good and evil, which scientists are no more competent to discuss than anybody else. I am perhaps too optimistic to believe that sinister forces will prevail. It could be argued, and one of the previous speakers mentioned this, that it may be dangerous to acquire too much scientific knowledge at too early a stage of the development of humanity. By this argument we might claim that science is advancing at too rapid a pace.

On the other hand, we should also consider the reverse, namely, the impact of society on science. It seems quite conceivable that the social evolution will retard and finally perhaps stop scientific advance. This might occur quite soon, and as I believe that science is a human value in itself, I would rather argue that those interested should advance science as far as possible while there is still time. It is also true that crucial advances in science or in biology depend on extraordinarily talented people. If young talented persons should decide not to take an interest in science, advances would stop. As an analogy I offer you the Gothic cathedrals. A considerable number of these were built in the twelfth and thirteenth century and then social conditions became prohibitive. Some centuries later people started to build baroque cathedrals. Similarly, we cannot predict how long research in immunology or in molecular biology will continue. Maybe the very fact that we feel urged to discuss the value of scientific advances is an early sign of an approaching decadence of this human style.

SEYMOUR S. KETY: Somehow the aspect of the front of this auditorium through this morning's procedures reminded me of the Last Judgement, with each

Lord Todd inspecting the stairs leading from the auditorium to the platform.

speaker coming before the Divine Hosts and each of them ascending the stairs after he passed. It is therefore with some trepidation that I take this position here, although I am somewhat relieved to see that the architect had failed to put a staircase downwards from this auditorium!

Neurobiology is a broad and a burgeoning field, and I have not attempted to review all its aspects. As a matter of fact Alfred Gilman told me last night that mine was the only recent paper that he has read on neurobiology which did not mention cyclic AMP. What I have attempted to do is to emphasize the unique features of the organization and the plasticity of nervous systems, and to outline the fundamental difference between the biological machinery, which processes and utilizes information, and the information itself. This I feel is necessary to a useful recognition of the strengths and the limitations of the biological sciences in comprehending and modifying behavior. This distinction is tremendously important, because although genetic engineering, if it ever achieves that degree of sophistication, may alter the biological machinery of behavior, it will never be able to alter the informational content of a mature nervous system, which distinguishes this nervous system from another one, even one identical in terms of its genetic constitution. Here we come to the real limitation of the biological sciences in understanding, in modifying and in controlling behavior. Psychopharmacology is perhaps one example of those limitations in terms of possible modification of behavior, granting the efficacy of some of the newer agents in the major mental illnesses such as schizophrenia, depression and mania.

What can one say about the possibilities of improving the mental state or the mental function of the vast majority of human beings, who are presumably, or by definition, normal in terms of their mental state? There is the old axiom in pharmacology that drugs can only act upon biological substrates and they therefore can only suppress or modify functions; they cannot introduce new ones. There is little doubt that drugs can suppress many normal states. Pain and anxiety would, I think, be two of the most important of the mental states that drugs

Seymour S. Kety: '...although genetic engineering, if it ever achieves that degree of sophistication, may alter the biological machinery of behavior, it will never be able to alter the informational content of a mature nervous system, which distinguishes this nervous system from another one, even one identical in terms of its genetic constitution.'

may be able to attenuate. But we must consider whether this is in fact desirable. Pain and anxiety subserve extremely important adaptive functions, as Dr Hersch has emphasized at a more thoughtful and more philosophical and ethical level. But even at the most pragmatic level it can be shown that attenuating normal anxiety impairs most effective behavior. There is no doubt that before I got up to speak I was tense and anxious. There is equally no doubt that there are a number of drugs that I might have taken to alleviate that anxiety. But I have little doubt, although I have not made the experiment, that had I taken one of these tranquillizing or anxiety-mitigating drugs, my performance would have been even less effective than it is at the present time.

How likely are we to improve upon mental function in the future? This is an even more difficult task, and the examples of drugs that improve normal function in any area of the body are extremely rare. Does amphetamine increase mental efficiency? In certain isolated instances and studies it appears possible that it improves mental efficiency when that efficiency is impaired by fatigue. Do the dysleptic drugs, the hallucinogens, LSD, increase the scope of consciousness, do they increase creativity, as some ten or fifteen years ago a group of artists believed? Only where we have no objective measure of creativity; but it would be extremely difficult to show by any kind of controlled or acceptable procedure that these dysleptic drugs improve any of the aspects of human consciousness. Will we be able to improve memory? Perhaps, especially where it is impaired by suboptimal operation in one or the other of the many facets that comprise it. But I do not believe that we are, in the foreseeable future, about to discover a drug that will make a normally bright youngster even brighter in terms of memory and efficiency of his cognitive processes.

The recognition of the fact that human behavior depends not only upon the biological machinery, but even more upon the information content, which is based upon life experience, attenuates somewhat our feelings of concern or of guilt about the biological manipulation of behavior, which is another one of these easily popularized metaphors or clichés that Dr Lederberg spoke about. Recently, two of the national periodicals in the United States carried full front-page pictures portending the evils of controlling human behavior by biological mechanisms, the implantation of electrodes or the administration of drugs. I had a conversation with one of the journalists involved in one of these periodicals, in which I told him that I felt relatively little guilt about my ability to manipulate behavior with the tools at my command, but if I were in his position, I should feel very concerned about the ability of the press to modify human behavior. That, however, did not alter his motivation to produce the copy.

As a biologist I am somewhat concerned about the sometimes far-fetched harm that biomedical science is supposed to make possible, but as a member of society I am concerned even more about the failure of society to utilize the rather commonplace and sometimes classical contributions that science has offered. I am much more disturbed about the lack of use of methods of birth control, which are 98 to 99% efficacious at the present time, really a remarkable degree of efficacy for any kind of agent in any kind of disorder. I am much more concerned about the failure of society to utilize these methods to control the frightening problem of overpopulation, than I am about the possibility that medical science may keep some people alive longer than nature would have permitted them to remain alive. I am much more concerned about our failure to use the knowledge that we acquired decades ago about sanitation, about infectious diseases and, more recently, about nutrition, our failure to apply more adequately these means of providing human health and well-being. I am much more concerned about the failure of our society to recognize the important deprivations that occur in poverty, not only in terms of nutrition and sanitation but also in terms of intellectual and social stimulation and motivation, than I am about the possibilities that something neurobiologists will discover will some day permit us to manipulate the behavior of human beings.

Discussion

PHILIP HANDLER: In my new and unaccustomed role as St Peter, let me permit you to ascend. Welcome to the Archangels!

Gentlemen, you have raised a number of questions of considerable interest. I believe that, at least for this audience, you have lowered the level of apprehension that society generally seems to be expressing concerning the evils we have let loose upon the world.

I noted that Dr Luria originally raised a point on which Dr Jerne then concluded: Whether the freedom to do scientific research is indeed a freedom which our society should cherish, or whether it is conceivable that society would ever deliberately take a decision not to know something, deliberately forego experimentation so as not to learn something.

I confess that my own prejudices are very strong. I consider that such a decision is analogous to book-burning and is not tolerable. Moreover, it is totally misleading since even if you decide not to know something, sooner or later someone else, somewhere, will decide to learn it. Hence, the most such a decision can do is stall. Meanwhile, one would do dreadful damage to the value structure of society by the very act of taking such a decision.

Truth is truth, even if it be viewed differently at different times and places and is ever subject to challenge. But what purpose can be served if humanity, organized humanity, deliberately chooses not to seek it? What nobler purpose is there in life than the search for truth? But the matter is discussed frequently, and two of you found it necessary to touch upon it. I wonder whether the two who did not would like to comment.

JOSHUA LEDERBERG: 'Deliberately forego experimentation' is a process that may take more subtle forms than book-burning. A society whose historical roots and flourishing industrial economy are so well founded on science will never state a decision in such black-and-white terms. It is rather a question of whether sustaining a budget for the National Institutes of Health of less than two billion dollars a year is the equivalent of book-burning; whether it will be less fashionable and less prestigious for a young man to go into scientific work. Will there be a continued din of attributions of malevolence about the nature of the scientific career?

For scientists to react defensively and polemically is of no use whatsoever. For scientists to claim that there is no possibility that their work may be of harm to man is manifestly false. It may be harmful for reasons that are beyond the control of the scientists, but that is the name of the game, the nature of the world in which we live.

We need to understand the problem much better than we do today; many glib remarks are made on all aspects of these questions which do not bear up under cross-examination. For example, we must expose the latent implicit assumptions under which a scientist in fact operates in defending the search for truth as his primary goal. In saying that, he is obviously setting aside some other goals, displacing some other aspects of the value structure. Furthermore, much of the opposition to science is based on the refusal to confront the issue of responsibility, just as much as on the explicit harm that may be attributed to scientific activity. This is the problem of bureaucracy: no one is responsible although all kinds of things may happen that we regret. We all regret the overpopulation of the world. Some of us have incidentally contributed to it, but it was not our fault. It was somehow the 'system' that is not operating properly. If there were a more clear-cut nexus of responsibility; if we knew whom we are talking about when we say 'society has not learned'; if we could say '*you* have not made the correct decision', and '*you* have lined your pockets instead of serving your fellow men'; and if we openly accepted responsibility – we might live better lives with the issues out on the table; certainly more effectively than we do in the rather vague bureaucratic framework of non-responsibility in which we operate at the present time.

SEYMOUR S. KETY: As Dr Lederberg said, we do channel science today, we do in many inchoate ways permit some kind of planning of scientific endeavor to go on, largely in terms of the budgetary allocations which legislators make for one goal or the other. And individually, of course, we choose areas of research that best suit our training, our motivation and our ethical considerations. I am sure that there are not many of us who would deliberately work upon a military invention, especially if we have been trained in the biomedical sciences where the motivations and traditions are for quite other ends. But what Dr Luria was probably speaking about was the theoretical possibility of turning off research in certain areas which seem to be dangerous. Here my own reaction is that this presumes that we can predict the final path that research will take. In many ways this contains the fallacy, of which some of our benevolent legislators have been the victim for some time, that one can predict what lines of research will eventually solve cancer or what lines of research will be relevant to other social problems. In the same way it is going to be extremely difficult to decide in advance what paths of research are likely to cause harm – just as difficult as it is to decide in advance precisely what lines are going to lead to social good.

SALVADOR E. LURIA: I would like to get back to the problem of genetic intervention, and specifically cloning, because this was what I had in mind when I mentioned in my paper that one might even cautiously consider the possibility of slowing down, or not encouraging, research in certain areas. First of all, one has to keep clearly in mind the distinction between basic scientific research, the finding of new facts of nature, and technological developments and applications to certain purposes. To me, as a biologist, the problem of cloning human beings has as little scientific interest as, let us say, the exploration of space. There is nothing of biological interest that can be learned by finding out how to clone human eggs which cannot be learned by cloning mouse eggs. The technology, however, is very different, and this is the point at which the question of controls should be considered. But even in a very ill-organized society – and ours is by no means so ill organized – I would be very careful about advocating in any form the principle of slowing down the progress of fundamental research.

The real problem is that of deciding whether to develop new technologies. How are new technologies going to be utilized in societies whose values are divided, whose values are changing? What we need is to develop a methodology for regulating the development of technology.

NIELS K. JERNE: Dr Handler started by asking whether we could imagine that a decision would be made to stop acquiring further knowledge.

PHILIP HANDLER: You implied at the very end of your remarks that some such decision was in the offing.

NIELS K. JERNE: No, I did not imply that decisions would be made deliberately. I would think that there are in society probably 'feed-back' factors we don't understand which will, not deliberately but in effect, turn off science, if science becomes distasteful to too many people. I think this has happened.

PHILIP HANDLER: Dr Lederberg has described the mechanism of cutting down the financial support.

NIELS K. JERNE: I am not thinking of that. I am thinking, for example, of the culture and science of Greece which stopped developing at a certain stage of the early Middle Ages, or even earlier, for some reason that is not well understood. But the acquisition of knowledge – the path that had been indicated and followed very successfully in mathematics, astronomy and so forth – came to a stop. This may very well happen again.

JOSHUA LEDERBERG: In fact the love of geometry has been described as one of the fatal diseases of Greek civilization! But without it, would we remember the Greeks?

May I respond to Dr Luria's remark about the scientific yield of experiments like cloning. From a narrowly dispassionate and scientific viewpoint, one might judge that the capacity for cloning in man and the observation of the effects of differential environments on the development of identical genotypes was potentially one of the most important approaches to the scientific understanding of human nature. This, however, is not a sufficient foundation to advocate cloning before weighing the ethical and social problems. We do not use man primarily as the animal for an experimentation. We may sometimes do experiments as a by-product of other purposes where some specific human need might be served. This may be very immediate, or part of the general framework of medical progress. Of course we must minimize intrusions on, or damage to, the specific individual. At this point, assuming that all reproductive decisions remain in the hands of responsible parents, we do not have a clear picture of the ethical values involved in cloning as distinguished from sexual reproduction.

To use the metaphor 'identical persons' for a clone is to say that a man is absolutely predestined by his genes. Do we really believe that? Are two twins 'identical persons'? Many important human and scientific questions are involved. Without postulating 'identity', we ought to know better the role of hereditary and of environmental factors, for example in musical or mathematical genius. This will be very difficult to answer without such natural experiments as twins, or their contrived counterpart, cloning.

In my paper I discussed a few other rather restricted circumstances that might lead parents to consider artificial renucleation of the egg as a technical answer to some medical problem. This would serve to relieve some distress, but in almost every case there are probably better alternatives available. This is the reason why I don't think cloning is ever going to be a terribly serious social problem. I simply do not see the pressures likely to lead to it. A state that is capable of resisting the advantages of multiplying Dr Luria's genes by demanding that he be the father of his country should also be able to resist the temptations of cloning the nuclei of any other particular individual. The same ethical and evolutionary issues are involved, with only minor technical distinctions.

SALVADOR E. LURIA: What I meant was that learning to clone human beings is not a process of scientific concern. I did not mean that some problems of human biology could not be attacked successfully if instead of having identical twins by the pair you could have them by the hundreds. What I was specifically referring to was that the process of learning to clone is a technology and as such is not scientifically interesting.

PHILIP HANDLER: I think the prospect is likely to be thrust upon us in a different way. Even now we are transplanting fertilized cattle ova into rabbit uteri which are flown all over the world and then inserted into the uteri of rather unproductive strains of cattle. In this way we are improving the strains of cattle in many areas where milk and beef production has been limited by the genetics of the available stock. Patently, if one wanted to go one step further, one would decide to clone, using the cell nuclei of the very best beef cattle and the very best milk cow available. Once that has been done, we will have come a long way down the trail to the technology that could be used for humans. Then society will require a decision.

SALVADOR E. LURIA: That is my point. It can be done on cattle.

PHILIP HANDLER: But the problem will be presented to society in the language of the publication to which Dr Kety was referring. *Time Magazine* made much of this prospect, found it repugnant and deplorable and took very seriously the idea of assuring that no federal funds may be made available for any research that will ever lead to the eventuality of a functional technology for cloning mammals. It is that decision not to do something, which I think we may have to face as a society, because if it can be done in one species, it can be done in other mammals as well.

SALVADOR E. LURIA: You are coming close to the central problem. What Dr Kety meant was that the press has much greater power than the scientists. This focuses attention on the central problem of today's technological society, the way decisions are made. As long as scientists passively accept the present situation, as long as they feel that it's regrettable but that one has to make the best of it and that after all it could be worse, scientists are resigning part of their responsibility. That responsibility is something more than doing our work well and look-

Salvador E. Luria: '...responsibility is something more than doing our work well and looking with a certain detached spirit at the fact that after all things have not been so badly misused. We have the responsibility to question the ways society is organized and to make use of this knowledge.'

ing with a certain detached spirit at the fact that after all things have not been so badly misused. We have the responsibility to question the ways society is organized and to make use of this knowledge. I am always surprised that there are not many more radicals among practising scientists than there are. And I have never been able to understand why. I suspect that one of the things that our young radical friends tell us, namely, that we have been too well treated by society in the last thirty years, may be true.

SEYMOUR S. KETY: I wanted to support Dr Luria in his statement that human cloning would not lead to any great advantages in scientific knowledge. Dr Lederberg, although he recognized the ethical considerations, has failed perhaps to see the possibilities of using identical twins for exactly the same kinds of studies on the relative weights of environmental and genetic factors in human personality. Here again it is the ethical consideration that prevents one from doing an experiment which deliberately separates identical twins and rears them in two quite different environments. One can get this information by empirical resort to those twins who have been inadvertently separated or to other mechanisms of indirect approach.

I would tend to agree with Dr Luria that some of these areas of research do not deserve support because they are too trivial in terms of scientific knowledge. I am not too concerned about the possible harm they may produce. This kind of scientific attitude is a valuable one because the public, which ultimately makes a decision as to how many dollars or francs or pounds are going to be allotted to this or that area of research, are very easily beguiled by some metaphors. It is important for the scientist to keep in mind what are the scientific or social values that may emerge from his work.

Heart transplantation is another instance which caught public fancy, and many cardiac surgeons moved into the field perhaps prematurely. On the other hand, there were equally competent cardiac surgeons who deliberately avoided doing cardiac transplantations in man because they felt there was nothing this would teach us that we could not learn from more fundamental studies in animals and that, furthermore, our technology was not yet advanced to the point where we can use cardiac transplantation effectively. But the public has nevertheless poured huge amounts of money into the development of cardiac transplantation and of artificial hearts. Many scientists would question, like Dr Luria, what increase in fundamental scientific knowledge or in social good will come about from this research.

PHILIP HANDLER: We have now had a fine demonstration of superlative scientists behaving as amateur philosophers and theologians. Later in the program we are going to watch professional philosophers demonstrate how they behave as amateur biologists.

One reason, however, for asking you to be here, is to ask what your crystal balls, as scientists, reveal as positive human benefit to be derived some time in the not too distant future from the kinds of science in which we are now engaged.

NIELS K. JERNE: Could I make a remark about cloning and heart transplantations? It is quite illuminating that we spend so much time discussing these particular items. Here we are faced with the whole of biology and the possible bad effects of knowledge of biology; and what do we come up with? Cloning, which I think is trivial – as in any case very few people would ever be cloned – so that this will never become a human problem of any dimension, neither will heart transplantation. If that is all we can come up with, the discussion is not really relevant to the issues we are considering.

PHILIP HANDLER: I think human values override scientific ones and since those who do science are human, one need have little concern about scientific villainy to be deliberately foisted upon the larger society.

But, let me turn you back to your crystal balls. You are the scientists, you do the world's work at the bench. There is great concern in the world at large that science may be more evil than good, a notion that none of us would have discussed only a few years ago. This could lead to the kind of decisions Dr Jerne was talking about, perhaps not as formulated specific decisions but as a reflection of the behavior of society generally. Dr Lederberg put it into dollar terms for those of us who live in the United States when he raised the spectre that the National Institutes of Health might stop paying for research and we would all find ourselves driving taxis.

But for now we are certainly going to go right on doing science. It is the possibilities of human benefit that prompt the larger part of society to pay for it. We scientists enjoy the doing of science itself. We deeply enjoy the illumination of the nature of life which our variety of science provides, and that is sufficient personal satisfaction. But society invests in it very heavily on the assumption that there will be forthcoming human benefits at least as great as those we have known in the past when the conduct of science was relatively cheap. Would you care to make any forecasts that you want to have in the record, so that when they celebrate the hundredth anniversary of Hoffmann-La Roche some of us may return to see how that record looks in retrospect.

SEYMOUR S. KETY: Since neurobiology is the youngest of these sciences and since its contributions to medicine and psychiatry are only beginning, it is relatively easy to point to some of the prospects in the field of psychiatric application of the neurobiological knowledge which has been or will be acquired in the next several decades. I would be willing to predict with considerable conviction that the major psychoses will be much better understood. Large steps will be made in the prevention and even in the eradication of some of these psychoses on the basis of neurobiological knowledge and the inferences one is beginning to make from psychopharmacology. If a disorder like schizophrenia could be attenuated that would be a major contribution, since schizophrenia, in terms of its human and financial cost, is perhaps the most costly of our major diseases, and, like depression, has already shown signs of yielding to pharmacotherapy.

But more important than simply the symptomatic relief are the fundamental concepts that are emerging from pharmacological and neurobiological findings which may lead to an understanding at least of the biological substrates of these disorders. It may then become possible to correct these substrates and thus prevent another outbreak of the disorder, even though a person's experience also plays an important role in the development of such mental disorders.

Niels K. Jerne: It is pretty easy to name some prospects in the pursuit of immunology. There is first the increasing understanding of the functions of the body, of cellular differentiation for instance, which is a value in itself, and may perhaps have many applications that we cannot foresee. More direct aims are to get rid of very numerous and prevalent diseases such as asthma and hypersensitivities, allergies, and even to find a way of preventing leukaemia and other cancers. The aim is very clear, and the prospect is excellent, as long as we get a chance to continue working.

Joshua Lederberg: I should like to respond on the issue of 'technopathy' – the diseases of culture induced by science. The biomedical field is perhaps less aggressively attacked by the critics of science than most of the other fields. The central issue has been that of industrialization and mechanization of modern society; so we biologists and physicians have a certain complacency. But we should be very careful not to be defensive. There is a great deal of ambiguity about the nature of the human values at stake. Some of the things that we regard as good others regard as evil; and perhaps *vice versa*. Not everyone will agree that the pursuit of immunology for its own sake is an unmitigated good – some people would regard it as an unmitigated evil – and neither of you can prove which of you is correct. This is an unprovable axiological assumption.

Self-congratulation would be premature; there is one very close shave about the undoubted grotesque misapplication of biology which we may be able to escape, and that is *biological warfare*. At the Disarmament Conference, a few hundred kilometers from here, in Geneva, there have been discussions for the last few years on the negotiation of a world-wide treaty to control the development, the stockpiling, the availability of instruments of war that would use microbes for hostile purposes. Most recently the Soviet Union, the United States and the United Kingdom have reconciled their divergent views and agreed upon a new draft treaty proposal. Prohibiting the use of any biological weapon in war is already implicit in the Geneva protocol (1925) which has had a somewhat dubious success in some aspects of chemical warfare, but has not been significantly violated in biological warfare. The new treaty seeks not only to prevent the use of such agents but also to forestall the possibility of using biological weaponry by prohibiting their development and their stockpiling. Paradoxically the Geneva protocol encouraged such developments, for it established a system of mutual retaliation. Each of the parties had indeed agreed not to use such agents; but the only way of enforcing this was to stockpile them in very considerable abundance; and so the major powers all had large stockpiles of viruses and bacteria that they threatened to use if the other side ever did. The hazardous potential of that kind of arrangement and the possible breakdown of stability based only on the prohibition of *use* is very obvious.

A second important element is of course the newly expressed interest of the Peking regime in joining into international arrangements, which would be rather meaningless if China were not involved. We may still face a time when biological weapons are re-introduced despite these treaties. Other treaties have had a limited lifetime on a global scale, and I think there remains a potential threat of enormous dimensions. Nevertheless, this new treaty is a magnificent positive step.

For the most part, biology and medicine are attacked because they have failed to meet infinite expectations rather than because of the explosive harm they may do. Look, we have not solved the problem of population! We have remarkable therapeutic drugs, but they are not all as usable in the field as they might be! We have not solved the global problems of nutrition. We have introduced new crops – but India now has a grain surplus and yet they may have less protein than ever. We have also introduced a 'drug culture'; while we may have helped to alleviate the anxiety of parents by giving them tranquillizers, we have in fact aggravated it by teaching their children the habits of using such drugs. We have also problems of iatrogenic disease; some of the most wonderful advances in medicine for the treatment of disease have had their own side-effects. I would not say that therapeutic drugs have killed more people than they have cured; but the balance is not so totally on one side as some of us may have believed.

The introduction of other environmental additives surely has done much good. We have pesticides, fuel additives, food additives and so forth, but there has never been sufficient critical attention to what the possible harmful side-effects may be.

I would say that biomedical scientists are perhaps criticized most widely and most realistically for their failure to pursue more broadly and more critically the total implications of the positive introductions that they and their colleagues have made.

SALVADOR E. LURIA: I was glad that Dr Lederberg mentioned the agreement on biological warfare prevention because this illustrates what I said before, that without interfering with science you can regulate technology. One reason why the regulation of development of biological weapons is being achieved successfully is that there had been lots of public outcries. I do not have any illusion that abolishing or banning biological weapons is a great advance, but it is an advance nevertheless, and it was done in what I would call an antagonistic way, i.e. by the pressure of an opposition, at least in the United States.

My second point concerns the question of prospects for medical applications of molecular biology. Until recently, the work of molecular biologists has contributed little that can be applied to the treatment of disease. Right now, however, we may see the prospect of practical applications stemming from the recent discovery that many viruses causing cancer reproduce by means of enzymes that appear to be unique to the viruses and not to be present in normal cells. This opens the possibility for a rational approach to cancer chemotherapy by developing inhibitors of these enzymes. Whether this approach will be successful or not will probably be known by the hundredth year of Hoffmann-La Roche.

PHILIP HANDLER: I am going to turn the session over to the other active participants. To find some logic in the way we are going to do this, let me start by inverting the alphabet and call on Lord Zuckerman first.

LORD ZUCKERMAN: I am sorry you have inverted the order of the alphabet. But since you have, I might as well give some of my reactions to many of the extraordinarily interesting issues ventilated this morning. In general, the discussion seemed to focus on possible constraints on the development of basic scientific knowledge on the one hand, and on the uses to which those advances would be put on the other. Reference was made to disillusionment and the possibility of funds being cut off, and to the fears we have for the future.

When you summed up the discussions, Mr Chairman, you said this was in effect a new issue which had come about during the last few years. This is no new issue; it is the oldest issue I know. There have been corresponding hinges before. George Gissing said, 'I hate and fear science'. What he was really saying was that he feared the uses to which new scientific knowledge would be put. But because of this slant to the discussion, you have necessarily adjusted the focus and put the question who is to decide what must be done, who is to decide how science grows or how science is used. And Dr Lederberg, reflecting a thought that Dr Luria had also expressed, said that he himself would advocate a natural caution. He also said that the scientific process is one that is dominated by truth, and he did not want to see it diluted by whatever it was that exercised politicians in the pursuit of their vocation.

One has to remember that we can't see into the future in any precise fashion. Science, basic science, determines its own fashion at any given moment. One does not know how many Miltons are blushing unseen in the scientific world, because they are not encouraged to pursue what may be their own unique ideas, how many are being suppressed by the fact that certain fields of science are made overwhelmingly fashionable by the influence of the successful scientists.

Science not only opens, it also closes options; technology always closes more options. Reference was made for example to the population problem, to how it came about. There was talk of the green revolution. The cloning of cattle was referred to as a possibility that might benefit man. If it benefits man in the sense that was suggested, it could make the population problem worse. Dr Jerne said that who amongst us would advocate we should not have vaccination. No sane man, he suggested, would ever say that. In point of fact, I have heard sane men say it. I have heard sane men say that the unthinkable must be thought about when one considers the population problem. If the eventual increase in population is such that one cannot deal with it, all sorts of things may have to be thought about.

The industrial revolution closed options. We are sitting here today because of a few small critical discoveries which in our eyes would look trivial today, but which brought about vast changes in the organization of society, in production – trivial things, like the ability to bore a cylinder of steel accurately.

The point I want to make here, to return to what I understood from Dr Lederberg's statement, is that the scientist has no political franchise as such. He has no special franchise when it comes to the declaration of value judgements and current beliefs. It is current beliefs that have the 'playback', of which I think Dr Luria has spoken. Value judgements as such – the good, the true and the beautiful, whatever the form in which values may be described – have remained quite eternal in their own way. It is our social beliefs of the moment that have a 'playback' which brings about transformations in public attitudes.

Reference was made by Dr Lederberg to the fact that he saw – so far as the future of his subject is concerned – one good thing, in that negotiations are now taking place in order to try to outlaw the concept of biological and bacteriological warfare. But he said that this came about through public pressure and that governments were reluctant. There I must correct him. Public pressure undoubtedly had a major effect. The views expressed by some scientists, and in particular certain scientists on the other side of the Atlantic, were immensely powerful. But the governments had already taken the initiative. I say this with knowledge. I was involved in many of these negotiations as an official.

Scientists, if they are to prove able to translate into action their fears, their wishes and their hopes for the future, should operate in the political arena. We have not got the time to do otherwise. We seem to have woken up from a deep sleep which has been going on only since the end of the thirties. In the thirties, dare I say it, there was as sophisticated a discussion of these matters as we are enjoying today. We have got to engage in those processes that affect our democratic decisions.

The power of the press can be influenced by scientists. Scientists who bring genetic engineering, cloning, heart transplantations and all the rest before the public are as much to blame for distorting issues as those who remain silent. We must modulate our messages. Science cannot go on giving man the impression that he can enjoy everything, and in the particular field about which we are talking, that he can be assured in the future of a healthy, happy and eternal life. Instead scientists should help transform public attitudes in a sensible way, or become politicians using their scientific knowledge to form and translate political sentiments into a reality.

PHILIP HANDLER: I suppose since I used several of those phrases I should qualify them. First 'the hinge of history'. Those who use that term, and I who share their belief, are well aware that man has always lived with a sense of crisis, always thought that 'this moment in time is the critical moment in time'. The increasing awareness of this being a particularly momentous period comes about because of the continuing acceleration of the rate of change. Because of our increasing human numbers, of the galloping drain on the planet's resources, there is the sense that time may be running out, in that major undesirable trends, if not already irreversible, can soon become so.

We are burning petroleum at a perfectly incredible rate. It took three and a half billion years to accumulate all the petroleum there is on this planet. We are now using it primarily as a source of energy. By most projections, in another century or century and a half there will be none left; a few generations of men will have taken it upon themselves to have burned up all the petroleum it took all these billions of years to produce. The problem is not that we may deprive our successors of an energy source, as they will surely find others, the sun, fusion or fission energy, etc. But we may well deprive them of a unique raw material for the chemical industry, while thoughtlessly depleting a number of minerals already known to be in short worldwide supply. When the world population becomes so great that all of us are tightly packaged in one sense or another, that too will change the nature of society in an irreversible way, short of a cataclysm to which none of us can look forward as a solution to man's problems.

One cannot but wonder what fraction of our individual human and societal problems reflect the fact that, in an evolutionary sense, we are but a few generations removed – hence little changed – from our ancestors who were clustered in small, free-roving hunting bands. Whereas today, most of humanity is close-packed in ever growing metropolises.

You stated flatly, Lord Zuckerman, that science closes options. But surely, most of the options that have been made available to us were created by science. May we not hope that science, tomorrow, will continue to create options rather than close them?

LORD ZUCKERMAN: Obviously science creates the options, it creates the world in which we live. I was merely trying to make the point that there are fashions in science. These create the options but in so doing they close others.

PHILIP HANDLER: Dr Lederberg, I think that Lord Zuckerman's statements were directed to you.

JOSHUA LEDERBERG: They were also directed to Dr Luria; some of the remarks attributed to me should be his responsibility. I made no remark about the role of scientific agitation in respect to BW (bacteriological warfare). That was Dr Luria's, but, at least as far as the United States and its policy are concerned, I must agree with him that the agitations, if you wish, in which microbiologists had a significant role without a doubt played an important part in making this a hot is-sue. Of course governments responded. There was a remarkable example of uni-lateral disarmament. At a certain point I'm not so sure I would have advocated going so far. My concern was that with the promulgation of the doctrine that the United States would unilaterally eschew biological weaponry, we might lack the lever by which to extract a corresponding concession from the Communist side. But all is well that ends well, and I think we are approaching a satisfactory con-clusion on that specific issue.

PHILIP HANDLER: The facts of United States behavior in this matter were really somewhere between your position and that of Lord Zuckerman. This matter arose during my first term on the President's Science Advisory Committee (PSAC). Melvin Calvin and I were on a special panel with oversight of the United States BW/CW research endeavor. Although we were both university profes-sors, we were also, in a sense, government officials. At that time, we filed a leng-thy report which analysed the current status of such activities and summarized the basis of our recommendation that the United States limit its activity to pure-ly defensive measures and that the United States government formally proclaim that it would totally eschew biological warfare. This was endorsed by the PSAC, and shortly thereafter the United States Ambassador to the United Nations made such a statement on the floor of the United Nations, thereby formally committing the United States to the *de facto*, albeit not *de iure* adherence to the 'Geneva Protocol'. As you noted, about two or three years later the Nixon Administration took the next step. My point in recounting this is that, in this instance, initiative came from scientists whose leverage derived from their special position in being both inside and outside the government. Withal, this entire episode is, as Dr Luria noted, an excellent example of a process wherein science provided understanding that led to a new technology which society – formalized as a government – examined, found undesirable and took the decision not to permit its utilization. It is an example of technological assessment at its very best.

JOSHUA LEDERBERG: I did not advocate that scientists in particular undertake the political franchise. In fact, I'm probably more modest on that question than most of my colleagues and I sometimes wonder why. What I did say was that – given that scientists share the wish to preserve the truth-oriented vocation – it was absolutely essential that they understand the nature of the objections being lodged against the scientific process. I also meant to say that one of the most se-rious of these objections was the problem of the non-responsible bureaucracy, i.e. there is no particular place where one could lodge one's complaints about this, that or the other having happened. If we could explore the framework of technological decision-making, we could understand better than we do now the actual process in which such decisions are in fact effected, and there might be a better basis for conciliation. We would all understand one another's roles more appropriately, rather than the myths that surround them at the present time.

Regarding the nature of the 'hinge of history' I have a somewhat different view as to the foundations of the crisis, although I am obviously borrowing from Toynbee and many others on this score. But it seems to me that since World War II we have discovered the colonies, or what was then called the colonies. We discovered that the earth consists of rather more than a few hundred million Europeans and their values. We have made a political and ethical decision, that I think all of us would avow, about the brotherhood of man and the right for an equal opportunity on the part of all the peoples of the earth. We don't really know quite how to implement that humanitarian decision. The disparity between our own hopes – not to mention the political and eventually military pressures – and those of the other peoples of the earth is at the center of that hinge. I could enlarge on this with respect to the technological and scientific crisis, of which it is a part. In the States we have our colonies at home about which we could make exactly the same kind of remark.

PHILIP HANDLER: That can be roughly quantitated if it is true that the course of population growth is now inevitable for at least the next two or three decades. If one then asks what would be required if all the peoples on earth in the year 2000 were to live as well as Americans did in the year 1950, the drain on most of the major minerals that we extract from the earth must increase by a factor of 70. Since this is not even remotely feasible, there is the dilemma to which Dr Lederberg was just referring. Dr Luria, would you care also to respond to Lord Zuckerman?

SALVADOR E. LURIA: Just one more thing about the matter of value remaining constant and only belief changing. I think it is slightly a matter of semantics. Some of these major problems that arise from the population explosion will require, and are already beginning to show, the development of a more adaptive set of values. I believe more people, certainly young people in the United States, even though they still hold to the value of being alive, are beginning to feel that the value of wealth has lost some significance. I do not know how long it will last, but many people have begun to ask whether it is not better to live in a world with fewer goods and gadgets but free from poverty and war. I consider this a change in values and not only a change in beliefs. I hope that this change continues and may even enroll some of my generation.

ALFRED SAUVY: Cet avis qui a été exprimé, on l'entend partout et dans tous les pays. Bien des gens vous disent: je préférerais avoir une vie plus simple et avoir moins de tracas de la société de consommation. Seulement, quand on passe à l'application, même sur le papier, il n'y a plus rien, plus de compétition. Tout le monde veut garder ce qu'il a. Il y a donc une divergence, une opposition profonde entre cette attitude individuelle et même, dans une certaine mesure, collective, et les comportements. Et il ne semble pas qu'il puisse y avoir un changement, tout au moins dans notre système de relative liberté démocratique.

JEANNE HERSCH: J'ai l'impression que vous, entre savants, ce matin, vous vous sentiez à certains moments comme sur la défensive devant une société qui semble menacer vos travaux. Il a paru, à certains moments, que vous preniez les devants. Certains disaient que les savants devaient s'engager dans la lutte politique pour la défense de la science, et d'autres invitaient leurs collègues à mettre en évidence les petites récompenses que le *vulgum pecus* qui paie des impôts peut attendre de la recherche scientifique, dans le domaine spécifique de chacun d'entre eux.

On nous promet, par exemple, la guérison de certaines formes de cancer et on nous dit: «Payez gentiment vos impôts qui vont faire vivre le laboratoire, parce que nous allons peut-être vous guérir lorsque vous serez malades.» Je crois qu'il y a dans cette attitude quelque chose qui ne correspond pas au rapport véritable de la science au monde dans lequel elle se développe. En effet, c'est un peu traiter le monde ambiant, malgré toutes les doctrines démocratiques professées, comme s'il était peuplé de petits enfants à qui on promet un sucre, alors que les savants obéissent à des impulsions tout à fait différentes. Je crois que le savant qui travaille par exemple en chimie ou en biologie moléculaire et qui fait des recherches pouvant aider à vaincre le cancer est mû par des impulsions qui n'ont pas grand-chose à voir avec le désir véritable de guérir un malade du cancer.

Il fait de la science, et je crois que c'est cette impulsion-là qui est décisive. La science, qui cherche une certaine forme de vérité, un certain langage de vérité, les savants doivent arriver à en communiquer le sens et l'amour à l'ensemble du monde dans lequel ils travaillent. Alors on sera sur un terrain de vérité. On parlera de la même chose, et non pas à travers un écran de prétextes qui, à la longue, ne peuvent être que percés à jour. Il me semble donc essentiel que les savants découvrent mieux la nature propre de leur travail et trouvent le moyen de la communiquer aux autres, non pas avec un prétexte, non pas avec un bonbon – si bienfaisant qu'il soit d'une part, si nocif qu'il puisse être de l'autre – mais dans la vérité de la nature de ce travail, car le jour où l'humanité renoncera à la science, elle renoncera actuellement à elle-même. Non qu'il n'y ait pas d'humanité sans science, mais quand la science est née, on ne peut plus y renoncer sans cesser d'être un être humain. Ce qui ne veut pas dire que les recherches ne connaissent de limites, et ici je voudrais reprendre la question de M. Luria, car elle m'a semblé extrêmement sérieuse: celle de savoir si n'importe quelle recherche expérimentale possible, parce qu'elle est possible, doit être faite.

SALVADOR E. LURIA: As regards the impression we may have given of trying to justify the work of science through its results, first let me say that the matter of the possible applications came out this morning. I was requested by the Chairman to say something and being the last one to speak on this subject, I distilled my mind and I finally came up with this possibility of an approach to cancer therapy. But there is really very little to say as far as applications of molecular biology are concerned. On the other hand – Dr Handler's point is very well taken – the motivation of scientists is to do science. However, as long as the motivation of scientists to do science had remained uncoupled with the consciousness of the uses to which the products of science may be put in society the situation was somewhat anarchistic. We could afford such an anarchistic situation of doing anything that could be done at a time when there was no risk that the consequences of science might be of such magnitude that they could change the situation on the earth. The two major risks, of course, are nuclear weapons and the population explosion, both of which have become possible through the application of scientific knowledge.

To go back to what Lord Zuckerman was saying earlier it seems to me that the hinge of history comes in when the order of magnitude of the perturbations brought about by a certain technology is the same as the intrinsic parameters of the phenomena. Once we begin to use up the resources of the earth within the space of one generation then is the time when history begins to be upon us. That's why I would agree with every single thing you said concerning the need for scientists to be aware of, and for society to control to some extent, the application. But I would not agree, at least not without much more discussion, that society at this moment would do well to control basic science. As far as basic science is concerned, we can still afford to have as much of it as possible, as much as we can afford to finance.

NIELS K. JERNE: I should like to make a remark to Dr Hersch. I agree with practically everything you said, except for what I believe you said about communication, namely, that scientists should communicate to others what they are doing. I find this point is not well taken, because scientists do in fact publish the results of their thoughts and investigations. You may say, 'well, but I can't understand the language they talk, why don't they say what they are doing in a different way?' But this is unreasonable. It can't be done in a different way. You cannot popularize science. Scientists are communicating in the way they think the results of their activity should be communicated. And if there are persons who don't understand it, this is not the concern of the scientist. You could just as well ask Picasso, 'why don't you paint differently, so that we could understand what you are saying'.

KARL LÄMMLI: Es scheint mir ein prinzipieller Aspekt zu sein, daß die Wissenschaftler gar nicht eine volle Wahrheit bringen können, sondern nur immer einen Teilaspekt. Dies nicht nur, weil ein jeder Wissenschaftler auf seinem Spezialgebiet arbeitet, sondern vor allem darum, weil die wissenschaftliche Forschung immer unter vereinfachten Bedingungen, unter Laborbedingungen, arbeitet. Das Resultat: Wir können nicht alle Interdependenzen, die in der Natur oder in der Gesellschaft vorkommen, im Labor berücksichtigen, sonst käme kein Experiment zustande. Die Resultate der Forschung zeigen also nur eine Teilwahrheit, einen Teilaspekt der Natur. Wenn man nun diese Resultate technologisch anwendet, kommt es zu den bekannten Störungen, zum Beispiel als

Nebenwirkungen von Präparaten. Ähnlich steht es, wenn der praktizierende Arzt entscheiden muß, wen er dem Tod überlassen soll, wen er künstlich ernähren, bei wem er transplantieren, wen er reanimieren soll. Die Malaise der Gesellschaft gegenüber der Wissenschaft beruht eben darauf, daß diese nur Teilwahrheiten produziert. Darum dürfen wir nicht sagen, sie produziere Wahrheit an sich.

JAN WALDENSTRÖM: Dr Jerne, you speak about immunological memory, and Dr Kety talks about cerebral memory. It might be of interest to hear you discuss whether there are any similarities between the two kinds of memory. Of course, immunological memory is to be regarded more or less as a metaphor. Still, it is built on specific protein synthesis, and we hear from Dr Kety that by inhibiting protein synthesis you can damage part of memory, at least the retention of engrammata. You may say that this is a very sophisticated and specialized question. But I think it is one of the central questions of medicine and especially of gerontology.

SEYMOUR S. KETY: Dr Waldenström has touched upon an important controversy in the neurobiology of memory. Early in molecular biology, progress in genetic and immunological memory was so exciting that this became the model for cerebral memory. However, this is not the only model one can adopt, and my own personal feeling is that there are many more possibilities for the storage of information in terms of the networks of the brain than in the form of aminoacid sequences in molecules. In both cases protein synthesis would still be a crucial factor and, to the best of my knowledge, no experiment has yet demonstrated that memory is in fact encoded in the same way as immunological memory. It is still an open question whether the encoding possibilities of the network are of primary importance.

NIELS K. JERNE: As Dr Waldenström said, the use of the word memory in immunology is actually by analogy; it seems an analogy that we don't want to press too much, as Dr Kety has just explained. There is in immunology a phenomenon that once the immune system has recognized a foreign substance, an antigen, a vaccine, this immune system is changed in such a way as to be more capable of recognizing that same foreign substance when it occurs again. This phenomenon we describe as immunological memory. It also has another aspect in common with learning from experience. Neither the memory in the brain nor the immunological memory can be transferred to your offspring. These are the main analogies between the two systems. I agree with Dr Kety that probably, or very certainly, the nervous system is much more complicated. It will be much easier to manipulate the immune system than the nervous system.

ERNST VON WEIZSÄCKER: Ich möchte der Befürchtung von Dr. Jerne, daß in absehbarer Zeit der Wissenschaft ähnlich der Garaus gemacht wird wie früher den

Ernst von Weizsäcker: «Es ist eine Flucht, wenn Naturwissenschaftler sagen, daß es primär durch bösartige Wahl von negativen Alternativen zum Mißbrauch komme... Die politisch wirksamen Entscheidungen sind viel komplexer.»

gotischen Kathedralen, eine gewisse Rationalisierung geben. Es wäre verständlich, wenn man aus Furcht vor möglichen entsetzlichen Folgen der wissenschaftlichen Forschung in Erwägung zöge, die Ursachen, das heißt die Grundlagenforschung zu unterbinden. Denn es ist zu spät, erst bei der Technologie einzugreifen. Ich möchte das an dem Beispiel kurz erläutern, das Dr. Luria – allerdings im entgegengesetzten Sinn – verwendet hat. Er sagte, das Beispiel der biologischen Waffen zeige, daß man die böse Technologie verbieten kann, ohne eine Veränderung in der Grundlagenforschung anzustreben. Ich halte das für eine Illusion. Man kann erwarten, daß im Laufe der weiteren Entwicklung der Medizin und besonders der Immunologie das technologische Know-how für B-Waffen so anwächst, daß eines Tages auch jenen Gruppen, die sich an Moral und Völkerrecht und die Genfer Abkommen usw. nicht gebunden fühlen, eine desaströse Technologie zur Verfügung steht. In dieser Situation wird es nichts mehr nützen zu sagen: «Schaltet diese Technologie aus», sondern man wird sich dann fragen, warum wir nicht vor zwanzig Jahren die entsprechende Grundlagenforschung gestoppt haben.

Trotzdem, ich bin natürlich kein Verfechter eines Verbotes der Grundlagenforschung. Aber die Probleme sind nicht einfach. Die sogenannten Entscheidungen, wie sie Dr. Luria in seiner Eröffnungsrede genannt hat, sind nicht die Art von Entscheidungen, die wir in der Naturwissenschaft vorfinden und die wir auf einfache Alternativen reduzieren können. In der Regel sind diese Probleme sehr viel komplexer, sehr viel interaktiver. Es ist eine Flucht, wenn Naturwissenschaftler sagen, daß es primär durch bösartige Wahl von negativen Alternativen zum Mißbrauch komme. Die Utopie von bösartigen Diktatoren entspringt, glaube ich, typisch den Gehirnen derer, die in einfachen Alternativen zu denken gewohnt sind. Die politisch wirksamen Entscheidungen sind viel komplexer. Deswegen wäre meine ethische Forderung, daß wissenschaftliche Methoden für wesentlich komplexere Systeme entwickelt werden sollten. Damit meine ich nicht einfach Psychologie oder Soziologie, die die leicht entscheidbaren, quantifizierbaren Alternativen aus den unermeßlich komplizierten psychologischen oder soziologischen Gebäuden herausextrahieren, sondern ich meine neue Methoden, die die ganze Komplexität ernst nehmen. Dies aber ist eine interdisziplinäre Aufgabe.

RUDOLF SCHENKEL: Almost all the speakers expressed the opinion that biomedical basic research is purely truth-orientated and thus represents a human value of the highest order. But in fact, not a single biomedical experiment takes place in the dimension of truth alone; each is achieved by actual interventions affecting complex systems of life on earth. These experiments are only possible in a modern laboratory. They necessarily require today's 'technocracy' and thus involve our environmental system, already ravaged by countless interventions of mankind. Besides this the preparation and carrying out of every single experiment produces further impacts and provides the starting point for new experiments with new encroachments. Should indeed any intervention whatsoever be justified if it serves the search for truth?

Let us consider this relation to truth. The biomedical experimenter in research is interested only in an extremely limited facet of truth and not in *the truth*, not in the total effect his experiments have on the surroundings. In a negligent or ruthless manner he is blind to the importance of these implications of his work. He is trained accordingly: with a sensorium for an extremely selective aspect of reality. This makes him a suitable instrument of technology and industry.

In the field of technology and industry truth is no longer the question, not even partial truth, but only the power of technical and medical 'means'. The vast majorities of mankind are still fascinated by the 'miracles' of technology and medicine, i.e. very narrow aspects of their effects. This is why the situation is of the greatest interest both economically and politically. Yet, the effects of technology and industry on the entire system of life on earth, which have become both over-powerful and extremely dangerous, are still not fully recognized.

The same basic attitude is inherent in biomedical research, technology and industry:

- the demand that all the components of our environment, including all forms of life, should be at our disposal for any desired intervention;
- the selective character of the aims and the blindness and ruthlessness with regard to comprehensive global systems.

When today we rightly speak of the risk of mankind's situation, we must finally realize that the attitude I have described plays a decisive part in this.

Man is now the most powerful component in the sphere of life; all other components come within his grasp and are subject to his influence. In spite of this he is not independent. By degrading all spheres of life he also jeopardizes his own existence. Today more than this insight must be demanded from the researcher! Man as the most powerful component in the sphere of life must develop solidarity with all the other components and must learn to concede them their worth and dignity. Such consideration and the preparedness to self-restriction must above all be exacted from those engaged in research.

PHILIP HANDLER: The question under consideration is whether there should ever be any circumstances where we should forego seeking that understanding itself for fear of the possibility that we could not live with it when it is obtained. This is what Dr Luria and Dr Jerne were talking about earlier. That scientists must ever be aware of the potential consequences of their understanding has already been agreed to by all four gentlemen on the platform.

SALVADOR E. LURIA: I would like to say just a word in response to what I think Dr von Weizsäcker said and that is the following: The matter of keeping in mind all of the broader implications of science is one that is not very distant from the practice that is beginning to develop in the United States. We are now trying at the Massachusetts Institute of Technology to introduce in the teaching of under-graduate courses in biology or in physics certain lectures on the impact of that field on society, specifically describing some of the past applications, some of the potential applications and some of the responsibilities. This is a trend which, if it spreads, is going to have a very beneficial effect on the education of the scientists of the next generation.

PHILIP HANDLER: We had a literal demonstration a while ago of what Dr Jerne was saying. If non-scientists wish to have some appreciation or understanding of science, they will have to 'speak' the language of science, at least in some part. Witness the confoundment in this room when we cannot all listen to the same classical language and understand it. Similarly, it is very difficult to understand what immunologists are doing if you have no command of the language that they use, necessarily, to describe immunology. That is a non-trivial problem, indeed a very difficult one.

Some of us do work at it. Dr Lederberg writes a column for the newspaper, once a week, in which he tries to make available to the general American public some of the consequences of scientific understanding. Others have taken longer routes. I have edited a book on *Biology and the Future of Man*, which has been well received, but by only a relatively small sector of the public. It is a difficult task, Sir, and you must not ask too much of the scientific community. What Dr Jerne was saying was that the non-scientific community will also have to make an effort if the two cultures are to communicate.

MARGARET MEAD: In the early 1950's we, the social scientists, saw very clearly what was going to happen in the reaction to science in the United States. At that time the scientific community did not include any social scientists in any of their planning. We made a study of the image of the scientist which predicted accu-rately what has in fact happened. But they took no notice of that. Now the image of the scientists that has alienated our young people is the image of an elitist group working with their own problems unconcerned with the relevance of what they are doing.

There are some who say that it is not the business of the scientist to communicate with the others. But more important than this particular point is what biology can contribute. I want to speak in particular about the contribution of this panel to the sort of problem that the two or three last speakers have raised, i.e. how do we think about the surround, how do we cease to be fragmented and how do we integrate specialized science into a wider field? Biology is presenting us, we hope, with the living model for this type of thinking, with an ecological model in which we stop seeking for maxima and begin seeking for optima.

The phrase 'power over nature' is continually used in the old sense of a physical, chemical model vis-à-vis nature. What biology is introducing, however, is the idea that man is part of the system and must consider himself as part of the system, which seems to many of us the model we need. Not system theory that is again produced on a model of game theory, but a kind of system theory that is produced from the whole of biology and an attitude sufficiently complex to give the fragmented specialized scientists and the feedback from technology a place in our future understanding.

F. CLARKE FRASER: I would like to make three points, one about the population explosion and the quality of life. It is my experience that whenever I talk about this to businessmen or engineers or economists they say 'what nonsense, this is a snow job that the scientists are putting up', and it is very hard to talk to my friends in the Maritime Provinces or to someone who has just flown over the prairies and to convince them that there is not enough room. So, until we get the non-scientists, the grass-root people and the politicians really concerned, we are not going to get anywhere about doing something about the population explosion.

F. Clarke Fraser: '...until we get the non-scientists, the grass-root people and the politicians really concerned, we are not going to get anywhere about doing something about the population explosion.'

This leads to the question of what the population explosion and the possible remedies are going to do to our gene pool. It was Dr Lederberg, in his text rather than his talk, who said that all sorts of things are happening to people's genes. There are for instance the effects of economy and of industry influencing our gene pool, about which we do not really know anything. These alterations are much greater than those from relaxed selection resulting from improved medical care. Yet there seems to be little concern about finding out what is in fact going on. Some of the great resources of science should be turned to this end.

We are going to have to think about what happens if top family size does get reduced to, say, 2.5. A stable population level will remove a great deal of selection. In our present state of negative selection due to the differential family size, this might be a good thing for a while, but it will not continue to be so. One will have to start thinking about measures that could be introduced to encourage positive selection.

PHILIP HANDLER: Do you have in mind a mechanism for positive selection?

F. CLARKE FRASER: I think mechanisms could be worked out in terms of tax benefits, etc. For instance, our Government has just put in a regulation whereby women will receive health benefits when they take time off their jobs for pregnancy. Here is a place where one could impose a sliding scale which might have a directive influence on people's reproductive behavior.

PHILIP HANDLER: Picking and choosing amongst the population?

F. CLARKE FRASER: Choosing, yes. One has to admit that there are desirable qualities and undesirable qualities and that one is going to have to choose between them.

NIELS K. JERNE: Who is going to choose?

F. CLARKE FRASER: Society.

PHILIP HANDLER: This selection would be based entirely upon some measured attributes of the parents then?

F. CLARKE FRASER: I do not think one has to base it on specific individuals but on incentives.

PHILIP HANDLER: You are not talking about amniocentesis and the removal of the patently biologically undesirable individuals; you are talking about trying to increase in the population the distribution of those characteristics that you or someone in authority will find desirable?

F. CLARKE FRASER: There are certain aspects of performance, for instance, which one would generally agree are desirable. One could arrange benefits in terms of, say, educational scholarships that would encourage selective reproduction in relation to this kind of performance. Our 'baby bonus', for instance, acts in the opposite direction.

SALVADOR E. LURIA: It seems to me that what you have just said is the very strongest argument in favor of getting to work hard on population control in other ways, because one of the worst dangers of the population explosion is going to be exactly the acceptability of the kind of proposal that you have just put on the floor.

F. CLARKE FRASER: I agree! We must start to think about it.

SEYMOUR S. KETY: Actually mechanisms are in operation today for making value judgements in terms of the rearing of children. These could easily be applied not only to the adoption but also to the production of children. There is not much outcry about the processes by which adoptive parents are selected and yet one has to prove before a court of law that one has the ability and the right to adopt a child. The same kind of mechanism could be used in terms of the right to produce a child. I am not speaking now of how these value judgements are made or of what the values are, but in terms simply of the mechanisms by which they could be applied. As a matter of fact, horrifying as it may be that there be somebody who plays god on this issue, I would find it less reprehensible than permitting widespread procreation and the bringing forth of new individuals into environments that do not want them. The evils of not doing anything are perhaps greater than the possible inequities involved in trying to do something salutary about it.

F. CLARKE FRASER: People are making uninformed decisions that act dysgenically. Perhaps it would be a good idea to think about how people could learn to make informed decisions that would act eugenically. That is all I am trying to say.

PHILIP HANDLER: Dr Mead told us a while ago that we are an elite group desiring to establish ourselves as such.

F. CLARKE FRASER: I am not suggesting that the decision should be made within the confines of this room.
    My third point is that there seems to be rather great emphasis in our talk on the possibility of regulating science because of fear of what may happen. Perhaps there should be some talk about learning how to regulate society. We have to learn how to handle the things that science is doing and the things that lead from this. But we will get nowhere by trying to stop the scientists. We have to

figure out how the social scientists, the economists and politicians are going to handle these problems.

SALVADOR E. LURIA: For the record I should like to point out that there is a very great difference between the situation of adoption that Dr Kety mentioned and the situation of selective breeding. In one case you have a baby and the baby is there, and what you are trying to do is to provide for her or him the optimal circumstances that we wish we had the machinery to provide for everybody in society. The other situation is that, in an imperfect society, for anybody to take upon himself to decide which group is preferable or which character is preferable is exactly the kind of decision we ought to strive very hard to avoid, to avoid the need for doing so.

SEYMOUR S. KETY: Dr Luria, would you object to a court of law ruling that a family which was guilty of child battering did not have the right to produce more children?

SALVADOR E. LURIA: I would not say that I object. First of all, I would like to ask a few more questions about the court of law; whether it is in the Southern States of the United States, whether the family is black or white, and so on.

PHILIP HANDLER: The problem he presents us with is just as white as black, and it occurs in Boston, Massachusetts, just as much as in Atlanta, Georgia. You have ducked the question.

SALVADOR E. LURIA: No, I say that there are sociological elements to consider. So I would not like to have a court do that. The law in California which said that a woman who had had more than two children out of wedlock would have to be sterilized was a violation of fundamental human rights, or what I consider fundamental human rights. Certainly, there is no such thing as a fundamental human right in philosophical or in biological terms, but I really think that we are on very dangerous ground. We ought to be grateful to Dr Fraser for having brought us to this ground.

ERNEST BOESIGER: Plusieurs des rapporteurs ont parlé de la non-continuation de la sélection naturelle dans notre espèce et, par voie de conséquence, de l'arrêt de l'évolution biologique dans notre espèce. J'aimerais d'abord faire une remarque sur un point souvent discuté: il ne sera jamais possible d'empêcher la recherche de continuer. On peut la freiner en coupant les crédits, mais pas l'empêcher. Or ici, ce que nous pouvons et devons faire pour éviter les dangers, réels et grands, annoncés par plusieurs des rapporteurs, c'est de pousser les recherches beaucoup plus loin, notamment dans un domaine dont on n'a pas parlé jusqu'à présent et qui me semble très important: l'étude des structures génétiques de la population humaine et des mécanismes qui peuvent être responsables de cette dynamique des populations.

Revenons-en à la sélection naturelle: il est évident qu'elle continue à agir dans notre espèce, et ceci puissamment. Il est certain que la sélection naturelle a diminué quand il s'agit de techniques médicales qui permettent de maintenir en vie les porteurs de gènes délétères qui, autrefois, n'auraient pas survécu. Mais cela ne signifie pas que la sélection naturelle n'existe plus, car pour qu'elle cesse d'agir sur l'espèce humaine, comme sur toutes les autres espèces animales et végétales, il faudrait que la survie jusqu'à la fin de l'âge de la reproduction soit la même et que le taux de reproduction soit identique. Or, ce dernier – tout comme l'ensemble des pools de gènes – varie considérablement d'un pays à l'autre. Ces différences signifient que nous assistons à une modification importante, donc à une évolution de l'espèce humaine sous cette pression de sélection naturelle. C'est pourquoi nous n'avons pas encore réussi à réduire celle-ci. On dit souvent qu'il y a dans l'espèce humaine une mortalité prénatale par avortement spontané naturel, qui est estimée à environ 17%. Si on ajoute un faible pourcentage pour la part qui passe inaperçue, parce que la femme elle-même ne s'en aperçoit pas, c'est-à-dire une mortalité prénatale très précoce, on arrive à environ 20% de mortalité prénatale. C'est un chiffre qui signifie qu'il y a là une pression sélective très importante. Donc, il est certain que la sélection naturelle continue dans notre espèce.

Par ailleurs, les craintes qui ont été exprimées sont importantes. Il est certain que par tous les moyens puissants dont la technique dispose actuellement, c'est-à-dire par toutes sortes de produits pharmaceutiques qui sont mutagènes, par les drogues, par les radiations, dont le taux augmente, nous élevons rapidement le taux de mutation dans les populations naturelles de notre espèce. Bien sûr, nous savons qu'il y a de très nombreux gènes délétères dans notre espèce qui ne représentent aucun danger, car beaucoup d'entre eux se trouvent en situation d'hétérosis équilibrée et peuvent avoir des avantages. Il est d'ailleurs impossible de dire, dans l'absolu, qu'un gène est bon ou mauvais. Tout gène peut être bon ou mauvais dans une situation génétique ou dans un milieu donné. Prenez par exemple des gènes létaux, comme ceux de la thalassémie. Ils ont un avantage sélectif, bien qu'il s'agisse là de gènes létaux, donc hautement nocifs, quand il y a infestation de paludisme. Mais il n'y a pas de tri possible entre bons et mauvais gènes, ce qui rend d'emblée très dangereux tout projet d'eugénisme, du moins tel qu'il a été prévu de façon extrême, par exemple par Huxley et Muller qui, eux, préconisent un meilleur génotype. Il n'y a pas de meilleur génotype, comme il n'y a pas de bons et de mauvais gènes. L'espèce humaine, comme toutes les autres espèces, à des degrés divers, il est vrai, a besoin d'une très grande quantité de génotypes différents. De ce fait, les projets eugéniques qui voudraient uniformiser l'espèce humaine sont extrêmement dangereux. Mais la réponse à de tels dangers n'est pas de dire: «Il ne faut donc pas faire de recherches dans ce domaine», car il n'est pas possible d'arrêter la recherche. La réponse est: «Il faudrait que nous en sachions un peu plus que ce que nous savons – soit presque rien – sur la structure génétique des populations humaines et la dynamique des populations humaines.»

JOSHUA LEDERBERG: I agree with virtually all that was said here. Evolution is of course continuing in man. It will come to a stop only when there is a zero variance of reproduction; we are very far from such a situation at the present time. It is obvious, social factors play a much larger role in the present differentials in evolution than do the medical ones. Contemplate, for example, that the Negro component of the United States population has varied from 19% in 1800 to 9.7% in 1930, and then 11.2% in 1970. This is a rapid evolution of the gene pool under the influence of differential migration, as well as reproduction (natural selection). The extent of diffusion of racial genotypes is even more susceptible to social factors; we have however little quantitative information on this point.

We can see the same thing in a global context. If some parts of the world are undergoing a rapid population explosion and others hardly at all, this is a very rapid evolutionary change. We anticipate a greater uniformity of sampling from this total gene pool. But the greater mixing of previously isolated groups is by far the most important alteration in the evolutionary process.

A point that I must put simply as a question is the rate at which the environmental factors influence the accumulation of mutations. We do not know the answer. Radiation probably accounts for 10% – more or less – of the spontaneous mutation rate. Other environmental factors like chemicals, like drugs, like food additives and so forth may be negligible or may be immensely more important. My own speculative calculation is that they increase the mutation rate by factors of two to five; unfortunately our reliable information on this question is very limited.

PHILIP HANDLER: Is there reason to believe that the rate of spontaneous mutation in man has changed in the last century?

JOSHUA LEDERBERG: We have no way of knowing this. My views on the general eugenic questions are on the record and I won't pursue them here.

PHILIP HANDLER: I would like to support something that Dr Lederberg just said which offers a form of direct answer to what Dr Boesiger has been telling us. Again I must use the case of the United States for which I happen to know some relevant numbers. When the population of the United States was 100 millions, our agricultural labor force was just about 14 millions. But, when the population had grown to 200 millions, that agricultural labor force had declined to 4 millions rather than also doubling to 28 millions. That means there are now about 20 million individuals available to the labor force but no longer working on farms in relatively simple activities. Instead, they are living in urban settings, in a quite different social structure, indeed a violently different social structure.

Worse still, there are almost no positions available for this pool of unskilled labor and only a small fraction have proved to be easily educable to more highly skilled positions. Hence our dreadful ghettos and some part of our unemployment problem.

FRANZ BÖCKLE: Dr. von Weizsäcker und Frau Dr. Mead fordern etwas wie ein ökologisches System der Kommunikation zwischen den verschiedenen interessierten Wissenschaften, insbesondere zwischen den Geistes- und den empirischen Wissenschaften – wenn man diese Unterscheidung überhaupt hier machen darf. Ein solches Kommunikationsystem sollte dazu dienen, die Probleme zwischen Wissen und Förderung dieses Wissens einerseits und der Technologie andererseits in ein besseres Verhältnis zu bringen. Die Unterscheidung von Dr. Kety zwischen Informationsträger und der Information selbst scheint mir für unsere weiteren Überlegungen von größter Bedeutung. Eine solche Unterscheidung bietet grundsätzlich den Ansatz für eine unterschiedliche Art der Steuerung. Bei dieser engen Verbindung zwischen dem Informationsträgersystem und der Information wird einerseits eine Steuerung dieses Systems und über dieses System von größter Bedeutung sein. Andererseits wird auch eine Steuerung der Information notwendig sein. Dr. Kety deutete an, daß der Presse größere Machtmittel zur Verfügung stehen als dem Wissenschaftler.

Wir dürfen nun aber nicht etwa der Meinung verfallen, wie sie hier einige Male angeklungen ist, daß die Information durch eine rein äußere Steuerung gelenkt werden dürfte, also mit dem Hilfsmittel des Verbotes oder der Gesetzgebung. Vielmehr werden wir darauf hinpeilen müssen, die verschiedenen Möglichkeiten der Steuerung mit der Bewußtseinsbildung immer breiterer Schichten zu verbinden; einer Bewußtseinsbildung, die das Subjekt selbst anspricht und die es ihm ermöglicht, immer mehr in die Entscheidungsprozesse einzugreifen. Das lag doch, wenn ich recht verstanden habe, Dr. von Weizsäcker, auch Ihrer Frage zugrunde, ob die Steuerung schon bei der Wissenschaft anfangen sollte oder ob wir kraß zwischen Wissen und Technologie unterscheiden und die Steuerung erst bei der Technologie beginnen dürfen.

KENNETH J. ARROW: I wish to set forth some axiological schemes which are common enough property of economists and which bear on some distinctions made here. There has been much reference today to the population explosion as one of the great evil consequences of scientific progress. This opinion seems to have aroused the least dissension of any expressed here. There are however some different opinions as to the measures that might be taken.

Obviously, if we have a model in which population is expanding in an exponential or sometimes even superexponential rate and an earth of finite size, there is at some point going to be a conflict, and there can be no question that in a very, very long-run equilibrium sense you have to achieve zero population growth. I don't mean to dispute that point, nor do I want to dispute the argument that even in shorter periods population growth may be a deleterious factor. But I want to ask, deleterious how and to whom, to what, and I want to use these questions to illustrate the point I am making.

It is useful to distinguish between values, opportunities and behavior. These have been run together in some of the discussions here. I agree that values are in some sense relatively permanent characteristics. What does change over time are the opportunities for exercising those values. The behavior of society or the individual in society at any moment of time is really the interaction between the values and the opportunities. I think of values as being the rules by which choice of behavior is made. The opportunities are the set of alternatives of choices available at the individual or the social level. Examples of behavior are how many children you have, how people work, how they distribute their time, what is produced. The choice among various alternatives is made in such a way as to achieve as high a level as possible on the value scale of the individuals in society. Interpreting Dr Luria's remarks on adaptive behavior one could say that as the opportunities change, even with a fixed set of values, the behavior will change. I don't want to push this to the limit. In some sense values at any level do change over time, but they change relatively slowly.

The values are the point of view of the chooser, the 'we', whoever 'we' are, whether 'we' is the state, the public or the scientific community. However we make our choices we must think in terms of a definite set of values. I prefer therefore to think that the changes that have taken place have occurred mainly in the opportunities available to us.

Take the example of family size. From the point of view of the individual, obviously it has been much changed by developments in contraception techniques. These change the opportunities open to the parents to vary the size of family. A slightly more subtle example is the decreased mortality of children. This changes the opportunities in a different sense. Assuming the values of the family are geared to something like completed family size rather than to simply having children as such, then clearly the decreased mortality of children does mean that, other things being equal, there will be a tendency to reduce the number of births. We have a feedback mechanism which has, of course, been much discussed.

Values are primarily inherent in the individuals. These cherish values of desiring children. They cherish economic values such as food, housing, space and the like for the children as well as for themselves. I don't think the family is quite dead as a desirable objective of human society, and I don't see why the value for having children should not be included in the scale of values important to individuals. And since society is nothing but individuals this value is inherent in social values. Like Dr Luria, I was disturbed by some of the suggestions and the language used in dealing with who should have children and how the numbers should be decided, which parents should have them and the like. They reflect to my mind a certain lack of care about the values of individuals.

When I say social values rather than individual values I of course include the idea that this means not only a respect of one's own values but a respect for

Kenneth J. Arrow: '...I was disturbed by some of the suggestions and the language used in dealing with who should have children and how the numbers should be decided, which parent should have them and the like. They reflect to my mind a certain lack of care about the values of individuals.'

the values of others. There is to be, in Kantian language, a symmetry of individuals, a respect for the other people as ends rather than means. How do you achieve this? It is one thing to establish a value scheme in which, when we evaluate alternatives, we turn to individual values. It is another thing to establish a social choice mechanism by which these individual values are given a play. The natural way is to let the individual make the choices as well as determine the values.

To give an example, the family size in this view would be an individually chosen proposition. This is subject to several clarifications. One is that the individual should be as fully informed as possible of the consequences of his actions and of the technologies available to achieve his ambitions. In other words the question of, say, education on contraceptives has by now gone over the hill of public acceptance though it may not be followed. Knowledge on family planning methods should in any case be disseminated as much as possible as it increases the scope of individual choice.

Individual choice is also subject to a clarification concerning respect for values of others. The achievement of my values may be at the expense of somebody else's. This is presumably at the logical root of the idea that there is a population problem at all. The only reason is that presumably other people are going to be hurt by having a larger population. If I choose to have children and am not hurting anybody else what difference does it make? It might worry one group, the children themselves. Supposing I am the only family on an island and choose to have 25 children who then cannot be supported on that island, I have perhaps overindulged in my responsibility. But this is, in a sense, part of my individual choice and presumably an individual responsibility to the extent that I care for the welfare of the children. If we think of food supply, now recognized not to be the crucial factor as Malthus claimed, then the answer is twofold: First, the cost of acquiring that food is going to be borne by the parents first and by the children themselves later on, and a parent who has any responsibility to his own children as part of his family already accounts for this in his decision to have or not to have children. Secondly, of course, almost every mouth is accompanied by a pair of hands so that the net loss is not quite what it is sometimes made out to be. On the contrary, throughout the world, and increasingly so, as modern methods of agricultural technology are adopted, this has ceased to be the basic issue. Individuals, on the whole, have the ability to produce more than is the minimum necessary for their upkeep.

It is true that society is very complex, and we do not easily have ways of making sure that individuals bear all the costs of their actions. By costs I mean deprivation of other people's values. In the case of ordinary commodities, i.e. things that you can appropriate and that if I have, you don't have, we have worked out a price system which, while far from perfect, nevertheless offers a certain degree of calculus useful in these contexts. But there are many aspects of social intercourse for which the price system is not a technically possible regulator. Education affords an interesting example. Although we could exclude children from education and thereby have a price system, we tend to regard education, for reasons we need not examine, as a social responsibility. Therefore, parents are not required to bear the entire costs of their own children's education. They may bear it in the form of taxes, but these are not specifically related to their children's education.

To this extent my argument about individual choice has to be modified. But if one keeps it in mind, a certain amount of clarification can be achieved as to where society has to step in. I repeat: providing the costs to other people of your behavior, whether it be genetic intervention, whether it be sheer number of children, are in fact borne by you, then the only problem is one of information or counselling. On the other hand, to the extent that there are costs of which society does not readily bear the burden, there is ground for social control.

However, there is a paradox here. The better the social externalities (to use the term that economists use; pollution is a classic example for what I mean) are recognized, the larger the bureaucratic apparatus apparently that is going to be needed to do the recognizing. We have various devices for trying to minimize the size of the state apparatus, e. g. the use of taxes instead of regulations; these have minimized the issue but have not completely avoided it. It seems hard to see a way by which you can enlarge the role of the state, whether it be a scientifically or democratically dominated state, without impairing to some extent individual freedom. It is an unavoidable paradox like other things in life, and it is one that has to be recognized.

Let me conclude with one other somewhat paradoxical remark. If we take respect for individual values we are presumably accepting in social matters some kind of democratic egalitarian society and a democratic egalitarian determination of the forms of social control. I certainly agree with those who repudiate the elite of scientists as I do the elite of economists in economic policy (of course our standing is not so high and we are not nearly so much of a problem). But it does happen to be a rather peculiar fact that many of the measures that have been advocated and that have been mentioned here favorably as progressive steps are definitely the results of an elite determination which has impressed itself upon the organs of society and the state against public opinion. A very conspicuous example of this is abortion. Repeated polls have shown that the majority of the population of the United States, 60–70%, are strongly opposed to more liberalized abortion laws, particularly among the lower classes. In fact it seems to be only upper class men, for some reason or other, who are in favor, and even they tend to be something like fifty-fifty on this issue. It is an elite group which has put forth the liberalization of the abortion laws in places like New York State. In many respects we have a contradiction, also seen in the environmental field, between an elite determination of values, which I do believe to be superior, and another ideal, which I think most people here cherish strongly, that of the democratic co-participation of all members of society.

All the sessions of the Symposium were transmitted by short-circuit television to several other rooms in order to allow the interested members of the Roche staff to follow the discussions.

During the Symposium, informal buffet lunches were offered in the Roche-Personalhaus. Below: Active participants, guests, representatives of the press joined members of the Roche staff and continued the discussions. Above: Monsieur et Madame Pichot helped themselves at the buffet.

Session II

Impact of Biomedical Progress on Society
and the Individual

Introduction

René König: Ich habe mich seit 1958 sehr viel sowohl mit der Soziologie des medizinischen Systems als auch mit der Soziologie in der Medizin beschäftigt. Die Soziologie des medizinischen Systems befaßt sich zum Beispiel mit dem Problem der Kommunikation zwischen Arzt und Patient, die nicht immer ganz einfach zu realisieren ist, oder mit dem Problem Droge als Arzt versus Arzt als Droge. Die Soziologie des Medizinberufs selber hat sich stark verändert. Er ist heute nicht mehr ein einheitlicher Beruf, wie es noch vor ungefähr dreißig Jahren der Fall war. Neben den zentralen medizinischen Beruf des Arztes ist eine Fülle von paramedizinischen Berufen getreten, die eine ganz neue Situation schaffen.

Ich war heute morgen aufrichtig überrascht, zu hören, wie unsere medizinischen und naturwissenschaftlichen Kollegen von sozialen Tatbeständen sprachen. Noch vor dreißig Jahren hätte jeder Naturwissenschaftler sich seine eigene Soziologie, seine Privatsoziologie, zurechtgemacht. Das wäre etwa so, als wollte ich mir meine eigene Mikrobiologie zurechtmachen. Heute verwenden unsere naturwissenschaftlichen Kollegen weitgehend eine Sprache, die wir Soziologen verstehen. Vielleicht gibt es auch eine Möglichkeit, Wissenschaften in popularisierender Weise allen zugänglich zu machen. Ich bin kein Feind der Populärliteratur, wenn sie von seriösen Wissenschaftlern gemacht wird.

Jetzt zur Sache. Der Titel unseres Symposiums heißt «The Challenge of Life – Biomedical Progress and Human Values». Er zerfällt eindeutig in zwei Teile: «Biomedical Progress» und «Human Values». Nun, es werden mehrere Redner die Probleme aufzeigen, die tatsächlich als Folge des biomedizinischen Fortschritts entstanden sind. Aber man kann den Titel auch umkehren. Dr. Moltmann hat in seinem Bericht auf die umgekehrte Möglichkeit hingewiesen, das heißt die «Human Values» an die erste Stelle zu setzen und anzufangen mit menschlichen und sozialen Motivationen für die biomedizinische Forschung. Über den Einfluß des Fortschritts der Naturwissenschaften auf die Gesellschaft zu reden, ist fast eine Banalität geworden. Es ist viel wichtiger zu wissen, was aus den Menschen im Laufe dieser Entwicklung wird.

Als es heute morgen um die Frage ging, Forschung um jeden Preis oder Zu-

René König: «Das Herantragen einer Moral von außen ist allzu oft nur der gelungene oder auch mißlungene Versuch der totalen Knebelung der Forschung.»

rückschneiden der Forschung, sagte Dr. Handler sehr richtig, jede Behinderung der Forschung komme den nationalsozialistischen Verbrennungen von Büchern gleich. An diesem Satz ist nichts zu rütteln. Aber man muß andererseits auch zugeben, daß jeder Versuch, die menschliche Dimension auszuschalten, ebenso unmöglich ist, das heißt, wir müssen uns hier auf eine neue Moral einigen. Es kann sich natürlich nicht darum handeln, jetzt von außen her eine Moral an diese Probleme heranzubringen, sondern diese Moral muß als eine professionelle Moral entwickelt werden. Das Herantragen einer Moral von außen ist allzu oft nur der gelungene oder auch mißlungene Versuch der totalen Knebelung der Forschung. Da sind diejenigen, die am liebsten alle Forschung sofort aufhören lassen möchten. Aber wenn wir vom Professionellen ausgehen, etwa im Sinne des medizinischen Eides, dann wissen wir sehr wohl, daß es die Möglichkeit gibt, zu fragen, wozu etwas gut ist. Dr. Sauvy hat einmal vor Jahren den Satz geprägt: «Nous vivons toujours plus longtemps et plus mal.» Das war eine klare Bewertung. Wir werden immer älter und dabei immer seniler. Ist es befriedigend, 95 Jahre alt zu sein und total «gaga»? Die Biomedizin kann diese Frage nicht übergehen; sie muß sich für medizinische Artistik oder für ein menschliches Maß entscheiden. Es genügt nicht, einen Menschen um jeden Preis am Leben zu erhalten. Das kann eine sinnlose Quälerei sein. Es kommt vielmehr darauf an, ihn unter erträglichen Verhältnissen am Leben zu erhalten.

Weiter bleibt bei der ganzen Problematik des biomedizinischen Fortschritts die Frage der Selektion. Dr. Sauvy hat in seinem Bericht geschrieben «le problème de la contre-sélection reste posé». Schaffen wir wirklich eine Auslese, indem wir Leben unter allen Umständen bewahren? Oder schaffen wir damit neue Schwierigkeiten, denen wir im Augenblick vielleicht noch gar nicht gewachsen sind?

Ich möchte Ihnen aus der Sicht des Soziologen sagen, warum diese Probleme heute so wichtig sind. Unser ganzes Arbeitssystem hat sich geändert. Das alte Industriesystem war für die Masse der Arbeitenden auf physische Tätigkeit ausgerichtet. Menschen, die physische Arbeit leisten, sind heute in der Industrie kaum mehr vorhanden, da mit den neuen Steuerungstechniken eine völlig neue Arbeitsweise eintrat, die diese Arbeit äußerlich viel angenehmer macht. Sie besteht im Beobachten, Entscheiden und verlangt Präzision und Sinn für Zusammenwirken im Betrieb, aber sie hat die unerwartete Folge, einen dauernden Streß auf die Arbeitenden auszuüben, den sie früher nicht kannten. Die frühere Belastung war physischer Natur, dementsprechend war die frühere Krankheit Alkoholismus. Heute haben wir mit einem psychischen Streß zu rechnen, der nach anderen Heilmitteln ruft. Hier beginnen die Probleme aufzutreten, die mit den psychotropen Drogen gegeben sind.

Dr. Mead wird ein Problem hervorheben, das mit der Lebensform des Menschen zusammenhängt. Es ist die durch die erhöhten Ausbildungsanforderungen verlängerte Abhängigkeitszeit der jungen Menschen. Sie schafft ein Gefühl der ungenügenden Integration in die heutige Gesellschaft, ein Gefühl der Fremdheit, ein Gefühl der Distanzierung, das ebenfalls wieder eine ständige Bereitschaft erzeugt, zu psychotropen Drogen zu greifen. Das sind nicht mehr individuelle Reaktionen, sondern Massenreaktionen von Menschen, die der gleichen Situation gegenüberstehen.

Presentation of topics

ALFRED SAUVY: Je ne veux pas reprendre le texte qui vous a été distribué. Il ne fait d'ailleurs que rassembler des constatations assez banales. On disait, il y a deux jours, que le système monétaire a plus changé depuis le début du siècle que depuis 2000 ans. Il en est de même, et bien plus, des conditions de multiplication de la vie humaine. Il s'est passé en deux siècles beaucoup plus de changements qu'en 200000 ans avant, ou même davantage. Le mécanisme physiologique de la reproduction est resté le même, mais l'homme intervient avec des efficacités diverses. Pendant des centaines de milliers d'années, l'homme a eu une pierre sur la tête, et sa longueur de vie a été limitée à 25 ou 30 ans. La démographie préhistorique qui commence nous renseigne assez bien là-dessus. Aujourd'hui, il y a une véritable explosion, puisque le mot est à la mode. La longueur de la vie humaine a plus que doublé en deux siècles. La première conséquence, c'est qu'il faudrait que la population en ait conscience. Ces changements sont-ils connus de l'humanité dans son ensemble? Malheureusement, la population ne connaît pas la population. Il n'appartient pas aux scientifiques, à mon avis, d'exercer des choix, mais il leur appartient d'éclairer les choix qui seront pris.

Nous assistons à un accès des masses à la vie politique. Partis d'une société verticale, nous voudrions arriver à une société horizontale. Mais cela suppose une diffusion considérable des connaissances. Or, les faits les plus patents ne sont pas toujours connus, même de l'élite culturelle. Il y a des domaines où la science est respectée, et d'autres où elle est ignorée, donc maltraitée. Il en résulte, dans tout notre système social, des déformations, un écartèlement, qui ne peut que s'accentuer avec des risques d'explosion ou d'ensevelissement. Nous avons tous vu la liberté éclairant le monde, mais nous ressemblons plutôt au tableau des aveugles de Bruegel, qui, bien enchaînés, se jettent dans le précipice*.

Je prends un exemple tout à fait contemporain, du moins dans mon pays. Il est beaucoup question de retraites de vieillesse, problème très important. Et cependant, la plupart des gens qui en parlent, non seulement ne connaissent pas les tables de survie, mais ne connaissent même pas leur existence. On peut bien penser que les décisions prises ne seront ni conformes aux intérêts de la population, ni même aux objectifs de ceux qui les prendront. Or, il est inconcevable d'avoir une dictature de la culture. Voilà par conséquent une question parmi bien d'autres.

Sur l'évolution future de la vie humaine et la longévité, il y a de grandes divergences de vues. Les Soviétiques voient très volontiers l'homme vivre plus tard à 120, 130 ans ou davantage. Il y a cette semaine en Suisse un congrès où des hommes discutent des possibilités de prolonger la vie humaine de dix ou quinze ans. D'autres sont beaucoup moins optimistes sur ce point, et on peut constater que la mortalité sénile, je veux dire à partir de 55 ans, remonte en divers pays depuis une quinzaine d'années. Le docteur Crick, Prix Nobel de médecine, a proposé de fixer l'âge légal de la mort à 80 ans. Un institut de recherche contre le cancer en France me disait ces jours-ci qu'il ne rencontrait qu'incompréhension, même en dehors des questions financières. C'est un problème propre aux pays développés. De tout temps, la société a cherché à éliminer les indésirables, et les moyens qu'elle a employés ont été de plus en plus subtils. Nous voudrions les éliminer, sans en avoir conscience, en toute irresponsabilité. On peut assimiler cette élimination, que beaucoup souhaitent sans le dire, à une sorte de défense de l'organisme.

Quant aux pays en développement, dont la croissance est très rapide, où le progrès médical a largement précédé le progrès économique, le problème est assez bien connu dans les chiffres; il l'est beaucoup moins dans les possibilités de changement. L'attitude de la Chine est significative, puisqu'elle s'est fixé comme objectif la famille de deux ou trois enfants, ce qui était tout à fait contraire à la doctrine marxiste jusqu'à ces dernières années. Mais enfin, quand on parle, comme ce matin, d'autoriser ou d'interdire d'avoir des enfants, je pense que nous n'avons pas la possibilité, nous Blancs, de commander à des nations d'autres pays, et je dois répondre: «Allez voir les hommes de l'Inde ou du Pakistan et demandez-leur si la chose est possible. Vous verrez ce qu'il vous répondront.» En matière de population, il y a toujours eu, dans l'humanité et en dehors de tout calcul, deux réactions affectives, deux angoisses: la peur du vide, du néant, de la dépopulation, du désert, et la peur de la faim, sur le *Radeau de la Méduse***.

*Ce tableau de Bruegel le Vieux illustre le proverbe latin: *Si caecus caecum ducit, ambo in foveam cadunt.* (Si un aveugle conduit un aveugle, tous deux tombent dans le fossé).

**Allusion au tableau peint en 1819 (musée du Louvre) par Théodore Géricault (1791–1824) après le naufrage de la frégate *Méduse* survenu en 1816. Le radeau sur lequel s'étaient entassés 150 rescapés fut le théâtre des scènes épouvantables causées par la famine et la soif.

Alfred Sauvy: «En matière de population, il y a toujours eu, dans l'humanité et en dehors de tout calcul, deux réactions affectives, deux angoisses: la peur du vide, du néant, de la dépopulation, du désert, et la peur de la faim, sur le *Radeau de la Méduse*.»

Toutes les populations du monde se trouvent devant le dilemme, croître en nombre ou vieillir. C'est une simple constatation arithmétique. Ce n'est pas forcément un choix entre deux catastrophes, mais c'est un choix qui existe et qui est ignoré, même dans les pays développés, parce que l'on n'aime pas les dilemmes. Dans les pays en développement le problème est moins actuel, mais il sera beaucoup plus poussé. Le nombre des vieux dans ces pays va, en effet, augmenter environ de un à sept en un demi-siècle. Dès lors, ou bien toute la population suit à ce rythme ou bien elle ne suit pas à ce rythme et il y aura vieillissement important. Ce qui n'est pas moins sûr, c'est que les populations, en particulier peu développées, ont en elles un potentiel d'accroissement, une sorte de vitesse acquise. Pas plus qu'on ne peut arrêter une voiture brusquement sans causer des catastrophes, on ne peut arrêter une population. Et il est extraordinaire qu'une théorie aussi simpliste que le *zero growth rate*, lancée il y a deux ans, ignore les éléments les plus frustes de l'arithmétique démographique. L'arrêt d'une population est impossible, mais si par hasard on y arrivait, si on interdisait effectivement aux gens d'avoir des enfants, il se produirait des perturbations dans la population par âge qui dureraient un siècle ou deux. Au début, les gouvernements devraient recommander aux familles, pendant une ou deux générations, de n'avoir qu'un seul enfant. Ensuite, pendant encore une ou deux générations, les gouvernements annonceraient: «Maintenant il faut avoir quatre enfants.» Ce sont des puérilités.

Ce que nous constatons récemment, c'est le recul du stérilet intra-utérin qui semblait être le moyen le plus adapté aux populations très pauvres et ignorantes. Il recule, notamment, dans l'Inde, chaque année. Et nous constatons aussi une stagnation des stérilisants hormonaux, sur lesquels on fondait beaucoup d'espoirs il y a dix ans et même il y a cinq ans. Le progrès est très lent, peut-être parce que l'homme ou les organismes de contrôle ont peur de livrer à l'humanité des produits qui entraîneraient des conséquences inattendues. On peut poser la question: «Le vieillissement d'une population est-il un mal? Est-ce un mal que d'avoir 25 % de vieux, de sexagénaires?» Le moins qu'on puisse dire est que cela pose des problèmes socio-politiques. Il faudra que les sociétés s'habituent à la vieillesse. Il y aura une nécessité de pleine conscience. Après avoir beaucoup réfléchi sur la révolte des jeunes, que j'avais d'ailleurs annoncée il y a douze ans, je persiste à penser qu'une des causes les plus profondes est une réaction contre le vieillissement. L'âge de l'orphelin a augmenté de 22 ans depuis la baisse de la mortalité, et sur les épaules de la génération jeune, il y a une génération de plus. Bref, dès que le démographe pur sort de ces problèmes de comptabilité d'hommes, il débouche dans un immense domaine complexe, chargé de périls, d'angoisses et de doutes. Dans certains cas, il est épouvanté et il referme les fenêtres, pour revenir à sa chère démographie pure. Dans d'autres, il essaie de poursuivre et tout au moins de transmettre les connaissances qu'il a acquises. Je conclus donc à nouveau sur la nécessité d'une intense diffusion. La société telle que nous la concevons n'est pas démocratique; elle ne le sera que lorsqu'elle se connaîtra elle-même. Pour le moment, elle découvre des quantités de choses, mais l'ensemble de la population ne les connaît pas. Et elle est prête à faire prendre ou à suggérer des mesures de suicide. L'instrument existe cependant, l'instrument de diffusion nous l'avons, c'est la télévision. Il faudrait arriver à l'employer sans agression envers le public tout en lui donnant du spectacle, parce qu'il en veut, la science s'y glissant avec une certaine discrétion. C'est toute une technique à créer. Je la considère comme absolument vitale au sens le plus strict du mot. Voilà quelques réflexions, non certes désabusées, mais sans béatitude.

PIERRE PICHOT: Le problème des rapports entre la disponibilité des drogues psychotropes et l'attitude de la société envers les troubles du comportement peut être schématiquement posé sur deux plans.

La biochimie et la pharmacologie créent à un rythme rapide des drogues psychotropes dans le but de traiter les troubles du comportement. Leur emploi, en médecine, a entraîné des modifications considérables de la pratique médicale, de l'attitude des médecins envers certains problèmes théoriques de la médecine et de l'attitude du public envers la maladie mentale.

Mais, à côté de ce qu'on peut appeler le versant thérapeutique licite, la disponibilité des drogues psychotropes a entraîné une augmentation de leur consommation à des fins dont la nature thérapeutique peut être contestée, ou bien qui sont absolument étrangères aux applications médicales. La limite est difficile à fixer, car aussi bien on passe insensiblement de la prescription médicale d'une drogue tranquillisante chez un malade présentant une anxiété pathologique, à l'auto-administration incontrôlée de ce même tranquillisant afin de supprimer un état psychologique déplaisant résultant d'un conflit normal de l'existence, et finalement à l'abus entraînant pharmacodépendance et troubles du comportement nuisibles à l'individu et à la société. Bien que le problème soit très antérieur à l'expansion psychopharmacologique et que certaines des drogues soulevant les controverses les plus actuelles sous l'angle sociologique, tel le haschich, soient des produits naturels, de connaissance et d'usage très anciens, les progrès biomédicaux lui ont donné une dimension nouvelle, et l'attitude de la société se trouve aujourd'hui dans une phase évolutive cruciale à leur égard.

En pratique, on rassemble sous le terme de drogues psychotropes des substances qui, par leur origine et par leur utilisation, peuvent être classées en trois catégories :

1⁰ Des substances découvertes en vue d'application médico-psychologiques, employées uniquement comme médicaments, sur prescription médicale, et ne donnant pas l'occasion d'abus : par exemple, ce que nous appelons les neuroleptiques ou les antidépressants.

2⁰ Des substances découvertes en vue d'application médicale, employées comme médicaments, mais également utilisées spontanément par certains sujets, à cause de leur action psychotrope, sans que le but en soit de lutter contre un état pathologique. Cette classe, très nombreuse, comprend aussi bien la morphine, l'héroïne, que certains anxiolytiques, les hypnotiques barbituriques, les amphétamines, etc.

3⁰ Des substances dont la valeur thérapeutique est actuellement considérée comme faible ou nulle et dont l'emploi est non médical. Il faut distinguer là trois sous-variétés :

a. Celles d'origine naturelle (habituellement végétale) dont la consommation est considérée comme normale depuis très longtemps dans une culture définie. De ce fait, elles ne sont généralement pas incluses parmi les « drogues », à tort d'ailleurs. L'exemple le plus typique dans notre culture occidentale est l'alcool ingéré sous forme de boissons alcoolisées.

b. Celles de même nature mais qui, provenant d'une culture où elles étaient « normales », sont introduites dans un milieu différent. Au XVIᵉ siècle c'était en Europe la situation du tabac. Le tabac était normal dans la culture indienne précolombienne ; il a été introduit en Europe et, finalement, est devenu, au cours des siècles, une drogue normale. Sans discuter ici des dangers éventuels que peut présenter son emploi, il est manifeste que sur le plan de la sociologie historique, le cannabis, c'est-à-dire le haschich, se trouve aujourd'hui, en Europe, dans la situation du tabac au XVIᵉ siècle. Ce qui ne veut pas dire que je recommande la vente officielle du haschich.

c. Celles nécessitant des manipulations chimiques pour leur extraction, voire entièrement synthétisées. La cocaïne, qui n'a pratiquement plus d'utilisation thérapeutique, constitue à cet égard un premier exemple. Un deuxième exemple est la lysergamide (LSD), qui est intéressante au point de vue de la science théorique, mais qui n'a pratiquement jamais eu d'application thérapeutique.

Ces trois catégories de drogues psychotropes posent des problèmes d'ordre différent. La première catégorie, celle des substances thérapeutiques qui ne donnent pas occasion d'abus et qui sont des drogues qui toutes concernent le traitement des anomalies mentales graves, c'est-à-dire des psychoses, de la schizophrénie, des dépressions, cette première catégorie lors de son emploi a entraîné des conséquences médicales que l'on peut ainsi schématiser.

Chez les malades qui sont hospitalisés, ces drogues diminuent notablement l'intensité des anomalies du comportement. Ensuite, elles ont, de ce fait, diminué en moyenne la durée d'hospitalisation. Et, enfin, le nombre de malades traités en milieu extra-hospitalier, soit entre les périodes d'hospitalisation, soit de manière permanente chez ceux auxquels la chimiothérapie permet le maintien d'un niveau adaptif convenable, a entraîné la modification des structures médicales, des structures de soins.

Au total, ceci a modifié l'attitude des psychiatres et celle du public et, par voie de conséquence, les mesures législatives. D'une manière générale, on assiste actuellement dans tous les pays de culture industrielle à une libéralisation progressive des dispositions qui tendent à rapprocher le statut légal du malade mental de celui du malade somatique. Alors que le nombre des malades traités augmente constamment, celui des malades internés, c'est-à-dire traités à l'hôpital avec privation de liberté, diminue, et ceci dans des proportions considérables. L'admission à l'hôpital psychiatrique n'apparaît plus comme une mort sociale, ce qu'elle était il y a peu dans la représentation populaire. L'augmentation du nombre des malades soignés contrastant avec la diminution des internements ne peut s'expliquer que si l'on admet que nombre de malades acceptent volontairement de se soumettre au traitement. L'image que le public se faisait des troubles majeurs du comportement, c'est-à-dire cette image d'affections incurables nécessitant la séquestration à vie, tend désormais à se rapprocher progressivement de celle que les gens ont de la maladie en général, soit d'un état éventuellement curable par un traitement médical.

A propos de la deuxième catégorie de drogues – celles qui engendrent la pharmacodépendance – il me paraît important de souligner que c'est essentiellement la nature des modifications du comportement provoquées par ces drogues qui conditionne l'attitude du public à leur égard. En effet, on a bien souvent fait remarquer que la tolérance extraordinaire de notre société vis-à-vis de l'alcool –

Pierre Pichot: «L'admission à l'hôpital psychiatrique n'apparaît plus comme une mort sociale, ce qu'elle était il y a peu dans la représentation populaire.»

bien que celui-ci soit à lui seul à l'origine de faits nocifs individuels et sociaux, physiques et psychiques plusieurs fois supérieurs à ceux de toutes les autres drogues réunies – tenait en partie au fait que la consommation de l'alcool produisait une augmentation de la sociabilité. On pourrait faire une remarque analogue à propos d'une série de drogues qui sont également très bien tolérées par la société. Ce sont les hypnotiques barbituriques qui, à l'heure actuelle, font l'objet d'une toxicomanie dont les proportions sont considérables. On a calculé que 371 000 kilos de barbituriques ont été fabriqués en 1960 aux Etats-Unis, ce qui donne, pour chaque citoyen de ce pays, une moyenne de 60 capsules de barbituriques par an, enfants, vieillards et femmes compris. Il y a donc une énorme toxicomanie mondiale aux barbituriques qui est parfaitement tolérée et qui, dans une certaine mesure, est même encouragée par la pratique des prescriptions médicales.

A l'opposé, notre société tend à avoir une attitude très hostile envers trois variétés de drogues: les dérivés de l'opium, le cannabis et les hallucinogènes, et enfin les amphétamines. La consommation des alcaloïdes de l'opium entraîne une désinsertion sociale rapide; celle des amphétamines à hautes doses favorise un comportement agressif et souvent criminel. Quant aux hallucinogènes, il est inutile de rappeler dans quelle mesure ceux qui en préconisent la consommation la justifient en tant que moyen de protester contre la culture actuelle et d'échapper à ses contraintes. Ainsi d'une manière générale, il semble bien que la société tende à développer des attitudes hostiles envers les drogues qu'elle perçoit comme favorisant des comportements qu'elle juge asociaux ou antisociaux, c'est-à-dire contraires à son système de valeurs et que, par contre, elle soit relativement tolérante pour des drogues peut-être même plus dangereuses, mais qui entraînent des modifications qui vont dans le sens de son système de valeurs, par exemple la sociabilité pour l'alcool. Ainsi la disponibilité des drogues psychotropes entraîne une double modification des attitudes. Elle tend à libéraliser celles qui étaient jusqu'ici relativement coercitives, en ce qui concerne les troubles psychotiques du comportement, dans la mesure où ceux-ci, du fait de leur accessibilité à la chimiothérapie, se rapprochent du modèle médical général. Elle tend au contraire à imposer des mesures de contrainte contre les sujets consommant des drogues psychotropes et surtout dans la mesure où celles-ci favorisent des comportements en contradiction avec les modèles culturels. L'évolution actuelle de la législation dans la plupart des pays, aussi bien que l'attitude de la presse et du public, en témoignent.

Enfin, je voudrais insister sur une catégorie de drogues qui posent au maximum le problème des rapports entre le progrès biomédical et celui des valeurs humaines, sujet de notre réunion. Il s'agit de drogues telles que les hypnotiques et les tranquillisants surtout, c'est-à-dire de drogues pour lesquelles les limites d'une prescription légitime et d'une administration abusive sont difficiles à tracer. Ce matin, le Dr Kety a, avec beaucoup d'humour, rappelé que l'anxiété normale améliore la qualité de la performance de celui qui l'éprouve. Dans le même ordre d'idées, je voudrais terminer cet exposé en citant un passage d'un récent ouvrage très technique, publié en Belgique, sur les toxicomanies. L'auteur, que je cite, y condamne: «La propension caractéristique pour notre époque qu'ont les gens de vouloir immédiatement pallier leurs troubles physiques ou psychiques par une automédication impromptue, tellement ils sont devenus incapables de supporter un ennui ou des sensations désagréables et d'y remédier par des moyens peut-être moins radicaux, mais de toute façon moins dangereux, mais plus hygiéniques et plus naturels.» Cette citation de l'auteur, qui s'appelle Varenne, est caractéristique, car bien que provenant d'un médecin, elle fait appel à des notions qui appartiennent à la représentation populaire de la santé et de la maladie (par exemple la supériorité des procédés naturels sur les drogues) ou à des jugements portant sur des valeurs éthiques, par exemple la valeur morale de la résistance à la souffrance. C'est là un domaine où, en tant que psychiatre, je n'ose pas trop m'engager. Je voudrais simplement dire que la question fondamentale de l'extension de l'emploi des drogues psychotropes à des états qui ne diffèrent pas qualitativement du comportement normal pose un problème très difficile de philosophie de la médecine, qui est celui des limites de la santé et de la maladie. C'est en définitive la réponse que la société donnera à cette question qui déterminera, pour cette catégorie de drogues psychotropes, l'orientation du progrès biomédical.

MARGARET MEAD: I think it is necessary to emphasize that the anthropological approach permits us first to study a very complex whole in a great many of its aspects taking into account the interrelationships between all the parts of small communities tightly locked into their physical environment and their level of technology. We can then use this as a method for looking at much larger and more complex situations. It is still an apprenticeship method on the whole and not one that we have been able to generalize to the point of a method that is separable from those who practise it.

As I listened to my predecessors this afternoon I was surprised, especially when Dr Sauvy said that recognition of the problems that are facing us today was not widely disseminated. Three weeks ago in a village where people forty years ago were in the 'Stone Age', I heard as intelligent a discussion of the consequences of children finishing the sixth grade at twelve when they are physically not strong enough to do the work of men and they no longer fit in their village, as I have heard in any civilized country. Today everywhere in the world, people are taking account of the problems we are discussing here.

I would like particularly to distinguish between two things: Distinguish the 'generation gap' that we are experiencing at present, which is different from any other gap between generations that we have ever had, from the perennial problems of changing relationships between youth, middle age and old age. These two phenomena have been heavily confused, because about six years ago, when the world 'generation gap' first came into being, the oldest members of the new generation, who were born after the world-wide and dramatic changes around World War II, were only 20. These 'senior citizens' of 19 and 20 were all minors, students and the sons and daughters of middle-aged people, and it looked as if what we were faced with was a conflict between youth and age.

We are now beginning to realize that this is in fact a conflict between generations born in different periods. The senior members of the new generation, who are now 26, in ten years will be 36, and in 20 years 46 and they will still be on the other side of the 'generation gap' from those of us who grew up before World War II. The inter-generational friction in the United States is moving from friction between undergraduates and their professors and adolescent children and their parents, to friction between young doctors and older doctors, young lawyers and older lawyers, young teachers and older teachers, which dramatizes the fact that this is one phenomenon that is not primarily youth versus age.

At the same time there have been enormous shifts, due to the biomedical revolution in its wider sense, in the relationships between youth and age, which are likely to continue, but have to be separated from this particular 'generation gap' itself which occurred only once. These other conflicts are partly due to the much longer period of apprenticeship and learning that is required of youth today.

But we also have to take into account the falling age of puberty. It is falling four months a decade and is threatening to obliterate the period between childhood and puberty, on which we have depended in the past for young people to learn a good part of their culture, before they were confused by endocrinological changes. It is, of course, probable that this is due to the greater vulnerability to poor nutrition of the faster growing child. Since I wrote my paper I have had an opportunity to go over the work of Laurence Malcolm in New Guinea, where he is demonstrating that the slow-growing child survives better in cases of extreme protein deficiency, and when these children are moved into towns and their diet is changed, their growth is speeded up. But the falling age of puberty, and the increasing height which has also been an aspect of modern societies, introduce another series of problems into the relationships between youth and age.

However, the most drastic change that has occurred may well be the change in the relationship between men and women. If we think of the agricultural revolution as having begun the emancipation from work to provide daily subsistence and from the tasks of parenthood of a few men now being free to pursue statesmanship, religion, art and matters of the intellect, and ultimately science, while the bulk of men and all women were still tied to the tasks of subsistence and parenthood, then we can look on the biomedical revolution as having done the same for women and incidentally for a large number of men. With the decreased infant death rate and even more with the demands for smaller families as a response to the population explosion, women will no longer be supported all their lives, because they will have their two or three children in their early twenties. This is having a drastic effect. Women will demand that, if they are not to be first seduced into the belief that being a homemaker is the best thing in the world, and then supported for accepting the homemaker's role, they must have an opportunity to act as individuals contributing to society not as parents, but as individuals.

Of course, for every woman who is permitted to contribute as an individual, some man is liberated from the task of support and from compulsory parenthood also. This will make it possible for parenthood to become a vocation. Actually, family size is one of the most volatile ideas in the history of the earth. I saw it change in Bali, in Indonesia, in twenty years, with people who detested having children, and every possible method had to be invented to get them to have children, including threats of horrendous punishments in purgatory where men who did not have children were followed continuously by female pigs, and women had to breastfeed scorpions. Twenty years later the same people wanted eleven or twelve children under the impetus of Sukarno's new nationalism. In the United States, we moved from the 1920's, when an Ivy League college woman had, on the average, six-tenths of a child – which worried everybody, and we had something called 'status babies', which meant you had one to show you could – to the 1950's, when one graduating class at Annapolis wanted an average of ten children. These were people from the same social class. It is abundantly clear that it is within our powers, with the use of the mass media, to change the style of parenthood around the earth without recourse to the various forms of social assault and battery that have been suggested and repudiated this morning. We have the possibility that parenthood can become a vocation, no longer being the by-product of behaving like your neighbors, which it is at present. This would again alter the power of individuals to make choices in their own lives.

It is much more important at present, when our methods are not sufficiently refined to take into account anything like the complexities that are going to result from these very massive changes, to consider what's happening everywhere now in terms of an awareness of what might happen, than to make single projections into the future that are so single and so linear that they are almost always doomed to be proven untrue. Although we have heard a great deal about the 'self-fulfilling prophecy', this in itself is a rather linear idea. So now it becomes important to watch what is happening in the whole of society, as different parts of society attempt to adjust to this new awareness, the new changes in the age pyramid, in the relation between young and old and in the relation between the sexes. When we do this we find a tremendous number of contradictions. We find young people who insist on manipulating themselves chemically, so that they have instant access to the sorts of prophecy and visions that it used to take twenty years of discipline to produce. But we also have young people who insist on eating natural foods, rejecting every form of chemical, and even well-shaped pestles, and moving into the desert to pound things up with poorly shaped stones that no well-behaved savage would think of using. We find both of these attitudes existing at the same time.

We have the contrast in women's liberation movements between women who are demanding free abortion and those who are objecting to abortion as a male-induced attitude and demanding that, instead, whatever biological intervention occurs should take place in the bodies of men as not endangering the foetus so much. We have women who are demanding breastfeeding and emphasizing feminine functions, and we have also in parts of the women's liberation movement an emphasis on obliterating every distinction between man and woman, ironing out the menstrual cycle and going in for test-tube babies. It's impossible to know how these attitudes are going to balance each other out without paying a great deal of attention to what is happening now.

In the same way, when we included birth in hospitals, and hospitals were no longer places for people to die, they became associated with life. This seemed a very good thing until we realized that it also made birth into a surgical procedure under the control of men and so transformed a natural process into a pathological process. In the past, women who had given birth assisted other women to give birth and didn't treat it as a medical emergency. So what we gained on the one hand we lost on the other.

It may be worthwhile also to consider that as parenthood becomes more of a vocation we get a shrinkage of the universality of the obligation towards parenthood. We are getting something rather different in our relationships between physician and patient from what we had in the past when the physician shared with the priest and the legislator and the parent the position where all knowledge came down from those who knew to those who didn't, from the past to the present. The more experienced person could dictate to the less experienced, and of course children, patients, students, clients and welfare mothers were all in this general category of the less experienced.

With the occurrence of the generation gap particularly, and with the acceleration of change, we now have the phenomenon that there is much wider experience on the part of those who were once the recipients of all this well-intentioned and authoritative care. We are getting a demand for participation from those who were once the grateful and passive recipients of our highly experienced expertise. Students are demanding a part in deciding what they are to be taught, and patients are, of course, in many parts of the world now beginning to demand to have something to say about their therapy – which is very awkward!

But even more important is the increasing capacity of the average citizen to take care of himself. There has been a great deal of discussion here about the ratio of doctors to patients and the question of the right to health. I think we should discuss also the question of the capacity to be healthy, the capacity which is expressed in a greater knowledge of personal hygiene and the knowledge, e. g. of what to do when you get a cut. You only have to look at the kind of populations that I work with in New Guinea to see that their health has improved over the last twenty-five years, not only because of diseases like malaria being removed, but because the people themselves know a great many things they had not known before and are able to take charge of many parts of their lives that in the past they were helpless to improve without an imported expert from the developed world.

JÜRGEN MOLTMANN: Wenn wir die ethischen Fragen des biomedizinischen Fortschritts in ihrer vollen Breite diskutieren wollen, müssen wir das Thema dieser
Session II auch umkehren und nicht nur nach dem Einfluß des biomedizinischen
Fortschritts auf Mensch und Gesellschaft, sondern auch nach dem Einfluß von
Mensch und Gesellschaft auf den biomedizinischen Fortschritt fragen. Wissen-
schaftlich-technische Fortschritte und menschliche Interessen stehen immer in
einem Prozeß wechselseitiger Beeinflussung und Veränderung. Es gibt im menschlichen Leben keine Fakten ohne Bewußtsein, Interesse und Entscheidung, wie
es auch kein Bewußtsein ohne Fakten, ihre Entdeckung und ihren Gebrauch
gibt. Die ethischen Fragen entstehen darum nicht erst in den Reaktionen von
Mensch und Gesellschaft auf die neuen Möglichkeiten, die der biomedizinische
Fortschritt eröffnet, sondern sie stecken schon in den Aktionen von Mensch und
Gesellschaft im biomedizinischen Fortschritt selbst. Das heißt: Der biomedizinische Fortschritt ist nicht wertneutral, so daß man erst hinterher nach der
menschlichen Verwertung seiner Errungenschaften fragen müßte, sondern er
stand von Anfang an im Auftrag bestimmter menschlicher und sozialer Interessen, Wünsche und Hoffnungen. Solange sich diese Interessen von selbst verstehen, werden sie nicht diskutiert. Heute aber sind sie durch ihre fortschreitende
Erfüllung fraglich geworden. Jedes Jahr sind wir besser gerüstet, zu erreichen,
was wir wollen – aber was wollen wir eigentlich? Welche menschlichen Interessen motivieren den biomedizinischen Fortschritt?

In der Einladung zu diesem Symposium heißt es: «Die Stellung des Unternehmens (Hoffmann-La Roche) in der medizinischen Welt wurde in der letzten
Zeit dadurch verstärkt, daß es den Kampf gegen die Krankheit als ein unteilbares Ganzes betrachtet.» So liegt das erste menschliche Interesse an diesem
Fortschritt im Kampf gegen die Krankheit und für die Gesundheit, im Kampf
gegen den Tod und für die Verlängerung des Lebens. Das klingt so lange
selbstverständlich, als Menschen durch natürliche Mängel beherrscht werden,
die sie durch Kulturleistungen kompensieren müssen, um zu überleben. Was
aber heißt Gesundheit, wenn Krankheiten nicht mehr naturgegeben sind? Was
heißt Leben, wenn der Tod nicht mehr von selbst kommt? Worin liegt der Sinn
des Lebens, wenn das nackte Überleben nicht mehr im Vordergrund steht?

Bis in die Gegenwart hinein entstehen menschliche Interessen, Moral- und
Sozialsysteme aus dem, was Darwin kurz den *Kampf ums Dasein* genannt hat. In
diesem Kampf liegt der Sinn des menschlichen Lebens in der Überwindung von
Hunger, Armut, Krankheit und Todesbedrohung, also im Überleben des Einzel-
nen wie der menschlichen Gattung. Je mehr aber der Mensch in diesem Kampf
erfolgreich wird, um so mehr wird nicht das nackte Leben, sondern die
Menschlichkeit dieses Lebens fraglich. «Was kommt nach dem Kampf ums
Dasein?» fragte Sir Julian Huxley und meinte, daß dann das «Streben nach
Erfüllung» der menschlichen Möglichkeiten in den Vordergrund treten werde.
Um aber herauszufinden, welche Möglichkeiten realisiert werden sollen und
welche nicht, braucht man eine Vision der menschlichen Zukunft des Menschen.
Ich möchte dafür versuchsweise den Begriff des *Friedens im Dasein* einführen.

Der Kampf ums Dasein war durch das bedrohende Negative bestimmt, durch Nahrungsmangel, Krankheiten, feindliche Umwelt und konkurrierende Gruppen. Selbsterhaltung und Überwindung des Negativen im Dasein ergaben den Sinn des Lebens. Je mehr aber diese Nöte des Daseins überwunden werden und eine künstliche Fülle von neuen Möglichkeiten produziert wird, um so mehr werden Bestimmungen des Sinnes des menschlichen Lebens wichtig, die jenen Kampf ums Dasein transzendieren, weil sie sich nicht von selbst aus ihm ergeben. Die Evolution des Menschen geht dann über die Negation des Negativen hinaus in den Entwurf des Positiven, das aus dem Überfluß an neuen Möglichkeiten gewonnen werden soll.

Gemessen an diesem Übergang vom Kampf ums Dasein zum Frieden im Dasein, werden eine Reihe von biomedizinischen Hoffnungen und Zielen fragwürdig. Aus dem Kampf gegen Krankheit und Tod entstanden konkrete Visionen, wie zum Beispiel die Vision einer keimfreien Welt, eines schmerzfreien Lebens und durch beginnende Technik der Organtransplantation die Idee eines vielleicht endlosen Lebens. Sollte ein schmerzfreies, endloses Leben in einer keimfreien Welt möglich werden, dann erfüllte sich ein Traum, der aus dem Kampf ums Dasein geboren wurde; es wird aber zugleich fraglich, welchen Sinn ein solches Leben haben kann. Wird ein Leben ohne Schmerz und Schmerzgefühl, ohne Angst, nicht auch ein Leben ohne Interesse am Leben, das heißt ohne Liebe? Ist ein Leben ohne Widerstand nicht auch ein Leben ohne Erlebnis des Lebens? Wird einem endlosen Leben nicht der Charakter der Einmaligkeit und die Möglichkeit der Identifizierbarkeit fehlen? Monotonie, Langeweile und Erlebnisarmut sind heute schon Humanprobleme der Industriegesellschaften, die durch neue Psychopharmaka und Psychotechniken mühsam verdrängt werden müssen. Es ist wohl kaum befriedigend, biochemisch Gebilde zu konstruieren, die akustisch die Formel «Ich bin glücklich» ausstoßen.

Wichtiger aber ist, daß, gemessen am Übergang vom Kampf ums Dasein zum Frieden im Dasein, schon heute das Problem entsteht, wie Teilfortschritte und die Balancen eines Lebenssystems ausgeglichen werden können. Jeder Fortschritt auf einem Gebiet des Lebens bringt das Lebenssystem im ganzen aus der Balance. Alle Fortschritte, auch der biomedizinische Fortschritt, sind ungleiche, ungleichzeitige und meistens nichtkoordinierte Fortschritte. Sie zerstören die Gleichgewichte und erzeugen Spannungen und Konflikte. Darum sagte Dr. Sauvy: «Der Fortschritt der Medizin hat den Fortschritt der Wirtschaft überflügelt, er ermöglicht ärmeren Menschen länger zu leben.» Dieser Fortschritt hat ferner die Balance von «Altern und Wachsen» der Menschheit zerstört und durch Überalterung auf der einen Seite und verfrühte Reife auf der anderen Generationenkonflikte produziert. Er hat das Verhältnis zwischen Mann und Frau in den mittleren Jahren verändert, worauf Dr. Mead hinwies. Er hat endlich das Verhältnis der menschlichen Person zu ihrem Körper in Unordnung gebracht und Identitätskonflikte heraufbeschworen. Eine Ethik des Friedens im Dasein muß nach dem ökologischen Gesetz darauf drängen, daß Eingriffe in natürliche wie in soziale Systeme durch Ersatzleistungen kompensiert werden, so daß bei allen

Teilfortschritten die Balancen des Lebens neu geordnet werden. Biomedizinische Eingriffe in natürliche Systeme müssen durch vom Menschen regulierte Sozialsysteme ersetzt werden. Das gilt auch für den Ersatz der natürlichen Selektion durch eine soziale – man wird darum nicht herumkommen. Biomedizinische Veränderungen von Sozialsystemen müssen durch die Erfüllung des Nachholbedarfs auf den Gebieten der Wirtschaft, des Rechtes, der Politik und der Moral ausgeglichen werden. Der wissenschaftliche Fortschritt kann also nicht gestoppt werden, aber er muß verbreitert werden auf immer komplexere Systemeinheiten, zum Beispiel ein System, das Biomedizin, Wirtschaft, Politik und Öffentlichkeit umfaßt. Nicht die Reglementierung der Wissenschaft, auch nicht ihre Freiheit, sondern ihre Integration in größere geistige, soziale und politische Systeme der Kommunikation und Kooperation ist wichtig. Kam der biomedizinische Fortschritt bisher vornehmlich den Völkern und Schichten zugute, die ihn produzierten, so käme es nun darauf an, ihn auf die Benachteiligten einzustellen, auf die speziellen Krankheiten der nichtindustrialisierten Völker. Anders sind die notwendigen Systembalancen nicht wieder herzustellen, die durch Teilfortschritte verzerrt sind.

Wird der Sinn des Lebens im Frieden im Dasein gesehen, so müssen auch jene Moralsysteme abgebaut werden, die den Kampf ums Dasein stilisiert haben. Es müssen Lebensformen entwickelt werden, die in rationalen Weltverhältnissen Kreativität, Liebe und Menschlichkeit ermöglichen. Das Prinzip der Selbsterhaltung gegen andere muß zum Prinzip der Selbsterfüllung im anderen und mit anderen, also zum Prinzip der Solidarität, gewandelt werden. Die Angst- und Aggressionssysteme, die zur Selbsterhaltung notwendig waren, müssen in Systeme der Kooperation gewandelt werden. Der Gruppenegoismus, der aus Selbsterhaltung entspringt und zu Konkurrenz- und Machtkämpfen führt, bedroht heute die Menschheit mit kollektivem Selbstmord. Selbst wenn dieser vermieden wird, führt der Drang nach Selbstbestätigung («gleich und gleich gesellt sich gern») heute schon zu Segregationsgesellschaften: die Alten in die Altersheime, die Kranken in die Krankenhäuser, die Geisteskranken in die Verwahranstalten. Die Liberalisierung der öffentlichen Einstellung zu Geisteskranken wird durch die Intoleranz unserer städtischen Sozialstruktur unwirksam gemacht. Zur neuen Selbsterfahrung und Selbsterfüllung des Menschen gehört darum das moralische Prinzip der Anerkennung des anderen, so daß Ungleichartige zusammen leben mögen und ihre Spannungen und Konflikte für fruchtbar halten. Frieden im Dasein ist ein Leben, das die Widersprüche in sich enthält und die Kraft findet, Spannungen und Konflikte in sich zu fassen und auszuhalten. Dazu gehört endlich eine neue Einschätzung von Krankheit, Alter und Tod. Im Kampf ums Dasein wurde Gesundheit mit Arbeits- und Genußfähigkeit identifiziert, weil Menschlichkeit mit Lebendigkeit gleichgesetzt wurde. Jetzt aber käme es darauf an, zu erkennen, daß Krankheiten ebenso wichtige Lernprozesse der Person sein können wie das aktive Leben, und daß das Alter seine eigene Würde hat, die nicht nach dem Leistungsprinzip gemessen werden kann, und daß endlich das bewußte Sterben

Jürgen Moltmann: «Menschliches Leben ist angenommenes und anerkanntes Leben, sonst fehlt ihm seine Menschlichkeit, auch wenn es lebendig ist.»

für die Menschlichkeit eines Menschen ein ebenso wichtiger Vorgang ist wie seine Geburt.

Wir werden Lebendigkeit und Menschlichkeit zu unterscheiden lernen. Ich möchte eine Definition versuchen: Menschliches Leben ist angenommenes und anerkanntes Leben, sonst fehlt ihm seine Menschlichkeit, auch wenn es lebendig ist. Zur Geburt eines Kindes gehört seine Annahme durch die Eltern und die Gesellschaft. Die Zumutbarkeiten solcher Annahme bestimmen dann die Geburtenkontrolle. Die Heilung von Krankheiten findet ihren Sinn nicht schon in der Gesundheit selbst, sondern in der Fähigkeit des Menschen, sich den Verwundbarkeiten und Schmerzen der Liebe, des Interesses am Leben zu öffnen. Biomedizinische Eingriffe finden ihr Ziel und ihre Grenze in der Kraft ihrer menschlichen Verarbeitung durch die Person und die Gesellschaft. Wenn das nicht mehr möglich ist, werden sie sinnlos. Endlich werden für die Bestimmung des Todes als des «Todes des Menschen» die Erlebbarkeit des Lebens und die bewußte Annahme des Sterbens vordringlich.

Nachdem der biomedizinische Fortschritt im Kampf ums Dasein der Menschen erfolgreich war, kommt es darauf an, die Menschlichkeit des Menschen im Frieden im Dasein zu finden.

RENÉ KÖNIG: Dr. Goldstein hatte einen Bericht eingereicht, der direkt Stellung nimmt zu dem Beitrag von Dr. Pichot.

AVRAM GOLDSTEIN: When I viewed the program as a whole it seemed to me that there was a lack of a certain practicality which should be brought out here. Since my own field of interest is in the area of drug abuse and since this is an area in which the question of the progress of biomedical science in relation to society has come to the fore very acutely in the last few years, I thought it important that we concentrate upon the practical question of what the community of biomedical and social scientists can in fact do about this problem. The answer has to be that, as scientists, we have a certain capacity to bring objectivity and analytic capability to a problem and therefore to offer society this objectivity and the facts that we are capable of uncovering, as a sound basis for decision in areas where often decisions are made on an irrational or emotional basis.

In the area of drug abuse we need a great deal more research than we have accomplished, both at the basic level and at the applied or clinical level. This is an area in which I would take strong exception to remarks that Dr Hersch made this morning to the effect that many scientists worked only for the sake of abstract intellectual curiosity and then offered, as a pretext for their work, the idea like a candy bar that society might gain something from it. In fact, to make intelligent decisions about what to do in relation to a major problem facing society – in this case the problem of drug abuse – one does not really know what to do in the absence of an understanding of what the problem is. To gain that understanding it is necessary to do research at the most basic level.

Although perhaps some members of the public do not realize this yet, we have virtually no understanding of how psychotropic drugs act at the most fundamental level. We do not understand anything about the biochemistry of the 'reward systems', as the psychologist calls them, which are certainly involved in the process of drug abuse and of its perpetuation. We know nothing of the underlying mechanisms involved in the relief of anxiety, which is a prominent component of the drug abuse picture. We know almost nothing about the development of tolerance and of physical dependence, both of which play a major role in the abuse of certain drugs.

Surprisingly, we know very little even about treatment efficacy where the research would have to be done at a clinical level. Indeed this is an area where there is a positive duty to experiment. We have heard a lot about the right to experiment and whether possibly sometimes experiments should not be done. But if one is attempting to treat conditions for which the treatment is unknown, then there is a duty to experiment, that is to say, to design all treatments in a fashion that can be properly evaluated. This is not the case in relation to any drug abuse problem of which I know, treatments for which have until now been based entirely on presuppositions or upon unproved psychiatric theories.

Sometimes the statement 'we need more research' is a cover-up for doing nothing to change the status quo. We hear from politicians and others in the public, who don't want to face the necessity for changing an absurd situation, that we need more research before we can do anything about it. The classic example for this is the case of the greatest non-problem in the drug abuse field and that is the cannabis non-problem.

As any pharmacologist who has studied the literature and looked at this drug knows, it is a non-problem because in relation to other drugs of abuse and indeed on the same standards by which we evaluate drugs in general for use in the human population, cannabis would pass the test. That is not to say that it is a harmless drug. There are no such things as harmless drugs. But it is quite clear that on a relative scale cannabis is a fairly innocuous recreational drug. But

Avram Goldstein: 'If I were to devote the appropriate time to the various drugs of abuse in a ten-minute talk, I would have to devote nine minutes to alcohol and one minute to all the rest.'

when research studies show this, politicians and others say, 'you had better go back and do some more research'. In fact, the biomedical community in particular, and the community of scientists in general, have the significant opportunity to study this problem and then to influence society's attitude toward it, so that we can achieve a more rational outlook in respect both to legislation and to the general attitude of society toward drug use.

First, let me take a completely consistent position toward the abuse of all drugs and abolish once and for all the absurd distinction that throws alcohol, cigarettes and coffee out of the drug category, so that when one speaks of drug abuse one automatically is supposed to be talking about amphetamines, barbiturates, LSD and so on, saying nothing about the other drugs, and particularly alcohol, which is the number one drug abuse problem on any criterion. If I were to devote the appropriate time to the various drugs of abuse in a ten-minute talk, I would have to devote nine minutes to alcohol and one minute to all the rest. We must not lose sight of this anomaly. One way to do it is not to be drawn into the trap as scientists, particularly biomedical scientists, of commenting, speaking, participating in sessions or symposia on drug abuse without insisting that alcohol and tobacco be included where they belong.

Secondly, it is essential that we transform attitudes toward drug abuse from present ones to non-punitive ones that emphasize compassion, medical help, in the best tradition of medicine. This means changing laws; changing laws means changing the attitude of society and of legislators. There is hope in the very rapid changes that happen nowadays in the public attitudes, as e. g. the change in attitude toward abortion and contraception. We have seen the change in attitude toward alcohol in a period of ten to twenty years. Alcoholism was regarded as a vice – it is now regarded properly as a medical illness. The same should be true of the use of heroin, amphetamine and barbiturates, as these are conditions that destroy the lives of individuals far more than they affect society as a whole. In this area of so-called victimless crimes, i. e. crimes in which the user himself is the only victim or largely the only victim, it is essential that we get rid of the legal approach, which in any case has been highly ineffective.

We should offer treatment to those who wish treatment; we should consider carefully how to deal with those who do not wish treatment, how to protect society from the spread of a certain epidemic quality in drug abuse and at the same time preserve individual freedom. That is a difficult problem and requires study and perhaps experimentation. And we require lastly honest education of young people, honest in the sense of explaining the facts as we understand them, especially when they seem to be in conflict with legal structures, so that we can gain the respect of the young people and so that they will listen to us when we tell them about drugs that really are dangerous.

Drugs are here, they are part of the environment. No wishful thinking, no legal structure, no enforcement, even if it involved one law enforcement officer for every member of society, could possibly eliminate drugs as a presence of the latter part of the twentieth century. Like industrialization, like computers, like rapid transportation, like the mass media, they are here, and the problem, especially for young people, is how to live with them. Some of the drugs are old and have been here for a long time; some are new on the scene and the direct products of modern biomedical science. The young have to learn to live with them, that means to learn which drugs are safe recreational drugs that can be used in moderation and which drugs have a high danger of enslaving the individual, turning his life pattern into an unsatisfactory one. In all these matters the community of scientists have a special obligation to educate the public, to educate the law makers to bring about these essential changes.

Discussion

ALFRED SAUVY: J'ai dénoncé tout à l'heure l'insuffisance des connaissances de l'opinion. Je n'ai pas contesté qu'il y a eu de grands progrès dans ces connaissances, mais ces progrès sont très inégaux. Il y a des choses que l'opinion connaît très bien, d'autres qu'elle connaît très mal. Il en résulte des distorsions. Je ne vais pas jusqu'à dire qu'il vaudrait mieux qu'elle ne connût rien du tout, mais je crois que ces inégalités de connaissances peuvent être dangereuses: je l'ai constaté sur divers problèmes les plus vitaux.

RENÉ KÖNIG: Heute morgen wurde über das Recht der Einschränkung der Forschung gesprochen. Keiner von den hier Anwesenden, der irgendeinen Fachzweig vertritt, ist der Meinung, daß es in seinem Gebiet zu viel Forschung gibt. Auf dem Gebiete der Sozialwissenschaften habe ich mich mit einem Problem beschäftigt, das indirekt in unseren Diskussionen eine Rolle spielt, der Ehescheidung. Auch heute verfügen wir nur über elementarste Kenntnisse, welche über die juristischen Aspekte des Ursprungs der Voraussetzungen für die Ehescheidung nicht hinausgehen. Wir erfahren von einer scheidungsreifen Situation immer erst dann, wenn sie durch den Klärungsprozeß der Individuen gegangen ist. Das ist aber schon sehr viel später. Die Frage ist, wann hat dieser Prozeß wirklich begonnen. Das ist auch für den Juristen wichtig, denn er kann dann erst entscheiden, welches Scheidungsgründe sind, sofern man im Gesetz überhaupt Scheidungsgründe anerkennen will.

JÜRGEN MOLTMANN: Meine Frage war, wie man mit der Ungleichzeitigkeit und Ungleichheit von Fortschritten in den einzelnen Lebensbereichen fertig wird, denn hier kommt es auf eine ethische Gegensteuerung an. Dr. Sauvy stellte die Frage des Ausgleichs zwischen dem Altern einer Generation und dem Wachsen. Das ist eine Frage der Entscheidung zwischen dem Wert der Gegenwart und dem Wert der Zukunft. Eine ähnliche Frage stellte Dr. Pichot: wenn die Einstellung zu Geisteskranken liberaler wird, zugleich aber die Sozialstruktur unserer Städte so ist, daß die Geisteskranken nicht in Familien aufgenommen werden können, wie finden wir dann aus diesem Widerspruch einen Ausweg? Das gleiche gilt für das Verhältnis zwischen Mann und Frau, das vielleicht in der Geschichte nie gut geordnet war. Wie Frau Dr. Mead gezeigt hat, ist es verzerrt, wenn der biomedizinische Fortschritt der Frau im mittleren Alter zugute kommt, aber nicht entsprechend dem Manne.

MARGARET MEAD: It is important that we don't set these things up as either/or. For instance, when we are looking at the population distribution in different countries. If we continue to condemn countries that have too many children or, on the other hand, condemn those that have too few, or set them up in a hierarchical order, we get into continual difficulties. If, instead, we use something like a ratio, looking at the relationship of the resources and the degree of education of a given country at a given time in terms of their whole age structure, then it will be possible to say that what is a good choice for one country is not such a good choice for another, and we can compare ratios instead of absolute figures, and still protect national sensitivities.

My second point concerns the terrible results of aging populations. I was asked on the radio today whether it wouldn't be better to get rid of the old blood and have young blood. (It's interesting to note that every time people mention blood in a social context you know something has gone wrong.) In the old kind of society the aged were a resource for experience as long as they stayed mentally fit, but then they became a terrible burden on the initiative of the young. In the present type of society it is true that instead we have too many aged who are incompetent because they have been kept alive far beyond their usefulness, but we also have the fact that it is the oldest competent people who know more about change than anyone else. If we recognize that we need those who can teach the younger people how to change and to trust change instead of being frightened of change, it is those who have experienced the greatest change and survived and found change beneficial, who are in the best position to make that kind of contribution.

To say that for a population to get older is inevitably a penalty that a society may have to pay is again much too simple. We are living in the kind of society that puts the aging population, who have made no adjustment to change, on the shelf, and which says that no scientist is worth anything after he is thirty-five. Instead of making older people into a burden we should again integrate them. Instead of retiring and segregating them we could make them again actively useful in society. There is very good evidence that one of the principal factors producing the kind of aging we have today is the segregation of the old and the gradual diminution of their participation in this society.

There are illustrations of this in the Caucasus. One of my younger colleagues, Dr Sula Benet*, has been studying such a society where people of up to 125 years are still active, and this not because they have been dodging the draught. They get old by shrinking their pattern of activity but not changing it. They eat a little less, drink a little less, make love a little less, participate a little less and walk a little less, but they still do everything. It is quite possible that our present horror of old age is due to the one-sided truncations of life that our modern society has introduced.

PIERRE PICHOT: Je ne pense pas qu'il y ait une contradiction entre, d'une part, les problèmes particuliers que posent l'urbanisation et l'industrialisation de la société à la santé mentale et, d'autre part, la libéralisation des législations et des attitudes envers les malades mentaux. En réalité, il se produit actuellement une modification du centre de gravité dans ce domaine. C'est-à-dire que les transformations sociales entraînent une intolérance croissante à certains types de maladies mentales qui autrefois n'étaient pas considérées comme nécessitant une hospitalisation. Essentiellement deux variétés: les insuffisances intellectuelles, les débilités mentales d'une part et, de l'autre, les affaiblissements intellectuels du vieillard. Ces deux catégories de sujets étaient autrefois tolérées par la société dans un milieu rural de civilisation rurale avec une bonne intégration. A l'heure actuelle, dans une civilisation industrielle et urbaine, il est impossible, même matériellement, de garder dans une famille un vieillard dément, parce qu'il mettra le feu à la maison, ou un enfant débile parce que le père et la mère travaillent. Si bien qu'on assiste à une augmentation considérable du pourcentage d'hospitalisation. Des études très précises avec extrapolations, faites en particulier en Suède, fixent la date proche où tous les déments séniles de ce pays seront hospitalisés. Ce n'est pas là une question de libéralisation, c'est une question

* After the Symposium I received the following information from Sula Benet who had just returned from a second field trip to Soviet Abkhasia. According to the official consensus, in 1954, there were 2,144 people aged 90 or more within a population of 300,000. Of these 300,000, 100,000 were ethnically Abkhasian, and it was among these that the old people were found. Almost all were village dwellers, and over 70% of them were women. Sula Benet studied a group of old people aged between 90 and 119 whose general appearance was that of a 60-year-old. Ages of up to 135 have been reported. It is her impression that after about 70 the aging process appears to be arrested.

d'intolérance, d'impossibilité matérielle de notre société de conserver ce type de malades dans le milieu familial. Mais, inversement, il est manifeste que la société est plus tolérante pour un autre type de maladies, les psychoses, et en particulier la schizophrénie. La représentation populaire du «fou», pour employer un mot populaire, était celle ou bien d'un individu qui se prenait, en France, pour Napoléon ou bien surtout d'un individu dangereux. Or, actuellement cette représentation tend à se modifier et en grande partie à cause des progrès biomédicaux, car il ne faut pas oublier que la représentation que l'on trouve dans les caricatures des journaux du malade mental qui s'habille comme Napoléon correspond à une maladie que le progrès biomédical a fait disparaître complètement: la paralysie générale syphilitique, affection qui remplissait les hôpitaux du XIXᵉ siècle. D'autre part, l'idée du fou furieux – le terme est employé, en France, dans les vieux textes légaux – diminue parce que les progrès biomédicaux et la psychopharmacologie ont rendu ce type de malade beaucoup plus rare. Il y a donc une balance et non pas une contradiction: la société devient plus intolérante à certains déficits qui font que le sujet ne peut plus être conservé à l'extérieur, mais plus tolérante à l'égard d'un autre type de malade mental qu'on accepte maintenant de voir en dehors d'un hôpital. Et la même remarque concerne les troubles du comportement des toxicomanes à l'égard desquels la société devient nettement plus intolérante. Il y a une modification générale du sens de gravité qui est due à la fois aux modifications des conditions de vie par l'industrialisation et l'urbanisation, et au progrès biomédical par l'effet du traitement sur les symptômes.

RENÉ KÖNIG: Wir haben eine vergleichende Untersuchung abgeschlossen über die Rehabilitation von ehemaligen Psychosepatienten der Landesheilanstalt in Düsseldorf und einer sehr teuren Privatklinik an einem anderen Ort. Dabei hat sich folgendes herausgestellt: Die Patienten aus dem teuren Institut hatten keinerlei Schwierigkeit, sich zu Hause wieder einzugliedern, weil ihre Familien und auch ihre Arbeitgeber informiert waren über die Fortschritte der klinischen Behandlung der Psychose. Hingegen hatten die anderen aus der Landesheilanstalt die allergrößten Schwierigkeiten. Es hieß einfach: «Der ist verrückt. Warum kommt er nach Hause?» Ein sehr merkwürdiges und sehr zu denken gebendes Ergebnis, andererseits aber auch zu Optimismus verleitend, denn wenn diese Dinge bekannter sind, werden vielleicht auch die einfachen Leute verständiger darauf reagieren, und nicht der Rehabilitation eines Mannes, der aus einer Anstalt kommt, so enorme Widerstände entgegensetzen. Anders liegt die Front natürlich bei Senilität; da ist ein einfacher Abbau vorhanden.

COUNT D. GIBSON: In anticipation of topics to be discussed tomorrow I'd like to offer a brief comment on a new kind of relationship between hospital, patient and family, in response to some of the remarks of Dres Mead, Pichot and König. As we move to the application of biomedical knowledge in society, the absolute necessity of grasping the setting of the patient becomes obvious. Let me cite two developments in the United States that are related to home care. One is mainly disastrous; the other has an implicit pattern of helpfulness.

The first relates to the great pressures on our state-supported mental hospitals due to the development of the psychoactive drugs, which have made possible the rapid discharge of patients from the institution. This has been viewed by the legislator and in turn the tax payer with great satisfaction. But the professionals in the institutions who have administered the drugs have all too often discharged the patients too rapidly into home settings about which the professionals knew nothing. In this setting the fool is no longer a *furious* fool, but he is still a fool. Particularly the discharge of young parents into homes where the professionals have provided no kind of support may have very distressing effects on their small children even though the parent's psychiatric disorder is suppressed by the drug. The institution has failed to grasp the realities of the home setting.

On the other hand, for 25 years now there has been a very slow but steady development of organized home care for patients with physical and psychical illness and for patients with mental retardation, which has been accompanied by great success. A family willing to care for a relative upon his return from an institution can show itself capable of the most remarkable, compassionate, perceptive and sensitive ability to care for the patient and does it far better and far more cheaply than any of the institutions that had been set up. The family can do this, provided there is a carefully organized support system. The professionals are no longer the custodians but the support. When the family setting is one in which this is no longer a wise procedure, the support system stands ready and willing to take the patient back. These things do not happen simply and easily but precisely by carefully considering the many facets of a family situation and the needs of the patient. There are signs that we will perhaps be able once again to free ourselves from the hospital as the automatic place in which all care is rendered.

Count D. Gibson: 'A family willing to care for a relative upon his return from an institution can show itself capable of the most remarkable, compassionate, perceptive and sensitive ability to care for the patient and does it far better and far more cheaply than any of the institutions that had been set up. The family can do this, provided there is a carefully organized support system.'

JEAN BERGIER: J'aimerais poser une question très concrète à M. Pichot, une question plus directement médicale que sociologique. La toxicomanie ou la pharmacodépendance présente dans notre civilisation souvent un double aspect ou est conçue sous un double aspect. D'une part, pour le médecin, il s'agit d'une maladie que l'on doit traiter et si possible guérir, et, d'autre part, pour les pouvoirs publics, il s'agit souvent d'une infraction, voire d'un délit, qu'il s'agit au contraire de punir et de réprimer. Ma question est donc la suivante: dans quelle mesure la punition ou la menace de punition est-elle favorable ou défavorable au succès du traitement médical de la toxicomanie considérée en tant que maladie?

PIERRE PICHOT: La réponse est assez facile à donner. On peut comparer la toxicomanie à une maladie infectieuse, et la lutte contre les maladies infectieuses est surtout efficace quand on en supprime l'agent. En réalité, je ne pense pas que les sanctions contre les toxicomanes aient une efficacité quelconque et, personnellement, je considère un toxicomane comme un malade. Mais je considère aussi que le meilleur moyen de lutter contre la toxicomanie est de supprimer le toxique et, par conséquent, éventuellement de prendre des sanctions contre ceux qui apportent les toxiques et non pas contre le toxicomane, car ce n'est pas le toxicomane qui produit le toxique, en général.

ERNST VON WEIZSÄCKER: Ich habe heute früh davon gesprochen, daß die Wissenschaft sich von der Technik nicht einfach trennen läßt. Man kann sie auch nicht von der Politik trennen. Daraus hat sich die Forderung nach einer Methodologie für eine interdisziplinäre Wissenschaft von den unvergleichlich viel komplexeren Systemen ergeben. In einer solchen Wissenschaft sind bestimmte komplexere Fragen anzugehen, die einer nicht mit Computern ausgerüsteten wissenschaftlichen Welt gar nicht zugänglich waren. Das ist selbstverständlich. Außerdem muß man bereit sein, auch das Offenhalten von Fragen und von Situationen zu tolerieren. Das heißt nicht nur, daß es manchmal gar nicht möglich ist, bestimmte Fragen zu klären, weil es zu schwierig oder zu komplex ist, sondern unter Umständen, daß es moralisch gar nicht zulässig ist. Beispiele dafür sind in vielen Beiträgen dieses Symposiums gegeben worden. Es ist sicher nicht ratsam oder moralisch zulässig, empirisch die 50%-Letaldosis von Autoabgasen beim Menschen zu bestimmen. Wir müssen, wenn wir in diesen komplexeren Systemen arbeiten und denken, die Offenheit von solchen wissenschaftlich stellbaren Fragen aushalten und nach politischen Lösungen suchen. Das klingt hoffnungslos und kann auch als Alibi dafür dienen, daß man in Wirklichkeit nichts tut.

Ich möchte noch einmal auf das Beispiel der B- und C-Waffen zurückkommen. Wenn die politischen und technischen Kontrollen von B- und C-Waffen so weit gehen wollten, daß sie ausschließen, daß irgendwo auf der Welt B- und C-Waffen hergestellt werden, dann würden diese Kontrollen eine totale Veränderung unserer gegenwärtigen sozialen Systeme implizieren, und das ist sicher nicht das, was wir wollen. Es ist also eine furchtbar triviale Feststellung, daß in diesen komplexen Systemen ständig mit einem gewissen Vertrauensvorschuß gearbeitet werden muß, einem Vertrauensvorschuß auch gegenüber jenen Personen oder Sachen, denen die Wissenschaft eher mit Mißtrauen oder mit Skepsis begegnet.

TALCOTT PARSONS: Dr Handler this morning referred to the possibility of a cessation of the process of evolution and possibly a dead-end as the status for man. Some of us social scientists who have been concerned with the evolution of societies and cultures and with their continuities with organic evolution wonder whether this fact, which I know has been well established in biology, isn't connected with a certain transition of the primary processes of the evolution to the behavior on social and sociocultural levels, rather than to the genetic constitution of the species. This is very much an open question, and I doubt whether very much clear evidence on it exists. At any rate, such an idea emphasizes a continuity between the two sets of sciences, and this continuity can be picked up in many different areas. For instance there are prehuman prototypes of virtually all the human social institutions and cultural entities. Obviously the human family is grounded in the functions on the one hand of biosexual reproduction, which genetically speaking is very ancient indeed, and on the other hand of the care of the young. There is an evolutionary trend toward increasing importance of the latter, especially in the mammalian order.

   Another very important field concerns the use of knowledge in intelligent behavior to define the kind of enterprise that the biomedical progress represents. Our friends, the animal psychologists, have studied intelligent behavior at prehuman levels very exhaustively indeed, and there is certainly definite continuity in that respect. I am not proposing to suggest that the eminent biomedical scientists here are rats running in mazes, but some of their very remote ancestors, as intellectual investigators, were on a rat-like level.

   My decision to stand up here was promoted by Dr Moltmann's remarks when he spoke of the contrast between the picture of the evolutionary process as Darwinian struggle for existence levels, and what tend to be the ideals at least of relatively civilized humans. This is an extremely complicated subject. But I would be rather sceptical of the fundamental character of the differences, if this is interpreted to mean that we are moving toward a social utopia, in which the distressing phenomenon of struggle will virtually have ceased to appear. Particulars have fundamentally changed. Many human beings survive to, if not very old age, a normal life cycle through the application of biomedical knowledge, who would not have survived under struggleful existence conditions. Yet, I am of the opinion that the main tendency is for some kind of balance between the factors of new order, new control, better adaptation on the one hand and of the emergence of new tensions, conflicts and sources of distress on the other. We live in a period when the latter factor is, shall we say, not inconspicuous.

MARGARET MEAD: We should recognize that we are in a transitional period, where the ameliorating effects of medicine have kept alive a large number of people who in childhood faced rather devastating diseases but survived. What we have at present in civilized countries is a population of surviving people who as infants were taught that they had to stay alive under any circumstances and gain weight. As a result we have now a fairly large population of people who, if they were able to make a choice, would choose not to go on living. But we put them in a position where they can't make the choice, because the medical profession has been faithful to its task of preservation of life, and because they themselves are unable to give up after their experience as children of learning to live under any circumstances. Another reason is that they never saw in their childhood senile, helpless old people being kept artificially alive. The only old people they saw, and the only old people one sees under primitive conditions, are very hale and hardy old people who may be a little deaf and a little arthritic, but they are, you know, like Cambridge dons riding bicycles at eighty, and Cambridge dons riding bicycles at eighty don't give anybody a horror of old age.

In the next generation in civilized countries, we are going to have children who won't have had to make such a fight for life, who won't have had croup over and over again, gasping for breath till the neighbors come in, and who will have seen many old people being kept alive against what they know would have been their intention. And we will begin to have people who will elect the conditions under which they will stay alive and elect the right to die. But they will do this individually under their own power, with a 'living will', as it's called in the United States. They will not ask doctors to kill them, as many people would like to do – people are always trying to get doctors to kill somebody. We will not ask the state to intervene, because any state that can keep any life alive and sacrifices it pays a dreadful price ethically. Instead we shall develop individuals of a type who can make their own choice at a sufficient distance from their own death, so that they can cope with it a long time off and free the medical profession from the present demand that keeps them alive.

MARIE-PIERRE HERZOG: Devant le nombre de problèmes qui ont été discutés ici et qui mettent en question des options si fondamentales, je voudrais faire deux remarques très brèves. La première concerne les irrationalités que nous constatons dans l'acceptation des vérités scientifiques. Ce problème a été évoqué ce matin par M. Fraser et ce soir par M. Sauvy. Ils ont signalé l'un et l'autre que certaines vérités ou certaines prévisions scientifiques extrêmement probables n'étaient pas acceptées par la masse du public ou des collectivités dans lesquelles vit la communauté scientifique. Je crois que ceci est dû à la profonde influence – que nous méconnaissons toujours – des facteurs culturels profonds qui animent ces communautés. C'est un lieu commun de le dire, mais dans la mesure où, à l'Unesco où je travaille, je suis en contact avec 125 pays, je m'aperçois de plus en plus que la revendication de l'identité culturelle, le maintien de cette identité sont absolument fondamentaux. Et je ne dis pas seulement cela pour les peuples du tiers monde, je dis cela également pour les pays développés desquels il s'agit aujourd'hui. Il me semble que notre discussion à cet égard est très frappante. Nous constatons dans la discussion de ce matin et de cet après-midi qu'il y a un conflit dans notre collectivité entre une culture de type judéo-chrétien où l'homme a des relations personnelles avec Dieu et a toujours pensé qu'il en avait, et une vérité de type scientifique qui tend à dépersonnaliser nécessairement par sa recherche d'objectivité les problèmes de l'individu dans sa singularité. Premier point.

Deuxième point: le problème des valeurs que M. König évoquait il y a un instant. J'ai été très frappée ce matin, en écoutant les grands savants qui nous parlaient et qui ont dans leur curriculum de si prestigieuses récompenses, de voir avec quel embarras et avec quelle prudence ils s'approchaient du problème des valeurs. D'abord je me suis félicitée qu'ils s'en approchassent parce que ceci signifie que la coupure maudite entre la science et la philosophie, qui est une coupure récente, est en train enfin de se combler. Mais d'autre part je ne me suis pas étonnée, parce que la formation scientifique telle qu'elle a été donnée et reçue, ces trois derniers siècles en Europe occidentale et aux Etats-Unis, est une formation qui vous met en face d'un certain type de vérité.

Il est difficile quand on a été formé ainsi d'appréhender le type de vérité qui peut être celui par lequel nous saisissons des valeurs. Une valeur n'est pas quelque chose qu'on saisit et qu'on peut démontrer scientifiquement. Une valeur est quelque chose qui nous appelle, et la valeur de la valeur est toujours en discussion, de sorte que la question est toujours posée de savoir si cette valeur est encore valide ou bien si cette valeur a véritablement «valeur». Cela c'est le problème de la nature des valeurs qui donc introduit un autre mode de vérité, et c'est pour cela que nos collègues scientifiques hésitent. Il ne faut pas qu'ils s'étonnent d'hésiter, leur recherche serait fausse s'ils n'hésitaient pas. D'autre part, et pour conclure, il n'y a pas de spécialistes des valeurs. Nous avons pu croire un certain temps que les philosophes ou bien les théologiens ou bien cer-

Marie-Pierre Herzog: «Une valeur n'est pas quelque chose qu'on saisit et qu'on peut démontrer scientifiquement. Une valeur est quelque chose qui nous appelle, et la valeur de la valeur est toujours en discussion, de sorte que la question est toujours posée de savoir si cette valeur a encore valide ou bien si cette valeur est véritablement valeur.»

tains sages étaient des spécialistes des valeurs, et certains de nos collègues scientifiques donnent l'impression qu'il y aurait quelque part des gens qui sauraient
mieux qu'eux. Non, ni mieux ni plus mal, les valeurs sont à tout le monde, l'esprit souffle où il veut; ce que l'on peut dire, c'est que de temps en temps une voix
se fait entendre, la voix d'un grand sage, la voix d'un grand savant, la voix d'un
grand saint, et qui réactive généralement les valeurs que nous connaissons déjà.
Ce qui est important finalement, c'est de savoir comment ces valeurs que la
sagesse des différentes cultures a petit à petit mises au point peuvent se réin-
carner dans de nouvelles manières de vivre et ainsi comment on vivra la nouvelle
vie et la nouvelle mort et les nouvelles dimensions de la famille en fonction de ce
qui s'est toujours appelé la sagesse, la compassion ou la fraternité.

ROBERT REICHARDT: Ich möchte nochmals auf die sehr abstrakte Frage der
Werte eingehen, da mir scheint, daß dies ein Bereich ist, bei dem es ganz besonders wichtig ist, die Kommunikation zwischen den verschiedenen Wissenschaften überhaupt funktionsfähig zu machen. Ich möchte von der Frage Dr. Plet-
schers ausgehen, wer sich die übermenschliche Weisheit anmaßen werde, zu
sagen, welche wissenschaftliche Entwicklung gut oder schlecht sei. Nun könnte
man sagen, daß wir durch unsere Situation dazu verdammt sind, diese Weisheit
in Anspruch zu nehmen, da wir Prioritäten setzen müssen für die verschiedenen
möglichen wissenschaftlichen Entwicklungen. Man müßte daher grundsätzlich
die Frage stellen, was denn überhaupt voraussehbar gemacht und wieviel ge-
plant werden kann.

Es wurde heute vormittag von der Notwendigkeit gesprochen, ein möglichst komplexes und weites System von Interaktionen, von Interdependenzen
ins Kalkül zu ziehen. Nun wissen wir, daß bei primitiven Gesellschaften, bei
Agrargesellschaften, ein gewisses Gleichgewicht zwischen sozialen und tech-
nologischen Faktoren vorhanden ist und daß sehr viele Entscheidungen, die für
das Funktionieren und Überleben der Gesellschaft notwendig sind, eben durch
die Eingespieltheit dieses Systems zwischen Natur und Gesellschaft abgenommen werden.

Man darf nicht übersehen, daß auch in unserer Gesellschaft ein großer Teil
des Funktionierens, auch in bezug etwa auf das Akzeptieren medizinischer Tat-
bestände und medizinischen Wissens, auf eingelebten und von uns noch nicht
verstandenen Mechanismen beruht. Man ist vor die Frage gestellt, ob die bewußte Entscheidung über bestimmte Entwicklungen der Wissenschaft und der
Technologie nicht grundsätzlich zu einem Ungleichgewicht führt, das möglicher-
weise unabsehbare Konsequenzen haben kann. So hat die Einführung des Auto-
mobils eine solche Entwicklung ausgelöst und zu Konsequenzen geführt, die bei
der Einführung dieser Technologie noch völlig unvorhersehbar waren. Es wäre
aber falsch, hier von Irrationalität zu sprechen, denn die Anschaffung des Auto-
mobils kann, vom Individuum aus gesehen, ein rationaler Akt sein, wobei nur
die kollektive Konsequenz unter Umständen in unerwünschten Nebenwirkungen bestehen kann.

Das gleiche ließe sich natürlich auch von biomedizinischen Fortschritten sagen. Wir stehen also vor der schwierigen Frage, wie weit überhaupt etwas voraussehbar und planbar ist. Unsere Reaktion darf nicht Resignation sein, die alles einer angenommenen metaphysischen oder organischen Entwicklung überlassen würde. Auf der anderen Seite ist es auch gefährlich, die Möglichkeit der Vorausschau und der Planung zu überschätzen. Daher sind neuartige Ansätze der Wissenschaft, wie sie Dr. von Weizsäcker angesprochen hat, zur Entwicklung notwendig. Man könnte die Metapher brauchen, daß der Wissenschaftler, der Entscheidungen fällt, besonders auch auf dem Gebiet der Anwendung der Technologie, sich etwa so verhält, wie wenn in einer Kristallstruktur ein einzelnes Atom begänne, die Gesamtstruktur zu begreifen.

Robert Reichardt: «Man könnte die Metapher brauchen, daß der Wissenschaftler, der Entscheidungen fällt, besonders auch auf dem Gebiet der Anwendung der Technologie, sich etwa so verhält, wie wenn in einer Kristallstruktur ein einzelnes Atom begänne, die Gesamtstruktur zu begreifen.»

Noch kurz einige Überlegungen zur Entwicklung einer Wissenschaft von den Werten, wobei ich durchaus nicht meine, es müßten Spezialisten dafür ausgebildet werden, vielmehr ist dies als interdisziplinäre Aufgabe zu sehen. Dennoch können wir bereits jetzt einige grundsätzliche Aussagen über Werte machen, zum Beispiel, daß jede Entscheidung hinsichtlich der Werte multidimensional ist. Es gibt also nicht eine einfache Entscheidung für oder gegen Sterblichkeit, für oder gegen Gesundheit, sondern es werden bei solchen Entscheidungen gleichzeitig auch andere Wertprobleme berührt. Ein Beispiel ist die Antibabypille, die nicht nur Bevölkerungsprobleme, sondern auch die ganze Problematik des Hedonismus beziehungsweise der Triebrepression tangiert.

Eine zweite Aussage ist, daß die Beziehung zwischen Werten nicht als konstant angesehen werden kann, nicht einmal in ihrer Abhängigkeit. Ich möchte dafür ein Beispiel bringen: der Zusammenhang zwischen Gesundheit und ökonomischer Entwicklung, wobei wir noch diskutieren müßten, wieweit ökonomische Entwicklung an sich ein Wert ist und wieweit sie nur instrumentell ist für andere Werte. Bei technologisch primitiven Gesellschaften besteht eine positive Korrelation zwischen Gesundheit und ökonomischer Entwicklung, während in unserer technisch hochentwickelten Gesellschaft eine negative Korrelation besteht, das heißt, wenn wir ökonomisches Wachstum forcieren wollen, müssen wir dies mit gesundheitlichen Nachteilen erkaufen und umgekehrt. Auch hier kann der Zusammenhang zwischen verschiedenen Wertbereichen nicht als konstant angesehen werden.

Meine dritte Aussage betrifft die von Dr. Luria heute früh angeschnittenen Feedback-Prozesse zwischen Werten. Auch hier würde ich sagen, daß ein solcher Feedback-Effekt nicht nur zwischen Werten und der sich entwickelnden Technologie entsteht, sondern auch zwischen dem sozialen Bereich, den Werten und wiederum der Technologie, so daß mehrere Systeme hier gleichsam interagieren. Ein Beispiel wäre etwa der wachsende Skeptizismus gegenüber der Forschung, wo aus einer Freiheit der Forschung gleichsam als Rückwirkung des Erfolges eine Skepsis gegen die Forschung vom sozialen System her entsteht.

Meine Überlegung angesichts der Komplexität dieser Probleme ist die, daß wir schon sehr viel gewonnen hätten, wenn wir mehr darauf ausgingen, Entscheidungstechniken oder Entscheidungsvorgänge zu entwickeln, die das Schlimmste verhüten, anstatt zu glauben, wir könnten bereits optimale Strategien der Entwicklung voraussehen.

SIR ROGER ORMROD: I have a bone to pick with Dr Mead, if I may be allowed to. The bone I should like to pick with her is her statement that the generation gap between those of us who grew up before the Second World War and those of us who grew up subsequently is greater than any generation gap in history. I wonder why she says that. I have always felt a greater gap between myself and those who grew up before the First World War, than I feel with those who grew up after the Second World War. This is a purely introspective observation, and I cannot validate it, but it seems to me to be a great mistake to say that this gap between the generations is in some way unique, because it only serves to encourage all sorts of ideas which do no good to anybody.

The discussions that we have had today have been extremely interesting, profound but, may I say, vague. I should like to narrow the focus a little and try to look at some specific matter and see where we get. The one I shall take up is the easy one for me, because I am a divorce judge, Mr Moderator, and so am interested in the relations between men and women, particularly husbands and wives, but also people who are not husbands and wives. My question is this: With the introduction now of 95% safe contraception with the pill, with the legalization of abortion – which means in effect abortion on request no matter what the legal format may say, because there is no stopping point between either no abortion, abortion on grounds of serious ill health or abortion on request – what does Dr Mead think the effect on the relations between the sexes will be as a result of the biomedical research in these two fields? It cannot be very long before we have an abortion pill. And once we have an abortion pill, the power to control conception and the power to control the birth of children will be wholly and completely in the hands of the female. The male will have ceased to have any control over this situation at all. If one adds artificial insemination, one begins to ask oneself, is one really necessary?

It is highly important that when great advances in medical research are made, it should be the task of some competent group to be thinking about where this is going to take us. Has anybody worked out, or even thought about, the impact on the relationship between men and women of the various drugs and measures I have mentioned? I do not want any artificial suggestion that we should not investigate these matters in order to protect the status of the male. But it is a good idea that we should at least know what might happen to us. Clearly, also, someone ought to be thinking about what the effect may be on marriage, although marriage itself, I realize, means a great deal of different things to many different societies. But is it going to be a permanent companionship for life? In which case we shall be asking the psychiatrists and the marriage guidance counsellors for one kind of therapy. Or is it to be an intermittant association, here today and gone tomorrow? In which case we shall need another set.

SALVADOR E. LURIA: I was struck very positively by the as usually provocative remark of Dr Mead about the generation gap. It seems to me that the significance of what we are observing now, at least in some countries, may be the fact that this generation gap continues when people graduate from college, or finish some other experiences. They continue to have the spirit of dissent when they are already in their adult work as young doctors, young lawyers or young engineers. As far as we can anticipate now, there is a chance that a substantial part of this generation may refuse to be corrupted by the traditional society in the way every previous generation has been corrupted.

I do believe that if these people refuse to be corrupted, they may be the ones who are going to find the proper way of regulating the developments and uses of science and technology in society without having recourse to coercion. If similar symposia are held in the future, I hope that we shall have many more active participants who are young people, directly out of our colleges and universities, beginning in their professions, and who are the ones who are going to have the power of making the decisions in the future. I hope that they are going to make wiser decisions than our fathers did; we have done as best as we could.

MARGARET MEAD: There have indeed been generation gaps between particular groups of people, in particular countries. Certainly the generation gap that occurs in a country like the United States or Israel, where you have illiterate immigrants speaking another language and their children speaking the language of the country but not their parent's language, is enormous. This is the first time in history that such a gap is going right around the world.

There is no one in your and my generation, Sir Roger, who has ever been or ever can be young in the present-day world. We are old in it, you know, though we do that quite well. The people who grew up since World War II have an experience that no older person has, anywhere; so nowhere in the whole world can the young look for a model, for someone who has lived the life they live. The same is true for our generation, yours and mine – I hope I am not insulting you by putting you in the same generation. We belong to a generation which will never be repeated. And the young people we look at will never be anything like us.

Now this is what I am talking about. Such gaps never before included the whole world. The world became one in the mid-1940's, when communication went around it and everybody simultaneously experienced the changes that are occurring. That's the reason why I regard the gap as unique. It is not a matter of opinion, it is a matter of rather careful study.

In the second place the effect of putting contraception in the hands of women. We have given this a great deal of thought and realize that it is on the whole very disadvantageous; but I would like to point out that it has been invented entirely by men! And why did they do it? Because they are extraordinarily unwilling to experiment with their own bodies. And they are extremely willing to experiment with women's bodies. There are whole groups of women today who feel very strongly that even if we are to consider only the future of the offspring, and not the differential conveniences to men and women, it would be much safer to monkey with men than it is to monkey with women. The major objection to the pill at present is that we do not know what the effects will be on the children. We have not had it long enough. Now the ideal contraception undoubtedly would be a pill one half of which a man and the other half a woman would have to take simultaneously. But I do not think we are going to get such full equality. All I would hope for until we have such a pill is some cooperative participation in contraception.

We have thought about the effect of contraception on the family. Our type of family was designed for early death, and anyone who was unhappily married had great hope. Today, he has very little. We have to take into account that life-long marriage was set up in the stable society where we did not expect a great deal of development to take place within personalities, where women were expected to bear children throughout their reproductive period and die of the last one, and then permit their husband to marry somebody else. It was a totally different picture from what we have today, and we are considering this also. So the probability is that the most we can ask if we have adequate and appropriate contraception is that those who enter parenthood voluntarily, as there are no longer any social insistences on parenthood in our Western countries, will try to stay together until their children are grown. For people who do not mean to do that, this should be one of the ethical reasons for not having children. It may be possible to establish this.

I do not think, Sir Roger, that we are going to do men in very badly. It is more important to realize that every time you liberate a woman, you liberate some man from giving his life to supporting her. If most women have had to devote their entire life to parenthood, with high risk of death and risk of illness in many countries, most men have had to give their life to parenthood too, and neither of them have had very much chance to develop as individuals. We belong to a special group here – but for the bulk of mankind throughout history, men and women have lived and died as parents, devoting their whole time to subsistance activities, so that there could be another generation of children, and nothing else.

In reply to what Dr Luria said, I think he has got the point that the generation gap was such that it has permitted the young to really challenge the existing system. I saw this happen on another scale in a small island community that I have studied for forty years, where the children used to hate society, but were regularly co-opted back into it, just as the bright boys who went to English public schools always hated it but sent their children there just the same. In Manus Island the young men were left out of their own system an extra few years due to the war, and when they came back they were old enough to challenge it, which was helped by other events in the world. What we are facing today is a new set of values from the young people. They are holding to them even though they apparently go into the establishment; they are not being co-opted as they were before, as they were fifteen years ago. This is certainly true in the United States and in New Guinea and in a good many other places.

However, as to the fact that you wished there were more young people here, I too share this wish, except that the experience we have been having recently with young people points towards one precaution. We must recognize that the only young people who can stand up in such a gathering as this are our own children. I do not mean they have to be our biological children. But they have to be children of people like us. Then they are not overcome by Nobel prize winners or any the rest of it, because they saw father at breakfast, and they know he is human. They can stand up, they do not have to use four-letter words, throw temper tantrums, or talk in the same jargon from Stockholm to Tokyo, because they have had that extra-generation of familiarity with a certain style of thought.

All that the others do, you know, is write something so stereotype that you cannot even recognize what country it was written in. We tried that a the Nobel Foundation Conference in Stockholm, but the young people contributed almost nothing; they spent their time being angry and rude because they were overwhelmed.

So we need a new strategy now for the inclusion of young people. I think that we should include them down to 14; there is no reason at all, why a bright 14-year-old would not have made a real contribution to this meeting, provided he was a son of a physicist, or a biologist or an anthropologist, and was used to standing up to somebody of his own kind. Now in case anybody thinks that's elitist, I would say the same thing for the children of 'Hard Hats'. If you want to talk to them, get children of 'Hard Hats' to work with you when you talk to them.

ALFRED SAUVY: Je voudrais compléter quelques observations de ce matin. Je n'ai pas été contredit, il me semble, ce qui ne veut pas dire approuvé. Mais je voudrais reprendre la question de l'avenir et, en particulier, démographique. On a reproché à nos propos leur caractère vague : je veux donc insister sur une réalité, celle du potentiel démographique, qui nous donne une quasi-certitude avec une base solide, qu'elle soit agréable ou non. Dans les pays peu développés, la population, sauf catastrophe, va quadrupler avant de se stabiliser. C'est une chose qui est à peu près écrite et, par conséquent, tout ce qu'on fera en ignorant ce phénomène sera bâti sur le sable. Devant la perspective d'une multiplication inégale entre les régions et qui aura des répercussions politiques internationales considérables, que faut-il faire ? Avant tout, ne pas chercher à y échapper par des expressions commodes comme « apocalypse » ou « effondrement », c'est simplement un moyen d'évasion. Nous pouvons très bien continuer dans les difficultés sans effondrement. Imaginez qu'on ait consulté un expert au temps de Tibère ou de Caligula en lui demandant combien de temps cet Empire Romain des Prétoriens allait durer. Cet expert aurait dit : « Tout au plus quarante ans. Cet empire n'a pas quarante ans de vie. » Il a duré quatre siècles, et il a fallu encore les Barbares de l'extérieur pour le tuer. Et si ce même expert avait été appelé devant Byzance au Ve siècle les Goths étant à Andrinople, il aurait dit : « Ce n'est pas quarante ans, c'est dix ans ou cinq ans que Byzance va durer ». Et Byzance a duré dix siècles. Dix siècles dans la corruption, dans les difficultés, mais il a duré. Et cela, nous ne voulons pas souvent nous l'imaginer ; nous cherchons à nous débarrasser des tourments par des mots extraordinaires. L'angoisse elle-même est sinon un toxique, du moins une façon de ne pas regarder.

En fait, ces progrès médicaux, sociaux, biomédicaux qui sont notre sujet, dans les débuts disons au XVIIIe siècle, c'était le Bien en soi, c'était le Progrès, il n'y avait aucune question. Et même au temps de la recherche absolue de la guerre, au début du XIXe siècle, on croyait encore au Progrès en soi.

Aujourd'hui, nous avons grand-peur de la guerre, nous ne la cherchons pas, mais nous ne savons plus ce qu'il faut appeler le progrès. Nous doutons et nous avons peur des autres hommes. Dans les pays développés, les hommes se concentrent aux mêmes points jugés les plus favorables, qu'il s'agisse d'emploi ou d'espace, ce qui crée une impression, un complexe de surpeuplement et d'animosité les uns contre les autres, mais particulièrement d'animosité contre les jeunes qui semblent des intrus.

Depuis que les jeunes ont lancé leurs invectives et qu'elles n'ont pas été vraiment contredites, nous avons tous, quand on a parlé de société de consommation, été chargés d'un certain remords, et nous avons plongé le nez dans notre assiette plus ou moins bien garnie. Mais depuis ce moment, nous n'avons rien fait pour tenir compte de ces reproches, qui sont évidemment violence sans solution, mais qui sont justifiés et dont nous reconnaissons le fondement.

Il est à craindre que l'humanité utilise de plus en plus des moyens cruels. Cruels envers qui ? Envers les faibles évidemment ! Ils sont menacés de partout. Ces cruautés seront certes baptisées de termes élogieux ou absolutoires et habillées de parures convenables. Je pense, au contraire, qu'il faut essayer de voir clair le plus loin et le plus longtemps possible.

CYRIL KOUPERNIK: It seems to me that in such a diversified language as English it is very unfortunate that the same word 'drug' should be applied to the different categories which Dr Pichot has described today. This is one of the reasons why there is a lack of understanding on the part of the general public. Maintenant je passe au français. Comme vous savez, la langue la plus utilisée en France à l'heure actuelle est ce que nous appelons le «franglais»; c'est ainsi que ce mot de «drogue», qui était parfaitement clair en français avant, a maintenant la même ambivalence. Ceci n'est pas uniquement un problème sémantique. Il y a, à l'heure actuelle, notamment en France, mais également en Angleterre et en Italie, un mouvement fait surtout de ces jeunes dont nous parlions tout à l'heure, mais aussi de jeunes psychiatres. Ce mouvement, que je n'hésite pas à qualifier de criminel et de stupide, est le mouvement d'antipsychiatrie. Il compromet, d'une façon parfois tragique, tous les progrès réalisés grâce au développement prodigieux de la psychopharmacologie. Et si j'ai un vœu à émettre, c'est que le rapport, tellement clair et si convaincant, du Dr Pichot puisse être diffusé en dehors de cette enceinte.

ALBERT PRINZ: A considerable amount of discussion has been devoted to the question of whether it is desirable or not to manipulate society by interfering with the natural process of selection. Hence the corresponding amount of controversy. Dr Moltmann advocated, if I have understood correctly, artificial selection with a view to levelling out the differences in a pluralistic yet very unequal society and thus improving human relations.

It seems to me that there are certain other conceivable models visualising a totally different society from the depicted ideal one, and this futurologic aspect of society has, in my opinion, as yet not been considered. That is a society based on and governed by a numerically small technocracy. I remember reading an American paper some time ago, which was accompanied by a graph representing a pyramid which did not slope gradually but had a very broad base rising steeply until topped by a fine needle of selected technocrats. In other words, a society where fewer and fewer people possess more and more knowledge and the vast majority less and less. This might well be a rather dreadful vision of the future.

RENÉ KÖNIG: Wir haben jetzt das Ende unserer Zeit und unserer Diskussionsvoten erreicht. Als Ergebnis scheint mir die von allen geteilte Überzeugung sehr wichtig, eine professionelle Moral sei für den Wissenschaftler, ob Natur- oder Sozialwissenschaftler, notwendig. Dabei finde ich es höchst erfreulich, daß wir uns praktisch nicht über Methodenfragen unterhalten, sondern nur zur Sache geredet haben. Zur Sache, das heißt zu bestimmten Werten, zu bestimmten Problemen des Menschseins heute.

Session III

'The Right to Health'

Introduction

JAN WALDENSTRÖM: Our subject today will be 'the right to health'. In his introductory speech Dr Pletscher states three problems which are relevant to our topic.
First, the question of setting limits to research, which was one of the topics yesterday, and the second problem, treated by Dr Hersch today, whether it is necessary to treat minor ailments or whether they should be borne with stoicism.
Should the pharmaceutical industry differentiate between illnesses that seriously
endanger health, and others that only make life more burdensome? In this
connection there is a need for a new definition of the term 'health'. Perhaps the
philosophers may help us with that. The third problem is how our medical priorities are going to be decided. The financial cost of care with mechanized medicine is great. But the shortage of manpower may be a still more important obstacle than money.

DrHersch in her very stimulating paper has expressed an idea which, I
think, is of great significance: «A supposer que l'homme puisse un jour vivre très
longtemps en étant toujours au meilleur niveau de sa santé, cela signifierait qu'il
aurait subordonné toute sa vie à cette santé, qu'il refuserait de se fatiguer au service d'aucune tâche, qu'il ne se donnerait désormais à rien. Une telle «option»
ne serait plus humaine. Il aurait perdu sa libre conscience pour retomber comme
un fait parmi les faits, parmi les seules nécessités d'hygiène parfaite. La parfaite
santé aurait perdu sa raison d'être.»

This statement reminds me of a story about a man who wanted to become
old. As DrKönig said yesterday, to become 95 and completely 'gaga' is nothing
to look forward to. The man did not share this opinion but went to his doctor
and said, 'Doctor, if I do not drink and if I eat very little and if I never have anything to do with women, don't you think that I shall live very long?' The doctor
answered, 'I could not guarantee that your life will be longer, but I am sure, it
will seem much longer.' Perhaps we should not forget this story. There is the old
Roman expression *Vixit dum vixit laetus*. He lived happy as long as he lived. Isn't
that also a human value we have to accept? At least we should remember it
when we talk about prolonging life more or less indefinitely. In modern mechanized medicine, you have so many means of prolonging life artificially with arti-

ficial respiration, with intravenous drips, with pacemakers that you can keep many people alive for a long time, yet very often without doing them or their relatives any real favour. I am telling my students that when mechanized medicine will be fully developed, half of the Swedish population will work to keep the other half alive. And that is nothing to look forward to.

Then there is the other side of the picture. We see terrible car accidents happen to very young people. 21% of the driving population in the United States are between 15 and 24 years of age, but they have 34% of the accidents: In 1969 17,700 youngsters were killed in automobile crashes in the United States and a still larger part were injured. This is one of the big medical problems about which we do not talk nearly enough.

Presentation of topics

JEANNE HERSCH: Pour parler du droit à la santé, je vais être obligée de commettre deux hérésies. Non pas que j'aime les hérésies particulièrement: elles seraient très aimables dans une époque de grande orthodoxie, mais ce n'est pas notre cas aujourd'hui. Je vais commettre deux hérésies, qui ont d'ailleurs été déjà commises avant moi, je crois, par presque tous ceux qui ont parlé, mais ils ne l'ont pas déclaré.

La première, c'est que je suis obligée de recourir à quelque chose qui est *au-delà des faits*. Quand on a parlé de valeurs, on a aussi recouru à quelque chose de tel, mais on ne l'a pas dit en autant de termes. C'est un fait que dans certaines sociétés il existe des valeurs. Ça oui! Mais ce qui fait qu'une valeur commande des comportements, ce n'est pas le fait de la valeur, c'est autre chose dans ce fait.

Eh bien, je suis obligée d'aller au-delà des faits et de recourir à une dimension qu'on pourrait éventuellement appeler de ce mot tabou qu'est «métaphysique». Je ne vais pas faire de métaphysique, et pourtant il y en aura dans ce que je dirai. Et je le déclare exprès, cela comporte une part, je crois, de courage et presque de bravade. Pourquoi est-on obligé de recourir à une dimension de cet ordre? C'est qu'il n'existe aucun droit dans les faits. Ceux-ci ne fondent pas un droit à la santé. Pour qu'il y ait un droit à la santé, il faut qu'il y ait quelque chose par-delà les faits qui exige absolument que quelque chose au niveau des faits soit respecté ou accompli. On se réfère donc à des valeurs ou si vous voulez à un *sens*. Mais les faits en eux-mêmes ne parlent pas et n'ont pas de sens. Quand nous parlons des faits, nous leur donnons un sens par notre parole, toute imprégnée de sens et de valeur, et nous ne pouvons pas faire autrement. Je dirai même davantage. Cette dimension métaphysique si honnie par la science est une condition de la science même, parce que la science aussi est un langage qui veut avoir un sens et que ce langage serait exclu, s'il n'y avait pas cette dimension par-delà les faits. Telle est ma première hérésie.

Deuxième hérésie: je vais recourir à quelque chose de *permanent*. Je crois que le permanent est absolument indispensable lorsqu'il s'agit de comprendre et de juger des changements. En effet, on est obligé de se référer à quelque chose qui n'est pas ce qui change. Pour que le changement ait un sens, on est obligé de se référer à quelque chose de permanent. A moins qu'on dise, comme on a l'air de le supposer souvent aujourd'hui, que le seul fait du changement est en soi une valeur. Auquel cas évidemment, on se réfère à une valeur: celle du changement. Reste à savoir si véritablement le simple fait de se passer après quelque chose d'autre implique que ce qui se passe après est meilleur que ce qui est avant, ou bien si quelque chose peut venir après et être pire, et s'il ne faut pas se référer à autre chose qu'à l'ordre de succession pour juger le changement.

Si on parle de droit à la santé, c'est qu'on se réfère à quelque chose qui justifie et qui porte ce droit. Je n'ai jamais entendu parler, par exemple, du droit à la santé des poulets. Ce qui fait qu'il y a un droit des hommes à la santé, c'est probablement ce qui fait de façon permanente que l'homme est un homme et non pas un poulet. Ce à cause de quoi on préfère expérimenter avec des animaux plutôt qu'avec des hommes, bien que l'homme soit aussi – mais pas seulement – un animal.

Qu'est-ce qui fait que l'homme est un homme? C'est, je crois, quelque chose de permanent et qui probablement fonde le droit à la santé. Ce quelque chose de permanent me paraît être la capacité de l'homme d'avoir une conscience claire. Elle n'est jamais absolument claire, mais elle cherche à l'être, elle se veut ainsi dans toute la mesure du possible. Cela signifie que l'homme cherche à *connaître* avec le maximum de clarté possible et à prendre ses *décisions* avec le maximum de clarté possible, car il est orienté du côté de la connaissance vers la vérité et porté du côté de l'action par sa liberté, celle-ci étant inséparable de la vérité.

C'est pourquoi cette conscience claire, cette condition proprement humaine, est une condition de l'existence de la science, et c'est la raison fondamentale pour laquelle je crois que l'humanité doit se défendre contre l'invasion des drogues psychotropes – indépendamment de toute autre considération de nocivité relative au niveau de l'hygiène physique pure et simple. Cette conscience claire paraît aujourd'hui submergée dans une assez large mesure par les nouveaux pouvoirs que les hommes ont créés dans tous les domaines. Et il semble qu'actuellement, à force de constater et à force de prédire comment les choses sont et comment elles vont probablement ou certainement être – ce qu'on fait dans la dimension scientifique –, on se trouve constamment placé devant des perspectives extrêmes, inhumaines, des menaces de fin du monde ou bien des promesses de paradis immédiat. Et on demande aux hommes non pas de se comporter envers le monde tel qu'il est aujourd'hui, mais «qu'est-ce que vous feriez au seuil de la fin du monde» ou bien «qu'est-ce que vous voulez faire pour avoir le paradis tout de suite»?

Ces deux dimensions sont inhumaines. L'homme ne sait absolument pas quoi faire devant la fin du monde ou devant le paradis, pour la bonne raison qu'aussi bien dans la fin du monde que dans le paradis il n'y a plus d'hommes. Les hommes au paradis ne sont pas proprement des hommes. Adam et Eve au paradis terrestre ne l'étaient pas encore. L'homme a commencé avec Eve et la pomme. Là commence l'humanité. Et par conséquent, si nous voulons sauvegarder l'homme, il s'agit de ne pas le placer dans ces perspectives extrêmes, mais dans les perspectives réelles de l'humanité. Sinon l'homme perd son identité. Il démissionne de sa condition, il nie les limites qui le constituent, les limites sans lesquelles il n'est plus un homme; il essaie d'être un ange ou une bête ou un robot, mais pas un homme.

Lord Todd dans son introduction nous avait parlé de ce désir que l'homme a d'être sain, riche et sage. Ces trois termes ont un sens quand aucun des trois n'est pris comme un absolu et quand ils continuent à se limiter les uns les autres. Mais si vous prenez l'un d'entre eux dans un sens absolu et total, c'est la fin de l'être humain. Par exemple, si la santé doit être un droit absolu en soi, on aboutit à cette situation, dont nous parlait tout à l'heure notre président d'aujourd'hui, à savoir que toute la vie est vouée à l'entretien de la santé, c'est-à-dire qu'on est un détraqué mental, un malade, et qu'on a perdu la vraie santé humaine.

Ni l'information, à laquelle on fait si souvent appel quand on ne sait plus quoi décider, ni la prévision à laquelle on recourt aussi quand on ne sait plus décider, ne peuvent remplacer dans la condition humaine les décisions de la liberté. C'est pourquoi des décisions doivent être prises, dans le domaine médical et dans celui de la législation de la santé, ce que M. von Weizsäcker appelait l'autre jour des « décisions politiques ». Je ne les appellerai pas nécessairement politiques. Ce sont des décisions qui doivent être prises avec la part de doute et de culpabilité qu'implique toute décision, parce qu'aucune décision ne se prend avec une connaissance totale et exhaustive de toutes ses conséquences. Et toutes les décisions médicales sont de cet ordre. Seulement, les nouveaux pouvoirs sont devenus tellement considérables qu'il me semble qu'un médecin isolé ne peut pas prendre aujourd'hui, parfois, seul, les décisions qui s'imposent.

C'est pourquoi il me paraît urgent que s'élabore, en l'absence d'un consensus social général, au moins un consensus professionnel minimum devant les nouveaux pouvoirs de la médecine. Nous l'avons vu, au cours des exposés d'hier, on se trouve constamment non pas devant des valeurs et des non-valeurs, mais devant des valeurs opposées, par exemple: la valeur de l'individu, cette valeur incomparable, qu'on ne peut pas multiplier par deux, par cinq ou par un million, et la valeur du grand nombre. Peut-on subordonner l'une à l'autre? Quelqu'un a dit hier qu'en s'occupant de la santé de l'individu, on risque de camoufler les grandes injustices dont est victime le grand nombre. Mais l'inverse est vrai aussi. Quand on veut s'occuper de tout le monde, on ne soigne personne.

Ce qui rend donc un consensus difficile, c'est que des valeurs opposées coexistent et s'affrontent lors des décisions à prendre: d'un côté, le devoir d'une thérapeutique pure, de l'autre, les intérêts de la recherche et de l'expérimentation; d'un côté le bienfait du soulagement physique, ou psychologique, ou social, de l'autre, la dignité de l'indépendance, de la responsabilité et de l'intégrité personnelles. C'est encore l'opposition des valeurs qui rend ambiguë et en quelque sorte paradoxale «l'humanisation» de la morale et du droit sous l'influence de la médecine: ceux qui veulent être le plus humains, c'est-à-dire le plus indulgents envers l'homme, le plus pleins de compassion médicale, sont aussi ceux qui réduisent le «coupable» ou le «délinquant» à n'être plus qu'un malade innocent, irresponsable, qu'ils dispensent d'être un homme en lui en déniant la dignité. De l'autre côté, il y a ceux qui font preuve de rigueur, de dureté, mais qui respectent dans l'autre, et même chez le malade mental gravement atteint, son irréductible liberté responsable et personnelle, et qui conservent le respect que cette irréductibilité implique.

Devant toutes ces valeurs contradictoires, il nous faut tout de même repérer lesquelles sont des conditions de sens de toute l'activité médicale. J'avais constamment envie de demander aux grands savants et aux grands médecins qui ont parlé devant nous: «Mais *pourquoi* faites-vous tout cela? Quel est en vous le moteur lorsque vous cherchez à guérir quelqu'un?»

On ne peut pas médicaliser toute la vie, ni individuelle ni sociale. La condition humaine, la condition dans laquelle l'homme est l'homme, exige nécessairement que l'être humain supporte toutes les données et tous les niveaux de cette condition. Et tous à la fois. Il ne peut pas découper, il ne peut pas exclure. La recherche d'un consensus professionnel minimum devrait tenir compte de tous ces aspects, sinon le découpage entraînerait la disparition de l'être humain comme tel. Leur complexité, leurs contradictions rendent les décisions à prendre bien trop difficiles et trop lourdes de conséquences, je crois, pour qu'aucun médecin conscient de l'enjeu accepte de trancher tout seul.

On a touché au problème des limites de l'expérimentation sur l'homme. Je pense que ces limites se trouvent là où l'expérimentation contredit le sens même de la recherche, c'est-à-dire où il y a attentat contre l'humain en tant que capacité de conscience claire, de connaître et de décider. On rencontre une autre limite lorsqu'on veut planifier le planificateur, planifier l'homme lui-même, de sorte que la finalité de tout le plan s'effondre. Il se produit alors une perte de sens.

Jeanne Hersch: «On ne peut pas médicaliser toute la vie, ni individuelle ni sociale. La condition humaine, la condition dans laquelle l'homme est l'homme, exige nécessairement que l'être humain supporte toutes les données et tous les niveaux de cette condition. Et tous à la fois.»

A ce qu'on a dit des jeunes hier, je voudrais ajouter que, quant à moi, j'ai l'impression que les jeunes souffrent beaucoup plus d'une perte de sens que de l'injustice sociale. Ils protestent contre l'injustice sociale, et ils ont raison de le faire. Là, les slogans ne manquent pas. Mais ce dont ils souffrent en profondeur, c'est beaucoup plus de la menace qui pèse sur le sens même de la vie, sur le sens de la condition humaine.

BERNARD BARBER: My main assignment concerns the problem of proper ethical treatment of the human subjects who are what has been called 'the animals of necessity' in nearly all of our clinical experimentation. This is an old problem, as all medical treatment has an element of experiment about it, but the problem is now very much enlarged because of a series of new conditions.

First of all, there has been a very large increase in scientific development and the necessary clinical experimentation that goes along with it. The problem has also been defined by disasters such as the thalidomide catastrophe and even more strongly, resulting in the Nuremberg code, by the use of human guinea-pigs by some Nazi doctors. Finally, there have been expressions of concern from within the biomedical community itself. In the United States very distinguished moral influence has been given by Dr Henry Beecher, and in England Dr Pappworth has made somewhat similar kinds of statements about shortcomings in this area.

I want to emphasize two points: First, as to values, I agree with Dr Hersch that very often the problem is not a lack or a confusion of values in human affairs, but a multiplicity of values that have to be reconciled with one another. I don't quite like her way of putting it, of opposed values, as if necessarily there were no ways of having a combination of two values that would be perfectly satisfactory to everybody. It isn't an either/or situation. Still, there are these potentially conflicting values. For example, in the biomedical area there are two very clear sets of values. One is the physician's value of humane therapy and the second is the fact that the researcher is a scientist and wishes to be an original and distinguished discoverer. There is the value of science. This is what I call the dilemma of therapy and science. Let me use this as a shorthand for this potential conflict.

My second point is that there is a strong need for social research, using the best available research techniques and studying representative samples of experience for this problem and indeed for many other social problems that we have talked about today. The patterns of behavior revealed by such research and also the analyses of the social sources of this behavior are essential both for satisfactory understanding and for wise policy. I'm pleading, of course, a case for certain very important new developments in social science. It is terribly important for natural scientists to get the message that there is something new in the world and that social scientists should be called upon much more often concerning social problems caused by medical progress.

My colleagues and I have done two studies: One is on a nationally repre-

Bernard Barber: 'It is terribly important for natural scientists to get the message that there is something new in the world and that social scientists should be called upon much more often concerning social problems caused by medical progress.'

sentative sample of institutions that do biomedical research in the United States, and another study is on 350 active researchers, 300 of them in a large university hospital in a research center, another 50 in a community and teaching hospital. The two key issues involved were the questions whether proper informed consent was obtained and whether the risk-benefit ratio was reasonable.

We were interested first in finding out the expressed standards that researchers actually have about these two issues. We did this by presenting them with very detailed hypothetical research proposals taken from the literature and elaborately pretested on active researchers. Our subjects were asked to inform us on their concern about informed consent in response to these research proposals and on their decisions, hypothetical, about risk-benefit ratio.

In our second study we again used the hypotheticals, but in this case we asked each researcher to tell us for each of the studies that he was doing – we have a total of 424 studies – to estimate the risk and the benefit for the present subject and the benefit for future patients. There are no absolute risk-benefit ratio values, but we have his estimates of risk-benefit ratios.

The patterns we find are encouraging. The majority have what we call a strict pattern; they are concerned about the consent issue; they are concerned about the risk-benefit ratio, and in their own research do not do studies in which the risk exceeds the benefit.

However, there is a permissive minority, who on one or more of these matters are somewhat less strict, or more permissive, who are not concerned about consent, and who do studies where the risk exceeds the benefit.

What are some of the sources of this permissiveness? I may recur to the matter of the potentially conflicting values. Apparently, in most cases the physician researcher or the clinical researcher has it both ways. He can be a humane therapist and he can try for some degree of originality and discovery. Most scientific research is relatively trivial, both scientifically and ethically. But we find that this potential value conflict in some cases is at the source of the trouble.

For example, we find certain people, whom we came to call the mass producers, who produce a number of studies, but who are not cited in the literature at all. Incidentally, this citation measure has been well validated by some of my colleagues; it checks out beautifully against such things as award of prizes or distinction of the university they are connected with. These are people who are, in effect, doing science and not getting any reward for it. Our inference is that they are pushing a little bit harder still on the science value, trying to compete, and therefore sacrificing somewhat the humane therapy value.

The same conflict comes out in another way. We discovered that certain people are what we call locally underrewarded. These are people who are as productive as certain of their colleagues at their local institution but who are lower in academic rank. Again our assumption is that these are people who feel that they have to work somewhat harder and cut a few corners to get promoted and are thus pushing the science side at the expense of humane therapy.

So what this analysis amounts to is in effect this: Under certain conditions, the conflict between the value of science and the value of humane therapy is resolved. Under other conditions, where there is relative failure in the competitive situation or unjust treatment in the local situation, the science value is stressed.

What are some of the other sources of possible inadequate solution of this dilemma? We studied what we sociologists call socialization patterns or training patterns, and it became evident that the biomedical research community is laggard in this respect. The situation is not a very good one; only one out of 350 researchers had even a short course dealing with ethical questions. Our view is that all this could be considerably improved at a relatively small cost in the medical schools.

What about the peer review committees which in the United States are now mandated for all research that has been supported since 1966 by the National Institutes of Health? No institution can afford not to have those grants. We find that the situation has considerably improved since the late 1950's. At that time there was a small minority of institutions who had peer review committees, but since 1966 practically all institutions have such committees. However, about 15% of the institutions don't review all research, and many of the researchers themselves told us that some of the research they were doing was not being peer-reviewed, even where allegedly all was supposed to be.

We also find that there is some control within the collaboration groups. For example, we could score individuals as either permissive or strict. So we compared, for the research collaboration groups, whether like were associating with like. We indeed found that the strict were with the strict and the more permissive with the more permissive, but it also turned out that people consult unlikes; the strict were consulting the permissive and the permissive were consulting the strict, so some control was coming about in that way.

Our research shows overall that there has certainly been a large improvement since the late 1950's in this whole area, but there is still some need for improvement, especially given the high moral standards and the high moral claims of the biomedical research community. This is an area in which even a small minority of permissive studies is not something that people will tolerate.

On the basis of our data we can recommend specific changes in a number of areas, e. g. in the ways of adjusting these potentially conflicting values, in the methods of training and in the structures and processes of the peer review committees and the collaboration groups. Such changes will better realize the values of what our legal friends call 'all the parties at interest'. With certain knowledge and certain changes in policy, the researchers, the present subjects and the future patients will all be better off.

ARNOLD BURGEN: I chose a rather dramatic title for my presentation. But much of what we are talking about today has arisen because of the philosophical idea of magic bullets. It is an old one from the Middle Ages but really took fire at the end of the last century and the beginning of this. The most famous proponent of the idea was Paul Ehrlich, who thought that one might be able to find specific chemical substances that would produce immediate and dramatic improvements in health. The magic element in it has remained in the popular literature because indeed such things have been found and have been so dramatic as still to carry the connotation of magic with them.

I would contrast against the magic bullets some of the more recent developments in health; a heart transplant is the one that comes to mind, where the visible machinery of creating health has been so evident as to contrast very unfavourably with the magic bullet. The magic bullet was the pill that you swallowed and then you were better. It did not cost much, and the idea of it was that it could be spread throughout the world, whereas the transplant gives rise to quite different problems because cost and the manpower element become important.

It is still worth our while to recall what enormous effects the magic-bullet approach has had on our lives. I don't think any of our social science colleagues could deny that this has had as large as, or perhaps larger social consequences than, almost any political creed that we have seen in our lifetime.

Bacterial diseases, which accounted for perhaps halving of the current life span in the last century, have virtually disappeared. They are so easily treatable that one hardly talks about them. I should be accused of being trite if I were to go on about them, but I pick out one because it is connected with Hoffmann-La Roche, and that is isoniazid, which has turned out to be much the most potent drug against tuberculosis and has changed a pattern in which tuberculosis was a source of misery and death to a very considerable part of the population, not only in the developed world but also in the underdeveloped world, to one in which the treatment is easy.

I should also like to challenge some of my colleagues who have, I think, been sniping at what I regarded almost as a truism, i. e. that the improvement of health leads to an improvement in human happiness. It is true, as Dr Hersch has argued most cogently this morning, that if one is too obsessed with the improve-

Arnold Burgen: 'Community values show up as improvement in health statistics but these are not the things that matter. The things that matter are how the individuals feel, and the individuals nearly always are happy that their health has been improved and not the other way round.'

ment of health, this becomes an ill in itself. But if the improvement of health comes relatively painlessly as it does through magic bullets, then the moral consequences are almost wholly beneficial. Again, one has to contrast the human values and the community values.

Community values show up as improvement in health statistics but these are not the things that matter. The things that matter are how the individuals feel, and the individuals nearly always are happy that their health has been improved and not the other way round.

One can ask whether this approach has come to an end. There are signs that it is slowing down, that it is becoming more difficult to find things and that the first easy crop has been harvested. One can certainly point to the very serious failures to find drugs to treat virus diseases or cancer. There are many people who feel that the chemotherapeutic approach to these diseases is not going to be successful. I would suggest that it is too early to abandon it. One just has to become, as science does become, more sophisticated and look for more subtle ways of tackling the problem, rather than seek approaches that are obviously hopelessly crude in terms of what we know about the biology of these processes, which is still very little.

If one goes beyond dealing with intercurrent disease of that kind one should ask whether there are any major objectives that might be tackled by the magic-bullet type approach. I would emphasize again that the advantage of the approach is that, if it is successful, it is universal, cheap, simple and the social manipulations involved are often rather minimal.

It seems to me that the top target on anyone's list ought to be ageing. When we are trying to deal with ageing there are two quite distinct problems. One is to increase the total life span of the population, making everyone live to 150! The other is, not to attempt to change the life span but trying to make life more livable during the latter part of the life span. This means that one has to tackle the degenerative diseases, most of which seem to resolve themselves into vascular disease of old age. One has to deal with problems, which are perhaps among the most distressing problems of ageing, and that is of uneven ageing, of the man who has a perfectly sound body but has mental deterioration or of the man who is physically totally incapacitated but is still mentally fit. So little is known even about how to evaluate these problems that one certainly cannot make any prediction about them.

We know that life span in animals can easily be shortened by various agents and there is evidence from epidemiological studies that in man one of the toxic agents that has been referred to previously – tobacco – shortens life span. In animals the means of prolonging life – usually again life span rather than improved life status – have so far been rather few. The one that seems to have the best authentication is starvation from early after birth or perhaps even starvation of the mother before birth which can lead to very considerable prolongation of life in rodents. I'm not recommending this as a socially desirable form of treatment. It is one that qualifies absolutely for the strictures that Dr Hersch has made about medical treatment. But one has to proceed on the scientifically hopeful line that if one undesirable way of prolonging life is already known then more desirable ways of prolonging life may well be found.

This introduces a category of research that needs positive encouragement, being socially desirable, since the problems of the ageing population are probably the most serious ones we have to deal with in our society. If even a fraction of the effort which has been put into cancer research had been put into research of ageing we might know more about it now.

The second problem that is a socially desirable line of research is learning. This is perhaps related to the first. Anyone who looks at our educational processes or watches a child learning realizes that this is a horribly inefficient process. It seems to proceed by fits and starts and there are long periods when no apparent learning is occurring although there must be physiological and neurological changes that are preparing for the next step of acquisition of skills. There must be some way of accelerating this process. Again, what we know from our medical experience is that it is easy to do the opposite, i.e. to reduce learning. The natural experiments that we have in conditions like cretinism and phenylketonuria show how learning can be impaired and then restored by correction of the condition.

Lastly I want to touch on the problem of intelligibility of scientific ideas. We all know that there is a great deal of antagonism to science and scientists in the general community at the present time. This has been particularly well stated by George Steiner in a recent book, where he says that it is because of unintelligibility that people are afraid of scientists.

Science is indeed an extremely complicated and highly developed subject, and intelligibility is a problem. It is a great problem even for scientists working within one particular field to be able to talk to each other. For a biologist to talk to a physicist implies another level of intelligibility. If you ask a biologist, what he thinks of the work going on in nuclear physics of a certain kind, or astrophysics, or space exploration, he will usually be able to give you a very fair opinion. He won't say, 'It's terrifying what the space scientists are doing', instead he will say, 'Yes, I know so-and-so, who has talked to me about this, and it seemed a very reasonable affair.' The people concerned will know a good scientist and have faith in him. In other words, between branches of science there is a communication network which depends on trust in each other. The scientists know the unreliable people, they know the reliable people, and they know where to get an opinion as to what is good, what is safe and what isn't. We have got to set up a similar network for the communication between the layman and the scientist. All too often it operates the other way round, i.e. the layman hears from the bad scientist, the man who is trying to get publicity amongst lay people, because he fails amongst his fellow-scientists, as they know him too well. How can we redress the balance?

CHARLES A. BERRY: It is impossible to summarize for you in detail the many things that I would like to say. So I would refer you to the actual printed paper for most of this material.

I was asked to look at health as a physician sees it. This prompted me to ask myself whether I look at it differently from others. Health has generally been defined as a normal condition of body and mind and normally functioning body organs. This implies that we know what 'normal' is. The first thing we have to admit as physicians and scientists is that we frequently do not know what this is. We say something is normal, and relate it to a very large group of people about which we have been able to collect some information. Nonetheless we still have difficulty in being sure what normal is for a given individual.

During the last ten years I have been dealing with a very special group of people who have been selected for a demanding task, and, as such, have been subjected to a very high degree of controlled health care. We have been trying to define the normal for the individual in our very small population. This immediately raises the question whether we could do the same for a very large population. As Dr Hersch rightly says in her paper, those who try to safeguard social life, or even life at all, are in a very difficult situation. Those of us who try to control the health of a group of people find immediately that what we feel is necessary for them is not viewed in the same manner by the people whom we are trying to help.

There is a sort of dichotomy today between preventive medicine and therapeutic medicine. If all of you think for a moment you will realize that the bulk of people who are engaged in providing medical care or health care are really involved in therapy: they take care of people who are already ill. We have not been able up to now to put the same kind of emphasis on the preventive aspects of medical care. We are indeed preoccupied with illness.

In the space program, we were faced with a difference. We did not have patients come to us except for some of the minor illnesses that usually plague all of us. Basically these were people who were well. We were trying to devise a medi-

Charles A. Berry: 'If all of you think for a moment you will realize that the bulk of people who are engaged in providing medical care or health care are really involved in therapy: they take care of people who are already ill. We have not been able up to now to put the same kind of emphasis on the preventive aspects of medical care.'

cal program that would allow us to see that they stayed well and were thus able to do a job. We could further utilize these individuals as their own control so that we could measure very small deviations from that base line from which they started and which we called their 'normal'. We started out with a great deal of anticipation and speculation as to what would be the worst that could happen. Then we saw what really did happen to the individual as he was exposed to the environment or as he went about his normal activities and preparation for his occupation. If an individual did indeed become ill we looked upon this as a preventive medicine failure. We tried to take the page from the engineers' notebook and did a 'failure analysis' to see whether we could improve the system.

I want all of you to realize that health care is certainly more than just trying to create a normally functioning set of body organs, including the mind. You cannot separate it from economics, nor can you separate it from social and other pressures that impinge upon the individual and threaten his health. We have all met cases where we gave medical treatment that was very correct and exact, and still that patient was no better off in the long run, for the situation to which he returned was one which utterly destroyed everything that had been done on a medical basis.

I firmly believe that there is a right to health. We have to try to render adequate health care to the population at large. I realize this is an awesome task that we are undertaking. It challenges our current delivery systems and it certainly challenges the number of people available to render that kind of health care.

One of the things that have been very valuable in our efforts has been the activities to utilize technology, to be on the frontier not only of medicine but on a frontier utilizing engineering capability to convert part of technology for use in medicine. Our task within the space program was not only to get people into space, but to monitor them from distances of 240,000 miles and have some idea about their medical status. This gave an impetus to the development of a number of things that are of great benefit in other areas of medicine.

I would mention two major kinds of advance derived from this: First, it provided a more scientific basis for measurements. Instead of having individuals make these measurements and put their own interpretation into obtaining them we had a scientific basis allowing much better comparison of measurements. We do realize that there is a tremendous amount of art in medicine and we don't attempt to eliminate it. But it certainly is an advantage to have a greater scientific basis.

Secondly, it freed us, as physicians, from some of the tasks that we had normally been doing. It allowed us to utilize paramedical people and it meant that we could do other jobs. We had to educate both the individuals who were a part of our group and the physicians. Physicians, in general, tend to be conservative in that they want nothing to interfere with their patient–doctor relationship, and I firmly agree with this. But we have to ask ourselves how many physicians are able to maintain a good patient–doctor relationship today with the way medicine is practised. I would say there are not many. Therefore we must educate the physician to the fact that the machine is not going to interfere. It will on the contrary give him the opportunity to put some humaneness back into medicine. The machine will enable him to meet the patient with medical information in his hand, all within the same day and thus to be much more the physician that he should be. The patients certainly want some time with the physician so that they can learn to understand what is happening to them.

In order to utilize technology you have to try to apply it to all the various areas where one can reasonably think that you might have to render medical care. This would start with very remote areas in which, with space flights, we have certainly had a great deal of experience. But on the surface of the earth too, remote medical care can be provided by some of these techniques.

The basis for this type of activity is an adequate communication system. You must also provide a system to store the information as a part of this communication system. This we can do on a world-wide basis just as well as in a very small area.

Dr Jerne yesterday made a statement with which I have to take very serious issue, and I certainly hope it is not what he sincerely believes when he says that you cannot popularize science. With this attitude, if we stick to it and mean that we cannot explain to people in a manner they can understand what we are doing, we have lost the entire ball game of what we are trying to accomplish.

I have lived in an engineer's world for the last ten years and I realized very early that I must learn to speak their language as they must learn to speak some of mine. You have to do this if you want to sell your programs so that with their help you can accomplish what you set out to do. You need them as team-members as medicine today is a team-effort and is becoming more so.

The patient too must understand. You must educate him to his illness so that he can be a help to you. We might end by saying that the drug companies have been very excellent in this regard, in that they have helped us educate both patients and physicians.

Discussion

ARNOLD BURGEN: May I ask you a question, Dr Hersch. You talked about the two contrasting states of instant paradise in the end of the world. It seems to me that these are too simplified because instant paradise has many elements to it. What we have been discussing particularly in this meeting is that element of paradise which is medical. It seems to me that the creation of good health by itself is not instant paradise because there are a great many other elements to human nature that are not being modified by this. On the other hand the denial of that part of paradise perhaps reduces some of the other elements of human nature.

JEANNE HERSCH: Bien sûr, l'expression de fin du monde et de paradis était simplifiée. Mais ce que j'ai voulu dire, c'est que cela rejoint ce que l'un des conférenciers avait dit hier, à savoir que la science devait cesser de faire des promesses totales. Dans le domaine de la santé non plus, on ne peut pas faire une promesse totale. Il n'y a pas de santé totale. Il n'y a pas d'état de santé paradisiaque. J'ai écrit dans mon papier, mais je n'ai pas répété aujourd'hui, qu'à mon avis la capacité de supporter certaines choses fait partie de la santé. Un être en bonne santé est un être capable de supporter certains inconvénients, certains désagréments, certaines peines, et même certaines angoisses. Cela fait partie de la condition humaine.

C'est donc pour cela que j'ai dit qu'on ne devrait pas se placer dans des perspectives totales, parce qu'elles sont trompeuses, elles suscitent des espoirs et des attentes qui doivent être déçus, et qui le sont par nature, nécessairement. Alors ces espoirs déçus entraînent une aggravation de l'état en question, parce qu'au lieu d'être supporté, il est rejeté, l'indignation bouillonne, et toute la situation se trouve de ce fait aggravée, et par conséquent le bonheur, si vous voulez parler de bonheur, s'en trouve diminué.

Je crois d'ailleurs que le bonheur est une de ces bonnes choses qu'on vise le mieux indirectement. La plupart des choses très précieuses ne peuvent pas être visées directement. On peut bien viser la suppression de telle ou telle maladie ou l'atténuation de telle ou telle peine, mais jamais viser l'état de santé totale qui serait l'état paradisiaque, où finalement le corps serait à la fois oublié et source de plaisir.

CHARLES A. BERRY: In your written paper you say that you feel doctors should be given a greater burden in the decision between life and death. You put this as a question actually, and the thing that interested me is this, do you feel that doctors should be given that choice? Or do you feel, as I gathered you did, that this is a personal choice of the individual concerned?

JEANNE HERSCH: Je vous remercie de me poser cette question. Je pense que, dans des décisions aussi importantes, on ne décide jamais pour soi tout seul. Cela, c'est un premier point. Si véritablement un être humain pouvait décider pour lui tout seul, je dirais que chacun a le droit de décider pour lui tout seul. Mais ce n'est pas le cas. Nous sommes, qu'on le veuille ou non, interdépendants. Un comportement a une influence sur les comportements d'autrui. Si, par exemple, on opte pour sa propre mort, on n'opte pas seulement pour sa propre mort, on opte aussi pour celle des autres, et c'est pourquoi je ne crois pas qu'on ait dans ce domaine, comme d'ailleurs dans d'autres aussi importants, un droit strictement individuel, délimité et absolu. C'est pourquoi je crois qu'il est essentiel que se crée progressivement quelque chose qui n'existe pas actuellement: un minimum de consensus social général dont puisse s'inspirer ensuite le corps médical dans son ensemble, avec certaines règles, certains critères, certaines normes. Voilà le chemin dont je crois que nous avons besoin et dont nous ne pouvons, à vrai dire, pas nous passer dès maintenant.

JAN WALDENSTRÖM: I should like to ask Dr Barber what we should mean by informed consent. This has been discussed many times at different meetings. The National Academy of Sciences had a meeting to discuss the ethical aspects of experimentation with human subjects. There, Dr Jonas made the very essential remark that we should not try to hide our responsibility behind consent, not even behind informed consent.

Still, it is necessary to inform the patient as well as we can, and that brings up a question that Dr Berry started: Do we speak the same language? Are we able to explain to a patient what it is all about? I strongly doubt it. During all these years I have talked to a great many patients and found that some might understand while others don't. What I want to stress is that if we have given a lecture in our own language to the patient and he nods consent, then we may not just go and do that experiment without taking the final responsibility upon us. I would not be too much impressed by this beautiful expression 'informed consent' – its validity all depends upon how good a doctor is at explaining and on the educational level of the patient. Also, we must remember that the patient is usually in a rather perturbed state of mind and probably not very much inclined to judge his own situation objectively.

To sharpen the sense of responsibility in our young investigators it is important to teach them more about problems connected with human experimentation. I am sure that to say this is to tread on toes that are very sensitive – at least mine are – as it is true that we do not discuss ethical problems enough with our people.

The mass production of scientific papers is an interesting phenomenon. I have a friend, and I may well say I admire him, though I have my doubts. Even his friends, and of course his enemies, state that his goal in life is to have produced one thousand papers. He is in fact on his way now – not being very old and having produced 600 already. This is a serious disease in medicine. I am sure it has to do with medical funds: You get more money from research councils and what not if you are very productive, and so a vicious circle is started.

BERNARD BARBER: 'Informed consent' is a phrase that refers first to a value and secondly to a process of interaction between researcher and patient subject. We certainly must be very careful in scientific research never to seem to call into question the value. The value derives from some of the larger values of our society that are indeed sweeping the world, such as the notion that a man must as much as possible be treated as an equal under any conditions, that he must have a measure of active participation in all affairs that concern him, that he has a right to express his interests in the matters where he is involved.

As to the actual process of interaction unrealistic levels of communication obviously cannot be achieved. First of all, a great deal of research knowledge is esoteric, is hardly communicable even to other medical specialists, let alone to the ordinary layman. Secondly, very often in research, one is attempting to penetrate the unknown, and certainly one cannot be expected to say what one might find with any degree of precision.

Yet, it would be a mistake for the medical research community to stand on that idea. All that is expected is that the value be acknowledged and that the actual process of interaction be one where some reasonable attempt is made to achieve this value in so far as this is possible. Indeed the members of the medical research community might do well to try to explore this. So we want to agree that an attempt should be made to communicate to the patient something of the degree of risk and something of the degree of possible benefit to him and to other people.

Let me repeat that there could be attacks on the biomedical research community if they are not going to sponsor the necessary investigations into medicosocial problems. A great many of the extreme criticisms that the biomedical research community is subject to could easily be forestalled.

CHARLES A. BERRY: I am concerned, Mr Chairman, about your statement on informed consent. If you explain to the patient in your own language you will be in the same spot we are in right now. It is very important that you try to put your information into the patient's language. This can be done even though it is difficult. What the patient needs to understand is whether there is any risk to him, and if so, what kind of risk. If you start interpreting details of the research project you will carry it to the ridiculous and make a mockery of the whole thing. But it is important to outline risk and possible benefit of a study in the patient's language so that he can have a final say on whether or not he wants to participate.

JAN WALDENSTRÖM: I may not have expressed myself quite clearly. What I mean to say is that even if you try your best to explain it to the patient and even if as a result you have what you would call consent, you have to be just as critical as without it because you should not hide behind the patient's consent with a good conscience about having informed him. There is another important rule: There should be no experiments on a patient that is unrelated to his own disease.

ARNOLD BURGEN: I want to ask Dr Barber about his second item, i.e. risk–benefit ratio. Obviously potential benefits can be dressed up. Risks, I should have thought, are very difficult to evaluate because they really fall into two main classes of risks: those you know about from past experience and those you cannot foresee.

BERNARD BARBER: As I said, we quickly discovered that most research, according to the researchers' own statements, involves both very little risk or discomfort and very little benefit. In a very small minority of cases the researcher's own statement indicated that he estimated a considerably larger risk to the patients involved than benefit. In some cases this was compensated for by the estimate that there would be considerable benefit to future subjects.

Regarding the point that Dr Waldenström just made I wonder whether we do want to go so far as to say we should never use any patients who do not have the relevant condition or ailment. Dr Parsons, at the Daedalus conference, suggested that research can be viewed as a communal enterprise. This is in fact the reason why the patient has the right to informed consent, i.e. the researcher and the subject are both engaged in something of common interest. It seems to me there is an ethical obligation for any given individual, and certainly for the total population, to provide subjects for research.

JAN WALDENSTRÖM: And that subject, if I may interrupt you, will be a patient?

BERNARD BARBER: Perhaps so. Perhaps you should use normals; but under certain circumstances the patient may have a condition in which he can easily tolerate something else. Let me give you a trivial example. A great deal of research simply involves taking a bit of blood from patients who are in the hospital. No great discomfort or danger is present in that situation, but the blood is essential. Certainly, one cannot deny oneself the opportunity to say to this patient, 'may we have some of your blood, this is part of your contribution to the ongoing enterprise of scientific research'. In some cases there might be somewhat more serious contributions that the patient who is otherwise ill could still tolerate. It would seem to me that this is something one may ethically ask, in fact one has a right, an obligation even, to ask, if one defines the interaction as a communal enterprise. In this enterprise, the biomedical research community always has to be aware of the fact that it is likely to have superior knowledge, hence superior power, and that it must not abuse this superior knowledge and this superior power. In any case it will be a good sociological model to keep in mind that we are parties in a common enterprise and that we can under certain conditions rightfully expect contributions to be made by normals and by patients.

JAN WALDENSTRÖM: One of the reasons why we are a little hesitant to use patients is that to a certain extent they are dependent upon the doctors.

JEANNE HERSCH: J'ai l'impression que si on entre dans les considérations que M. Barber vient de faire, il n'y a plus aucune limite nette. C'est-à-dire qu'on pourra toujours dire, dans tous les cas, que n'importe quoi qu'on a fait se trouve entrer dans la catégorie qui vient d'être décrite. M. Barber a dit: « under certain circumstances », mais ces circonstances sont impossibles à préciser. Alors là, on ouvre la porte à l'arbitraire total, et comme vous avez vous-même décrit la force des impulsions qui poussent à aller tout juste trop loin, à partir du moment où cette limite s'efface ou se brouille à ce point, il n'y en a plus.

BERNARD BARBER: The abstract possibility is always there that the line beyond which one would want to go may be overstepped. This is why we do need control mechanisms. First of all, there are general ethical prescriptions if nothing else, some version of the Hippocratic oath, that the physician researcher has. Many of our people pick up some kind of crude awareness of the effects of research at medical school and later in their training. But it is clear that the training could be improved. Scientific training is very well done so that good socialization goes on in medical school for being a good scientist, but the ethical side is neglected.

Of course, the peer review committees have been quite effective though outsiders should be involved somewhat more than they now are. This word 'outsider' gives horrors to many people in the biomedical research community. They see one or another variety of the wrong kind of outsiders, the moral absolutist, the ignorant person. But here is the place for a new social role. People should be sitting on the peer review committees who are specially trained to know something about biomedical research, who know which specialists to consult for the relevant problem, who know something about the principles of fair procedure, and who know how to discern public opinion. One of the grossest mistakes in this area is for the review committee to pick up a person almost at random. The typical case in the United States is to have a minister, who is not necessarily the person to know best what the public is thinking.

If we had people in this new social role, they might form a professional association. I would also welcome circuit judges, circuit courts, where specialist outsiders from other institutions sit on the committee, because very often the insiders are simply blinded to other considerations.

MARGARET MEAD: I would like to follow up several points of Dr Berry. We already have various private entrepreneurs in the United States setting up ways of computerizing health data. You wear a bracelet round your wrist on which it says 'telephone so-and-so', and when you telephone you get your medical life history. But we are in the same sort of situation that lead to the dreadful confusion of measurements two hundred years ago and which we have had since with the American, British and European systems of measurements confusing things. So it is very important not to start on this technology unless we have a system that can be expanded until it includes the whole world. This means that we need some transitional situation before we launch it globally. Also, it should not be launched in one country. If it is launched in one country the idiosyncrasies of that country are bound to be expressed in the system in some peculiar way, from which we will suffer for the next hundred years. So every effort should be made to encourage and support the World Health Organization in working out a universal system of computerized health histories.

But, we need something in the interval to bridge the gap, something that would advance the cause of modern medicine vis-à-vis the prejudices and superstitions of a large part of the public, and would be especially valuable to the pharmaceutical industry. People today have been frightened to death by stories of how one drug does not like another, of how some drugs do not like cheese, so that if you combine a particular drug with cheese – or bananas – you die. These stories have been blown up very disproportionately but they make wonderful horror stories. Then there are the stories about the people with penicillin allergies who are still given penicillin, or about hasty blood transfusions with blood types that do not match. These are some of the bugaboos and nightmares of the partly educated public; but of course their fears are founded. Today the average physician, even of the very highest caliber, does not ask what other medication you are taking.

This means that we need a universal card that is properly designed on an international basis on which every prescribing physician enters the drugs he is using – most patients are not even told what drugs they are given nor whether they

Margaret Mead: 'People today have been frightened to death by stories of how one drug does not like another, of how some drugs do not like cheese, so that if you combine a particular drug with cheese – or bananas – you die. These stories have been blown up very disproportionately but they make wonderful horror stories.'

are sensitive to certain blood types or allergic to certain drugs. These cards should be so designed that they can be handled on a computer.

This would allay a great many of the fears, protect a great many persons from the cross-fire between rare allergies and rare combinations of drugs and relieve the physician of taking the life history, which anyhow virtually nobody takes anywhere today.

It would also be a means of educating the patients. We can't emphasize enough that the way to more universal health care is by the education of the patients, so that they can understand what is said to them, and use the instructions of doctors. There is a historical tradition of treating patients as imbecils. Somebody said we were treating them as innocents, but I think we treat them as imbecils, in addition to innocents. Such a new system will need the backing of international agencies, of international pharmaceutical companies and of the whole world associated with health.

My second point concerns the question of research on human subjects. At the conference to which Dr Barber referred, Talcott Parsons and I came up with more or less the same solution from our separate disciplines. He called it collegiality and I called it treating informants as collaborators. In both cases we advocated treating the human subject as a co-experimenter, admitting him to the purposes of the experiment and making his consent a consent either in the community sense or in terms of his specific disease.

This works very nicely as long as people want to be part of the scientific world and want to be treated as if they were baby chemists. It is rather like the way in which we integrated negroes in the United States in the 1940's when we said, 'if you cut your hair the way we do and dress the way we do and talk the way we do, we will pretend you are almost like us'. But there is a very large part of the emerging peoples who do not want to be treated just like us. And the same is true for human subjects who are not highly appealed by being treated as if they were almost as good as scientists. In this case we are going to need ways in which the communities that back up health centers can also take part in research in which they can set the goals. This means in some cases that they will not accept pieces of research that are accepted in other places. But with one serious mistake of uninformed consent you can build up a resistance to experimentation that is extremely costly to science and therefore to the human race.

It should be mentioned that it's the Western developed countries that are using the populations of undeveloped countries as guinea-pigs because they are debarred from doing so in the developed countries by law. This will not stand up. This will compromise our own ethics.

My final comment concerns the allocation of rare skills or rare supplies of drugs or rare equipment and the ethical questions involved. The criterion for allotting scarce skills, scarce drugs and scarce equipment should be whether the patient who gets it will thereby make a contribution to science for the benefit of mankind and not whether he is head of the Boy Scouts. This may sound puzzling but we have a city in the United States where a committee of laymen allot kidney machines, and if you are head of the Boy Scouts this is one of the better ways of getting one. If the criterion was based on these considerations we should advance our total ethics more than we have done so far.

CHARLES A. BERRY: The idea of an international health card is an excellent interim position. Our goal should be to have medical histories available wherever you might be in the world, so that your history could be retrieved if you were seen medically, e.g. in an emergency. The minute you say this you bring up the problem of the privacy of a medical record that is in a computer system. In fact, there are ways to make that private.

However, it is a problem if you decide to develop such a system with the use of technology, while at the same time there are large areas of the world where there is not even the simplest type of medical care available. You emphasize the differences if you go ahead with it. What we would like to try is to bring everybody as much as possible up to our own level. But it will be a while before we achieve it.

BERNARD BARBER: The ethical situation to which Dr Mead referred with regard to the use of human subjects in countries other than the United States but under some form of American auspices is a little bit more complicated than she has indicated. I am in consultation with the Population Council which sponsors a great deal of research in reproductive biology in other countries of the world, the developing countries but also European countries. They informed me that it is the physicians in the European countries and in the developing countries who refuse to have the peer review, i.e. they say 'we can do without it in our country; why should we follow your standards'.

NIELS K. JERNE: My comment concerns the introduction by Dr Berry where he took issue with something I said yesterday about the way scientists communicate, and there were other discussions which also took issue with what I said. I may perhaps have been misunderstood as I do not think that there is an essential difference of opinion. I am of course not against the popularization of scientific ideas and results. On the contrary, I have tried myself on several occasions to make immunological concepts and results understandable to a larger public and sometimes not without success.

But my point yesterday was that scientists cannot be accused of not communicating. I feel that the proper communication of a scientist is by the publication of scientific papers. All popularization implies to some extent a distortion, a dilution and I think that philosophically it is not possible. Popular exposition has to leave out doubts, experimental restrictions, will too easily feel inclined to generalize whereas generalizations are dangerous, and may even have to leave out fundamental ideas because the readers will most often not be capable of understanding those fully.

I could illustrate this with some extreme examples. If a mathematician finds properties by his analyses, say, of cyclic functions, or if a physical chemist finds certain solutions to the thermodynamics of irreversible systems, he will find impenetrable barriers to a general understanding of the essence of his propositions, even by an educated public.

I therefore favour popularization but want to point out that this has fundamental limitations. As I said yesterday, similar situations exist in art. Poets and painters cannot be asked to do a work once more to popularize it for their general public who do not understand poetry and painting.

JOSHUA LEDERBERG: Regarding the question of communication it is of the utmost importance to reverse the process of alienation between the scientific worker and the general public. Most of us are well aware that scientific research demands sacrifice on the part of the public having taxes extracted out of their pockets, at the point of a gun – as someone characterized government – for the benefit of the scientific investigator. This is a process that certainly requires some justification and some understanding on the part of the public. In the field of medical research one easily justifies this in terms of a cost–benefit analysis. There is also the problem of basic scientific work. I feel that the public is well able to sympathize with the general cultural importance of scientific investigation, quite apart from any concrete utility. But it must be made available to them for their understanding.

Obviously not every scientific problem, not every piece of research, is a good example to illustrate the flavor of scientific inquiry. One often does not choose certain topics because they are too premature. Those issues that are least well understood are often the most difficult to explain and it is only when a line of work has reached a certain conclusion that it becomes simple enough to be explained to the public at large.

The second problem, however, is the alienation of the scientist himself. I think the scientist must recall that he is part of the community of people whence he comes, to whom he is responsible and that the communication in a certain sense is always reciprocal. One cannot attempt to formulate one's own ideas in a form that others can understand without deriving some profit in terms of the setting, in terms of the meaning of one's own work for the entire cultural process.

However, it is often difficult to ask scientists themselves to act as popularizers, as communicators; this in itself is a specialized role. What many of us would ask is not that many scientist should stop working in the laboratory in order to popularize but that they should give more encouragement and more respect to those who do this. As there are many scientific journalists who do not meet our standards of veracity and fair dealing we often tend to condemn the entire community of scientific journalists. We don't give the communicators a very high place of esteem or prestige or respect. We have no particular institutional arrangements by which to afford a general high standard. I try to think how this could be done at the university, but it is rather difficult there. At least the professional societies ought to take a more aggressive role in establishing positions for this very important function of communication.

I'd like to comment on some remarks that have come up now and then about what molecular biology can do for medicine. I agree with Dr Luria that it is very difficult at this stage to point to any specific therapeutic utility derived from molecular-biological investigations, although a few are appearing, e. g. in the field of virus therapy. It is much more likely that molecular biology will have an absolutely indispensable role in preventive medicine. It will presumably lead to an understanding of the mechanisms by which mutation occurs and the genetic damage that can result, e. g. from environmental hazards and chemical carcino-genesis.

This is much more subtle as one does not point to a specific drug that has been developed on the basis of scientific investigation, but rather to a general understanding of a process and a general sensitivity to the role of biochemical and environmental factors for a large number of diseases. I don't have to tell you that the patient who has not had cancer is not nearly as spectacular an ex-ample of the medical victory as the patient who may have to undergo the most radical surgery or other treatment and be barely salvageable after most of the harm has been done. Yet it is exactly in the preventive mode – if one is to speak of a crusade against cancer – that most of our efforts should intelligently be spent, since one can estimate that at least half of cancer is of definable environ-mental origin.

Since there are many people here from Hoffmann-La Roche, I would like to pursue this theme just slightly. It has to do with the general problem of the side-effects of environmental additives of which drugs are an extremely important consideration. I am very sympathetic with the burdens that the pharmaceutical industry has had to fall under, especially in the United States, with the bureaucrat-ic machinery of the FDA, which often poses what seem to be the most irrational kinds of responsibilities for testing. This diverts a great deal of effort that could be better spent. But companies like Hoffmann-La Roche have an opportunity and a responsibility to show some leadership in what would constitute the most rational, the most effective, the most efficient methods of testing of drugs for side-effects. I am very much disturbed that so little attention is paid to pursuing in very great detail the biochemical metabolic fate of drugs before they are intro-duced widely, as a method of eliciting suspicions about what may happen to them. In my own field too little attention is paid to possible genetic hazards of drugs that are used very widely, perhaps because of the distraction by the bu-reaucratic requirements.

Just one brief remark on some of the points of Dr Barber. We must ob-viously exhibit gratitude to a social scientist, who has been able to give us an ex-ample of good empirical research on the relationships of medicine and medical research in an important component of the social order.

There are serious problems regarding informed consent. For example, the legal view of the matter would hold that no one would rationally give up anything for nothing and that if a patient ever gets into any difficulty, retrospectively he must have been under coercion. He could not have been properly informed or he would not have accepted any risk. If one pursues this to its logical conclusion, it would be necessary for every patient to be accompanied by a legal counsel before he could competently give his informed consent. This would be precisely what is required in the judicial process and there is no reason in the world why the same doctrine might not eventually apply here.

What is missing is the element of compensation. In what way is the patient being compensated for his willingness to participate in the scheme? The communal interest has been mentioned and it is obviously of the utmost importance. Perhaps we should consider formal compensation to a subject to undertake research for the general good. It is the reverse of taxation. At the very least some form of insurance is needed that does not go into questions of negligence or of liability, but makes certain that, if ever a patient is injured as a consequence of a medical experiment, he does not have to accuse anyone of negligence but can indeed be compensated in full.

ARNOLD BURGEN: Regarding Dr Jerne's comment I think there are two levels of understanding and communication in science and he is only considering one of them. If you take a mathematical proposition, there are two levels at which you can consider it. One is the mathematical result and how you can use it. The second is how you obtained it and whether the necessary rigour was applied in getting there. The mathematician is much more concerned with the rigour. He cares much less what the answer is than how it was derived, whereas people who want to use mathematics are concerned with the result. This is true all the way along. If I want to understand a bit of physics, I want to know broadly what it means. It doesn't matter to me exactly what kind of piece of hardware is used to obtain the results or even what computer programme it needed to process the results. I want to know what its general significance is. The public want to know – e.g. if Dr Luria is working on a virus – what a virus is, what potential it has for human beings and how it can be controlled. They want as honest information as they can get, not down to the finest detail nor down to all the doubts and certainly not with all the precision that is needed to follow this on a professional level.

JEANNE HERSCH: Exactement. J'ai été très contente de la distinction que M. Burgen vient de faire, mais je voudrais renverser les deux termes auxquels il a abouti. Parce que je crois, pour ma part, que l'intérêt du public est exactement l'inverse. Ce qu'il lui importe essentiellement de savoir pour comprendre ce qu'est la science, c'est beaucoup moins le résultat obtenu que précisément la nature de la démarche, la méthode employée, le chemin suivi. C'est ça essentiellement qu'il importerait de lui faire comprendre.

SIR ROGER ORMROD: May I take up three points: The first is the title of today's part of the Symposium, 'the Right to Health'. So far as any lawyer is concerned, when the word 'right' is used, there always is implied a correlative obligation; the right to health implies an obligation by somebody to provide the health. It may well be misleading if we talk about the right to health without at the same time considering where we think the obligation lies to supply that right. Of course it may be either the patient himself who should take steps to obtain health or to preserve it, or the community. To use the words 'right to anything' loosely is a highly misleading use of language, one that could have unfortunate results.

The second point I want to discuss is 'consent'. To a lawyer the phrase 'informed consent' is wholly redundant and is unfortunate. If once you introduce the word 'informed', you seem to be implying that there is something like an 'uninformed consent'. As a lawyer I don't recognize its existence. Regarding the question of informed consent, the situation strikes me as a lawyer as very strange. Here in the second half of the 20th century the medical profession is poised on this dilemma of informed consent. The jurists of the world since the dawn of history – if there were jurists at the dawn of history, which I doubt – have been debating this question of when consent is 'consent' or not. They have never come up with an answer; they have spent years of thought, and mountains of paper have been used, in an attempt to explain what it means, and the answer is nil. The lawyers, however, have evolved over the years a pragmatic solution to this question. In one sentence it can be put in this way: The degree of information required to make a consent valid varies with the gravity of the matter in issue. I can only speak in terms of English law. But if anyone seeks to suggest, after having gone through a marriage ceremony, that they did not consent to the ceremony, because they were not informed about some aspect of it, they get what in England we call short shrift. You have got a tremendous burden to establish that your consent was not informed.

On the other hand there are whole series of relationships, which are recognized by lawyers, in which higher and higher degrees of integrity and trust are called for. We have a classification in English law of the relationship which we call a relationship *uberrimae fidei*, a relationship requiring the utmost faith and frankness. This is exactly comparable and exactly applicable to the problem we are discussing today. It is quite ridiculous to suggest that any research worker should set about explaining to a patient whose consent he wants, what he is going to do in scientific terms. He can do this very easily, but the patient, of course, derives no benefit from it whatever. What the patient wants to know is two things: What is the degree of risk that he is undertaking when he accepts to enter into this experiment? What is the likely benefit to him or to others?

May I also make this plea to all biomedical scientists: Please treat patients as adults. They are adults. They have a great deal of sense if you will allow them to use it. If, however, you treat them as just slightly more intelligent than your

Sir Roger Ormrod: 'May I also make this plea to all biomedical scientists: Please treat patients as adults. They are adults. They have a great deal of sense if you will allow them to use it.'

guinea-pigs, then I'm afraid you will be in trouble. But if all scientists in dealing with patients will bear in mind that the patients too have a responsibility when they consent, then we shall get a better balance.

My third point concerns communication. As a lawyer, particularly as a judge, I have from time to time to hear cases involving expert evidence both medical and non-medical. It is a very surprising fact that of all the varieties of experts who give evidence before the Courts it is only the doctors who appear to resent it, so far as my experience goes. Doctors have a pathological detestation of the witness box. It is a pathological detestation of saying what is in their mind. I suspect that physicians have always been in this superior position, like priests, in which they are never called upon in the ordinary intercourse of daily life actually to say what is in their mind. A scientist who is advising a large company is exposed to argument and criticism in a boardroom or in an office, and an architect is subject to criticism by his clients. A doctor is never subject to criticism by his patients or if he is, there is no crosser doctor in the world. Witness boxes are an institutionalized form of criticism. But this emerges: The better the doctor, the better the witness he is. Those who are really expert in their subjects can make the most complex medical ideas and concepts plain to the lawyer, so that the rival lawyers or even the judge can debate them.

I recently tried a case in which the sex of a particular individual had to be determined. This involved a study of the chromosomal sex and the whole lot. The debate was conducted on the highest level by doctors of great competence; yet I don't think that any of the people in that room of adequate and average intelligence had difficulty in following the arguments that were put forward. Well, the doctors were real experts.

But it can sometimes work the other way. Years ago I was engaged in a case of the utmost complexity involving pathology of the nervous system. All the experts in London were called upon but none of them could understand it. Sir Charles Simmons, a very great neurologist, was giving evidence. The case lasted for many days before a very distinguished judge summed up the case for the jury. The poor jury went out to try to decide this insoluble neuropathological problem. In the corridor Sir Charles Simmons said to me, 'That's the first time I have really understood this case'.

JOAQUÍN RUIZ-GIMÉNEZ CORTÉS: Like Sir Roger I am a lawyer, a jurist, but it is always difficult for a lawyer to speak after a judge, especially when it is not to contradict him, but to agree essentially with what he has said. This is my first difficulty. The second is to have to speak in a foreign language. I choose English but am Spanish. I would have tried to do it in French, but English-speaking people are so much more tolerant with the mistakes made in their language! To speak a non-correct French is almost a sin against the Holy Ghost!

It appears we have reached a 'consensus' that biomedical research needs the respect and the backing of all of us. Speaking from a professional point of view it is obvious that, as lawyers, we must struggle to ascertain that social groups and politicians respect and grant the largest possible area of freedom for authentic scientific research. Law must not be used to restrain objective scientific research. Scientific freedom is mainly a problem of the personal conscience and responsibility of those who are dedicated to research. We must stimulate this sense of responsibility and conscience through education, the mass media, the scientific press, and at the same time stimulate respect for free investigation as one of the human values and human rights. The task of the law is to restrain and punish any interferences by political powers, by economic or social 'pressure groups' with fair freedom of research and especially with the proper use of the fruits of investigation.

The second point – implicit in the first – is that we ask all those who are dedicated to biomedical investigation to respect certain 'fundamental values'. I know it is very difficult to speak of values in a symposium of experts dedicated to the empirical sciences, but I am sure you accept that there are certain human

Joaquín Ruiz-Giménez Cortés: 'Law must not be used to restrain objective scientific research. Scientific freedom is mainly a problem of the personal conscience and responsibility of those who are dedicated to research. We must stimulate this sense of responsibility and conscience through education...'

values that cannot be denied. I will not enter into the fundamentals of this statement. I would only mention that there is a certain 'world agreement' on a minimum of human values, at least on those that were consecrated in the *Declaration
of Human Rights* in the United Nations and that were the object, in 1966, of the
pacts or covenants of the United Nations. I insist on underlining as an empirical
fact that there is a certain 'consensus' on this set of values. I take up three ideas
and requirements from it:

(a) *Respect of the right to life*. It is true that the word 'right' here is ambiguous compared with other classic 'human rights'. It is rather an appeal to society to afford the objective conditions that would make possible the satisfaction of
man's need to be healthy. The creation of these conditions is expressed as a
'right to life' in the text of the declaration and the pacts of the United Nations.
But to me the point underlined by Sir Roger is much more important, i.e. to
treat the patient as an adult, though I would rather say 'to treat the patient as
you yourself would like to be treated if you were a patient'. To measure the other's needs through our own needs and feelings is an equalitarian way of ruling
human relations.

(b) *Respect of the personal conscience of the patient*. Some of the speakers
have already mentioned this point. However, it is essential to insist on respect of
the personal conscience of every man, not only of religious conscience, or moral
conscience based on a rational ethics. Here I mean the personal conscience of a
man who feels himself 'a human being', a being free and responsible.

It is very important that the physician in his relation with the patient take
care of him with comprehension and inform him very honestly of all the risks of
a surgical intervention or an experiment. This leads us to the question of communication. Communication is essential, in particular the democratization of
knowledge, in this context of knowledge on biomedical progress. What must be
avoided is 'propaganda', the wrong kind of communication. Unluckily, during
the last two or three years there has been too much 'propaganda' or noisy 'publicity' on certain biomedical experiments and applications, which has brought
discredit on that kind of thing.

(c) Moreover, I would ask *to respect the equality and solidarity of all human
beings*. This concerns especially the problem of genetics. Equally important is the
problem of providing the medical care that biomedical progress has made available to all those who belong to other continents, to underdeveloped countries or
areas even on our continent. Of course, this requires the cooperation of society
(even, I would say, of the State, if the word 'State' is properly understood). It is
necessary to establish an order of priorities in public expenses. Nowadays,
biomedical research and education have top priority for human beings.

But it must be said that all this would require – I can only mention the problem as it is too close to political implications – a very deep reform of social and
economic structures. With the actual structures of many of our countries it is
practically impossible to obtain this ideal health care for everybody.

Very near here, in the Münster, the Cathedral, you will find the grave of a man who, like ourselves, lived in a moment of great crisis in the world. The man was Erasmus of Rotterdam. At a moment when the world was changing very deeply, as it is changing now, that man had faith in the possibility of freedom and peace for men. Let us hope that Erasmus will be a guide for us in our future work.

MICHAEL F. J. MARLET: Gestern wurde uns erklärt, daß der Mensch das Lebewesen ist, das sich selber erkennt und akzeptiert beziehungsweise zu erkennen und zu akzeptieren hat. Seine Gesundheit als sein leib-geistiges Wohlbefinden ist zwar einerseits in seiner leiblichen Kondition verwurzelt und kann durch sie beeinflußt werden, hat daher auch eine leibliche Beziehung zur Umgebung und zur Kulturstufe, andererseits aber wird die Gesundheit bestimmt durch seine Erwartungen, und diese Erwartungen sind wieder von seiner Information, von seinem Wissen und von dem entsprechenden Anerkennen seines Wesens abhängig. Persönlich hat mich die Bemerkung von Dr. Kety getroffen, daß wir uns bei diesem Symposium allzusehr auf die neuesten Kenntnisse konzentrieren, während diejenigen, die schon zehn oder zwanzig Jahre den Gang der Weltgeschichte in fast allen Ländern bestimmen, zu ungenügend kommuniziert sind, als daß der Mensch ihnen in seinen Erwartungen und in seinem entsprechenden Handeln Rechnung tragen könnte. Andererseits werden diese Erwartungen des Menschen bestimmt durch seine Grundhaltung, auf die gestern Dr. Moltmann hingewiesen hat, eine Grundhaltung der Anerkennung, des Akzeptierens und der Bereitschaft zur möglichen Veränderung der dilemmatischen Kondition des Menschen.

Inwiefern beeinflußt dieses Verständnis der Gesundheit die Beziehung zwischen Arzt und Patient? Es war im Referat von Dr. Burgen die Rede von zwei Grundrichtungen in der Erwartung des alternden Menschen. Nämlich einerseits die Erwartung, möglichst lange zu leben (und die entsprechende Haltung des Arztes, den Menschen möglichst am Leben erhalten zu wollen), andererseits aber der Wunsch des Menschen, vom Arzt Hilfe zu bekommen in seinen Schmerzen, in seinen Lebensängsten und in seinem körperlichen Leiden. Er möchte wahrscheinlich lieber möglichst intensiv menschlich leben als möglichst lange leben.

Zwar könnten wir diese Frage in der Schwebe lassen, wie es auch Dr. Burgen heute morgen getan hat. Ich möchte aber doch konkreter darauf eingehen, weil gerade diese Erwartung, die zu den Grundkomponenten des Verständnisses der Gesundheit gehört, auch das Handeln einer pharmazeutischen Firma beeinflußt. Welche Art Pharmaka sollen vermehrt produziert werden? Solche, die uns möglichst lange am Leben erhalten, oder solche, die uns dazu helfen, die Toleranz zu schaffen, die wir in der dilemmatischen Struktur des menschlichen Lebens immer mehr und immer tiefer brauchen? Ich meine keine Tranquillizer, mit denen unser Denken gleichsam ausgeschaltet wird, sondern vielmehr solche Mittel, die uns helfen, die Schärfen weniger zu spüren, und die uns dadurch die Möglichkeit geben, intensiver an dem eigentlich menschlichen Leben teilzunehmen, oder, wie Frau Dr. Hersch gesagt hat, mit deren Hilfe wir unsere Freiheit und unsere Erkenntnis tiefer erleben können.

ALFRED GILMAN: Before turning to my more serious discussion I would like to introduce just a bit of levity that relates to 'informed consent'. Dr Louis Lasagna, Clinical Professor of Pharmacology at the University of Rochester, decided to do an experiment on 'informed consent' and he chose as his drug – the reason for his choice will soon become apparent – aspirin. He consulted a certain textbook of pharmacology and carefully outlined all of the potential toxic reactions to aspirin. He then went to his subjects, indicated to them that he would like them to participate in a study of an analgesic and then read to them the toxic potentialities of aspirin, whereupon practically 100 % of the subjects refused to participate in the study. He followed this immediately by telling them that he had been describing aspirin, whereupon the subjects said, 'Aspirin! I would be delighted to participate'.

There have been two topics that have continually recurred during the course of our discussion. The first is the population explosion and its associated problems and the realization that this planet cannot accommodate an infinite number of people.

The second topic deals with life expectancy and beyond that life span. Dr Moltmann spoke of infinite life, of immortality, although he said it might become rather boring and repetitive. Dr König took 95 years of age as a reasonable objective, provided that one remain in tolerable condition, and the bible gives us three score ten.

Now, all drug companies that I know of are studying the aging process. Their stated objective, and I think Dr Burgen's stated objective, is not to increase the life span, but rather to avoid the premature aging of a given organ system, be it the cardiovascular system or the central nervous system. But I am

Alfred Gilman: '...the question that I am raising, assuming success in the study of aging and the ability to expand the life span to 95 years, is whether we are willing or selfish enough to sacrifice one generation in order to enjoy 25 more years of life.'

positive that in the back of their minds is the hope that they can achieve more than this, the hope that they can actually increase the life span.

Let us consider the fact that the most productive period for most scientists is in their thirties and forties, and in some disciplines as early as in their twenties. Now let us do some arithmetics. Take Dr König's 95 years and the biblical three score ten or seventy years, and subtract 70 from 95 and you come up with the very interesting number of 25 years. In these days of early marriage this essentially represents one generation. So the question that I am raising, assuming success in the study of aging and the ability to expand the life span to 95 years, is whether we are willing or selfish enough to sacrifice one generation in order to enjoy 25 more years of life.

JAN WALDENSTRÖM: There seems to be a general consensus here that the ageing problem is a major one. A British clinician has coined the phrase that the important thing is to add life to years, not years to life. That was the reason why I asked Dr Kety about a really good pill for memory. I feel sure that a significant part of the ageing of the central nervous system may be a problem of molecular biology and not only a problem of circulation. We talk so much about atherosclerosis of the brain. It may just as well be that some enzymatic processes are ageing.

ROBERT JUNGK: Eines der Hauptthemen dieses Symposiums ist die Kommunikation zwischen Wissenschaftlern und Öffentlichkeit. Sie haben sehr viele Sprecher der Wissenschaft gehört. Ich betrachte mich als Sprecher der Öffentlichkeit, als Kommunikator, und ich möchte Kritik nach beiden Seiten und Vorschläge nach beiden Seiten für eine Verbesserung dieser Beziehung unterbreiten. Ich meine nämlich, es genügt nicht, daß ein allgemeines Klagen anhebt. Auf der einen Seite ein Klagen über den Hochmut der Wissenschaftler, auf der anderen Seite ein Klagen über die Unzuverlässigkeit der Kommunikatoren. Wir sind in einem Zeitpunkt, wo die Verhältnisse zwischen Wissenschaft und Öffentlichkeit genau studiert werden müssen und wo wir auf Grund solcher genauen Studien uns überlegen sollten, ob wir nicht neue Institutionen brauchen, mit denen diese Beziehungen verbessert werden.

Als Kommunikator ist mir in meinen Begegnungen mit Menschen der Wissenschaft aufgefallen, wie wenig sie verstehen, daß die Sprache der Kommunikation eine ganz andere sein muß als die Sprache der Wissenschaft. Sie ist weniger präzise, dafür ist sie effektvoller. Sie ist weniger eng, weniger genau auf einen Punkt gerichtet, dafür versucht sie, breitere Probleme, breitere Komplexe zu sehen. Leider ist Kommunikation in einer Gesellschaft, die auf Konkurrenz aufgebaut ist, sehr stark abgestellt auf das Ereignis, die Sensation. Das ist nicht die Schuld der Kommunikatoren, sondern der öffentlichen Kommunikationsmittel, die heute noch weitgehend auf dem alten und überholten Konzept der sensationellen Nachricht aufgebaut sind.

Was kann geschehen? Etwas, was wir ganz ernsthaft überlegen müßten, was sich auch Hoffmann-La Roche überlegen sollte als Konsequenz dieses Symposiums, wäre, daß an allen Schulen, wo Professionisten ausgebildet werden, das heißt Techniker, Wissenschaftler, Mediziner, ein Lehrstuhl sowie ein Seminar für Kommunikation eingerichtet werden sollten. Das bedeutet nicht, daß nun diese Techniker, diese Wissenschaftler, diese Mediziner dort schreiben lernen – Schreiben ist eine Gabe, etwas, was man kaum lernen kann –, aber sie könnten zumindest etwas Verständnis für Kommunikation erlernen und vielleicht auch neue Haltungen zur Öffentlichkeit.

Man sollte nicht von oben herunter sprechen; man sollte den anderen ernst nehmen. Ich habe gefunden, daß noch heute 80 % der Menschen über 50 in diesen Berufen eine olympische Haltung einnehmen. Sogar von Joshua Lederberg, den ich als einen der Pioniere auf dem Gebiet der Verständigung zwischen Wissenschaft und Öffentlichkeit sehe, hörten wir Worte, die mir ein bißchen herablassend schienen zum Beispiel, als er sagte, wir sollten nur genau berichten.

Nun meine ich, daß die Rolle des Kommunikators nicht nur die des genauen Berichters ist. Er ist nicht nur der Hofmaler, er ist nicht nur das Instrument des Wissenschaftlers, sondern er hat selber ihm auch etwas zu geben. Er ist nämlich in gewissem Sinne der Vertreter der Öffentlichkeit. Er hat die Ansprüche, die Sorgen, die Wünsche derer, die schweigen müssen, an den Wissenschaftler heranzubringen. Er darf also nicht nur ein Übersetzer sein, sondern er muß auch ein Kritiker sein. Ich frage mich, ob nicht die Jugendrevolte zum Teil daraus entstanden ist, daß die Journalisten, die Kommunikatoren, ihre Arbeit gegenüber der Wissenschaft nicht getan haben, daß sie nicht kritisch genug waren, daß sie zu sehr in der Tasche der Wissenschaftler steckten, sich von ihnen zu sehr imponieren ließen und nicht den Mut hatten, vom Standpunkt der Öffentlichkeit aus mit kritischen Fragen an die Wissenschaftler heranzutreten.

Vielleicht noch wichtiger ist die Aufgabe des Kommunikators, außer Übersetzer, außer Kritiker auch noch «Integrator» zu sein. Die Gesellschaft leidet

Robert Jungk: «Der Kommunikator... ist nicht nur der Hofmaler, er ist nicht nur das Instrument des Wissenschaftlers, sondern er hat selber ihm auch etwas zu geben. Er ist nämlich in gewissem Sinne der Vertreter der Öffentlichkeit. Er hat die Ansprüche, die Sorgen, die Wünsche derer, die schweigen müssen, an den Wissenschaftler heranzubringen.»

nämlich unter einer Krankheit: der «Atomisierung». Wir müssen also Menschen haben, die versuchen, das Ganze zu überblicken. Was ihnen an Tiefe fehlt, kann ihnen an Weite gegeben sein. Der Wissenschaftler muß anerkennen, daß es nicht nur vertikale Denker gibt, die einen Punkt vertiefen, sondern auch horizontale Denker, die versuchen, eine Fülle verschiedener Daten zusammenzufassen, um daraus Ganzheiten zu formen, die dann der Kritik offenstehen können. Mir scheint die Rolle des Kommunikators als Integrator, der versucht, in der Fülle der Ereignisse das Ganze noch zu sehen und dann zu erfassen, wohin der Weg geht, außerordentlich wichtig zu sein. Wenn man den Kommunikator mit diesen drei Eigenschaften anerkennt, dann wird man ihn auch nicht mehr so sehr als Dienstboten behandeln, wie es heute die meisten Wissenschaftler noch tun.

KARL GROEGER: Ich habe als Mitarbeiter der Hoffmann-La Roche die Möglichkeit erhalten, dieses Symposium teilweise mitzuverfolgen. Als Laie auf den hier vertretenen Wissensgebieten kann ich auf manches Gesprochene keinen Bezug nehmen. Doch ist mir das eine aufgefallen. Es wurde gesprochen vom Wert des Lebens, von der Disharmonie zwischen den Generationen, vom Überbevölkerungsproblem und anderem mehr. Auf einen möglichen Sinn oder ein Ziel des Menschen wurde bis jetzt nicht eingegangen. Dr. Sauvy erwähnte kurz die Selbsterkenntnis des Menschen, und da glaube ich den Ansatzpunkt zu finden, von dem man ausgehen kann: Die Biochemie kann sich vom sich selbst erkennenden Menschen Bestimmung und Wert geben lassen. Hier ist dann auch das Maß enthalten, wie die Biochemie in eines Menschen Lauf eingreifen soll und darf.

DOUGLAS CAMERON: I should like to comment briefly on the matter of informed consent. This morning, Dr Waldenström, you pointed out, that even informed consent did not absolve the physician from his own personal responsibilities. Dr Barber's reply left me wondering whether the implications of your remark were fully understood. We have heard some disparaging comments about physicians; that they are overly sensitive to criticism, that their attitudes are in many ways inappropriate and it has even been suggested that they are quite incapable of taking a proper family and social history, let alone using this information meaningfully in the management of their patients. I can assure you that most American physicians are quite capable in this regard, and can only conclude that Dr Mead had extremely bad luck when she was ill in the United States. I think it's about time that a physician stood up and made a few comments.

This issue of informed consent raises considerations that in many ways go to the core of what this Symposium is all about. As a physician I have not the slightest doubt that your comment, Sir, was prompted by your own dedication to the ethics of medicine, and that in dealing with a patient, you have never had any doubt that your responsibility as a physician took priority over your responsibility as a scientist.

Either this position is valid or it is not. The position of course rests on the moral values enunciated long ago by Hippocrates and Maimonides and in contemporary times by the World Health Organization. A value accepted by mankind all these millennia and one which has transcended considerations of race, creed and political affiliation qualifies, I should have thought, as an enduring value in Dr Hersch's terms. Perhaps too a value by which, as Dr Luria suggested yesterday, we might do well to judge change; and certainly an example of an enduring human value deviations from which we should do well to avoid or undertake with the greatest caution.

I am not suggesting in any way that there is anything wrong with peer group review or with laymen, clergymen or even lawyers sitting on review committees. I am suggesting that the need for this has arisen because of a tendency to deviate from an enduring value code. Moreover the results of peer group judgment to date tend to confirm decisions taken in the first place on the basis of these enduring values.

Finally, I should like to suggest that the staggering implications of Dr Berry's vision, from which everybody seems to have shied off, can indeed be approached with confidence, provided there is a firm consensus regarding the enduring human value of the ethics of medicine. As the future unfolds the hardware, the tools, the techniques, the drugs will change, and mankind should make giant strides in the historic struggle for freedom. And let us in this audience never forget that freedom from disease is an important element in that struggle.

BERNARD BARBER: I am grateful to Dr Cameron for stressing that point. Indeed, in one critical case, the case of Southam and Mandel in the State of New York, where the charge was made that proper consent was not obtained for injecting live cancer cells into geriatric patients, there was a model proceeding held by the Board of Regents, a quasi judicial procedure with expert testimonial by lawyers, doctors and other kinds of people. One of the principles laid down was that the physician experimenter who is acting as therapist may not use any of the especial privileges and immunities that are his as a physician, for example to maintain certain kinds of secrecy that he thinks would be beneficial to the patient. So as Dr Cameron says and as was laid down in this quasi judicial proceeding, the role of the physician has priority.

JAN WALDENSTRÖM: Even with the excellent drugs that the pharmaceutical houses are giving us at the present moment, there is hardly an effective treatment that has not something of an experiment in it, since you can never be perfectly sure that the effects of the treatment will be what you hope. This of course adds to the difficulties of informing a patient.

Presentation of topics

KENNETH J. ARROW: I was asked to present a paper on the problems of the United States medical care system. As I began to write, this became somewhat more alive as a topic because of various political developments, much greater discussion and the introduction of various bills in Congress for a national health insurance system. I'm not going to duplicate the paper because as it has turned out it falls a little outside the discussions in this Symposium. I shall rather try to stress those aspects that fit most closely the issues that have been faced here, and neglect those devoted more specifically to the mechanics and economics of a health insurance system.

The question to be discussed is how medical care is in fact distributed to the population. As Sir Roger Ormrod remarked, a term like 'right to health' is at best a very ambiguous one and must be interpreted with due care. Medical care is a scarce commodity like most of the commodities that we buy and sell. It requires physicians, requires hospitals and in modern days requires a good deal of heavy technical equipment, all of which are expensive. The use of medical care necessitates that society give up other things. There is the whole question of the level of provision of medical care, which varies to a considerable extent from country to country. There is the question which people are to receive care, what kind of illnesses are to be given priority, what kind of treatments have to be given preference. In the paper by Lord Zuckerman there has been a suggested conflict between organ transplants and common colds, if I may desperately oversimplify.

We have experience in the world with the scarce commodities to which we are accustomed in our daily life. For better or worse, we have a rather standard method of handling their disposition. When we ask who gets different cuts of meat, the answer lies in the workings of the economic system, and particularly in what we call the price system. You have to pay for what you get. If you want something very much, you'll be willing to pay a high price. If it is expensive and you don't care for it very much, you'll forego or limit consumption and spend your resources, such as they are, on something else.

In terms of medical treatment this would mean that more treatment goes to the rich than to the poor, although not so much more as one might suppose, because medical care appears to be what economists call a necessity (not to be confused with the use of that word in daily life), i.e. proportionally the rich spend less of their income on medical care than do the poor. Nevertheless there will be some tendency to go by income. The price system means in particular that very expensive treatments will tend to be rarely used or used only by the very rich. This is not the place for a lecture in economics, but there is a general view that the price system creates great pressure for efficiency in the use of resources. If things are expensive, they are not going to be wasted, to put the matter bluntly.

However, medical care, considered as a commodity, is not very typical. It suffers from certain differences from the usual run of commodities, which make the price system less than perfectly applicable. There are a number of reasons why this may be so, but the most important is that the need for medical care is very uncertain. On the other hand, when it occurs it may be very important. So it is not a minor uncertainty that can be absorbed within the fringes, so to speak, of one's economic activity.

I want to distinguish between two kinds of uncertainty that occur here. One is the kind we think of most usually in connection with health insurance, i. e. the uncertainty of the incidence of illness. We don't know whether we are going to be sick or how sick we are going to be. We don't know what the costs of the medical care we are going to require are. The second kind of uncertainty is that we don't know the outcome of medical treatment. This is an important explanatory factor in the organization of the medical care systems throughout the world.

Let me take up the implications of these two types of uncertainty. First of all the uncertainty of incidence. Here, health insurance of one form or another has come to be a standard reply, where actually we are buying the services of 'risk avoidance', creating a new commodity in the world, which of course has many parallels in other fields of activity. However, insurance, and this is true anywhere, weakens, or even eliminates, the effect of the price system in rationing demand. In fact, when carried to the extreme, as in some of the American proposals or in the British system, there is no effective constraint upon the individual as far as his purse is concerned or as far as the price he has to pay, since the price is zero. He may pay an annual fee of some kind in the form of taxes, but this is irrelevant because it doesn't affect his decision to buy medical care on any particular occasion. To the extent then that demand for medical services is strong and will tend to outweigh the supply that society sees fit to provide, we have a problem of allocation.

One particular aspect of this, which is closely related to biomedical innovation, is the question of extremely expensive, sometimes called catastrophic, medical treatment. Renal dialysis has been a much discussed example in the United States and I suppose elsewhere since it is so conspicuous. Costs in the United States run to 25,000 dollars a year per person, and it is a prolonged treatment with no particular end in sight. The question how this burden shall be borne is obviously a severe one. The organ transplants raise the same problem, and presumably on the horizon there are other forms of extremely expensive medical treatment to be considered.

A first reaction is concern that this may turn out to be catastrophic not only for the individual, but also for the medical care system. If we adopt a system in which the purse and the price system play no controlling role, then what is to prevent the medical system from being swamped by demands for these expensive treatments? Research on this is beginning – I am engaged in one project but am not yet ready to give a full answer – and I am inclined to believe that overall this effect will turn out to be negligible. This may be surprising. One large insurance company in the United States now offers companies group insurance policies with an essentially unlimited coverage. For this they charge something in the order of $ 1.30 per year extra. This is their estimate of what these costs are going to be. One may assume that they are not foolish. In fact there is already empirical evidence. In one plan with an essentially unlimited ceiling, in ten years' experience, the highest figure reached for any year was 29,000 dollars and there were very few such cases. In other words, this is where the principles of insurance operate very well indeed.

The catastrophe to the individual is negligible on the scale of society, and when averaged over a large number turns out to be unimportant. It may be that deeper analysis will show more troubles here. In particular there may be a problem of demands for specialized kinds of resources. If a field requires highly trained specialists, then, even though in some overall sense very few doctors are tied up in this, these few may be swamped by the demand. Again one tends to feel that if the skills involved are not unduly scarce and if the demands are great, more physicians will be drawn into these fields and, over a period of time at least, the problem is solvable.

Let me turn to the other kind of uncertainty, the fact that the outcomes of treatment are uncertain. They are not only uncertain to individuals; they are differently uncertain to the physician and the patient. Presumably what makes the physician the physician is that he has less uncertainty about the outcome of disease than the patient. At least the patient thinks so. Many special phenomena of medical care can be explained in terms of an awareness of this differing uncertainty and a desire to guard against it.

But I want to call your attention to one aspect, i.e. that the demand for medical care is partly determined by the physician, as it is he who recommends how much medical care is required, say in the form of referring to specialists, or of utilizing his own services more extensively. This gives rise to a situation in which the desire for medical care is not completely controlled by the patient. You find that in areas where medical supplies are abundant they are also utilized more, controlling all other possible factors, income, population size, anything you can think of. When the doctors are there they make themselves busy, well, they make each other busy. So, the demand as registered, e.g. on waiting lists, is in fact a reflection of the operation of the medical system. When the medical system is tightly used of course, doctors make fewer referrals. Statistically there does not appear to be such a great demand.

This reaction introduces a certain kind of indeterminacy in the responsiveness of the medical care system to the needs of the populace. It means that in important respects the allocation of medical resources to different uses is controlled not by response to demand and to needs but by the desires of the medical service industry itself. Similarly, we have the question of locality. The distribution of physicians by geography is by no means commensurate with the needs, even the needs as expressed by dollars. Physicians go to places where they enjoy living. The same problem may arise again in the question of the type of medical service provided. There is a recurrent feeling that there is a tendency toward the sensational operation, toward the advanced technique, which attracts attention among the peer group and among the public, rather than concentration on the more mundane matters, which are much cheaper and would provide help to a large number of people. This is the sort of thing that is widely alleged and very hard to document. It does suggest that if we have a more centralized health system than we now have in the United States, a more direct kind of control over the doctors' activities will be needed. I think of this as supplementing the control by consumers' demand, not as supplanting it, since the ultimate demand is still a very strong factor.

A second aspect arising from uncertainty as to the outcome is a need for more stringent control over the quality of medical care. We actually have very little effective control in this regard. There have been studies by reputable sources suggesting that there are a good many unnecessary operations, a good deal of general practice that is well below the highest possible standards – I am not talking about the highest possible standards in the sense of standards obtainable only under ideal conditions, but standards obtainable even in routine practice conditions. In some cases physicians have been willing to cooperate to the extent of having observers around who were far from flattering to the doctors observed. Although this has not become a matter of public outcry, I think it ought to be. There is going to be a need for systematic sampling checks, as within hospitals. I would like to see lay participation in this. Also, the consumer should be assured, here as elsewhere in the economy, a sufficient degree of control of the kind of products he receives. Actually, demand for quality control in medicine is very old and is the psychological basis for licensing of doctors and for the other kinds of restrictions on entry. However, licensing a man at the beginning of his career does not guarantee a very effective check on his subsequent development, particularly in a world in which there are rapidly advancing techniques, in which a man, no matter how competent, may become obsolete.

Let me conclude with a question the answer to which I do not know. I talked about the distribution of medical care, and obviously implicit in this has been the idea that medical care is desirable because it promotes health. However, the evidence is not all that overwhelming. For one thing, the mortality table of the United States, certainly over the age of two or three, has remained essentially unchanged from 1955 to the present. During that period there have been great changes in medical care. There has been an increase in the amount of medical care per capita, the number of hospital beds per capita, paramedical service per capita and I believe even physicians per capita (I am not sure about the last). Certainly, there has been an increase in specialization among physicians. Yet in fifteen or sixteen years there has been no change in the mortality table. Now, we are very poor in morbidity data, and it is difficult to make them comparable over time. Still, I suppose there is some relationship between the two.

The same thing occurs very conspicuously in interstate comparisons. There is no relation whatsoever between the death rates in different states of the United States and the number of physicians per capita. They are completely unrelated phenomena.

The same is true if you make international comparisons. The United States has roughly twice as many physicians per capita as England or Sweden, and both of these countries have considerably better mortality rates than the United States. I am told that Israel is a country nearest in the number of physicians per capita to the United States, and it ranks quite a bit below the United States in mortality. So whatever these observations are worth, I call your attention to the fact that there seems to be some slippage between the idea of merely increasing the volume of medical care, at least at the present stage, and improving the health of the country.

AXEL STRØM: My theme, how to relieve the physician of unnecessary burdens, might seem a trivial one compared with the great and serious themes that have been presented by the previous speakers. Yet, from a practical point of view it is an important issue, as the 'right to health' implies the most effective use of the doctors' skills.

Lord Zuckerman has described in his paper in an excellent way the dilemma that confronts modern medicine: The demand for health services has increased much faster than our capacity to satisfy it, and there is no reason to believe that the demand will be reduced in the years to come. Faced with this problem the question arises how we use our doctors' skill and time.

However, the problem of how to relieve the doctor of unnecessary burdens cannot be dealt with separately; it must be seen in a broader context. The time has passed when practically all health work was done by doctors. A constantly increasing part is now done by other categories of health personnel. And paramedical institutions and social agencies play a more and more important role. But are the services organized in such a way as to ensure that the best use is made of the various categories of health personnel and institutions, according to their skills and qualifications, and that the best cooperation between them is secured?

Investigations have shown that most doctors spend much of their time in non-professional duties and in tasks that could be performed by others. As an example I mention the clerical work which social insurance systems and other kinds of social legislation impose upon the doctors. At least in some countries, such as mine, the regulations are such that completion of medical forms and certificates takes much of the doctor's time, thus reducing his productivity. In order to prevent any abuse of the health services, the legislation has introduced a mass of control measures. In forming the regulations the authorities have paid more attention to the question of control than to the load upon the doctor's time.

This is merely one example of how highly qualified professionals are used in tasks that could be performed by others. Many more examples could be found if we examined how other categories of health personnel spend their time. It is very easy, too, to find examples of lack of cooperation between the various categories of health workers and institutions: how patients are referred from one institution to another, and how different social agencies may work with problems of the same family, almost without knowing about each other.

The main reason for this situation is that the organization of the health services has not kept pace with the rapid progress of medicine. The advance in the biomedical field has been immense. The spectrum of disease is another than it was some decades ago. The psychological and social problems are of far greater importance than before, and the societies are undergoing rapid changes. Yet, in most countries comprehensive analyses of the impact of all these changes upon the organization of the health services are lacking.

The time has now come to analyse and evaluate the total situation. We must not confine ourselves to examining some small sectors of the problem, but take up the total situation for study. How shall we today organize the health services in our societies? How much of our resources shall be allocated to preventive health work and how much to therapeutic medicine? What categories of health personnel do we need? What type of work shall each of them do, and how shall their work be organized? How shall we train them adequately for their jobs and how shall we secure the best cooperation between them? The answers to these questions will of course differ from one country to another, depending upon the political system, traditions, economy, population density, etc.

There is the question whether medical students are adequately trained for the problems with which they will be confronted in practice, and similar questions could no doubt be asked also for other categories of health workers. We expect the various categories of health personnel to work together as a team in practice. Nevertheless, we train them separately, not in teamwork. Therefore the medical schools and the schools for other types of health personnel should reconsider their curricula and change them in a way to meet the requirements of today. It will not be easy to have a medical curriculum changed in a radical way as old traditions are very difficult to overcome. Formation of adequate health teams is the most effective way to relieve the doctor of some of his burdens. In the future much more attention should be paid to such teams.

There is, however, one great obstacle to the effectiveness of any reorganization of the health services: Some of the other categories of health personnel are in as short supply as doctors. In Norway shortage of nurses is a more important obstacle to an effective use of our health resources than the shortage of doctors, although we are in short supply of them, too. If we cannot solve this personnel-shortage problem, it will be very difficult to carry through any plan for a better health service. The solution will not be found in the creation of a new category of health workers, such as the feldshers of the Soviet Union. We should have to draw them from the same manpower pool, with the effect of augmenting the shortage of the present types of personnel.

A much debated question is the role of the doctor in the fight against the many social problems in modern society, whether they are labelled medical or not. Shall we accept that it is the duty of the doctor to handle such problems too, or shall we leave them to other professions and let the doctor concentrate

Axel Strøm: 'In modern society medical and social problems are very closely knitted together, and many patients cannot be given adequate medical care unless the social and environmental factors are taken into consideration. Such problems are not an unnecessary burden of which the doctor can be relieved.'

upon the specifically medical problems? In my view the doctors must accept the responsibility for such problems too. In modern society medical and social problems are very closely knitted together, and many patients cannot be given adequate medical care unless the social and environmental factors are taken into consideration. Such problems are not an unnecessary burden of which the doctor can be relieved.

I also raise the question whether it is possible to reduce the demand for health services, thus creating a better balance between the demand and our capacity to satisfy it. I doubt very much whether this will be possible. We have for many years taught people that they must protect their health and that they shall seek medical advice whenever they feel a need for it. We have been successful so far. Protection of health and medical care are today regarded as human rights, regardless of social class, economy, occupation, etc. It will be very hard, even unwise, to try to reverse our education of the public.

Self-medication is, as far as I see it, no solution. Of course, not all medication can be carried out through a doctor; some preparations must be available to individuals for their own treatment. But in view of the hazard of abuse we should not encourage an extension of self-medication.

My point is that the question of relieving the doctor of unnecessary burdens must be seen in a broader context: What changes are necessary in the organization of the health services in the societies of today? This is a problem very difficult to solve. But even if it were solved, I am rather pessimistic as to the possibilities of attaining a significant reduction in the burdens of the doctors.

LORD ZUCKERMAN: I was invited to prepare a paper to the title 'Choices and Priorities in Research and Development in the Biomedical Field'. It deals mainly and centrally with the issue of the relation of the resources available for health to popular expectations and to actual demand – on the assumption, which I accept, that there is an unquestioned right to health or that people have been brought up to believe that they have that right.

I began the paper – to which I shall not refer in what I am going to say to-day – by quoting from what Bernard Shaw said in 1906. It is still very relevant today, and indeed I doubt very much whether he would be satisfied with the existing position if he were still alive. I am tolerably certain that he would be adding new prefaces to the last one which he produced in 1936. What he said was that until the medical profession becomes a body of men trained and paid by the country to keep the country in health, it will remain what he saw it to be, a conspiracy to exploit popular credulity and human suffering. And he went on to say that however scientific a treatment may be, it cannot hold its place in the market if there is no demand for it, nor can the grossest quackery be kept off the market if there is a demand for it. Medical treatment, to Bernard Shaw, is governed by fashion in the same way as are clothes.

In my paper I emphasized the increased expectations of the public, and I concluded that there was a need for the establishment of medical priorities. And let us not make any mistake about this. These priorities are in fact recognized by the governements of those countries that manage health services. In the United Kingdom 5% of our Gross National Product (GNP) – which is 2,000 million pounds (roughly equal to 5 billion dollars) – goes to our National Health Service, only a trivial amount going to health through the private sector. In the world at large all medical services amount to no more than 80 billion dollars at current values, out of a world GNP of some 4,000 billion dollars. Medical research and development account for 4 billion dollars. For comparison – defence research and development consume some 20 billion dollars, five times as much.

Since Bernard Shaw wrote his play there have been major changes in the United Kingdom and in several other countries. The biggest change in the United Kingdom was the establishment of the National Health Service during the few years after the end of the Second World War.

The motivation which led to that service was the belief that social justice demanded that the health services available to the country should be better distributed than they were by the market mechanism. Nothing that I have heard here so far – or indeed read in Dr Arrow's paper – makes me believe that the health insurance approach is ever going to touch the real problem. Even though we have a National Health Service provided by exchequer funds, it has not succeeded in distributing health services evenly around the countryside, not even in London.

I have the figures for some of the specialist hospitals in London, in comparison with the cost of the big general teaching hospitals of the kind that have made medical education in England so celebrated. I take as my example of a specialist hospital the National Heart Hospital – to which not everybody goes for a heart transplant. The average cost per case are 407 pounds. In the London teaching hospitals it is less than a third of that, in the provincial teaching hospitals a quarter, in London non-teaching hospitals well below a quarter, and in provincial non-teaching hospitals it is one sixth of what it is in the National Heart Hospital.

I mention this point to indicate that there has not yet been achieved, and probably never will be, a totally 'fair' distribution of our medical resources. Equally, the money spent in the United Kingdom on research and development in medicine is not distributed according to need. If a brilliant research worker uses the resources he is given successfully, he will produce new discoveries. These will be applied – and then follows a new pattern of demand for the particular advance that he has made.

We have been talking a great deal at this meeting about values. It is a vital question. But all our talk will nonetheless be overtaken by facts – regardless of our values. Values and beliefs, ethics and demand – these are the issues. Public demand for medical services is going to overtake our debate. There won't be time for us to be certain that we have got our ethics or our beliefs up to date. And we have not answered Dr Pletscher's questions.

Dr Pletscher put three questions to us: 'Can we set limits to research?' Can we demand that medical research workers take the Hippocratic Oath, which traditionally the doctor swore? Can we suppress publications? His second was, 'Is there any justification for pharmaceutical houses to produce drugs for minor ailments' and, as it were, encourage the spread of a taste for drugs. Finally he asked, 'Is there a justification for therapeutic measures that are costly in money and manpower?'

I think I recognized all his questions in the paper that I produced. But I must confess that I did not take myself over the final hurdles, providing clear answers. But I shall try now in a series of propositions. First, resources, whether medical or otherwise, are limited in all countries. Secondly, one cannot possibly take the problems of the United States as a model for what is happening in the world at large – or what is likely to happen – in terms of their arguments about the provision of medical services.

There are well over a thousand million people in the world with an average income of under 200 dollars a year. While it is not the purpose of this Symposium to deal with the problems of this third world or with those of the Communist countries – Lord Todd made this plain at the outset of this meeting – the presence of that vast 'other' world nonetheless casts a shadow over everything we are going to do, for the simple reason that that world has claims on our richer world for money and aid. They, more than 1,000 million people, are as accessible as we are to messages about medical miracles, messages that are spelled out in newspapers, shown on television and which always, always promise a better tomorrow.

As I said, talk about values will be submerged by demand. The World Health Organization is there to see that underdeveloped territories know about modern developments in medicine. Those who saw television pictures of what has happened recently in India and in Pakistan, in particular in the east of Pakistan, will remember those horrifying pictures of people, young children, queuing up for cholera injections, for this, that and the other. That is an illustration of the immediate demand.

There is also a vast growing demand. Our very distinguished demographer colleague, Fred Sauvy, yesterday provided us with a picture of the current rate of growth of population, and of its projection to the end of this century, the year 2000. In this sort of discussion the year 2000 is a kind of myth. But population is growing now. Ten years hence there are going to be hundreds of millions more people in the world than today, and if the population of the world has not reached somewhere between six and seven billion people by the year 2000, it will certainly do so by the year 2010. Time is an abstraction here.

We were asked whether or not the economy is going to keep pace with advances in medicine. The answer is, it never could, because of the insatiable demand for more medical service. It is the wrong question to ask. What we have to ask is whether or not economic growth can keep up with all social demand, for medical services, for educational services to eliminate illiteracy, for the eradication of poverty and starvation, for housing and security.

The world is not yet up against the stops, certainly not the Western world. There is a major population problem; major changes are taking place in the age structure of society, creating new problems. But the world is not yet up against the stops. Yet, solutions to our problems won't wait while we debate the place of ethics in medicine. The green revolution alone won't solve the problem of population and poverty.

We can already see the nature of the world clientele that is going to demand its right to health. The theoretical statement that we need not worry about the food problem since we know how to make food synthetically means very little. It takes our mind off the real problem – that at this moment maldistribution is responsible for starvation, for poverty and for a host of other pressing political problems. No amount of abstract talk about the possibilities of science

Lord Zuckerman: '…solutions to our problems won't wait while we debate the place of ethics in medicine.'

and about providing food is going to solve these. They will exert new and more powerful political pressures upon all our existing resources.

Priorities have therefore to be set in medicine, given that the amount of money that can be made available for medical services has to be accommodated within the total sum that can be allocated for social purposes. Lord Todd referred to the fact that in spite of the previous independence of the medical research worker, he could see pressures coming on him because of social demand. I remember Lord Rosenheim writing not so long ago that even if medical research were to be stopped now, there could still be a major improvement in health.

Concepts of social justice will undoubtedly influence our ideas about priorities. For that reason it is necessary not to shirk the question, or an answer to the question, that was put in the first session. Broadly speaking, there are two kinds of demand. First of all new knowledge that can be applied provides new options which may increase man's standard of living. That is one way new demand comes about. The other way is when you identify a need and the need leads to new knowledge which can be applied. Gunnar Myrdal, the very distinguished Swedish economist, said that knowledge can be steered for a purpose. We all know that. But he added that ignorance can also be steered for a purpose.

In the United Kingdom we are already imposing – to a certain extent – a pattern of social justice on the pattern of medical research. Doing so does not in any way infringe the independence of the medical research worker. In the United States, President Nixon has also taken a major step in this direction by demanding an additional one hundred million dollars for research into cancer. There, he was following an earlier call for action by President de Gaulle. Maybe it is the nature of the Heads of State to make this sort of remark. Earlier today we were told by Dr Burgen that research into the diseases of old age represents another need. In my paper I gave my own choices, which certainly included old age but also the common cold.

But who is going to decide what areas of need should be selected for research. In my paper I suggested three possibilities. The one is the medical research worker. I dismissed him because he often creates a costly demand regardless of social priority. I dismissed the public and the client, because the client will absorb anything he is given, any pill, any medical service. And therefore I came down on government. But I am also frightened of government, and I do not want to see government setting the priorities in medical research. Nonetheless, we are committed to the democratic process. Public opinion is a vital step in that process.

I should like to take up this point. We have to talk to the public. Scientists, unfortunately, when they popularize, appear to learn more from the journalists than the journalists learn from the scientists – as far as manner is concerned. They dramatize, they exaggerate, they distort, and they create illusions.

In fact we have not been free from that guilt in this meeting. I hope Dr Mead will not mind if I refer to her because she likes 'speaking in headlines'. But some of her headlines are highly dangerous. What she said about male and female with respect to the pill is not correct. When this morning she said we were using the underdeveloped people as our guinea-pigs in medical research I was frankly horrified. I am not sure either that I accept her explanation of the generation gap. These examples may be dramatic ways of putting issues, but unfortunately they do lead to distortions in understanding.

It is possible to discuss these things in a balanced way. Before the National Health Service was introduced in the United Kingdom there had been many enquiries into the nature of medical service in England. In the thirties one organization, called Political Economic Planning, spent two or three years doing an independent study of all the various aspects of the British health services, and they came up with a plan. It was not the plan that was finally adopted, any more than was another plan produced by Government Officials during the war. What I am getting at is that if scientists and doctors wish to be the people who themselves determine what priorities should be established for medical research, then they have got to speak straight and fairly without distortion about what it is they are doing. They must not dramatize, they must not exaggerate, and they must not get the bad habits of film stars.

If they want to exercise any real influence they have got to understand what other pressures, social pressures, prevail within a country – what process it is that is undertaken by the exchequers all over the world when they decide what resources to put where. I should like the government hand to be held by the medical hand when it comes to the setting of medical priorities. They should in fact be set by the medical profession itself, within a sophisticated framework of governmental information, which takes into account not just the money that can be made available either from public or private sources for the direct application of the fruits of new knowledge, but also the consequential social costs which may have to be borne, given a successful breakthrough in the control of some particular disease. I do not think that if this is done, it will impinge in any way upon the freedom of the individual medical research worker to give his genius full play.

Discussion

COUNT D. GIBSON: I would like to share with the group the experiences that several of us in the United States have been privileged to have during the past ten years. To many of us the multiple problems that have been discussed in the last two days flow out of two bases: It is quite clear that the crisis in health care is directly the fruit of success in biomedical research. When there was very little medical care available it really did not make much difference whether it was maldistributed. It is precisely the brilliant results that have created many of the crises we now have.

In the mode of delivery we have continued in a basically entrepreneurial fashion at a time when specialization has become more and more constant. The waste aspects of the entrepreneurial mode on the one hand and of specialization on the other are with us in the United States. We certainly know that the patient approaches the physician with the terrible concern inside, 'I hope he can treat what I have got'. All too often the physician, as he sees the patient come near, thinks 'I hope he has got what I can treat'. I believe the fact that we now have individual physicians more and more specialized, being unable to respond to all the problems of the patients, has created one of our dilemmas.

Several of us felt that a new form of health care institution needed to be put together that could respond both in the preventive and in the curative and rehabilitational mode, that could also relate itself to education. We therefore formulated the notion of comprehensive health centers, learning a great deal, in this case, from developing countries. Within the past five years a number of these health centers have been established (there are now some hundred in the United States). They began of course in areas in which medical care was virtually absent, in rural areas, and in urban areas for low-income people. We felt that it was important to define a basic unit geographically and also in numbers, not less than about 5,000 people and not more than about 25,000. It was hoped that by restricting itself to this community the health center would be able to develop a pattern of care that reached into the preventive area and not merely in the curative mode. This has indeed been happening, and we now see that more and more care is being rendered within the community and less and less in the hospital.

The initial centers embraced quite a gap between the predominantly white middle-class professional physicians on the one hand and the community, predominantly poor and black or Chicano (Mexican-American), on the other. It seemed reasonable that the community should have some advisory role. I found it an extremely dramatic experience initially and I think so did the patients as they banded together in a representative group. As they began to talk to each other they discovered the depth of their distance from physicians. I have come to the conclusion that the great bulk of people had been taught upon throughout history because they had little alternative. They were lucky if we fetl compassionate, not so lucky if we were not that thoughtful about their needs. And so we found in these communities a profound suspicion of teaching and of research. I myself began to question the belief I had previously held that the best care was in teaching hospitals. For the right disease at the right time with the right research grant this is true. All too often, however, for many of our patients these criteria are not fulfilled.

So we had to go through a profound period of redeveloping confidence in each other, and now, rather than being an entrepreneur in a role taking care of a particular incident, we found ourselves increasingly functioning as servants of the community. This is a very different experience for a physician to have, and I have become persuaded that it is an appropriate one in the health care delivery system.

Within this new framework the community board together with the staff now develop a budget on what the allocation of resources will be. The staff proposes the program for the next year, and the community reviews whether it concurs that this program represents the full spectrum and a proper allocation of effort for the next year. This new way of working is one that fits in well with the aspirations of many of our medical students. I can merely summarize this different way of functioning as follows: In the past physicians have done many things, have rendered care *to* people, sometimes care that people did not understand or that came all too often in a paternalistic fashion. Of course it is the very nature of the care process that we do things *to* people. I believe we can care *for* people and we can render care *to* people in this new kind of representative relationship of a community board if in effect we do establish it together *with* them.

KENNETH J. ARROW: I have first of all to speak on Lord Zuckerman's paper. I am afraid that I at least was unable to follow the links between the different parts of his oral remarks and his written paper. He spoke very eloquently of lack of social justice in several dimensions, the inequalities within the medical system, a point on which Dr Gibson just made certain constructive observations. The inequality is among the nations of the world in terms of the medical resources and in terms of their economic resources in general. There are justified pressures from the poor, internally and externally, for greater aid as a competition to the allocation of resources to the medical field. With these values I fully concur. I think the decline in foreign aid among the leading nations of the world, my own especially, is a disgrace. However, the policy implications that followed seemed to bear little relation to these observations. They really came down to the discussion of certain priorities in the research and development field and, as I understood them, there tended to be an emphasis on certain specific fields of application.

We have heard some dissent from this opinion on priorities on the grounds that the outcome of scientific research is never predictable. I remember my distinguished philosophy professor, Morris Cohen, observe that if in 1830 the British Admiralty had announced it was willing to award some research grants on safety at sea – one proposal was an expedition to Brazil to look for certain very hard woods, another the design of rigging, and a third, by Dr William Rowan Hamilton, was to investigate the properties of the square root of minus one – it is unlikely that Hamilton would have gotten the contract. And yet Clerk Maxwell used Hamilton's method of quaternions to develop the theory of electromagnetic radiation, from which radio was eventually discovered and turned out to be indeed the most important contributor to safety at sea.

Basic research is certainly one on which ideas on predictability and direction in terms of application cannot be seriously entertained. It is also true that there are certain points at which basic research becomes ready to be translated into applied research. Obviously it is at this stage that decisions on priorities are possible. Lunar exploration is the most obvious recent case. The fact that it could be done was clearly demonstrable but did not mean that there was not ten years of hard work needed to translate this into actuality. So I partly agree with Lord Zuckerman in terms of the priorities. However, I am lost in seeking the logical connection with the much bigger issues that he raised suggesting almost the abolition of all research because compared with other needs, it seemed to be an exceedingly small and unimportant matter.

One of the difficulties of raising deep issues is that they make other things seem unimportant and that they may be unresolvable while something can be done with the others. With this in mind, let me refer to the observations that Dr Hersch and, to some extent, Dr Moltmann made yesterday. I may do them an injustice, but there seemed to me to be an attempt to plead for pain as a desirable characteristic of life, to object essentially to interferences with it, as you would be reducing humanity in the process. I myself hold the view that health is a good. I am not prepared, within the present possibilities of improving health in the near future, to accept that anything damaging is likely to occur to the humanity of the individuals. On the contrary, the individual racked with pain has had his humanity very seriously diminished; an individual deprived of faculties through preventable diseases is certainly no longer the same human being.

It seems to me we were worried to some extent by the increasing power through increasing knowledge. It means more choice and reduces the realm of necessity. So long as we have to do things to survive, it is pretty clear what our values are. Once we get beyond that realm, as we have in advanced communities, the nature of the situation does not restrict our choices so much. It is not easy to argue convincingly why one value is preferred to another, because you cannot logically demonstrate it. The situation of a wide area of choice – over reproduction, over death, over various matters that had previously been regarded as inevitable – does increase the responsibility of the individual. Dr Hersch regards this as a very good thing, and I tend to concur with that position. We all want to increase the freedom of the individual, but I am not sure whether the majority of people would agree with us. In fact I wonder whether some of our generation gap problems may not be the result of a difficulty in handling the increased degree of freedom available. This is fairly clear in the behavior of the young, in the sense that they do not have the same compulsive forces that people had in earlier generations, economic compulsions as the most obvious example. The result is that they can take different attitudes freely. There is a multiplication of possible life styles.

Dr Berry has outlined very interesting and obviously solidly documented work on the possibilities of making medicine more capital-intensive, economizing especially on the time of the patient and of the physician through the continuous or at least frequent monitoring of bodily processes. However, is there any evidence that preventive medicine is useful to any considerable extent? This is an empirical question, not a theoretical one. Obviously preventive medicine is desirable. The man who doesn't get cancer is much better off than, as Dr Lederberg says, the person who gets it and recovers. But preventive medicine at the individual level has to be proven to be effective, because you are referring to very large capital investments, and there is going to be a need to justify these investments on some basis before they are made.

PHILIP HANDLER: May I offer a single comment which has to do with the combined thrust of what Drs Arrow, Zuckerman and Gibson have put before us. My point relates to 'resources' and whether or not even the industrialized societies of the world can pay for the kind of care the people of those societies seem to demand at the present time. Lord Zuckerman was indicating that perhaps we never could. Perhaps our appetite for care will always outrun our ability to buy it because, somehow, the wealth must be generated elsewhere in society with which to pay for it.

There is another aspect of his argument. It seems to me that he made a superlative case for support of research, were his own arguments pursued. So, too, did the presentation by Dr Gibson. When Lord Zuckerman and I were little boys the chances that we would positively benefit by an encounter with a physician were rather small. He could hold your mother's hand, but not much more. Calomel and Argyrol in my throat are my memories of pediatric medicine, surely not very effective procedures. Practically everything that can be done in medicine today and that is truly useful to the patient is the consequence of research done during the period in which most of the people in this room have been alive. All of the history of medicine before that, glorious, well-intentioned, compassionate as it was, was relatively ineffective in terms of the benefit for the patient. The Caduceus is an ancient symbol, but it is a symbol of goodwill, love and much pain. Not much more than that.

Now what is it that we mean by medical care? What process are we describing? Who is it that comes to the physician? Who fills our hospital beds? Please notice how much the hospital population has changed. When I first entered the faculty of a medical school, pellagra was the leading cause of death in eight South Eastern American States. There is not one case of pellagra to be found in those eight States at the present time. I admit that this was accomplished in an era before the National Institutes of Health were making 'the right grants', Dr Gibson, but it was the result of research, and be it said, by a great physician in the United States.

What we really mean by 'medical care', the kind that is so expensive, that commits our resources of personnel, doctors, nurses, technicians, beds, is all representative of what Ivan Bennett called 'half-way medical technology', i.e. what we do for patients who have diseases they shouldn't have had in the first place if we had the wisdom to prevent them, diseases for which we do not have definite treatment but have developed supportive physiological measures. The classic of these, of course, was polio. When a polio patient, only a few years ago, arrived in hospital, he required the total resources of the hospital; the cost per day was just about as dreadful in its time, per patient, as is the cost of a cardiac transplant at this moment.

Or consider the years when almost all hospital beds were filled with patients with infectious diseases. As I sat there, a moment ago, just off the top of my head, quickly, I wrote down typhoid, infantile diarrhea, cholera, tuberculosis, pneumonia, the various streptococcal disorders, polio, smallpox, measles, meningitis. Which of you have seen a patient with a mastoid scar recently? Your surgical housestaffs don't even know how to perform a mastoidectomy. Bacterial endocarditis was a perfectly fearful disorder (my young sister died of it), but relatively few need die of it any more. Pneumonia was a dreaded diagnosis, and a strep throat could be a death sentence. Yet, thanks to research, few of these are problems in the industrialized societies of our time.

There is another group of disorders which we have now brought under control with definitive therapy and prevention so that they no longer tie up our resources. These are the acute nutritional deficiencies and again I speak only of the Western world, the industrialized nations. Pellagra, as I mentioned, has disappeared from the United States. There is still some in Rumania, in Italy and in Egypt; but it needn't be there, it is easily prevented and cured. Beriberi, iron deficiency anemia, pernicious anemia, scurvy, sprue, xerophthalmia and rickets are all disorders that cost the advanced countries very little to control. That they exist at all in the world is a disgrace to humanity. Like kwashiorkor these are diseases of maldistribution of the collective resources of mankind, and their elimination will require social and economic measures designed to improve the quality of life. But they need not be a drain on the health care system.

Then there are the endocrinopathies, the disorders of the sex organs, diabetes, various pituitary disorders, thyroid disorders, adrenal disease, parathyroid disease. For each of these we have rather definitive therapy. When a patient presents himself or herself, the physician knows what to do, does it fairly well and the patient rapidly returns to a normal role in society. Please understand that I have no illusions that their diagnosis is always successful, their treatment always effective. For example, we know that the death rate due to diabetic ketotic acidosis in small community hospitals is almost four times that in major hospitals affiliated with medical schools, just as the anesthetic death rate, low as it is, is also two or three times greater in such hospitals. My point is that, as compared with the past, the huge improvements in diagnosis and therapy made possible by yesterday's research have drastically reduced the cost – in all types of resources – of management of individuals with these various disorders.

What then is it that so seriously burdens the health care system; what is the medical care for which society clamors the world round? It is the management of those diseases for which we can offer no definite therapy or prevention but the victims of which are offered supportive physiological measures, the so-called half-way medical technologies. Among them are the various forms of neoplasia, vascular diseases, major psychoses, disorders of connective tissue, autoimmune processes, most neurological diseases, most virus diseases for which we lack immunizing procedures, most of the hereditary diseases of metabolism, and certain infestations such as schistosomiasis. Our debate on the moral proprieties of cardiac transplants is well taken – but it can only help assess for us the material value of a specific human life – such procedures are a small part of medical practice. This list of diseases – and I know how much it can be extended – reflects our ignorance of a wide variety of normal and pathological processes. Moreover, I venture to predict that each must pass through a phase in which the supportive measures will become yet more successful – and, thus, more costly in all senses.

Our only hope in this direction is to seek with renewed vigor the ultimate understanding which – if we are fortunate – may lead to rational preventive or therapeutic procedures as successful as those we have gained for the variety of infections, nutritional and endocrine diseases mentioned earlier. I can hold out no promise, much less a guarantee of success. But I can certainly guarantee that if we do not pursue such a course these diseases will continue to take their toll in human suffering and life, and will continue to confront organized society with the dilemma of decision as to the fraction of each nation's GNP we are willing to devote to the enterprise we now designate as 'medical care'.

In the United States and in Britain the annual investment in research is about 5% of the bill for medical care. In my view, there can be no more noble, no more human endeavor than the research enterprise. At the same time, in the economic sense of allocation of national resources, there can be no better investment, since success does mean ultimate reduction in the cost of medical care per capita. Admittedly, success also means an aging population with all its attendant problems, but those are for another discussion.

Finally, let me note that it is not merely medical understanding and capability that limits our fight with man's oldest enemy – disease. The level of general education and economic well-being may well remain a limiting factor. Witness the disgraceful prevalence of acute nutritional deficiency to which I referred earlier. Witness the fact that more than a century after Jenner there were 31,000 cases of smallpox reported around the world last year. But admitting all of that, my point remains, organized society can hope to cope with disease only when we

Philip Handler: 'In my view, there can be no more noble, no more human endeavor than the research enterprise. At the same time, in the economic sense of allocation of national resources, there can be no better investment, since success does mean ultimate reduction in the cost of medical care per capita.'

have the biological and medical understanding required to make that effort successful. And we do not yet have that degree of understanding. Those who state that we now spend too much on research and who wish to deflect such funds into the medical care system could not be more wrong! As are those who decry fundamental exploratory research and insist upon 'targeted research' directly addressed to specific diseases.

LORD ZUCKERMAN: Mr Chairman, I think Dr Arrow is quite correct. I did not, in fact, link together as well as I could the various steps of my verbal presentation. I failed because strangely enough I slipped a page of my notes, and I also didn't do the last page.

The argument is quite simple. Before a National Health Service was founded in the United Kingdom, resources were being spent in the medical services and also in medical research. Efforts were then made to get a measure of the scale of these resources, but this proved extraordinarily difficult. There were, as I said, several exhaustive studies in the thirties, and then Mr Willink accepted a plan for a medical service for the Conservative Party which was ready to be put into operation given that the Conservative Party would win the election in 1945. They did not. The Labour Party came in, and so it was their concept that was introduced and still operates, although it has gone through several modifications. But it was only when the National Health Service was established that its demands on national resources became evident. It was then that one realized that medical services had to be rationed.

So far as research is concerned new medical practices derive from the adventitious advances made by medical research workers. They have, as Dr Handler said, been phenomenal as regards the successes they have had in practice. Nonetheless the pattern of expenditure for medical research today is not necessarily in conformity with the remaining needs within the spectrum of health in the United Kingdom. Indeed, our chief medical officer, Sir George Godber, said that the only single measure that can conduce to another big improvement of health is to stop smoking.

ANOTHER SPEAKER: But not cigars!

ANOTHER SPEAKER: Méfiez-vous, Monsieur le Président, des austères!

LORD ZUCKERMAN: What I mean to say is that there are two kinds of approach to basic research: either new knowledge comes adventitiously and is then applied, thus creating a new demand for medical service, or there is an appreciation of what further needs there are, with a consequent effort to direct the attention of the scientists to those fields, which if research is successful will be improved. That is why I referred to the fact that President Nixon suggested that much more money should be spent on cancer research. Others, we know, proposed that much more effort should be put into gerontological research. I am quite certain

that Dr Burgen, in making this proposal this morning, did not have in his mind
that scientists should be dragooned and deprived of their liberty as scientists,
but rather that they should have their attention directed to a particular field.
What I wanted to suggest – and this is where I slipped the page I'm afraid – was
that it would be better if the resources available for medical research, which are
certainly insufficient in relation to the demand on the part of medical research
workers, were preferentially given to those fields to which Dr Handler referred a
few minutes ago.

I should like the decision to be taken by a consensus, to use Dr Hersch's
term, of medical people who are well informed about all the pressures there are
on the sum-total of resources available to a government. I certainly did not want
to suggest – although I quoted Lord Rosenheim – that medical research should
end.

JAN WALDENSTRÖM: Everybody is very much interested in what the newspapers
called 'the cancer crusade' in the United States, possibly the most important
programme of a scientific nature today. I quite agree with Lord Zuckerman that
the common cold is a nasty disease and does deserve priority in research, but
cancer is also bad.

The problem with the cancer research programme launched in the United
States is that it is not easy to administrate the large amount of money devoted to
it. Sir Alexander Haddow, who, until he became seriously ill, was the director of
the Chester Beatty Institute, gave us many of the useful drugs that we have for
neoplastic diseases. In an Editorial for the *New England Journal of Medicine*, he
puts forward a warning about the dangers of too much administration. We
should indeed be aware that although lots of money is good, freedom for the research worker to think is equally or perhaps still more important.

Jan Waldenström: 'Sitting at your desk at
fixed hours, leaving when the clock strikes,
being paid overtime if you stay another
half hour, that will not lead to a cure for
cancer; I'm pretty sure of that.'

In this context *The Double Helix** is an interesting story, Lord Todd. I believe that the atmosphere you and others are creating in Cambridge, being allowed to drink beer and look at girls' legs, while also working at making models of the double helix is just what science needs. Sitting at your desk at fixed hours, leaving when the clock strikes, being paid overtime if you stay another half hour, that will not lead to a cure for cancer; I'm pretty sure of that. Three years ago I attended a meeting of the Association of American Physicians and at the after-dinner talk I had to invent a new interesting disease. I said the most deadly disease that I knew of was hyperadministration.

Perhaps we should first talk about the possibilities of health control. Prophylaxis is usually cheaper than treatment and Dr Handler gives spectacular examples of what prophylaxis can do. Now it all depends upon how many cases you will find in a general health examination of a population that is thought to be healthy.

CHARLES A. BERRY: I will summarize for you some of the things that we do with our particular group of people. As you know we have had some fifty astronauts involved in our program. Some of these were selected as long ago as eleven years. Now this group has been followed up on an annual basis with a fairly detailed exam that was upgraded as we developed new techniques and new capabilities. We have constantly added more to their schedule and tried to keep them interested in what we were adding to an examination. This again is a matter of education. They have to understand why we are trying to do all these things, as it should not be just a matter of running through a mill.

The examinations they get on an annual basis are supplemented in many cases by particular examinations that occur at a time when they may be exposed to a particular stress; they may for instance be in a training program where they are put on a centrifuge. The information is then collected and added to a follow-on program which is stored in a central computer file allowing us to recall that information if we are going to fly a particular astronaut on a flight.

It is quite obvious that there is a great deal of physical examination, but equally of dynamic testing for which I should like to make a plea. Most of the examinations that tend to be done on patients are of a static type. You study the patient on an examining table, on a bed or on a chair. These examinations are not really testing the true function of the patient's organs and their capability to function. We have been deeply involved in dynamic testing for a number of years. This is an important change, one that is needed also for medicine here on the ground. But the question always arises whether it makes any real difference. As I mentioned earlier, it certainly makes a difference in that it gives us a base line allowing us to tell whether something is going wrong with a patient, since we know exactly what his normal is. We actually had this happen in conjunction with a particular flight mission, where we had an 8,000 white blood cell count as

---

* WATSON, J. D.: *The Double Helix*. London: Weidenfeld and Nicolson, 1968.

the only abnormality found. Any physician will immediately say 'that's not abnormal'. And that is true for the general population. But for this particular person it was grossly abnormal. It was 100% greater than his normal blood count.
As it turned out this was an early infectious disease which manifested itself within a period of about eight hours following the time that we had this as the only
finding on examination.

There has been consistent concern by critics about screening or continuing
preventive-medicine-type examinations. They focus on the absence of long-term
proof that the early detection of an illness can materially influence the course of
that particular disease. This has been raised as a matter of fact even in such diseases as hypertension, where we do have methods of therapy available. However, if you do detect an illness and thus initiate treatment, that is what medicine is
all about.

More to the point is if you try to utilize this system to *maintain* the person's
health. Now you have a healthy individual, you don't find disease; does doing
this examination in fact maintain his health? I firmly believe this is so. If you ask
me for research evidence to prove it, this is very difficult to come by. Obviously,
there is no examination that will absolutely guarantee that a person is not going
to have an illness. Even with the detailed exams in our group, we had a couple of
gall bladders removed, we had an operation performed to remove a wedge on a
cervical vertebra that caused some pressure on the spinal cord. But we need
these exams in order to get the information that will allow us to establish
sensibly and on a solid research basis whether or not screening will make a
difference.

Dr Arrow mentioned that it was very difficult to tell whether there was a
need for medical care, that the determined need was uncertain. I disagree with
that totally. This is saying that there isn't any need for preventive medicine and
that you only have a need when a physician is called for to take care of a person,
when hospitalization is necessary or when there is some emergency. In my view
everybody has a need for medical care and therefore that need is obviously there
all the time.

Lord Zuckerman mentioned that the requirement for medical care was
going to overrun us. I think it already has overrun us. What we have to do today, and here I thoroughly agree with what he said, is for people in the medical
field to join hands with government. You cannot stand off and hope that something is not going to happen. This has gone on too long. We have to join hands
with government and guide what is going to happen in order to provide the best
possible health care with the resources that we have.

There is an opinion held generally that NASA is an organization that has
had unlimited funds. They were not unlimited, but there certainly was ample
money to do the task because it was a very special task with a very close deadline,
a task that looked unsurmountable at the outset. In attempting what we did in
the form of technology, we tried to develop techniques that could be utilized
in many different ways. It happens that people, on seeing one of our brochures

showing our technology utilization procedures, say 'you can use them at NASA but we couldn't'. Well, we have to show in the form of a demonstration that they can be used everywhere, even in underdeveloped countries. We can utilize screening techniques and remote medicine techniques there because that is the place where these techniques are needed, maybe even more than in some of our own countries.

AXEL STRØM: Concerning health examinations of the general population it is very important to differentiate between health control of children and pregnant women, i.e. persons in growth, and grown persons. For the first group it has been proved many times that health control and health examinations are valuable. For the other group I am not quite sure.

Of course, if you examine a group of the general population, e. g. the labourers in an industrial firm, you will discover many defects and you can make some very nice statistics of it. But the question arises, how many of these diseases would not have manifested themselves very shortly afterwards and then come under treatment. It is impossible to answer this. Yet I have done so many of these health examinations in a firm that I doubt whether the labourers had much benefit from it. I then tried to find out whether health examinations influenced the rate of absenteeism in the firm, but am sorry to state that according to my experience they had no influence whatever. Absenteeism is caused by so many factors other than poor health that health control cannot do very much.

SEYMOUR S. KETY: Dr Arrow and Lord Zuckerman made a few provocative remarks that I thought worthy of some attention because they are distinguished scientists and experts in their field. Their statements would however tend to support a rising belief held by less learned individuals, at least in our country. Dr Arrow raised the question of the inability to demonstrate a clear relationship between the quality of, and the expenditures for, medical care of the population. But unfortunately he used life span and average national figures to support the contention. These are indices which may be rather insensitive to the quality of health in a community or in a nation. Had he instead used other indices like the incidence of premature birth, of birth complication, of infant mortality in different social and economic classes as compared with per-capita expenditure for medical care in those different classes he would have found a better correlation between community health and cost or quality of medical care.

Dr Handler already very adequately answered the questions of whether one can show ineffectiveness in the case of prevention and prophylaxis. In the field of psychiatry, which is a valuable example because psychiatric illness is so costly in terms of human resources as well as in terms of public expenditures, I was reminded that pellagra had once accounted for 10% of the population in mental hospitals. General paresis had been responsible for at least an equivalent fraction of the chronically mentally ill in a previous generation. Although one cannot use this as proof or crucial evidence, it is highly suggestive that in recent times the number of hospital beds and the occupancy of these beds for mental illness has shown a remarkable and very highly significant decrease since the advent of phenothiazines and other psychopharmacologic agents.

Statements made by Lord Zuckerman raised some questions in my mind. Lord Zuckerman showed a surprising and in my opinion unwarranted acceptance of the effectiveness of targeted research in his statements on the needs for channelling funds into those areas that seem to be the most pressing ones in terms of social requirements. I mention this simply because there is a fear in the minds of many of us that targeting of research prematurely may be a way of diverting funds from their most effective use in terms of social achievement. The new research crusade against cancer which has been vigorously stimulated in the United States by both President Nixon and Senator Kennedy may very well be followed by some remarkable achievements in the control and the understanding of cancer. However, there is a danger that when this happens, it will be credited to targeting of research. It is important to point out that it is unlikely that either one of these two men would have chosen cancer research as their major thrust in the health research field, were it not on the basis of expert advice showing that the basic research of the past twenty-five years seems now close to the time of harvesting. In this instance the targeting came after it was apparent to the scientific community that a major breakthrough is likely to occur in the field of cancer. It will not occur simply because of the millions of dollars that are being put into the field at this time, but it will be equally, if not more, on the basis of the expenditure of funds and the effort of many scientists extending over long periods of time, contributing to knowledge in many fundamental areas. Much of that research which would not have been considered relevant to cancer at the time it was carried out is now, in the wisdom of hindsight, recognized as crucial.

My other comment concerns the apparent competition between research and the needs of the communities for health care. This unfortunate juxtaposition has occurred in the United States; and there are many who feel that we cannot afford both the great needs for medical care and a continued expenditure of research funds and research training. I was impressed that thoughtful men at this Symposium were making statements that seemed compatible with this point of view. Lord Zuckerman indicated in his written paper that if all new medical research were to stop now and the resources it uses put into the further application of the knowledge we already have, enormous gains could still be achieved in the public health of the world. This comes alarmingly close to a proposal for a moratorium on research. The thing that really concerns me is the haphazard, inadequate and incompetent way in which we have taken advantage of medical research in terms of social application. But I would like to emphasize what Dr Handler said. The research expenditures in the United States in the biomedical field are $2^1/_2$ billion dollars a year. The costs of adequate health care in the United States, which we desperately need, and which I would support most actively, will be between 50 and 70 billion dollars a year. I do not see how we can generate those 50 to 70 billions of dollars by any kinds of cutback in the $2^1/_2$ billion dollars that we spend for research.

JEANNE HERSCH: Je voudrais dire que je n'ai pas reconnu ma pensée dans l'exposé qu'a fait tout à l'heure M. Arrow. Je n'ai à aucun moment dit que la souffrance était une chose désirable, qu'il fallait sauvegarder dans la vie humaine. Ce que j'ai dit, et que je suis prête à redire sous une autre forme, c'est que prétendre éliminer toute souffrance de la vie humaine, c'est en éliminer également toute espèce de signification. La raison en est que ce qui remplit la vie humaine et lui donne un sens, c'est la capacité de s'attacher à quelqu'un ou à quelque chose. Quand on est attaché à quelqu'un ou à quelque chose, on s'expose à des coups. On s'expose à perdre ce quelque chose ou ce quelqu'un à quoi on est attaché. Si on s'expose à le perdre, cela veut dire qu'on s'expose à en souffrir. Mais si cette souffrance doit pouvoir être immédiatement détruite par une drogue ou un tranquillisant quelconque, il ne reste que le vide de la vie humaine. Et c'est exactement de processus de cet ordre que souffrent actuellement les jeunes. Cela ne signifie en aucune façon qu'il ne faille jamais employer de remèdes pour diminuer la souffrance. Bien au contraire. Mais que les remèdes, les pilules et les tranquillisants ne peuvent pas être des solutions pour ce qui compte dans la vie. Et que, par conséquent, il faut apprendre à supporter, et que la santé comporte la capacité de supporter. C'est un des aspects de la santé. Voilà ce que j'ai dit.

Je voudrais profiter de ce que j'ai la parole pour dire combien je suis en désaccord avec ce qu'a dit hier M. Goldstein au sujet de la drogue. Il s'agit d'un point si dangereux et si sensible. J'ai été très surprise par la méthode comparative qu'il a utilisée, et qui me paraît doublement inadmissible quand il a comparé les effets de l'alcool par exemple, d'une part, et du cannabis de l'autre. Il a comparé un usage, qu'il a dit lui-même récréatif, en somme modéré, du cannabis (dont il a déclaré qu'il n'était pas un problème), avec un usage invétéré de l'alcool ou du tabac, et toutes les suites nocives que cela comporte. Je ne crois pas qu'on puisse comparer ces deux choses.

Deuxièmement, il a comparé deux phénomènes qui comportent dans notre civilisation occidentale des échelles totalement différentes. On ne peut pas comparer l'ampleur des conséquences du tabac ou de l'alcool avec les conséquences de la consommation actuelle du cannabis. Et j'espère que le ciel nous préservera de faire l'expérience d'une civilisation envahie par le cannabis, je préfère que nous en ignorions les effets.

Ensuite M. Goldstein a dit que nous ne savions presque rien dans le domaine des drogues, mais il veut déjà changer les lois. Il me semble que ce n'est pas un bon ordre dans la manière de procéder. Puis il a déclaré que le cannabis n'était pas un problème. Or, le moins qu'on puisse dire, c'est que sur ce point les psychiatres sont partagés. Je connais des psychiatres qui considèrent que le cannabis est l'antichambre des autres drogues et que, vu la forte proportion de ceux qui, après avoir pris du cannabis, passent ensuite aux autre drogues, cela comporte effectivement un très grand danger.

MARGARET MEAD: I want to point up the significance of the model that Dr Gibson described for meeting the rising demands for medical care in the rest of the world, care that would be comparable to our own, and to reinforce what Dr Handler said in terms of resources. Also, I want to support Lord Zuckerman's warning that any new technology we develop in our own countries will be noticed in the rest of the world thanks to the mass media and the WHO, and consequently there will be a demand for it in those parts. This is one of the very serious problems we are confronted with.

The kind of situation that Dr Gibson described can be put into operation in our own countries, and with good results even in homogeneous countries without the ethnic differences and the great discrepancies that we have in the United States. There are fishing communities, remote peasant communities or rural populations newly arrived in cities, there are foreign workers in Switzerland and other parts of Western Europe who all constitute divergent populations that are unfamiliar to most practising physicians. There is at present a tremendous gap between our practices and their understanding and ability to use them.

At the other end of civilization, in New Guinea, we are experimenting with the same model that Dr Gibson described, with local health councils who are given responsibility for spending a budget and who learn the costs of different kinds of medical care. Patients for whom nothing remains but support and comfort as there is no treatment left for them are no longer sent to hospital but are being comforted at home and looked after by local practitioners. Meanwhile the hospital facilities have been used much more wisely. There is every possibility that by establishing this kind of health center we can meet many of the needs of the emerging countries with more paraprofessionals who are indigenous and with better use of physicians. Moreover, if we establish them, this will have prestige and other countries will be glad to imitate us, instead of seeing, as in the last twenty years, hospitals demanding the most high-falluting equipment that nobody knows how to use or extravagant techniques such as organ transplantation. We can set up a model showing that the physicians who are the servants of the local community are also members of the faculty of Stanford University; I don't think Dr Gibson quite emphasized that enough. A key part in the question of medical care, population size and standard of living is that it is up to the developed countries to simplify and redesign our practices so that they are available to the rest of the world.

JOSHUA LEDERBERG: First a point of personal privilege. Having been advocate of better scientific communication I was rather distressed that the press carried a story about some remarks which I did not make concerning cutting off of funds for genetic research in the United States. I don't know where these came from.

I would like to comment on the question that was in debate between Dr Arrow, Dr Berry and others about the efficacy of multiphasic screening and other systems of monitoring. In my view it would be very unfortunate if this approach to preventive medicine were judged in the context of present-day technology. The methods available now are very crude, and the time sequence in which they can be afforded presents a serious theoretical difficulty. After all, a routine check-up made only once a year has a very small chance of picking up the progress of a disease unless it is one with a very protracted time course. These are just the ones where we have the least capacities for therapeutic intervention.

I would rather put up the model of, for example, prenatal care where very close monitoring of symptomatic cases has been of value in protecting maternal and child health. I would also advocate monitoring in situations like venereal disease, particularly for the military, where asymptomatic cases can be detected and treated. Monitoring can also play a very important role in cases of specific occupational hazards. To emphasize the point I would suggest that if we had a way in which, for patients at risk, we could detect cardiac dysrhythmias within periods of minutes prior to fibrillation, we could save ten- or hundredthousands of lives by being able to get there, but we need methods that have time scales of minutes rather than of months before we can feel that we have appropriately tested the technology of monitoring.

LORD ZUCKERMAN: I should like to make one comment on what Dr Kety said. I agree with him completely that one can't order breakthroughs in the biomedical field any more than one can do it in another field of enquiry. Equally I would agree that if resources were freely available, men of genius should be allowed free play and ought to carry on, follow their own inspiration, whatever the results. But resources are limited, and while I am not going to suggest for one second that what you called targeted research should be the sole criterium, I do believe that in any rational system it should be given proper weight.

The other part of Dr Kety's remarks to which I think reference should be made is the competition between funds for research and development and funds for medical care. It is very sad, but this competition exists. It is just one of the facts of life. Governments are inclined to cut research and development funds in times of stringency. This is another reason why scientists should be there, not just on the side lines, to see that so far as possible the future is not sacrificed to the present. This is true for all fields, and I believe it to be true for all countries.

JAN WALDENSTRÖM: I hope that Dr Handler is going to say a few words about the big cancer programme in the United States.

PHILIP HANDLER: I really hoped to escape this task, Mr Chairman. Dr Lederberg was more intimately involved with the beginnings of this matter than I was. In any case the problem, as a problem for the United States, has been seriously exaggerated. The scientific community and a large part of the medical community of the United States are at odds with the proposal of our Government with respect to the administrative machinery for government management of the cancer research program. The money itself, that increment of 100 million dollars for the first year of this program, had been placed into the next year's budget before the administrative problem revealed itself. To the extent that this is merely a domestic American political problem, it has no place on this program.

With respect to the problem itself as you described it earlier and the article by Dr Haddow, I think that too has been exaggerated. What is proposed is a program which begins at an incremental level of 100 million dollars above that previously available to our National Cancer Institute and is to increase to a billion dollars with time. In the United States Government we have two processes, authorization and appropriation; we frequently authorize very large sums which never materialize. So exactly how much of that will be made available, I don't know. But 100 million dollars has been added to the budget of the National Cancer Institute for the present year. Some of that money will be directed into the kind of research activities Dr Kety referred to as being targeted. Some of it will be used specifically to support rather large cancer clinics with their surrounding laboratory facilities, drug-testing facilities and the like. What fraction will find its way back to the kind of research Dr Kety meant, and which I advocate, I'm not quite certain. But it will surely be a very substantial fraction.

The National Institute of Health has shown its wisdom and flexibility in a remarkable way for twenty years. Funds are provided by the Congress in what are called 'categorical terms', that is to say to a series of Institutes each of which bears the name of a few major, related types of diseases – mental health, cancer, cardiovascular diseases, infectious disease, metabolic disease and so forth.

The Cancer Institute was the very first of those. The administration of the National Institutes of Health, all these years, has shown its wisdom in utilizing a large fraction of those funds to support all the diverse sorts of research which, by some stretch of their imagination, might reasonably be designated as 'relevant' to the disease problem at hand. I see no reason to think that this will not continue. My fears in that regard are rather minimal. I can worry about the possibility of directing too much money into areas where the leads don't really exist, into rather feckless testing of drugs in screening procedures when there is no rational basis for trying them in the first place. I confess that we have operated just such a cancer chemotherapy screening program, I think for fifteen years, and to the best of my knowledge it has never been rigorously and publicly examined to find out how well it has done.

Nevertheless, the report of the Committee of Consultants, originally a committee to advise Senator Yarborough and later a committee to advise Senator Kennedy, on which Dr Lederberg sat, is a beautiful statement of why it is thought by some that our understanding of cell biology, of many aspects of genetic mechanisms, of cell-surface and immunological processes and of the virology of cancer now give reason to think that the time may be propitious to direct a much heavier effort in this area. I hope that nothing more than that is intended and my concern is not very great. My fears were really alleviated by an episode in which I participated which deals with a certain piece of science.

I have personal reasons to know that the following study was made known to President Nixon and has clarified his thoughts with respect to the very problem we are discussing, the appropriate nature of this cancer crusade. The story deals with the origins of an exciting aspect of research in the United States, directed to the treatment of sickle-cell anemia. For those of you who don't know it, sickle-cell anemia is a disease limited to blacks, both in Africa and the United States. It is a disease which is the result of a genetic replacement of one amino acid in one of the two chains of about a hundred amino acids which form hemoglobin. When that sickle-cell hemoglobin loses its oxygen, which is what it normally should do in a capillary, then ten molecules of such hemoglobin collapse upon each other forming an insoluble crystal. As it comes out of solution, it distorts the erythrocyte which becomes very fragile and may rupture. This is a very serious problem; 'sickle-cell crises' in young people are extraordinarily difficult to manage, and the death rate is very high indeed.

It was recognized some time ago that in the presence of large concentrations of urea, the simple organic compound we all excrete in our urine, the hemoglobin molecules cannot associate; they don't become insoluble, the cell isn't distorted and it isn't fragile. So an attempt was made to utilize this fact as the basis of therapy in two quite different institutions. To do this required maintaining something of the order of one molar urea, and it seemed simply unbelievable that one could do this under clinical circumstances. They fed literally 2 kg urea per day to these people, which induced various other troubles. But a significant number of children in sickle-cell crisis were pulled through successfully.

In another laboratory (the Laboratory of Drs Stein and Moore at the Rockefeller Institute) where they heard this tale, they were as sceptical as I was that the urea could be the basis of the seemingly successful therapy. Like me, they said, 'well, they've undoubtedly done the right experiment for the wrong reasons'. If we accept the clinical judgment that the children were pulled through sickle-cell crises, we must conclude that something useful happened, but it just could not be due to that urea. This laboratory, five years before, had completed the determination of the structure of an enzyme called ribonuclease. In the course of that research they had reason to expose that ribonuclease to urea, and became aware that the terminal amino acid in the chain was carbamylated, if you will excuse the word, and they didn't know why. Finally they recognized that the oldest reaction in organic chemistry was the cause. The historic beginning of organic chemistry was a reaction in which cyanate was converted to urea. But that reaction is a reversible process, and in any solution of urea allowed to stand for a time some cyanate will be formed. That little bit of cyanate is the carbamylating agent – responsible for the carbamylation of ribonuclease in this early experience. Hence, they suspected that it might also be responsible for the effect of urea in sickle-cell anemia. They then treated pure sickle-cell hemoglobin with a small amount of cyanate and found an analogous reaction.

At the moment, that seems to be the basis of therapy for sickle-cell anemia! It is now being tested in the Rockefeller Hospital on a group of sickle-cell patients and, in due time, we will know whether truly this will work and can be successful therapy.

We are particularly interested because we may prove to our black population that research really has something to do with them. But more than that, the point is that no one in his right mind would ever have done that experiment. There was no way anyone could ever have arrived at the idea that the way to get at the sickle-cell anemia problem is to treat hemoglobin with cyanate. I cannot imagine any chemist or pharmacologist attempting that experiment. This story has its origins back in 1828, when Wöhler first synthesized urea. The next step was taken in a laboratory totally unconcerned with the problem of sickle-cell anemia. Nevertheless, in this way, a potential drug was found which, at this moment at least, bids fair to be a means to maintain the health of those genetically afflicted with sickle-cell anemia. Similarly, we do not know where cancer cures are going to come from, if at all. The only thing I can guarantee is that if we do not do the necessary fundamental research, there never will be any cancer cures. The only hope we have is to explore not only cancer itself, not force a limited directed program, but to continue to explore all opportunities as science itself reveals them. Mr Chairman, although I know I have taken much too long, that really is where I come out on our crusade against cancer.

In the Concluding Session nine representatives of different disciplines elaborate a synopsis of the preceding sessions. From left to right: Lord Zuckerman, René König, Talcott Parsons, Lord Rosenheim, Lord Todd, Franz Böckle, Salvador E. Luria, Philip Handler and Jan Waldenström.

Concluding Session

A Synopsis

Introduction

LORD TODD: We begin our final session with literature.
'Habe nun, ach Philosophie,
Juristerei und Medizin
Und leider auch Theologie!
Durchaus studiert, mit heißem Bemühn.
Da steh' ich nun, ich armer Tor!
Und bin so klug als wie zuvor.'

On Tuesday evening, in making some introductory remarks, I selected as my text an old English proverb about being healthy, wealthy and wise. I'm sure that as a social anthropologist Dr Mead at least will approve if I base my further remarks today on another old piece of folklore, even though it comes from old England and not from New Guinea. There is a game much beloved by little children in England in which all join hands in a circle and then dance round, singing 'Here we go round the mulberry bush, the mulberry bush, the mulberry bush, here we go round the mulberry bush on a cold and frosty morning'.

We have been going round the mulberry bush for two days now; so it might be desirable to move on to the second verse of that children's game, where, having finished the ritual dance, they proceed to action games: 'This is how we bake a cake, bake a cake, bake a cake.'

To that end I have today with me here on this platform – you will notice that we have all started as angels straightaway – four of our colleagues, each of whom will give us about a ten-minute talk in which he will put forward his views on matters that either have been discussed or should have been discussed. We have Dr Luria who is going to present the scientist's and Lord Rosenheim the physician's viewpoints while Dr Böckle and Dr Parsons will in some measure present the non-scientific viewpoints. Then I have asked to join us here the moderators of each of the previous sessions: Dr Handler, Dr König and Dr Waldenström. Again, a biologist, a sociologist and a physician. And I have further invited Lord Zuckerman to come up here because he is a man who loves an argument.

SALVADOR E. LURIA: I shall speak in English although some of you may believe that I am talking Italian. Let me just waste two minutes of your time on an anecdote. In the first lecture of my course in general biology at the Massachusetts Institute of Technology, there was, among about four hundred students, one who got up after the first thirty minutes and left the room. As he walked to the door I asked him, 'Is anything wrong?' And he said, 'O no, I just realized that this is not Electrical Engineering 205!'

I have tried to condense rather than collect my thoughts at the end of these two and a half days of the Symposium. What we have done is to explore, on the one hand, the frontiers of biological research, and on the other, the present status of medical research and the applications of medical knowledge in the community. As regards the frontiers of biological exploration, e. g. in molecular biology, in immunology, in neurobiology and in fields that have not been dealt with here, like the biochemistry of development or the phenomena of regulation in the mammalian and specifically in the human body, we have a situation in which the process of acquisition of knowledge is very rapid, but in which applications of a practical nature to the biomedical sector are slow in coming about. The prospects for medicine from these areas lie certainly in the possibility of control over cancer, over certain types of autoimmune diseases or certain conditions of the nervous system.

There are many other areas in which application has to be expected. But one can never tell what kind of application one is going to find until the knowledge is available to the informed and curious mind. We heard yesterday from Dr Handler a very beautiful example of how what may be an approach to the therapeutic control of sickle-cell anemia started through a series of half-informed, half-accidental processes in the area of biochemistry and protein chemistry.

One of the points that have not been mentioned very much is the matter of aging. There is a group of biologists who believe, though there is no solid evidence for this, that at least one of the mechanisms involved in aging may be a progressive accumulation of errors in proteins. In protein synthesis in the body accumulation of errors in proteins and errors in the mechanism of protein synthesis may lead to a progressive dysfunction of more and more cells of the body. An exciting model for this has come from some recent work done in England on the bread mould neurospora. Nobody knows yet whether aging in neurospora is a good model for aging in man. At least this here is another example of how basic research may serve to elucidate problems in medical and applied research.

Finally, one word about the possible applications of the new powers that biological research may put at the disposal of mankind and about which some of us have expressed concern. I would like to reiterate simply that what is required is not so much control over how much research or which research is done. What is required is wisdom in the decisions-making process of how the results of research are going to be applied.

Regarding medical research, it strikes me that, except for some remarks by Dr Handler, relatively little was said about the very large number of medical problems that remain unsolved. We talk and feel very elated about having more or less conquered bacterial diseases. Yet many of these bacterial diseases are still with us at what appears, at the time being, to be some irreducible basal number, for reasons that we do not understand. We have viral diseases completely uncontrolled except by preventive methods. We have problems such as cancer, and all the degenerative diseases, which are responsible for an enormous amount of suffering even if they are not responsible for the large number of early deaths. Therefore, any optimism about relaxing research for possible approaches to the treatment of these diseases, both at the biological and the biomedical research laboratories, would be greatly premature.

Then we have another limitation to the optimistic picture of the biomedical situation, and that is the problem of distribution of medical care, of drugs and other forms of treatment that are potentially available. Apart from the many diseases that we do not know how to treat, there are those that we know how to treat but often do not treat because we do not know how to distribute the short supply of certain commodities. This is a very important social aspect, which again should give us some sober thought before we paint too rosy a picture.

It is surprising to hear people who are not actively involved in biological or medical research talk about the possible impact on society or on the individual of the elimination of pain and suffering. As we look around us, whether in the developed or in the underdeveloped countries, we see very little of a surfeit of well-being, but an enormous amount of suffering, of sorrow caused by illness, by nutritional deprivation, or by poor conditions of living. Even if these conditions are not illness itself, they lead to illness and compound the suffering from illness. So we ought to go easy before giving the public the illusion or the misguided opinion that medicine and biology have come as far as they can get and that humanity has to resign itself to, or even enjoy and congratulate itself on, a certain amount of suffering.

When we think in terms of the suffering we have now and project it to the future we have to be even more sober. What will be the situation when the population pressure, which is beginning to mount, is going to be here in its full effects? If as little should be done as has been done so far, we may expect to have seven and a half billion people by the year 2000, and in the order of fifteen to eighteen billions by the year 2050. Under these conditions, very minor illnesses that may seem to us trivial are likely to become suddenly again relatively major scourges.

My last remark concerns the problem of communication. We have discussed the matter of the scientists communicating with the public, whether it can or cannot be done or should be done in terms that can be understood and that translate the excitement of science and explain what science can do. We certainly need to explain what science can do and to make a plea for more support for our research, not for selfish reasons, but because without research in biology and in medicine there is not going to be any further progress.

However, more important is that we know what the threats are. And here I feel a little bit guilty myself. In my paper which was directed to ethical values I have stressed some rather vague dangers connected with cloning and other forms of genetic intervention. But the fact is that scientists, demographers, medical people have not fulfilled their responsibility to explain to the public the implication of what is going to be upon us when the population pressure develops. We have a major responsibility for getting the public and the elected representatives to understand, not only in words but in real operational terms, the kind of things that need to be done if life on this planet is to continue to resemble the relatively happy life that some of us enjoy today.

LORD ROSENHEIM: I should like to look at some of the problems associated with the speed of biomedical progress through the eyes of a practising physician and a teacher of medicine. There can be no doubt in my mind about the need for team-work in medical practice, both within and outside the hospital, and I was most interested in the schemes outlined by Dr Strøm and by Dr Gibson. We are rapidly moving in this direction in Great Britain where health centres, manned by a number of doctors together with auxiliary personnel, are springing up rapidly. As our general practitioners, who still survive and flourish in Great Britain, are given greater opportunities for obtaining laboratory, radiological, electrocardiographic facilities for their patients, the use of hospital beds may very well undergo a change. And if multiphasic screening comes in on a large scale, then again the general practitioner making use of this and of the continuing records of patients may well be able to look after patients outside the sphere of hospital.

It is, however, extremely important, whether within or outside the hospital, that one doctor should be identified as looking after the patient, should know the patient's history, his worries, and his family, and should explain illness, treatment and prognosis to patient and family. We must at all costs maintain the personal doctor-patient relationship, the more so as investigation and treat-

Lord Rosenheim: 'We must at all costs maintain the personal doctor-patient relationship, the more so as investigation and treatment become increasingly complex and as patients living on borrowed life, if I may use this term, survive for many years, requiring regular medical attention.'

ment become increasingly complex and as patients living on borrowed life, if I may use this term, survive for many years, requiring regular medical attention.

This brings me to the vital problem of communication. There is a very great and growing need for properly informed health education. We must carry the public with us and if we do produce evidence that the cigarette is responsible for cancer of the lung then only broad health education is going to push this information home and to lead to the prevention of this very serious condition. I'm also greatly concerned, just as is Dr Luria, that advances in basic knowledge should be rapidly disseminated to practising doctors so that patients may benefit as soon as possible.

From this follows the vital problem of continuing postgraduate education of the general practitioner, the surgeon and the specialist. We are trying to tackle this problem in England, where we now have a Council for Postgraduate Medical Education and Training and regional postgraduate committees. Almost every large hospital has its postgraduate centre, its clinical tutor and a programme of lectures and demonstrations both for doctors working in the hospital and for general practitioners.

In the continuing education of doctors the pharmaceutical firms play an important role and bear a heavy responsibility. I welcome this opportunity to pay tribute to the excellent work done by pharmaceutical firms who not only produce the goods but disseminate excellent information about them. The increasing cooperation between the medical profession and the pharmaceutical industry is a very welcome feature of the present age and I hope it will develop even more in the coming decades.

Communication then in all directions is essential. Dr Mead referred to a Cambridge don aged eighty, riding his bicycle through the streets of Cambridge. I wonder whether this was the same don who had a puncture on his bicycle and was seen pumping air vigorously into the back tire which looked as if it might burst at any moment, while the front tire was completly flat. One of the students with some daring went up to him and said 'Excuse me, Professor, but I think you will find the puncture is in the front tire!' The Professor looked up and said, 'I always thought they communicated'. Unfortunately all of us often take communication for granted.

In this rapidly changing world in which we are faced with such an accelerating increase of knowledge there is a growing appreciation by the public of the aims of science, there is a growing half-understanding of medical problems engendered by the press, television and the radio and there is, of course, an increasing permissiveness and a changing code of ethics. The subjects of abortion, contraception and homosexuality are now freely discussed by the press in a manner that would have been quite unthinkable twenty or thirty years ago. And the recent introduction of abortion on a major scale in Great Britain and more recently in New York represents a great change in social and medical ethics. It is worth considering how such changes can come about. I would suggest that they can never be introduced by the medical profession but occur in response to a public demand or, to use Dr Hersch's term, as a result of a consensus from the informed public. Family planning is preventing the birth of an infinite number of healthy children while we spend our dwindling resources of young woman power and much money in maintaining the life of mental defectives, hydrocephalic children and those with spina bifida. The medical profession will certainly not change this at the present time, but public opinion may well do so during the next decades when this paradox becomes fully appreciated. At the other end of the scale old people, the really old, are no longer afraid to die. In fact they often want to die. One has always to consider to what sort of life one is bringing the person back. Most practising doctors have by now made up their mind on problems of resuscitation of the severely ill and the use of antibiotics to prolong the life of the bedridden paralytic old person.

Doctors are trained to take vital decisions. They have for many years decided whether a cancer was operable, whether a prostate gland should be removed, whether very expensive treatment was indicated, whether a patient had passed beyond medical care. I do not believe that the practising doctor should abdicate such decision-making to the lay, whether it be a minister of religion or a sociologist. Peer review of experiments on man is to my mind essential, but in daily practice a doctor, probably after consultation with his colleagues, must make decisions himself and this is what his patients expect of him.

New procedures such as renal dialysis, renal transplantation or the replacement of hip joints must in the early days be rationed not only by financial considerations but by the number of doctors trained in the new techniques. But any doctor who has seen the reincarnation of a uraemic patient following dialysis and/or transplantation or has seen a severe cripple walk with a new metal hip joint must wish for rapid availability of these new procedures. However, priorities have got to be decided because there is not money for everything at the present time. I recently had to open a new psychiatric wing in a large non-teaching hospital on the outskirts of London. They had put up a very fine prefabricated building with some twenty to twenty-five beds for psychiatric patients, with a day-room, with room for psychiatric social workers, for the psychiatrists, with the object of keeping patients out of mental hospitals with all the stigmata that are attached to this and with the object of returning them speedily to their homes. As I opened this wing, I wondered whether this was not perhaps of higher priority than a unit for renal dialysis for patients with chronic nephritis.

Finally, what of the future? I do not share Dr Hersch's fear of an imminent utopia resulting from biomedical progress. Each new advance brings with it its own difficulties, and at the present time renal dialysis, a wonderful advance, has been widely complicated by the occurrence of hepatitis associated with the newly discovered Australia antigen. Our discussions have high-lighted great advances and many great foreseeable difficulties but have shown that while we can guess some developments, we cannot predict the future. One must probably be either an optimist or a pessimist. Seeing the great advances that have occurred in my life-time I am a confirmed optimist about the future.

FRANZ BÖCKLE: Das eigentliche ethische Problem, vor das uns der naturwissenschaftliche Fortschritt stellt, liegt nicht in den Mitteln und Methoden als solchen, sondern in der Bestimmung der Ziele, der Interessen, also der Werte. Hier kam zum Ausdruck, daß sich in dieser Zielbestimmung die Naturwissenschaften nicht selbst genügen, sondern auf die Kooperation mit den Humanwissenschaften angewiesen sind. Wir haben vom Neurophysiologen gehört, daß wir zwischen Struktur und Information unterscheiden müssen. Das Triebverhalten ist nicht nur durch das hormonale und behavioristische Center im Hypothalamus bestimmt, sondern auch durch Lernprozesse in den kortikalen Schichten. Gerade in diesem Zusammenspiel liegt wohl die Grundstruktur, die auch für den Informationsprozeß aufgegriffen werden müßte. Sartre sagte einmal: «L'essentiel n'est pas ce qu'on a fait de l'homme, mais ce qu'il fait de ce qu'on a fait de lui.»

Der Mensch erfährt sich als ein Wesen, das ist, das um sich selbst weiß und das sich in der Geschichte seine Freiheit schafft. Er strebt und will und weiß sich in seinem Streben und Wollen gespalten. Er erfährt sich als der, der in dieses Streben Ordnung bringen muß und der seine Zukunft schafft, aber auch als der, der durch seine kulturgeschichtliche Entwicklung geformt ist. Er ist zwar heute durch die Kultur aus den Naturzwängen befreit, aber dadurch ist er um so mehr in soziale Zwänge hineingekommen. Freud hat das Über-Ich stets zum Erben des Ödipuskomplexes gemacht und darin die Wurzel der Kulturbildung gesehen. Es ist verwunderlich, daß der Name Freuds nie gefallen ist, der uns gerade über das Triebverhalten doch einiges zu sagen hätte.

Was ist Freiheit? Welches sind der Gehalt, das Ziel und die die Freiheit bestimmenden Werte? Ist es die Gesundheit? Ist es die Freiheit von physischem Schmerz? Oder ist es die Freiheit von menschlichem Leiden in einem weiteren Sinne des Wortes? Ist es das nackte Überleben, oder ist es die permanente Wendung des Übels? Oder ist es das in einem dialektischen Prozeß zu schaffende operationale Ziel einer klassenlosen Gesellschaft?

Was kann der Theologe dazu sagen? Negativ kann er bestenfalls sagen, daß niemand, selbst er nicht, den umfassenden und total bestimmenden Sinn des menschlichen Daseins in einem System verfügbar hat. Diese Feststellung von einem Theologen mag erstaunen, aber auch die Theologie hat eine revolutionäre Entwicklung durchgemacht. Richtig verstandene menschliche Autonomie fordert Respekt vor den immanenten Grenzen des Menschen. Und das führt den Theologen zu einer positiven Aussage. Der Theologe ist überzeugt, daß das menschliche Dasein von einem Grund und Sinn getragen wird, der den tiefsten Erfahrungen sowohl der menschlichen Ohnmacht wie der menschlichen Größe entspricht. Die Erkenntnis nämlich, daß der Mensch Freiheit nur finden kann, wenn er bereit ist, sich selber Grenzen zu setzen. Jetzt aber nicht, wie Sie vielleicht denken, Grenzen wie «das darfst du nicht forschen» und «diese Methode darfst du nicht anwenden», sondern vielmehr eine grundsätzliche Grenze: Dem Begehren wird die unmittelbare Befriedigung untersagt, soweit sich dieses Begehren selbst zerstören würde. Ist das nicht die Grundsituation des

Franz Böckle: «Der Mensch kann Freiheit nur finden, wenn er bereit ist, sich selber Grenzen zu setzen. Jetzt aber nicht, wie Sie vielleicht denken, Grenzen wie ‹das darfst du nicht forschen›, und ‹diese Methode darfst du nicht anwenden›, sondern vielmehr eine grundsätzliche Grenze: Dem Begehren wird die unmittelbare Befriedigung untersagt, soweit sich dieses Begehren selbst zerstören würde.»

Ödipus? Der Verzicht auf die Mutter und letzten Endes das Sichnichtidentifizieren mit dem Vater.

In seinem praktischen Handeln, also in der Ethik als einer praktischen Wissenschaft, ist der Mensch ganz auf eine Handlungsvernunft angewiesen. Diese Handlungsvernunft, die nicht einfach zusammenfällt mit der positiven Vernunft, muß realitätsbezogen und kommunikabel sein. Dazu muß sie, vom System her gesehen, kohärent und konsequent sein. Lassen Sie mich zu dieser Handlungsvernunft nun ein paar Deutungen geben.

Der Mensch kann seine Freiheit immer nur in seinen eigenen Grenzen erobern; er ist immer an seine eigenen Strukturen gebunden. Es ist nun immer mehr möglich, auch Verhaltensweisen, die wir mit dem Prädikat gut oder böse, gerecht oder ungerecht beschreiben, also Verhaltensweisen ethischer Art, durch die Veränderung der Strukturen zu beeinflussen. Und warum sollten diese Möglichkeiten nicht eingesetzt werden, soweit dadurch tatsächlich gewisse menschliche Aufgaben besser gelöst werden können. Es wurde von Dr. Burgen darauf hingewiesen, daß er eine große Priorität in einer Verbesserung der Lernprozesse sehen würde. So etwas meine ich damit.

Oder ein zweiter Aspekt: Überall, wo dem Menschen durch die Manipulation die Verantwortung unmöglich gemacht wird, dient sie nicht dem Aufbau des Menschen und kann daher unter keinen Umständen gerechtfertigt werden. Aber wo beginnt nun tatsächlich die Manipulation? Wie weit ist hier eine Aufklärungspflicht gegeben? Die Juristen haben uns darauf aufmerksam gemacht, daß diese in adäquater Information liegt. Hinsichtlich des Experimentes mit dem Menschen müssen wir die Information viel stärker dahin lenken, daß dem Menschen die Angst vor dem Manipuliertwerden genommen wird, indem er auf die Mitverantwortung über die individuelle Gesundheit hinaus für die Gesundheit der gesamten Population aufmerksam gemacht wird. Es wäre falsch, zu fragen, welchen Sinn es habe, für eine Transplantation an einem einzigen Menschen viel Geld einzusetzen, während noch so viel Not auf der ganzen Welt herrscht. So würde das Problem der Transplantation zu isoliert nur in bezug auf dieses individuelle Heil betrachtet. Jede Operationstechnik wird einmal an einem einzelnen Beispiel beginnen müssen, um dann zu den großen Fortschritten wachsen zu können. Allerdings tritt hier das Problem des richtigen Proportionierens dieser Mittel auf.

In der Disposition auf eine humanere Zukunft hin ist der Mensch mit seinem vernünftigen Handeln und Planen auf wirkmächtige Strukturen und deren gesetzmäßige Gestaltung angewiesen. Wir müssen uns also hüten, die Utopie eines völlig frei sich entscheidenden, mündigen Subjektes aufzustellen. Sosehr eine immer größere Mündigkeit angestrebt werden muß, so sehr müssen wir erkennen, wie gebunden der Mensch ist. Der Mensch hat sich zwar aus den herkömmlichen autoritären Strukturen befreit, läßt sich aber auf der anderen Seite ebensosehr oder noch viel intensiver führen, wenn er auf den Grundmechanismus des menschlichen Handelns, die Selbstentscheidung, hin angesprochen wird. Wenngleich es also das Bestreben sein muß, derartige Mechanismen transparent zu machen und die Manipulation durch eine wachsende Rationalität einzuschränken, müssen wir uns der Grenzen dieser Transparenz bewußt bleiben. Gerade darum ist es gefährlich, wenn wir allzu kurzschlüssig auf die normative Kraft des Faktischen absetzen. Obwohl Werte sich kulturell angleichen, ist dieser Anpassungsprozeß viel komplizierter, als man sich vorstellt. Was getan wird, ist nicht gleich auch schon normativ. Eine normative Kraft des Ethos entsteht erst dadurch, daß ein immer größerer Kreis in einem bestimmten Punkt zum Konsensus kommt. Nur so sind Prozesse möglich, die unter entsprechende Kontrollen gebracht werden können. Hier werden Experten, hier werden Politiker und hier wird auch das Publikum kritisch mitdenken müssen.

TALCOTT PARSONS: My assignment lies somewhere inbetween Dr Böckle's talk and those of the scientist and the physician who preceded him. Namely, what are the relevances of the social world and the intellectual disciplines in the health field which try to deal with it. Dr Handler, in his opening remarks, spoke of biomedical research as a 'child' of the industrial revolution, though he did not use this word. If we continue the metaphor, I would suggest that it was an ancestor two or three generations removed. There have been a number of crossings and possibly rather considerable mutations between the industrial revolution of the late eighteenth century and the biomedical research phenomenon of the nearly late twentieth century. Dr Ruiz-Giménes Cortés yesterday made the interesting statement that socially speaking the top priorities in modern society seem to be health and education.

The social organization of which all of us here are a part has come to be in the last generation a very notable, distinctive and new kind of organization. It combines in various complicated ways academic science (in the narrower sense as manifest in the teaching functions of the universities), the pharmaceutical industry and the complex of health-oriented professions whose primary function is the provision of service rather than the pursuit of knowledge. All these different components, with government as a source of support and as an actual potential regulator and setter of priorities, as well as the more diffuse pressures in the background from the general public, form a complex of social structures which, by nature, is shot through with potential conflict. It has both a basis of common interest and cooperation and a basis of tension and conflict. One way of looking at the conflicts is to ask what are the values that have the highest priority in each of these different sectors?

Dr Lederberg referred to the 'truth orientation' of the research communities. In the practising professions, 'service orientation' takes precedence over 'truth orientation'. But the two have to be very closely affiliated. In the educational sector, where teaching and training is fundamental, truth is important but cannot take full priority because the formation of character and the development of competence have to be a central orientation. In the industrial world which, of course, has to be concerned with orientation to the market and, on some level or other, to financial solvency if not profit, Hoffmann-La Roche conducts a great deal of very pure research. But this research has to be subsidized by

Adolf Walter Jann, Chairman of the Board of Hoffmann-La Roche, follows the deliberations. Behind him on the right, a grandson of the founder of Hoffmann-La Roche, Lukas Hoffmann, who works in France as a biologist for the World Wildlife Fund. In front of him Urs Hochstrasser, Professor of applied mathematics and Head of the Division of Science and Research (Federal Government Office).

the other activities of the firm, just as universities have to be subsidized by other parts of society – increasingly, in our time, by governments. This is a complex of social structures that is quite different from the classical picture of the early industrial system.

We have brought into the discussions of this Symposium a relatively recent phenomenon that has created very severe problems for this sector. Lord Zuckerman yesterday spoke of the enormous demand coming from the public and impinging on government for the services of the health professions, and the tendency of government in turn to put pressure on the research sector of the biomedical complex.

One very important aspect of what we might call the health complex is that it is a particularly central focus of the articulation between the individual and his social-cultural system. It is obvious that in order to perform the kinds of services directly or indirectly required for the health of individuals the health profession has to be involved in a very complex social organization. No collection of isolated researchers and practicians could perform these services.

Talcott Parsons: 'We, in the social sciences, are far behind the most advanced sectors of the biomedical science. I think it is incumbent to be very cautious and careful indeed about not rushing into premature applications.'

Dr Kety on Wednesday morning hit upon another particularly crucial key point of articulation. Namely, that the content of what we know and learn as human individuals and what gets organized, codified and institutionalized at cultural and social levels does not come primarily from the organism. Regarding information processing the central nervous system is the principal single point of articulation. If the biomedical sciences, particularly their neurological branch, are to articulate with problems of content and the organization of content they have to have theoretical relations to the behavioral and social sciences, to psychology, sociology and economics. I am thinking also of linguistics as an important, rapidly developing discipline.

It seems to me this is going to require much more than collaboration between the biomedical sciences and the psychosocial sciences. It is going to require genuine integration. This means that at some level there has to be a common theory, as well as much improved empirical research on our side of the fence. We, in the social sciences, are far behind the most advanced sectors of the biomedical science. I think it is incumbent to be very cautious and careful indeed about not rushing into premature applications.

Discussion

LORD TODD: Dr Handler, you were called slightly in question for saying that biomedical science came from the industrial revolution.

PHILIP HANDLER: I do not think it is seriously in issue, Lord Todd. The process may have mutated a few times, as we have been told, but quite clearly without the industrial revolution we would never have had any human beings freed up to do the research, we would never have had the physical plant that is required, nor the immense apparatus that makes modern research possible. We would never have had the physical tools, and so we would not have had the intellectual tools. If Dr Parsons chooses to think that we have mutated and crossed over several times, I would not dispute the point, but the facts of the industrial revolution are real. That is when the opportunity began.

It was what Dr Böckle was saying that seemed furthest from my views. I have tried to be among those who, somewhat defensively I suppose, occasionally attempt to deny the existence of 'two cultures'. Unhappily, I have rarely seen a better demonstration of the truth of that concept than this meeting, including this last hour. We have attempted to interpenetrate, if you will. The scientists and physicians on our panels have attempted to think through moral judgements, ethical values and to understand the attitudes of those who are not scientists. But we have not really interpenetrated at all, and I fear that the barriers seem to remain intact. Dr Böckle is at a disadvantage in that when he seeks for real examples he is not familiar enough with our kind of world to find precisely the examples he requires. That puts us at a disadvantage because we don't know precisely what he has in mind. This makes the discussion very difficult and again this is the two-cultural kind of problem for us.

I don't believe the problem of manipulation is a serious one. Human beings are not manipulated by scientists and physicians in any way to damage their individuality in the years that will follow their exposure to experimentation. Now physicians – those whom I have known and I know many – have been extremely conscious of this problem and have done their very best to see to it that there is no damage to their patients. By and large they are over-aware of the problem so that these patients are probably, in a purely medical sense, getting the best care of anybody in the hospital at the time they are there. I share your concern that one should make sure that human beings are not being manipulated for any end that does not at the same time serve society at large. If the experiment is not completely compatible with the welfare, and in fact the improvement of that patient, you should not be doing it. But you need controls.

FRANZ BÖCKLE: Ich glaube, daß ein grundlegendes Mißverständnis zwischen uns aufgetreten ist. Ich habe auf zwei Dinge hingewiesen. Einmal, daß der Mensch in seiner Handlungsvernunft nicht einfach identisch sei mit dem, was man die rein positive Erfassung von Fakten nennt. Dadurch, daß der Mensch Bewußtsein hat, kann er das bloße Feststellen von Fakten übersteigen, indem er sie durch sein Denken zueinander in ein Verhältnis bringt. Ich würde es begrüßen, wenn Handlungen, die Werte einschließen, durch wissenschaftliche Methoden, zum Beispiel Sozialkybernetik, verbessert werden könnten.

Ein weiteres Mißverständnis ist aufgetreten, als ich auf die Manipulation zu sprechen kam. Ich meinte, der Mensch sollte dazu gebracht werden, bei Experimenten zur Verbesserung der Gesundheit positiv mitzuspielen, konkret etwa bei der Arzneimittelprüfung. Wir alle sind uns im klaren, daß die pharmazeutische Industrie ohne dauernde Kontrolluntersuchungen in den Kliniken nicht auskommt, daß diese Untersuchungen zum Teil mit Placebos durchgeführt werden müssen, daß wir Blindversuche machen müssen usw. Ich sehe darin in keiner Weise eine schlimme Manipulation des Menschen. Aber fragen Sie einmal das Publikum. Wenn die Öffentlichkeit von Blindversuchen und von Placebos hört, dann geht sie hoch. Ich meine, man müßte solchen Dingen auf den Grund gehen und eben durch eine geschickte Information zeigen, daß der einzelne für das Gesundheitswesen mitverantwortlich ist.

LORD TODD: We are manipulating the public not in the narrow sense that you are referring to, but in the broad sense, by the effects that biomedical research has on the whole social structure.

LORD ZUCKERMAN: I was much interested in what Dr Böckle had to say, because he began with a particular concept of liberty, of which we heard an illustration from Lord Rosenheim who told us that, partly as a result of public pressure, we are now contracepting the birth of what might be millions of normal human beings while the medical profession is directing the energies of a vast number of the semi-professionals in the medical services to keeping alive children with spina bifida (I forget the two other illustrations that he gave). It is worth pursuing this further, but I would not pursue it in precisely the same way as Dr Böckle, because I presume that my reading on the subject of liberty is somewhat different from his. I am more influenced by the empiricist views of the earlier part of the nineteenth century. The simple idea of liberty is the freedom of the individual to operate without constraint. But you know that no individual can operate without constraint because when he does so he infringes the liberties of other individuals. At that moment the state, as it were, society, steps in and makes codes of behaviour.

We, the medical profession, are infringing this liberty. In the first session I remarked that science opens up enormous avenues for the future, it gives us the basic knowledge on which we build, and which we apply through technology. At the same time it closes other options because it sets fashions. This happens in the medical profession with new drugs and new procedures or as a result of public pressure. Society has for the moment decided that the particular liberty of an individual to put an end to his life through euthanasia should not be exercised. Nonetheless Lord Rosenheim can see the day coming when public pressure, perhaps because of intolerable conditions of living due to the population explosion, or, more correctly, because the medical profession has prolonged the lives of individuals into a helpless senility, may call for euthanasia. If that happens it will mean the restoration to the individual of a liberty that is now denied by social convention.

But when we look to the future we can see that as knowledge advances, opportunities will be opened up for a greater measure of enjoyment and consumption. At the same time there will be a closing of other options because the new knowledge will be directing the advance of society, humanity, along paths that it might otherwise not have taken. There will be more potential freedom, more goods available, more services theoretically available. Yet in point of fact there may well be less actual freedom in the world with another billion or two human beings in it.

LORD ROSENHEIM: I should just like to mention one minor point about what Dr Böckle said regarding double-blind trials and the public raising their hands in despair. This is in fact not the case. When one approaches people in order to do drug trials on them, one is always surprised by their willingness to take part and their understanding of the importance. One has to remember that every time one gives a drug to a patient, one is in fact doing an experiment, and it is very easy to explain to the patients the need for a double-blind trial. I don't regard this as manipulation or raising any difficulties. If there is any doubt in the mind of the person doing the trial and if there is any bias, then the trial cannot be carried out. But if one doesn't know which is the better drug, then the only way to find out is by a double-blind trial.

LORD TODD: In continuing the discussion I would remind you that on Tuesday evening we had an extremely interesting address from Dr Pletscher. He posed three questions which I think are the backbone of this Symposium.

His first question was, should there be, or should one contemplate, any limitations on, or control of, research in the biomedical field. The second question he put was to what degree the pharmaceutical industry should devote its efforts to the production of drugs for quite minor ailments. This was tied in by him with the questions of drug abuse and self-medication. His third question touched on medical priorities. It was what priority we should give to complex forms of medical treatment in the face of the rising universal demand for medical care. I think we should address ourselves to these three points now because we have been touching on a number of them here and there during our discussions; but have any of them been answered? Or, if the complete answer has not been given, has the way ahead been pointed for any of them?

There was a fairly general consensus of opinion that research as such should not be controlled. Of course, research might nonetheless be subject to a measure of what is not quite control but is near it. After all if there is not unlimited money to be spent, some decisions will have to be taken as to where the weight of effort shall be put in research. The degree to which you influence the major directions in which you spend your money does not simply affect the economic situation, but also determines the kind of scientific manpower supply that the country is going to produce. And the question that comes up again there is who makes the decisions?

LORD ZUCKERMAN: As I said before, there can be no question that the resources available for research and development will ever be adequate in relation to the claims made by researchers and potential researchers for assistance in the work they wish to do. The man of genius will always find the resources with which to fulfill his own inspiration. I do not see a problem there. Let him continue in his ways and afterwards let us see whether or not what he has done – insofar as the biomedical field is concerned – can aid the physician and the surgeon in dealing with the residual problems of medicine.

On the other hand, I am one of those who believe that you ought to beam research funds at certain fields in relation to social need. Let me just use an illustration. Macfarlane Burnett stated that molecular biology had not yet yielded anything that was of any use in practical medicine, nor was it likely to. He was of course sticking his neck out, but he was quite clear in his meaning. Molecular biology has however become highly fashionable, it has been a very adventurous field and has received considerable support. But it has not yet yielded what people had presumably hoped it would, apart from improving our basic understanding of cellular processes.

Now if another Macfarlane Burnett or six other Macfarlane Burnetts were to share that view, shouldn't the Medical Research Council in the United Kingdom start reducing the funds going to that field and divert them to fields which at the present moment do represent clearly defined needs, even if this went away from the principle 'back the man, not the project'? For example, several people at our meeting have suggested that the disabilities of old age are receiving too little attention, with which I agree. I also chose a few topics as matters that require more attention. By the simple device of distributing the available funds differentially one could change a fashion.

Still, I do not see how we can get out of this difficulty. The demand for funds to carry out research is more or less infinite. At the present moment medical practice, certainly its esoteric parts, is largely the result of fashions created by a few individuals. They have produced the problem Lord Rosenheim talked about – prolonging the life of children who are committed, as a result of the condition in which they are born, to real hopelessness. Since resources are limited, I should have no hesitation to say that I would illuminate with funds certain fields in accordance with need and make other fields less attractive.

You raised the question who is to judge. My own view is that if this is a question now, it will become much more acute very soon. Time is not on our side. The medical world moves very slowly. You, Lord Todd, were chairman of a royal commission on medical education, which published a voluminous report. But it has now been some five years since it was published, five years since it was accepted by the government and acclaimed. I should like to know how many medical schools have altered their curriculum in accordance with your recommendations. As I said, the medical world moves slowly. Who is to judge therefore as public pressures mount. If we do not seize the opportunity ourselves, if we do not realize what is coming, somebody else will choose for us.

I therefore believe that whether or not some people would call it elitist – this is a ridiculous term anyway – people who have a sophisticated view about resources and about needs should be the ones to decide which fields should be illuminated with funds and resources. And to a certain extent, let me say chauvinistically, we are doing this in the United Kingdom with our very limited resources today.

FRANZ BÖCKLE: Abstrakt gesehen, kann es natürlich keinen Zweifel daran geben, daß man das menschliche Erkennen nicht irgendwelchen Begrenzungen unterstellen kann. Sobald Sie das aber nicht mehr abstrakt, sondern in konkreten Modellen sehen, wird dieses Erkennen in soundso viele Zusammenhänge gestellt, in denen es nun zu Güterabwägungen kommt. Für gezielte Forschungen im Laboratorium, die entsprechende Geldaufwendungen erfordern, müssen die zur Verfügung stehenden Mittel in Relation zu sozialen Werten gesetzt werden.

SALVADOR E. LURIA: It seems to me that the distinction I made several times between basic research and development of technology is an important one. In the United States we have a paradoxical situation. The majority of basic research, at least in the biomedical field, is funded through agencies such as the National Institutes of Health and the National Science Foundation under peer review. On the other hand, a substantial amount of developmental research in these areas, apart from the one that is done by industrial firms, is supported by contract funds which are not subject to peer review. This is a most unfortunate situation. In fact, I expect to testify next month in Washington at hearings connected with the new cancer agencies, to make a strong plea for extending the peer review to all activities, including those directed more specifically to treatment. Somehow the situation has become upside-down from what it should be.

PHILIP HANDLER: I begin where Lord Zuckerman does, in agreeing that clearly, on the scale on which research is now done, only governments can pay the bill. Secondly, I agree that governments must allocate their resources and decide what fractions of their available tax revenues they will invest in various kinds of endeavor. No one of them may be limitless, no matter what the particular clientele and constituency may believe.

But then we part company. After the decision concerning the total sum allocable to medicine or to medical research, the subfractionation may not be a function of the highest reaches of government. If you ask that we make a list of the major medical problems that now defy us and that, in terms of yesterday's conversation, devour our medical and human resources, it is rather easy to do. But the reason why we don't have cures for many diseases right now is that nobody knows where to find them.

We can agree that cancer is a problem that all of us would like to attack, because clearly death due to cancer is abhorrent. But I don't know where the real clue to an effective cancer cure is. If you mean by 'targeted' research for cancer any exploration of how cells really function, and what might then go wrong with them in the neoplastic transformation, that's all right with me. But if you mean something narrower than that, I disagree.

If you want to say that cardiovascular disease is one of the greatest afflictions of mankind, but then say that, although some renal disease is of cardiovascular origin, renal dialysis is too expensive and must be foregone, let me point out that if we don't run those renal dialysis machines today and continue to improve them, we will not pursue the line of research that will one day give us a nice handy-dandy little pocket renal dialyser that will be cheap and effective, exercising little drain on society, and yet take care of sick people.

If we agree that cardiac transplants are foolish, then what you must admit is that a likely approach to dealing with this problem is to learn more about lipid metabolism than we know today, more about the metabolism of arteries and arterioles and how that changes with time. If that is what you mean by cardiac research, fine, but if you ask that we take any more narrow view than that, then you are making a very serious error.

LORD TODD: I am sure Lord Zuckerman did not mean what you were talking about at all. He means that if a country has six million pounds, francs, what have you, which it feels can be devoted to research and development, it is entitled to say, given that the right people are there, that four million might go into the medical field and two million into heavy engineering.

PHILIP HANDLER: No, I thought that he went further. I conceded all of this when I began. I said that I understand that the level of allocation is an absolute necessity and there is no way of avoiding it. The next step, once it has been decided how much money will be made available for biomedical research, becomes the critical one. I say we should not attempt to determine how much money should be allocated to research on multiple sclerosis, cystic fibrosis or the nephritides, etc. Rather must we, within the available allocation, follow where research opportunities beckon. And the best possible guide is the sum of the individual decisions of knowledgeable, competent biomedical investigators.

LORD TODD: However, I would say that that decision, insofar as anybody would wish to take it, is something that stands with the medical scientist. This is where the biomedical scientist must choose his priorities.

PHILIP HANDLER: Let him follow the leads of opportunity.

LORD ZUCKERMAN: Let me widen the cultural gulf between myself and Dr Handler then – and provocatively. First of all, let me say that Dr Handler is merely re-stating the basic principle by which our Medical Research Council operates – as written by successive secretaries into their annual reports, 'back the man and not the project'. I also want the men backed. But where resources are limited, priorities have to be agreed.

Somebody just suggested that this applied even in the cancer field and that what you call 'peer review' should be extended to all cancer research. But I want the peers to know something about what is happening over the whole field. Agreeing priorities is always difficult, not only priorities in allocating big resources to different fields of public expenditure in accordance with social pressures and political pressures, but also the priorities within a given field where only a certain amount of money is available for disbursement.

Let me tell you why I am frightened of the 'peer review'. I know of one peer review of a field where only one peer is involved, and he in effect decides who is to get money for research, whatever the channel through which it flows. I am not certain I like that. We do not have an unlimited range of options.

Some biomedical problems are more easily solved than others. At least some medical research workers are opportunists who obviously have a run at the easier problems. I can imagine a man without much idea about the field of research in which to engage, being directed to a problem, and being so successful that in due course he won the Nobel Prize. At the start he may have had no more interest in the subject he was given than in any other, and having won his prize, his intellectual motivation might well run out of steam.

Some problems are, as I said, much more easily solved than others. Some are probably insoluble. But I agree with Dr Handler that it is all but impossible to direct some genius to go and solve that problem to make a breakthrough at that particular point. That is where we agree. But now let me part company.

In the United Kingdom we have something like a thousand hospitals. Physiotherapy costs a great deal, yet in every hospital you will find your expert physiotherapists, but you will also discover that no two hospitals do the same thing. I speak as a victim. If you were to go with a bad back to the medical school where I was trained you would be told to rest. If you didn't like that advice and went to another hospital, you would be put through a very vigorous course of treatment. But that also doesn't help. If you then went to a third, equally eminent teaching hospital, you would be tortured by heroic treatment. But when it comes to finding out what causes backache and all the rest of the simple troubles, which are responsible for any amount of loss of time in industry, you won't find many men prepared to do the necessary research. These troubles seem very simple on the face of it, but in point of fact, they are probably extremely difficult. That is presumably why they get very little attention. I should like to illuminate that field of enquiry with research funds, so as to improve the likelihood that an apparently simple ailment like backache could be dealt with adequately. There then is one field, to which men as brilliant as are many in this room could have turned their attention, but didn't. They might have done, had they been directed by the denial of funds to other areas and the provision of funds to this one.

TALCOTT PARSONS: There is another aspect to the problem of whether there should be control of research, namely control of *how* research should be done – as distinguished from *what* research should be done – with reference to the standards of scientific competence and objectivity. Dr Lederberg said that we had a tempestuous time ahead and one of the types of storms would concern objectivity. I know this is true for my own discipline and I suspect that the biomedical sciences will not be totally immune to such tempestuousness.

JAN WALDENSTRÖM: As a physician I should like to disagree for a moment with Lord Zuckerman. I have a strong feeling that molecular biology will be the only type of science that will offer the possibility of a solution to the problem of cancer. It may be easier for the audience to understand this, if I give an example. There is an old skin disease called Sailor's skin, and people who have that develop skin carcinoma when they get exposed to ultraviolet light. Nobody knew what it really was until Dr Cleaver, a molecular biologist in the United States, working together with dermatologists, could show that this is a hereditary deficiency of a repair enzyme of the DNA. Ultraviolet light breaks up DNA molecules and this is continuously repaired in every cell, but if that enzyme is hereditarily defective, then you may get cancer.

I think you can never predict how these interesting new discoveries will come about. Dr Handler yesterday closed the session by telling us a most exciting story about a series of happy accidents, but which of course could happen only to prepared minds who are trained in molecular biological thinking. This discovery will probably alleviate an enormous amount of suffering in human beings who have malformed haemoglobin molecules.

RENÉ KÖNIG: Bis jetzt ist immer nur von Formen direkter Kontrolle der Forschung gesprochen worden. Ich möchte Ihnen jetzt einen konkreten Fall von indirekter Kontrolle vorlegen. Es genügt ja nicht, durch die Forschung neue pharmazeutische Wirkstoffe zu finden, sie müssen auch verkauft werden. Und hier stehen als Kontrollinstanz die praktizierenden Ärzte. Wie kommen sie zu neuen pharmazeutischen Produkten? Ich möchte auf eine Studie hinweisen, die bei uns im Institut in Köln über die von Ärzten gelesenen Zeitschriften gemacht worden ist. Die Ärzte verlieren genau wie jeder andere Mensch sehr schnell den Kontakt mit der Wissenschaft, so daß sie Schwierigkeiten haben, die wissenschaftlichen Zeitschriften zu lesen. Sie greifen in Deutschland also vorwiegend zu den Hauszeitschriften der großen pharmazeutischen Firmen mit der Begründung, daß diese viel klarer geschrieben seien und viel besser und in kurzer Form das Wesentliche zusammenfaßten. Wir haben in dieser Hinsicht etwa fünfzig bis siebzig Hauszeitschriften großer pharmazeutischer Firmen untersucht. Es hat sich gezeigt, daß die Ärzte eine sehr negative Einstellung gegenüber der Werbung haben und damit skeptisch sind, ob diese Hauszeitschriften ihnen etwas einreden wollen, was in Wahrheit gar nicht so gut ist. Andererseits übernehmen sie manchmal Anregungen, und entsprechend empfehlen sie die Pharmazeutika ihren Patienten. Ich möchte anregen, daß man die Rolle des Arztes in der indirekten Kontrolle der Medikamente untersucht.

LORD ROSENHEIM: In our country we now have a Medicine's Commission, and in the very near future when the Medicine Act goes into operation no new drug can be introduced without a licence. This too will be an important means of control. I should like to support what has been said about limitations on the control of research. Control is very often the consequence of no one knowing how to set about dealing with a certain topic. The thought did cross my mind that there might be a Nobel prize floating round for anyone who could deal with Lord Zuckerman's backache, and I wonder whether this is something that I should look into. In the Harveian Oration which Lord Platt gave a few years ago, he pointed out the great need for research into psychiatric problems. He said this in a way which he hoped would provoke a great deal of discussion. However, one of the only letters that appeared in the *Lancet* – or was it the *British Medical Journal*? – following its publication was from an expert in human metabolism who said that he preferred to do research on topics in which he could see some lead. If Lord Platt would kindly suggest leads in psychiatric research, he was sure that people would take this up.

If I might now pass on to Dr Pletscher's second question, i.e. the degree to which the pharmaceutical industry should devote energy and finance to drugs for relief of minor symptoms. I would hope that the pharmaceutical industry will continue to devote energy and finance to developing drugs for symptomatic relief, as I believe this is where their finance comes from; it certainly does not come from producing high-powered immunosuppressive agents or antiviral agents, which we need extremely badly and on which a lot of capital has to be sunk. They must make their money in other products. The relief of minor symptoms is therefore desirable not only from the point of view of those who have the minor symptoms but also of industry.

JAN WALDENSTRÖM: I quite agree with Lord Rosenheim that it is very important to combat what Freud has called 'das Unbehagen in der Kultur'. People feel dysphoric and they resort to all sorts of means in order to keep going. Of course, we have had much help from the pharmaceutical houses. There is however one great danger in self-medication though there is also one great positive side to it.

An example of the dangers is the phenacetin story. From clinics in Switzerland we heard that phenacetin, when taken for headaches excessively for decades, may damage the kidneys. We, in Sweden said, 'it cannot happen here; we have never seen it'. Then a fortnight later we found that there were a number of such patients in the city of Malmö. After a few years it was found that this was the most common single cause of chronic renal disease in this city. Americans, if I may be a little rude, still have not realized how important this problem is. I have been preaching this many times and they still say it cannot happen there.

On the other hand, if people took more care of those minor ailments, as Dr Pletscher calls them, this would certainly reduce the queues of people who come with all sorts of small complaints to the doctors' offices and thus cause shortage of doctors and stand in the way of people who need medical care much more.

PHILIP HANDLER: I offer one warning with respect to the operation of national commissions on drugs. The overreaction, if you will, with respect to placing new drugs (I mean as therapeutic agents) into society has been greater in the United States than anywhere else in the world. In consequence, at this point it has been almost a year since last a new drug application was filed before our Food and Drug Administration involving a new chemical entity. I have a strong suspicion that we have overdone it.

SALVADOR E. LURIA: May I add one point in connection with what Dr Waldenström and Dr Handler said. There is an interesting area of research. I am not aware whether the pharmaceutical industry is pursuing it. It is the question of the statistical analysis of the evaluation of drugs that may have counter-indications in a very small proportion of individuals. We tried to look into this at the Massachusetts Institute of Technology recently in connection with the evaluation of the possible consequences of small doses of radiation. It turned out that the necessary mathematical procedure is not available. I'm wondering whether this would not be an interesting area for the pharmaceutical industry to look into.

FRANZ BÖCKLE: Alle Redner haben darauf hingewiesen, daß die Entwicklung von Medikamenten zur Behandlung leichter Erkrankungen als ambivalent zu betrachten ist. Einerseits weil sie in die finanzielle Problematik hineinwirkt, und andererseits weil Nebenwirkungen auftreten können. Ich möchte aber einen positiven Aspekt herausheben. Das menschliche Zusammenleben kann durch die Erkenntnisse der modernen Sozialwissenschaften, zum Beispiel der Konfliktforschung, und die Erkenntnisse der biomedizinischen Forschung verbessert werden. Neue Behandlungsmittel für leichtere Beschwerden, die ihre negativen Auswirkungen auf das Zusammenleben haben, können das Gemeinschaftsleben wiederum menschlicher gestalten. Unter diesem Aspekt würde ich es bedauern, wenn man die Entwicklung solcher Hilfsmittel nur wegen der Nebenfolgen negativ sehen wollte.

LORD TODD: Dr Pletscher's second question is not so much whether the pharmaceutical industry should produce drugs for minor ailments, it is rather what degree of effort should be put into this. I think it is fair to say that a good many of the very successful tranquillizer drugs were obtained not in searching for tranquillizers but were noticed in testing for other purposes. That is the way many drugs for minor ailments will arise.

Regarding self-medication it has been said on many occasions during this Symposium that there is a very big forward drive in education. But as you get a drive in education, it is going to become increasingly impossible to prevent self-medication by people.

LORD ZUCKERMAN: May I ask whether the people with kidney trouble resulting from abusive intake of phenacetin were in any way helped by the drug before developing their trouble. I should like to link this question to what Dr Luria said, when he referred to a lack of certain mathematical and statistical techniques for determining the effects of low doses of radiation. How can we take time into account, so that one could predict, e.g. whether the F_1 and F_2 generation have been affected by the pill? The pill suppresses the oocytes. Oocytes are not being formed all the time in the ovary. How will statistical techniques tell one in advance that there are no side-effects on the oocytes as opposed to the side-effects with which we are concerned at the present moment.

JAN WALDENSTRÖM: I can certainly say that phenacetin is an excellent drug for headaches if you use it in reasonable quantities. After it became obligatory to have a doctor's prescription for even limited quantities, the serious results of self-medication have disappeared. I'm quite convinced that, as Lord Todd said, self-medication is here and will develop further. But with increased education the dangers will decrease. As the dangers of the drugs sometimes come out very late, many of the new legal arrangements for testing drugs are just stopping progress.

LORD TODD: No advance can ever be made in this world without some risk. It's a question of the degree of risk that you are prepared to face to get a certain benefit.

SALVADOR E. LURIA: I agree that the statistical problems on the side-effects of drugs are even more difficult if I want to have some information in advance. I don't know whether it is feasible to estimate what the minimum size and the distribution of the sample must be in order to evaluate whether the drug X, which is not yet in use, will have any contraindications. However, one should not be overcautious about drugs that are needed.

LORD TODD: I suggest we move on to the question of priorities. It has been touched upon quite a number of times but I doubt whether we have reached any real consensus. We have had it put to us that there is an immense need for medical care in areas much simpler than, e.g. the complex series of transplantations. We have had accounts given and pleas put forward for particular forms of medical care provision, for a new and improved multiphasic screening approach to medicine. We have had it said we should not waste money on complicated types of treatment.

On the other hand, Dr Handler pointed out that not so very long ago we were spending vast amounts of money on diseases now regarded as almost non-existent or at least trivial and that some of the very complicated techniques may well become cheap and easy to look after, if we go ahead with them and learn to handle them properly.

LORD ROSENHEIM: I agree with Dr Handler that we cannot stop research on techniques such as renal dialysis and transplantation. These are feasible and if a thing is feasible people will go on doing it. As I said earlier, if one sees a patient who has had a renal transplant, leading an active life, it is very difficult to believe that this is not a good line of treatment.

I wonder whether I might put the record straight, as I was quoted yesterday when I had not even opened my mouth, about something that I had said about research some years ago, namely, that if there were a moratorium on research – and I did not think that this was feasible – the health of developing countries would continue to improve for a long time by the application of what is known at the present time. I still believe that we could narrow the gap between the developing countries and our own very markedly by the application of existing knowledge to the developing countries.

Unfortunately, of course, since the developing countries have modern medical schools, they learn about cardiac surgery and about renal dialysis, and there is a growing demand in these countries for these esoteric methods of treatment, while there are many simple infectious diseases still requiring to be controlled. This is one of the major problems of the developing countries at the present time. Yet I would not stop complex and expensive research and methods of treatment. But I would try to develop treatment overseas to the standards of the Western world of up to ten years ago, when dialysis first started.

LORD TODD: The point about the underdeveloped countries is that public health measures alone could make tremendous differences.

PHILIP HANDLER: I was thinking that if I were an inhabitant of one of those countries I would be far more interested in a new drug that might be effective in schistosomiasis than in doing cardiac transplantations.

LORD TODD: Yes, of course, but you are up against the problem that when one offers a new technology it will be seized upon. After all, one of the troubles in underdeveloped countries is that if you show a television set to somebody in the remote Congo, he will thereafter be just as keen to have a TV set as the peasant in the Canton de Valais. As far as he is concerned, it is the government's problem to think of how it is to be paid for. You certainly get the same thing in medicine. I should like to get an answer to the question of the desirability of integration of the biomedical sciences and the social sciences, calling, as Dr König put it on Wednesday, for a new kind of professional morality. I do not quite understand just how this integration is going to be brought about.

TALCOTT PARSONS: I doubt whether with integration we have the same situation that was suggested yesterday for cancer, where things are right for a crash program. I am inclined to think that much development will be necessary on both sides, but especially on the social science side.

I might give one example where some genuine progress in integration has been made. Starting from certain phenomena that link what has traditionally been called mental illness with somatic illness, the so-called psychosomatic field, required the extension of analysis of the mechanisms involved in those kinds of illness. Conversely therapeutic possibilities had to be linked with certain themes that have emerged as prominent in psychology, anthropology and sociology.

One way of putting it is that in the psychological sense, a substantial part of illness is motivated. This can be demonstrated in many different cases. The concept of 'secondary gain' has been widely used in psychiatry. In my own case as a sociologist it would seem to me possible to use the concept of 'social role' and to treat illness as the focal point in the structure of one type of role. It is possible to delineate some of the primary features of the sick role, as for example the exemption from normal performance obligation for a very substantial part of the field of illness and the obligation at the same time to try to recover. It is an apparently paradoxical concept that you are obligated to try to recover while not held personally responsible for your condition, in the sense that will-power alone will not bring about recovery from most illnesses, both somatic and psychic. One can go a step beyond and suggest that somatic illness may have certain functions. The concept 'secondary gain' is virtually a label for that.

On the social side too illness probably has certain important functions. One is that motivated illness, or the motivated component of illness, may be an alternative to modes of socially unacceptable behavior. From the social point of view, some of the consequences of psychological tensions in social relationships may be diverted into illness and thereby in a certain sense be neutralized.

This example is good evidence for a beginning of integration. But if it is to be solid and have far-reaching consequences, it must go to deeper theoretical levels.

RENÉ KÖNIG: The French sociologist, Marcel Mauss, who died immediately after the Second World War, postulated this very integration already in the early twenties. He thought that it was impossible to develop social psychology without going back to endocrinology. He then came in a very narrow alliance with the French school of psychiatry and also with Jean Piaget from Geneva. So, this was an early attempt at integration.

ERNST VON WEIZSÄCKER: Lord Todd asked us to bake the cakes! But the cultural gaps we have faced during this meeting are hindering us. It is not that there is an insufficiency of our scientific knowledge that is preventing us from coming to grips. It is rather, as we heard now, especially from Dr Parsons, that the integration of the Two Cultures is the practical problem.

Dr Parsons provided evidence for what he said. I will cite further evidence by some clinicians in Germany. They looked at what happened to people who left the hospitals presumably cured, and found that only two, sometimes five, years after the patients had left the hospital they had developed almost the same illness, sometimes with the same, sometimes with other symptoms. So one comes to the conclusion that it was not so much the physiological condition that prevented the people from being healthy, but much more their family or working environment.

Our medical faculties have managed to escape all these problems almost entirely. There is practically no social training for physicians, and even if there were, they would have no opportunity to use it. Therefore I am greatly encouraged by what Dr Gibson told us of the United States where the patient, who knows of his shortcomings in his environment, plays an important and active role in the curing process.

Every physician should have some training, some experience, practical and theoretical, in social problems. The social scientist, on the other hand, should have some experience with medical and natural science problems. Due to pronounced specialization it is no longer necessary that every physician has the whole range of medicine present. He can therefore afford to take some notice of social questions.

TALCOTT PARSONS: The one direction which seems to me to hold out great promise for integration is a mode of theoretical thinking that in fact goes beyond the life sciences – I would include the social behavioral sciences among the life sciences – and for which the developments of the last two or three decades in the microbiological fields, especially genetics, are the primary examples. This is the concept of phenomena involving control of vital processes through codified structures. The genetic code, which in a sense was a great culmination of this development in genetics, is an example. A parallel kind of development has been very conspicuous in linguistics. There seem to be certain parallels between linguistic codes and codes at the microbiological level. Similar things are found, though not well understood yet, in many areas of culture. My own feeling is that the following-up of cybernetics and information theory are of prime importance to this kind of development. The following-up of the relations of the different sets of disciplines in terms of a model structure and process – it has to have both – and in terms of very careful, very detailed research on strategic problems may be a very promising path towards integration.

LORD ROSENHEIM: I look forward to some combined research into psychosomatic or somatopsychic disorders. This is a field in which there is common ground between the sociologist, the behavioural and the clinical scientists.

PHILIP HANDLER: The problem will of course find a home in the university historically. The invasion of one discipline by the practitioners of another has indeed come about and reflects recognition of the possibility of applying the skills one already has to solve problems which, classically, fall within the purview of some other discipline. That is why there are scientists called bio-chemists and bio-physicists. By and large, this integration has occurred in the heads of individual human beings who have taken it upon themselves to gather the essence of yet another discipline to add to the one they already have. In American universities there have been many experiments with rather contrived packages which are supposedly multidisciplinary. Very few have found success. It may be that they were not attractive to the brightest of the students, who continued to be attracted to the classical disciplines, rather than that the package itself was 'unnatural'.

But I have my own feeling about this form of 'integration'. Practitioners of the brilliance of Dr Parsons can manage this for themselves. Dr von Weizsäcker explained how it is being attempted in another setting, and more and more of this is occurring. But most such institutional attempts seem to have resulted in failure so far.

LORD TODD: I wonder whether this difficulty is not a specific feature of the universities. It has always struck me that the pharmaceutical industry is where essentially interdisciplinary research was developed, i.e. in chemotherapy, taking chemotherapy in its broadest sense.

Why has that happened? The reason is that in the universities the traditional classical disciplines were (a) too separate, and (b) the practitioners were all too concerned with their own honour and glory within their discipline, so the interdisciplinary work never got off the ground. The industrial position is quite different. Industry could get many different people and could say to them, 'Here is the problem we are trying to solve', and they were all prepared to solve one problem. This was very difficult to achieve in the universities.

SALVADOR E. LURIA: I would like to turn your argument round, Lord Todd. I do think that the success of interdisciplinary endeavor, for example in the pharmaceutical industry, is exactly the result of the absence of it in the university. The university, by keeping to a tight, precise and solid training in one field, makes it possible for the individual to be so well trained that later and displaced to another situation he will be an effective member of the group. But every time one tries to create interdepartmental or interdisciplinary training programs one comes out with people who are bad electrical engineers, bad economists and bad political scientists. Instead of being first-class engineers who then learn some political science and some economics. It seems to me that the function of a university is very much that of giving superior training to people who then can cooperate effectively.

PHILIP HANDLER: I entirely agree. I doubt whether we can solve human problems by pooling our ignorance.

MARGARET MEAD: I was very cross a while ago because we seemed to be spending our time saying how we did not understand each other, part of which was due to different nationalities, and part to the word 'values', which is a pestilential idea anyway. So those who are concerned about the well-being of mankind did not understand those who talked about man. You know, man and mankind are two different concepts. The Europeans who were talking about the necessity of grief were understood by the Americans as talking about not giving anesthesia for surgery, or possibly not even using psychotropic drugs for the cure of mental disease. And this went right on. Dr Hersch made an attempt at rectifying this misunderstanding yesterday – it did not take. I would like to mention again – making a cross-cultural comment in my role as an anthropologist – that Europeans, when they talk about the necessity of human suffering, are not talking about sticking needles into people or operating without anesthetics.

Also, separating our values and labelling them, and then dealing with preferential lists of values contrasts very strongly with the statements made here by both social and natural scientists on the tremendous concern about what is happening with the people on this planet, about the dangers of biological and chemical warfare and about the implications of the population explosion. All of these are values but they do not get labelled as such.

A second point, and this is important for any future conference, is that the way in which people trained in different disciplines learn to understand each other is by dealing with a common problem, or a common body of data, or a common example. Dr Handler made that point when he mentioned that there were no examples for communication between himself and Dr Böckle.

I would like to stress that the key point in this whole conference, which has made perfectly clear the attitudes that we have to take towards the importance of basic research, towards our inability to be certain what the outcomes will be of a variety of procedures, was Dr Handler's instance of the therapy for sickle-cell disease, which was concrete, definite, clear, and related to a variety of 'values'. We could conclude therefore, that you must not restrain basic research, you must not assume that when you target research – if you target it narrowly – you will get what you want.

Dr Handler's instance said something else, namely, that one of the ways we communicate with the rest of mankind is in the priorities that we set. Dr Handler said – and that little incident is just packed with everything – that it gave us an opportunity to assure our black population that we were doing something for them. Now, only a very limited number of our black population have sickle-cell disease as compared with primary malnutrition. But we cannot communicate our nutrition programs as well. This does not mean we should do more research on sickle-cells than on the effect of malnutrition. But it means that research on sickle-cells was a form of communication from the medical establishment to the people, which said 'We are concerned with what we know you are concerned with'. The sort of enterprise Dr Gibson talked about is again a form of communication, a social organization that mediates between the health establishment and the community.

A negative example is the attempt of the Kefauver Committee and its successor to exploit the very real fear in the United States that our children may use drugs, by putting up excessive regulations. I do not doubt that a good many of the regulations that are now hampering research in the pharmaceutical industry can be traced to this sequence of events. We need new forms of communications telling the public what the pharmaceutical industry is doing that is relevant to their problems.

We must not be discouraged by the cultural differences between ourselves and European theologians with their tendency to talk about something called 'man', which is only one step better than when European psychoanalysts talk about 'woman'. Instead, we must all work together on common problems and place our concerns in the widest possible context so that it doesn't seem as though we were particularly obsessed by our own discipline, or as Lord Todd calls it, our own honor and glory. We must be able to communicate to people that we are deeply concerned about what is a very critical period in the history of mankind.

ROBERT REICHARDT: I want to suggest possible lines of inquiry by which an integration of the biological, social and psychological sciences might be possible. For this reason I have to fall back on the detested term 'values'; it might be my European bias to do so. There could be much more communication on what is meant by values by the social scientist with the help of the biological scientist.

There are several kinds of problems that apply in this direction. The first is simply a semantic one. We have to clarify the terms; what do we mean, e. g. by 'identical persons'? As Dr Lederberg pointed out, this is no longer a trivial problem after the recent advances in genetics. The biologist has also much to say about the term 'normality'. Dr Berry mentioned that this was quite difficult to define and was a term more properly applied to individuals than to the whole of population.

A second line of inquiry would be what one could call 'biologistic rationalization for norms'. A good example is sexual behaviour, especially in European culture, where the sexual norms during the nineteenth century were motivated by health consideration. Masturbation and frequent sexual activity, e. g., were regarded as unhealthy. This view is not shared by the majority of contemporary biologists.

Another problem are racial prejudices based on biologistic ideas which were then turned into normative statements. Here, the biologist could certainly help the social scientist to resolve these prejudices and racialisms by bringing in clear and basic facts.

A third line would be for the natural scientist to explain the opportunities. If there is talk about 'manipulation', for instance, the social scientist should know much more about feasible technologies and how likely or unlikely they are, so that he could alleviate, e. g. the great fear among the public of electrodes put into the brain, a technology that has been largely overestimated.

There is a fourth question, touched upon by Dr Hersch, of what is constant or permanent in man. This can be approached not only from philosophical science but also from natural science.

I don't mean by these statements that all the burden lies with the biologist. But here is a way of bringing in the basic facts, which is very important for the social scientist and the ethical philosopher as it gives him a clearer concept of what he is talking about when he makes normative statements.

JOSHUA LEDERBERG: The question of the optimization of the spectrum of research, of its harmonization, has been opened up by various speakers making incorrect and incautious remarks. I thought it important to have some further comments.

Too many of my good friends have back troubles, for me not to express sincere sympathy with the remarks of Lord Zuckerman. One can postulate an array of many other problems that have this characteristic of being of very great human importance but where no one exactly knows how to approach them. The problem is that we would like to find out how to improve the social utility of the overall spectrum of research without diminishing its general quality. We would of course have to consider not just one but all the various priorities.

I strongly suspect that if you made up a shopping list of the problems that you wanted to be solved, and then weighed the items with respect to their accessibility and to the kinds of supporting research that would be needed in order to get anywhere you would end up with a pretty reasonable approximation to the lines of work we do at the present time. It would be wonderful to say, 'let us concentrate on solving the back problem, there will be great social utility in doing it'. But you have to take into account the disutility of diverting resources from productive areas to others that might be futile at this time. And worst of all would be to hamper the growth of *basic* knowledge which is constantly opening new opportunities for insight and for mastery. To be sure, there may be unperceived fascinations at a biochemical, a metabolic, a psychosomatic and an endocrinological level in this particular problem of backache. Perhaps it has never been framed in a sufficiently intelligent or attractive way to induce the

Joshua Lederberg: 'I strongly suspect that if you made up a shopping list of the problems that you wanted to be solved, and then weighed the items with respect to their accessibility and to the kinds of supporting research that would be needed in order to get anywhere you would end up with a pretty reasonable approximation to the lines of work we do at the present time.'

interest of the kinds of people who might be able to make a pertinent contribution to it. Most of us tend to think of it as something more akin to architecture than to biochemistry, and I am sure this is wrong.

We have to ask ourselves how fashions in research are produced at the present time. It is a phenomenon about which we have little understanding. There are probably many utilities and some disutilities to the band-wagon effects. I myself would be very suspicious of central planning. It has not proven to be successful in any interesting way. In areas of this complexity it is much more likely to lead to such excesses as the space program. The fundamental proposition on which I would rely is that if not in density at least in total sum there is more intelligence and more good will and more humanity outside the political establishment than inside it. The scientists at the laboratory bench know more about how to do good experiments and probably in the aggregate have no less a social conscience than the planner who might wish to say, 'you must work on this rather than on that'.

Now, there is a negative side too. There are fashions and some of them may be directed in ways that are purely artefactual. The attention of many scientists may not yet have been appropriately drawn to a set of problems to which there may be avenues of solution. For example, the science of nutrition was believed by many to have been completed around the year 1915 or 1920, with a few spectacular additions. It is only in the last few years that it has again become a fashionable subject for scientific investigation. In part because of a great deal of social interest, the malnutrition problem was rediscovered in the United States.

I can point to many other examples that would compete with the bad backs. In relation to the human misery that is involved I would submit that there is less work going on right now on schistosomiasis globally than on back problems. It is not difficult to visualize that more focussed research on these organisms, using already existing methodological approaches, as e.g. those of molecular biology, would be likely to lead to some very interesting solutions.

Another example would be a more rational application of new knowledge in molecular biology to the problems of food crop production, as regards not only the development of more carbohydrate products, but also the genetic improvement of crops. There have been the so-called 'miracle strains' of wheat and rice, but every geneticist knows that the scientific basis and the techniques to develop these strains existed already forty years ago. Absolutely no use whatever has been made of the new findings in molecular and cell biology in relation to this very pressing world problem. I am not advocating that there should be a shift of funds. But funds should be available when good and interesting projects are presented for review by peer groups who are able to evaluate their quality.

As regards the problem of integration there would be very great value in occasional interdisciplinary sessions that are problem-oriented rather than discipline-oriented, in which, e.g. biochemists might hear what are the important problems in medicine, in agriculture, in the social sphere. They could then use better their own imagination in deciding what are the available issues to which

their energies can fruitfully be addressed. We will thus have a free market in
ideas and in the availability of intelligence to solving human problems which most
of us believe to be superior to any systems of central planning.

JÜRGEN MOLTMANN: Herr Vorsitzender, Sie haben am Anfang dieses Symposiums gesagt: «A man should be healthy, wealthy and wise.» Wir haben gesprochen darüber, wie man gesund wird und seine Gesundheit erhält und wie man
wohlhabend wird. Wir haben auch darüber gesprochen, wie man gesund wird,
wenn man nicht wohlhabend ist, und wie man wohlhabend, aber nicht gesund
sein kann. Auf dem Gebiete der Weisheit sind wir aber noch nicht weit vor-
angekommen. Wenn mit dem biomedizinischen Fortschritt zwar die Leiden der
Menschheit gemildert werden können, aber keine Glücksgarantie damit verbunden ist, brauchen wir eine Ethik, die diesem Fortschritt gewachsen ist. Sie gehört für den Arzt zur menschlichen Beratung des Patienten und für die Erziehung des Patienten zur Weisheit im Umgang mit Medikamenten und ärztlicher
Behandlung.

Ich glaube, es ist weise, zwei Ordnungen zu unterscheiden: eine Ordnung
des Körpers und eine Ordnung der Person. In der Ordnung des Körpers heißt
Gesundheit die Funktionsfähigkeit des Organismus, in unserem Falle Arbeits-
fähigkeit und Genußfähigkeit. Krankheit ist dann eine Störung des Organismus.
In der Ordnung der Person aber zeigt sich die Gesundheit eines Menschen auch
darin, *wie* er Schmerz und Leiden, Verlust und Enttäuschung menschlich verarbeitet. In der Ordnung des Körpers ist der Tod ein Exitus. In der Ordnung der
Person aber ist der Tod mit der Hingabe des Lebens verbunden, mit dem Verlust
des Objektes der Liebe und mit Trauer.

Wenn diese beiden Ordnungen nicht ausgeglichen sind, kommt es zu Störungen in der Ethik. Es gibt eine Reaktion auf den biomedizinischen Fortschritt,
die romantisch und reaktionär ist. Man sagt: «Die Ordnung der Person ist alles.
Medizin und ärztliche Künste haben uns verführt. Wir wollen zurück zu natürlichen Heilmitteln. Wir müssen den Körper neu entdecken als unseren eigenen
Leib. Stoppt also den medizinischen Fortschritt, stoppt die genetische Forschung.» Ich nehme nicht an, daß die Kirchen sich zu Agenten solcher Reaktionen machen werden.

Viel gefährlicher aber scheint es mir, wenn die Ordnung des Körpers domi-
niert und die Ethik des Menschen bestimmt, denn es entstehen dann Verhaltensweisen, die mit Gleichgültigkeit gegenüber dem eigenen Leben und Tod und
dem Leben und Tod anderer Menschen verbunden sind. Manche der selbstver-
ordneten Medikamente haben Eigenschaften, die zu einem Leben ohne Leidenschaft, ohne Hoffnung und ohne Furcht, ohne Liebe und ohne Haß führen. Dann
ist der Fetus nur ein Appendix, und der Tod ist nur das Ende. Daraus kann
eine Gefühlskälte entstehen, die sich ausdrückt in Äußerungen wie «play it cool.»
Sozial entsteht daraus die Verdrängung von Alten und von Kranken, von Sterbenden und von Schwachen.

Es kommt darauf an, diese beiden Ordnungen in einen weisen Ausgleich zu bringen und den biomedizinischen Fortschritt zu integrieren in einer Ordnung der Humanität, die das Leben lebenswert macht. Aber das entsteht nicht einfach aus den schon vorhandenen Werten in der Gesellschaft, sondern es muß zuerst bewußt gemacht werden. Was wir verändern können, das muß mit menschlicher Kraft verändert werden zum Wohl des Menschen. Aber man muß auch aus der langen Geschichte unserer Kultur, unserer Religion und Ethik lernen, daß und wie das Unveränderliche mit Würde getragen wird.

Concluding remarks

LORD TODD: So much has been said in these two and a half days of discussion that when I also take into account what has been written and precirculated by the participants it seems well-nigh impossible to sum it up. The best I can do in the circumstances is to indicate those areas or questions about which there is some consensus of opinion and those on which we seem to be seriously divided – although I think there are less of the latter than might have been expected.

In many ways the three questions posed by Dr Pletscher at the outset really epitomize the subject matter of our discussions. These questions I paraphrase as follows:

(1) Should there be some control or limitation of research?
(2) Should we refrain from putting major effort into producing remedies for minor complaints? This, of course, bears on problems of drug abuse, self-medication, etc.
(3) What is to be done about the provision of very expensive medical and surgical treatments in the light of the overall need for medical care? In other words, what are our priorities in medicine?

In our opening session Dr Pletscher's first question was debated at length, and it has come up as a recurring theme in almost every session. It seems to me that there is substantial agreement that biomedical – like all other scientific research – should not be restricted save in so far as, when in any given country resources are limited, choices may have to be made as to those areas of science in which major efforts shall be mounted. Such choices must be made on economic and political considerations since they will affect technological development and, what may be equally important, they will determine the nature and the scale of scientific manpower supply. It is often forgotten that the most important aspect of research in universities is its training function – directly for postgraduates and indirectly for undergraduates. But direct control of science or even of technology is virtually impossible because of its inherent unpredictability.

Given that choices must be made who shall decide what technologies should be developed and on what scale? I think we are agreed that this is a function of government; decision is a political and not a scientific matter. In the world of today and tomorrow it is essential that the politician be given the best available scientific advice; but his must be the decision. Hence Lord Zuckerman's important plea for the scientist to concern himself with politics while bearing in mind Dr Lederberg's comment that scientific ability is, of itself, no guarantee of political wisdom. The social responsibility of the scientist is exactly that of other members of society – to ensure that the evidence available to him as a scientist is given appropriate consideration by governments before decisions are made. He should always remember, however, that his ability to predict the future consequences of any discovery or even the uses to which it might be put is really very limited.

In the background of the opening discussion of possible new technologies and their implications the problem of world population was frequently mentioned. Population problems occupied a large part of our second session and their magnitude was underlined by Dr Sauvy. There were differences of opinion about the real nature of the so-called generation gap and on whether the present crisis in society is without previous parallel. We were all agreed on the menace of the inevitable huge increase in world population during the next hundred years and the disastrous consequences that will ensue from a continuation of our present thoughtless depletion of our non-renewable natural resources. There is here an enormous challenge to science and technology, and in the biomedical and social sciences population control must be a prime concern. We must both think and act quickly for in these matters time is not on our side. The important issue of the degree to which legal action should be taken to control population growth was indeed raised, but my impression is that it was regrettably, if understandably, evaded by most speakers. It was in this and similar connections that the non-scientists made an urgent plea for an integration of the natural and the human sciences and I hope this plea will be heeded; it is, of course, relevant to the whole issue of communication between scientists, doctors, and the public.

On Dr Pletscher's second question about drugs for minor ailments there was much confused discussion which I can hardly deal with in detail. Broadly speaking, speakers were divided on what exactly was expected by a human being in the way of health, wealth and wisdom. Some of us felt that a totally pain- and trouble-free existence would be a little boring after a time, and that perhaps it was not something that should be ardently sought for, even in the unlikely event that it could be achieved. This being so, some at least felt that too much effort should not be devoted to minor disabilities. At the same time, if I may refer back to something I said earlier this afternoon, drugs to deal with minor ailments will turn up willy-nilly in the course of other work. The major efforts of the pharmaceutical industry in the immediate future are likely to be in areas like virology, allergy, the ageing process and degenerative disease and perhaps, as Dr Burgen so interestingly suggested, the processes of learning.

Self-medication, I gather, is not favoured by our medical colleagues, and, no doubt, with good reason; but it seems to me that, with rising levels of education, self-medication will increase whatever view the doctors hold. The question of drug abuse was hotly debated and quite different viewpoints were given by Dr Hersch and Dr Goldstein. There must inevitably be differences of opinion on the degree to which drug abuse is a menace to society rather than merely to the individual and hence on the degree to which legal prohibition is appropriate. It was, however, generally felt that medical rather than punitive treatment of addicts was desirable.

We have had a lot of discussion on the degree to which there is a right to health. My own conclusion from our discussion is that even if – as Sir Roger Ormrod pointed out – the expression is legally meaningless, the general public does in fact believe that it has what it calls 'a right to health'. We must recognize this even if neither the public nor we here can really define the word 'health' in this context. This 'right to health' is very relevant to our discussions on systems of medical care. On this we had interesting contributions from Dr Berry on space medicine, from Dr Gibson on community medicine, and from Lord Rosenheim today on physician–patient contact. There was a consensus of opinion that, whatever system we adopt for medical care, it must be based on social justice. In other words, however care is provided, whatever system is used, and to whatever degree medical care is rationed – for rationed it must be since demand will always far outstrip supply – it must be equally available to all without financial restriction. On the third of Dr Pletscher's questions it was, I think, very properly agreed that at the present time medical priorities can only be decided by the doctor. Nevertheless there is reason to hope that with further progress in biomedical research and the help of the pharmaceutical industry the determination of these priorities may become a more straightforward matter than it now is.

I do not claim that I have given you a good summary of our discussions; indeed, I have only presented in a rather broad way some thoughts that came to me today and others I have been jotting down during our earlier sessions. But if time does not permit a more detailed discussion of the conclusions we may have reached, it most certainly does permit, and indeed demands, a few words from me on behalf of all participants to thank our host Dr Jann, Chairman of Hoffmann-La Roche & Co. 'The Challenge of Life' as you have interpreted it in this Symposium, Dr Jann, is not only a broad but a very difficult topic, and it certainly has no very obvious commercial relevance. That you should have chosen this subject to mark your company's anniversary is itself a tribute to your farsightedness, to your concern for human welfare, and to the way in which you and your predecessors have led Hoffmann-La Roche along a path of which you can justifiably be proud. I can only hope, Dr Jann, that you have found our discussions interesting, that they may prove to have been worthwhile and that, in some measure at least, they may have repercussions of value not only in your Company but in a much wider sphere, for the problems we have talked about are those of all humanity. For us, your guests, this has been a wonderful opportunity, and for that opportunity I should like, on behalf of all my colleagues, to thank you most profoundly. We wish you in the future the same spectacular success that your Company has had in the past. And with your faith in research I have no doubt that success will indeed be yours.

Farewell address

by ADOLF WALTER JANN

Mr Chairman, Ladies and Gentlemen,

On behalf of all of us at Roche I should like to thank Lord Todd most sincerely for his very kind words.

Before the Symposium began, we knew that the main objective was to clarify the problems. We hoped that in the course of the exercise, certain pointers would emerge towards possible solutions. Where do we now stand?

Over the last three days the problems have certainly been analysed and presented in a most competent manner, but many of the big question marks which have always hung over their solution are of course still with us. Much has been said about life and death and who should bear the burden of taking the decision in *individual* cases. But in the wider sphere of whole communities and peoples, in which the allocation of scarce resources means life for some and death or misery for others, who then should take the decision and how is it to be communicated?

Lord Zuckerman made it clear that, as a matter of practical politics, those who hold the purse-strings will be the policy-makers, but he hopes that the medical profession will be able to exert some influence on governments in the matter of getting their priorities right. I share his opinion and his hopes.

We have therefore reached the position where most of the questions are now clear, but the answers to those questions will only emerge in the course of time as we cautiously proceed, step by step, to meet the obstacles and difficulties which lie in our path.

Somewhere along that path, we might well feel the need to offer our hospitality once again for a resumption of the dialogue, perhaps within a smaller circle and on more specific subjects.

As far as research is concerned, I have always held very firmly to certain basic beliefs. I believe that the force of human nature is such that the enthusiasm and momentum engendered by research could never be halted by mere government command. Dedicated scientists would always feel compelled to strive for further progress. Furthermore, I believe that it is equally impossible to put research – and especially medical research – under state control and still expect it to be successful in spite of a tremendous bureaucratic apparatus.

It only remains for me to thank all of you who have participated in the discussion as well as those who were patient enough to follow the proceedings for three days as listeners. I have to thank particularly the speakers, the moderators and our chairman, who have provided the basis and shape of this gathering.

We are especially grateful to Lord Todd for this afternoon's exercise in cake-baking. It is said that the proof of the pudding is in the eating, and I am sure the same applies to *that* cake, which will be sampled by our scientists in the weeks and months ahead, slice by slice.

Now that you are about to disperse, I wish you, and especially those of you who have far to travel to your homes, a pleasant journey and happy landings. I hope that you will take back with you agreeable memories of your short stay with us in Basel. As we may feel the need to resume our dialogue, I shall not say 'good-bye', I say 'so long', which in French is 'au revoir'; in Germany they say 'auf Wiedersehen', in Austria 'Servus', and in our Swiss language we say 'uf Widerluege'.

SECOND PART:
PAPERS AND CURRICULA OF THE ACTIVE
PARTICIPANTS

In a preliminary Symposium near Geneva in November 1970 the topics were discussed and the programme for the Roche Anniversary Symposium was outlined. From left to right: Philip Handler, Lord Todd, Alfred Pletscher, Robert M. Kunz, Hans Fehr, Ernst Sorkin and Pierre Pichot.

Individual discussions played an important role at the preliminary Symposium. Margaret Mead and Jacques Monod who unfortunately was unable to attend the Symposium in Basel.

Papers

Ethical aspects of the new perspectives in biomedical research

by SALVADOR E. LURIA

The interplay of ethical considerations with almost every aspect of biomedical research and practice has been very much in the minds of the planners of this conference, as evidenced by the number of experts in the field of ethics who are among the participants. I interpret my task, as one of the speakers in the first session, to comment on ethical problems and conflicts as seen from a biologist's point of view.

Ethical problems arise, in the biomedical field as in all other areas, when decisions are influenced by conflicting sets of values. Such conflicts are often unrecognized or at least not explicitly formulated, especially when one set of values is so prevalent in society that it is taken as an absolute while conflicting values are considered as 'deviant'. This is often observed in sociopolitical affairs: for example, some of the values of liberal democracy, such as free speech and due process, proclaimed originally by a revolutionary bourgeoisie and widely assumed since then to be 'intrinsically good', are sometimes experienced as artificial restraints by radical groups bent on changing again the structure of society and, more frequently, are violated by the instruments of a now dominant class.

Another example, this one closer to medicine, is the conflict between the demand for optimal care for individual patients, including costly major surgery, and the demand for adequate care on a broad social front – a conflict that may persist as long as medical services continue to be available in scarcity rather than in plenty. Both examples illustrate the simple truth that, in political as well as in medical affairs, values change as the situation changes. Conflicts arise, at first implicit and unrecognized, then seen as oppositions between 'valid' and 'deviant' values, finally as the expression of new human needs or aspirations or opportunities. Nowhere is this more evident than in the influence of modern technology on ethical values.

Can this view of ethics, that is, the awareness of the existence of conflicting sets of values, provide guidance for the practical resolution of specific conflicts, especially those that may face the biologist in his experimentation, or the pharmaceutical chemist in drug testing, or the physician in his daily practice? Are there any grounds for choice between guidelines, except one's personal convictions or prejudices or interests?

One thought I would like, as a biologist, to offer is that ethical values are not only the product of social and cultural history, but exert in turn a profound effect on the rate and direction of change in human affairs. Man is a unique species, whose current evolution, cultural as well as biological, is in good part directed by its own activities, which alter the natural, social, and intellectual environment and thereby change the human species itself. But this quasi self-domestication is, of course, experienced at the conscious level. Man's reactions to the situations created by his own activities are embodied in sets of values, which in turn exert regulatory functions. These functions are sometimes homeo-static (negative feedback), tending to prevent or delay the exploration of new options but also to avoid premature commitment to dubious courses of action. At other times, the regulatory functions of ethical principles are evolutionary (positive feedback), tending to accelerate the rate of change by removing cultural constraints that impede new explorations.

My argument is that not only does ethics evolve but it has an *adaptive* evolutionary history, in the sense that the 'validity' of its principles is tested by their consequences as regulatory mechanisms on the course of human events in a changing world. Ethical rules are part and parcel of human culture at a given stage, tested and validated by their effects on that culture. This argument re-jects, of course, any metaphysical justification of ethical principles; it also rejects the relativistic or anarchistic views of ethics, by which any set of values is equally tenable and suitable as a guideline. (The existentialist view, of unlim-ited individual freedom coupled with individual responsibility, falls outside this discussion because it is not concerned with guidelines for collective choice in social situations.)

Let us now consider briefly, from the point of view outlined above, a few examples from the biomedical sciences. A simple case is that of vaccine and drug testing. Here the relevant and often conflicting values involve the demand for disease prevention or cure, the corporate interests of drug and vaccine manu-facturers, and the concern for safety of experimental human subjects (and, especially in Great Britain, also of animal subjects!). Public opinion and govern-ment regulations reflect changes in the balance of values due to a variety of factors. Practices acceptable in 1900 in search for prophylaxis or treatment for pneumonia or yellow fever, or even in the 1950's in fighting poliomyelitis, may be unacceptable in 1970 or 1980, when the diseases to be cured have differ-ent morbidity or mortality or even different visibility to the public eye. Thus quantitative and emotional values may influence public opinion, and so may sociopolitical values such as the attitude of the public and of governments to-wards industrial initiatives.

Similar problems and analogous conflicts of values are encountered in the area of medical practice. The use of substantial amounts of medical skills and hospital facilities for complex procedures like organ transplantation, especially in near-terminal patients, might not have been questioned until the maldistribution of health care became more evident and more effectively articulated due to the changing urban situation, leading to a true revolution of health expectations. This aggressive concern for distribution of medical care is certain to change the pattern of distribution greatly; but the conflicting value, the concern for quality care and for the continuing advance in medical and surgical technology, must continue to play a valuable regulatory role. It is even possible, and greatly to be desired, that the tension in the conflict situation will result in a really significant evolutionary step – an expansion of investment in medical facilities that would permit satisfying the demands for both quantity and quality.

A different situation is presented by legalized abortion (and, less acutely, by birth control). Here the new set of values – improved status of women, concern about overpopulation, and other sociological considerations – meets long-standing religious and emotional values about the sanctity of human life, the status of the fetus, etc. as well as technical concerns about the possible demographic consequences of sex choice following sex diagnosis by amniocentesis (not to mention social patterns of differential availability of abortion to different social classes). The conflict is not only between old and conservative versus new and progressive. Each of the two sets of values plays useful roles in the transition period, the new one by fostering social experimentation and testing its effects, the old one by preventing a rash shift to a new situation that presents great possibility of abuses. It is interesting to consider in terms of mechanisms of social evolution the situation in the United States, where a few progressive states have passed legislation that legalizes abortion. Sociologically, we may think of the population of these states constituting itself into a tester group for implementation of the new practice – a social experiment carried out, not by sociologists or anthropologists, but by the people of a democracy.

Still different is the situation with regard to what has been called genetic intervention – the modification of the genetic endowment of individuals through the introduction of foreign cells (chimerism) or of genetic materials such as chromosomes or genes. The techniques to carry out such operations are not yet at hand and, according to some, may not be forthcoming. Even more distant appears to be the possibility of genetic intervention on the germ line, whether on the intact human being or on eggs fertilized *in vitro* and then implanted into the womb of a mother or foster-mother. Yet, despite the lack of immediate prospects, discussion of promises and dangers has been heated, if inconclusive. The conflicting values are not easily discerned. On the one hand, the extent of prospective medical benefits is difficult to evaluate; on the other hand, the fears are based mainly on a distrust of powerful technologies becoming available in a society whose power structure and institutional mechanisms make a misuse of such technologies only too likely – as was the case for nuclear fission or fusion. In fact, the possible creation of genetic weapons, especially through virus research, is one of the fears most often expressed. The misgivings reflect the fact that our society cannot trust its own mechanisms to provide adequate guidelines for handling the new power that may be offered to it. Here we encounter another ethical question, that of whether not only the development of some technologies, but even the pursuit of certain lines of scientific research should be discouraged or stopped, either voluntarily or by legislation. Again no solid guidelines are available for choosing between the 'traditional' (but only three centuries old!) ethics of freedom of research and what may prove to be a new ethical demand for restraint till the social implications of certain kinds of research become clear. Note how in this case it could be the prevalent values rather than the 'deviant' ones that play the role of troublemakers.

Even more heated, because of the less remote feasibility of the practice, has been the discussion concerning the 'cloning' of human beings by transplant of nuclei into enucleated human eggs, followed by implantation of the eggs into the womb. The case against cloning and the objection to experimentation on cloning of humans – an objection in which I personally concur – have often been presented in a confusing way because the arguments have been based on ethical misunderstanding. Theologians and medical scientists alike have upheld against cloning *the right of the individual to be unique*, that is, to be the product of the genetic lottery of meiosis and fertilization, as if this were an intrinsic biological and metaphysical right. But this argument, even when presented with a garnish of psychological jargon, reflects only a special set of values, that of the individualistic, puritan ethics of capitalist democracy. I suspect that anthropologists could cite a number of societies in which identity with other individuals, if possible, would be a highly prized value. Would the champions of uniqueness deny the members of those societies the right to be cloned?

A sounder argument is that cloning would reduce the genetic variability of human populations. This, however, would hardly be a significant effect unless the practice were to become widespread. The real ground on which many people, including myself, would like to prevent cloning of humans (and even regulate research in this and other similarly delicate areas of reproductive biology) is a concern for the social and biological consequences of untested interference with the process of human reproduction. This judgment is not based on any metaphysical belief in the sacredness of certain genetic rights, but on the ethical principle that steps that may affect masses of human beings ought not to be taken until one has some idea of what they entail. Like all principles, this is no doubt a debatable principle, but one defensible in terms of the concept of adaptive ethics. It simply means that when it comes to tampering with the genetic endowment of mankind (and also of individual men) a great deal of conservatism is wise and justified.

In relation to the series of problems discussed above – abortion and birth control, genetic engineering, and cloning – we must entertain, however, the possibility that future generations, bred under new conditions and new stresses, may evaluate the choices differently and develop and prize alternative values. Thus population pressures may tend to diminish the respect for individual life and may even make palatable certain forms of coercive restraints on procreation which are now abhorrent to most of us (incidentally, this seems to me a very good reason for trying to prevent the development of such pressures by voluntary limitation of the birth rate). On the other hand, any coercively enforced limitation of population size may increase the appeal and danger of a 'selective' ethics, encouraging the preferential breeding of certain human types or social groups. In opposition to this we have – and, I believe, should uphold and defend – the value of individual freedom tightly coupled with individual reproductive responsibility.

A more direct challenge to freedom, outside the area of reproductive biology, could come from the discovery and use of psychotropic drugs that influence choices and decisions, and even values. All sorts of threats to freedom could arise, from a consumerism based on drug-induced desires to a tyranny founded on manufactured docility. In view of the desperate need to understand more about the chemistry of the brain for medical and psychological reasons, any suggestion of restraint in research in psychopharmacology would clearly be inappropriate. We have here some very difficult questions of ethical choice, questions that concern the whole subject covered in this paper.

Medical science progresses through the acquisition of knowledge. This knowledge can be the source of powerful technologies, in the same way as physical and chemical knowledge can. On the one hand, we have the intrinsic demands of scientific progress proclaiming an ethics of knowledge and, for biomedical research, an ethics of maximal development of potentially beneficial medicines and techniques. On the other hand, we have an imperfect society, whose use of the products of science may be wise or unwise, depending on its consequences for the biological and cultural success of the human race, and also depending on the set of values by which it is judged – wise meaning profitable, or conducive to individual freedom, or maximizing welfare, happiness and choice among a range of options. The new ethical stricture facing scientists today compared, say, with the past turn of the century is the changed magnitude of the consequences of science in an increasingly crowded and rapidly changing world, the increased awareness of the power of science, and the widespread questioning of the wisdom with which society has used that power. For the time being, scientists have not yet succeeded in formulating a program of constructive contribution to the decision-making process and have limited themselves by and large to proclaiming the benefits of science, disclaiming responsibility for its occasional misuses, and upholding the pre-eminent demands of the progress of knowledge – each of these claims based on convenient, but challengeable values. The few demands for restraint in research have, not surprisingly, been directed to fields other than those of the proponents. The recently heightened pace of discussions on the role of science in society may help bring some illumination. Organizational forms may emerge through which scientists, by educating society as well as themselves, will participate in promoting a wise, adaptive utilization of the fruits of science.

Summary

Ethical problems arise in biomedical research because of conflicting values and interests, for example, the patient's rights and scientific goals. Values are not constant, but vary with changes in society. Changing values influence, in turn, the course of societal history, including the course of scientific research. A series of examples from the biomedical sciences provide illustrations of the above generalization. The principle that existing values exert a regulatory effect on the course of events is used to recommend caution in introducing new, untested practices, such as cloning, which may have profound effects on the attitude of society towards the worth of men and women as individuals.

Zusammenfassung

In der biomedizinischen Forschung entstehen ethische Probleme durch Konflikte zwischen Werten und Interessen, zum Beispiel zwischen den Rechten des Patienten und den Zielen der Forschung. Die Werte sind nicht konstant, sie ändern sich mit den Wandlungen in der Gesellschaft. Sich wandelnde Werte beeinflussen ihrerseits den Gang der Gesellschaftsgeschichte, also auch den Lauf der wissenschaftlichen Forschung. Eine Reihe von Beispielen aus den biomedizinischen Wissenschaften dienen als Illustration für obige Verallgemeinerung. Auf Grund des Prinzips, daß bestehende Werte eine regulierende Wirkung auf den Gang der Ereignisse ausüben, wird Vorsicht empfohlen bei der Einführung neuer, unerprobter Methoden, wie zum Beispiel des «Cloning», welches tiefgreifende Auswirkungen auf die Haltung der Gesellschaft gegenüber dem Wert der Menschen als Individuen haben kann.

Résumé

Les problèmes éthiques naissent, en recherche biomédicale, du conflit opposant les valeurs aux intérêts, par exemple les droits du malade et les buts de la science. Les valeurs ne sont pas constantes, mais elles varient en fonction des changements qui se produisent dans la société. A leur tour, les valeurs en fluctuation influent sur le déroulement de l'histoire de la société, y compris celui de la recherche scientifique. Une série d'exemples tirés des disciplines biomédicales vient illustrer la généralisation précitée. Se fondant sur le principe que les valeurs existantes exercent un effet régulateur sur le cours des événements, l'auteur recommande la prudence au sujet de pratiques nouvelles qui n'ont pas encore été mises à l'épreuve – tel le clonage – mais qui peuvent avoir de profondes répercussions sur l'attitude de la société à l'égard de la valeur de l'homme en tant qu'individu.

Resumen

Los problemas éticos que se plantean en la investigación biomédica surgen de la coexistencia de ciertos valores e intereses contrapuestos, por ejemplo: el derecho del paciente y los objetivos de la ciencia. Los valores no son inmutables, sino que varían a medida que cambia la sociedad. Al modificarse los mismos, a su vez influyen en la evolución histórica de la sociedad e incluso en el curso de la investigación científica. Una serie de ejemplos tomados de las ciencias biomédicas ilustran esa aserción.

Se aduce el efecto regulador que los valores vigentes ejercen sobre los acontecimientos para recomendar cautela en el caso de introducir nuevos procedimientos que aún no hayan sido puestos a prueba, como por ejemplo la creación de clonas, que pueden influir hondamente en la actitud de la sociedad con respecto al valor del hombre y de la mujer como individuos.

Biomedical frontiers: genetics

by Joshua Lederberg

From time to time during the past decade, I have been challenged to collect my thoughts about the human implications of advances in genetic research. My first reactions were typical of those of many of my colleagues when they first looked up from the laboratory bench. Suddenly all things seemed possible – and on an earth which lies between heaven and hell, this prospect is at best ambivalent.

One can catalog the most plausible technical options, and I will not shirk this part of my task (see Table 1). However, to do only this almost inevitably leads to misunderstandings and misattributions. Furthermore, our forecasts will be factually wrong if they do not take account of the cultural setting, as well as the scientific bases, of health research and its applications.

For example, I once offered what I thought was a safely ironic formula: 'given sufficient time, any enterprise (including the renovation of man) would become possible, provided it did not violate some basic law of physical nature'. Long before we had mastered interstellar transportation and taught computers to write good poetry, we would surely have eliminated death; and genetic engineering would be a closer step on the same path. *Given sufficient time* made the formula safely tautologous. Even so, it conceals latent assumptions – that the human enterprise will continue, and that it will encompass an enduring commitment to scientific inquiry and its application to health and economic efficiency.

I did not then seriously doubt that scientific work would continue to double every twelve or fifteen years. Its internal information flow might nevertheless be overloaded, and the integrity and efficiency of the careers of individual scientists might become the limiting factors in the overall growth of knowledge. (Innovation cannot outpace the rate at which basic tools are formed and shared with the oncoming generation. Thus, if a language were to evolve with accelerating speed, we should perforce end up with Babel, or no language at all.) I did not foresee the extent to which the underlying commitment to progress would be rejected by a significant counterculture.

Science and technology are among the pre-eminent targets of this nihilistic revolution, and with good reason. The movement is a revolt against large-scale social organization (held responsible for imperialism, war, pollution and dehumanization), and this is inextricably interdependent with science and technology. The modern industrial state, east or west of the Elbe, rests upon efficiency of production by scientific techniques. And science can hardly be funded except from the surplus. Yet scientific criticism is also the most revolutionary source of skepticism of the values of industrial capitalism.

Medical progress is by no means immune to similar criticisms. We will hear that it is fundamentally immoral to waste resources on the development of new treatments in the face of world-wide needs for elementary hygiene and nutrition. (The same critics may even attack programs for eliminating smallpox, on the grounds that this will simply expose more children to kwashiorkor). At a more sophisticated level, many physicians approach a philosophy of therapeutic nihilism, wondering at what point new drugs may be doing more harm, overt or unsuspected, than good. In this vein, it is likely that there will be fewer drugs in tomorrow's repertory than today's; that much more pharmacological effort will go into more complete validation of existing agents, including many that are widely used with or without the benefit of professional prescriptions.

Against such a backdrop of existential confusion, it is hard to generate much enthusiasm for a brave new world – but the same skepticism also helps to reduce the odds that innovations in the genetic sphere will be rapidly and uncritically adopted. We need no longer repeat the caveats about rigidifying human values that the early eugenicists had taken for granted. Like it or not, we face a world that is almost perversely pluralistic in its basic values. Even in the most intellectualized communities, genes for genius are likely to be as little sought after as special schools for gifted children – perhaps out of folk wisdom about the little we know, and the less we do, about the ideal education for a given child.

The insularity of the eugenic advocates is equally quaint. The evolutionary impact of the most ambitious programs of selective breeding, sperm banks, or other plausible technologies, could not begin to compare with the shifts of global population that are connected with political and economic development. Those who are concerned about the future of man will have to pay more attention to the condition of the overwhelming majority of contemporary men. The human gene pool is very poorly represented in this room.

Although the powers of scientific wizardry are too often exaggerated, the present congregation does have a special leverage on global health, nutrition and some aspects of population control, and world peace. We are part of the most nearly bona fide international community – of health and scientific workers. And if, by our personal example, we cannot demonstrate alternatives to the nation-state as a medium of personal growth and expression, who will?

The remaking of man is then an impossible and inappropriate framework for the application of genetics. Genetic science could shed light on the evolutionary diversification of the species. But what has emerged so far is the almost enigmatic lack of reliable evidence for consequential systematic, biological differences – related or comparable to the diversity of culture – among the races of man. This may say more about the crudeness of our tools than the realities of differences in temperament. But it is mainly a testimonial to the wide variation of types that make up every culture, and make every generalization dangerous.

A few critics of objective research have criticized the very effort to discover genetic differences between races. In part, this is a reaction to the indefensible prejudgments about such research that have been offered by SHOCKLEY[3,4], with which I need hardly say I am in violent disagreement. These critics go further in suggesting that inquiry into racial difference can have no humanitarian justification – but this is also an implicitly racist prejudgment. Much of the controversy is based on mere ignorance of the significance of the term 'genetic', which is misrepresented as 'irremediable'. Nothing would be more helpful in achieving equality in opportunity and in education than an understanding of *specific* genetic and developmental mechanisms in intelligence and in the learning needed for survival in modern society.

For an extreme example, until we knew how to teach the congenitally deaf to communicate, the deaf-mute was de facto an idiot. We have only the vaguest knowledge of the subtler variations in cognitive style among children, including the all-important factors of timing and balance. Hypothetically, a child who might be an excellent reader if taught by a particular technique at age eight may now be labelled a failure and discarded at age six.

Racial variations – so heavily overladen with confounded environmental factors – are the least promising material for such investigations. Studies *within kindreds* of F-2 hybrids would be advocated by any geneticist, but have not yet been taken up.

The principal task of genetics is scientific *understanding*; and the principal target for its applications to man is the alleviation of individual distress – which the physician cannot repudiate no matter what the general state of the world. In pursuing his goals, it should go without saying that the geneticist is bound by the same set of ethical restraints that apply to other innovative branches of medicine. The surgeon does not use his scalpel by whim; and even in the chase after potential knowledge he is, above all, accountable by law and ethical tradition to the needs of his patient. There is of course some risk that a totalitarian regime will find it convenient to lobotomize its captives, or perpetrate the equivalent through controlling and disseminating genes, or drugs, or circuses, or even songs (as Plato boasted). This fear may be one of the impelling motives of the anarchistic movement. But liberal paralysis and self-denial have an unenviable history of failure against totalitarian ruthlessness.

Table 1 catalogs a number of potential techniques that may relate to the prevention or therapy of genetic disease, or which may influence genetic constitution. This is not a well-bounded arena, for all of medicine – indeed all of culture – is potentially euphenic. That is they may (1) ameliorate the actual development and expression of genetic predisposition, and (2) thereby indirectly influence the relative frequency of different genes in the population. This discussion must also overlap the medical applications of embryological knowledge, for many genetic defects will have to be prenatally diagnosed and treated to forfend irreversible failures of development, which then result in lifelong impairment.

The boundaries of genetic disease are also uncertain, for every pathology must have both a genetic and an environmental component. Many common diseases, as well as overall longevity, have a significant heritability. About five percent of overall morbidity can be related to specific genetic defects with a relatively simple basis; if we also take account of the heritable component of prevalent diseases like schizophrenia, diabetes, cardiovascular disease, and so on, at least a fourth of total morbidity (in medically advanced communities) must be attributed to genetic imperfections.

Genetic load, mutagenesis and environmental hygiene

The genetic load is therefore a formidable part of the problems that must be faced by medical practitioners and their patients. Plainly, preventive measures should have a high priority, if we could thereby prevent the intrusion of genetic defects in the first instance. This may not always be possible – an unknown part of the genetic load is 'segregational', that is, it derives from a relative disadvantage of either of the homozygotes compared with a fitter heterozygote. Natural selection then tends to keep both of the alternative alleles in the population, notwithstanding the inevitable quota of impaired homozygotes that must recur at every generation.

However, the 'mutational' part of the genetic load must be considerable, and this is related to the rate of mutation (informational deterioration) in the genetic material. A certain level of mutation is an inevitable byproduct of molecular accidents in cell metabolism. However, if we argue from the relative incidence of environmental compared with intrinsic carcinogenesis, which may be a parallel phenomenon, we may judge that four fifths of our ambient mutation rate is of environmental origin, and could be eliminated by environmental hygiene (relating to drugs, food additives, and possibly some natural foods, water and air pollutants, certain virus infections). About ten percent of that quota can be attributed to the natural radiation background, which is essentially not avoidable, and an equal proportion to artificial radiation (mostly incidental to diagnostic X-ray), much of which is avoidable.

This issue has been prominently displayed as an argument against the frivolous use of LSD (especially of 'street grade'); but equally cogent evidence against cyclamates and trenchant suspicions about many other widely used drugs have been ignored.

Here is a field full of confusion with respect both to policy arguments and to the technical assessment of mutagenic hazards. I believe environmental hygiene may be the most fruitful area of application of more sophisticated molecular genetic analysis.

Options for genetic therapy

Among these options, a few stand out for offering the most realistic opportunities for health benefits. They include:

Antenatal diagnosis. An increasing number of diseases will be reliably diagnosed by cytological and biochemical studies on cell cultures derived by amniocentesis. We have already made exciting advances in the understanding of several neurochemical disorders, which rely upon the identification of specific enzyme defects. The techniques of cell-fusion and of chromosome identification with fluorescent stains will strengthen our ability to trace mutant genes and similar methods will also help to identify high-risk parents. We can also visualize more direct assays for specific information content of DNA with techniques for the isolation of specific messenger RNA, and then of the homologous genes. The DNA segments can then, in principle, be tested in cell-free systems for protein synthesis, or perhaps even subjected to direct analysis of their nucleotide sequences. This level of sophistication in the analysis of gene effects should, in many cases, lead to deeper understanding of the disease, and may provoke explicit therapies. Meanwhile, our main recourse is voluntary abortion of the impaired fetus, to allow a mother the best chance available to her of delivering a child free from malignant defect.

Our experience with the antenatal diagnosis of sex should help correct overanxious predictions about the anticipated misuse of 'genetic engineering'. This has allowed a reliable method of voluntary control of the sex of offspring for some years. Whether the sex of the fetus has ever been a controlling factor in a decision for abortion, without more persuasive indications, it simply has not surfaced as a significant social problem to warrant any special regulatory controls. The common-sense and patient-oriented values of the medical profession remain the most effective bulwark against nonsensical distortions of its tools.

It has been suggested, quite seriously, that voluntary control of the sex of offspring might encourage a limitation of family size (e.g. one boy, one girl) consistent with the social interest in overall moderation of population growth, and that a balanced sex ratio would be maintained even under voluntary choice. In any case, keeping the state out of reproductive decisions altogether is a safeguard against undue interference.

Geneticists are perhaps fortunate that the revolt against 'sexist chauvinism' has taken hold before their techniques could be blamed for these cultural shifts in life-style, which so outweigh the influence of medical practice.

Transplantation. Many genetic defects involve cell populations as metabolic units that could be supplanted or restored by transplantation. For example, complete transfusion plays an important part in the therapy of Rh-hemolytic anemia (but is associated with a danger of graft-versus-host immune disease when applied to the fetus). The scope of tissue transplantation should not be judged by its present limited application, which is constrained by the hazard of graft-rejection. Specific ways of mitigating rejection are bound to appear as a fruit of immunobiological and immunogenetic research. We will then have a simple, practical way, for example, to deal with sickle-hemoglobin disease, namely by transplantation of normal erythropoietic marrow to the newborn, or perhaps the fetus. We will also surely find that many other diseases, genetic or not, are amenable to relief by tissue and organ transplants – e.g. hepatocytes for phenylketonuria and for galactosemia, or insulin-secreting cells for diabetes. The last example illustrates the opportunities for therapy even where the transplanted organ may not be the primary seat of action of a defect.

Transplanted immunocytes are also likely to play a key role in the treatment of auto-immune disease (perhaps after systemic elimination of offending cells) and in the prevention and treatment of neoplasms.

In cell biology research, we have just begun to move into the arena of systematic work on the genetics of somatic cells. The discovery by Henry Harris (Oxford) of powerful methods to induce the fusion of cells has attracted enormous interest in the consequences of mixing chromosomes of different genotypes and species, and in their reassortment in various combinations. The way is then open to genetic analysis (and genetic engineering) of mammalian and human cells in a way that would have been technically and ethically impossible otherwise. We can then also expect that domesticated lines of somatic cells will be important inputs to therapeutic applications of transplants.

Vaccination and virogenic therapy. Since 1798, vaccination has constituted an important medical application of the genetic modification of somatic cells by viruses, though its practitioners to this day are often oblivious to it. Jenner found that inoculation with infectious lymph caused a mild disease, cowpox, immunity to which also protected against the dangerous smallpox.

Many aspects of vaccination are still scientifically obscure; but we can now describe the process in terms of molecular genetics.

The DNA of the cowpox virus is purposely introduced into certain cells which adopt the genetic information contained therein. These cells thereupon produce new gene products, encoded by the viral DNA, which stimulate other body cells to produce antibodies against them. The cross-immunity is then a byproduct of the virogenic alteration of some cells of the host.

Live viruses are now widely used for vaccination against many other diseases, including polio, measles, and in special cases or in the near future, rubella, mumps, rabies, and so on.

Vaccination can be regarded as if it were a therapy to replace the functions of hypothetical genes not normally present in the human organism, those that would endogenously stimulate the formation of antibodies. This idea can be extended, in principle, to other gene products, for example enzymes that may be missing in certain gene-defect diseases like phenylketonuria and perhaps diabetes. Laboratory models for this kind of virogenic therapy are being perfected, and rational trials for human disease can be anticipated shortly. Although basic genetic principles underlie this technique, and the genetic apparatus of somatic cells is altered, it is classified as euphenic because the germ cells are left unchanged and there should be no effects in future generations. This is a matter of empirical observation, rather than a necessary principle in biology, and it is quite conceivable that some inoculated virogenes might also be inherited, as has already been postulated for certain tumor viruses in rodents. This reservation applies with equal force to vaccination against infectious diseases, about which we have little information in proportion to the enormous numbers of children involved.

The recent discovery of 'reverse transcriptases' which copy RNA information back to DNA promises to simplify some of the technical problems of developing virogenic agents. Differentiated cells should, under certain conditions, produce multiple copies of active, messenger RNA molecules, and it will be easier to purify and test these than to attempt to dig out a single DNA gene from the complete chromosome set. (In due course, however, this should also be facilitated by knowing the chemical signals that distinguish the active from the inactive genes in a given cell.) Reverse-transcription would then allow the recording of the RNA-message into DNA, which would then be spliced to a virus for facilitated re-integration into chromosomes.

Virogeny will be in competition with cell transplants for the restoration of genetic defects; but each may have special advantages in particular cases. For example, the transplantation of neurones is not likely to be very helpful except at the earlier stages of development.

The introduction of virogenic therapy should reawaken our concerns about vaccines intended for immunization against infectious disease. As we become properly attentive to the problems of unexpected side effects, we may find it necessary to devote more careful attention to the prophylactic agents used on a mass scale than to virogenic therapeutics applied even at some risk to a few badly impaired children.

Renucleation (cloning). From the work of BRIGGS and KING[1], and of GURDON[2], we know that an activated egg may be renucleated with a nucleus taken from a somatic cell of an existing frog. From a genetic standpoint, the new embryo is comparable to a cutting, or clone, of a rose plant.

The technical possibility of renucleating the human egg may then be an achievable extrapolation of work in progress with laboratory animals, and is likely to be reinforced by emerging utilities with livestock. Does its potential availability for human reproduction pose any special difficulties or opportunities?

This question was introduced first to make a rhetorical point. Many speculations had been forwarded about the possibilities of 'genetic surgery' of a kind that would require fantastic innovations in our knowledge of molecular genetics. Renucleation had, however, been demonstrated long since in frogs; and it was also very plain that it would be available in man as a necessary prerequisite to more incisive techniques of genetic manipulation. It follows that, *if* one wishes to agonize about the likelier directions of futuristic change, one should attend to renucleation.

If it could be done today, it is hard to see where renucleation would have very important applications; but this is precisely the kind of anticipatory study that needs to be done. On the positive side, it may give some otherwise sterile mates the opportunity of parenthood. An anovulatory woman might borrow an otherwise wasted egg cell, renucleate it with one of her own, or her husbands, somatic cells, and have it reimplanted into her own uterus. Or a fertile wife might offer an intact egg for microsurgical fertilization with a haploid spermatocyte nucleus from her azoospermic husband.

We can properly understand the moral objections and justifications of such procedures only if we explore the whole continuum of technical interventions in human reproduction. Ever since primitive man discovered the connection between sexual intercourse and conception, human reproduction has entailed deliberate exercise of purpose and intelligence, an unavoidable power and responsibility for the next generation. The guarding of such responsibilities against external intrusions is the essence of personal freedom. It goes without saying that we would abhor state-enforced reproduction of any kind. Conversely, to what extent should individual patients be deprived of the possibility of using technical devices they, and their professional counselors, believe to be in their own and their offspring's interest?

Many unanswered questions remain on the ethical or technical merits of renucleation. Popular discussion of cloning has probably overemphasized the significance of a common genotype: monozygotic twins are not copies of an identical personality, especially if they have been reared separately. They do resemble one another more closely than other relatives, to be sure; and renucleation could be a means of avoiding certain genetic defects that arise from segregation. If, for other valid reasons, renucleation is ever practised, we can clean up many uncertainties about the interplay of heredity and environment; and students of human nature will not want to waste such opportunities. So many developmental hazards may be associated with renucleation, that very extensive animal studies would be the minimum prerequisite to ethically justifiable trials in man, and the interval gives us ample time to ponder the values in balance. It is easy sport to write fantasies about the possible extrapolations of any scientific advance. What fantasies could be derived from the surgical division of a brain into several barely communicating parts! Useful counsel to policy makers should go beyond these explorations. Special attention must be devoted to the social factors that must prevail to launch a technology, then for this to 'go out of control'. The nuclear arms race is the prototype – but the pressures of international conflict make this an egregious example. No other technology can command more than a fragment of the military budget, and biology will have a long way to go to approach the auto industry and market. In my own view, the struggle to prolong life at all costs, and our partial successes are already creating ethical and social dilemmas far more grievous than the innovations of quality control of births. The economic impulses for life-prolongation are theoretically unlimited, empirical evidence of carelessness in personal hygiene notwithstanding.

Our consensual standards of an ethical medical experiment require that it serve a reasonable humanitarian purpose and that it have the informed consent of the individuals concerned. The problem of renucleation sets into relief the general problem of parenthood. Who else can speak for the welfare of the individual not yet in being? Should parents be held in contempt if they procreate by natural means in the face of risks of a significant deformity in their offspring? Should they be encouraged to undertake artificial measures that will give their young an easier start? And where is the boundary-line of the responsibility of the parent, and of the community, for manipulating a child's development – the socialization and education, that predestine him to function as a particular kind of human being?

These questions are properly applied to the destinies of particular individuals born day by day. Gloomy predictions about the long-range future of the species might be substantiated as a side effect of medical care and other welfare measures that avert the pain of natural selection. However, the pace of discovery in genetics is so rapid compared with that of biological evolution that we can afford to wait another fifty or a hundred years before we tackle the species problem. We will then have sharper tools, and at least as much wisdom about how to use them. Meanwhile we have enough to do in trying to minimize the enormous burden of personal distress and anxiety that attends our genetic load as it is manifest birth by birth, death by death.

Table 1. Potential technologies of eugenics and euphenics

A. *Selective mating*

    (1) By phenotype of parents (assisted by biochemical and cytological assay)
       (a) negative – distracting, discouraging or sterilizing the 'unfit';
       (b) positive
           (i)   encouraging select pairs,
           (ii) with artificial insemination, donor ('rational germinal choice'),
           (iii) with oval or ovarian transplant,
           (iv) both, or fertilization in vitro, followed by implantation,
           (v)   extracorporeal gestation (test tube baby) – see also euphenics (i–v are not very different in their *genetic* consequences).
    (2) By genotype of parents – as above, with deeper analysis of parental constitution. Except for specific aberrations very little can be said at present about genetics of *desirable* traits.
    (3) By relationship of parents
       (a) inbreeding. The main impact is to expose recessive, usually deleterious genes; increase phenotypic variability of F_1; decrease the genotypic variability of later generations;
       (b) outbreeding – antithesis of (a). Most cultures strongly encourage outbreeding.
    (4) By age of parents – to forfend accumulation of deleterious mutations and chromosome anomalies which increase with parental age.
    (5) By phenotype or genotype of the zygote or of fetus (antenatal diagnosis and voluntary abortion). Earlier selections would avoid the trauma of aborting an established fetus.

(6) By genotype of the gametes, e.g. separation of X from Y, or normal from defect-bearing sperm.

(7) With sperm of other species (compare 1b iv). Nothing is known of the consequences among primate species. All contemporary races of man appear to be freely interfertile.

B.   *Innovations in zygote biology*

Vegetative (asexual) propagation. Cloning.

(1) Parthenogenesis – development of an unfertilized egg. (This might be genetically identical to the mother, or might be a product of meiosis, which would be an intense form of inbreeding).

(2) Regeneration – development of whole individual from somatic tissues (as in some plants and lower animals like earthworms).

(3) Differentiation of gametes from somatic tissues previously subject to extensive genetic manipulation.

(4) Somatic reduction in gamete-forming cells in culture (somatic inbreeding) – would allow predictable outcome of further matings from a given parent which is not now assured.

(5) Nuclear transplantation – renucleation of a fertilized, enucleated egg. Genetically equivalent to cloning from the source of the nucleus.

(6) Embryo-splitting to produce twins or multiples. Not to be confused with multiple ovulation (occasionally induced by fertility-promoting drugs). About one third of spontaneous twins are monozygotic, i.e. arise from the splitting of one embryo. Note also the opposite phenomenon.

(7) Embryo fusion (chimerism) so that one individual comprises two or more genotypes. This grades into tissue transplantation at later stages. It should allow different genotypes a new latitude for mutual complementation, e.g. *mens sana in corpore sano*. Somewhat less than one thousandth live births are spontaneous chimeras, but some of these arise by other mechanisms.

C.   *Adjuncts from somatic cell biology*

For eugenic applications these would be coupled with procedures like B (5). For euphenic effects, altered cells can be grafted back to a host or some manipulations done directly on his tissues.

(1) Algeny – directed alterations of genes
   (a) controversial claims of effects of DNA uptake in mammalian cells following a long tradition of genetic work with DNA in bacteria;
   (b) incorporation of viruses
       (i) experimental tumor viruses,
       (ii) use of specially modified viruses,
           (α) vaccination to induce immunity to viruses,
           (β) virogenic therapy to replace missing genes,
           (γ) virogenic enhancement for superior performance – if we but knew the biochemistry thereof;
   (c) specifically induced mutations. No plausible approaches are now apparent.

(2) Random mutation and specific selection of cells with altered properties has full precedent in strain selection in microbes. Many uncertainties relating to possible cancer potential of such implants.

(3) Cell fusion to form somatic hybrids. These cells may then lose various chromosomes to give many new forms. Extends scope of (2). Can be readily applied to fuse *cells* from 'distant' species, e.g. fish and human.

(4) Development of symbiotic strains of lower species, with habitats that grade from the external world (e.g. crops) to internal, to intracellular. Parasitic worms in man have evolved in this direction with the help of adaptations to thwart immunological rejection. In principle they might be domesticated. So also might algae be trained to an intracellular habitat in man where they might photosynthesize essential nutrients, if not bulk calories, as they already do in primitive animals.

References

1.   BRIGGS, R., KING, T.J.: Transplantation of Living Nuclei from Blastula Cells into Enucleated Frog Eggs. *Proc. nat. Acad. Sci. (Wash.) 38*, 455–463 (1952).
2.   GURDON, J.B.: Transplanted Nuclei and Cell Differentiation. *Science 219*, 24–36 (1968).
3.   SHOCKLEY, W.: Is Quality of U.S. Population Declining?, interview; in: *U.S. News and World Report*, 22. 11. 1965.
4.   SHOCKLEY, W.: A 'Try Simplest Cases' Approach to the Heredity-Poverty-Crime Problem. *Proc. nat. Acad. Sci. (Wash.) 57*, 1767–1774 (1967).

Further reading

ARON, R.: *Progress and Disillusion*. New York: Præger, 1967.
CARTER, C.O.: Genetics of Common Disorders. *Brit. med. Bull. 25*, 25–57 (1969).
DAVIS, B.D.: Prospects for Genetic Intervention in Man. *Science 170*, 1279–1283 (1970).
HANDLER, P.: *Biology and the Future of Man*. Oxford: University Press, 1970.
LEDERBERG, J.: Orthobiosis: the Perfection of Man; in: *The Place of Value in a World of Facts*. (Nobel Symposium XIV.) New York: Wiley (interscience), 1970. This Nobel Symposium XIV paper includes a comprehensive bibliography.

Summary

Advances in molecular biology promise to enlarge our technical capacity to intervene in genetic problems. Social and ethical factors are therefore likely to play an increasingly important role in determining the application of new scientific advances in man. This is no cause for great alarm, for the same principle already applies to the use of surgery and of other medical interventions that could, in theory, also be applied for extraordinary 'renovations' of human nature.

The evolution of wise policies for the use of genetic advances, and the surveillance of existing practices for compliance with consensual ethical standards, and for the anticipation of social injury, of course requires a widely disseminated understanding of the probable potentialities of various types of genetic intervention.

The most important influences on the genetic composition of the human species are likely to remain side effects of other global policies: the movement of populations, transportation technology, the effects of war and of discrepancies in economic development and attention to welfare, and the level of education and understanding of reproductive processes.

Geneticists can help to bypass difficult moral problems involved in the calculated reduction of the genetic load from deleterious genes by encouraging more effective attention to preventive genetic hygiene, especially through the identification and elimination of principal environmental sources of gene mutation.

Specific options for genetic therapy include the rapidly developing field of antenatal diagnosis (coupled with elective abortion of threatened fetuses); cell and organ transplantation; and virogenic therapy. The latter would entail the introduction of desired DNA segments into domesticated strains of viruses; these would then serve for the vaccination of patients lacking a critical metabolic function, which would then be restored under the influence of the added DNA.

The renucleation of eggs (cloning) is also a theoretical possibility, likely to be of more metaphorical than pragmatic interest. The discussion of cloning may help to illuminate the ethical problem of parenthood, generally: what is the responsibility of each generation for the biological and educational predetermination of its successors?

In any event, the central responsibility of the geneticist qua physician is to the welfare of his individual patients.

Zusammenfassung

Fortschritte in der Molekularbiologie bieten gute Aussichten für vermehrte technische Möglichkeiten, in genetische Probleme einzugreifen. Soziale und ethische Faktoren werden daher eine zunehmend wichtigere Rolle bei Entscheidungen über den Einsatz neuer wissenschaftlicher Erkenntnisse beim Menschen spielen. Das ist kein Grund zu übertriebener Sorge, da das gleiche Prinzip bereits für die Anwendung chirurgischer und anderer medizinischer Maßnahmen gilt und sich theoretisch auch zu ungewöhnlichen «Renovationen» der menschlichen Natur verwenden ließe.

Die Entwicklung wohldurchdachter Grundsätze für die Anwendung genetischer Fortschritte, für die Überprüfung bereits bestehender Verfahren in bezug auf ihre Vereinbarkeit mit den allgemeinverbindlichen ethischen Grundsätzen und zur Verhütung sozialer Ungerechtigkeit erfordert natürlich ein stark verbreitetes Verständnis der wahrscheinlichen Auswirkungen verschiedenartiger genetischer Eingriffe.

Die wichtigsten Einflüsse auf die genetische Zusammensetzung der menschlichen Spezies werden vermutlich auch in Zukunft die Auswirkungen anderer weltweiter politischer Entwicklungen haben: Bevölkerungsbewegung, Transporttechnologie, Folgen von Krieg und von Diskrepanzen im wirtschaftlichen Wachstum und in der Fürsorge, im Bildungsniveau und im Verständnis der Fortpflanzungsmechanismen.

Die Genetiker können helfen, schwierige moralische Probleme im Zusammenhang mit der gezielten Reduktion der durch schädliche Gene entstehenden erblichen Belastung zu umgehen, indem sie der vorbeugenden genetischen Hygiene größere Aufmerksamkeit zuteil werden lassen, besonders durch das

Erkennen und das Beseitigen primärer umweltbedingter Ursachen von Genmutationen.

Spezifische Anwendungsmöglichkeiten für eine genetische Therapie bieten unter anderem das sich rasch entwickelnde Gebiet der pränatalen Diagnostik (kombiniert mit elektivem Abort gefährdeter Feten), die Zell- und die Organtransplantation sowie die virogene Therapie. Die letzterwähnte Methode würde in der Einführung gewünschter DNS-Segmente in domestizierte Virusstämme bestehen, die zur Impfung von Patienten benutzt werden könnten, denen eine kritische Stoffwechselfunktion fehlt und die dank dem Einfluß der zugesetzten DNS wiederhergestellt würde.

Eine weitere theoretische Möglichkeit, die allerdings vermutlich von eher symbolischem als pragmatischem Interesse ist, bietet die Renukleation oder das «Cloning» von Eizellen. Die Erörterung des Cloning-Verfahrens mag helfen, das ethische Problem der Elternschaft in einem umfassenden Sinne zu beleuchten: welche Verantwortung trägt jede Generation für die biologische und die bildungsmäßige Prädeterminierung ihrer Nachkommenschaft?

In jedem Falle besteht die wichtigste Pflicht des Genetikers als Arzt darin, auf das Wohlergehen jedes einzelnen seiner Patienten bedacht zu sein.

Résumé

Les progrès de la biologie moléculaire promettent d'accroître les moyens techniques dont nous disposerons pour tenter de résoudre les problèmes génétiques. C'est pourquoi les facteurs sociaux et éthiques joueront probablement un rôle de plus en plus déterminant pour l'application à l'homme des nouvelles réalisations de la science. Il ne faut pas voir là de grands motifs de s'inquiéter, car le même principe intervient déjà en chirurgie ainsi que dans toutes les autres formes d'intervention médicale qui pourraient en théorie être aussi mises en œuvre pour «rénover» de façon extraordinaire la nature humaine.

Mettre au point des lignes directrices prudentes applicables aux progrès de la génétique, surveiller les méthodes actuelles pour s'assurer qu'elles sont conformes au consensus éthique en vigueur et qu'elles ne porteront pas, à longue échéance, tort à la société – autant de mesures qui exigent, bien sûr, qu'un public très étendu comprenne les possibilités qu'offrent les différentes formes d'intervention génétique.

Il est probable que les influences principales qui s'exerceront sur le patrimoine génétique de l'espèce humaine ne seront jamais que des sous-produits d'autres politiques d'application plus générale: mouvements de population, technologie des transports, conséquences des conflits armés et des disparités du développement économique, souci du bien-être social, niveau d'éducation et compréhension des processus de la reproduction.

Les généticiens peuvent contribuer à la solution des problèmes moraux difficiles à résoudre qui interviennent lorsqu'il s'agit de réduire de façon calculée le nombre des gènes nuisibles dans le profil génétique de l'homme en encourageant l'application d'une hygiène génétique préventive plus efficace, moyennant en particulier la détermination et l'élimination des principales sources écologiques des mutations génétiques.

Parmi les options précises de la généticothérapie, nous mentionnerons le domaine en évolution rapide du diagnostic prénatal (associé avec l'avortement volontaire des fœtus génétiquement menacés), les greffes cellulaires et organiques et la virogénéticothérapie. Cette dernière méthode pourrait comporter l'introduction de certaines fractions sélectionnées d'ADN dans des souches virales acclimatées qui serviraient ensuite à vacciner les patients à la fonction métabolique déficiente, qui serait ainsi rétablie sous l'influence de l'ADN apporté de l'extérieur.

La renucléation des œufs (clonage) constitue aussi une possibilité théorique qui présente probablement un intérêt plus abstrait que pratique. Le débat consacré au clonage contribuera peut-être à éclairer le problème éthique de la procréation dans un contexte plus général, en d'autres termes le problème de savoir dans quelle mesure chaque génération assume la responsabilité de la prédétermination biologique et pédagogique des générations qui lui succéderont.

En tout état de cause, la responsabilité fondamentale du généticien en sa qualité de médecin est de travailler au bien-être de chacun de ses patients.

Resumen

Es de suponer que los progresos de la biología molecular nos proporcionarán nuevas posibilidades técnicas de intervenir en los problemas genéticos. Por consiguiente, es probable que los factores sociales y éticos desempeñen un papel cada vez más determinante en la aplicación al hombre de los nuevos adelantos científicos. Esto no debe alarmarnos demasiado, pues lo mismo vale ya para la cirugía y otras formas de intervención médica que también podrían, teóricamente, llevarse a cabo para realizar extraordinarias «renovaciones» de la naturaleza humana.

La adopción de una línea de conducta adecuada que rija la aplicación de los adelantos en el campo de la genética, así como la vigilancia de las técnicas disponibles, al objeto de garantizar su conformidad con las normas éticas de la sociedad en que vivimos e impedir cualquier abuso social, requiere naturalmente un amplio conocimiento de las posibilidades que entrañan las distintas formas de intervención genética.

Es probable que las mayores influencias que se ejercerán sobre la constitución genética de la especie humana sigan proviniendo de otras decisiones de mayor alcance, como son: los movimientos demográficos, la mecanización de los medios de comunicación, las consecuencias de los conflictos armados y de las discrepancias del desarrollo económico y del bienestar social, así como el nivel de educación y la comprensión de los procesos de la reproducción.

Los investigadores en genética pueden ayudar a soslayar los espinosos problemas morales que implica la corrección de defectos mediante reducción de los genes mutables, haciendo que se conceda más importancia a una higiene genética preventiva, especialmente determinando y eliminando las principales causas ecológicas responsables de mutaciones genéticas.

Entre las opciones precisas de la «geneticoterapia» cabe señalar el diagnóstico prenatal (inclusive el aborto provocado de fetos genéticamente amenazados), campo que está tomando gran incremento; el trasplante de células y órganos; finalmente, la terapéutica virogenética. Este último método supone la introducción de segmentos seleccionados de ADN en cepas cultivadas de virus, las cuales servirían posteriormente para vacunar a pacientes que carezcan de una función metabólica importante, para restablecerla mediante el aporte externo de ADN.

La renucleación de un óvulo *(cloning)* constituye otra posibilidad que presenta un interés más teórico que práctico. La polémica suscitada por el «cloning» quizás contribuya a elucidar el problema ético de la paternidad en un contexto más general: ¿Hasta qué punto ha de asumir cada generación la responsabilidad de la predeterminación biológica y formativa de las que le seguirán? De todos modos, la primera obligación del especialista en genética, en su calidad de médico, es la de velar por el bienestar de cada uno de sus pacientes.

Newer knowledge of immunobiology and its applications

by NIELS KAJ JERNE

In considering the biomedical frontiers of immunology, we must distinguish between the medical frontiers and the biological frontiers. The main point I wish to make in this brief discussion is that the interaction between these two frontiers is not a one-way flow. It might be claimed that medical applications of immunology must necessarily be based on biological knowledge and that therefore the medical frontier will always have to lag behind the biological frontier. This is not true, however, and hitherto the situation has often been the other way round. I think that it is one of the attractions of immunology that medical observations have had, and continue to exert, a direct impact on our fundamental immunological concepts and understanding, and on the other hand that the possibility of direct application in medicine is never very remote from fundamental immunological studies. This can be illustrated by many examples; thus, vaccination, which is the oldest exploitation of immunological processes in medicine, or rather in prophylaxis, was utilized long before there existed a science of immunology and even long before antibodies were known to exist. The enormous benefit of smallpox vaccination to human health resulted from the observation that persons infected with cowpox appeared to have acquired immunity to smallpox. The assumption and subsequent demonstration of the general validity of this phenomenon has led to two types of activity. One was to try to understand how it works, the other was simply to use the fact that it works in prophylactic procedures. It is clear that the latter is most immediately useful, and that this medical application preceded biological understanding.

The fact that skin can be transplanted from one region of the body to another region, but not from one person to another person, except for identical twins, was known long before it was known that these phenomena involve an immune response of the recipient. When this became clear, it followed that a deeper study of the immune system and of the way it can be manipulated would be necessary to make the procedure of transplantation successful. This insight did not prevent surgeons, however, from going ahead with kidney transplantation and from succeeding in many cases, contrary to what an immunologist would have predicted. This second example of medical procedures which are applied in spite of the lack of biological knowledge has some other interesting aspects. Only a few years ago, many immunologists considered the phenomenon of transplant rejection to be of only limited interest for basic immunological studies. By transplantation, foreign substances are introduced into a recipient. It appeared obvious that the recipient responds as to any other foreign antigen, and that it was simpler, for basic experimentation, to use well-defined antigens instead of the complex tissue antigens involved in transplantation. Only recently, after innumerable studies of the basic elements in transplant rejection had been conducted, did it become clear that the polymorphism within a species with respect to the histocompatibility antigens that a given individual possesses, is of fundamental importance to the biological understanding of the immune system. Some remarkable facts have emerged, namely that the immune system is much more readily capable of responding to histocompatibility antigens possessed by other individuals of the same species than it is to respond to unrelated foreign antigens and, furthermore, that the capability of an individual to respond to foreign or synthetic antigens is to a considerable extent determined by the set of histocompatibility antigens that this individual happens to possess. It would thus seem that antigens of the individual itself, to which the immune system of this individual does not respond, govern the range of immune responses of which this individual is capable. The understanding of the relationship between histocompatibility antigens and the potentiality of the immune system for responding to certain antigens may therefore be crucial for the solution of the antibody diversity problem, which has always been the most fundamental problem in basic immunology. Thus, medical frontiers in transplantation have initiated major biological advances in immunology, which are not restricted merely to their usefulness for transplantation.

Many other medical observations have influenced the ideas of those that study immunology mainly as a biological subject. For example, it was shown that children suffering from certain forms of agammaglobulinaemia, that is to say, children that are genetically incapable of producing circulating antibodies, can be immunized against smallpox by vaccination. This observation called into question the actual importance and function of circulating antibodies. Likewise, the medical recognition that, in certain diseases, antibodies are produced against constituents of the individual himself cast doubt on the ancient concept that, no matter how large the range of different antibodies is that a given individual can make, he might be intrinsically incapable of making antibodies against his own antigens.

Another recent example of medical and biological interaction in immunology is the discovery and utilization of so-called 7S antibody inhibition. Experimentalists engaged in laboratory studies observed that an animal is incapable of responding to a given antigen with antibody formation, if this animal receives a simultaneous injection of specific 7S antibody obtained from another animal that has been previously immunized. Almost at the same time, obstetricians made a similar observation independently and made use of this knowledge to prevent the occurrence of erythroblastosis neonatorum – the often fatal haemolytic disease of the newborn caused by maternal antibodies – in the children of rhesus-positive fathers and rhesus-negative mothers. It became clear that most often the mother becomes immunized against rhesus-positive red cells during birth of the first child and that her production of antibodies that would be fatal for the second child could be prevented by injecting human 7S anti-rhesus antibodies into the mother at the time of the first birth. This procedure will largely eliminate the 'rhesus disease' of babies.

The last fifteen years have witnessed an enormous expansion in immunology, not only in regard to the number of research workers and laboratories that are devoted to the study of immunological problems, but also in regard to the range of problems that have been recognized to belong to this subject. This rapid development partly reflects the medical recognition that further improvements of immunization and transplantation procedures will require deeper understanding of the immune system, and that an ever expanding number of diseases which are badly understood, including many degenerative diseases and cancer, have important immunological components. The other impact has come from molecular biology. The fact that both the genetic code and the synthesis of proteins are similar in all living cells, has led molecular biologists to the study of multi-cellular organisms, including man. One of the objects of these ambitious attempts is to understand cellular differentiation, that is to say, the mechanism by which cells are induced to assume certain limited, definite tasks. The remarkable phenomenon of the production of specific antibody molecules by lymphocytes has appeared particularly attractive and promising in this respect, as it can be invoked simply by the injection of antigens of known chemical composition.

Since the discovery of antibodies, biologists have always been both astonished and fascinated by the fact that one individual is capable of making fitting antibody molecules to practically every foreign substance that is introduced into its tissues. The question arises how many different antibody molecules one individual or one animal species can potentially make. Among those scientists that have expressed an opinion in this matter, the difference in estimates is enormous. Some contend that several thousand antibody molecules of different specificity might suffice to constitute an effective immune system, whereas others claim that the number must be rather in the range of many millions. This question involves the meaning of antibody specificity. It is clear that a given antibody molecule that reacts with a given antigenic determinant can also react with certain related antigenic determinants, so that we must envisage that one antibody molecule can, with different degrees of fit, combine with any of a large number of different antigens. Conversely, one given antigen may find, among a large number of antibody molecules that are presented to it, a considerable number of different antibody molecules that can attach to it, again with different degrees of fit. Thus, there is no one-to-one relationship between antigen and antibody, and it is at present impossible to estimate from this type of considerations how many different antibody molecules an individual would need for producing the effects that are measured by serological assays. There are arguments tending to show that this number need not be so enormously high. On the other hand, recent studies on so-called idiotypic properties of individual antibody molecules have shown that in certain situations when, say, 50 rabbits are all immunized with the same antigen, they will all make specific antibodies to that antigen, but the molecules that each rabbit makes will be different from those made by any of the remaining 49 rabbits. This type of observation argues for an enormously large number of different structural possibilities for making antibodies of similar specificity. It seems probable from these observations that one individual can potentially make an enormous number, perhaps of the order of one million or more, of antibody molecules that differ in their specificity and therefore in their molecular structure. The question of understanding the basis for this synthetic potentiality is called the problem of antibody diversity. In the early days of immunology, the solution to this problem seemed to lie in understanding the actual mechanism by which a cell synthesizes antibody. This is no longer so, because it has now become clear that antibody molecules are synthesized basically by the same mechanism by which enzymes and other proteins are synthesized, namely by a process that builds up linear sequences of amino acid residues as directed by the nucleotide sequences of structural genes in the nucleic acid of the cellular genome. As it has been shown that the specificity of an antibody molecule is determined by the sequence of amino acid residues in its polypeptide chains, the problem of antibody diversity has shifted to the problem of how the genome of our lymphocytes can be endowed with sequences of nucleotides that determine millions of different antibodies. An impressive amount of evidence has accumulated supporting Burnet's original postulate that one given antigen-sensitive lymphocyte can produce antibody molecules of only one specificity. The population of lymphocytes which makes up the immune system must therefore have the same range of diversity as the antibody molecules that this individual can produce. In other words, our population of antibody-producing lymphocytes must possess a very large number of different genes for this purpose, and the central question at the moment is whether all these genes are already present in the germ-line, that is to say, in the DNA of a single sperm or egg cell (and therefore in every lymphocyte), or whether the genes for the particular antibody that any given lymphocyte can synthesize are genes that have arisen from a small number of germ-line genes by somatic modification during lymphocyte differentiation in the ontogeny of a multicellular individual. It seems to me that the latter possibility is the most likely and also the most intriguing. Instead of covering all expectation by a complete dictionary of antibody genes in the germ cells, nature may have solved the problem for an individual to be able to produce antibodies to any of a large number of foreign substances it may happen to encounter, by permitting the population of lymphocytes to build up a dictionary of genes by a random mechanism. The fact that a previous encounter with foreign antigen greatly enhances the response of the system after a second encounter with the same antigen would reflect the selection by antigen of those randomly arisen cells of the lymphocyte population that happen to be capable of producing a fitting antibody, and their subsequent multiplication. The term 'immunological memory' that is used for this phenomenon seems well chosen, because its features include learning from experience and the impossibility of transmitting this learning to the offspring.

We should like to know more of the main task of the immune system, that has made it evolve in the phylogenic pathway towards the vertebrates. Not so long ago, the main purpose of the immune system was thought to be obviously the defence against invading microorganisms. Now we believe that it may represent a more general surveillance system capable of removing effete cells and of destroying cells which are escaping control, such as cancer cells. It is likely that a greater insight into these matters will be gained as soon as the mechanisms by which antibody diversity is generated will have been uncovered. Many immunology laboratories in the world are, therefore, placing a great part of their efforts into attempts to advance this present essential frontier in immunology, and there can be no doubt that such an understanding will have a great impact on advances in medicine, as well as in all fields of biology where questions of cell differentiation are paramount.

The second crucial problem in the biology of the immune system is the question of the signals to which lymphocytes respond. An adult person possesses about 10^{12}, or a million times a million, of these cells. Though the lymphocytes are concentrated densely in certain parts of the body, such as bone marrow, thymus, spleen, and lymph nodes, they are also circulating in the blood, in the lymph and in the tissue fluids. This scatter presents a certain difficulty in studying the system, whereas on the other hand the fact that the lymphocytes do not form a tissue of adhering cells but move around freely, offers certain experimental advantages, particularly for in-vitro studies. A given lymphocyte can secrete into its surroundings about 2,000 antibody molecules per second, and it has become almost certain that all antibody molecules produced by one cell are identical. It would be most simple to imagine that a foreign antigen entering into the organism attaches to those lymphocytes that can make a more or less well-fitting antibody, and that this attachment of the antigen represents the signal that induces these selected lymphocytes to multiply and to produce their antibody product. Numerous studies of these matters in recent years have shown, however, that the problem of the adequate signals is much more complex. First of all it is easy to understand that the organism must possess not only the ability to respond to certain antigenic signals with antibody formation, but that it must also be capable of stopping antibody formation to a given antigen. In other words, there must be some feedback mechanism in the response. The discovery of which I spoke earlier, that the presence of specific 7 S antibodies can inhibit the cells to produce antibodies to the corresponding antigen, probably represents one of such feedback signals. Furthermore, it has been shown that the immune system is made up of two classes of lymphocytes. The lymphocytes of one class are potentially antibody-secreting cells or precursors of such cells. They are, however, not capable of responding directly to some antigens, but require the help of lymphocytes of the other class which do not secrete anti-body but which appear capable of assembling antigen molecules at their sur-face. Though the nature of this interaction between cells has not been suffi-ciently clarified, it has become clear that we cannot regard the lymphocytes as a population of independent cells, but must envisage interaction and communi-cation between them. No matter how complex the actual effective signals and their ultimate pathway within a cell may turn out to be, they must be of at least two radically different kinds, namely signals that turn on antibody formation and cell proliferation, and such that have the exact opposite effect, namely of stopping all responses to this particular antigen. This latter type of signals leaves the animal in an unresponsive state which is called immunological tolerance or paralysis. A large part of the work that is being done at the present frontier of immunology is concerned with the study of these matters, in trying to disen-tangle cell-to-cell interactions, as well as intracellular communications by the variety of factors which the lymphocytes secrete. The laboratory studies of the nature of these signals, and of the feedback circuits that can turn the cells of the immune system on or off, are increasingly being conducted in cell cultures in vitro by which certain complexities of working with intact animals can be cir-cumvented. One problem for this approach is to be able to maintain lympho-cytes in culture without loss of the functional properties in which we are inter-ested. Another is to develop methods for separating lymphocytes into popula-tions of different type and function.

The immune system as a whole appears to have evolved to deal with sev-eral different tasks by different forms of immune response. The system can pro-duce about a dozen different classes of antibodies that have different size, structure and physiological properties. Moreover, several important tasks, such as transplant rejection, and target cell destruction, involve the class of lympho-cytes that do not secrete antibodies, but that appear to incorporate antibody molecules into their cell membranes. As there is a complex interaction of the various forms of immune response, a medical manipulation of the system with the purpose of eliminating certain responses whilst retaining others requires more knowledge than we possess at this moment. Further advances in our under-standing of the genetic, molecular, cellular and regulatory components of the system are therefore needed before basic immunology can deal decisively with various medical desiderata, such as the provision of vaccines against protozoal infections, the immune elimination of cancer cells, the therapy of allergies and auto-immune disorders, and the induction of specific tolerance to transplants.

In my brief summary of the biological state of affairs in immunology, two crucial problems have been stressed. One, the generation of antibody diver-sity is of a genetic nature. The other concerns the signals and the communi-cation between cells that enable the system to mimic certain characteristics of learning from experience and of memory.

Summary

A distinction is made between the medical and the biological frontiers in immunology. Several examples are given of fruitful interaction between these two. This continuing interaction is one of the great attractions of immunology.

Two crucial problems of present basic immunology are described. One concerns the generation of antibody diversity, i.e. the genetic basis of the potentiality of an individual to produce an enormous number of different antibody molecules. The other concerns the signals to which lymphocytes, selected by antigen, respond.

Medical manipulations of the immune system have advanced to a remarkable extent during this century, though basic mechanisms are not understood. These advances have had a great impact on public health. Decisive further progress cannot be expected, however, before some of the biological problems outlined have been solved.

Zusammenfassung

Es wird ein Unterschied zwischen der medizinischen und der biologischen Forschung in der Immunologie gemacht. Etliche Beispiele für eine ersprießliche Wechselbeziehung zwischen den beiden Wissensgebieten sind angeführt. Diese fortgesetzte wechselseitige Beeinflussung verleiht der Immunologie großen Reiz.

Zwei Kernprobleme der modernen Grundlagenimmunologie werden beschrieben. Das eine betrifft die Entstehung der Antikörperdiversität, nämlich die grundlegende genetische Voraussetzung der Fähigkeit eines Individuums, enorme Mengen unterschiedlicher Antikörpermoleküle zu synthetisieren. Das andere behandelt die Signale, auf die durch Antigen selektionierte Lymphozyten reagieren.

Medizinische Eingriffe in das Immunsystem sind während dieses Jahrhunderts in bemerkenswerter Weise vervollkommnet worden, obwohl man die grundlegenden Vorgänge noch nicht vollständig versteht. Diese Fortschritte haben die Volksgesundheit erheblich verbessert. Weitere entscheidende Fortschritte sind allerdings erst zu erwarten, wenn einige der angeschnittenen biologischen Probleme gelöst sein werden.

Résumé

Lorsque l'on traite de l'immunologie et de ses limites, il faut établir une distinction entre les aspects médicaux et les aspects biologiques. Nous donnons ici plusieurs exemples d'interactions fécondes entre ces deux aspects. Ce sont ces phénomènes d'interaction continue qui, pour les chercheurs, constituent l'un des principaux attraits de l'immunologie.

Nous exposons deux problèmes capitaux de l'immunologie fondamentale de notre époque. L'un concerne la diversité des anticorps formés, autrement dit la base génétique à partir de laquelle un individu peut élaborer une quantité considérable de molécules d'anticorps différentes. L'autre problème a trait aux signaux auxquels répondent les lymphocytes, sélectionnés par les antigènes.

Bien que l'on n'ait pas encore élucidé tous les mécanismes de base du système immunologique, les applications médicales de l'immunologie ont fait, au cours de ce siècle, de remarquables progrès dont les conséquences sont très importantes pour la santé publique. Toutefois, on ne peut escompter de nouveaux résultats aussi fructueux tant que certains des problèmes biologiques que nous avons brièvement exposés n'auront pas été résolus.

Resumen

Cuando se habla de la inmunología y de sus límites, conviene distinguir entre los aspectos médicos y biológicos. Se señalan varios ejemplos de interacción fructuosa entre ambos. Esta estrecha correlación constituye, precisamente, uno de los mayores atractivos de la inmunología.

Se exponen dos problemas capitales de la inmunología fundamental en la actualidad. Uno estriba en la diversidad de anticuerpos formados, es decir la base genética a partir de la cual un individuo es capaz de formar una multitud de distintas moléculas de anticuerpos. El otro problema concierne las señales a las cuales responden los linfocitos seleccionados por los antígenos.

Las posibilidades de acción médica sobre el sistema inmunitario han progresado enormemente en nuestro siglo, a pesar de que aún no se han elucidado del todo sus mecanismos fundamentales. Dichos adelantos tuvieron importantísimas repercusiones en el campo de la salud pública. Nuevos progresos decisivos dependerán del esclarecimiento de algunos de los problemas biológicos esbozados en este trabajo.

Progress in neurobiology and its implications for society

by Seymour S. Kety

Within this generation an unprecedented change has occurred in the relationship between man and his environment. Technological progress, which was at first a means of protecting him against environmental hazards and vicissitudes, became through most of civilized history a means of exploiting, but not harnessing, the land, sea, wind, rain and sun for human benefit. The great strides which physics and chemistry have made in only the past three decades have unleashed natural forces and generated artificial hazards of a type and magnitude capable of altering the face of the earth and of extraterritorial domains as well, disturbing the ecological balance of nature, overriding the slow processes of evolution and threatening the survival of many useful and familiar species including man himself. The problems of thermonuclear war, environmental pollution and the paradox of overpopulation brought about by partial control of famine and disease without a concomitant diminution of the birth rate are more serious than any problem which nature ever thrust upon terrestrial creatures – and all are the products of a unique evolutionary development – the human brain.

So great is the leverage which these modern technologies have given to human society and to individual men that there has come of late the realization that in the individual or collective judgment of man resides the crux of these forces and their potential for benefit or harm. The solution of these problems, the control of these forces and their alignment to serve rather than thwart human survival and evolution depend upon the study and elucidation of the biological processes, but more significantly, the experiences and values which determine human behavior.

The two kinds of determinants of human behavior

It is useful to distinguish between the machinery which mediates behavior and the stored information which is necessary to the evaluations and decisions which govern it. While the first of these determinants can admirably be investigated by the biological disciplines and modified by chemical or physical intervention, the informational content and the system of values can be examined and influenced only by the disciplines and techniques that deal with the social and psychological context of experience. The over-simplifications of reductionism are readily refuted by any word in any language – like *home* or *house* or even *cat* – whether in the form of the component letters or sounds, or in the special perturbations in neuronal activity induced in the brain which perceives them. None of these is susceptible of much further reduction without loss of meaning. They can be explained and understood only in terms of the phenomenology and human experience that is condensed in them.

This inability to reduce informational content to structure, if not unique for the nervous system, is exaggerated by orders of magnitude there in comparison with the translational facility which appears to be attainable in genetics or immunology. The linkages between a gene, an enzyme and a function have been made comprehensible over the past two decades by the intellectual triumphs of molecular biology as have the specificities of antigen-antibody complementarity. But in the case of the human brain, despite remarkable achievements in neurobiology, its behavioral output remains largely inexplicable in molecular terms. One need not invoke the transcendentalism of free will to account for the hiatus; sheer complexity offers a sufficient explanation.

It is not merely the number of neuronal units, variously estimated in the tens of billions, which creates this complexity, but the connections between them. Whereas the functions of muscle, liver or lymphatic tissue may, to a large extent, be comprehended as an addition of the functions of their component cells, the function of even a primitive brain depends predominantly upon the organization of its components and the static properties of their activity. The role of each of these neurons depends in turn upon its location, its connections (which may number in the thousands), the present activity and the history of the network of which it is a part. In only the simplest neural networks, such as the nine-neuron cardiac ganglion of crustacea, have these interconnections and interactions been well defined. It is quite likely that the information storage, the comparisons and discriminations involved in a human decision are distributed over millions of neurons, making its description or comprehension at that level extremely remote.

At other levels of the central nervous system, however, there is considerable specialization and convergence of function, and the close clustering of units with similar functions into apparent control centers. Techniques for recording from individual units have revealed the presence of neurons which respond, not to the simplest elements of sensory input, but to particular patterns or combinations. In the visual cortex are found cells which respond only to lines, or to angles, corners, or contours presented in particular orientations and positions to either eye. These more complex cells apparently receive inputs from numbers of simpler cells and from both retinas from which they extract particular patterns or binocular representation. Other cortical cells have been described upon which more than one sensory modality converges, while in the brainstem recordings have been made from cells which respond only to inputs of special significance in the previous experience of the animal. From studies such as these one can begin discern the mechanisms whereby pattern and significance are extracted from the continous barrage of environmental stimuli, even though representing the neural counterpart of the perception of a particular face or scene would clearly be impossible.

At various levels of the central nervous system neurons subserving a particular modality or function are often packed together, sometimes in characteristic arrays, the axons leading from them tending to form definite tracts. Changes in electrical activity which can be recorded from such regions can sometimes be correlated with behavior, and particular behavioral changes can be evoked by electrical stimulation of the region. Such behavioral responses have included: alterations in heart rate, blood pressure, respiration and temperature, sleep or arousal, rage, attack, fear, withdrawal, exploration, eating, drinking, sexual activity, and positive reinforcement or pleasure which is inferred from the animal's tendency to effect a repetition of the stimulation of certain areas, especially the region of the medial forebrain bundle. There have been some reports of vague pleasurable sensations associated with stimulation of similar areas in man. Since it is not possible to duplicate the complex tempero-spatial patterns of activity in the networks responsible for the cognitive activity which normally precedes and accompanies such behavioral or emotional responses, it is not surprising that these artificially evoked states lack an appropriate cognitive basis, abruptly interrupting the normally motivated activity of the animal at the onset of stimulation and permitting an equally abrupt return at its termination.

An area of great current interest is the chemical differentiation which exists in nervous systems. It has been recognized for some time that the impulse transmitted along the length of a neuron is electrical in nature but that, except in rare instances, the action of one neuron upon another, or upon a muscle fibre or gland cell is brought about by the release of a chemical substance at the axonal ending. This traverses a thin gap or synaptic cleft and acts upon a receptor site in the postsynaptic membrane which is responsive to a particular chemical transmitter. At least two transmitters have been established in the peripheral nervous system: acetylcholine at myoneural junctions and parasympathetic nerve endings, and norepinephrine at the endings of the sympathetic nervous system. Considerable information has been acquired in recent years regarding the synthesis of these transmitters at the nerve endings, and the mechanisms involved in their storage, release and inactivation at the synapse. Since these substances, among others, are synthesized at axonal endings in the central nervous system and some evidence exists for their release and action upon specific receptors, it is a reasonable inference that they act as neurotransmitters there as well.

By means of histofluorescence techniques, neurons containing serotonin or the catecholamines – dopamine and norepinephrine – have been demonstrated in the brain, their cell bodies grouped in the medial and lateral regions of the brainstem, respectively. A majority of the axons of both types of neurons pass through the medial forebrain bundle and are widely distributed throughout the brain, with fairly dense endings on neurons in the hypothalamus, the hippocampus and other parts of the limbic system, the cerebral and cerebellar cortex.

Evidence is accumulating from studies of their turnover in various regions and of their behavioral effects when applied directly to specific loci that the biogenic amines – norepinephrine, dopamine or serotonin – are transmitters in the neural pathways which mediate certain affective or behavioral states. One pathway – the nigrostriatal tract, the axons of which contain dopamine – has been shown to be deficient in the disorder of movement known as Parkinson's disease. Such knowledge has led to the effective use of the dopamine precursor, L-dopa, in that condition. Less definitive but fairly compelling evidence implicates norepinephrine in pathways that mediate arousal, emotions and appetitive responses.

A reduction in the store of norepinephrine or an increase in its rate of turnover has been found in certain parts of the brain when animals are stressed or when rage is induced. The administration of a drug which specifically blocks the synthesis of catecholamines interferes with arousal, motivation, exploration, conditioned avoidance responses, and reward-seeking behavior. The last effect has been reversed by restoring norepinephrine in the brain. Satiated rats will feed when small doses of norepinephrine are applied to a particular region of the hypothalamus. When the brain is depleted of serotonin by specific interference with its synthesis, an increased sensitivity to pain and other external stimuli occurs and wakefulness replaces the normal periods of sleep.

Some drugs which produce euphoria in man and others which are effective in the treatment of depression may act by enhancing the concentration of norepinephrine at central synapses. Conversely, depression may follow the administration of drugs which deplete the brain of norepinephrine, and agents which are useful in the treatment of acute manic states may act by reducing the concentrations or effects of norepinephrine at certain synapses in the brain. Although there is no direct evidence, observations such as these suggest the possibility that norepinephrine, as well as other biogenic amines, play important roles in the mediation of normal mood via processes or pathways which, when disordered, result in manic-depressive or other affective mental illnesses.

Quite recently, one of the biogenic amines, dopamine, has been implicated in some interesting pharmacologic effects of relevance to schizophrenia. Of the numerous drugs capable of inducing a toxic psychosis in man, amphetamine is unique in that the psychosis produced by large or chronic dosage most closely resembles, and is often confused with, schizophrenia. Conversely, two classes of chemically unrelated drugs, the phenothiazines and the butyrophenones, have been found to be most effective in the treatment of schizophrenia, relieving not only disturbed behavior but often affecting the thought disorder as well. Although these pharmacologic effects have been known for some time it was only in the past two years that evidence was adduced to indicate their action on the dopamine-containing systems of the brain, amphetamine appearing to exaggerate the release of dopamine at nerve endings while both the phenothiazines and butyrophenones block dopaminergic receptors. These findings have directed attention to the possible involvement of the dopamine-containing neural systems in schizophrenia.

The realization that genetic information was encoded in the specific nucleotide sequences of DNA suggested the possibility that a similar process of macromolecular coding was responsible for the storage of experiential information. Although that hypothesis has not been convincingly supported nor generally accepted, it has had considerable heuristic value. Much of the research which derived from it developed evidence that RNA and protein synthesis was important in the memory process. A substantial number of investigators have shown that while animals may learn under the influence of actinomycin or cycloheximide which severely depress the synthesis of RNA or protein respectively, they are unable to retain or 'consolidate' the experience. These findings are compatible with the widely held concept that neurons and the synapses between them are involved in the storage of information as well as its processing. That concept would regard consolidation as the process whereby a brief excitation of a neuronal network becomes more permanently established under appropriate conditions by an increase in the conductance of each of its synapses. This could occur by the development of new or the enlargement of existing synapses or by an increase in the mechanisms for generating or releasing transmitter, in all of which processes protein synthesis would be required.

The well-known importance of arousal, affective state, reward and punishment in the establishment of memory suggests a facilitative action of biogenic amines on protein synthesis at synapses, if, in fact, these substances and that process do represent substrates of the psychological phenomena. The peripheral autonomic and humoral components of affective states have well-recognized functions in the anticipation, facilitation and maintenance of a number of crucial adaptive responses to environmental hazards or opportunities on which the survival of the individual or the species depends. Although the central components of these affective states are not well defined at present, it is quite possible that they subserve equally important adaptations – reinforcing significant inputs, suppressing trivial or familiar ones, evoking or facilitating aversive or appetitive responses, which, in the experience of the individual or the species, have had the greatest survival value, and so influencing the neuronal processes involved in memory as to permit the reinforcement and persistence of the most appropriate responses. The dependence of learning on arousal and on reward and punishment suggests the existence of a mechanism which consolidates not all experience equally but only those experiences which are significant for survival.

It is not difficult to see how, as a result of selective pressure, certain primitive affective states and behavioral responses could have become genetically endowed – discomfort and aversive behavior to noxious or threatening stimuli, pleasure and appetitive behavior to stimuli associated with safety, food and mating. It is possible that some affective states, by an interaction between their neurochemical substrates and those involved in memory may favor the persistence of the particular patterns of neuronal activity which subserved the sensory configurations and behavioral responses leading to and from the affective state. Some such concept of polarized plasticity would help to explain the development of perceptions, values and exquisitely tuned behaviors arising out of the genetic *anlage* of the species but elaborated by and specifically adapted to the idiosyncratic experience of the individual.

It may be useful to examine the social implications of present neurobiological knowledge and that which may accrue in the foreseeable future in the light of the discontinuity which exists between the biological mechanisms of the brain and the information it contains. If that information is stored in the complex interactions of millions of neurons, it is obvious that the neuronal structure of a decision or a voluntary act is vastly more complicated than the amino acid sequence of any protein and its reconstitution or synthesis in neurobiological terms equally remote. Those who are enthusiastic about the possibilities or concerned about the hazards of cloning or other types of genetic manipulation in man must surely recognize that in the case of the brain what will emerge from even the most successful of such attempts would be an organ similar in potential but also in sophistication to that of the newborn.

Prosthetic devices are now capable of development for the blind or deaf which can convert aspects of the environment into neuronal signals, but these can assume meaning only on the basis of a laborious process of education.

Where learning or some of its components like attention, memory, affect, motivation or performance are impaired by disease, metabolic defect or nutritional inadequacy, it is quite possible that continued research will be able to specify the deficits, so that the biological if not the experiential causes of retarded intellectual maturation may be corrected. Impaired cerebral circulation accounts for a substantial segment of the senile dementias and it is not unreasonable to expect that arteriosclerosis of the brain as well as the heart will eventually yield to biochemically based comprehension and therapy.

Although learning may be speeded up and made more efficient by present knowledge of its attributes, there is no foreseeable substitute for it in the elaboration of the apperceptive mass which resides in the human brain and to a significant extent determines human behavior.

Turning from cognitive to affective processes, one finds considerably greater promise of effective biological restitution. Tumors or focal lesions involving particular centers or pathways may account for some states of disordered behavior or emotion which appropriate surgical treatment may alleviate. More important, perhaps, is the likelihood that as the chemical transmitters involved in particular emotional states are more definitively elucidated, more specific pharmacological agents will be developed to alter their activity and the functions they subserve. In the past decade pharmacology has contributed significantly to psychiatric treatment of depression, mania and schizophrenia which constitute the most prevalent and incapacitating of the mental illnesses. It is likely that agents of greater efficacy and specificity will be developed as their neurochemical disturbances are further elucidated. The physical dependence on certain chemical substances like alcohol and the derivatives of opium is most likely to be a biochemical process. Present knowledge is fragmentary and inadequate, but continued and expanding research on the nature of drug-receptor interaction, on the feed-back from synaptic activity to neuronal metabolism and enzyme induction, and a greater understanding of the mechanisms and transmitters involved in appetitive responses, cannot help but contribute to the elucidation and correction of the biochemical derangements which underlie the syndrome of addiction.

In addition to the prospects of further significant advances in the treatment of the seriously disabling mental illnesses, one may with confidence predict the development of improved drugs useful in the alleviation of symptoms which are less serious but even more widespread. Analgesics, sedatives, and anti-anxiety agents with fewer side effects will probably continue to be developed or discovered as will euphoriants and hallucinogens with little therapeutic value. For all of these drugs it will be the responsibility of science to ascertain and point out their indications and contraindications, and the dangers inherent in their indiscriminate use. It will also be incumbent on society to develop effective means of regulating their manufacture and distribution in order to gain the advantages of their appropriate use and minimize their harmful effects. It is noteworthy that among the agents most widely abused today, the most important – alcohol and preparations of opium and cannabis – were discovered long before the advent of modern pharmacology or technology.

The amelioration of behavior disordered by disease and inappropriate to the life experience of the individual may increasingly be achieved by physical or chemical correction of the machinery of the brain but does not necessarily presage a corresponding danger that other aspects of behavior will be manipulated with comparable tools.

Most of the meaningful behavior of man is determined not by the machinery of the brain but by the values, motivations, thoughts and prejudices which are based upon the experience and education of the individual. No drug I can think of can add new information to that store and no possible placement of electrodes can create the necessary circuits. Those who have wanted to control human behavior in the past have not waited for drugs or electrical stimulation, but have found it disconcertingly effective to manipulate education, information, rewards and punishment to suit their ends. The greatest technological contribution to the control of human behavior was made over 500 years ago in the invention of the printing press. In modern times comparable achievements will be found in the development of radio and television.

One would not wish to imply that the net of these great contributions has been other than salutary, despite the fact that they have been used at times for ulterior ends. Even there, does the fault lie with the technological achievement or with our failure to develop the political sophistication and the social will to assure its beneficial use? Manipulation of the brain by biological techniques would involve such drastic invasions of the privacy, integrity and rights of the individual, that in their application, behavioral control would have been accomplished even if the electrodes carried no current and the pills were placebos!

The biological sciences are beginning to provide understanding of the machinery of the mind as well as the body, and where it is defective, to improve it. While we await with impatience or with concern the identification of a new biochemical process or the development of a new drug or technique which will improve or control our minds, the intellectual development of each individual, like his risk of illness or death, is constantly being influenced and largely determined, by fairly commonplace, understandable, and modifiable processes that affect where and how he is born, under what conditions he develops, what he is fed and taught, and what physical, chemical and intellectual components he finds in his lifelong environment.

Summary

Recent progress in the biology of the nervous system and behavior is distinguished by contributions to the mechanisms by which information is encoded, transmitted and processed in the brain, by elucidation of the biochemical and physiological processes involved in synaptic transmission in the peripheral nervous system and the accumulation of histochemical, neurochemical, pharmacological and behavioral evidence that several chemical transmitters are involved in particular pathways and synapses in the central nervous system with functions which mediate or modify arousal and sleep, motivation, and a variety of affective states. This information has furthered the understanding of the action of a number of recently developed drugs of considerable value in the treatment of the affective illnesses and schizophrenia and may well lead to the discovery of the biological substrates from which some of these disorders arise.

It is important, in considering the social implications of neuro- and psychobiology to recognize the distinction between the mechanisms which encode, process, store, and utilize information and the information itself. There will some day be a biochemistry and a biophysics of memory – but not of memories. Where these biological processes are impaired by disease, one may expect that continued research may lead to their restitution. Only rarely will means be found to improve upon normal function.

Much of human behavior depends upon the informational content of the brain, based upon the experience of the individual and his cognitive functioning. Although these may be distorted by drugs they cannot be predictably created, altered, or replaced by biological techniques. Although neurobiology should constantly be concerned with the possibilities of the harm as well as the good of which it is capable, it seems quite clear that it will be a long time before the biological sciences approach the power and responsibility of affecting human behavior which reside today in the press, radio and television, parental attitudes, social values and education.

Zusammenfassung

Die jüngsten Fortschritte auf den Gebieten der Biologie des Nervensystems und des Verhaltens sind dreifach gekennzeichnet: einmal durch neue Einsichten in die Mechanismen, mittels deren Information im Gehirn fixiert, übertragen und verarbeitet wird, dann durch Klärung der biochemischen und physiologischen Vorgänge, die bei der synaptischen Übermittlung im peripheren Nervensystem eine Rolle spielen, und schließlich durch die Häufung histochemischer, neurochemischer, pharmakologischer und verhaltensmäßiger Hinweise darauf, daß verschiedene chemische Übermittlungssubstanzen in speziellen Bahnen und Synapsen im Zentralnervensystem mitwirken, und zwar in Funktionen, die Erwachen und Schlaf, Motivation und eine Vielfalt affektiver Zustände vermitteln oder verändern. Diese Information hat das Verständnis für die Wirkung einer Anzahl kürzlich entwickelter, bei der Behandlung der affektiven Erkrankungen und der Schizophrenie wertvoller Arzneimittel gefördert und könnte gut zur Entdeckung jener biologischen Substrate führen, von denen einige dieser Störungen herrühren.

Wenn man die sozialen Folgen der Neuro- und Psychobiologie betrachtet, ist es wichtig, den Unterschied zwischen den die Information fixierenden, verarbeitenden, speichernden und freisetzenden Mechanismen und der Information selbst zu erkennen. Eines Tages wird es eine Biochemie und eine Biophysik des Gedächtnisses geben, nicht aber der Erinnerungen. Wo diese biologischen Vorgänge durch Krankheit gestört sind, darf man erwarten, daß kontinuierliche Forschung zu ihrer Heilung führt. Nur selten werden sich Mittel finden lassen, welche die normale Funktion noch übertreffen.

Im menschlichen Verhalten hängt viel vom Informationsgehalt des Hirnes ab, der auf der Erfahrung des einzelnen und dem Funktionieren kognitiver Mechanismen basiert. Wohl können diese durch Drogen entstellt werden; sie lassen sich jedoch nicht in absehbarer Weise durch biologische Techniken hervorbringen, verändern oder ersetzen. Wenn sich die Neurobiologie auch ständig mit den Möglichkeiten sowohl des Schadens als auch des Nutzens, dessen sie fähig ist, befassen sollte, so ist doch offensichtlich, daß es noch lange dauern wird, bis die biologischen Wissenschaften auch nur annähernd jene Macht und Verantwortung in der Beeinflussung des menschlichen Verhaltens erreicht haben, welche heute Presse, Radio und Fernsehen, Einstellung der Eltern, gesellschaftlichen Werten und Erziehung gegeben sind.

Résumé

Les progrès récents de la biologie du système nerveux et du comportement se distinguent par les contributions à la connaissance des mécanismes de codage, de transmission et d'utilisation de l'information dans le cerveau, d'une part, par l'élucidation des processus biochimiques et physiologiques qui interviennent dans la transmission synaptique au niveau du système nerveux périphérique, d'autre part, et enfin par l'accumulation de preuves histochimiques, neurochimiques, pharmacologiques et comportementales de l'intervention de plusieurs transmetteurs chimiques dans des parcours et synapses déterminés du système nerveux central, où leur fonction consiste à modifier ou à causer l'éveil et le sommeil, les motivations et divers états affectifs. Ces acquisitions, qui permettent de mieux comprendre l'action de nouveaux médicaments présentant une valeur considérable pour le traitement des troubles affectifs et de la schizophrénie, pourraient fort bien conduire à la découverte des substrats biologiques où siègent certains de ces dérèglements.

En considérant les implications sociales de la neurobiologie, il importe de concevoir qu'il existe une distinction entre les mécanismes de codage, d'assimilation, de mémorisation et d'utilisation de l'information et cette information elle-même. Il existera un jour une biochimie et une biophysique de la mémoire – mais non des souvenirs. On peut s'attendre à ce que les recherches qui se poursuivent permettent un jour de restaurer les processus biologiques altérés par la maladie. Mais c'est uniquement dans des cas très rares que l'on parviendra à trouver les moyens d'améliorer les fonctions normales.

Le comportement de l'être humain dépend pour une bonne part de l'information contenue dans le cerveau, elle-même fonction de l'expérience de l'individu et du fonctionnement de son mécanisme cognitif. Bien que ces données puissent être modifiées par des substances pharmacologiques, elles ne peuvent très probablement pas, par contre, être créées, altérées ou remplacées par l'application de techniques biologiques. La neurobiologie doit certes constamment se préoccuper du bien ou du mal qu'elle peut faire, mais il est bien évident qu'il s'écoulera de longues années avant que les sciences biologiques acquièrent le pouvoir d'influer sur le comportement humain, pouvoir que détiennent à l'heure actuelle les *mass-media* (presse, radio, télévision), les parents, les valeurs sociales et l'éducation.

Resumen

Los recientes progresos de la biología del sistema nervioso y del comportamiento se distinguen: por haber contribuido al conocimiento del mecanismo mediante el cual las informaciones se codifican, transmiten y asimilan en el cerebro; por su aporte al esclarecimiento de los procesos bioquímicos y fisiológicos que intervienen en la transmisión sináptica al nivel del sistema nervioso

periférico; y por la acumulación de datos histoquímicos, neuroquímicos, farma-
cológicos y referentes al comportamiento que demuestran la intervención de
varios transmisores químicos en determinados recorridos y sinapsis del sistema
nervioso central, cuya función es la de inducir o modificar la vigilia o el sueño,
crear motivaciones y varios estados emotivos. Gracias a dichos hallazgos, hoy
se comprende mejor el mecanismo de acción de ciertos nuevos medicamentos,
muy valiosos para el tratamiento de los trastornos de la afectividad y de la
esquizofrenia y que bien pudieran conducir al descubrimiento de los substratos
biológicos de donde surgen algunos de esos desórdenes.

Si se consideran las implicaciones sociales de la neurobiología y de la
psicología, es importante distinguir entre los mecanismos encargados de codi-
ficar, asimilar, memorizar y utilizar informaciones y la información misma.
Algún día existirá una bioquímica y una biofísica de la memoria – pero no de
los recuerdos. Cuando estos procesos biológicos están alterados por la enfermedad, es lícito esperar que la continua investigación permitirá su restablecimiento.
Pero, será muy raro que se encuentren medios para mejorar la capacidad
normal.

El comportamiento del ser humano depende en gran parte de la información
contenida en su cerebro, fruto de la experiencia del individuo y de su capacidad
cognoscitiva. Aunque éstas puedan ser deformadas por medio de sustancias
farmacológicas, no parece ser posible crearlas, alterarlas o reemplazarlas a
voluntad merced a técnicas biológicas.

La neurobiología siempre debe ser tan consciente de las posibilidades
perniciosas de las que es capaz, como de las benéficas. Sin embargo, transcurrirá
todavía mucho tiempo hasta que las ciencias biológicas adquieran el poder y la
responsabilidad de influir sobre el comportamiento humano que hoy detienen
la prensa, la radiotelevisión, los padres, la sociedad y los educadores.

Preliminary Symposium in Geneva. The various aspects of the topics were discussed in small interdisciplinary groups. Above, the panel directed by Philip Handler, below the one under the chairmanship of René König.

Changements quantitatifs et qualitatifs des populations humaines, sous l'influence des progrès biomédicaux ou biomédico-sociaux

par Alfred Sauvy

I. Présentation et limites du sujet

Nous nous proposons d'abord de voir en quoi ont consisté ces progrès, à quelle époque ils ont commencé, comment ils se sont manifestés et répandus, quel a été leur domaine.

Les progrès médicaux

On peut estimer que, jusqu'au XVIIIe siècle, disons même jusqu'à l'inoculation de la variole vers 1760, suivie de la vaccination Jenner, la thérapeutique était, en dépit des progrès réalisés en anatomie et en physiologie, à peu près inopérante, tout au moins en termes de mortalité. Il existait, certes, des remèdes traditionnels ou relativement récents (quinine par exemple), mais, en revanche, nombre d'actions médicales étaient contraires à la santé et à la vie des patients.

La vaccination contre la variole a été suivie, lentement d'abord, puis plus rapidement, d'une série de progrès biomédicaux, d'abord discontinus (anesthésie, auscultation, etc.), puis à peu près ininterrompus depuis l'ère pastorienne, stimulés et accélérés, il faut bien le reconnaître, par les deux guerres (chirurgie, antibiotiques, etc.).

Les progrès en médecine préventive, ou même en hygiène, ont été sans doute plus efficaces que l'action curative. Les conditions de l'accouchement, l'allaitement et l'élevage des nourrissons, la distribution d'eau potable, etc. ont bénéficié de progrès considérables.

Ces progrès, à peu près réservés, au début, aux populations blanches et même aux classes les plus favorisées de ces populations, se sont ensuite étendus peu à peu à l'ensemble des populations du globe, le mouvement étant encore en cours.

Progrès économiques et sociaux

Depuis le jour où s'était instituée une hiérarchie dans la société, il y a eu des hommes bien nourris, bien vêtus, bien logés et bénéficiant des commodités permises par les connaissances de leur temps, à côté d'hommes, beaucoup plus nombreux, souvent privés du strict nécessaire.

Le changement social ne s'est fait que graduellement et partiellement. S'il faut fixer une date, un point de départ des progrès économiques et sociaux, c'est encore le XVIIIe siècle qui s'impose à l'esprit. Jusque-là, il s'agissait essentiellement de charité, pour soulager les misères les plus criantes et non d'action vraiment sociale.

Laissant de côté les utopies (Th. More, Harrington, etc.), qui promettent la félicité générale dans l'abondance, nous voyons en France, en Italie naître des projets de sécurité sociale, plus paternalistes que révolutionnaires, qui ne prendront corps qu'à la fin du XIXe siècle. En Angleterre, la loi des pauvres (ou plutôt les lois des pauvres) donne aux miséreux un certain droit, contre lequel s'insurgeront Townsend et Malthus.

En 1789, la Déclaration des droits de l'homme a précisé ces notions nouvelles, qui se sont concrétisées plus tard.

En même temps, la production de subsistances, alimentaires notamment, a suffisamment augmenté, toujours dans les pays avancés, pour permettre d'améliorer le sort des classes inférieures. Les dernières famines véritables datent dans ces pays du XVIIIe siècle (le cas de l'Irlande est spécial).

Cette amélioration des conditions d'existence, nourriture, logement, etc., ne s'est faite que graduellement et n'est pas encore commencée dans divers pays.

En résumé

Sous leurs diverses formes, les progrès n'ont débuté vraiment qu'au XVIIIe siècle. Comme c'est aussi à ce moment que l'on commence à disposer de statistiques, c'est cette époque que nous retiendrons. Cependant, dans certains cas, il faudrait remonter à la découverte de l'Amérique. Ces progrès ont consisté en:
une meilleure thérapeutique,
le progrès des connaissances, en matière d'hygiène et de prévention,
une nourriture plus abondante et des conditions économiques plus satisfaisantes,
une diffusion de ces progrès à l'ensemble des classes sociales et des populations, diffusion qui est encore loin de son terme.

Nous parlerons plus loin des facteurs génétiques.

II. Changements quantitatifs

Les progrès biomédicaux et biomédico-sociaux ont agi sur le nombre des hommes, sur les conditions de leur multiplication et sur leur multiplication elle-même, enfin sur leur répartition dans le monde.

Ce progrès a été aidé par le facteur économique, suivi de près de la baisse de la mortalité, à laquelle il a, lui aussi, contribué.

La baisse de la mortalité

On peut estimer, grossièrement, que, des temps préhistoriques à l'époque moderne, la vie moyenne de l'espèce humaine n'a guère changé, si l'on fait abstraction des catastrophes (épidémies, guerres, famines) nécessairement très inégales dans le temps et l'espace. Cette vie moyenne s'établissait aux environs de 25 ans (ou même davantage), durée au-dessous de laquelle une population n'aurait pas pu subsister. Les durées supérieures à 30 ans, constatées au XVIIIe et au XVIIe siècles, ne concernaient que des populations favorisées.

Cette pierre, qui pesait sur la tête de l'humanité, s'est soulevée au XVIIIe siècle, si bien que, dans les pays avancés, l'espérance de vie à la naissance a sensiblement augmenté. Voici à peu près les principales étapes:

vers 1775	30 ans	vers 1900	48 ans
vers 1830	36 ans	vers 1940	62 ans
vers 1860	41 ans	vers 1970	70 ans

La baisse a été beaucoup plus forte pour la mortalité infantile que pour la mortalité aux âges élevés. La première (12 premiers mois) a baissé de 25% environ à 2% et même moins. De ce seul fait, l'espérance de vie à la naissance a augmenté de plus de 10 ans.

Quelques étapes

Voici, pour plusieurs tables types des Nations-Unies, les quotients de mortalité pour 1000, à divers âges (sexe féminin):

	Espérance de vie 25 ans ($e_o = 25$)	Espérance de vie 50 ans ($e_o = 50$)	Espérance de vie 70,2 ans ($e_o = 70,2$)
0 an	268,15	123,75	23,37
15–19 ans	64,32	21,65	4,17
35–39 ans	122,47	35,73	9,70
55–59 ans	212,56	86,36	43,37
75–79 ans	593,79	407,31	299,75

Pour ces mêmes tables types, voici les nombres de survivants (sexe féminin):

	$e_o = 25$ ans	$e_o = 50$ ans	$e_o = 70,2$ ans
Naissance	100 000	100 000	100 000
1 an	73 185	87 625	97 663
20 ans	47 638	77 615	95 926
40 ans	30 940	67 981	93 136
60 ans	14 709	53 076	83 642
75 ans	3 854	27 141	55 662
85 ans	385	7 123	21 690

Accélération après la Seconde Guerre

Depuis 25 ans, la baisse de la mortalité s'est, grâce à la diffusion des techniques antimortelles de base (eau potable, vaccin, etc.), étendue à un grand nombre de pays, jusque-là non touchés. En effet, ces techniques:

n'entraînent pas de fortes dépenses financières,

n'exigent pas un important personnel médical de haute qualification,

ne nécessitent pas le concours actif de la population.

C'est pourquoi elles se sont répandues plus vite que les techniques anti-natales et que les techniques économiques.

On peut, assez conventionnellement, distinguer quatre groupes de pays:

Dans les pays très attardés (Afrique noire, Bolivie, Haïti), l'espérance de vie ne dépasse guère 40 ans et est souvent plus basse encore. C'est le niveau de l'Europe occidentale vers 1850, avec un niveau de vie trois fois plus faible.

Dans les pays qui ont un service médical apte à utiliser les techniques préventives de masse, l'espérance de vie dépasse 50 ans, niveau de l'Europe occidentale vers 1914, avec un niveau de vie, ici aussi, trois fois plus faible.

Dans les pays pauvres, mais bien organisés, l'espérance de vie dépasse 60 ans, niveau de l'Europe occidentale vers 1939, mais le niveau de vie est deux fois plus faible.

Enfin, dans les pays avancés, le chiffre de 70 ans est souvent dépassé.

Dans les trois premiers groupes, le niveau de vie est très inférieur à celui qu'avaient les populations avancées, du moment où elles avaient la même espérance de vie. Ainsi, le *progrès médical a devancé le progrès économique; il permet de faire vivre, plus longtemps, des hommes plus pauvres.*

Dans la plus grande partie du monde, un bébé de famille modeste trouve, dans son berceau, une espérance de vie supérieure à celle d'un noble du XVIIIe et même d'un riche européen du début du XXe siècle.

Les taux de mortalité

Les taux de mortalité qui, de tout temps, étaient compris entre 35 et 40 pour 1000 habitants, vont aujourd'hui de 5 à 35 pour 1000.

Dans les pays avancés, la mortalité s'élève aux environs de 10 pour 1000; elle est donc plus élevée que celle de certains pays peu développés, à cause du vieillissement de la population, dont nous parlons plus loin. Dans les pays peu développés, on trouve, à côté de taux très bas de 5 à 6 pour 1000 (Hongkong, Singapour, etc.), des taux très élevés en Afrique noire.

Pour l'ensemble du monde, le taux est de 13 pour 1000, le tiers environ du niveau traditionnel et naturel.

Jusqu'où?

Jusqu'où se poursuivra le recul de la mort? Les avis divergent largement.

Selon les uns, de nouvelles étapes seront franchies, la vie humaine s'allongeant peut-être au-dessus de 100 ans.

Selon d'autres, les gains réalisés ont été plus destructeurs que créateurs (microbes et virus, chirurgie) et n'ont guère touché les affections endogènes, de sénescence notamment. La vie moyenne pourrait alors buter sur le plafond «biologique» de 77 ou 78 ans. A l'appui de leur thèse, ils font valoir la légère reprise de la mortalité au-dessus de 55 ans, en divers pays très avancés, depuis quinze ans.

D'autres encore parlent d'une revanche de la mort, sous l'effet de diverses saturations (abus des antibiotiques, résistance des virus, etc.).

En tout état de cause, un ralentissement est probable.

Fécondité, natalité

La *fécondité physiologique* ou *fertilité* de l'espèce humaine ne semble pas avoir changé à travers les siècles et les millénaires. Elle n'a pas davantage été modifiée par les progrès biomédicaux.

Il n'en est pas de même de la fécondité effective, laquelle a varié sous l'influence de divers facteurs:

mœurs matrimoniales (âge au mariage notamment),

baisse de la mortalité et notamment de la mortalité puerpérale,

pratiques antinatales.

Celles-ci, signalées dans divers pays, à diverses époques n'étaient le plus souvent ni générales ni efficaces (cependant une stérilité physiologique pouvait résulter de la dégradation des organes).

C'est aussi au XVIIIe siècle que se place la diffusion de pratiques contraceptives (limitée à peu près à la France). Il ne s'agit guère encore de progrès médicaux. Mais, à partir de 1875, l'influence de ceux-ci se fait sentir de trois façons:

accroissement du nombre d'enfants par famille, du fait de la baisse de la mortalité aux jeunes âges,

progrès économique, social et culturel, incitant à abandonner la fécondité physiologique,

perfectionnement des techniques antinatales: pour la contraception, diaphragme en 1882, stérilet en 1928 (Gräfenberg), puis à nouveau, en 1962, produits stérilisants, diffusés à partir de 1960 environ. En outre, le perfectionnement des techniques abortives a incité plusieurs pays, notamment les pays européens socialistes, à recourir à l'avortement libre, plus efficace que la contraception.

La baisse de la fécondité s'est, jusqu'à ces dernières années, limitée à peu près aux pays développés. Le taux de reproduction brut (remplacement d'une génération féminine par la suivante, dans l'hypothèse d'une mortalité nulle jusqu'à la ménopause) est supérieur à 3 dans la plupart des pays peu développés et compris entre 0,95 et 1,3 dans les pays évolués.

Exigeant le concours actif de la population (sauf toutefois le stérilet) les techniques antinatales se sont répandues beaucoup moins vite que les techniques antimortelles de base. Le stérilet lui-même a donné des mécomptes.

Dans une «population naturelle», ne bénéficiant d'aucune thérapeutique efficace et ne recourant pas aux pratiques antinatales, un couple, uni de la puberté à la ménopause, doit avoir en moyenne 12 naissances vivantes. Mais ce chiffre subit une série de déchets:

Au XVIIIe siècle, la mort suffisait à réduire ce nombre à 4. Le célibat et le mariage après la puberté ramenait encore ce nombre à 2,1 survivants à la puberté, ce qui donnait un taux de reproduction nette très peu supérieur à un.

Aujourd'hui, en Europe, c'est la prévention des naissances qui ramène ce nombre à 4; la mortalité ne joue plus qu'un rôle très faible.

Dans une population type du tiers monde, le déchet dû à la mort n'est guère plus de 30%. Il reste finalement 4,5 enfants, ce qui correspond à un taux net de reproduction de 2,25.

Ces données nous fournissent un aperçu général des changements survenus sous l'influence de la baisse de la mortalité et de la fécondité, dans la reproduction des populations.

Le nombre des hommes

Nous touchons là le point le plus important: les progrès médico-sociaux ont permis aux hommes de se multiplier ou plus exactement d'accélérer leur multiplication. En effet, la baisse de la mortalité a, dans presque tous les pays, précédé la limitation des naissances. En simplifiant quelque peu, cette augmentation s'est faite en deux temps:

1. Au XIXe siècle (et même au XVIIIe), ce sont les populations européennes qui ont bénéficié du décalage. En dépit d'une intense émigration vers le Nouveau Monde, la population d'Europe occidentale a augmenté au XIXe au rythme de 1 % par an environ. Les progrès médico-sociaux ont, en somme, profité d'abord aux pays qui les ont inventés.

2. Lorsque cette exubérance s'est quelque peu ralentie, sous l'influence de la baisse de la natalité, le relais a, en quelque sorte, été assuré par les populations des autres régions, qui, depuis 25 ans, ont augmenté à un rythme beaucoup plus rapide encore.

Le décalage des techniques évoqué plus haut a joué dans les deux cas en faveur de l'accroissement de la population.

La multiplication naturelle dépassée

Le pouvoir multiplicateur naturel de l'espèce humaine peut être estimé dans des conditions normales, sans misère excessive, à 1 % ou 1,5 % par an; mais, dans la pratique, une telle progression n'a jamais été atteinte, avant les temps modernes, du moins sur une assez longue durée. Depuis le Christ, cette augmentation a dû être, en moyenne, de l'ordre de 0,1 % par an dans les pays constituant l'Empire romain.

Combinant les effets d'une fécondité presque naturelle et d'une mortalité réduite par le progrès scientifique, les pays peu développés bénéficient aujourd'hui d'une progression de 2 à 3 % par an; des taux supérieurs à 3,5 % ont même été enregistrés. Jamais à aucune époque, la population d'un pays n'a augmenté à un tel rythme, sauf certains cas d'immigration intense. Pour la première fois, le pouvoir multiplicateur naturel de l'espèce humaine est dépassé.

Pour l'ensemble du monde, Chine comprise (avec l'aléa d'une telle inclusion), la progression est estimée à 1,8 % par an, taux inédit lui aussi, qui assure un doublement en 45 ans.

Voici la répartition de la population du monde à diverses époques (en millions):

	1750	1850	1900	1970	2000 (perspectives)
Afrique	99	99	137	354	602
Amérique	12	59	144	511	912
Asie	466	715	905	2059	3860
Europe	140	260	401	465	575
URSS	*	*	*	242	326
Océanie	2	3	7	19	30
Total	719	1136	1594	3650	6305

Dans la dernière colonne figurent les perspectives des Nations-Unies dans l'hypothèse moyenne, corrigées pour tenir compte des résultats jusqu'en 1970.

Traduit en pourcentages, ce tableau devient, après répartition de la population soviétique, entre Asie et Europe:

	1750	1850	1900	1970	2000
Afrique	13,8	8,7	8,6	9,7	9,6
Amérique	1,7	5,2	9,0	14,0	14,4
Asie	64,8	63,0	56,8	57,9	62,5
Europe	19,4	22,8	25,2	17,9	13,0
Océanie	0,3	0,3	0,4	0,5	0,5
	100,0	100,0	100,0	100,0	100,0

L'accroissement, puis le recul de l'Europe sont particulièrement nets. Celui de l'Amérique du Nord est également accentué.

Un important potentiel d'accroissement

En l'absence de catastrophes, une augmentation importante de la population du monde est une certitude, en particulier en Asie, en Afrique et en Amérique latine, à cause du potentiel existant, ignoré ou sous-estimé de nombreux auteurs. En effet:

Les générations déjà nées fourniront, aux divers âges, des effectifs plus importants que ceux d'aujourd'hui, pour deux raisons:
elles sont au départ supérieures en nombre aux générations précédentes, à chaque âge;
elles bénéficieront, au cours de leur vie, de taux de mortalité inférieurs à ceux qu'ont eus ces générations antérieures.

Quant aux générations à naître, elles seront issues de générations aux effectifs presque doubles, au début, de ceux des générations précédentes. Pour que le nombre des naissances diminue ou reste constant, il faudrait donc une forte baisse de la natalité, qui, dans certains pays, devrait être de moitié en une génération.

Les Nations-Unies ont risqué quelques projections, qui sont de simples trajectoires possibles. Selon que la baisse de la fécondité sera rapide, moyenne ou lente, le nombre des hommes sur la terre se stabilisera à 9 milliards en 2050, 14 milliards en 2100 ou 30 milliards en 2150. Le premier de ces chiffres est très optimiste.

Non seulement il serait illusoire de croire que la population de pays même développés puisse s'arrêter brusquement de croître, mais un tel arrêt serait chargé de risques. Si la natalité tombait soudain au niveau de la mortalité, il en résulterait des perturbations violentes dans la structure par âges et dans diverses caractéristiques démographiques et économiques, et cela pendant plusieurs siècles.

Croître ou vieillir
Dès l'instant que l'augmentation du nombre de personnes âgées, pendant une assez longue période, est une certitude, toutes les populations du monde se trouvent devant le dilemme «croître ou vieillir». Nous étudierons plus loin le phénomène du vieillissement. Bornons-nous à souligner ici que les conditions de la croissance ne peuvent pas être séparées de l'évolution de la répartition par âges.

En conclusion
Les progrès biomédicaux et biomédico-sociaux ont, avec l'aide du support économique, entraîné, du point de vue quantitatif, des changements quantitatifs profonds. Le nombre des hommes sur la terre a considérablement augmenté, augmenté aujourd'hui à un rythme jusqu'ici inconnu, et continuera à augmenter, au moins pendant trois générations. Il ne s'agit pas d'un simple changement, mais d'une véritable mutation. Nous nous bornons à citer, sans les traiter, les considérables problèmes économiques, sociaux, politiques posés par cette exubérance, qui risque de déborder les capacités de la planète et les techniques des hommes.

III. Changements qualitatifs

Les changements qualitatifs qui ont pu résulter des progrès biomédicaux et biomédico-sociaux sont de multiples sortes. Nous distinguerons ici:
les caractères démographiques (sexe, âge, activité),
les caractères physiques (taille, poids, puberté, répartition des races),
les caractères intellectuels, culturels (intelligence, langue, religion, etc.),
les caractères physiologiques ou pathologiques (santé, morbidité).
Il s'agit de constatations plus ou moins précises, mais se prêtant plus ou moins bien à la mesure. Par contre, nous ne jugerons pas les changements d'ordre social ou moral, sur lesquels les appréciations sont fatalement entachées de subjectivité.

La répartition par sexe
Si importants qu'ils soient, les progrès biomédicaux ne semblent pas avoir affecté sensiblement la répartition par sexe. La masculinité des naissances vivantes n'a pas subi de changements notables, et les quelques changements qui

ont pu survenir ont pu résulter d'autres facteurs (âge des parents, par exemple). La baisse de la mortalité infantile a accru très légèrement le nombre de garçons; d'autre part, à l'âge adulte, la baisse de la mortalité puerpérale a augmenté un peu le nombre de femmes.

Il faut cependant accorder quelque attention à la surmortalité masculine aux âges mûrs. Son augmentation, dans plusieurs pays, semble résulter de causes sociales (alcoolisme, tabac, genre de vie), plus que de facteurs biologiques.

Nous laissons de côté naturellement l'influence des guerres, comme aussi des morts accidentelles.

Aucun moyen n'a été trouvé qui permette d'agir sur la masculinité à la conception, mais des possibilités apparaissent, dont les conséquences pourraient être notables, en particulier sous forme d'un abaissement de la fécondité.

La répartition par âge

Bien plus importante est l'influence des progrès sur la répartition par âge. Contrairement à une idée très répandue, l'allongement de la vie (baisse de la mortalité) n'a pas contribué jusqu'ici au vieillissement des populations (mesuré le plus souvent, par la proportion des personnes de plus de 60 ou de plus de 65 ans, dans la population totale). Telle qu'elle s'est produite jusqu'ici, la baisse de la mortalité a, en effet, porté surtout sur les premiers âges. Or, une baisse de la mortalité infantile exerce évidemment un effet de rajeunissement, tout en contribuant à l'allongement de la vie. Il se trouve que, dans les pays ayant connu une baisse de la mortalité, sans baisse de la natalité, la répartition par âges n'a pas subi de changements notables.

Au contraire, en sapant la pyramide des âges à sa base, la baisse de la natalité est la cause propre du vieillissement; l'émigration a pu jouer, en outre, un rôle accessoire dans certains pays. Le vieillissement a donc touché en premier lieu la France, puis les autres pays d'Europe et anglo-saxons, mais les populations de haute natalité ont conservé la jeunesse «naturelle».

Voici, pour 100 habitants, le nombre de sexagénaires dans quelques pays d'Europe:

	Angleterre, Galles	France	Allemagne	Italie
1850	7,5	10,1	7,8	8,7
1880	7,5	12,3	7,9	8,8
1900	7,5	12,6	8,0	9,6
1930	11,6	13,8	11,0	10,7
1970	18,7	17,8	18,0	15,3

A la fin du XVIIIe siècle, la proportion de sexagénaires devait être d'environ 6 à 7%. Elle a donc presque triplé; celle des octogénaires a été multipliée par 4 ou 5.

Mais, comme nous l'avons vu, la baisse de la natalité a résulté directement ou indirectement des progrès médico-sociaux, notamment de la baisse de la mortalité qui a eu pour effet l'augmentation du nombre moyen d'enfants par famille.

Perspectives de vieillissement

Non seulement le vieillissement des populations n'est pas terminé, mais il n'en est encore qu'à ses débuts.

Dans les pays évolués, si le taux net de reproduction tombe aux environs de l'unité, comme c'est déjà le cas en Suède, la population tendra vers l'état stationnaire. Si l'espérance de vie à la naissance est portée à 77 ans (suppressions des causes de décès exogènes), la proportion de sexagénaires passera à 25 % environ.

Dans les pays peu évolués, où le dilemme «croître ou vieillir» se pose en termes particulièrement sévères, un vieillissement très important est à prévoir. La proportion de sexagénaires, qui souvent ne dépasse pas 3 %, atteindra et dépassera un jour 20 %.

Nous ne pouvons nous étendre ici sur les problèmes de tous ordres posés par le vieillissement présent ou à venir, bornons-nous à souligner leur grande importance.

La population active

Bien que l'activité professionnelle ne soit pas une notion proprement démographique, il est intéressant de voir dans quelle mesure les progrès biomédicaux influent sur la répartition générale des hommes.

Laissant de côté l'évolution générale dictée par le progrès économique et social (marche du secteur primaire vers le secteur tertiaire), nous nous attachons particulièrement aux professions médicales et paramédicales. Comme la consommation médicale augmente désormais plus vite que le revenu national, et comme les progrès de productivité sont relativement faibles, dans ces activités, essentiellement de services (en dehors de la fabrication de produits pharmaceutiques et d'appareils médicaux), nous voyons s'accroître la proportion de personnes actives employées en vue de la santé, à un rythme qui doit approcher 5 % par an, dans les pays les plus avancés et qui est loin de couvrir les besoins.

Le nombre de personnes directement affectées aux soins de santé, dans les pays avancés, ne dépasse pas 2 ou 2,5 %, mais, si l'on tient compte de toutes les activités indirectes (administration, fabrication de produits, transports, etc.), la proportion est beaucoup plus forte, peut-être de l'ordre de 6 à 8 %.

Taille, poids, puberté

Depuis les premières données biométriques, fournies par Buffon, nous pouvons avoir une idée des changements survenus dans l'espèce humaine. Cependant, les renseignements sur ce point sont limités, discontinus, souvent non comparables, de sorte qu'il n'est pas possible de fournir une véritable série statistique. Au reste, pour la plus grande partie des pays, les données sont presque inexistantes.

Tous les auteurs s'accordent en tout cas à reconnaître, pour les pays avancés:

une augmentation de la taille,

un accroissement du poids,
une puberté plus précoce.

Voici, de 1880 à 1960, l'augmentation de la taille dans 5 pays :

	1880	1960
Norvège	1,69 m	1,77 m
Pays-Bas	1,65 m	1,76 m
Allemagne du Sud	1,66 m	1,72 m
France	1,65 m	1,70 m
Espagne	1,62 m	1,65 m

L'augmentation va de 3 à 11 cm, selon les pays ; laissant de côté l'Espagne, moins développée, nous trouvons (en moyenne arithmétique) une augmentation de 7,5 cm en 80 ans. Selon une autre source, la taille moyenne a augmenté, au cours du XXᵉ siècle, de 7 à 10 cm. Ces chiffres semblent peut-être un peu élevés et ne valent en tout cas que pour les pays avancés.

Harvard admet, en 80 ans, un allongement de 8 cm, soit 1 cm par 10 ans. La taille des fils est le plus souvent supérieure à celle des pères.

Non seulement la taille s'est allongée, mais la croissance d'un individu est plus rapide qu'autrefois. La taille moyenne des nouveau-nés a augmenté de 1 cm en 40 ans, le poids s'accroissant en proportion. Après la naissance, le poids s'accroît plus vite qu'autrefois ; le tour de poitrine a augmenté, lui aussi, plus vite que le tour de tête.

La puberté est plus précoce : pour les filles, l'âge est passé de 16 ou 17 ans à 13 ou 14 ans. La croissance finit d'ailleurs plus tôt qu'autrefois (17 à 18 ans pour les garçons). Voici la taille de garçons de 13 ans, à deux époques :

	1877	1957
Hambourg	1,42 m	1,58 m
Varsovie	1,36 m	1,49 m
Stockholm	1,44 m	1,55 m
Léningrad	1,38 m	1,49 m
Tokyo	1,38 m	1,48 m

Selon Vladimir Vlastowski, biologiste soviétique, la presbytie n'apparaîtrait que 5 à 8 ans plus tard qu'au XIXᵉ siècle.

La cause principale de ces changements paraît être la meilleure alimentation. L'expérience de l'Autrichien Kassowitz, en 1921, sur 14 enfants de condition modeste, a été concluante : taille et poids ont augmenté plus que la normale.

Une autre explication possible est génétique et réside dans l'éclatement des isolats ; elle ne semble pas aussi certaine que la précédente.

Quant à l'accélération de la puberté, elle est attribuée aussi à d'autres causes qu'on ne peut assimiler à des progrès biomédicaux : stimulation de l'urbanisation, excitation de l'hypophyse, mode de vie, etc.

Les groupes ethniques

Il est difficile de donner une répartition correcte selon les races, en raison des croisements nombreux et des incertitudes de définition ; mais les données figurant plus haut sur les diverses parties du monde nous indiquent au moins le sens du mouvement: dans une première phase, qui a duré jusqu'à la Première Guerre et même à la Seconde, le nombre des blancs d'origine européenne et leur proportion ont augmenté de façon sensible. Le mouvement est aujourd'hui inverse, alors que la population blanche européenne s'accroît à un rythme inférieur à 1% par an, les autres races (Japonais exceptés) progressent à un rythme de l'ordre de 2,5 ou 3% par an, réserve faite pour la Chine.

Caractères intellectuels et culturels

Il est fort difficile non seulement de mesurer l'intelligence, mais de la définir. Au début du siècle, à la suite de Galton, des doctrines pessimistes ont vu le jour: les classes supérieures ayant moins d'enfants que les autres et les individus intelligents ayant tendance à monter dans l'échelle sociale, le niveau de l'intelligence humaine devait aller, disait-on, en se dégradant continuellement. Le nivellement de la fécondité selon les classes sociales suffirait à dissiper ces craintes, mais rien de positif n'apparaît, pour le moment, permettant de parler d'une amélioration.

Il est à peine besoin de souligner l'élévation du niveau culturel, aujourd'hui générale, conséquence des progrès économiques, plus que des progrès médico-sociaux.

L'accroissement considérable des populations européennes, par baisse de la mortalité, a permis concurremment avec la domination politique une extension importante de certaines langues européennes, portugais, français, espagnol et surtout anglais.

Quant aux religions, un changement analogue à celui des races s'est produit, à l'avantage des religions chrétiennes au début. Mais il faudrait aussi tenir compte du degré de pratique, observation fort difficile. Les religions musulmane et hindoue semblent en vive progression.

Santé, morbidité

L'état de santé et la morbidité se prêtent beaucoup moins à la mesure que la mortalité. Trop souvent, l'augmentation du nombre des malades traduit plutôt le développement des services médicaux et sanitaires qu'un changement pathologique; l'interprétation est alors à l'opposé de la réalité. Il est difficile de savoir dans quelle mesure le progrès biomédical a transformé des morts en malades et des malades ou des morts en bien-portants. La réponse diffère largement selon les affections et les thérapeutiques.

Parmi les facteurs ayant contribué à une amélioration sanitaire, nous pouvons citer:
caractère décisif de nombreuses interventions chirurgicales;
progrès importants accomplis dans le traitement de certaines maladies, endémiques ou chroniques comme la malaria ou la syphilis;
progrès réalisés, grâce aux techniques préventives (vaccin, etc.);
pratiques d'hygiène (eau potable, etc.) et connaissances de la population;

diminution du nombre des enfants de mères relativement âgées, la baisse de la fécondité a porté surtout sur les mères de plus de 30 ans, mais la proportion de femmes de plus de 30 ans par rapport aux femmes de 20 à 30 ans étant un peu plus élevée qu'autrefois, l'avantage est en partie compensé;
forte réduction des carences alimentaires (rachitisme, etc.);
éclatement des isolats et réduction des tares dominantes.

Les facteurs détériorants sont plus difficiles à localiser et plus faciles à contester. Citons seulement quelques possibilités:
prolongation de la vie d'un malade sans guérison (affections pulmonaires, digestives, etc.);
affections résultant des thérapeutiques ou des abus de médication;
progrès possible (mais non certain) des affections mentales; en tout état de cause, certaines affections, supportables dans la vie rurale traditionnelle, deviennent socialement graves, du fait de la non-adaptation des personnes atteintes à la vie urbaine moderne;
sélection à rebours, nous reviendrons plus loin sur ce point délicat.

Sans qu'il soit possible d'établir un bilan d'ensemble, on peut estimer que *l'état sanitaire a été fortement amélioré à âge égal.*

Influence du vieillissement

Compte tenu du vieillissement de la population, la réponse est naturellement moins optimiste. Pour mesurer l'influence propre du vieillissement, nous pouvons appliquer à une population jeune (donc ancienne) et à une vieille (contemporaine) les taux de fréquence de maladie constatés aujourd'hui*. Nous trouvons ainsi, pour 1000 habitants, 61 malades, un jour donné, dans la population jeune et 89 dans la population âgée. Cela signifie que, si les populations européennes avaient la composition par âges du XVIIIe siècle, leur morbidité ainsi mesurée serait de 32 % plus faible.

Le problème de la sélection

Dès les premières étapes de la baisse de la mortalité, certains auteurs ont estimé qu'il en résultait une sélection à rebours, la nature n'ayant plus l'occasion de faire sa propre sélection positive.

Cet argument a été combattu, non seulement parce qu'il semblait reprocher à la médecine de mieux soigner les hommes, mais parce qu'il n'avait pas de fondement sérieux. Un enfant sauvé, dans son jeune âge, par un vaccin antidiphtérique, par exemple, n'est pas moins vigoureux qu'un autre.

La réponse générale n'est plus aussi certaine aujourd'hui. Peut-être l'accroissement de la mortalité aux âges élevés signalé plus haut, résulte-t-il, en partie, d'une contre-sélection, les plus faibles à l'âge adulte ayant été poussés

---

* La fréquence des maladies à chaque âge est donnée par un sondage auprès d'un échantillon de 1600 médecins, fait en 1966/67 par l'*Institut européen de documentation et de recherche sur les maladies.* Il s'agit des consultations et visites en clientèle privée. Ce qui importe d'ailleurs, dans ce résultat, c'est la comparaison des deux populations plus que les nombres absolus.

à un âge avancé. D'autre part, les efforts s'exercent aujourd'hui pour combattre les maladies exogènes, jusqu'ici rebelles, notamment dans la première année, ce qui permet la vie d'enfants mal conformés. Certaines tares héréditaires (diabète infantile, hémophilie, etc.) peuvent se propager, du fait que les sujets atteints peuvent désormais parvenir à l'âge de procréation. C'est un sujet extrêmement délicat qui peut prendre facilement une figure inhumaine, mais qui demande à être étudié sans préjugé.

IV. Conclusion

Nous sommes loin d'avoir abordé, dans cet aperçu, tous les aspects des changements survenus sous l'influence des progrès biomédico-sociaux. En particulier, nous avons volontairement écarté les difficultés résultant du mode de vie, des conditions sociales telles que l'extension de l'alcoolisme, du tabac, des stupéfiants et hallucinogènes, le surmenage de certaines professions, etc. Ces dégradations viennent le plus souvent du progrès économique et non des progrès biomédicaux.

Résumons les conclusions auxquelles nous sommes parvenus :
le fait essentiel est la baisse profonde de la mortalité, aujourd'hui à peu près générale dans le monde ;
la baisse de la fécondité résulte directement ou indirectement des progrès biomédico-sociaux, mais n'est pas aussi générale ;
le décalage entre les deux mutations a entraîné une *augmentation importante du nombre des hommes ;*
cette augmentation a porté *d'abord sur les populations évoluées, puis sur les autres populations ;*
l'accroissement rapide de la population du monde, qui est loin d'être achevé, pose *d'importants problèmes économiques, sociaux et politiques ;*
la population des pays en avance a vieilli de façon importante, et *ce vieillissement s'étendra à l'ensemble du monde*, le dilemme impérieux est : *croître ou vieillir ;*
la population active s'est modifiée de façon importante, le nombre de personnes occupées directement ou indirectement par les soins de santé augmente en valeur absolue et en valeur relative ;
la taille et le poids des hommes ont augmenté dans les pays avancés, notamment du fait de l'amélioration alimentaire ;
la puberté est plus précoce ;
l'inégalité d'accroissement des diverses populations a entraîné des *changements de répartition selon le groupe ethnique, la langue, la religion, etc. ;*
l'état sanitaire s'est notablement amélioré à âge égal, mais le vieillissement a joué en sens inverse, en augmentant la morbidité de l'ensemble de la population ;
l'éclatement des isolats et la réduction de la consanguinité ont été un facteur génétique améliorant ;
le problème de la contre-sélection reste posé.

La valeur des résultats exposés dans cette étude est très inégale; la précision et la fiabilité sont supérieures pour les changements quantitatifs, car les changements qualitatifs sont plus difficiles à mesurer et à interpréter.

Résumé

Une importante mutation, qu'on peut placer au XVIIIᵉ siècle, a touché l'humanité. Le fait essentiel est que la lutte contre la mort, sans efficacité générale jusque-là, a bénéficié de thérapeutiques nouvelles, suivies de résultats. Aux progrès de la médecine et de l'hygiène se sont ajoutés des progrès économiques et sociaux.

Changements quantitatifs

De 25 ans environ, chiffre multimillénaire, la vie moyenne de l'homme est passée, en deux siècles, à 70 dans les pays évolués. Le nombre de survivants à 20 ans, pour 100 naissances, a doublé passant de 48 à 96. A 75 ans, le nombre de survivants a été multiplié par 14 et à 85 ans par 56.

Dans la plupart des pays peu évolués, le progrès ne s'est manifesté, de façon notable, que depuis la Seconde Guerre; les techniques antinatales et les techniques économiques se sont répandues dans ces pays moins vite que les techniques antimortelles, ce qui a posé des problèmes difficiles.

Sans qu'on puisse annoncer son arrêt, après deux siècles aussi bien employés, on peut estimer que la baisse de la mortalité va subir un net ralentissement.

La fertilité ou fécondité physiologique n'a pas changé (réserve faite sur les meilleures conditions de grossesse et d'accouchement), mais, dans les pays avancés, la fécondité a fortement diminué sous l'influence des progrès des techniques antinatales et de leur diffusion.

Ces changements ont eu une grande influence sur les populations, en nombre et en structure.

En termes de *nombre*, un accroissement considérable s'est produit, qu'on peut schématiquement diviser en deux temps: Au XIXᵉ siècle, la progression a concerné surtout les populations d'origine européenne, alors qu'au XXᵉ siècle, elle a touché davantage les pays peu évolués. Pour ceux-ci, le rythme de la multiplication naturelle (qu'on peut estimer à 1 % environ) a été très largement dépassé, des rythmes de 3 %, ou même 3,5 %, par an étant couramment observés.

En termes de *structure*, les populations avancées ont subi un vieillissement sans précédent, la proportion de sexagénaires ayant à peu près triplé, passant de 6 % environ à 18 %.

Du fait de la baisse de la mortalité, tous les pays du monde se trouvent devant le dilemme, purement arithmétique, «croître ou vieillir».

Changements qualitatifs

Laissant maintenant l'âge de côté, nous voyons de sensibles changements physiques, augmentation de la taille, du poids, avancement de la puberté, toujours dans les pays avancés, et d'importantes transformations intellectuelles, culturelles, professionnelles.

D'autre part, l'accroissement de nombre a été inégal selon les groupes ethniques, modifiant la proportion des langues, des religions, etc.

L'amélioration sanitaire est fort nette, à âge égal, du moins dans les pays évolués, mais le vieillissement agit en sens inverse. L'éclatement des isolats a joué génétiquement un rôle favorable. Longtemps contesté, à juste titre, le phénomène de la contre-sélection due au recul de la mort n'est plus à exclure totalement aujourd'hui.

Summary

The 18th century witnessed important changes in man's condition. In a nutshell, efforts to combat disease, largely unsuccessful until then, benefited from the application of new forms of treatment. Indeed, progress was made not only in medicine and general hygiene but also in economic and social spheres.

Quantitative changes

In 200 years, the life expectancy of man has risen from 25, the average throughout thousands of years, to 70 in developed countries. The number of people surviving until 20 has doubled from 48 to 96 per 100 births, while the number living till 75 has multiplied 14 times, and those living till 85, 56 times.

In most underdeveloped countries, there was, until after the Second World War, little evidence of this progress. In the meantime, however, birth control and relative economic prosperity have spread to these areas too, although less rapidly than methods of keeping people alive, a discrepancy that has given rise to certain difficult problems.

Without prophesying a complete halt in the decline of the mortality rate after two such rewarding centuries, it is possible to foresee a slight falling-off in the tendency.

The fecundity of the human race has not changed (though there has been an improvement in conditions governing pregnancy and confinement), but in developed countries, the extensive application of modern methods of birth control has considerably reduced fertility.

These changes have had a marked influence on the structure and numbers of all races.

Numerically, the world's population has shown a substantial growth at two particular times in history: the 19th century, when numbers rose increasingly among peoples of European origin, and the 20th century, when it was the turn rather of the underdeveloped countries. There, the natural birthrate, estimated at about 1 %, has been exceeded by a wide margin and now lies between 3 % and 3.5 % per annum.

Structurally, the populations of advanced countries have aged to an unprecedented degree, the percentage of sexagenarians having almost tripled from about 6 % to 18 %.

And now, owing to the low mortality rate, all countries are faced with the same, purely arithmetical dilemma: to have a growing or just an ageing population?

Qualitative changes

Apart from changing age patterns, we may also observe marked physical changes in the populations of advanced countries, e.g. an increase in average height and weight, and earlier puberty. There have also been important shifts in intellectual, cultural and professional patterns.

On the other hand, not all ethnic groups have grown at the same rate. Consequently, there has been a modification of the numerical importance of certain languages, religions, etc. Comparatively speaking, there has been, at least in advanced countries, an indubitable improvement in matters of health, but the greater age of today's population has tended to counteract this development. The elimination of barriers surrounding social and geographical isolates has had distinct genetic advantages. The idea of counter-selection, inspired by the low mortality rate and so long and so justly called in question, can no longer be totally excluded nowadays.

Zusammenfassung

Das 18. Jahrhundert ist für die Menschheit durch eine entscheidende Wende gekennzeichnet. Wesentlicher Faktor dabei ist, daß der bis dahin im allgemeinen aussichtslose Kampf gegen den Tod von der Erschließung neuer therapeutischer Mittel profitieren konnte, die zu entsprechenden Resultaten führte. Und im Zuge der sich einstellenden Fortschritte in der Medizin und Hygiene folgten solche auf wirtschaftlichem und auf sozialem Gebiet.

Quantitative Veränderungen

Von etwa 25 Jahren (eine für etliche Jahrtausende gültige Zahl) ist die durchschnittliche Lebenserwartung des Menschen in den Ländern der zivilisierten Welt innert zweier Jahrhunderte auf 70 Jahre angestiegen. Die Anzahl Überlebender bei 20 Jahren, bezogen auf 100 Geburten, hat sich von 48 auf 96 verdoppelt; diejenige für das Alter von 75 hat sich um 14 und jene von 85 Jahren um 56 vervielfacht.

In den meisten weniger entwickelten Ländern hat sich der Fortschritt erst seit dem Zweiten Weltkrieg in bemerkenswerter Weise manifestiert. Da die Techniken der Geburtenverhütung und der Ökonomie eine langsamere Verbreitung fanden als die Errungenschaften der Medizin in der Bekämpfung der Sterblichkeit, ergab sich eine Reihe schwer lösbarer Probleme.

Wenn auch ein Stagnieren nach zwei derart erfolgbringenden Jahrhunderten nicht abzusehen ist, so läßt sich doch erkennen, daß der weitere Rückgang der Sterblichkeit einer merklichen Verlangsamung unterworfen sein wird.

Die Fertilität, das heißt die physiologische Fruchtbarkeit, ist unverändert geblieben (vorbehaltlich der verbesserten Bedingungen für Schwangerschaft und Entbindung), doch dank der Wirksamkeit und Verbreitung moderner Techniken der Empfängnisverhütung hat die Fruchtbarkeit in den hochentwickelten Ländern erheblich abgenommen.

Diese Veränderungen nun haben einen großen Einfluß auf die Populationen ausgeübt, sowohl hinsichtlich Zahl wie Struktur.

Hinsichtlich der *Zahl* fand eine beträchtliche Bevölkerungszunahme statt, welche sich schematisch in zwei Zeitabschnitte unterteilen läßt: Waren es im 19. Jahrhundert in erster Linie die Völker europäischen Ursprungs, die der Fortschritt betraf, so erfuhren ihn im 20. Jahrhundert mehr die unterentwickelten Länder. Für diese ist der Rhythmus der natürlichen Vermehrung (den man auf etwa 1% schätzen kann) weitgehend überschritten. Für gewöhnlich wurden Rhythmen zwischen 3% und 3,5% pro Jahr beobachtet.

Hinsichtlich der *Struktur* zeigten die hochentwickelten Völker eine bislang unerreichte Alterungsquote. Das prozentuale Verhältnis der Sechziger hat sich von 6% auf ungefähr 18% fast verdreifacht.

Das Absinken der Mortalitätsrate konfrontiert in der Tat alle Nationen der Erde mit dem gleichen, rein rechnerischen Dilemma: «Wachstum oder Überalterung».

Qualitative Veränderungen

Neben dem gerade angesprochenen Altersfaktor lassen sich spürbare Wandlungen in der Körperkonstitution des Menschen erkennen, zum Beispiel Zunahme der Körpergröße, des Gewichts und früheres Eintreten der Pubertät. Es gab aber auch Umgestaltungen intellektueller, kultureller und beruflicher Art. Dies alles stets in bezug auf die fortschrittlich entwickelten Länder gesehen.

Andererseits war die zahlenmäßige Zunahme nach ethnischen Gruppen ungleichmäßig, wodurch die Verhältniszahlen bestimmter Sprachen, Religionen usw. modifiziert wurden.

Obwohl der Gesundheitszustand der Bevölkerung gleicher Altersgruppen, zumindest in den hochentwickelten Ländern, einen deutlichen Aufschwung erfuhr, wirkt sich doch das Altern eher im umgekehrten Sinne aus. Das Erschließen von Isolierungsbereichen hat sich genetisch günstig ausgewirkt. Lange Zeit wohl zu Recht bestritten, ist das Phänomen der Kontraselektion auf Grund der rückläufigen Sterblichkeitsziffer heute nicht mehr gänzlich von der Hand zu weisen.

Resumen

El siglo XVIII marca una nueva etapa en la historia de la humanidad. Lo esencial fue el hecho que la lucha contra la muerte, generalmente vana hasta entonces, se benefició de terapéuticas nuevas, dando el consiguiente resultado. Al avance de la medicina y de la higiene añadióse el progreso económico y social.

Cambios cuantitativos

La vida media, que durante varios milenios duraba unos 25 años, pasó en dos siglos a 70 años en los países adelantados. El número de sobrevivientes, por 100 nacimientos, duplicóse a la edad de 20 años, aumentanto de 48 a 96, multiplicándose por 14 a la edad de 75 años, y por 56 a la de 85 años.

En la mayoría de los países menos avanzados, este fenómeno no se hizo manifiesto sino después de la segunda guerra mundial; las técnicas tendientes a disminuir la natalidad y el progreso económico cundieron con menor rapidez en esos países que los avances de la medicina contra la mortalidad, planteando así difíciles problemas.

Aunque no es de suponer que esta evolución se detenga un día, sí cabe afirmar que después de dos siglos, tan bien aprovechados, la mortalidad decrecerá a un ritmo sensiblemente más lento.

Si bien la fecundidad fisiológica no ha sido afectada (salvo la debida a mejores condiciones durante el embarazo y el parto), la natalidad, en los países adelantados, ha disminuido considerablemente con los progresos de la contracepción y de su difusión.

Estas modificaciones han influido grandemente sobre la estructura y el número de la población.

Numéricamente, el incremento ha sido notable, y a grandes rasgos puede decirse que éste se ha efectuado en dos tiempos: primero, en el siglo XIX, afectando principalmente a los pueblos de origen europeo, luego, en el siglo XX, más a los países en vías de desarrollo. Estos, cuyo crecimiento natural aproximadamente de 1%, sobrepasaron en mucho dicha ṭasa, llegando a ser corrientes índices de 3% e incluso 3,5% por año.

En lo que atañe a la *estructura*, los pueblos adelantados experimentaron un envejecimiento sin precedentes; la proporción de sexagenarios, por ejemplo, triplicó casi, pasando de 6% a aproximadamente 18%. Este descenso de la mortalidad ha colocado a todos los países del mundo ante el dilema: aumentar en número o envejecer.

Cambios cualitativos

Aparte de la edad, nótanse en los países avanzados modificaciones importantes de los caracteres físicos – aumento en la talla y en el peso, pubertad más precoz – y también de los de orden intelectual, cultural y profesional.

Con el crecimiento desigual de los diversos grupos étnicos, varió asimismo la proporción y extensión de las lenguas, religiones, etc.

Si la salud ha mejorado en forma muy notable en la población de igual edad – al menos en los países desarrollados –, el envejecimiento ha influido más bien en sentido inverso. La apertura de los grupos aislados ha sido favorable desde el punto de vista genético. Con el descenso de la mortalidad no se puede descartar ya del todo el fenómeno de la contraselección, mucho tiempo negado, quizás con razón.

Disponibilité des drogues psychotropes et attitudes de la société envers les troubles du comportement

par Pierre Pichot

Existe-t-il une relation entre la disponibilité des drogues psychotropes et l'attitude de la société envers les troubles du comportement? Dans le cadre d'une réunion consacrée au progrès biomédical, il nous paraît d'abord nécessaire de restreindre la discussion, pour l'essentiel, d'une part à la culture que l'on peut appeler occidentale ou industrielle, et d'autre part à la période contemporaine, c'est-à-dire à celle où la chimie et la pharmacologie ont mis à la disposition du public un grand nombre de drogues psychotropes actives. Il reste entendu que les termes de cette limitation ne doivent pas être considérés de manière trop rigide. Lorsque nous parlons de culture «occidentale», ceci inclut un pays tel que le Japon, qui a fourni des données importantes sur le problème lors de l'«épidémie» de toxicomanies aux amphétamines, qui a suivi la dernière guerre mondiale. Nous nous réservons de plus de nous référer à des faits antérieurs à la période que l'on fait habituellement débuter en 1952, date à partir de laquelle le terme de drogue psychotrope et celui de psychopharmacologie ont été introduits. Ces réserves faites, la question peut être schématiquement posée sur deux plans.

La biochimie et la pharmacologie créent à un rythme rapide des drogues psychotropes dans le but de traiter les troubles du comportement. Leur emploi a entraîné des modifications considérables de la psychiatrie. Du fait des résultats thérapeutiques obtenus, elles ont poussé à une transformation graduelle des cadres institutionnels d'exercice de cette branche de la médecine. L'apparition chez les psychiatres d'attitudes théoriques divergentes vis-à-vis du comportement, renforçant chez les uns une position médico-biologique, poussant les autres vers une conception purement socio-génétique, qui débouche à l'extrême sur la négation même d'une pathologie du comportement chez les tenants de l'antipsychiatrie, bien que leurs sources soient anciennes et multiples, peuvent être reliées par des voies diverses au développement de la psychopharmacologie. Enfin, bien que la représentation populaire des maladies se modifie en général avec une extrême lenteur, il ne fait pas de doute que la découverte de drogues psychotropes efficaces joue un rôle dans l'évolution des attitudes du public, telles qu'elles peuvent s'exprimer directement dans les demandes présentées par les malades eux-mêmes, par leur famille ou leur entourage et indirectement dans les articles des journaux non spécialisés et dans les mesures législatives proposées, reflets plus souvent d'attitudes sociales générales que d'éléments strictement techniques.

Mais, à côté de ce qu'on peut appeler le versant thérapeutique licite, la disponibilité des drogues psychotropes a entraîné une augmentation de leur consommation à des fins dont la nature thérapeutique peut être contestée, ou qui sont absolument étrangères aux applications médicales. La limite est difficile à fixer, car aussi bien on passe insensiblement de la prescription médicale d'une drogue tranquillisante chez une malade présentant une anxiété pathologique à l'auto-administration incontrôlée de ce même tranquillisant afin de supprimer un état psychologique déplaisant résultant d'un conflit normal de l'existence et finalement à l'abus entraînant pharmacodépendance et troubles du comportement nuisibles à l'individu et à la société. Bien que le problème soit très antérieur à l'expansion psychopharmacologique et que certaines des drogues soulevant les controverses les plus actuelles sous l'angle sociologique soient des produits naturels, de connaissance et d'usage très anciens, les progrès biomédicaux lui ont donné une dimension nouvelle et l'attitude de la société se trouve aujourd'hui dans une phase évolutive cruciale à leur égard.

1. Définition et classification des drogues psychotropes

Les drogues psychotropes sont des substances dont l'introduction dans l'organisme modifie le psychisme. Sont exclues en principe de ce cadre: a. les substances qui ne provoquent des modifications psychologiques qu'au cours d'intoxications graves: l'insuline en surdosage entraînant des troubles de la conscience allant jusqu'au coma ou l'oxyde de carbone induisant des troubles de la mémoire particuliers par l'intermédiaire de lésions cérébrales spécifiques; b. les analgésiques type aspirine; c. les drogues dont l'action essentielle se situe dans un autre domaine et qui n'ont que très accessoirement, et à titre d'effets secondaires, une action sur le psychisme. Cependant ces limites sont difficiles à fixer. Ainsi les anesthésiques généraux, employés normalement pour induire une perte de conscience, ont pu être utilisés à dose infra-anesthésique pour provoquer l'ivresse: éther, chloroforme, protoxyde d'azote. Certains analgésiques-antipyrétiques sont susceptibles d'engendrer une dépendance appelée par Wilson (1965) «type aspirine» et ont éventuellement, dans le cas de la phénacétine par exemple, des propriétés psychotropes telles qu'il existe une *Phenacetinsucht* (Kielholz, 1957). Enfin l'action psychotrope secondaire de drogues ayant un domaine d'action très éloigné est attestée par leur emploi par les toxicomanes: certains antiparkinsoniens de synthèse.

En pratique, on rassemble sous le terme de drogues psychotropes des substances qui, par leur origine et leur utilisation, peuvent être classées en trois catégories:

1° Des substances découvertes en vue d'applications médico-psychologiques, employées uniquement comme médicaments, sur prescription médicale, et ne donnant pas l'occasion d'abus: par exemple la chlorpromazine ou les antidépresseurs (tricycliques et inhibiteurs de la MAO).

2° Des substances découvertes en vue d'application médicale, employées comme médicaments, mais également utilisées spontanément par certains sujets à cause de leur action psychotrope, sans que le but en soit de lutter contre un état pathologique. Cette classe, très nombreuse, comprend aussi bien la morphine que certains anxiolytiques, des hypnotiques barbituriques, les amphétamines, etc.

3° Des substances dont la valeur thérapeutique est *actuellement* considérée comme faible ou nulle et dont l'emploi est non médical. Il faut là distinguer:

a. Celles d'origine naturelle (habituellement végétale) dont la consommation est considérée comme normale depuis très longtemps dans une culture définie. De ce fait elles n'y sont généralement pas incluses parmi les «drogues». L'exemple le plus typique dans notre culture occidentale est l'alcool ingéré sous forme de boissons alcoolisées. Il n'a pratiquement aucune valeur thérapeutique, bien que celle-ci ait été affirmée (les codex actuels contiennent encore des préparations à base de vins). Sa consommation n'est généralement soumise à aucune restriction bien que les conséquences de son abus puissent être considérables pour l'individu et la société. Les essais de contrôle de l'emploi de cette classe de drogues sont relativement inefficaces en raison de l'ancienneté de leur implantation dans les modèles culturels (par exemple les diverses prohibitions totales ou partielles par mesures législatives). Seule une transformation culturelle profonde obtient un résultat: l'introduction de la religion musulmane a pratiquement supprimé l'usage du vin dans une zone géographique où il était «normal». Dans notre culture occidentale les boissons contenant de la caféine (café, thé), le tabac appartiennent à cette classe.

b. Celles de même nature mais qui, provenant d'une culture où elles étaient «normales», sont introduites dans un milieu différent. Au XVIe siècle, c'était en Europe la situation du tabac. Elément de la culture indienne précolombienne, présenté initialement comme médicament puis, devant l'extension de son emploi manifestement non thérapeutique, objet d'interdictions diverses et inefficaces, il est aujourd'hui autorisé malgré sa nocivité indirecte pour la santé de l'individu. Le cannabis peut être mis en parallèle: consommé en Asie et en Afrique par environ 200 millions d'individus (enquête des Nations Unies, 1950), son utilisation a été et est considérée comme «normale» dans certaines cultures (on peut rappeler que jusqu'en 1953/1954 sa vente en Tunisie et au Maroc était libre et dépendait d'un monopole d'Etat). Ce n'est pas que, dans ces pays, il n'y ait pas eu, comme pour l'alcool en Occident, des tentatives de prohibition: par les chefs de l'islam en Afrique du Nord entre le XIe et le XVe siècle, par Napoléon en Egypte en 1800, par les gouvernements tunisien et marocain en 1953/1954, mais ces tentatives ont eu une efficacité limitée. Le cannabis, depuis une dizaine d'années, a été introduit sur une large échelle dans les pays de culture occidentale où jusqu'alors il n'avait fait l'objet que d'une consommation épisodique de quelques éléments marginaux (certains artistes romantiques en

France), et ce malgré les mesures de prohibition prises. Sans discuter ici des dangers éventuels que peut présenter son emploi, il est manifeste que sur le plan historique le cannabis se trouve aujourd'hui dans la situation du tabac au XVIe siècle.

c. Celles nécessitant des manipulations chimiques pour leur extraction, voire entièrement synthétisées. Dans certains cas leur importance thérapeutique a pu être réelle, mais ne l'est plus. D'autres fois elle a toujours été nulle. La cocaïne constitue à cet égard un premier exemple. La mastication de la feuille de coca est culturellement «normale» chez les Indiens des Andes: le Pérou produisait en 1968 officiellement 9000 tonnes de feuilles de cocaïer. L'emploi de la feuille ne s'est jamais étendu à d'autres cultures. Mais l'isolement par les pharmacologues de la cocaïne, qui est un anesthésique de contact, a entraîné, à cause de son action psychotrope, son emploi non médical à partir de la fin du XIXe siècle. Aujourd'hui son utilité thérapeutique est pratiquement nulle. Elle peut donc être considérée comme un cas intermédiaire entre le groupe précédent (du fait qu'elle était «normale» dans une certaine culture et qu'elle a été introduite dans une autre) et le groupe que nous envisageons (du fait que son introduction en Occident a été lié à l'isolement du produit actif à partir de la préparation naturelle).

Un deuxième exemple est la lysergamide (diéthylamide de l'acide lysergique). Produit de demi-synthèse dont l'intérêt théorique en médecine expérimentale est indiscutable, mais dont les applications pratiques sont minimes ou nulles, il a rapidement été employé pour ses propriétés psychotropes en dehors de toute indication médicale.

Les trois catégories de drogues psychotropes posent des problèmes d'ordre différent. Schématiquement on peut opposer la première, celle des substances thérapeutiques ne donnant pas l'occasion d'abus, et les deux autres qui ont en commun d'engendrer éventuellement la pharmacodépendance. Alors que la découverte des substances appartenant à la première a eu pour conséquence de modifier très profondément les aspects institutionnels de la psychiatrie et, par voie de conséquence, certaines attitudes de la société vis-à-vis de la maladie mentale, la diffusion des drogues engendrant éventuellement la pharmacodépendance a aussi influé sur l'attitude sociale, mais dans un domaine différent, celui des troubles du comportement qu'elles engendrent. Le problème est particulièrement complexe en ce qui concerne la deuxième catégorie, du fait de sa position intermédiaire. Douées d'une utilité thérapeutique, mais susceptibles d'être utilisées à des fins non médicales, les drogues qui en font partie méritent de ce fait une discussion particulière.

2. Les drogues psychotropes à emploi uniquement thérapeutique

On fixe habituellement à 1952, lorsque fut introduit le premier neuroleptique, la chlorpromazine, l'origine de ce qu'on a appelé l'«ère psychopharmacologique» en psychiatrie. On peut certes faire remarquer qu'avant cette date existaient déjà des médicaments psychotropes, aussi bien sédatifs-hypnotiques que stimulants. On peut également rappeler que, dans le domaine des troubles majeurs du comportement, des psychoses, trois traitements biologiques indiscutablement efficaces avaient été introduits entre 1920 et 1940, la malaria-thérapie dans la paralysie générale, l'insulinothérapie dans la schizophrénie, l'électrochoc dans la dépression mélancolique. Mais il n'en reste pas moins que c'est à partir de 1952 que des drogues agissant dans les différentes variétés de psychoses, schizophréniques et affectives, apparaissent et deviennent d'un emploi généralisé, transformant en quelques années la pratique de la médecine mentale. Initialement les résistances sont très fortes. En 1960 encore, dans le *Handbook of Abnormal Psychology*, édité par H. J. Eysenck, le chapitre intitulé «The effects of drugs on behaviour» se termine par le paragraphe suivant: «Perhaps this brief and somewhat sceptical account has done less than justice to the latest «new era» in psychiatry. The reader may like to judge after consulting a recent paper by Little (1958), containing an account of a well-controlled «double-blind comparison of the effects of chlorpromazine, barbiturate and »placebo in one hundred and forty-two chronic psychotic inpatients». There were non-significant differences between the three treatments.» A la même époque de bons esprits soutenaient que les progrès constatés ne dépendaient pas de l'action des drogues, mais de l'introduction, qui avait été relativement contemporaine, de méthodes sociothérapiques. A l'heure actuelle il n'existe plus guère de voix discordantes. Tout le monde reconnaît le rôle éminent de la chimiothérapie par les neuroleptiques et les antidépresseurs en psychiatrie. Leur action est certes purement symptomatique, et les mécanismes neurophysiologiques qui la sous-tendent restent en partie conjecturaux, mais les conséquences pratiques suivantes sont désormais bien établies:

a. Chez les malades qui restent hospitalisés, les drogues diminuent notablement l'intensité des anomalies du comportement, supprimant en grande partie l'agitation (et par conséquent la nécessité de contention), les anomalies de l'humeur et les manifestations délirantes. De ce fait se trouve transformée l'atmosphère générale des services, se trouvent augmentées les possibilités de contact psychothérapique et favorisées les tentatives de resocialisation par thérapeutique occupationnelle.

b. La durée d'hospitalisation est en moyenne diminuée. Si, dans certains cas, une hospitalisation prolongée reste nécessaire, les malades bénéficient néanmoins à l'intérieur de l'hôpital d'un niveau de fonctionnement supérieur à celui qui aurait été le leur en l'absence de chimiothérapie; pour d'autres il est possible d'atteindre un niveau compatible avec un retour dans la société, quitte, lors de rechutes, à envisager une réhospitalisation de durée limitée. Statistiquement cette évolution s'est traduite par les faits suivants: arrêt de la croissance constante du nombre de lits occupés par des malades mentaux dans les pays industrialisés, puis, dans certains cas, régression légère de ce nombre; diminution de la durée moyenne de séjour à l'hôpital; augmentation du pourcentage de réadmissions par rapport au nombre de premières admissions. L'aspect évolutif des psychoses chroniques, qui constituent la masse de l'hospitalisation psychiatrique, s'est ainsi transformé: l'évolution d'une seule tenue, autrefois habituelle, a été souvent remplacée par une évolution par poussées entrecoupées de périodes d'adaptation satisfaisantes dans le milieu social normal. L'augmentation de ce fait des réhospitalisations (qui a fait parler de manière critique de *revolving door policy*) ne doit pas dissimuler le fait que le temps total passé par le malade dans son milieu social normal a été notablement allongé.

c. Le nombre de malades traités en milieu extra-hospitalier, soit entre les périodes d'hospitalisation, soit de manière permanente chez ceux auxquels la chimiothérapie permet le maintien d'un niveau adaptatif convenable, a entraîné la modification des structures de soins.

Bien que ces effets ne se soient fait sentir que depuis une dizaine d'années, les conséquences qu'ils ont eues sur les attitudes vis-à-vis des troubles du comportement sont sensibles et nombreuses.

Les unes concernent les psychiatres.

L'idée que les troubles majeurs du comportement peuvent être envisagés suivant le modèle médical général, qu'ils dépendent en dernière analyse d'une perturbation biochimique du système nerveux central, est ancienne et a déjà été soutenue avec autorité à la fin du XIXᵉ siècle par Kraepelin (et aussi, paradoxalement, par Freud). Mais ceci restait une prise de position théorique, non confirmée par les résultats empiriques. Les effets de la chimiothérapie des psychoses ont apporté un argument difficile à réfuter, fourni un point de départ à des hypothèses précises et stimulé l'intérêt pour les recherches. Il était habituel de considérer jusqu'alors une position organiciste en psychiatrie comme associée à un conservatisme pessimiste – ce qui était partiellement vrai au XIXᵉ siècle et au début du XXᵉ lorsque postuler une base organique aux troubles mentaux équivalait pratiquement à leur attribuer une origine lésionnelle et, par conséquent, à admettre leur incurabilité. Désormais, et du fait de la disponibilité des médicaments psychotropes, admettre l'existence de perturbations fonctionnelles biochimiques – position organiciste – va au contraire de pair avec l'optimisme thérapeutique. Peut-être est-il possible de trouver un parallèle à ce phénomène dans le domaine de la génétique avec l'accent désormais mis sur la biochimie moléculaire.

L'augmentation de la proportion des malades pouvant sortir de l'hôpital, mais devant pourtant continuer à recevoir un traitement continu a entraîné un déplacement du centre de gravité des structures de soins. Il est compréhensible que ceci amène les centres psychiatriques à n'être plus des «asiles» éloignés des agglomérations urbaines, mais des services actifs au même titre que ceux des autres spécialités, installés dans le cadre d'hôpitaux généraux. Il est également certain que la proportion des médecins et des personnels paramédicaux (infirmières, travailleurs sociaux, etc.) engagés dans les traitements ambulatoires (en dispensaire ou à domicile) doit augmenter. Tout ceci entraîne des problèmes administratifs et financiers d'une très grande ampleur dans la plupart des pays industriels. L'abandon des «asiles psychiatriques» (parallèle à celui des sanatoriums depuis l'ère de la chimiothérapie antituberculeuse) et l'installation d'organismes actifs proches des populations concernées en sont les éléments essentiels. Cette évolution a poussé, par un mouvement naturel et sans doute excessif, ceux qui se trouvent à la pointe des tendances dénommées aux Etats-Unis *community psychiatry* (qui existent sous d'autres noms dans les autres pays) à prévoir la disparition totale de la psychiatrie hospitalière. Paradoxalement se trouve souvent passé sous silence dans ces plaidoyers le rôle de la chimiothérapie dans le déclenchement de cette évolution. Les extrapolations sont dangereuses en ce domaine. Dans les conditions actuelles, une part importante des troubles du comportement est inaccessible à la chimiothérapie et est difficilement modifiable. Si l'on se réfère aux statistiques françaises d'hospitalisation publique pour l'année 1968, on trouve, sur un effectif total de 116000 lits psychiatriques, les pourcentages suivants d'occupation pour les catégories les plus importantes:

		Hommes	Femmes	Moyenne et total	
Accessibles à la chimiothérapie	psychoses thymiques	5%	11%	8%	47%
	psychoses schizophréniques et délirantes	36%	42%	39%	
Non accessibles à la chimiothérapie	démences	5%	13%	9%	28%
	retard mental	23%	16%	19%	
	alcoolisme	15%	5%	10%	

Si, grâce aux progrès de nos connaissances dans la biochimie des psychoses fonctionnelles, toutes les psychoses thymiques et schizophréniques quittaient les hôpitaux psychiatriques, ceci laisserait encore en place 50% des effectifs. Les troubles du comportement à base en général lésionnelle (démences et retard mental) occupent à elles seules 30% des lits (non comptées les institutions pour enfants). Or leur nombre aura certainement tendance à augmenter, d'une part, du fait de l'intolérance croissante des structures sociales urbaines à leur égard et, d'autre part, en ce qui concerne les démences, du fait du vieillissement de la population. Malgré ces réserves, la période qui dure maintenant depuis 150 ans et qui a été caractérisée par le «renfermement» des sujets présentant des troubles graves du comportement dans des établissements isolés touche certainement à sa fin, et ceci essentiellement grâce aux modifications des attitudes des psychiatres provoquées, souvent inconsciemment, par la disponibilité de drogues psychotropes. Les structures les mieux appropriées à la nouvelle situation ne sont pas encore clairement définies et évolueront probablement en fonction des découvertes ultérieures (il n'est pas *a priori* impossible que les progrès de la biochimie mettent à notre disposition des moyens de prévenir l'apparition des lésions cérébrales causes des démences, aujourd'hui strictement irréversibles). Mais de toute manière la période actuelle constitue un moment privilégié dans l'évolution des attitudes médicales.

Les autres conséquences des effets de la chimiothérapie des psychoses concernent le public.

Nous possédons très peu d'études objectives sur l'attitude vis-à-vis des maladies, et spécialement des maladies mentales, et il est toujours très dangereux de généraliser en ce domaine à partir de constatations isolées. On peut cependant considérer qu'elle peut s'exprimer dans les articles de la presse non spécialisée et dans les décisions des instances gouvernementales et judiciaires (celles-ci subissant en outre l'influence de l'opinion d'experts). Mais surtout on peut inférer les modifications d'attitudes à partir du comportement du public vis-à-vis des institutions médicales.

Le problème de la presse nous retiendra peu. Un relevé des articles montre qu'ils sont centrés sur deux thèmes d'ailleurs rigoureusement contradictoires: celui de la dangerosité potentielle qui incite, à l'occasion d'un crime dont l'auteur est un malade mental, à réclamer des dispositions plus rigoureuses de séquestration et celui du danger de privation de liberté sous prétexte de maladie, qui justifie les campagnes contre les internements arbitraires. Il s'agit là de positions anciennes et stéréotypées, dans lesquelles il est impossible de discerner une tendance évolutive.

Par contre il est manifeste que les mesures administratives et judiciaires nouvelles reflètent une transformation profonde des idées. D'une manière générale, on assiste à une «libéralisation» progressive des dispositions, qui tend à rapprocher le statut légal du malade mental de celui du malade somatique. Comme l'a souligné T. Parsons, le rôle du malade, corrélatif de son statut, comprend l'obligation de désirer guérir et celle de coopérer avec le médecin dans ce but. Or un des éléments définissant la maladie mentale grave est la perte de contact avec la réalité, donc pour l'individu la possibilité de voir où est son intérêt. La société est amenée, comme dans le cas de l'enfant, à substituer une volonté extérieure à celle du malade, à se passer de son consentement. La privation de liberté par décision sociale n'est dans cette perspective qu'apparente, puisqu'en fait le psychotique est déjà privé de liberté par sa maladie même. Telle est la justification de l'internement dans la majorité des cas (la notion de dangerosité est à l'origine d'une autre variété d'internement, beaucoup plus rare et dont le fondement social est radicalement différent). Il est remarquable qu'alors que le nombre des malades mentaux traités augmente constamment, celui des internements diminue, et ce dans des proportions souvent considérables. Ceci est lié évidemment à une modification des attitudes, qui se reflète dans les décisions administratives et judiciaires (Brill faisait remarquer en 1967 que dans l'Etat de New York la procédure d'internement était devenue très difficile à obtenir pour les psychoses). S'il est vrai que la tendance est ancienne, son accélération actuelle doit probablement beaucoup à l'introduction de la chimiothérapie. L'hospitalisation est désormais pour beaucoup de malades de brève durée. Parmi les 123000 admissions effectuées en France en 1968 dans les hôpitaux psychiatriques publics, 70% ont été suivies d'une sortie dans le courant de la même année. Cette proportion serait plus élevée si l'on tenait compte des malades mentaux hospitalisés dans les hôpitaux généraux.

L'admission à l'hôpital psychiatrique n'apparaît plus comme une mort sociale, ce qu'elle était il y a peu dans la représentation populaire. L'augmentation du nombre des malades soignés contrastant avec la diminution des internements ne peut s'expliquer que si l'on admet que nombre de malades acceptent volontairement de se soumettre à un traitement. Comme il est peu vraisemblable que l'internement, malgré des excès certains, ait été employé autrefois systématiquement alors qu'il était inutile, il faut bien admettre une modification de l'attitude des malades, reflétant la modification de l'attitude du public, et il paraît légitime d'en attribuer au moins partiellement la cause à la chimiothérapie. L'image que le public se faisait des troubles majeurs du comportement: affections incurables, nécessitant la séquestration à vie, tend à se rapprocher de celle qu'il a de la maladie en général: état curable par un traitement médical.

3. Les drogues psychotropes engendrant la pharmacodépendance

La fixation des limites de l'emploi légitime d'une drogue psychotrope est difficile, et cette difficulté est illustrée par les hésitations des textes officiels internationaux. Le comité qui, avant la guerre, s'intitulait dans le cadre de la S. d. N. «Commission consultative du trafic de l'opium et autres drogues nuisibles» est devenu successivement «Commission des drogues susceptibles d'engendrer la toxicomanie», puis, à partir de 1964, «Commission O. M. S. d'experts des drogues engendrant la dépendance». En 1969 cette commission a proposé une définition qui fixe le critère actuel, celui de pharmacodépendance: «La pharmacodépendance est un état psychique et quelquefois également physique résultant de l'interaction entre un organisme vivant et un médicament se caractérisant par des modifications du comportement et par d'autres réactions, qui comprennent toujours une pulsion à prendre le médicament de façon continue ou périodique afin de retrouver ses effets psychiques et quelquefois d'éviter le malaise de la privation. Cet état peut s'accompagner ou non de tolérance. Un même individu peut être dépendant de plusieurs médicaments.» H. Halbach, qui a contribué à l'introduction de ce terme, remarque (1968) qu'il ne contient en soi aucune indication quant au risque encouru par le sujet – et éventuellement par la société – et ceci volontairement. C'est d'ailleurs selon lui la raison qui rend sa diffusion lente: «La lenteur relative de l'incorporation générale de ce nouveau terme dans les textes de loi et dans des réglementations est due en grande partie au caractère formel de ceux-ci. Dès que l'attitude prévalant aujourd'hui envers la toxicomanie aura évolué de punitive vers une autre plus thérapeutique, ce phénomène sera reconnu partout comme une question de psycho-socio-pathologie, et le langage des lois le reflétera.»

Il est possible d'évaluer la nocivité des drogues engendrant la pharmaco-dépendance suivant des critères différents. Les pharmacologues tiennent essentiellement compte de la facilité avec laquelle elles provoquent une dépendance physique et des réactions de tolérance. Les spécialistes des toxicomanies envisagent surtout l'intensité de l'action nuisible sur le psychisme – la psychotoxicité. Ainsi dans un travail récent, se basant sur ces trois critères, Varenne (1971) propose un classement général en fonction d'une échelle de dangerosité décroissante:

	Dépendance physique	Tolérance	Psycho-toxicité
1. Type opiacés	+ +	+ + +	+ +
2. Type alcool-barbituriques-tranquillisants	+	+ ±	+ ±
3. Type amphétamines	—	+ +	+ + ±
4. Type hallucinogènes	—	±	+ + +
5. Type cocaïne	—	—	+ +
6. Type cannabis	—	—	+ ±
7. Type phénacétine	—	+	±
8. Substances volatiles	—	±	+
9. Caféine	—	±	±
10. Nicotine	—	+	—

Mais ceci ne tient pas compte de deux aspects qui jouent un rôle important dans l'attitude de l'opinion. L'un est la toxicité somatique. Ainsi le tabac, qui est classé par Varenne au dernier rang en ce qui concerne la dangerosité, est en fait très nocif en tant que facteur de risque de cancer des voies respiratoires supérieures et d'affections cardio-vasculaires, alors que les boissons contenant de la caféine, qui le précèdent sur la liste (en raison des cas exceptionnels de toxicomanie observés en Afrique du Nord), n'influent pratiquement pas sur le développement d'affections somatiques. La même remarque peut être faite pour la phénacétine dont la place ne tient pas compte des lésions rénales que sa consommation abusive provoque. Or il est manifeste que l'attitude de l'opinion publique peut éventuellement être influencée par la divulgation de ce danger somatique. L'effet de l'affichage obligatoire des propriétés cancérigènes du tabac sur la consommation des cigarettes aux Etats-Unis peut être signalé. Plus frappante encore est la baisse constatée de consommation illégale de lysergamide à la suite de l'annonce que cette drogue aurait la propriété de favoriser les aberrations chromosomiques.

Mais l'aspect qui joue probablement le rôle le plus important dans l'attitude du public est la nature des modifications du comportement provoquées par la drogue. On a bien souvent fait remarquer que la tolérance extraordinaire de notre société vis-à-vis de l'alcool, bien que celui-ci soit à lui seul à l'origine d'effets nocifs individuels et sociaux, psychiques et somatiques plusieurs fois supérieurs à ceux de toutes les autres drogues réunies, tenait en partie au fait que sa consommation produisait une augmentation de la sociabilité. Moins connu est le problème des barbituriques. Leur consommation est considérable: en 1960 les Etats-Unis en ont fabriqué 371 500 kilos, «quantité suffisante pour préparer environ six milliards de capsules d'un grain»* (Fort, 1964). Un sondage en 1961/1962 a montré que ces drogues étaient prescrites dans 11 à 12% des ordonnances. Le nombre de sujets en état de pharmacodépendance est considérable: Varenne cite les statistiques suivantes concernant le Centre d'études de prévention et de traitement de l'alcoolisme et des toxicomanies de Gand (Belgique). Sur 100 sujets toxicomanes observés, 39 le sont aux barbituriques, 13 aux tranquillisants, contre seulement 48 à toutes les autres drogues réunies. (L'alcoolisme, non inclus dans cette statistique, correspondrait, à la même échelle, à 900 sujets.) Or ni les médecins, ni le public ne tendent à condamner cette pharmacodépendance. La Commission des Stupéfiants de l'O.N.U. le note depuis 1965: «Sur le plan professionnel et commercial, les dangers de la situation sont pris trop à la légère. Il est prouvé que certains médecins prescrivent et délivrent ces drogues inconsidérément, que les particuliers se livrent à une automédication injustifiée.» Varenne, comparant les attitudes d'hostilité vis-à-vis de la consommation du cannabis à celles de tolérance vis-à-vis de celle des barbituriques, pense expliquer cette discordance en notant que «les fumeurs de cannabis sont des jeunes qui se montrent tandis que les barbituromanes sont des adultes qui se cachent». Il note d'autre part: «Les femmes abusent plus fréquemment de barbituriques que les hommes. Cela s'explique entre autres par l'attitude tolérante de la société envers la consommation de ces drogues par les femmes, en proie au surmenage domestique ou professionnel, alors que, par contre, elles se verraient sévèrement critiquées si elles noyaient leurs soucis dans l'alcool; celui-ci reste toujours une drogue dont la consommation excessive n'est concédée par l'opinion publique qu'aux hommes. Pour la femme le recours à l'ingestion de pilules ne signifie donc pas tellement le franchissement d'une barrière sociale et n'est pas réellement censuré par la coutume.» Il nous semble qu'un des éléments de cette tolérance est que la pharmacodépendance aux barbituriques ne s'accompagne pas en général de modifications du comportement considérées comme socialement nuisibles. A l'opposé notre société tend à avoir une attitude très hostile envers trois variétés de drogues: dérivés de l'opium, cannabis et hallucinogènes, amphétamines. La consommation des alcaloïdes de l'opium – de l'héroïne en particulier – entraîne une désinsertion sociale rapide; celle des amphétamines à hautes doses favorise un comportement agressif délinquant (au Japon en 1955, au sommet de la vague de toxicomanies aux amphétamines, on comptait environ 250 000 toxicomanes, 50% des meurtriers arrêtés à Tokyo à cette époque abusaient de ces drogues); quant aux hallucinogènes, il est inutile de rappeler dans quelle mesure ceux qui en préconisent la consommation la justifient en tant que moyen de protester contre la culture actuelle et d'échapper à ses contraintes. Ainsi, d'une manière générale, il semble bien que la société tende à développer des attitudes hostiles envers

---

* Soit plus de 60 capsules par individu et par an, enfants compris.

les drogues qu'elle perçoit comme favorisant des comportements jugés a-sociaux ou anti-sociaux, c'est-à-dire contraires à son système de valeurs. La disponibilité des drogues psychotropes entraîne donc une double modification des attitudes. Elle tend à «libéraliser» celles, jusque-là relativement coercitives, qui concernent les troubles pathologiques psychotiques du comportement, dans la mesure où ceux-ci, du fait de leur accessibilité à la chimiothérapie, se rapprochent du modèle médical général. Elle tend au contraire à imposer des mesures de contrainte contre les sujets consommant des drogues psychotropes et surtout dans la mesure où celles-ci favorisent des comportements en contradiction avec les modèles culturels. L'évolution actuelle de la législation dans la plupart des pays aussi bien que l'attitude de la presse non technique en témoignent.

4. Remarques concernant les drogues à action thérapeutique pouvant être utilisées à des fins non médicales

Certaines des drogues engendrant la pharmacodépendance n'ont actuellement aucune utilité thérapeutique ou n'en ont jamais possédé. Mais d'autres, qui ont été préparées en vue d'un emploi médical, ont une valeur thérapeutique. Lorsque, comme dans le cas des alcaloïdes de l'opium, leur place dans la pharmacopée est indiscutée, et dans l'état actuel de nos connaissances irremplaçable, elles posent seulement des problèmes techniques de lutte contre leur emploi abusif, en attendant que le progrès biomédical mette à la disposition de la médecine des drogues ayant les mêmes propriétés thérapeutiques sans posséder de propension toxicomanigène. (Il suffit de rappeler que ce fut le cas pour les anesthésiques de contact qui ont privé la cocaïne de son utilité.) Par contre, le problème est beaucoup plus complexe pour les drogues telles que les hypnotiques et surtout les tranquillisants. Pour eux les limites entre une prescription légitime et une administration abusive est difficile à tracer. Aussi en est-on venu à mettre en doute la justification de leur emploi, voire même des recherches les concernant, en condamnant «la propension, caractéristique pour notre époque qu'ont les gens de vouloir immédiatement pallier leurs troubles physiques ou psychiques par une automédication impromptue, tellement ils sont devenus incapables de supporter un ennui ou des sensations désagréables, et d'y remédier par des moyens peut-être moins radicaux, mais de toute façon moins dangereux, mais plus hygiéniques, plus naturels». Cette citation de Varenne est caractéristique car, provenant d'un médecin, elle fait appel à des notions qui appartiennent à la représentation populaire de la santé et de la maladie (supériorité des procédés «naturels» sur les drogues), ou à des jugements portant sur les valeurs éthiques (vertu morale de la résistance à la souffrance). C'est là un domaine où la compétence du psychiatre s'arrête. C'est en définitive la réponse que la société donnera aux questions que pose ce problème qui déterminera pour cette catégorie de drogues psychotropes l'orientation du progrès biomédical.

Résumé

Les rapports entre l'augmentation de la disponibilité de drogues psychotropes due en particulier aux progrès de la chimie et de la pharmacologie, avec
les modifications de l'attitude de la société envers les troubles du comportement
doivent être posés sur deux plans, celui de la thérapeutique licite et celui de la
consommation à des fins extramédicales.

Les drogues psychotropes peuvent être divisées en trois classes: a. celles
découvertes en vue d'applications thérapeutiques, employées uniquement
comme médicaments et ne donnant pas l'occasion d'abus: type chlorpromazine,
antidépresseurs; b. celles découvertes en vue d'applications thérapeutiques,
encore employées comme telles, mais également utilisées spontanément à des
fins extramédicales: type opiacés, hypnotiques tranquillisants; c. celles de valeur
thérapeutique faible ou nulle et d'emploi uniquement non médical. Cette dernière classe comprend des produits d'origine naturelle, dont l'emploi est institu-
tionnalisé dans une culture: type alcool éthylique, des produits de même origine, institutionnalisés dans une culture et importés dans un autre milieu culturel: type cannabis actuellement en Europe ainsi que des produits nécessitant une
manipulation chimique: types cocaïne, lysergamide.

Les drogues à emploi uniquement thérapeutique, actives sur les psychoses,
ont été à l'origine d'une révolution en psychiatrie qui a provoqué des modifications de l'attitude des psychiatres et du public. La modification des structures de
soins, la transformation des «asiles» isolés servant au «renfermement» d'un
grand nombre de sujets «aliénés» à l'écart des villes en services médicaux actifs
dans le cadre des hôpitaux généraux, la multiplication des traitements extra-
hospitaliers sont l'expression institutionnelle des nouvelles attitudes des psychiatres. La modification de l'attitude du public, quoique plus lente, aboutit progressivement à enlever à la maladie mentale son stigmate social, ce qui se reflète dans
la généralisation des traitements acceptés volontairement tant par le sujet que
par sa famille. Le statut du malade mental tend à se rapprocher de celui du
malade somatique: la maladie mentale vue autrefois comme une affection incurable nécessitant une séquestration à vie tend à se rapprocher de la conception
de la maladie en général: état curable par un traitement médical.

Les drogues engendrant la pharmacodépendance, qu'elles aient ou non
parallèlement une valeur thérapeutique, entraînent dans le public des attitudes
qui dépendent en grande partie des modifications du comportement qu'elles
provoquent. Ceci rend compte de l'extrême tolérance de la société vis-à-vis de
drogues objectivement très nocives tel l'alcool, parce qu'elles sont considérées
comme améliorant la sociabilité, et de l'hostilité contre celles considérées
comme socialement nuisibles, soit qu'elles amènent une désinsertion sociale
rapide (les dérivés de l'opium), soit qu'elles provoquent des comportements
agressifs (les amphétamines), soit qu'elles favorisent un état de non-participation sociale (le cannabis).

Ainsi l'augmentation de la disponibilité des drogues psychotropes tend-elle à faire varier l'attitude de la société dans deux directions divergentes: plus grande tolérance envers les troubles mentaux graves, dans la mesure où ceux-ci sont, grâce à la chimiothérapie, réduits au modèle médical général; plus grande hostilité envers les troubles du comportement produits par les drogues engendrant la pharmacodépendance, dans la mesure où ceux-ci sont en contradiction avec le modèle culturel.

Un cas particulier est celui des drogues pour lesquelles les limites entre prescription légitime et emploi abusif sont difficiles à tracer, tels les hypnotiques et les tranquillisants. Ici se posent essentiellement des problèmes philosophiques et éthiques vis-à-vis desquels il appartient à la société de prendre position.

Summary

The relation between increased availability of psychotropic drugs, due in particular to chemical and pharmacological progress, and changes in the attitude of society towards behavioural disorders must be viewed on two levels – that of legitimate therapy and that of consumption for non-medical purposes.

Psychotropic drugs may be divided into three categories: (a) those discovered for therapeutic applications, used exclusively as medicaments, and giving rise to no abuse (of the chlorpromazine, antidepressant type); (b) those discovered for therapeutic applications, still employed as such but also used spontaneously for extramedical purposes (of the opiate, hypnotic, tranquillizing type); (c) those of low or non-existent therapeutic value used only non-medically. This last category comprises: products of natural origin, the use of which has been institutionalized in a culture (of the ethyl alcohol type); products of the same origin, institutionalized in one culture and imported into another cultural environment (of the cannabis type now found in Europe); and products requiring chemical manipulation (of the cocaine, lysergamide type).

The drugs for purely therapeutic use which are effective in cases of psychosis were at the origin of a revolution in psychiatry which brought about changes in the attitude of psychiatrists and the public in general. The modification of the structure of psychiatric care, in particular the transformation of isolated 'asylums' used for 'locking-up' a large number of 'outcast' subjects away from the towns into active medical services within the framework of general hospitals, and the multiplication of extrahospital treatment are the institutional expression of the new attitudes adopted by psychiatrists. The change in public opinion, although slower, has gradually led to mental disease losing its social stigma – and this has been reflected by the spread of treatment voluntarily accepted both by the subject and by his family. The status of the mentally sick now tends to resemble that of the somatically sick: mental illness, at one time considered an incurable disease requiring sequestration for life, now tends to be considered in the same way as disease in general: a condition that is curable by medical treatment.

Drugs that produce pharmaco-dependency, whether or not of concomitant therapeutic value, generate an attitude in the public which depends largely on the behavioural changes they elicit. This explains the extreme tolerance of society towards certain drugs that are objectively extremely harmful such as alcohol, because they are thought to improve sociability, and the hostility of society towards those drugs considered socially harmful because they lead either to rapid social withdrawal (opium derivatives), or to aggressive behaviour (amphetamines), or because they favour a state of social non-participation (cannabis).

Thus the increased availability of psychotropic drugs tends to modify society's attitude in two divergent directions: greater tolerance towards serious mental disorders, in such measure as, thanks to chemotherapy, they are reduced to the general medical model; great hostility towards behavioural disorders caused by dependency-inducing drugs to the extent that they are contradictory to the cultural model.

A special case are those drugs for which the line between legitimate prescription and abusive use is difficult to trace, such as hypnotics and tranquillizers. This is essentially where philosophical and ethical problems arise in the face of which society must adopt a position one way or the other.

Zusammenfassung

Die Beziehungen zwischen der zunehmenden Verfügbarkeit von Psychopharmaka – hauptsächlich bedingt durch die Fortschritte von Chemie und Pharmakologie – und der veränderten Einstellung der Gesellschaft gegenüber Verhaltensstörungen müssen auf zwei Ebenen gesehen werden: auf derjenigen der legitimen Therapie einerseits und auf derjenigen des Konsums zu nichtmedizinischen Zwecken anderseits.

Die psychotropen Präparate können in drei Klassen eingeteilt werden: a. für therapeutische Anwendung entwickelte Arzneimittel, die ausschließlich als Medikamente verwendet werden und keine Möglichkeit zum Mißbrauch bieten (Chlorpromazin oder Antidepressiva); b. Verbindungen, die für therapeutische Anwendung entwickelt wurden und als solche noch verwendet werden (Opiate, Schlafmittel und Tranquillizer); c. solche von geringem oder gar keinem therapeutischem Wert und für den rein nichtmedizinischen Gebrauch. In diese letzte Kategorie gehören Produkte natürlicher Herkunft, deren Anwendung in einer Kultur einen festen Platz gefunden hat (als typisches Beispiel der Alkohol); Produkte desselben Ursprungs, die in einer Kultur üblicherweise verwendet und in ein anderes kulturelles Milieu importiert werden (wie derzeit Cannabis in Europa); schließlich Produkte, die einer chemischen Bearbeitung bedürfen (Kokain und Lysergamid).

Die Präparate, die ausschließlich therapeutisch angewendet werden – und die bei Psychosen wirksam sind –, haben in der Psychiatrie zu einer revolutionären Entwicklung geführt, deren Folge eine Veränderung der Einstellung sowohl des Psychiaters als auch des Publikums ist. Die Veränderung der Pflegestruktur, die Umwandlung der isolierten «Asyle», in denen eine große Anzahl «Geisteskranker» fern von den Städten «eingesperrt» gehalten wurden, in aktive medizinische Abteilungen im Rahmen allgemeiner Krankenhäuser, die immer häufigere ambulante Behandlung sind der institutionelle Ausdruck für die neue Einstellung der Psychiater. Die Veränderung der Einstellung des Publikums führt – wenn auch langsamer – zu einer Befreiung der Geisteskrankheit von ihrem sozialen Stigma; Ausdruck dafür ist die Zunahme freiwillig akzeptierter Behandlungen seitens des Patienten, aber auch seitens seiner Familie. Der Status des Geisteskranken nähert sich langsam dem des körperlich Kranken: Die Geisteskrankheit, die ehedem als eine unheilbare Erkrankung betrachtet wurde, die eine Absonderung auf Lebzeiten notwendig machte, ist im Begriff, sich dem Konzept der Krankheit ganz allgemein zu nähern: ein Zustand, der durch eine medizinische Behandlung heilbar ist.

Präparate, die zu einer Drogenabhängigkeit führen – mit oder ohne therapeutischen Wert –, bewirken im Publikum eine Einstellung, die weitgehend abhängt von den Verhaltensveränderungen, die sie hervorrufen. Das zeigt sich einerseits in der außergewöhnlichen Toleranz unserer Gesellschaft gegenüber objektiv sehr schädlichen Drogen, wie zum Beispiel Alkohol, weil man glaubt, diese könnten geselliger machen; anderseits in der feindlichen Haltung gegenüber jenen Drogen, die sozial gesehen als schädlich gelten – sei es, daß sie eine rasche soziale Absonderung bewirken (Opiumderivate), daß sie ein aggressives Verhalten fördern (Amphetamine), oder daß sie zu einem Zustand sozialer Desinteressiertheit führen (Cannabis).

Somit beeinflußt die zunehmende Verfügbarkeit psychotroper Drogen die Einstellung der Gesellschaft in zwei divergierenden Richtungen: größere Toleranz gegenüber den schweren Geistesstörungen in dem Maße, in welchem diese dank der Chemotherapie dem allgemeinen medizinischen Modell nähergebracht werden; größere Feindseligkeit gegenüber den Verhaltensstörungen als Folge von Drogen, die zu Abhängigkeit führen, in dem Maße, in dem diese im Widerspruch zum kulturellen Modell stehen.

Einen Spezialfall bilden jene Drogen, für die die Grenzen zwischen legitimer Verschreibung und mißbräuchlicher Verwendung schwer zu ziehen sind, wie zum Beispiel bei den Schlafmitteln und den Tranquillizern. Hier stellen sich die philosophischen und ethischen Probleme, zu denen die Gesellschaft Stellung beziehen muß.

Resumen

Las relaciones entre la disponibilidad creciente de drogas psicotropas, debida en particular a los progresos de la química y la farmacología, y la nueva actitud de la sociedad ante los trastornos del comportamiento se sitúan en dos planos: el de la terapéutica lícita y el del consumo con fines ajenos a la medicina.

Se pueden distinguir tres grupos de drogas psicotropas: a) las descubiertas para fines terapéuticos, empleadas exclusivamente como medicamentos y que no se prestan a abuso: tipo clorpromazina, antidepresivos; b) las descubiertas para aplicación terapéutica, todavía empleadas en medicina pero igualmente utilizadas para fines ajenos a ella: tipo opiáceos, hipnóticos tranquilizantes; c) las de débil o ningún valor terapéutico, no empleadas en medicina. Este último grupo comprende: productos de origen natural, cuyo uso se ha institucionalizado en alguna cultura, v. gr.: el alcohol etílico; productos del mismo origen, institucionalizados en una cultura determinada e importados en otro medio cultural, como sucede actualmente en Europa con el cannabis; productos que requieren una manipulación farmacológica, v. gr.: la cocaína, la lisergamida.

Las drogas de empleo exclusivamente terapéutico, activas sobre las psicosis, originaron una revolución en psiquiatría que ha modificado la actitud de los psiquiatras y del público en general. La nueva estructura asistencial, v. gr.: la transformación de los manicomios aislados – destinados a recluir lejos de las ciudades a numerosos sujetos «alienados» – en servicios de asistencia médica activa integrados en los hospitales generales, así como la tendencia creciente al tratamiento ambulatorio, traducen bien la presente actitud de los psiquiatras. Si bien más lento, el cambio de actitud del público contribuye progresivamente a quitarle a la enfermedad mental su estigma social, lo cual es patente en el hecho de que tanto los sujetos como sus familias aceptan el tratamiento con menos reticencia. El estatuto del enfermo mental tiende a ser similar al del enfermo somático; así, el concepto de enfermedad mental, antes considerada como una afección incurable que hacía necesaria la reclusión perpetua del paciente, se aproxima al de la enfermedad en general: es decir, que se la considera como un estado capaz de ser curado con un tratamiento médico.

Las drogas que engendran farmacodependencia, con valor terapéutico o sin él, suscitan en el público una postura que depende, en gran parte, de las alteraciones del comportamiento que puedan causar. Ello explica, por un lado, la extrema tolerancia de nuestra sociedad frente a drogas de reconocida nocividad como el alcohol, por considerarse que facilitan la comunicación humana, y, por otro, su hostilidad hacia las conceptuadas como perniciosas socialmente, ya por conducir a una rápida desintegración social (los derivados del opio), ya por provocar un comportamiento agresivo (las anfetaminas) o ya por favorecer un estado en el que el sujeto rechaza la participación social (el cannabis).

Así pues, la disponibilidad creciente de las drogas psicotropas influye en la actitud de la sociedad en dos direcciones distintas: por una parte, mayor tolerancia frente a los trastornos mentales graves, con tal de que queden reducidos a un modelo médico general gracias a la quimioterapia; por otra, mayor hostilidad hacia las alteraciones del comportamiento producidas por las drogas que engendran farmacodependencia, en la medida en que se aparten del canon cultural.

Un caso particular es el de las drogas que no permiten trazar un límite preciso entre su lícita prescripción y su empleo abusivo, como los hipnóticos y los tranquilizantes. Aquí se plantean problemas esencialmente filosóficos y éticos ante los cuales la sociedad tendrá que adoptar una posición.

Changing life patterns and the consciousness of the individual*

by Margaret Mead

Massive changes in the condition of man can be seen as signalling, or as expressed in, manifestations of individual consciousness, with a resulting change in the position of the individual in society. Changes to come may be signalled many hundreds of years in advance of a change in the position of the common man and woman, or may be concomitants of shattering changes in the life of the many. In Euro-American culture we have been accustomed to draw sustenance from the expressed insights of religious leaders and philosophers before our era, and to see most of what happens in the world as merely a fulfillment of their prophecies and hopes – whether these be the prophecy of a Last Judgement or the promise or threat of Plato's Republic. The present, interpreted through the past, has regularly assumed a mantle of inevitability; man's state is described to him and then the articulate individual has lamented or welcomed a present-day condition over which he has had little or no control. Marxism, in spite of the dynamism which is part of its essential dogma, owes a great deal of its appeal to the belief that the diagnosis of capitalist society's ills and its collapse are inevitable.

Initially, the age of science offered almost the same promise as the prophets and the philosophers; an increase in knowledge was seen as inevitable, and with it an increase in control over nature; the course of knowledge could be charted and predicted. Those who opposed the deterministic view of science – that more knowledge and control would grow in an inevitable sequence from knowledge and control – did so by assertions of counter-beliefs, by attacks on rationality itself, and by apocalyptic statements of doom. Utopian scientific futures and rejections of the world of technology which science had made possible were essentially expressions of the same state of mind or certainty within which the individual might rejoice in a hope of a different fate, abso-

---

* While I have occasionally drawn upon conditions in other modern countries, and emerging countries, as in the definition of the world-wide generation gap, the description of contemporary responses to biomedical advances has drawn primarily on American behavior. Each country supplies its own culturally distinctive use of the new discoveries and its own distinctive resistances. But as intervention in human life through various biomedical means has proceeded so very far in the United States, it also provides useful material on the kind of possible social responses which we may expect.

lutely promised, or prepare for disaster, or nothingness, absolutely promised also. We have had very little tolerance for ambiguity, for totally uncertain outcomes, outcomes in which fear and hope were the components rather than emotions appropriate to the actual state of the world.

Yet, since the mid 1940's, man is being asked to work with a different set of premises, to include within his attitude towards life that attitude itself, just as the observer must now be included within the observations he makes, and the physician within the situation of treatment. After centuries in which thinking took its form from the written page, where symbols that had limited referrants followed each other across the page, and ordered our thought into linear sequences, the supplementation of script by multi-sensory records and immediate replications of actuality now gives us opportunities of a quite different sort. The present can be seen as a stage that cannot be predicted from the past and that forms the matrix of an unpredictable future, with quite different kinds of degrees of freedom, degrees of freedom conferred upon us by our awareness of what we do.

The task of the human scientist discussing the changing condition of man becomes a different one also. However much one may describe and diagnose, it is no longer possible to project ahead, except in terms of a series of alternatives, no one of which has the kind of certainty or preference which could generate either the advocacy or violent rejection possible in the past. For the question, *what will be the consequences of the biomedical revolution for man*, one has to substitute *what is happening to man now*, how does the perception of the possible outcomes change the present? In turn, this question leads not to speculation about the future, but rather to further questions about how aware mankind is now of such speculations.

One example. The age of puberty is falling by about four months a decade. A linear projection would involve us in a nonsensical prediction. But what other kinds of prediction are there? If we accept the fact and alter our institutions, or inaugurate direct experimentation towards control of this change, either type of recognition will itself alter the condition. But those whose rhythm of growth has been facilitated by new institutions – new forms of education, or marriage, or enjoined service to the community – or altered by biomedical intervention, will differ in ways which we cannot predict from those on whose behalf we thought we were intervening. The confession or rebellion of those whose earlier puberty is recognized neither by themselves nor by society and those who are aware of what is happening are different in kind in a fashion which we do not have, at present, any way to allow for.

Whether we consider the substitution of artificial infant feeding, the use of drugs to moderate and control mental states or the control of fertility by biochemical means, in every case the concomitants of such innovations are so complex that the next step can only be enacted rather than predicted. Older approaches to the question of breast feeding versus artificial feeding dealt, for example, with the differential health of the baby, its character formation, liability to depression or freedom from ambivalence, or with the effects on the mother, who would now be freed for new types of activity. No one included two generation effects, and so the revolt in favor of breast feeding, on the one hand, or the appearance of a grandchild generation, children of mothers who had not themselves been breast-fed, who demanded new forms of contact, tactile nearness in crowds, or who found contact impossible, was not foreseen. If it had been, there still remains the question of whether the prediction could have been acted upon within the climate of opinion that produced the original rejection of breast feeding.

Or, expressed another way, we have increased our ability to describe the probability of a massive earthquake on the California Coast of the United States but not the probability of the response to it by those millions who now make their homes on top of the well-documented fault. The relationship between increased documentation of a threat and the mobilization of refusal to believe in that threat's reality is not known, and with our present research methods, not yet knowable.

Any statement that I attempt to make about the present changes in life style must be made with these ambiguities in mind. To the extent that any diagnostic statement becomes part of our present awareness of our condition, that condition itself has been altered. (This situation is often dealt with under the cliché heading of the self-fulfilling prophecy, but the actuality is far more complex. The assumption of the self-fulfilling prophecy is in fact a linear statement.)

We may, however, attempt to locate some aspects of present-day life as intimately bound up with the biomedical revolution which made our present condition possible. The biomedical revolution may be compared to the agricultural revolution which occurred some 10,000 years earlier, in that it is introducing new degrees of freedom into human life. The agricultural revolution provided man with enough surplus to allow a few members of each generation to devote their time to activities other than subsistence and parental responsibilities. The biomedical revolution has enormously increased these possibilities for both sexes, as the proportion of the children who live to the children who are born steadily increases. The population explosion and the threats to the quality of life, which are now recognized, have altered the focus on the increase of population to a focus upon changing the ratio of number of adults to number of children, devaluing the continuous, precautionary production of larger numbers of children because many of them will die. It makes it possible for many women – and many men – to be relieved of the duties of parenthood and freed to devote themselves as individuals either to more individualistic lives or to more whole-hearted service to society. It makes it possible for both men and women to live longer, and to preserve their health to a later age, but by preserving the weak, and compensating for weaknesses, it also increases the threat and the fear of ending life as bedridden and senile.

So as we look at the wide horizons, at the possibilities of prevention and change opened up by the biomedical revolution, the simplest and clearest result is the increase in options for any society, for the individuals within it, and for the whole of mankind. With the increase in options comes, however, a situation in which unpredictable fluctuations are also more frequent and the burden of choice, for individuals and for social groups, becomes heavier and in some cases unbearable.

The recognition of the population explosion has meant increasing social tolerance for abortion; more experimentation with abortion methods, and safer methods of abortion. But the availability of abortion within societies where there are deep religious attitudes towards the unborn as individuals whose lives must be protected means that, as women are permitted to subject themselves to abortion, and mourning for an elective abortion is impossible, women are now displaying many psychological features formerly associated with uncompleted mourning, including failure in the very tasks that the abortion was supposed to free them to do. There are also reactions within the medical profession, committed for 2,000 years to the preservation of all life at all costs, against too large a proportion of their time being invested in performing abortions. The compensatory combination of abortion centers with contraceptive education may somewhat reduce the opposition to abortion, as the inclusion of birth within hospital settings otherwise associated with illness and death has to some degree softened the attitude towards hospitals. The hospital – in those countries where birth takes place within a general hospital setting – becomes a symbol of birth as well as of death. But, by placing childbirth within the medical setting, in which physicians are almost always men, childbirth itself has been defined as illness, and medico-surgical procedural style has severely interfered with the relationship between mother and child, anesthetizing women at the moment of birth and in many cases permanently impairing maternal responses. In the same way, the present movement of placing mental cases within a general hospital, made possible by the development of tranquilizing drugs, can be seen as a move towards the humanization of all illness by including mental illness within the accepted therapeutic institution. But such inclusion also leads to the attempt of psychiatrists to treat grief and mourning as forms of illness. The central ethic of the practice of medicine – the commitment to save life at any and all costs, that medical practice should be no respector of persons – has now led to the insistence upon prolonging the lives of those who are completely unrelated to their surroundings, and to the compensatory arguments that 'brain death' and not the failure of the heart should constitute death.

It seems probable that the disproportionate furor over heart transplants may be primarily a symptom of deep concern over the new kinds of decisions that are being introduced into men's lives. We are actually better equipped, culturally, to deal with the dangers of large-scale phenomena, such as the effect of hurricanes, the contamination of the environment, or war, than we are to face the decisions that are introduced into the lives of individuals, as men and women, as parents and children, as physicians, patients and legislators, by the newest biomedical advances.

The pill illustrates another area of increased choice and increased anxiety. Efforts, both social and individual, to prevent the birth of children and to dissociate sexual activity from pregnancy, are very old, probably as old as the understanding of physical paternity. All known methods, up to the development of the pill, have been somewhat inefficient and unreliable, partly because of the type of involvement required of individuals in preventive acts in close association with peaks of emotional excitement. The incompatibility of careful, calculating observance of precautions against the outcome of passion – a child – and the emotion from which children are born was in itself a kind of guarantee of failure in a large number of cases. The pill has introduced a whole series of new conditions, calculated care may now be taken far from the scene, and the kind of attention once necessary to preserve the life of a young infant is now required to be sure that no infant is born – unremitting vigilance. Furthermore, the onus has been placed entirely on women, just at a period when the permission to have fewer children seemed to be freeing women from the kind of responsibilities they had had in the past. At present, the widely distributed folklorish attacks on the pill reflect deep-seated uneasiness; the biological factors in comparison with the cultural factors in this uneasiness are not known. It may be argued that these attacks are only the responses of men and women reared within a different set of biomedical possibilities and that the new generation will be free of such anxieties, but studies of attitudes towards pain among third-generation Americans whose grandparents were European immigrants suggest that the transmission of cultural attitudes from one generation to the next is more complicated and latent attitudes may survive in variously distorted forms for a long time.

Biomedical advances, both because of the threat of overpopulation due to the control of epidemics and the preservation of infants, and because of the research on fertility now permitted, are offering men and women the most profound possibilities of shift in complementary roles that has occurred in recorded history. Society, from prehistoric times, has taken its form from the division of labor between men and women, and the relationship of adults of both sexes to children. Throughout history, the questions of age and sex identity have been primary pivots of identification. Now, neither one of these two sets of status absolutes may be primary. It is possible, that identification by methods yet to be developed, of temperament or gift, might become a primary determinant of expected social role, as infant mathematicians, e.g., of either sex are identified early and nurtured appropriately. Or, new methods, some biomedical, some cultural, for the evoking of hitherto unguessed potentialities may introduce the opposite kind of choice. No longer will children be looked at, first as boys or girls, then as certain kinds of boys or girls, but possibly as having potentialities for extremely different career lines. Such a choice is currently being made among the children of the well-to-do and the poor, as the children of the poor are fed so insufficiently that many are irretrievably stunted and damaged, while the children of the affluent are given the best nutrition and preventive care. When these distinctions are made in the name of traditional usage and prejudice, as foreign workers, or members of other races are badly housed and badly fed, the extent to which we are consciously producing different kinds of people is masked. But biomedical advances in knowledge of nutrition, and the effect of nutrition on the central nervous system, and the irreversible effects of some disease states, either in mother or young child, both threaten acceptance of traditional inequalities and make possible their eradication. This opens the door to improvements in the quality of the human race which are intoxicating – and frightening.

Traditional age relationships are also being altered. Although there have always been some elders who survived with their sensory abilities unimpaired, the proportion of such men and women has always been low. The generation in power has been the parent generation, in good physical health still, and more knowledgeable than their children, able to keep them under control, both by the extent of their superior knowledge and skill and the power that this gave them, and by superior physical strength. The checks on the power exercised by the grandparent generation, although institutionalized in some countries – like China – were compensated for by the difference in proportions. But today, this middle generation suffers from the weight of its parent generation, ill, failing in powers, an economic burden, and a dismal prophecy of what their own old age will be like. They suffer because present-day medical advances do least for mature men – while providing continuous care for women, as potential, actual, or past mothers – and because the physical and cultural development of their children is unprecedented in their experience. Medical advances in the postponement and amelioration of menopausal symptoms can now give a woman an almost symptom-free transition from her reproductive period to her period of post-menopausal zest. Men's failing powers and disappointments in life were once matched by periods of depression and instability in their wives. Today, men encounter less and less this kind of behavior in their middle-aged wives, which would make renewed demands upon their protectiveness. And as women are able to draw on physiological change now smooth and untraumatic, to provide them with a new impetus towards activity, men become more conspicuously dependent upon external sources of renewed zest – which if not provided by a new career success are very likely to be sought in new wives. Our traditional family style, with lifelong marriage and lifelong institutionalization of men's responsibility for women, was postulated on much shorter lives, and much greater health hazards for both men and women than they face today.

The challenge presented by healthy, zestful middle-aged women is compounded by the difficulty of bringing up children who have all the visible signs of greater maturity coupled with the disconcerting capacity to deal with the modern world as natives, and not as immigrants from an earlier age. The progress of civilization has meant that greater and greater power was placed in the hands of the middle-aged, who could force the retirement of the old, no longer able to do physical work, no longer able to keep up with change, and to keep the young in subjection, conscript them and send them to war, force them to postpone gratification of sex and demands for independence and autonomy. When this security and power is threatened from three sides, the greater health and drive in middle-aged women, the superior strength and familiarity with the modern world of children and the threatening model provided by an old age prolonged indefinitely into suffering, senility and dependency, stability in middle life becomes very difficult. Yet present-day society is postulated upon it. All of these considerations suggest that more attention to the health of middle-aged men is urgently needed to correct these imbalances. The falling age of puberty may be attributed, although the mechanisms are not known, to some aspects of the industrial revolution and the concomitant biomedical revolution. It seems likely that it is due to the greater vulnerability of those who grow faster under adverse conditions, who would once have died and are now being saved, or simply to the decreasing need for protective slower growth. But the fact is indubitable, and a falling average of four months a decade, one year every thirty years, presents very serious challenges, perhaps as serious ones as the population explosion and the environmental crisis. It has been the years between the end of early childhood and the onset of puberty that have given human beings the time to learn to use their tremendous brains, brains which without a long period of learning would be in the service of emotions instead of being able to discipline and control those emotions. It may be hypothesized that shortening the period of reproductivity – initially in females – resulted in this longer growth period or latency, as it is sometimes called. The loss of this period would present entirely new problems of how human beings were to learn during and after, rather than before, the onset of puberty. Alternatively, it would undoubtedly be possible to retard the onset of puberty, but we have no idea what the consequences of such drastic intervention would be.

A compensatory process may perhaps be found in that in a changing society it is the oldest, mentally still competent members who have incorporated the processes of change and who are those most, not least, welcoming innovations.

In these discussions there has been strong emphasis upon the individual, man or woman, old or young, vis-à-vis others in the society. Modern industrialization has fostered the independent individual member of an independent family unit, consisting of a married pair and their minor children. Such a family unit can move easily, as modern changing conditions demand. But with the increased emphasis on this two-generation – or nuclear – family, the extrusion of the old, the break in the tie between generations, the diversity of life attendant upon close contact between different age groups, and – increasingly – of class groups has been broken. In the past adaptation to change, just as adaptation to cultural constancies, was carried by exposure of all generations to each other, so that age and sex roles were learned reciprocally by old and young. There are now severe breaks in this process, begun by the emphasis upon the nuclear family as an ideal, and accentuated by the extent of the generation gap engendered by the simultaneous and world-wide changes of the mid 1940's – the bomb, space, television, computers, inauguration of wide-spread production processes which broke the natural cycle by introducing synthetic and non-biodegradable materials. Much of the present emphasis upon consciousness-expanding drugs can be seen as an attempt to restore the kind of sense of continuity that was once provided by the pattern of relationship between older and young, in the family and in the community. This search for a new kind of consciousness, search for self-abandon, search for self-manipulation, and search for the manipulation of others through eavesdropping devices and 'truth drugs' can all be seen as extreme reactions to the present state of enormous possibility and enormous uncertainty about how these possibilities are to be taken advantage of.

A second set of compensatory behaviors can be found in the various extreme positions that are being taken by and about women today. There is a demand for natural childbirth, an attempt to involve the husband in the birth of his child by his presence at the birth, rejection of anesthesia and emphasis upon breast-feeding. The rejection of the pill, as being a danger to the mother's capacity for successful gestation, and the insistence that biological contraceptive methods should be developed for males also constitute an emphasis upon the value of female maternal functioning and an attempt to weaken the dichotomy between male and female by greater involvement of the male in the parental process. This is strengthened by the post World War II experience of how deeply involved young fathers could become in the care of infants if their exposure to their children occurred within the first weeks after birth. Tapping and manipulating latent parental capacities of men is one response to the sense of change in the demands on parenthood in general.

A different response is found in the demands that the biomedical sciences wipe out all the differences between men and women, erase the vagaries of the menstrual cycle, develop extra-uterine gestation and/or methods of implanting the fertilized embryo in the womb of some other woman, eliminate the menopause, equalize the burdens of contraception or sterilization between men and women, and either provide absolutely free abortion – as such an equalizer – or attempt to eliminate any need for abortion, because it is seen as a male-induced method of dealing with unwanted children. Both of these sets of demands come as a consequence of the biomedical revolution and both make new claims on scientific research and practice to deal in new ways with the change in social demand that women accept a lifelong maternal role. It should also be added that an ability to predetermine the sex of offspring will result for the first time in history in female infants being chosen rather than being regarded as the by-products of the search for male offspring.

Similarly the young may demand better drugs, drugs that will admit them, without any of the previous long years of laborious preparation required for participation in Zen and Yoga, into an instant transcendence of everyday life, in fact into a biochemically produced paradisiacal or prophetic state. But other young people are rebelling against all of the products of scientific research, and

are going back to 'natural' foods, foods grown without benefit of artificial ferti-
lizers or pesticides, and free from chemical additives of any sort. Both are
responses to the same phenomena – our unprecedented capacity to intervene
at every stage, from choice of seeds to final preparation of food-stuffs.

The response of many young people to the removal of the fear of pregnancy
and to the relaxation or parental concern about their behavior – very easily
relaxed when there is little chance of offspring – has been initially towards increased sex freedom and often increased promiscuity. But this is also already
beginning to correct itself. One of the objections to the pill is that it removes all
responsible choice too far away from moments dictated by passion. And as
young people demand coeducational living quarters, new taboos are emerging
to outlaw sex from those who live together such as students or young workers.

The position of the aged is equally surrounded by ambivalences. Those
who have preserved the learnings of their childhood, when a good child fought
its way through croup and children's contagious diseases, choking and battling
to stay alive and gain weight, now fight on, years after consciousness has gone,
just trying to live. But among the next generation of aging people, the fear of
such years of useless, unproductive, burdensome dependency and loss of self
is leading to new demands on new medical definitions of the right to die. The
fear of suffering and loss of identity is replacing the older fear of death, but
again this takes different and apparently opposing forms. There is found among
the young – in those countries where the use of drugs has assumed the dimensions
of a cult, the United States, Japan, Scandinavia – a reckless promiscuous approach to drugs, a willingness to try anything, even with the information that
it may lead to death. But there are also serious flickers of interest in being frozen
for later revival, perhaps centuries hence, while one is young and strong – a
new bid for a kind of immortality, but an immortality in which biomedical
science is the power invoked. The future of biomedical research and the future
of man's continued expansion of choices is implicit in the way in which these
issues of the relationship between the sexes and between age groups, and between
those who are divided by birth into certain classes, races or ethnic groups are
solved. The preservation of different blood banks by race opens the door to
many other fears about the use of blood, and to abuses of the attempt to provide needed blood. The fear of any mood-altering substances leads to panic
reactions, like the cessation of the controlled manufacture of LSD, in the
United States, and the subsequent spread of poorly controlled and even more
dangerous drugs. Ambivalence towards the pill impedes proper experimentation and controlled observation.

Superficially, this would lead one to conclude that there are right decisions,
decisions that can be arrived at by the simple application of scientific logic which
should guide mankind's decisions about the preservation of the aged, the manufacture and use of drugs, the ways in which reproductivity is curbed, the age at
which puberty is reached, and that it is a reasonably simple matter to make such
decisions. Obstacles to such rational decisions then seem to be the politicians

who, because they are power-seeking, manipulate the irrational attitudes of the uninstructed populace.

It is true that very often we do lack the appropriate political decision-making mechanism to introduce a needed change in improving public health, in seeking a population balance, and in providing new therapies. But it is also true that through the imperfect political process there is an attempt, rough, uncalibrated, redundant, to try out and live through some of the unforeseeable concomitants of any change. The unregularized rebellions of this younger generation, the bitterness and reactionary excesses of groups recently dispossessed or recently optimistic in a population, the bizarre and horrendous response of artists to the modern world, to what has happened to the image of man, and to the image of the future, are all ways in which human beings are attempting to try out the options open to them. If we separate something called rationality and science from the stirrings of other, but equally valid types of response, we run the risk of setting up the sort of opposition within society, in which coercive rationality is confronted by anarchistic mysticism, and each threatens to destroy the other. A delicate awareness of the way in which each modern society is responding to the present apparent consequences and the future promises of biomedical science is one way of preventing such disastrous polarization.

In experimental communities contemporary young people are trying to build human situations, large enough and complete enough to try out some of the complexities and contradictions of modern life. They should be watched and protected. Here, as much as, and possibly more than, in the laboratory the future is being born.

Summary

Our present recognition of the nature of social processes suggests that attempts at linear predictions must be replaced by an acute awareness of, and attention to, multiple aspects of our present situation. A series of changes, in the relation of men and women, of the aged, the mature and the childless, are developing in direct relationship to advances in the biomedical field, and are expressed in: a lowered demand for large numbers of children and a freeing of men and women from the demands of parenthood, greater longevity and imposed survival long after consciousness and individuality are lost, new attitudes towards safety and the preservation of life, contradictory attempts to accentuate and even out differences between men and women, unstable relationships between the mature and the more rapidly maturing young. It is suggested that the future of mankind and the continuing invocation of biomedical advances are dependent upon the way in which some of these contradictions are resolved into new institutions and new forms of family and community living.

Zusammenfassung

Unsere derzeitigen Kenntnisse über die Natur der sozialen Fortentwicklung lassen vermuten, daß Versuche linearer Vorhersagen durch unmittelbare Einsicht und Verständnis für verschiedene Aspekte unserer gegenwärtigen Situation ersetzt werden müssen. Eine Vielzahl von Veränderungen in der Beziehung zwischen Mann und Frau, zwischen Alten, Reifen und Kinderlosen entwickeln sich in direkter Relation zu den Fortschritten auf biomedizinischem Gebiet. Sie finden ihren Ausdruck in einer Abnahme des Wunsches nach vielen Kindern und in einer Befreiung von Mann und Frau von den Pflichten der Elternschaft; größerer Lebenserwartung und aufgezwungenem Überleben lange nachdem Bewußtsein und Individualität verlorengingen; in neuen Einstellungen zu Fragen der Sicherheit und Erhaltung des Lebens; in widersprüchlichen Versuchen, die Unterschiede zwischen Mann und Frau zu betonen oder auch zu verwischen; in unstabilen Beziehungen zwischen den Erwachsenen und der schneller reifenden Jugend. Es wird die Meinung vertreten, daß die Zukunft der Menschheit und der fortdauernde Einsatz der biomedizinischen Fortschritte davon abhängen, in welcher Weise einige dieser Widersprüchlichkeiten eine Lösung in neuen Ordnungen und neuen Formen des Familien- und Gemeinschaftslebens finden werden.

Résumé

Ce que nous savons à l'heure actuelle de la nature des processus sociaux indique qu'il faut remplacer les prévisions linéaires par une observation et une prise de conscience aiguës des multiples aspects de notre situation présente. Une série de changements se dessinent dans les rapports entre les hommes et les femmes, entre les personnes âgées, les adultes d'âge mûr et les personnes sans enfants, en corrélation directe avec les progrès réalisés dans le domaine biomédical. Ces changements se traduisent par: l'abaissement du nombre des familles nombreuses, la libération de l'homme et de la femme de l'obligation de procréer, une longévité plus grande et une survie imposée à des sujets ayant perdu depuis longtemps conscience et individualité, une conception nouvelle de la sécurité et de la préservation de la vie, des tendances contradictoires visant les unes à accentuer, les autres à niveler les différences entre l'homme et la femme, des rapports instables entre les adultes mûrs et les jeunes parvenant plus rapidement à maturité. L'auteur pense que l'avenir de l'humanité et celui des progrès biomédicaux dépendent des moyens choisis pour résoudre certaines de ces contradictions, dans le cadre de nouvelles institutions et de nouvelles formes de vie familiale et communautaire.

Resumen

Nuestro conocimiento actual de la naturaleza de la evolución social nos induce a pensar que las tentativas de predicción linear deben ceder el paso a una toma de conciencia aguda de los múltiples aspectos de nuestra situación presente que requieren nuestra atención. Una serie de modificaciones en las relaciones entre hombres y mujeres, entre las personas de edad, entre adultos y jóvenes sin hijos, están en correlación directa con los progresos que se realizan en el ámbito de la biomedicina. Estas modificaciones se traducen por: un menor deseo de tener una familia numerosa, una liberación tanto del hombre como de la mujer de una gran parte de las obligaciones que incumben a los padres, mayor longevidad y supervivencia impuesta a los que desde hace tiempo han perdido la conciencia y su individualidad, nuevas actitudes frente a la seguridad y la preservación de la vida, tentativas contradictorias de acentuar o de allanar las diferencias entre el hombre y la mujer, relaciones inestables entre los adultos y los jóvenes que llegan más rápidamente a la madurez. Se opina que el futuro de la humanidad y la continuidad de los progresos biomédicos dependen de la manera como se resuelvan algunas de estas contradicciones dentro de nuevas instituciones y de nuevas formas de vida familiar y comunitaria.

Der Einfluß von Mensch und Gesellschaft auf den biomedizinischen Fortschritt

von Jürgen Moltmann

I. Wissenschaft und Interesse

Werden Wissenschaft und Ethik getrennt, so kommt die Ethik immer zu spät. Erst wenn die Wissenschaften uns die Methoden der Macht gelehrt haben, soll die Ethik uns zur Verantwortung der Macht bringen. Nachdem die Fakten und Daten aufgezählt sind, soll die Ethik sie für den Menschen deuten. Nachdem das Instrumentarium vorhanden ist, soll die Ethik ihren sinnvollen Gebrauch erkunden, um Mißbrauch zu verhindern.

Dieses Diskussionsmodell führt in eine Sackgasse. Sind wir von Jahr zu Jahr technisch besser gerüstet, zu erreichen, was wir wollen, so entsteht ethisch die hilflose Frage: Was wollen wir eigentlich? (Bertrand de Jouvenel.) Je mehr *mögliche* Zukünfte machbar werden, um so weniger scheinen Menschen sich auf eine gemeinsame, *wünschbare* Zukunft einigen zu können. Der Zwang zum Fortschritt in den Sciences scheint die Humanities kulturell immer beliebiger zu machen. Der Fehler in diesem Denkmodell liegt darin, daß man von der *Abstraktion* der Wissenschaften aus der Gesellschaft ausgeht und erst dann nach der ethischen und sozialpolitischen *Integration* wissenschaftlich-technischer Macht in die humanen Ziele der Gesellschaft fragt. Weil aber aus einer von Werten abstrahierten, «wertfreien» Wissenschaft keine Werte deduziert werden können, geraten die Werte, nach denen wissenschaftliche Ergebnisse verwertet werden, in die Beliebigkeit schon vorhandener sozialer, ökonomischer und politischer Interessen oder des persönlichen Geschmacks. Auf dieser Diskussionsebene lassen sich eine Fülle von ethischen Postulaten aufstellen und diskutieren, aber sie bleiben alle ohne Relevanz für die Praxis und sind meistens nur Dekoration für die Show öffentlicher Symposien. Ich glaube aber, daß dieses Diskussionsmodell aus einer optischen Täuschung entstanden ist.

Ich werde darum versuchen, den umgekehrten Weg einzuschlagen. Wir beginnen mit einer Analyse des vorhandenen Ethos der biomedizinischen Fortschritte und fragen dann nach der Rückwirkung jener Fortschritte auf dieses Ethos. Wir beginnen mit den menschlichen und sozialen *Motivationen* für die biomedizinische Wissenschaft und Technik, die bisher nicht sehr gut erforscht sind, und fragen nach ihren Veränderungen durch die Ergebnisse jener Wissenschaft. Damit kehren wir das Thema dieser Session um und fragen zuerst nach dem «Einfluß von Mensch und Gesellschaft auf den biomedizinischen Fortschritt» und dann nach dem «Einfluß des biomedizinischen Fortschritts auf Mensch und Gesellschaft». Erst wenn die erkenntnisleitenden Interessen dieser Wissenschaft und die praxisleitenden Interessen dieser Humantechniken erkannt sind, kann man begründet nach den *Wechselwirkungen von Interesse und Erkenntnis* unter den heutigen Verhältnissen fragen.

Die *Segregation* von Wissenschaft und Gesellschaft, von Science und Humanities, von Technik und Ethik, war und ist notwendig, um die Wissenschaft in Forschung und Anwendung aus den Grenzen vorhandener gesellschaftlicher Religionen und Moralsysteme sowie gesellschaftlicher Ideologien zu befreien. Die Erinnerung an die Konflikte zwischen Kirche und Wissenschaft in den Fällen Galilei und Darwin ist noch lebendig. Die Konflikte zwischen Staatsmarxismus und Wissenschaft in der UdSSR zeigen, daß jene Befreiung auch unter anderen Umständen notwendig ist[*].

Die *Integration* von Wissenschaft und Gesellschaft ist aber heute ebenso notwendig, um die Wissenschaften aus ihren neuen, quasi-religiösen Rollen zu befreien, in die sie durch vermeintliche Absonderung (= Heiligung) von gesellschaftlichen Interessen und Wertsystemen geraten sind. Hüteten früher die Priester das Herrschaftswissen gegenüber den Laien, so haben dies heute die Fachleute übernommen – der Laie bleibt der gleiche. Diese Rollenverteilung ist fortschrittshemmend. Sie überfordert Wissenschaftler mit Verantwortung und entmündigt den Laien mit Faszination und Horror durch Wissenschaft[**]. Die Aufgabe der Wissenschaft kann nur darin liegen, Entscheidungsmöglichkeiten und Entscheidungskonsequenzen offenzulegen, die sonst nicht erkennbar wären. Sie ist damit selbst auf den wissenschaftlich-politischen und den wissenschaftlich-ethischen Dialog angewiesen, in dem allein der Consensus über leitende Interessen, Werte und Wertprioritäten gewonnen werden kann. Die Vergesellschaftung der Wissenschaften kann dabei nicht ohne die Verwissenschaftlichung der Gesellschaft vor sich gehen. Man käme sonst in Zustände, in denen die Planer und die Geplanten, die Macher und die Gemachten nicht mehr gemeinsam «Mensch» sind, und die Objekte sich nicht mehr in den Subjekten der Wissenschaften und die Subjekte sich nicht mehr in den Objekten der Wissenschaft wiedererkennen[***].

[*] Wie am Symposium deutlich zum Ausdruck kam, wird niemand der wissenschaftlichen Grundlagenforschung Grenzen setzen wollen – am wenigsten haben die christlichen Kirchen dazu Anlaß –, obgleich auch die Grundlagenforschung natürlich immer abhängig ist von Budgetfragen und vom Interesse der wissenschaftlich begabten Jugend.

[**] Es zeigte sich auch an diesem Symposium, daß die bei manchen Wissenschaftlern übliche Rede von der «scientific community» gegenüber einer «non-scientific community» durch ihren elitären Anschein die Kommunikation erschwert. Sie gibt den Wissenschaften das Image einer «geschlossenen Gesellschaft».

[***] So wurde am Symposium gefordert, die Wissenschaften in größeren ökologischen Systemen zu sehen und sie besser als bisher in solche zu integrieren; zum Beispiel Biomedizin – pharmazeutische Produktion – Gesundheitspolitik – Öffentlichkeit. Der wissenschaftliche Fortschritt kann nicht begrenzt werden, sondern muß auf der Erforschung immer komplexerer Systeme verbreitert werden. Aus der Zusammenfassung von Genetik, Informationstheorie, Hermeneutik und Soziologie können neue Disziplinen entstehen.

II. Zum Ethos des biochemischen Fortschritts

Wissenschaft ist in Forschung und Anwendung Auftragsarbeit. Menschliche Interessen gehen ihr voran, sind mit ihr verbunden und in ihren Fortschritt eingebaut. Solange sich diese Interessen «von selbst verstehen», brauchen sie nicht diskutiert zu werden. Heute ist aber auf vielen Gebieten die Moral dessen, «was sich von selbst versteht», zum Problem geworden. Im Namen welcher menschlichen Interessen wird der genannte Fortschritt betrieben?

In der Einladung zu diesem Symposium hieß es: «Die Stellung des Unternehmens (Hoffmann-La Roche) in der medizinischen Welt wurde in der letzten Zeit dadurch verstärkt, daß es den Kampf gegen die Krankheit als ein unteilbares Ganzes betrachtet.» So liegt das erste menschliche Interesse im *Kampf gegen die Krankheit und für die Gesundheit*, im Kampf gegen den Tod und für die Verlängerung des Lebens.

Das klingt so lange selbstverständlich, als der Mensch durch seine natürlichen Mängel beherrscht wird, die er durch Kulturleistungen kompensieren muß, um zu überleben. Das wird aber zum Problem, wenn die unmittelbaren Lebensbedürfnisse erfüllt sind und nicht mehr den negativen Maßstab für seine Anstrengungen hergeben. Was kommt nach dem *Kampf ums Dasein?*

Mit dem «Kampf ums Dasein» ist das elementare *Interesse des Menschen an seiner Selbstbefreiung* von Naturabhängigkeit in der Umwelt und im eigenen Leibe verbunden. Es ist die Kehrseite seines *Willens zur Macht* über die Natur und sich selbst. Seit der Mensch aus der Naturabhängigkeit herausgetreten ist und in dem Maße, wie er der Natur mächtig wird, wird er zum «Menschen», das heißt zur handlungsfähigen Person. Immer mehr wird es ihm heute möglich, nicht nur seine geistige und private, sondern auch seine physische und soziale Existenz selbst zu bestimmen. Befreiung und Macht sind aber nur so lange von Interesse, als man sie nicht hat. Je mehr der Mensch sie gewinnt*, um so mehr wird das zu entwerfende und zu lebende Humanum fraglich. «Wozu sind die Menschen da?[1]» Sir *Julian Huxley* sprach davon, daß nach dem «Kampf ums Dasein» nun immer mehr das «Streben nach Erfüllung», das heißt nach Erfüllung der menschlichen Möglichkeiten, in den Vordergrund träte[2]. Doch welche Möglichkeiten sollen erfüllt werden und welche nicht? Er fügte hinzu, daß jetzt für den Menschen die Steuerung der Evolution der Natur, jedenfalls seiner eigenen Evolution, zur inneren Bestimmung seiner Macht und Freiheit würde.

Die biblischen Religionen haben seit 3000 Jahren in der Bestimmung zur Herrschaft über die Natur die Erfüllung der menschlichen Bestimmung gesehen, sie jedoch verbunden mit der Bestimmung des Menschen zum Ebenbild des schöpferischen Gottes. Er soll nicht Ebenbild der Natur und ihrer Mächte sein**.

---

* Darüber, daß mit steigendem Machtgewinn durch den Menschen das Problem der Beherrschung, der Kontrolle und des weisen Umgangs mit dieser Macht immer dringlicher wird, waren sich alle Symposiumsteilnehmer einig.

** Er soll nicht ein Ebenbild des vernichtenden Nichts werden und die Natur und sich selbst zerstören.

Als diese Erkenntnisse entstanden, waren die Möglichkeiten des Menschen gering, seine Abhängigkeiten von der undurchschaubaren Natur dagegen groß. Im Zuge des wissenschaftlichen und technischen Fortschritts ist dann, positiv gesehen, der Mensch in eine bisher ungeahnte Realisierung dieser Bestimmungen eingetreten – wenn er « Mensch » ist.

Aus den elementaren *Interessen* an Befreiung und Macht sind in der Kulturgeschichte eine Reihe von *Hoffnungen* entstanden, die in den biomedizinischen Fortschritt investiert wurden. Sie richten sich auf die Verbesserung der menschlichen Kondition, auf die Erweiterung des Weltverstandes, auf Steigerung seiner Glücksfähigkeit und die Anhebung seiner Moralität. Aus diesen Hoffnungen werden heute konkrete *Visionen* entworfen, wie zum Beispiel auf dem Ciba-Symposium 1962.

1. Die Überwindung viraler und bakterieller Infektionskrankheiten gibt Anlaß zur Vision einer *keimfreien Welt.*

2. Die Entwicklung der Psychopharmaka verbindet sich mit der Utopie eines *schmerzfreien Lebens.*

3. Die beginnende Technik der Organtransplantation führt zur Idee der auswechselbaren Körperteile und eines *endlosen Lebens.*

4. Die neue Eugenik läßt die Steuerung und *Beschleunigung der Evolution* des Menschen als möglich erscheinen. Sie wird mit der Vision verbunden, daß «in Zukunft Menschen bessere Generationen von Menschen schaffen werden» (Muller).

Auf dem Boden dieser menschlichen Interessen, Hoffnungen und Visionen ist der biochemische Fortschritt selbst ein großartiges ethisches Unternehmen der Menschheit. Doch bleibt er nur lebendig, solange sich diese Interessen und Hoffnungen der Menschheit von selbst verstehen.

III. Rückwirkungen des Fortschritts auf die ethischen Interessen

Jedes menschliche Handeln löst nicht nur vorhandene Probleme, sondern produziert auch neue. Es kommt meistens anders, als man gedacht hat. Diese neuen Probleme lassen sich in drei Gruppen einteilen:

1. Alles, was der Mensch gebrauchen kann, kann er auch mißbrauchen. Darum ist der biomedizinische Fortschritt so lange ambivalent, als der Mensch ein unzuverlässiges Wesen ist.

2. Hoffnungen können enttäuscht werden, wenn sie nicht erfüllt werden. Sie können aber auch durch ihre Erfüllung enttäuscht werden. Angesichts der genannten biomedizinischen Utopien ist nicht ihre vermutliche Unerfüllbarkeit, sondern eher ihre vermutete Erfüllbarkeit das Problem für die zugrunde liegende Ethik.

3. Jeder Fortschritt auf einem Gebiet des Lebens bringt das Lebenssystem des Ganzen aus der Balance. Darum muß bei Teilfortschritten die Balance immer wieder neu hergestellt werden. Die sprachliche Symbolik, die rechtlichen

Codes, die moralischen Verläßlichkeiten und die Produktionsverhältnisse müssen neu geordnet werden.

ad 1. Solange Machtzuwachs elementare Not überwindet, ergibt sich der Gebrauch von selbst. Geht er aber über das Notwendige hinaus, so kann er lebensfeindlich verwendet werden und neue Not produzieren.

Neben den genannten Positiv-Utopien gibt es heute eine gleiche Anzahl von Negativ-Utopien des biomedizinischen Fortschritts. Läßt sich mit ihm ein öffentlicher Gesundheitsdienst organisieren, so lassen sich auch biochemische Kriegführung und die Herrschaft einer genetisch hochgezüchteten Elite über biochemisch verblödete Massen produzieren. Auch ohne solche Spekulationen kann man zwar auf der einen Seite im Kampf gegen die Krankheit erfolgreicher werden und sich doch auf der anderen Seite fragen, ob das, was für das Wachstum der pharmazeutischen Industrie gut ist, auch gut für den Rest der Welt sein muß.

ad 2. Hoffnungen werden in der Regel enttäuscht, wenn etwas anderes herauskommt, als man gewollt hat. Die Befreiung des Menschen von Naturabhängigkeit hat nicht nur natürliche Mängel des Menschen überwunden, sondern auch eine Reihe natürlicher, sich selbst regulierender Systeme durchbrochen. Sie müssen durch von Menschen regulierte Sozialsysteme ersetzt werden.

Biologie und Medizin haben die Sterblichkeit gesenkt, doch dafür die Bevölkerungsexplosion eingehandelt. Sie haben eine gewisse natürliche Selektion überwunden, doch dafür eine Verschlechterung des Erbguts eingetauscht. Sie haben Bakterien und Schädlinge bekämpft, doch dafür durch DDT den «stummen Frühling» geschaffen. Sie haben Schmerzen bekämpft und ein weltweites LSD-Problem geschaffen. Die Befreiung des Menschen von der Natur zwingt zur sozialen Organisation dieser Freiheit, und diese bringt eine Fülle neuer sozialer Abhängigkeiten hervor. Die Visionen eines schmerzfreien, endlosen und verbesserlichen Lebens in einer keimfreien Welt sind abstrakt, weil sie die sozialen, politischen und ethischen Kosten einer solchen Welt nicht berücksichtigen*. Was früher die «Natur» durch Krankheit, frühe Sterblichkeit und Selektion regulierte, muß jetzt durch soziale Organisation übernommen werden: durch Geburtenkontrolle, durch Eugenik und vermutlich einmal auch durch passive Euthanasie. Eingriffe in natürliche Systeme müssen durch Ersatzleistungen kompensiert werden. Dieses ökologische Gesetz setzt vermutlich auch den Experimenten des Menschen mit sich selbst und seiner zukünftigen Selbstschöpfung gewisse Toleranzgrenzen, wenn die Kosten des Fortschritts seinen Gewinn übersteigen.

* Mit dem biomedizinischen Fortschritt ist keine Glücksgarantie verbunden. Die Fortschritte der Menschheit sind durchweg ungleich, ungleichzeitig und nicht koordiniert. Sie bringen natürliche und soziale Gleichgewichte aus der hergebrachten Ordnung und erzwingen damit Spannungen und Konflikte. *Räumlich* gesehen, hat der biomedizinische Fortschritt zu neuen Sozialkonflikten zwischen arm und reich, Mann und Frau, Kleinfamilie und Gesellschaft geführt. *Zeitlich* gesehen, hat er, wie besonders Margaret Mead betonte, die natürliche Generationenfolge durch Überalterung auf der einen und verfrühte Reife auf der anderen Seite zerstört. *Persönlich* hat er die Balance von Ich und Körper gestört und neue Identitätskonflikte produziert. Eine neue *Sozialpolitik* muß die Gerechtigkeit in der Teilnahme am Gesundheitswesen herstellen. Eine *Generationenpolitik* muß den Ausgleich zwischen Altern und Wachsen der Bevölkerung suchen, damit weder die Gegenwart der Zukunft noch die Zukunft der Gegenwart, das heißt weder die Alten den Jungen noch die Jungen den Alten, geopfert werden. Man kann die Verantwortung nicht mehr auf «die Natur» abschieben und auch nicht auf das sogenannte freie Spiel der Kräfte.

ad 3. Hoffnungen können aber auch durch ihre Erfüllung enttäuscht werden. Sollte ein schmerzfreies, endloses und verbesserliches Leben in einer keimfreien Welt möglich werden, dann erfüllt sich eine Menschheitshoffnung, und es geht zugleich ein Traum verloren, denn es wird dann fraglich, welchen Sinn ein solches Leben haben kann und wozu solche Menschen da sind.

Ist ein Leben ohne Schmerz nicht auch ein Leben ohne Liebe? Ist ein Leben ohne Widerstand und Kampf nicht auch ein Leben ohne Erlebnis des Lebens? Wird ein endloses Leben nicht ein langweiliges Leben, dem der Charakter der Einmaligkeit fehlt? Monotonie, Langeweile und Erlebnisarmut sind schon heute Humanprobleme der Industriegesellschaft, die durch neue Psychopharmaka und Psychotechniken mühsam verdrängt werden müssen. Je mehr menschliche Interessen und Hoffnungen durch den biomedizinischen Fortschritt erfüllt werden, um so mehr lösen sich jene ethischen Motivationen auf, die jenen Fortschritt antreiben. Menschen wissen nicht mehr, was sie meinen, wenn sie sagen: «Ich» oder «mein Leib» oder «Leben» oder «Tod». Damit kann endlich auch das allgemeine Interesse an diesem Fortschritt erlahmen und erlöschen. Warum soll der medizinische Fortschritt Menschen leistungsfähiger machen, wenn die meisten menschlichen Leistungen in dieser Gesellschaft formalisierbar sind und durch Maschinen übernommen werden können? Wie kann dieser Fortschritt Menschen glücksfähiger machen, wenn Glück nicht mehr definierbar ist? Es ist nicht befriedigend, Gebilde zu konstruieren, die akustisch die Formel «Ich bin glücklich» ausstoßen. Je mehr die Humanität, die man bisher suchte, möglich wird, um so mehr muß offenbar Humanität neu interpretiert und neu formuliert werden, damit man mit den Möglichkeiten auch etwas Sinnvolles anfangen kann. Das ist die Frage nach der neuen Balance im Lebenssystem angesichts der eminenten Fortschritte auf dem Gebiet der Biomedizin. Da ist aber zuerst die Frage nach den durch jenen Fortschritt selbst bewirkten Veränderungen der leitenden Interessen für Erkenntnis und Praxis.

IV. Veränderung der menschlichen Interessen

1. Vom Kampf ums Dasein zum Streben nach Erfüllung

«In der psychosozialen Evolution ist der Kampf ums Dasein ersetzt durch etwas, was man Streben nach Erfüllung nennen könnte. Der wichtigste Antrieb in dieser Phase der Evolution ist der psychosoziale Druck.» Wir nehmen diesen fruchtbaren Gedanken von Sir *Julian Huxley* auf, um die Veränderungen der menschlichen Interessen durch den biomedizinischen Fortschritt zu charakterisieren. Als Vision des evolutionären Humanismus bezeichnete er das Ziel: «Lebenserfüllung – größere Möglichkeiten der Erfüllung auf seelisch-geistigem Gebiet für mehr Individuen und größere Leistungen innerhalb der Gemeinschaften durch eine bessere Ausnützung der menschlichen Möglichkeiten und damit größere Freude an den Fähigkeiten des Menschen[3].»

Wird der Kampf ums Dasein durch das Streben nach Erfüllung abgelöst, so wandeln sich die Interessen und Moralsysteme der Menschen grundsätzlich. Der Kampf ums Dasein war ein Kampf ums Überleben. In ihm waren Menschen durch das bedrohende Negative bestimmt, durch Nahrungsmangel, Krankheit, feindliche Umwelt und konkurrierende Gruppen. Der Sinn ihres Lebens war durch *Selbsterhaltung* bestimmt. Je mehr aber Menschen Macht über die feindliche Natur und ihren eigenen gebrechlichen Leib gewinnen, um so weniger können Selbsterhaltung und das nackte Überleben der Sinn ihres Lebens sein. Je mehr sie die natürlichen Mängel überwinden und eine künstliche Fülle von Möglichkeiten produzieren, um so mehr wird das Leben in dieser Fülle der Möglichkeiten zum Problem. Was früher als Lebensnotwendigkeit selbstevident war, verliert seine Antriebskraft, wenn die Not des Daseins überwunden wird oder doch nicht mehr im Vordergrund steht. Die Evolution des Menschen geht darum über die Negation des Negativen im Kampf ums Dasein hinaus in den Entwurf des Positiven, das aus dem Überfluß der Möglichkeiten gewonnen werden soll. Damit wird menschliches Leben zum ersten Male de facto zur moralischen Aufgabe. Ist das Leben selbst gesichert, so geht es um das *gute* und *glückliche Leben* im *Frieden des Daseins*. Damit wird das Leben keineswegs leichter, denn ihm fehlen nun die klaren Fronten und Aufgaben aus dem Kampf ums Dasein. Die feindliche Umwelt und feindliche Konkurrenten geben nicht mehr die negativen Maßstäbe für die Existenzentscheidungen her. Das Ziel der Lebenserfüllung und die Freude des Menschen am Spiel seiner Fähigkeiten weisen noch zurück auf das unerfüllte und beschränkte Leben im Kampf ums Dasein und zehren von den dort entwickelten Hoffnungen. Sie verlieren heute aber ihre Kraft, wie die seelische Hilflosigkeit der Jugend in den Industrieländern jetzt schon zeigt. Der «Möglichkeitsmensch» wird zum «Mann ohne Eigenschaften» (Robert Musil).

Je mehr Macht der Mensch gewinnt, um so größer wird seine Verantwortung. Mit dem Interesse an Selbsterfüllung verbindet sich darum von selbst die Verantwortung für die beherrschbaren Bereiche der Natur. Und ihrer inneren Struktur nach ist «Verantwortung für etwas» immer verbunden mit der «Verantwortung vor jemandem». Die Instanz, *vor* der Herrschaft verantwortet werden muß, geht dabei über den Bereich dessen, *für* das man verantwortlich ist, hinaus und läßt sich darum nur als etwas Transzendentes erfahren. Ich glaube, daß an dieser Stelle heute für viele Menschen, besonders für Wissenschaftler, der «Schmerz einer Transzendenz» aufbricht, die Verantwortung fordert und sich zugleich den bisherigen Bildern und Symbolen entzieht. Dieser Schmerz der Transzendenz kann ein noch wichtigerer Antrieb werden als der «psychosoziale Druck». Auch das jüdisch-christliche Symbol des Menschen als Ebenbild des unsichtbaren Gottes im Sichtbaren muß im Blick auf die Macht- und Möglichkeitsfülle des Menschen heute neu interpretiert werden, wenn es ein wirksames Symbol seiner Verantwortung für die Steuerung der Evolution der Natur und sein genetisches Selbstexperiment werden soll.

2. Vom Sozialdarwinismus zum «Frieden im Dasein»

Wird der Kampf ums Dasein durch neue Bestimmungen des menschlichen Lebens ersetzt, so müssen auch jene Moralsysteme überwunden werden, die den Kampf ums Dasein stilisiert haben. Es können Lebensformen entwickelt werden, die in rationalen Weltverhältnissen Kreativität und Liebe ermöglichen.

Das Ethos des Kampfes ums Dasein muß zum *Ethos des Friedens im Dasein* verändert werden.

Das Prinzip der Selbsterhaltung gegen andere kann zum Prinzip der Selbsterfüllung im anderen und mit anderen, das heißt zum Prinzip der Solidarität verwandelt werden.

Die Angst- und Aggressionssysteme, die zur Selbsterhaltung notwendig waren, können zugunsten von Hoffnungs- und Kooperationssystemen abgebaut werden.

Der *Gruppenegoismus*, der aus der Selbsterhaltung entspringt und zu Konkurrenz- und Machtkämpfen führt, bedroht heute die Menschheit mit kollektivem Selbstmord. Selbst wenn dieser verhindert werden kann, führt jener Egoismus doch schon zu *Segregationsgesellschaften*. Wo immer heute Spannungen und Konflikte auftreten, wird der Friede nicht durch Versöhnung, sondern durch Trennung, Vertreibung, Spaltung, Apartheid und Gettos herbeigeführt. Auch ohne Rassen- und Klassenkämpfe produzieren wir soziale Trennungen: die Alten in die Altersheime, die Kranken in die Krankenhäuser, die Geisteskranken in die Pflegeheime usw. Dann sind die Tüchtigen und Arrivierten unter sich und können sich die Beute des Bruttosozialproduktes teilen. Nach ärztlichen Schätzungen brauchten etwa 50 % der Geisteskranken nicht in den Kliniken zu sein, wenn ihre Familien sie aufnehmen würden. Doch die städtische Sozialstruktur ist intolerant. Das gilt auch für die Alten in Altersheimen. Im nächsten Jahr werden 5000 koreanische Schwestern kommen, um deutschen Krankenhäusern Entwicklungshilfe zu leisten, die sonst schließen müßten. Wird in unserer Gesellschaft der Kampf ums Dasein auf diese, nur wenig zivilisierte Weise fortgesetzt, so werden auch die Tüchtigen nur für begrenzte Zeit überleben können, solange sie nämlich nicht krank oder alt werden.

«Gleich und gleich gesellt sich gern», so nannte Aristoteles das natürliche Gesellungsprinzip. Dieses Prinzip wirkt in unserer Gesellschaft heute lebensfeindlich, weil spaltend. Zur neuen Selbsterfahrung und Selbsterfüllung des Menschen gehört darum das Prinzip der *Anerkennung des anderen*, so daß Ungleichartige zusammenleben und ihre Differenzen und Spannungen für fruchtbar halten. Anders kann der Friede im Dasein nicht gewonnen werden.

Zur Ethik des Kampfes ums Dasein gehörte endlich jenes Ideal von Gesundheit, das Gesundheit mit Leistungs- und Genußfähigkeit identifiziert (S. Freud). Gesundheit läuft damit zuletzt immer auf die ungehinderte Teilnahme an der Produktion und die unverminderte Teilhabe am Bruttosozialprodukt hinaus. Krankheit und Alter sind dann nur Übel, die verdrängt werden müssen. Entsprechend werden unheilbar Kranke und Alte behandelt, ganz zu schweigen davon, wie und wo in unseren Krankenhäusern eigentlich gestorben wird. Zu einer Ethik des Friedens im Dasein gehört eine neue Einschätzung von Krankheit, Altern und Sterben. Krankheit kann ein ebenso wichtiger Lern- und Gestaltungsprozeß der Person sein wie das gesunde, aktive Leben. Nachdem die aktivistische Gesellschaft «Jugendlichkeit» bis hin zur Komik zum Ideal erhoben hat, ist es Zeit, die Würde des Alters wiederzuentdecken. Nachdem der Tod nur noch als leidiger Störenfried angesehen wurde, gibt es Gründe, die Ars moriendi wieder zu lernen, um mit Würde zu sterben. Der Kampf gegen Krank-

heit und für Gesundheit ist gut, wenn er Menschen bereit macht, sich für die
menschlichen Schmerzen der Liebe und für die produktiven Konflikte des Lebens
und Sterbens zu öffnen, um sie human zu verarbeiten. Die Ethik des Kampfes
ums Dasein würde sonst zu einer kranken Gesellschaft führen. Wo dieser Kampf
heute zu gewissen Graden erfolgreich ist, führt er oft zur Verödung des Lebens,
zu einer passiven Konsumentenhaltung ohne Leidenschaft für das Leben. Wo
er fortgesetzt wird, führt er zu Überflußgesellschaften in einem Meer von Elends-
gesellschaften auf der Erde. Erst wenn eine Ethik des «Friedens im Dasein» jene
Kampfethik überwindet, kommt es dazu, daß die Gesunden von den Kranken,
die Jungen von den Alten, die Lebendigen von den Sterbenden und die reichen
von den armen Völkern lernen, an ihnen Interesse zeigen und Solidarität aus
Interesse an ihnen empfinden.

V. Das Recht zu leben und das Recht zu sterben

Der biochemische Fortschritt hat eine Reihe natürlicher Systeme durchbrochen und sie für den Eingriff des Menschen zugänglich gemacht. Diese Systeme müssen durch von Menschen regulierte Sozialsysteme ersetzt werden.
Wir sprechen darum von Bevölkerungs*politik*, Gesundheits*politik* und werden
einmal auch die neue Genetik mit dem Wort *Politik* verbinden müssen. Ge-
störte natürliche Balancen müssen durch soziale Regulationen ersetzt werden.
Damit wird das Leben bewußter. Geburt und Tod, Inhalt und Gestalt des Lebens verstehen sich nicht mehr von selbst, sondern müssen vom Menschen verstanden werden, um sinnvoll gehandhabt zu werden. Das vollzieht sich in
sprachlicher Symbolik, rechtlichen Übereinkünften und einer neuen Moral.

1. Das Ich und der Leib

Das Selbstbewußtsein des Menschen zeigt sich darin, daß er «Ich» sagen
kann und damit sich selber meint. «Ich bin *somebody*», sagt er und identifiziert
sich damit leiblich. Wie ist das angesichts der Fortschritte in der Körpermedizin
und der Organtransplantationen möglich? «Seit es gelang, die Krankheit theoretisch vom kranken Menschen zu isolieren und die gesamte Kausalkette vom
Erreger bis zu allen wichtigen Bedingungen im Krankheitsprozess in den Griff
zu bekommen, ist eine gezielte Therapie möglich geworden[4].» Das aber setzt die
Distanzierung des Ich von seiner *Leiblichkeit* als dem *Körper, den es hat*, voraus.
Die spontane leibliche Identität des Menschen wird durch ein distanziertes
Eigentumsverhältnis des Menschen zu seinem Körper ersetzt. Wenn nun Organe
dieses Körpers – wie Maschinenteile an dem Auto, das er besitzt – ausgewechselt
werden können, dann entsteht eine Ich-Diffusion[5]. Was wird mit dem Symbol
«Ich» bezeichnet: die leibliche Existenz oder mein Körper oder ein austausch-
barer Set von körperlichen Systemteilen? Zur Organtransplantation gehört
auch die Domestizierung der eingesetzten Teile, wie bei Prothesen. Das gilt
nicht nur für den Körper, der ein zunächst fremdes Teil annehmen und integrieren muß, sondern auch für das Ich als das organisierende Zentrum des Leibes.

Zum schwierigen medizinischen Prozeß der Objektivierung des Leibes zum Körper gehört darum umgekehrt ein nicht weniger schwieriger und langwieriger Prozeß der Subjektivierung des Körpers zum Leib des Ich. Die Isolierung der Krankheit vom kranken Menschen ist ihrerseits angewiesen auf die Integration von Krankheit und Gesundung durch diesen Menschen. Medizinische Veränderungen am Körper und erst recht jede genetisch mögliche Veränderung der Conditio humana leben von der Wahrheit, «daß das Objekt ihres Verfügens ein Subjekt ist und bleiben muß» (W. Korff) oder werden soll. Das setzt den entsprechenden Eingriffen ihre Ziele und gewisse Grenzen. Lassen sich die Eingriffe nicht mehr von der betroffenen Person menschlich verarbeiten und nicht mehr an ihre Personalität rückkoppeln, so werden sie menschlich gesehen sinnlos. Die Interessen des Patienten, die Interessen der allgemeinen Volksgesundheit und die Interessen des wissenschaftlichen Fortschritts müssen darum an einer «Gesamtsicht der menschlichen Person in einer Personengemeinschaft orientiert sein[6].» Fortschritte in der Körpermedizin müssen darum durch die Entwicklung einer erweiterten Ich-Sensibilität ausgeglichen werden, wenn sie menschlich verarbeitet werden sollen. Es ist schon heute ein ethisches Problem für viele, den sinnvollen Ausgleich zwischen ihrem Leib-Sein und ihrem Körper-Haben zu finden. Wenn sich das Ich nicht mehr leiblich inkarnieren kann, sondern sich seinen Körper permanent in der Distanz der Auswechselbarkeit gewisser Körperteile halten muß, entsteht eine Gleichgültigkeit gegenüber dem eigenen und fremden leiblichen Leben; vom Body-counting in Vietnam angefangen bis zu Verhaltensweisen, die der Ausdruck «play it cool» beschreibt. Die Selbsterfahrung als eines Dinges macht zwar in gewisser Weise *unverwundbar*, macht aber auch *liebesunfähig* und unproduktiv. Je mehr Unverwundbarkeit und Schmerzlosigkeit medizinisch möglich werden, um so mehr sollte man sich auf die Verwundbarkeit durch sinnvolle humane Schmerzen der Liebe besinnen. Anwendung und Gebrauch von Medikamenten finden ihre Grenze an der drohenden Gefühlskälte des Menschen. Damit wird das bisher durch die Leiblichkeit gegebene Ich-Bewußtsein zu einer personalen Aufgabe. Man muß seine leiblichen Inkarnationen bewußt suchen und das Risiko seiner Verwundbarkeit wissend eingehen*.

2. Leben und erlebtes Leben

Ein zweites sprachliches Symbol heißt «Leben». Im Kampf ums Dasein heißt Leben *Überleben*. Heute kann das Überleben sehr weit ausgedehnt und der Tod hinausgezögert werden. Es können Menschen am Leben erhalten werden, ohne daß sie davon noch irgend etwas spüren. Damit wird fraglich, was wir meinen, wenn wir «Leben» sagen. Für die auf Lebenserhaltung verpflichtete Medizin ist aber sehr wichtig, wenigstens in Umrissen zu wissen, was menschliches Leben genannt werden kann. Man kann sich nicht mehr darauf verlassen, daß sich Leben von selbst versteht, daß es ohne menschliches Zutun hingenom-

---

* Darum sagte Jeanne Hersch: «Ertragenkönnen ist ein Teil der Gesundheit.» (Siehe Seite 351.)

men und hingegeben werden muß. Je mehr Menschen das Schicksal von Menschen bestimmen können, um so mehr brauchen sie eine menschliche Definition vom Leben. Das ist bei der Kontrolle von Geburt und Tod besonders prekär, wird aber in der Mitte des Lebens ebenso problematisch. Ohne die gefährlichen praktischen Fragen und rechtlichen Probleme aus den Augen zu lassen, möchte ich für die Diskussion eine vorläufige Definition vorschlagen: *Menschliches Leben ist angenommenes, geliebtes und erlebtes Leben*[7].

Wo Leben nicht angenommen, geliebt und erlebt werden kann, haben wir es nicht mehr mit menschlichem Leben zu tun. Erfährt ein Kind nicht, daß es angenommen wird, so wird es krank. Nimmt ein Mensch sich selbst nicht an, so verliert er seine Lebendigkeit. Kann ein Leben nicht mehr erlebt werden, so ist es tot. Man kann dann weiter sagen, daß menschliches Sein (esse) Interessiertsein (inter-esse) ist. Es ist lebendig, solange es an anderem Leben teilnehmen kann und von anderem Leben Teilnahme erfährt. Teilnahmslosigkeit und Verlassenheit nennen wir darum «totes Leben». Menschliches Leben ist lebendig, solange es in Beziehungen und Verhältnissen existiert. Verhältnislosigkeit nennen wir darum «Tod». In den Industriegesellschaften und den medizinisch gut versorgten Gesellschaften breiten sich schon heute in erschreckendem Maße Erlebnisarmut, Apathie und Desinteresse am Leben aus. «Es ist eine Welt von Eigenschaften ohne Mann entstanden, von Erlebnissen ohne den, der sie erlebt, und es sieht beinahe so aus, als ob im Idealfall der Mensch überhaupt nicht mehr privat erlebt würde und die freundliche Schwere der Verantwortung sich in ein Formelsystem von möglichen Bedeutungen auflösen solle» (R. Musil[8]). Die Monotonie des apathischen Lebens ist eine Krankheit, die sich nicht mehr medizinisch heilen läßt, sondern nur durch die Überwindung der Einheitskulturen, die wir produziert haben, durch eine kulturelle Vielfalt, durch das Zusammenleben mit Andersartigen und die bewußte Annahme der Schmerzen, die Differenzen und Konflikte mit sich bringen. Erlebtes Leben ist ein Leben, das den Widerspruch in sich enthält und die Kraft findet, Widersprüche in sich zu fassen und auszuhalten*.

3. Familienplanung und Geburtenkontrolle

Durch neuere medizinische Erkenntnisse und Mittel ist die Geburt eines Kindes nicht mehr Sache der Natur, sondern der Freiheit und Verantwortung von Menschen. Durch «die Pille» können geschlechtliche Vereinigungen der Liebe von solchen der Zeugung unterschieden werden. Die Zeugung und Geburt eines Kindes ist damit eine moralische und soziale Frage geworden. Zwar gehört bisher Elternschaft zur Erfüllung menschlichen Lebens ebenso wie Kindschaft. Aber die Verantwortung für ein Kind hat sich von dem Zeitpunkt nach der Geburt auf die Zeit vor der Zeugung verlagert. Sie ist damit wesentlich

---

* Ich stimme mit Jeanne Hersch überein, wenn sie sagt: «Der Mensch bleibt ein Wesen, dem es obliegt, während Krankheit und angesichts des Todes – durch die Art und Weise, wie er sie erträgt – den Sinn des Lebens, seines Lebens, aufrechtzuerhalten. Dieser Sinn ist nicht die Gesundheit. Die Gesundheit steht im Dienst dieses Sinnes.» (Siehe Seite 351.)

größer geworden. Die Zahl der ungewollten Kinder kann vermindert werden. Zur Geburt eines Kindes gehört also der bewußte Wille und die übernommene Verantwortung für das Kind. Sofern die Eltern als Bürger in einer Gemeinschaft leben, haben sie mit der Verantwortung für ihre Kinder auch eine Verantwortung für die Gemeinschaft übernommen, wie umgekehrt auch die Gemeinschaft an ihrer Verantwortung für die Kinder partizipiert. Zum menschlichen Leben eines Kindes gehört darum nicht nur der biologische Zeugungs- und Geburtsvorgang, sondern ebenso wesentlich die Annahme durch die Eltern und die Gemeinschaft. Das *Recht zum Leben* ist damit nicht mehr eine Naturgegebenheit, sondern eine Aufgabe der Eltern und der Gemeinschaft, die es zu erteilen haben. Daraus entstehen zunächst Rechte der Geburtenkontrolle durch Eltern und Gemeinschaft. Daraus können später auch gewisse Rechte der Eugenik entstehen, obwohl diese eine «humane» Gesellschaft voraussetzen würden, deren Auswahlkriterien den bisher begründeten Verdacht des Machtmißbrauchs entkräften würden. *Kinder müssen angenommen werden*, das ist meines Erachtens die wirklich menschliche Seite einer Geburt. Der Akt der Annahme geht der bewußten Zeugung eines Kindes seitens der Eltern voraus. Er folgt aber auch auf die Geburt des Kindes und muß in den Verhältnissen seines Aufwachsens immer wiederholt werden. Müssen durch Geburtenkontrolle auch der Gesellschaft Rechte eingeräumt werden, so muß auch von ihr die bewußte Annahme von Kindern erwartet werden. Man kann dann keine kinderfeindlichen Städte mehr bauen. Auch Kinderlose in der Gesellschaft müssen dann dieses Recht der Annahme und des Zugangs zu den Kindern bekommen. Das würde eine vorsichtige Entprivatisierung der Familien bedeuten, ohne daß die notwendigen personalen Verhältnisse von Eltern und Kindern aufgelöst werden müßten. Gehen wir davon aus, daß menschliches Leben *angenommenes Leben* ist, dann sind diese Fragen wichtiger als die Fragen nach dem Zeitpunkt für den Beginn des menschlichen Lebens, die bei Schwangerschaftsunterbrechungen noch wichtig sind, durch Fortschritte in der Familienplanung sich aber erübrigen werden.

4. Der Tod des Körpers – der Tod des Menschen

Es ist heute schwierig, das definitive Ende des Lebens zu bestimmen, denn der Mensch kann von Organen seines Körpers «überlebt» werden. Die Differenzierung verschiedener Organtode hat die Grenze von Leben und Tod unscharf gemacht. Das Sterben ist biologisch gesehen ein negativer Rückkoppelungsprozeß, der sich in mehreren Phasen über eine längere Zeit erstreckt. Es gibt Menschen, bei denen das Gehirn endgültig seinen Dienst nach langem Herzstillstand versagt hat, bei denen aber Herz und Atmung ihre Funktionen wieder aufgenommen haben. Ihr Körper lebt ein bewußtloses Leben weiter, aber lebendig, im Sinne eines seines Daseins bewußten Lebens, sind sie nicht mehr. Es ist ein nicht mehr erlebbares Leben. Weil das vollständige Erlöschen der Gehirnfunktionen nach dem heutigen Stand des Wissens irreversibel ist, kann man im empirischen Bereich den Gehirntod als « Realsymbol für das Ende des menschlichen Lebens ansehen[9].» Mit ihm erlischt die menschliche Rechtsperson, auch wenn gewisse Organe weiter am Leben erhalten werden können.

Wenn biologisch gesehen die Grenze von Leben und Tod unscharf wird und der Tod, je nach Stand des medizinischen Wissens und Könnens, seine klare Definition verliert, dann wird es um so wichtiger, den Tod als *Tod des ganzen Menschen* menschlich zu verstehen und durch bewußte Einstellungen auf den Tod in das erlebte Leben zu integrieren. Der Tod kann zwar durch das Absterben lebenswichtiger Organteile *festgestellt werden*, er wird aber vom Menschen *erfahren* an der Liebe, die die Seele verleiblicht und den Leib beseelt. Je mehr wir uns in der *Liebe* inkarnieren, um so verwundbarer werden wir durch den Tod; durch den Tod derer, die wir lieben und durch das eigene Sterben. Je mehr umgekehrt das *Interesse am Leben* erlischt, um so weniger spüren wir Trauer und Schmerz, weil wir den Tod seelisch schon vorweggenommen haben[10]. Viele Menschen haben heute mit Hilfe von Drogen Techniken entwickelt, im Ernstfall des Todes das Leben nicht mehr erleben zu müssen; Techniken der Gleichgültigkeit und Apathie. Eine Ethik des angenommenen, geliebten und erlebten Lebens muß darum ihrerseits Einstellungen auf den Tod einüben und das Sterben aus seiner Verdrängung oder Beschönigung befreien. Wie das Leben und die Liebe eine Kunst sind, so ist auch das Sterbenkönnen eine Kunst. Wir wissen zwar im doppelten Sinne, wie man sich «das Leben nimmt», wir wissen aber wenig davon, wie man es menschlich und mit Würde lassen kann. Der Mensch hat ein *Recht auf seinen eigenen Tod*, wie er ein Recht auf sein Leben hat. Die medizinischen Möglichkeiten, die Grenze von Leben und Tod zu verschieben und unbewußt zu machen, werden dann human benutzt, wenn der Mensch sich auf seinen Tod vorbereitet und sein Leben, wenn es so weit ist, bewußter als heute aus der Hand gibt. Diese andere Einstellung zum Tod fordert einen Erziehungsprozeß, der die Sperren der Verdrängung gegen Tod und Trauer aufhebt, damit das Leben wieder liebenswert wird. Gerade weil mit dem biomedizinischen Fortschritt keine Glücksgarantie verbunden ist, muß eine Ethik der Humanität, die ihm gewachsen sein soll, beides vor Augen haben: die medizinische Linderung des Leidens und die Abschaffung gewisser Krankheit sowie die menschliche Annahme und bewußte Verarbeitung von Leiden, Krankheitszeiten und Sterben. Wie die Ordnung des Körpers in die Ordnung der menschlichen Person integriert werden muß, so muß auch der biomedizinische Fortschritt in die Ordnung der Humanität integriert werden.

Anmerkungen

1.   Diese Frage wurde auf dem Ciba-Symposium in London 1962 mehrfach gestellt. Vergleiche: *Das Umstrittene Experiment: Der Mensch.* Ed. R. Jungk, J. Mundt. München: Desch, 1966.
2.   Ebenda, p. 33.
3.   Ebenda, p. 36.
4.   Franz Böckle: Ethische Aspekte der Organtransplantation beim Menschen. *Studium Generale 23*, 444–459 (1970).

5. JEANNE HERSCH: *Proceedings of the Symposium on Science Politica and Biomedical Research*, Nr. 16, p. 75.

6. MICHAEL MARLET: Medizinische Experimente am Menschen? *Orientierung 33*, 21 ff. (1969).

7. Vergleiche dazu ALFRED GIERER: *Die physikalischen Grundlagen der Biologie und das Selbstverständnis des Menschen*. München, 1969.

8. ROBERT MUSIL: *Der Mann ohne Eigenschaften*, p. 150. Hamburg: Rowohlt, 1952. Ähnlich ERICH FROMM: *The Revolution of Hope*, pp. 38 ff., 82 ff. New York: Harper & Row, 1968.

9. FRANZ BÖCKLE: Ethische Aspekte der Organtransplantation beim Menschen. *Studium Generale 23*, 457 (1970). Vergleiche dazu E. JÜNGEL: *Tod*. Stuttgart: Kreuz-Verlag, 1971.

10. JÜRGEN MOLTMANN: *Perspektiven der Theologie*, p. 51 ff. München: Kaiser, 1968, und: *Resurrection as Hope*, Ingersoll-Lecture, *The Harvard Theological Review 61*, Nr. 2, 129 ff. (1968).

Zusammenfassung

1. Wissenschaftlicher Fortschritt und menschliche Interessen stehen in einem Prozeß ihrer gegenseitigen Bedingung und Veränderung. Die ethische Frage ist die Frage nach den Motivationen, Gestalten und Veränderungen der in den wissenschaftlichen und technischen Fortschritt der Biochemie investierten menschlichen Interessen. Sie umfaßt darum nicht erst die Reaktionen von Mensch und Gesellschaft auf die Ergebnisse des biomedizinischen Fortschritts, sondern auch schon die Aktionen von Menschen und Gesellschaft im biomedizinischen Fortschritt.

2. Das bisherige Ethos des biochemischen Fortschritts liegt in den menschlichen *Interessen* am Kampf gegen die Krankheit und für die Gesundheit sowie in der Selbstbefreiung von der Natur und an der Macht über die Natur. Aus diesen Interessen heraus sind gewisse *Hoffnungen* auf die Verbesserung der menschlichen Kondition, die Erweiterung des Weltverstandes, die Steigerung seiner Glücksfähigkeit und die Anhebung seiner Moralität entstanden. Aus diesen Hoffnungen entstehen *konkrete Visionen:* die Vision einer keimfreien Welt, die Vision eines schmerzfreien Lebens, die Vision eines endlosen Lebens und einer Beschleunigung der menschlichen Evolution.

3. Der biomedizinische Fortschritt verändert die grundlegenden ethischen Interessen von Mensch und Gesellschaft. Der Fortschritt ist so lange ambivalent, als der Mensch ein unzuverlässiges Wesen ist. Er enttäuscht seine eigenen Hoffnungen, weil ihre Erfüllung mit sozialen Ersatzleistungen an die zerstörten natürlichen Systeme verbunden ist, deren Kosten größer als die Gewinne werden können. Er enttäuscht seine eigenen Hoffnungen durch ihre Erfüllung, sofern der Sinn des Lebens dann neu formuliert werden muß, wenn dieser Sinn sich nicht mehr aus dem Kampf ums Dasein von selbst versteht.

4. Die durch den biomedizinischen Fortschritt hervorgerufenen Veränderungen menschlicher Interessen können als Übergang vom *Kampf ums Dasein* zum *Streben nach Erfüllung* beschrieben werden. Bestimmungen des Sinns menschlichen Lebens, die den Kampf ums Dasein transzendieren, wer-

den dadurch aktuell. Die Veränderung des Ethos des Kampfes ums Dasein zum *Ethos des Friedens im Dasein* wird zur Aufgabe der Gegenwart. Das Prinzip der *Selbsterhaltung gegen andere* kann zum Prinzip der *Selbsterfüllung im anderen* gewandelt werden. Aggressionssysteme können durch Kooperationssysteme überwunden werden. Der Gruppenegoismus («Gleich und gleich gesellt sich gern»), der aus unseren Gesellschaften *Segregationsgesellschaften* macht, muß durch ein neues Interesse am spannungsreichen und konfliktgeladenen Leben mit anderen («Anerkennung des anderen») überwunden werden. Dazu gehört eine neue Einschätzung von Krankheit, Alter und Tod. *Krankheit* ist ein ebenso wichtiger *Lernprozeß* der Person wie das gesunde, aktive Leben. Das *Altern* hat seine eigene *Würde*, die nicht nach dem Leistungsmaßstab gemessen werden kann. Sterben ist ein menschlich ebenso wichtiger Vorgang wie Geburt und Leben.

5. Das *Recht zu leben* und das *Recht zu sterben* ergibt sich nicht mehr von selbst, sondern muß bewußt formuliert werden. Das verlangt eine neue Symbolik des Sinnes des Lebens. Angesichts der medizinischen Möglichkeiten muß der Mensch einen neuen *Ausgleich von Leib-sein und Körper-haben* finden. Medizinische Eingriffe finden ihr Ziel und ihre Grenze an der Kraft ihrer menschlichen Verarbeitung durch den betroffenen Menschen und die menschliche Gesellschaft. Die Heilung menschlicher Wunden hat ihren Sinn darin, den Menschen fähig zu machen, sich für die Schmerzen der Liebe und die Verwundbarkeit der Kreativität zu öffnen. – Ist Leben nicht mehr Überleben, dann können wir *menschliches Leben* als *angenommenes, geliebtes und erlebtes Leben* verstehen. Nichtangenommenes und nicht mehr erlebbares Leben ist nicht mehr menschliches Leben. – Damit wird für die Frage nach dem Beginn des menschlichen Lebens seine *Annahme* durch Eltern und Gesellschaft vordringlich. – Damit wird für die Bestimmung des Todes des Menschen die Erlebbarkeit des Lebens und die bewußte Annahme des Sterbens vordringlich.

Summary

1. Scientific progress and human interests are undergoing a process of mutual interaction and modification. Ethics involve the inquiry into the motivation, shaping and changing of the human interests that have been invested in the scientific and technical progress of biochemistry. They therefore include not only the reactions of man and society to the results of biomedical progress, but also their actions within this progress.

2. Until now, the ethical considerations in biomedical progress have been guided by human *interests* in the fight against disease and for health, as well as in man's liberation from the bonds of nature and in gaining power over nature. These interests have given rise to certain *hopes* for the improvement of the human condition, the expansion of world understanding, an increased capacity for happiness and a higher standard of morality. From these hopes, certain

concrete visions have arisen: the vision of a germ-free world, of a life without pain, of unending life and an acceleration of the evolution of mankind.

3. Biomedical progress alters the basic ethical interests of man and society. As long as man is an unreliable creature, progress is ambivalent. He disappoints his own hopes because, in order to fulfil them, social efforts have to be made to replace the natural systems that have been destroyed and the costs are greater than the profits that can be gained. He disappoints his own hopes even in fulfilling them, because the meaning of life must then be reformulated when this meaning is no longer self-evident from the struggle to survive.

4. The changes in human interests brought about by biomedical progress can be described as a transition from the *struggle to survive* to the *striving for fulfilment*. Thus the need today is to determine the meaning of human life in a way that transcends the struggle for mere survival. It is the task of the present time to change the ethos of the struggle for existence into an *ethos of peaceful existence*. The principle of *self-preservation against others* can be transformed into the principle of *self-fulfilment through others*. Systems of aggression can be replaced by systems of cooperation. Group egoism ('Birds of a feather flock together'), which makes our society a *segregated society*, must be overcome by a new acceptance of life with others with all its tensions and conflicts ('acceptance of otherness'). This must include a reassessment of illness, ageing and death. Illness is a *process of learning* that is as important to the individual as healthy, active life. *Growing old* has its own *dignity*, which cannot be measured by output and performance. Death is a human process just as important as birth or life.

5. *The right to live* and *the right to die* are no longer a matter of course but must be consciously formulated. This demands a new symbolism for the meaning of life. In view of the medical possibilities, man has to find a *new balance* between his mere *bodily existence* and his *physical embodiment*. The aim and the limits of medical procedures are set by the ability of the individual involved and of society to assimilate them in human terms. The healing of human wounds has the purpose of fitting the individual for experiencing the pain of love and the frailty of creation. If life is no longer mere survival, *human life* can be understood as *life that is experienced, loved and accepted*. Life that is not accepted or can no longer be experienced is no longer human life. *Acceptance* by parents and society is thus of prime importance in the question of what constitutes the beginning of human life. And the ability to experience life and the conscious acceptance of death are of prime importance in determining the death of a person.

Résumé

1. Le progrès scientifique et les aspirations humaines s'interpénètrent et se conditionnent mutuellement. Le problème éthique est celui des motivations, des

formes et des transformations des activités humaines engagées dans le progrès scientifique et technique de la médecine. Par conséquent, il englobe non seulement les réactions de l'homme et de la société aux résultats du progrès biomédical, mais déjà les actions des hommes et de la société qui contribuent au progrès biomédical.

2. Jusqu'ici, l'éthique du progrès biomédical résidait dans l'*intérêt* que l'homme porte à la lutte contre la maladie et pour la santé, ainsi qu'à l'autolibération de la nature et à la domination de celle-ci. De cet intérêt sont nés certains *espoirs* quant à l'amélioration de la condition humaine, à l'élévation du niveau intellectuel du monde, à l'augmentation de l'aptitude au bonheur et au relèvement de la moralité. De ces espoirs sont issues des *visions* concrètes: la vision d'un monde exempt de germes pathogènes, la vision d'une vie exempte de douleur, la vision d'une vie illimitée et d'une accélération de l'évolution humaine.

3. Le progrès biomédical transforme les aspirations éthiques fondamentales de l'homme et de la société. Le progrès restera ambivalent aussi longtemps que l'homme restera un être non fiable. Il déçoit ses propres espoirs, car leur accomplissement implique que la société substitue aux systèmes naturels détruits des mesures dont le coût peut alors dépasser les bénéfices qu'elles procurent. Il déçoit ses propres espoirs par leur réalisation, dans la mesure où le sens de la vie doit alors être à nouveau formulé, lorsque ce sens ne découle plus naturellement de la lutte pour l'existence.

4. Les transformations des aspirations humaines provoquées par le progrès biomédical peuvent être qualifiées de transition de la *lutte pour l'existence à l'effort tendant à l'accomplissement*. De ce fait, les définitions du sens de la vie humaine qui transcendent la lutte pour l'existence deviennent actuelles. La transformation de l'éthique de la lutte pour l'existence en une *éthique de la paix dans l'existence* devient la tâche du présent.

Le principe de l'*autoconservation opposant les uns aux autres* peut être transformé en un principe de *réalisation de soi dans l'autre*. Les systèmes d'agression peuvent être supplantés par des systèmes de coopération. L'égoïsme de groupe («Qui se ressemble s'assemble») qui transforme nos sociétés en «*sociétés de ségrégation*» doit être remplacé par un intérêt nouveau pour une vie où l'estime portée à autrui permettra de surmonter tensions et conflits. Cela implique une nouvelle évaluation de la maladie, de l'âge et de la mort. La *maladie* est un *processus d'apprentissage* aussi important pour la personnalité que la vie active menée en bonne santé. Le *vieillissement* a sa *dignité* propre qui ne peut pas être mesurée à l'échelle du rendement. Mourir est un processus humainement aussi important que la naissance et la vie.

5. Le *droit de vivre* et le *droit de mourir* ne sont plus acquis naturellement, mais doivent être formulés consciemment, ce qui exige une nouvelle définition du sens de la vie. En présence des possibilités médicales, l'homme doit trouver un nouvel équilibre entre l'*identité somatique et la somatognosie*. Les interventions médicales trouvent leur but et leurs limites dans la force de les assimiler

humainement que possèdent l'homme atteint et la société humaine. La guérison des plaies humaines sert à rendre l'homme capable de s'ouvrir aux peines de l'amour et à la vulnérabilité de la créativité. Si la vie n'est plus la survie, nous pouvons qualifier la *vie humaine* de *vie acceptée, aimée et vécue.* Une vie non acceptée et ne pouvant plus être vécue consciemment n'est plus une vie humaine. De ce fait, la question de savoir quand commence exactement la vie humaine implique en premier lieu son *acceptation* par les parents et par la société, et la définition de la mort de l'homme présuppose la vie vécue consciemment et l'acceptation consciente du passage de la vie à la mort.

Resumen

1. El progreso científico y los intereses humanos se condicionan y modifican recíprocamente. El problema ético concierne las motivaciones, la creación y el cambio de los intereses humanos implicados en los adelantos científicos y técnicos de la medicina. Por consiguiente, abarca no sólo las reacciones del hombre y de la sociedad ante los resultados del progreso biomédico sino también las acciones de los hombres y de la sociedad que contribuyen a dicho adelanto.

2. Hasta ahora, la ética del progreso biomédico radicaba en los *intereses* humanos que suponía la lucha contra la enfermedad y en favor de la salud, así como la emancipación del hombre de la naturaleza y su dominio sobre ésta. De esos intereses nacieron ciertas *esperanzas* de mejorar la condición humana, ampliar la comprensión universal, acrecentar la aptitud a la felicidad y elevar la moral. Esperanzas que, a su vez, dieron origen a *visiones concretas*: la visión de un mundo exento de gérmenes patógenos, la visión de una vida libre de dolor, la visión de una vida sin fin y de una evolución humana acelerada.

3. El progreso biomédico modifica los intereses fundamentales del hombre y de la sociedad. Dicho progreso será ambivalente mientras el ser humano sea imprevisible. El hombre decepciona sus propias esperanzas, porque para realizarlas tendría que sustituir los sistemas naturales destruidos por prestaciones sociales, cuyos gastos podrían exceder los beneficios que procuraran. Decepciona sus esperanzas realizándolas, por cuanto el sentido de la vida debe ser formulado de nuevo al no emanar más, naturalmente, de la lucha por la existencia.

4. La modificación de los intereses humanos provocada por el progreso biomédico puede ser considerada como una transición de la *lucha por la existencia* a la *aspiración de la plena realización de sí mismo.* De ahí que las definiciones del sentido de la vida humana que trasciendan la lucha por la existencia se vuelvan actuales. Convertir la ética de la lucha por la existencia en una *ética de la paz en la existencia* será la meta a la que debemos tender en la actualidad. El *principio de conservación que opone a unos contra otros* puede mudarse en un principio de *realización de sí mismo en el prójimo.* Los sistemas

de agresión pueden ser suplantados por sistemas de cooperación. El egoísmo de grupo que transforma nuestra sociedad en *sociedades segregadas* debe ceder el paso a un nuevo interés por una vida llena de tensiones y conflictos con los demás («reconocimiento del otro»). Esto supone una nueva apreciación de la enfermedad, de la edad y de la muerte. La *enfermedad* es un aprendizaje tan importante para la personalidad, como puede serlo la vida activa en buena salud. El *envejecer* tiene su propia dignidad, que no se deja medir con la escala del rendimiento, y el morir es un proceso humanamente tan importante como nacer o vivir.

5. El *derecho a vivir* y el *derecho a morir* ya no se dan por sí mismos, sino que tienen que ser formulados conscientemente. Esto supone un nuevo concepto de la vida. Ante las posibilidades de la medicina, el hombre tiene que establecer una nueva *relación entre «ser cuerpo» y «tener cuerpo»*. Las intervenciones médicas encuentran su justificación y sus límites en la capacidad del hombre y de la sociedad para asimilarlas. La curación de las heridas tiene un sentido en tanto haga al hombre capaz de abrirse a los sufrimientos del amor y de asumir la vulnerabilidad que entraña el acto creador. Si vivir ya no sólo es sobrevir, podemos concebir como humana la vida aceptada, amada y consciente. Una vida no aceptada y que no pueda ser vivida en plena consciencia, ya no es humana. – Por lo tanto, para determinar el comienzo de la vida humana, es primordial su *aceptación* por los padres y por la sociedad. – Del mismo modo, es primordial, para determinar la muerte de un ser humano, la vivencia y la aceptación consciente del tránsito de la vida a la muerte.

Comments on the drug abuse problem

by AVRAM GOLDSTEIN

These remarks are intended to supplement Dr Pichot's interesting contribution (see pp. 286–303). Organized society in every country is in a dilemma as to how best to deal with the growing problem of drug abuse. There are two aspects to this problem: the harm to the health of the individual, and the harm to the health of society. We have a right to be concerned with both. It is not sufficient for us to describe and attempt to analyse the causes and consequences of the drug abuse pandemic. We have a duty to devise humane and effective ways of preventing, controlling, and mitigating both types of harm caused by it. It is essential for the community of biomedical scientists and physicians to offer some rational guidance in the face of the general hysteria, and to exercise creative initiative in bringing about the necessary changes in the way society approaches this difficult problem.

The drug abuse pandemic and society's attitude towards it

The root causes of the drug abuse pandemic are obviously complex. They will probably remain obscure. One cause of the current alarm over drug abuse lies in the undeniable fact that a pattern of behavior that has long been present in certain subcultures is now being assimilated into the dominant cultures. Thus, in the United States types of addiction formerly confined to ghetto populations have recently spread to the white middle- and upper-class youth[1].

A significant contributor to the pandemic is unquestionably the fact that mind-altering drugs have become legitimized through their widespread (and often overenthusiastic) medical use. This point has been dealt with quite fully by Dr Pichot.

Another important factor is the availability of pure drugs, which are much more potent than natural products. Coupled with the more widespread acceptance of the intravenous route of administration, these afford the possibility of more powerful and immediate pleasure than could be achieved before. The contrast between distilled liquors and beer or wine comes to mind. Wine, which cannot exceed about 15 percent in alcohol content, has been known and used for millennia without great danger. The sudden introduction of the much more powerful pure intoxicant, ethyl alcohol, into a culture may produce dramatically disruptive social effects. A well-documented example is the introduction of gin into England in the seventeenth century[2]. Mohammedan prohibitions against alcohol may also reflect concern over spread of knowledge about distillation in a wine-using society. Likewise, the dangers of opium were greatly intensified by the advent of the pure alkaloids, morphine and heroin, only about one hundred years ago. The same arguments may be applied to the other important drugs of abuse, products of the chemical industry, namely amphetamines, cocaine, barbiturates, and (one may anticipate) pure tetrahydrocannabinol.

A relevant fact emerging from psychopharmacologic research of the past decade tends to discredit the idea that special personality disorders underlie the development of drug addiction. The studies of the Michigan group [14] with monkeys show that opiates, as well as other drugs of abuse, are in themselves reinforcing. Any monkey, without previous experience, given the opportunity to inject such a substance, will predictably develop a pattern of compulsive addiction. Eventually the animal will do this to the exclusion of the classical instinctive behaviors concerned with satisfying hunger, thirst and sexual needs. As shown by OLDS[12], moreover, electrical self-stimulation of certain 'reward' centers in the medial forebrain bundle and elsewhere in the brain also leads to a pattern of compulsive behavior. The stimulation is so powerfully reinforcing that it is indulged in to the virtual exclusion of all normal activities. Thus, one can easily create, in monkeys or in rats, a state of addiction without the use of drugs. Very likely the addicting drugs stimulate the same or similar 'reward' centers, which have the normal function of subserving appropriate adaptive responses to pleasurable inputs. WIKLER[17] has shown that many of the phenomena leading to relapse in ex-addicts can be understood in the context of classical and operant conditioning. The circumstances under which a drug relieved anxiety or stress or an abstinence syndrome in the past, if they recur, will again evoke a powerful drive to use the drug.

It is quite possible, therefore, that the only conditions required for the initiation of a drug addiction are access to the drug, a willingness to try it and instruction by someone already expert in its use. One may properly ask, then, 'Why do not all who have access to a drug try it and become addicted?' The form of the question suggests the need for research upon those who resist being swept into a pattern of drug abuse, as well as upon those who succumb. Probably important in avoiding the first steps in the addiction process are a certain determination not to become involved, a willingness to be guided by the mores of society and the ability to foresee the long-term consequences of one's actions.

With the increasing recognition that drug addiction can happen to anyone (i.e. even to the sons and daughters of the 'establishment'), and not only to some criminal types or those with 'character disorders', we have to re-orient our thinking about the problem. Radical changes of attitude will have to be implemented before significant progress can be made. Fortunately we are living in an age (as pointed out so well by TOFFLER[15]) in which change occurs so rapidly as to defy imagination, and in which attitudes, too – even those long ingrained in our culture – can change rapidly. This was evidenced a decade or so ago in the rapid transformation of public attitudes towards alcoholism, which now is generally regarded as a disease rather than a vice. Recent changes in attitude towards contraception and abortion have been even more revolutionary. There is hope, therefore, that if the biomedical community speaks now with a clear voice, we may be listened to. Then changes that seemed impossible only yesterday might occur with surprising speed.

Changing society's attitudes towards drug abuse

The attitude of society throughout most of the world towards drug abuse has been characterized by deeply ingrained fear, inconsistency and hypocrisy, leading to punitive policies ('If we strike it down or lock it up, it will go away'). These policies have been remarkably unsuccessful, as judged by criteria of prevention, cure, and rehabilitation. We shall discuss these attitudes and the changes that are required.

1. A consistent position towards all mind-altering drugs

Curiously, the legal system that attempts to regulate drugs of abuse classifies and deals with them in ways that are often irrelevant to the actual harm they cause either to the individual or to society. The prime example of this irrationality is our attitude towards alcohol. To the pharmacologist, alcohol is a drug. There is absolutely no basis for distinguishing it in principle from other drugs. It is a mind-altering agent. It is a psychotropic drug. It also happens to be, on medical grounds, the one drug that is more directly harmful to the individual and to society than any other[6]. Alcoholism incapacitates far more people than all other drugs combined. In the United States today the accepted estimate is of some 9 million alcoholics, or roughly 4 percent of the entire population. An alcoholic is defined, for the purpose of such an estimate, as one whose use of this drug is out of control, and whose life therefore is dominated by the need for alcohol. It includes those at various stages of the well-known progression – loss of reliability, loss of employment, loss of family, loss of income, loss of health, loss of self-respect – ending sometimes at 'skid row', the abode of the derelicts.

Not only in point of numbers of victims – and their families too – but also in other respects, alcohol is the worst drug of abuse. Its immediate intoxicating effects are particularly unpleasant (though not more so than the barbiturates, which resemble it closely). It causes a characteristic loss of judgment in the very early stages of intoxication, resulting in profound impairment of the performance of complex tasks, such as driving an automobile. Anyone who has measured such effects in the laboratory will not be surprised that alcohol is a factor in one half of the more than 50,000 road fatalities annually in the United States[18]. The release of inhibitions during alcohol intoxication also produces another kind of behavior that is especially dangerous to society – a boisterous, aggressive style, leading easily and frequently to physical violence and even to homicide.

The health hazards of alcohol to the individual are severe. There are nutritional disturbances associated with increased caloric dependence upon ethanol at the expense of a balanced diet. Hepatic cirrhosis and irreversible neurologic deficits are well-known outcomes of alcoholism. Less well recognized, even now, is the extreme gravity of the alcohol withdrawal syndrome, with its high mortality from delirium tremens and frank grand mal convulsive seizures – a far more serious withdrawal syndrome than is seen with any other drug (excepting again the barbiturates)[8,9,16].

We understand this, of course, in the biomedical community, but it is interesting to see how readily we ourselves are swept into the general tide. Usually, having made an appropriate acknowledgement of the existence of alcoholism, one goes on to wax eloquent over the dangers of cannabis or heroin, never again mentioning the most important drug of all. Only recently, a research article appeared in the journal *Science*[13] in which the authors, who certainly should have known better, speak about alcohol *in contradistinction* to 'drugs'. The public at large, of course, does not consider alcohol a drug at all, and this makes it almost impossible to engage in rational discourse with laymen and politicians (especially over a lunchtime cocktail) about the dangers of drug abuse. We should recognize how difficult it is, even for scientists and physicians, to avoid falling into such a trap. We are immersed in society's prejudices, as we are immersed in the atmosphere itself; we breathe and assimilate this milieu, without even noticing it is there.

Tobacco is another touchstone by which the sincerity of attitudes towards drug abuse may be gauged. Again we are dealing with an addicting drug that causes incalculable harm to individuals and society[19,21]. And again we find this dangerous drug consigned to a special category, as though it were not part of the drug abuse problem.

Finally, the absurd and irrational way marihuana has been dealt with is germane to this discussion[10]. Quite clearly, from the pharmacologic point of view, cannabis, at least in its crude form in marihuana cigarettes, does not present a very serious danger. Certainly the danger is less than the demonstrated hazards of alcohol and tobacco[7]. To say, in the face of the facts, that this is a menacing drug 'because we never know what we may discover about it' is to defend a hypocritical position under the guise of scientific objectivity. We are called upon constantly to make decisions about drug safety on the basis of existing knowledge and probable outcomes. Applying the same criteria by which we admit other drugs to general use, we have to rate cannabis as a relatively innocuous recreational intoxicant. This is not to say, of course, that excessive use is harmless. The crucial point about drug abuse is that, used in moderation, many mind-altering drugs may have an appropriate recreational role. Danger arises only if there is a quantitative and qualitative change from incidental, recreational use to immoderate use and an increasing preoccupation with the securing and self-administration of a drug. That is a difference of profound significance, which really distinguishes the addict from the drug user. It is the same difference that distinguishes the social drinker from the alcoholic.

I urge, as a first step towards closing the 'generation gap' and refuting the accusations of hypocrisy with which the young belabor the old, that biomedical scientists and physicians make a special and persistent effort to include in the category of drug abuse all those drugs, including alcohol and tobacco, which properly belong there, regardless of their current legal status.

2. Elimination of punitive attitudes towards drug abuse and substitution of compassion and help, in the best tradition of medicine

Drug abuse is bad, not because it is illegal, but because it destroys lives and threatens others. We are concerned with drug abuse as a medical and public health problem. The person who is entrapped in a behavior pattern that limits his choices in life, a behavior pattern with which he himself is often dissatisfied, is a person who needs medical help. There seems ample evidence that criminalizing drug users only makes matters worse, for a compulsion that is already so great as to supplant the normal satisfactions of life is unlikely to be suppressed by threats and legal actions. It is difficult to make a distinction between those who only use drugs and those who distribute drugs, at least at the street level, where these functions are intricately intertwined. Laws forbidding deviant behavior are especially subject to corruption in their enforcement. Particularly repulsive is the practice of entrapment, whereby police agents actually further the commission of crimes in order to make spectacular arrests. The instances that come to light, of corruption among those charged with enforcing the narcotic laws, make one wonder how atypical such corruption really is. The stricter the enforcement, the higher the black market price, so that a lucrative industry depends upon the law for its profitability[20]. And the more driven to crime is the user who is under a compulsion to support his habit. We must ask seriously if the entire attempt to control drug abuse through law, especially by penalties on the drug user, creates more problems than it solves, makes things worse rather than better[11].

I do not wish to be misunderstood. I am certainly not advocating that people be encouraged to use these potentially dangerous drugs, nor am I minimizing the serious harm that they can cause both to the individual and to society. I am simply expressing the pragmatic point of view that we may serve our purpose better by using alternative means of dissuading people from using drugs, means that may well be more effective than the punitive ones upon which we have relied with so little success.

I think it quite important, in this connection, not to draw the wrong lessons from the British experience[3]. For a long time the British system, in which addicts were able to obtain drugs freely upon prescription by a physician, was regarded by many as a noble example of how the spread of addiction could be limited without criminalizing the users. Abuses of this system developed, which did indeed permit the spread of addiction in England. It is significant, however, that with some administrative changes but without any change in principle, the expanded epidemic has now apparently been brought under control. The system again appears to be dealing with the problem in an appropriate medical fashion.

If we regard drug addicts as people in need of medical help, it is absolutely essential to keep the lines of communication and trust open, so that these victims of drug abuse can be brought into some kind of treatment. It may be argued – and quite properly – that our knowledge is still inadequate as to what the best treatments may be. Here is where carefully controlled clinical investigations are urgently needed.

3. Offering treatment to those who want treatment

I would like to discuss the treatment problem from the vantage point of my experience during the past year and a half operating a treatment program for hard-core heroin addicts[4,5]. We use oral methadone as a primary tool for stabilizing the addicts and bringing them into a therapeutic environment in which they can be helped to change their life styles and to learn alternative satisfactions to those obtained through heroin. Disillusioning experiences in other (especially compulsory) kinds of treatment programs have led many to conclude that most heroin addicts are incorrigible. I believe this is incorrect. The majority of all hard-core addicts, in our experience, are motivated to seek a better life for themselves if they are given the opportunity to seek treatment in a program they can trust. Naturally, motivation is often mixed, there is a high degree of ambivalence, and the danger of relapse is great. Nevertheless, in a program now treating over 400 addicts, we have been able to retain two thirds of all those admitted for at least one year. Of these, 95 percent have ceased using heroin, or use it only very rarely. Similar success rates have been obtained in other methadone programs. Our aim is to rehabilitate these patients to the point where they are ready to lead drug-free lives without methadone or other narcotic drugs. One of our most encouraging findings has been that, contrary to the expectations of those who believe drug addicts will simply turn from one 'high' to another, there has been a reduction rather than an increase in the use of other dangerous drugs. Thus, our patients move towards a completely drug-free life while they are stabilized on a constant dose of methadone, which in itself produces no 'high'.

Of importance in the rehabilitation of heroin addicts – and this will probably apply to abusers of other drugs as well – is the use of peer-group techniques, through employment of ex-addicts as staff members, and the intensive involvement of patients in their own rehabilitative treatment. What is essential is to strengthen a motivation that already exists among addicts for whom the use of drugs to alter the state of consciousness, and the associated state of dependence, have become an unrewarding style of life. These people, who have been incarcerated repeatedly and who have rebelled against society's emphatic 'We don't want you using drugs', are able to break away from drugs when non-judgmental, non-punitive medical and paramedical help is offered to them.

4. Prevention of drug abuse

An important question, requiring investigation, is how one can best isolate foci of infection in this epidemic disease. To what extent is it permissible to use compulsion to remove infective foci from the communities, so that others are not drawn into the pattern of addiction? A good model might be the public health approach to venereal disease, where a careful blend of medical help and compulsion to undergo treatment have been successfully employed in the past. Perhaps treatment programs should involve a certain degree of isolation from the rest of the community. On the other hand, isolation of the kind imposed through law enforcement procedures has been characterized by a high degree of failure. One learns from addicts that as they leave a jail or compulsory treatment facility after a long incarceration, the dominant feeling is that they have 'earned a fix', i.e. the war between them and society is to continue, despite periodic setbacks. A significant advantage of methadone treatment is that the addict can remain within his family and community, and retain his personal liberty, while at the same time abstaining from drug use. Since the focus of epidemic spread in a community is the group of active addicts there, elimination of drug abuse in a methadone program should effectively limit the recruitment of new addicts.

Education of the young is of course crucial. If people really understood the dangers of the most harmful drugs, would they nevertheless become involved with them? Certainly, a degree of risk-taking is common in adolescents and even among some adults. On the other hand, the risks have not been honestly explained in most educational efforts in this field. When young people are told things about drugs (especially cannabis) that they know to be nonsense, and when drug abuse education ignores or glosses over alcohol and tobacco, they are naturally prone to discount things they are told that may be true and important. Cannabis should be de-emphasized and placed in proper perspective in the context of honest educational efforts about such really dangerous drugs as alcohol, tobacco, barbiturates, amphetamines and heroin. It is necessary to explain frankly to young people that although the opiate narcotics are not intrinsically very toxic, the dependence produced by them truly enslaves the individual. More than with any other group of drugs, the powerful reinforcement experienced with intravenous opiates leads almost inexorably to a compulsive pattern of addiction.

Finally, we need to remove the issue of drug abuse from the realm of crusades and politics and to put it firmly under the public health and community medicine aegis where it belongs. The medical profession must again become involved in this problem. We must assert our right to do this, free of interference from the law enforcers. Fortunately, circumstances right now, at least in the United States, seem to be favorable. The epidemic of heroin addiction among our men in Vietnam is being viewed by the public and by government in a sympathetic rather than a punitive manner, just as morphine addiction after the Civil War was considered a 'soldier's disease' and not a crime. An important step along the same lines would be a faster re-orientation of the World Health Organization towards these newer and more sympathetic attitudes towards the victims of drug abuse.

References

1. BENTEL, D.J., CRIM, D., SMITH, D.E.: The Year of the Middle Class Junkie. *Calif. Hlth 28*, No. 10, 1 (1971).
2. COFFEY, T.G.: Beer Street: Gin Lane; Some Views of 18th-Century Drinking. *Quart. J. Stud. Alcohol 27*, 669 (1966).
3. EDWARDS, G.: The British Approach to the Treatment of Heroin Addiction. *Lancet 1969/I*, 768.
4. GOLDSTEIN, A.: Blind-controlled Dosage Comparisons with Methadone in Two Hundred Patients; in: *Proceedings of the Third National Conference on Methadone Treatment*, New York, 14. 11. 1970.
5. GOLDSTEIN, A.: Blind-dosage Comparisons and Other Studies in a Large Methadone Program. *J. psyched. Drugs*, 1971. (In press.)
6. HIRSH, J.: Public Health and Social Aspects of Alcoholism. Chapter 1; in: *Alcoholism*. Ed. G.N. Thompson, Springfield, Ill.: C.C Thomas, 1956.
7. HOLLISTER, L.E.: Marihuana in Man: Three Years Later. *Science 172*, 21 (1971).
8. ISBELL, H., FRASER, H.F.: Addiction to Analgesics and Barbiturates. *Pharmacol. Rev. 2*, 355 (1950).
9. ISBELL, H., FRASER, H.F., WIKLER, A., BELLEVILLE, R.E., EISENMAN, A.J.: An Experimental Study of the Etiology of 'Rum Fits' and Delirium tremens. *Quart. J. Stud. Alcohol 16*, 1 (1955).
10. KAPLAN, J.: *Marihuana: The New Prohibition*. New York: World Publishing Co., 1970.
11. LINDESMITH, A.R.: *The Addict and the Law*. Bloomington: Indiana University Press, 1965.
12. OLDS, J.: Hypothalamic Substrates of Reward. *Physiol. Rev. 42*, 554 (1962).
13. RUBIN, E., LIEBER, C.S.: Alcoholism, Alcohol and Drugs. *Science 172*, 1097 (1971).
14. SCHUSTER, C.R., THOMPSON, T.: Self-administration of and Behavioral Dependence on Drugs. *Ann. Rev. Pharmacol. 9*, 483 (1969).
15. TOFFLER, A.: *Future Shock*. New York: Random House, 1970.
16. VICTOR, M., ADAMS, R.D.: The Effect of Alcohol on the Nervous System. *Res. Publ. Ass. nerv. ment. Dis. 32*, 526 (1953).
17. WIKLER, A.: Some Implications of Conditioning Theory for Problems of Drug Abuse. *Behav. Sci. 16*, 92 (1971).
18. Alcohol and Highway Safety: A Report to the Congress from the Secretary of Transportation. U.S. Department of Transportation, August 1968.
19. Smoking and Health, Surgeon General's Report. Washington, D. C.: Public Health Service Publication No. 1103, 1964.
20. The Economics of the Drug Market: Heroin. Ford Foundation Drug Abuse Survey Project, July 1971.
21. The Health Consequences of Smoking. Washington, D.C.: Public Health Service Publication No. 1696, 1967.

Summary

The biomedical community has a duty to provide sane and rational leadership in combating the present pandemic of drug abuse. We need to approach the matter logically and in a spirit of medical compassion, especially since punitive methods have generally failed or even been counterproductive. We need to give greatest attention to drugs like alcohol, barbiturates and amphetamines, which cause the greatest harm to individuals and society, consequently assigning a low priority to relatively more innocuous drugs like cannabis. We need to offer treatment to those who seek it, as we would to the victims of venereal diseases, trying to minimize the social stigma in order to maximize the trust and confidence that can bring more patients into our clinics. We need to participate actively in honest educational programs to teach young people the difference between recreational use of mild intoxicants and compulsive use of dependence-producing drugs, in the hope that they will avoid the latter.

Zusammenfassung

Die biomedizinische Wissenschaft ist verpflichtet, die Bekämpfung der gegenwärtig grassierenden Seuche des Drogenmißbrauchs verständig und planvoll zu leiten. Das Problem müssen wir folgerichtig und im Geiste des ärztlichen Mitgefühls angehen, besonders, weil sich strafrechtliche Maßnahmen meist als unwirksam erwiesen oder sogar negativ ausgewirkt haben. Größte Aufmerksamkeit ist Drogen wie Alkohol, Barbituraten und Amphetaminen, die über den einzelnen und die Gesellschaft am meisten Leid bringen, zu widmen, weshalb relativ harmloseren Drogen wie Cannabis eine geringere Dringlichkeitsstufe zuerkannt werden sollte. Wir müssen jenen, die darum ersuchen, eine Behandlung anbieten, und zwar in gleicher Weise, wie wir es bei den an venerischen Erkrankungen Leidenden tun, und wir sollten versuchen, sie von der gesellschaftlichen Ächtung zu befreien und so bei ihnen möglichst viel Vertrauen und Zuversicht erwecken. Das könnte mehr Patienten dazu bewegen, unsere Kliniken aufzusuchen. Es ist notwendig, daß wir uns aktiv an der Ausarbeitung aufgeschlossener Erziehungsprogramme beteiligen, um die Jugendlichen über den Unterschied zwischen der angenehm entspannenden Wirkung leichter Rauschmittel und dem zwanghaften Bedürfnis nach süchtigmachenden Drogen aufzuklären, in der Hoffnung, daß sie die letzteren meiden werden.

Résumé

La communauté biomédicale a le devoir de prendre la tête de la lutte contre la toxicomanie qui règne de nos jours à l'état pandémique et de le faire avec bon sens et discernement. Il faut que nous abordions le sujet avec logique et dans un esprit de compassion médicale, d'autant plus que les méthodes répressives ont échoué d'une manière générale – quand elles n'ont pas produit l'effet contraire. Nous devons prêter toute notre attention à des drogues comme l'alcool, les barbituriques et les amphétamines, car ce sont elles qui nuisent le plus aux individus et à la société et, par voie de conséquence, reléguer à un ordre d'urgence moins immédiat les substances relativement moins dangereuses, tel le cannabis. Nous devons offrir la possibilité d'un traitement à ceux qui le cherchent, comme nous le ferions pour les victimes d'une maladie vénérienne, tout en essayant de réduire les stigmates sociaux afin de créer un climat de confiance qui nous permettra de secourir plus de malades. Nous avons le devoir de participer activement à l'élaboration de programmes éducatifs loyaux pour enseigner aux jeunes gens la différence entre l'emploi récréatif de toxiques légers et l'usage obsessionnel de substances toxicomanigènes, dans l'espoir qu'ils éviteront ces dernières.

Resumen

A las profesiones sanitarias en conjunto les corresponde asumir el papel de adalid, sensato y objetivo, en el combate contra la actual pandemia de abuso de drogas. Es necesario abordar este asunto con inteligencia y ánimo comprensivo, especialmente después del fracaso casi general de los métodos coercitivos empleados, que han llegado incluso a ser contraproducentes. Debemos prestar toda nuestra atención a drogas tales como el alcohol, los barbitúricos y las anfetaminas, que son las que causan el mayor perjuicio tanto al individuo como a la sociedad, y conceder, por consiguiente, una importancia secundaria a sustancias relativamente menos peligrosas, como el cannabis. Debemos ofrecer tratamiento a quienes lo deseen, como lo haríamos para víctimas de enfermedades venéreas, tratando de reducir el prejuicio social existente y crear un clima de confianza que nos permita socorrer más pacientes. Asimismo tenemos que participar activamente en los programas educativos con una información veraz que enseñe a los jóvenes a distinguir entre el consumo recreativo y moderado de sustancias tóxicas leves y el uso imperioso de drogas que engendran farmacodependencia, con la esperanza de que evitarán esto último.

Nouveaux pouvoirs de l'homme, sens de sa vie et de sa santé

par JEANNE HERSCH

Croissance non maîtrisée des pouvoirs humains et perte d'identité

Toute tentative morale ou légale pour délimiter l'exercice légitime d'un pouvoir humain se réfère d'abord à la nature de ce pouvoir, à son étendue possible et à ses conséquences prévisibles. Elle vise donc un pouvoir connu et actuel. Elle n'anticipe pas. Elle veut remédier à des abus dont la menace est déjà manifeste.

N'importe quelle forme de pouvoir nouveau existe donc d'abord à l'état sauvage et produit ses effets désordonnés jusqu'au moment où un consensus se constitue contre ceux-ci et contre leur cause, ajoutant une contrainte à toutes celles qui sauvegardent la vie sociale et la vie tout court.

Dans une époque comme la nôtre, où l'accroissement et la multiplication des pouvoirs humains a pris une allure vertigineuse, le retard ordinaire de la maîtrise par règles et lois sur l'exercice de pouvoirs nouveaux entraîne deux difficultés essentielles. D'une part, le retard s'accroît, et la perplexité qui en résulte, d'autre part, est d'autant plus grande que les enjeux sont neufs, les possibilités offertes sans précédent, les conséquences à la fois plus vastes et plus durables, imprévisibles, irréversibles, alors que sont mises en jeu des valeurs contradictoires. Dans la perplexité, les «opinions» s'émiettent, se singularisent, et le consensus indispensable devient impossible à trouver.

Les pouvoirs humains nouveaux encore à l'état sauvage sont nombreux et dramatiquement puissants dans les domaines les plus divers. Leurs effets, voulus ou indirects, se propagent, on ignore jusqu'où, au fond des mers, dans les sols, l'atmosphère et les espaces planétaires, dans les textures et les rapports des sociétés humaines, et jusqu'au plus intime de la sensibilité et du vouloir des personnes, là où se construisent ou se désagrègent l'amour du monde et le sens de la vie.

L'homme, hébété, regarde déferler, inextricablement mêlées, menaces de fin du monde et promesses de paradis immédiat. Il ne sait plus les distinguer. Il ne sait plus ce qu'il veut. Ou bien, s'il veut encore quelque chose, il ne sait plus au nom de qui ou de quoi il le veut. On lui dit à la fois qu'il a le droit et le devoir de disposer à ses fins propres non seulement de sa planète, mais de l'univers entier – et qu'il n'est que le dernier des singes, produit par le hasard et la nécessité de son héritage génétique, de son milieu social et du contenu de son inconscient. On lui dit que l'univers est à son service, car il est, jusqu'à nouvel avis, le plus évolué des mammifères et, malgré l'écrasante supériorité de mémoire, de tri et de calcul des machines électroniques, un ordinateur encore incomparable. Ces raisons d'asservir l'univers, il en use et en abuse chaque jour, sans pourtant leur reconnaître une évidence convaincante, car il ne sait plus *qui* il est, ni s'il est *quelqu'un*.

Cette ignorance ultime constitue, avec l'incertitude et la perplexité engendrées par l'accroissement torrentiel de ses nouveaux pouvoirs, un cercle vicieux dont il est prisonnier. Si un consensus social ou moral plus ancien le liait encore aux autres hommes, il y trouverait sans doute le relais, la sécurité provisoire lui laissant le temps de se reconnaître lui-même dans sa permanence essentielle. S'il savait encore qui il est, il pourrait rechercher, à partir de cette conscience, le dialogue avec autrui afin de reconstruire un consensus indispensable. Mais le cercle vicieux paraît sans issue et suscite obscurément l'attente d'une catastrophe massive, grossière, qui détruirait le jeu entier auquel il ne sait plus jouer. D'où une attente de la fin du monde, ou du moins de l'humanité, dont on guette les signes précurseurs – dont on s'efforce de multiplier les signes précurseurs par la violence ou l'angélisme, par la violence *et* l'angélisme.

Incertitudes et division du corps médical devant ses nouveaux pouvoirs

Parmi les pouvoirs nouveaux récemment acquis, ceux de la médecine (chirurgie, médication, psychothérapie), de la biologie et de la biologie moléculaire posent aux savants qui les détiennent et aux industries qui les multiplient les problèmes les plus immédiats et les plus brûlants. Les enjeux d'amélioration ou d'aggravation de l'état du patient sont évidents, mais d'autres sont souvent à peine entrevus. La chirurgie des greffes, par exemple, n'est guère discutée qu'au niveau des chances de réussite sous forme de durée de la survie, des probabilités d'échec dues aux processus de rejet et de la proportion à maintenir entre les risques courus par le donneur et par le receveur de l'organe d'une part, les intérêts de la recherche chirurgicale de l'autre. Or les progrès de cette chirurgie, qui lui permettent d'atteindre des organes de plus en plus centraux, risquent de détruire peu à peu, sournoisement, dans la sensibilité du public, le sens fondamental de l'unité de l'organisme, condition sous-jacente et secrète du respect de l'être vivant, et de le remplacer par une «image» mécanique, qui rejoindrait celle, mentionnée plus haut, de l'ordinateur très supérieur. En outre, ces progrès engagent la recherche et la pratique médicale dans des voies extrêmement coûteuses, imposant une application très restreinte et sélective et accentuant encore l'inégalité des êtres humains devant la maladie et devant la mort. Enfin, les banques d'organes risqueraient de ressusciter un esclavage d'un genre nouveau.

On a vu le corps médical radicalement divisé sur la question des greffes.

Il apparaît tout aussi divisé en matière de drogues, de tranquillisants, d'auto-médication, de régulation des naissances, etc. Sur les mesures à prendre là où les progrès de la médecine suppriment la sélection en multipliant certaines maladies héréditaires, la perplexité est totale, et plus encore sur le droit d'intervenir dans le patrimoine génétique lorsque cette possibilité existera réellement. Même le devoir le plus élémentaire, le plus universellement reconnu de la médecine: celui de lutter contre la mort et de prolonger la vie par tous les moyens disponibles, est devenu douteux dans nombre de circonstances, par suite des moyens prodigieusement accrus mis au service de ce devoir. Faut-il prolonger indéfiniment la vie de ceux qui souffrent ou dont la conscience réduite est tombée au-dessous du niveau humain? Faut-il accroître les ravages de l'explosion démographique, augmenter le nombre des bouches à nourrir là où la nourriture fait défaut, aux dépens des enfants qui ont toute la vie devant eux? Faut-il abolir la règle médicale millénaire et donner aux médecins la charge démesurée de choisir eux-mêmes entre la vie et la mort? Vaut-il mieux, là où ne peut vivre qu'une population limitée, favoriser son vieillissement? Faut-il que tous vivent le plus longtemps possible et qu'il y ait moins de naissances, ou vaut-il mieux que les vivants soient jeunes et en pleine force?

Ces questions, et tant d'autres, lorsqu'on les pose hors de tout consensus préalable, et sans pouvoir même se référer à quelque valeur commune que ce soit, il est devenu impossible de les poser en elles-mêmes, je veux dire en s'interrogeant sur la nature même de l'acte médical ou du choix qu'elles appellent. Une telle interrogation exigerait en effet le recours à une norme morale, permanente à travers changements et progrès, malgré eux, et leur donnant leur sens. Or il n'existe plus rien de tel. S'il est encore une valeur communément admise, c'est celle du changement lui-même. Mais alors: *quel* changement et *pourquoi?*

Le recours aux faits pour qu'ils commandent les actes

Faute de référence commune et permanente permettant d'apprécier moralement l'acte et le choix mêmes, on a recours à la science, aux sciences, pour obtenir une réponse aux perplexités qu'elles ont fait naître. On attend des faits qu'ils dictent la conduite à tenir. On demande en particulier aux sciences sociales et humaines des informations aussi étendues et précises que possible sur les *conséquences prévisibles* que va entraîner la mise en œuvre des nouveaux pouvoirs.

Ces conséquences seront considérées sous divers angles, par exemple: la qualité de l'espèce, telle qu'elle a des chances d'être par suite de la suppression de la sélection naturelle et par suite de l'explosion démographique; les effets économiques et militaires sur les intérêts nationaux; l'agrément, la commodité, l'hygiène, le plaisir, le bonheur de la vie collective ou individuelle; les chances données à des formes d'activité considérées comme désirables au moment particulier où nous vivons.

Dans tous ces cas, on ne s'interroge que sur des prévisions *de faits*, car on admet que les faits prévus ou prévisibles portent en eux, aux yeux de chacun et de tous, leur caractère souhaitable ou nocif. Les jugements de valeur sont sans cesse sous-entendus, si bien sous-entendus que tout se passe comme s'ils n'intervenaient pas du tout – comme si *la même compétence* qui permet de prévoir le développement futur des faits permettait du même coup d'apprécier, dans l'objectivité pure, leur *valeur*, positive ou négative, pour chaque être humain et pour l'humanité. Comme si, en dernière analyse, un ordinateur plus capable qu'un cerveau humain de tenir compte de la complexité des données et des probabilités statistiques du développement pouvait, mieux que quiconque, *choisir* les solutions les meilleures pour le genre humain.

Mais les faits ne fournissent jamais à eux seuls une orientation à l'action, une raison au choix, une valeur au jugement, un sens à la vie. Lorsqu'ils *paraissent* avoir cette efficacité, c'est qu'ils sont eux-mêmes éclairés, orientés, jugés, grâce à des valeurs à tel point communes, à tel point incontestées, qu'à force d'aller sans dire elles passent inaperçues et se cachent derrière les faits qu'elles imprègnent: ce qui prolonge la vie est un bien, ce qui la rend agréable et sans douleur est un bien, et ainsi de suite.

Les choses se gâtent lorsque les conséquences d'options qui paraissent aussi évidemment bonnes contredisent cet optimisme, lorsqu'elles comportent une nouvelle forme de douleur, d'inconfort, parfois de mort – ou lorsqu'elles contredisent les principes implicites de telle ou telle «bien-pensance» traditionnelle ou moderniste – ou encore lorsqu'elles font apparaître comme contradictoires des principes constitutifs (tacitement) d'une même «bien-pensance».

Alors plus personne ne sait ce qu'il convient de faire. Les nouveaux pouvoirs sont toujours là et continuent à provoquer l'émerveillement. Mais *ils n'ont plus de sens* parce que la vie même n'en a plus.

Une source de sens: conscience claire et liberté

Il faut bien alors en venir à la question essentielle. *Pourquoi* la santé, la vie de l'homme sont-elles si précieuses? Pourquoi leur consacre-t-on tant de soin? Pourquoi croit-on pouvoir leur sacrifier la nature, les plantes, les animaux, la vie des fleuves, la paix des forêts? En quoi l'homme diffère-t-il essentiellement d'un bipède sans plumes ou d'un ordinateur futur dont les capacités de mémoire et de sélection dépasseront de plus en plus les siennes?

Seule la réponse à cette question sera capable (si on laisse hors de jeu toute dimension proprement religieuse, comme il faut le faire aujourd'hui lorsqu'il s'agit de retrouver un consensus général) de fournir *une source de sens* pour toute l'entreprise médicale et biologique. Seule cette réponse, ce retour au sens, permettra de prendre les options indispensables là où les nouveaux pouvoirs l'exigent.

Ce n'est pas la recherche du bonheur ou le refus de la souffrance qui peuvent caractériser l'homme et justifier ses privilèges. Cette recherche, ce refus, on les retrouve, sous des formes diverses, chez toutes les espèces vivantes.

Ce qui fait que l'homme est l'homme, c'est qu'il est doué d'une conscience lui permettant de *connaître* et de *décider*, donc de chercher librement la vérité et de choisir sa conduite en saisissant toujours plus clairement le sens, les conditions et les conséquences de ses actes. Il peut ne pas chercher à connaître et se dérober devant toute décision. Mais par ce refus, il est encore un homme, car ce refus est un choix. L'homme n'est pas une donnée, et l'essentiel de lui-même n'est pas au niveau des faits, mais de l'ordre du possible et de la liberté.

Pour quelle autre raison, sinon pour celle-ci, aurait-on élaboré depuis tant de siècles des interdits aussi sévères autour de la profession médicale? Pour quelle autre raison le médecin devrait-il *absolument* lutter contre la mort tant que subsiste le moindre souffle de vie? Pour quelle autre raison ne ramènerait-on pas l'obligation médicale au niveau relatif que les faits semblent imposer – puisque après tout le malade, un peu plus tôt, un peu plus tard, finira bien par mourir? Et n'est-ce pas justement parce que nos contemporains, envahis par «les faits» et leur apparente rigueur, se refusent souvent à rien chercher ni reconnaître au-delà d'eux que nombre de médecins aujourd'hui ne connaissent ou ne reconnaissent plus de distinction nette entre thérapie et expérimentation?

Emmêlement de l'ordre des faits et de celui de la liberté

Tout serait simple si l'homme se laissait réduire à un ensemble de faits; simple, mais ennuyeux et vide de sens: la médecine, la science elle-même perdraient leur raison d'être. Tout serait encore assez simple s'il était possible, en l'homme, de séparer complètement ce qui est de l'ordre des faits et ce qui est de l'ordre de la conscience et de la liberté. Mais il n'en est rien. C'est pourquoi tant de problèmes concernant l'homme – et notamment ceux qui se posent aux médecins – ne comportent pas de solutions, mais seulement des choix, avec une part considérable de doute et de culpabilité. Par exemple: pourquoi ne pas exposer *un* patient à certains risques supplémentaires si le savoir ainsi obtenu doit permettre ensuite de soulager ou même de sauver *un grand nombre* d'autres malades? Au niveau des faits, et si le patient n'est qu'un ensemble de données de faits, l'argumentation est inattaquable, car alors le nombre règne. Mais si les hommes n'étaient qu'un ensemble de faits, pourquoi importerait-il de les soulager ou de les sauver? – Inversement, s'il y a en chacun cet absolu d'une conscience de vérité et de liberté qui le fait homme et où le nombre ne peut intervenir, chaque malade représente pour le médecin *la fin* ultime de son intervention, et il ne peut sous aucun prétexte en faire *un moyen* servant à une autre fin quelle qu'elle soit (science, guérisons futures sur une grande échelle, etc.). Mais la tentation renaît, car l'absolu ressurgit sous le nombre: chacun de ceux qui auraient pu être guéris au prix des risques courus par quelques-uns est, au-delà des faits, une conscience humaine.

Si l'on admet que l'homme est homme essentiellement par une conscience qui, par-delà les faits mais au milieu des faits, connaît et décide, toute une série de problèmes se posent sous un jour différent: ils exigent une information sans cesse plus approfondie, mais ils n'en attendent aucune solution. Ils se posent à la conscience individuelle et ils appellent un consensus social. Je voudrais en indiquer quelques-uns.

D'abord, il apparaît que la science en général, et la science médicale en particulier, sont de nature morale. Les décisions qui s'y prennent sont certes éclairées par l'information et l'expérience des experts et dépendent, sous cet aspect, de leur compétence. Mais elles n'en dépendent, en quelque sorte, que latéralement. Centralement, elles dépendent des *décisions* de ces experts. Or lorsque des experts prennent des décisions mettant en jeu le fondement de l'humain au-delà des faits, ils ne décident plus en experts, mais en hommes, avec leur conscience d'hommes. C'est pourquoi certains des problèmes posés dans la profession médicale par les nouveaux pouvoirs ne devraient plus aboutir à une décision individuelle d'un seul médecin, ni même à un consensus limité du corps médical; ils imposent l'élaboration d'un consensus social, si possible juridiquement énoncé. Pour le moment, ce consensus n'existe pas.

La santé et le droit à la santé

Ensuite, que signifient, dans cette perspective où l'homme est conçu comme conscience qui connaît et décide, les termes de «santé» et de «droit à la santé»? La santé ne sera pas comprise avant tout comme un état agréable et sans douleur, ni comme une possibilité d'insertion active dans la société. Ces deux aspects, si importants qu'ils soient, restent subordonnés à l'essentiel: la capacité d'être un homme qui pense, connaît et agit. Le bien-être de la santé, l'élimination de la douleur, l'insertion active dans la société trouvent leur sens essentiel dans le fait qu'ils favorisent la claire conscience et la décision. Il s'ensuit qu'il ne devrait jamais être question d'éliminer la douleur, ou de rendre possible l'intégration sociale, aux dépens de la conscience claire, comme on semble parfois le faire en psychiatrie.

Le «droit à la santé», dans la perspective de ce qui précède, se fonde non sur quelque «droit au bonheur» impossible à définir, mais sur ce devoir d'être un homme qui est constitutif de l'homme, devoir de lucidité et de décision dont la maladie et la douleur compromettent l'accomplissement. Dans ce sens, ce droit est *en principe* absolu, et c'est pourquoi il n'est rien de moins justifiable que l'inégalité des soins. Mais ici encore l'absolu et les faits sont inextricablement liés, et le devoir de lucidité interdit de méconnaître ces données essentielles de la condition humaine. Il y a toujours plus de gens qui sont toujours mieux soignés. Et pourtant, avec les nouveaux pouvoirs de la médecine et les méthodes thérapeutiques absorbantes et coûteuses qu'ils entraînent, jamais peut-être, malgré le progrès, l'inégalité des soins n'a été aussi grande et la sélection des malades privilégiés plus difficile à admettre. Même si nous supposons d'énormes progrès sociaux, le traitement médical se heurtera toujours à des limites théoriques et pratiques. Le «droit à la santé», fondé sur quelque chose d'absolu en l'homme, sera toujours limité et relatif, il ne saurait signifier l'abolition de la souffrance, de la maladie, de la vieillesse et de la mort. On a tendance à entretenir aujourd'hui, autour de ces évidences, un halo d'illusions verbales qui empêche les hommes de regarder ces vérités en face et de les assumer – c'est-à-dire d'être des hommes. Finalement, le mot *supporter* n'est pas et ne sera jamais, dans la condition humaine, un mot périmé. Il y a et il y aura toujours «à supporter». Ceux qui promettent et ceux qui réclament «le paradis, tout de suite!» mentent aux autres et à eux-mêmes.

Savoir supporter fait partie de la santé

Cela signifie, d'une part, que l'effort, au niveau des *faits* médicaux et sociaux, pour réduire, dans toute la mesure du possible, la douleur, l'angoisse, les incapacités, la dépendance, l'insuffisance et l'inégalité des soins doit être poursuivi sans cesse, et sans espoir d'atteindre un état paradisiaque. Cela signifie, d'autre part, que l'obligation et la faculté de «supporter» font partie de la condition humaine. A supposer que l'homme puisse un jour vivre très longtemps en étant toujours au meilleur niveau de sa santé, cela signifierait qu'il aurait subordonné toute sa vie à cette santé, qu'il refuserait de se fatiguer au service d'aucune tâche, qu'il ne se donnerait désormais à rien. Une telle «option» ne serait plus humaine. Il aurait perdu sa libre conscience pour retomber comme un fait parmi les faits, parmi les seules nécessités d'une hygiène parfaite. La parfaite santé aurait perdu sa raison d'être.

C'est dans une telle voie que la médecine préventive d'aujourd'hui semble parfois engager les gens quand elle recommande de multiplier les contrôles de tous genres et que les conseils savants ou pseudo-savants envahissent la publicité.

L'homme reste un être à qui il incombe de maintenir, à travers la maladie et devant la mort, par sa manière même de les supporter, le sens de la vie – le sens de sa vie. Ce sens n'est pas la santé. La santé est au service de ce sens. Elle tire de lui son propre sens et ses droits.

La santé, d'après ce qui précède, n'est pas et ne peut pas être parfaite. Elle est un état de relative aisance et de relatif bien-être. Elle comporte, même sans «maladie», des maux et des malaises passagers, périodiques ou chroniques, que souvent on ne sait pas guérir et qui doivent être supportés. Faut-il penser que le droit au bien-être ordonne de recourir aussitôt aux tranquillisants, euphorisants, etc.? Les médecins, surchargés, encouragent à cet égard l'automédication pendant de longues périodes. Les producteurs aussi. Au nom du droit au bien-être et de celui de disposer de soi, on recourt aux moyens chimiques pour fuir tout malaise. Mais on n'est pas seul. La fuite se propage, devient épidémie.

Je crois qu'il y a, à la source de ce processus, une idée fausse de la santé. Savoir supporter certains maux, certains malaises, certaines approches de l'angoisse, cela fait partie, dans la condition humaine normale, de la santé. En être devenu incapable, c'est méconnaître cette condition, exiger d'être un autre qu'un homme (un ange?), c'est entrer dans la maladie avant même que les effets nocifs des tranquillisants ne se soient fait sentir.

Je suis souvent surprise d'entendre comment des médecins, des éducateurs, des prêtres posent le problème des drogues hallucinogènes. Ils en comparent les effets plus ou moins nocifs au seul niveau des faits. On a l'impression que s'il existait une drogue hallucinogène totalement dépourvue d'effets médicalement nocifs, ils s'empresseraient de la recommander. Seul compte le plan de l'hygiène physique et mentale. Or l'essentiel est ailleurs. L'essentiel, c'est que l'être humain, perdu dans l'univers, possède dans sa boîte crânienne ce miraculeux pouvoir de conscience claire, qui lui permet de connaître et de décider. Obscurcir ce pouvoir volontairement, y introduire la confusion, le chaos, fût-il éclatant, par des corps chimiques, fussent-ils inoffensifs (ce qu'ils ne sont jamais), c'est un sacrilège. C'est offenser et mutiler en soi l'homme, à qui chacun en soi doit le respect. Et comme on n'est jamais seul, on entraîne les autres à la même offense, à la même destruction. On abolit la protection que les hommes se doivent les uns aux autres contre la défaite et la trahison de l'humain. On perd la raison d'être de la santé avant de perdre la santé elle-même.

Ici plus encore qu'ailleurs un consensus profond serait indispensable.

Résumé

L'homme a conquis, ces dernières années, dans les domaines les plus divers, des pouvoirs d'agir nouveaux, d'une puissance sans précédent.

L'exercice de ces pouvoirs n'est encore régi, dans la plupart des cas, par aucune règle morale commune, aucun système de lois cohérent. Il n'existe le plus souvent à leur sujet aucun *consensus* social, et même aucun consensus professionnel. Les nouveaux pouvoirs de l'homme sont encore *sauvages*, alors qu'ils déploient chaque jour leurs effets.

Le consensus indispensable est d'autant plus difficile à créer que l'homme, devant les menaces de fin du monde et les promesses de paradis immédiats, perd le sens de sa vie. Il ne sait plus ce qu'il est ni si ses conquêtes ont un sens.

Les progrès de la médecine, de la biologie et de la biologie moléculaire ouvrent à l'action des possibilités nouvelles face auxquelles le corps médical et l'opinion publique restent divisés. Aucune valeur commune n'apparaît sinon celle du changement même.

Faute de valeur commune, on se livre à des prévisions, dans l'espoir que les faits imposeront d'eux-mêmes les décisions les meilleures. Mais les faits à eux seuls ne livrent aucune norme et n'engendrent aucun *sens*.

Il faut donc poser la question essentielle: pourquoi la santé, la vie de l'homme valent-elles tant d'efforts? En quoi l'homme diffère-t-il d'un «produit», biologique ou mécanique? La réponse à cette question pourrait être *source de sens*.

L'homme est l'homme parce qu'il est capable de chercher la vérité et de choisir sa conduite – de connaître et de décider. L'essentiel en lui n'est pas de l'ordre des faits, mais du possible et de la liberté.

C'est là que la santé et le droit à la santé trouvent leur sens (et non dans quelque «droit au bonheur» impossible à définir): dans ce devoir d'être un homme, qui est constitutif de l'homme. Il y a un droit à la santé parce que la maladie et la douleur menacent la capacité de lucidité et de décision. Mais ce droit, ainsi absolument fondé, ne saurait faire disparaître la souffrance, la maladie, la vieillesse et la mort. Le verbe *supporter* n'est donc jamais périmé, et «savoir supporter» fait partie de la santé.

Le problème des drogues cesse alors de se poser au niveau de la simple nocivité. Celui qui en use tend à altérer la clarté de sa conscience; il offense et mutile l'homme qu'il est, perdant la raison d'être de sa santé *avant* sa santé même.

Summary

In recent years, man has conquered new fields and acquired unprecedented new powers.

In most cases, the use of these powers has not yet been regulated by any common moral standard or by any consistent system of laws. Usually, there is no *consensus* in society regarding those powers, not even within the profession. Man's new powers are still *uncontrolled*, whereas their effects are increasingly developing throughout the world. The consensus, although absolutely needed, is still more difficult to secure at a time when man, faced with warnings of imminent world destruction or promises of earthly paradise, is losing his sense of purpose. He no longer knows where he stands of whether his triumphs have any meaning.

Progress in medicine, biology and molecular biology has opened up new prospects of action on which the medical profession and public opinion remain divided. There seem to be no common values except change itself.

In the absence of any common values, man falls back on forecasts, in the hope that the facts will of themselves produce the best decisions. But the facts alone provide neither a standard nor a *meaning*.

The crucial question is therefore: why should human health and life be worth so much effort? How does man differ from any other biological or mechanical 'product'? The reply to this question might well suggest a *meaning*.

Man is what he is because he is capable of seeking truth and choosing his own conduct – of knowing and deciding. The essential thing about him is not what he is, but what he can be thanks to his freedom of choice.

This gives a meaning to health and to man's right to health (rather than some indefinable 'right to happiness') – the duty to be a man, a duty that makes man what he is. He is entitled to health because sickness and pain impair his capacity for clear thinking and decision. But this right, absolute though it is, does not prevent suffering, disease, old age and death. The word *endure* is never obsolete, and it is a part of health to know 'how to endure'.

The problem of drugs should therefore not be approached purely from the standpoint of the factual harm they cause. An individual who uses them reduces the clarity of his mind; he degrades and mutilates himself as a human being, and loses the justification for his health *before* he loses his health itself.

Zusammenfassung

Der Mensch hat in den letzten Jahren in verschiedensten Bereichen neue Macht des Handelns – von bisher ungeahntem Ausmaß – erworben. Meist ist die Ausübung dieser Macht noch durch keine gemeinsame moralische Übereinkunft – durch kein gesamtverbindliches Gesetzessystem – geregelt. In den allermeisten Fällen gibt es in dieser Hinsicht noch keinen sozialen *Konsens*, selbst keine professionelle Übereinstimmung. Die neue Macht des Menschen ist noch ungezähmt, obwohl sich ihre Folgen auf der ganzen Welt äußern.

Der unerläßliche Konsens ist um so schwieriger zu erreichen, als der Mensch – angesichts der Bedrohung durch ein Weltende und auch durch die Verheißungen unmittelbarer Paradiese – den Sinn seines Lebens verliert. Er weiß nicht mehr, was er ist, und ebensowenig, ob seine Errungenschaften einen Sinn haben.

Die Fortschritte der Medizin, der Biologie und der Molekularbiologie erschließen völlig neue Möglichkeiten des Handelns, über deren Gebrauch Ärzteschaft und Öffentlichkeit geteilter Meinung sind. Es zeigt sich kein gemeinsam anerkannter Wert – wenn nicht der des Wechsels an sich.

Angesichts des Fehlens gemeinsamer Werte sucht man in der Futurologie Zuflucht, in der Hoffnung, daß die Tatsachen aus sich heraus zwangsläufig die besten Entscheidungen ergeben werden. Aber die Tatsachen allein liefern keine Norm und erzeugen keinen *Sinn*.

Man muß deshalb die grundlegende Frage stellen: Warum eigentlich sind die Gesundheit, das Leben des Menschen derart viele Anstrengungen wert? Wodurch unterscheidet sich der Mensch von irgendeinem biologisch oder mechanisch hervorgebrachten «Produkt»? Aus der Antwort auf diese Frage könnte ein *Sinn* hervorgehen.

Der Mensch ist Mensch, weil er die Wahrheit suchen und sein Handeln wählen kann – weil er zu erkennen und zu entscheiden vermag. Das Wesentliche in ihm liegt nicht im Bereich des Tatsächlichen, sondern im Bereich der Möglichkeiten und der Freiheit.

Daselbst liegt der Sinn der Gesundheit und des Rechtes auf Gesundheit (und nicht in irgendeinem undefinierbaren «Recht auf Glück»): darin, daß Mensch-

sein keine Tatsache, sondern Aufgabe ist. Es gibt ein Recht auf Gesundheit,
weil Krankheit und Schmerz die klare Sicht und Entscheidungskraft beeinträch-
tigen. Aber dieses – derweise absolut begründete – Recht vermag nicht das
Leiden, die Krankheit, das Alter und den Tod aus der Welt zu schaffen. Das
Wort *ertragen* hat daher seine Bedeutung keineswegs verloren. «Zu ertragen
wissen» ist Teil der Gesundheit.

Das Drogenproblem ist daher mehr als nur eine Frage der Schädlichkeit.
Wer Drogen nimmt, gefährdet die Klarheit seines Bewußtseins. Er beleidigt und
verstümmelt den Menschen in sich; er verliert die Daseinsberechtigung für seine
Gesundheit, *bevor* er diese selbst verliert.

Resumen

En los últimos años el hombre ha conquistado, en los campos más diversos,
nuevos poderes de una magnitud sin precedentes.

En la mayor parte de los casos, el ejercicio de estos poderes no está aún
regido por ninguna regla moral común ni por ningún sistema de leyes coherente.
Por lo general no existe ningún *consenso* social con referencia a ellos; más aún,
ningún consenso profesional. Los nuevos poderes del hombre se encuentran
todavía un poco en estado salvaje, si bien sus efectos se extienden día a día.

El consenso indispensable es tanto más difícil de crear cuanto que el
hombre, frente a la amenaza del fin del mundo y a la promesa del paraíso
inmediato, pierde el sentido de su vida. Ya no sabe quien es, ni si tienen sentido
sus conquistas.

Los progresos de la medicina, de la biología y de la biología molecular
ponen en juego nuevas posibilidades frente a las cuales el cuerpo médico y la
opinión pública están divididos. No se da ningún valor común, salvo el del
cambio mismo.

La falta de un valor común da lugar a la adopción de conjeturas, con la
esperanza de que los hechos impondrán por sí mismos las mejores decisiones.
Pero los hechos solos no dan ninguna norma ni crean ningún *sentido*.

Es necesario, pues, plantear la pregunta esencial: ¿Por qué la salud y la vida
del hombre merecen tantos esfuerzos? ¿En qué difiere el hombre de un «pro-
ducto», biológico o mecánico? La respuesta a esta pregunta podría ser *fuente
de sentido*.

El hombre es hombre porque es capaz de buscar la verdad y de elegir su
conducta – de conocer y decidir. Su esencia no reside en el orden de los hechos,
sino en el de las posibilidades y de la libertad.

Es aquí (y no en un indefinible «derecho a la felicidad») donde encuentran
sentido la salud y el derecho a la salud: en este deber de ser hombre, que es
constitutivo del hombre. Existe un derecho a la salud, porque la enfermedad y
el dolor comprometen la capacidad de lucidez y de decisión. Dicho derecho,
absolutamente fundado así, no podrá, sin embargo, hacer desaparecer del

mundo el sufrimiento, la enfermedad y la muerte. El verbo «soportar», pues, no ha caducado nunca, y «saber soportar» forma parte de la salud.

El problema de las drogas ya no se plantea entonces simplemente con relación a su nocividad. Quien las utiliza tiende a alterar la claridad de su conciencia; ofende y mutila su condición humana, perdiendo la razón de ser de su salud antes que su salud misma.

Experimenting with humans: problems and processes of social control in the biomedical research community

by Bernard Barber, John Lally, Julia Makarushka, and Daniel Sullivan

During the last thirty years, a large number of discoveries have been made in biomedical science. Accompanying this rapid progress, indeed an essential prerequisite for it, has been a very large and very rapid increase in the amount of use of human subjects in biomedical research. A major consequence of all this successful research on human subjects has, of course, been enormous benefits to the health and welfare of those who enjoy modern medical care. However, as with probably all purposive social action, there have also been some unintended and undesired side effects, in both the medical and moral realms. Chief among the undesired moral side effects has been the failure to achieve the highest, and in a few cases even adequate, standards of professional moral concern for the human subjects being used in this necessary biomedical experimentation.

Although there is a small but longish history of attention to the problem of the abuse of the subjects of medical experimentation, during the last ten years or so attention to this problem has increased a great deal[1]. First of all, increased attention and concern has been expressed within the biomedical research community itself[2]. Biomedical researchers, joined by professors of law and social scientists, have organized symposia to compose a rounded view of the problem[3].

Second, increased attention and concern has been expressed in new governmental regulations, notably those of the National Institutes of Health and the Food and Drug Administration[4]. Because it has mandated peer review for all the biomedical research it has supported since 1966, which includes a considerable part of all the biomedical research done in this country and nearly every biomedical research organization, the National Institutes of Health have played an especially important role in the regulation of the use of human subjects[5].

Finally, increased attention and concern has been widely and continually displayed in the mass media. This concern has perhaps been especially focussed on three *causes célèbres* during the last ten years: the thalidomide disaster in Germany; the Southam and Mandel case in New York State in which live cancer cells were injected into geriatric patients without their informed consent; and the bitter controversy between Drs. DeBakey and Cooley of Baylor and

Houston over their own priority rights and the rights of patients in their artificial heart program[6].

Unfortunately, all this literature of concern, both past and present, has some important defects. Though often wise, it contains a paucity of hard and detailed facts based on representative samples of experience. Also, it lacks that understanding of some of the sources of ethical shortcomings in this area which can be provided by sociological analysis. Finally, because of inadequate facts and unsatisfactory analysis, the policy recommendations made in this literature have often been defective. The purpose of the studies and the work carried out by our Research Group on Human Experimentation, supported by grants from the Russell Sage Foundation, has been to make improvements in all these respects: to provide better facts, better analysis, and better policy recommendations. This paper is an exceedingly condensed synopsis of the findings, analysis, and recommendations we have made so far[7].

The two research studies: design and methodology

The data for our analysis were collected in two overlapping studies. The first one, our National Survey, obtained responses to a mailed questionnaire survey from a set of 293 biomedical research institutions which our analysis shows to constitute a nationally representative sample along several important dimensions of all American institutions of this kind. Those who filled out the questionnaires for their institutions, often with considerable help from their colleagues and administrative staff, are typically themselves both active researchers and members of their institution's peer-review committee. This is important, since what we chiefly sought to learn in this study is, one, the structure, processes, and efficacy of the peer-review committee and, two, the expressed standards of the individuals who filled out the questionnaires on such key ethical concerns in the use of human subjects as the importance of *informed voluntary consent* and the proper *balance between risk and benefit* in experiments done with human subjects.

The second study, our Intensive Two-Institution Study, obtained responses to lengthy personal interviews, using a different instrument from the first study, from the active researchers in two biomedical research institutions chosen by cluster analysis to be representative of a very large number of the institutions in our national sample. One of our two institutions, the one we call University Hospital and Research Center, measures very high on a whole cluster of characteristics that many biomedical research institutions have: a large number of researchers, a large research budget, highly productive researchers, a medical school with a teaching hospital closely connected with it, strongly encouraging research, doing research that is risky for the human subjects involved, research that is at the scientific frontiers, and receiving a high proportion of its research funds from the National Institutes of Health. Our other institution, the one we call Community and Teaching Hospital, is a teaching hospital that was loosely affiliated with a medical school when our study was conducted. Research is emphasized to a lesser degree in Community and Teaching Hospital as indicated by its lower rank on all of the variables by which University Hospital and Research Center were just characterized. In each of these two institutions, we sought to interview all researchers using human subjects, identifying such researchers first by published lists of research papers and then by the 'snow-ball' technique, that is, by referrals from one researcher to another whose work was not on the published list. We obtained 352 interviews, 298 at University Hospital and Research Center, 54 at Community and Teaching Hospital. In addition, we obtained some 35 completed short questionnaires from those who refused an interview. Our total response, then, was 387 out of 539 who were eligible. This is a response rate of 72%, and it is likely that, because the institutions were selected using the clustering technique, we do have here a set of representative responses from biomedical researchers who use human subjects.

In this second study, we were again interested in the expressed *standards* of our researchers on the two issues of voluntary consent and risk-benefit ratios. In addition, with these researchers, we collected data on their own *practices* with regard to risks and benefits in the studies on humans that they were conducting at the time of the interview. Beyond this, we added two new and important topics for study. One is their socialization or training into ethical standards and practices. The other is their involvement in collaboration groups and various informal social networks and the effects of these groups and networks on their ethical standards and practices.

Is there a problem? The patterns of ethical standards and practices

As even a cursory inspection of all the codes, regulations, and discussion of the ethics of the use of human subjects in biomedical research will show, the two key issues are informed voluntary consent and favorable risk-benefit ratios. The first goal of our investigations, therefore, was to try to find what expressed standards and what actual behavior with regard to these two issues prevail among the respondents in our two studies.

To get at expressed standards we asked biomedical researchers to respond to a battery of six extremely detailed research protocols which measure their concern with the consent issue and their willingness to do more and less risky studies. (Because of the length of time it took to consider and answer these questions, we used only two of them in our second study.) Our hypothetical research protocols, which we knew to be hypothetical-actual and not hypothetical-fantastic because we had constructed them out of the research literature, checked them with able researchers, pre-tested them with a dozen chiefs of research, and found them to be real to our respondents, include the following kinds of problems involving various degrees of salience of the consent issue and varying degrees of risk to the subjects: a study of the relation between hallucinogenic drug use and chromosome break, a test of alternate treatments for congenital heart defect in children, a test of new antidepressant drugs in a psychiatric hospital, doing unnecessary thymectomies on children to ascertain effects on tissue transplant survival, a study of the effects of radioactive calcium on bone metabolism in children, and a study of pulmonary function in adults under anesthesia for routine hernia repair and requiring the prolongation of anesthesia.

To get at actual behavior, as against expressed standards, in our Intensive Two-Institution Study we asked the researchers to give us their own best estimates, for the studies in which they were currently involved, of the amount of risk and the amount of benefit likely to accrue, first, to the patient-subjects being used, and, second, to future patients. Each respondent could list up to eight studies; a total of 424 studies varying greatly by substance, risk, and benefit were reported.

Now, using the data obtained in these two ways, what patterns of ethical standards and behavior among biomedical researchers does our evidence show? It shows two patterns. It shows, first and fortunately, that the majority of such researchers are very much aware of the importance of informed voluntary consent, that they express unwillingness to take undue risk when confronted with hypothetical research protocols, and that they do not themselves actually do studies in which the risk-benefit ratio is unfavorable for their patient-subjects. But the evidence also shows, unfortunately, that there is a significant minority that is more permissive in one or more of these three respects.

On awareness of the importance of consent, for example, some 23% see nothing wrong in doing the chromosome-break study without asking consent of the students involved, even though such students might be exposed to the danger of arrest if findings about their drug use were not kept sufficiently confidential. On response to the high-risk hypotheticals, 6% would approve the high-risk thymectomy study and 14% would approve the high-risk use of radioactive calcium in the bone-metabolism study in children even if the chances of success in the study were only one in ten. As to actual behavior, it is interesting to note that only 11% of the studies our biomedical researchers reported themselves doing involved more than 'very little' risk for the present subjects. Still, for those entailing any risk at all, which comes to 56% of all the studies, some 20% are reported as entailing greater risks than benefits to the subjects involved. Of course, some of these studies may be done for the benefit of future patients. But that raises other ethical questions. Finally, using other data we have collected, it is clear that not all patients are equally involved in studies involving unfavorable risk-benefit ratios. Studies where risks exceed the benefits, according to our scale, are almost twice as likely to be done using subject populations more than three fourths of whom are ward and/or clinic patients than are studies where the risk at least equals the benefits. In sum, to answer our question, yes, there is a problem in the use of human subjects. The patterns of ethical

standards and practices are not entirely satisfactory in the light of the high
aspirations and claims of the biomedical research community.

The dilemma of science and therapy:
the effects of competition in the national scientific community

How shall we account for these ethical shortcomings in the biomedical research community? That is our next problem, and we have tried to give some
different kinds of answers to it. For one thing, we have examined the structure
and functioning of various social control mechanisms – socialization structures,
collaboration and other informal groups, and peer-review committees – to
see how well or poorly they conduce to satisfactory ethical behavior. For another thing, though, and this is what we shall pay attention to immediately, we
want to see how the possible *conflict of different values* which are held to be
important in the biomedical research community can be the source of ethical
shortcomings. It is not so much the lack of all values, or hypocrisy about proclaimed values, we hypothesize, that is responsible in part for ethical inade-
quacies but rather the occasional putting of one important value too much ahead
of another that is important also but that has to give way in certain circumstances.

We are talking about what we have come to call, in the case of the biomedical research community, *the dilemma of science and therapy*. Ethical biomedical
research requires the successful balancing of two important values. As physician, the researcher holds the value of humane therapeutic treatment. As
scientist, he holds the value of scientific success through priority of discovery[8].
Very often, these two values can both be achieved fully, or in some ethically
satisfactory balance, in a given piece of research using human subjects. Our
data show this clearly. Sometimes, however, emphasis on one value may make
the achievement of the other difficult. For example, too great a concern for patients in general, or for some particular patients, may prevent a researcher from
carrying out a piece of work that might lead to an important discovery. Con-
trariwise, as some researchers themselves have alleged, an ambitious researcher
may press too hard with his 'new' ideas and his quest for scientific recognition
to the detriment of his human subjects[9].

What our data and our analysis show is that the competition in science for
priority of discovery and for the recognition and prestige that go with it is indeed one of the sources, first and directly, of too much emphasis on the value
of science as against therapy, and, second and indirectly, of more permissive
behavior in the use of human subjects. It is the unsuccessful scientist who keeps
on striving for competitive recognition who, at least in our sample, is most
likely to be more permissive with regard to both expressed standards about
the consent and risk-benefit issues and actual behavior on the risk-benefit
ratio. We discovered this by comparing our *high quality* scientists, those who

made discoveries for which they have received a great deal of scientific recognition as measured by citation of their work by peers in the national scientific community, with our *extreme mass producer* scientists, those who have published many papers but who have received no recognition from their peers in the form of citations[10]. It is these 'extreme mass producers', and especially the younger ones, our data show, who express less awareness of the importance of consent, more willingness to do studies without therapeutic benefit, and who report themselves as more likely to do studies in which the risk exceeds the benefit. Caught up in the competition system of science, unsuccessful in it, but still pursuing the prize of peer recognition, they are more likely to overvalue science as against therapy and therefore to display more permissive standards and practices.

The dilemma of science and therapy: the effects of local-institutional reward

Scientists get their recognition and reward not only from the national peer community but also from their colleagues in the local institutions where they carry on their research. Presumably, in a universalistic system such as science aspires to be, achievement and recognition in the former community would be correspondingly recognized and rewarded by appropriate promotion and rank in the latter. Where this is not so, where certain scientists are under-rewarded in their local institutions, we should expect them, in addition to feeling some sense of injustice, to strive for still further recognition in the national peer community and thereby to compel the particularistic local institution to give them their due rank and reward. Such anxious striving, we felt, would make the under-rewarded somewhat overvalue science as against therapy and lead them into more permissive behavior.

And that is indeed a pattern we find in our data. When we compare the biomedical researchers in our Intensive Two-Institution Study with one another on both national scientific recognition and local-institutional rank and reward, we find some who are indeed locally under-rewarded. That is, they have lesser local-institutional rank as compared with some of their colleagues who have only an equal or lesser amount of national scientific recognition. It is these under-rewarded researchers, we found, who are more likely to do studies where the risk-benefit ratio is unfavorable[11]. Just as relative failure in competition in the national scientific community may lead men to overvalue science as against therapy and so lead to permissive behavior, so may lack of just reward at the local-institutional level lead to anxious scientific striving and to permissive behavior.

Social control: the structures and processes of socialization

We turn now from the conflict of values, from the dilemma of science and therapy and its consequences for ethical standards and practice in biomedical research, to an analysis of certain structures and processes of social control and how they produce good and bad standards and practice in this area. Among sociologists, the concept of social control is construed quite broadly and includes structures and processes which are both formal and informal, both manifest and latent. It refers to such diverse structures and processes as those for instilling necessary knowledge and values into social actors, those for bringing the pressures of informal social interaction to bear on behalf of conformity or deviance, and those for applying the punishments and rewards that various private and governmental organizations have defined as necessary for ensuring satisfactory social performance in any given sphere. Social control is what produces the mixture of conformity and deviance in society, the balance of order and disorder.

The first of the three sets of structures and processes of social control that our Research Group on Human Experimentation has investigated are those having to do with socialization of biomedical researchers, that is, those that are supposed to instill in these researchers the knowledge, values, and norms necessary for satisfactory ethical performance with regard to the use of human subjects. Although we also studied the socialization that occurs during internship, residency, and the actual research career, we will here report only on the patterns and consequences of ethical socialization during the medical school years. That is the time when basic professional values and knowledge are supposed to be instilled; that is when profession's central and most serious concerns are given time and place[12].

We turn first to the formal medical school curriculum and ask, how much socialization into research ethics is given there? A summary answer is, not much, but let us look at some detailed data. Of the more than three hundred researchers in our Intensive Two-Institution Study who responded to our questions in this area, only 13% report that they had a seminar, a lecture, or part of a course devoted to the issues involved in the use of human subjects, and only one researcher says that he had had a complete course dealing with these issues. Thirteen per cent of the respondents say that the issues of research had come up when, as students, they did practice procedures on one another, and 24% say that they became aware of the issue of the risk-benefit ratio when they were doing experimental work with animals.Thirty-four per cent remember dicussions with instructors or with other students of the ethical issues involved in specific research projects which they read about or learned of in class. But 57% of the physicians interviewed report not a single one of these socializing experiences. Obviously, the medical school has not been taking the problems of research ethics as one of its central concerns. There is some slight hope, however, in the finding that the younger respondents report somewhat more of these experiences than the older ones, though this represents only slight improvement and does not begin to cope with the need that nearly all physicians now have for competent knowledge in this area. It should be remembered that even non-researcher physicians have to confront these issues when they are requested, as they often are, to ask their patients to serve as subjects in research.

Our second question is, how effective is even this small amount of formal socialization? So far as expressed standards are concerned, the answer is, not very. Those researchers who report any formal socialization experiences in medical school are only slightly less permissive in response to the hypothetical questions posing the risk-benefit ratio issue than their colleagues who report no such experiences, that is, there is a smaller proportion of the former who would permit the risks of the bone-metabolism study, for example, to be taken at all. Fortunately, the formal socialization experiences do have an influence so far as the issue of informed consent is concerned. On the hypothetical protocol where this issue was involved, some 35% of those reporting formal socialization experiences recognize that the issue was not handled by the researcher in the protocol, as against 22% of those not having such experiences. In both cases, of course, it is only a minority that shows itself sensitive to the consent issue.

At the same time that formal socialization into research ethics in medical schools is inadequate, there seems to be a kind of socialization into the value of research science which leads to more permissive standards and behavior. In addition to our questions about specific socialization experiences, we asked our respondents an open-ended question: 'Was there any other experience during medical school which made you aware of the issues involved in the use of human subjects in research?' About one third of the sample mention other experiences of various kinds. These we grouped into three categories: (1) the 'negative reaction' group which report experiences connected with the endangering or harming of research subjects; (2) the 'clinical orientation' group which report experiences connected with a growing awareness of the obligation of a doctor to respect his patients and be responsible for them; and (3) the 'value of research' group which report experiences connected with learning the importance of research on human subjects in acquiring new knowledge. The three groups, we found, vary in their permissiveness in response to the protocols involving the risk-benefit ratio issue. Our data show a continuous increase in the percentage of those willing to accept the risk in, for example, the bone-metabolism study, as we move from the 'negative reaction' group to the 'clinical orientation' group to the 'value of research' group. The last group also shows itself least alert to the consent issue. Finally, this group is also most likely to be doing a study where there is an unfavorable risk-benefit ratio. Apparently, socialization into the science value is more effective for some medical students than socialization into the humane therapy value. And it is clear that it is not that professional socialization cannot be effective, but that it may be of the wrong kind or in the wrong proportions.

Social control: the effects of collaboration groups

The second set of social control structures and processes we have investigated are the collaboration groups and other informal social networks in which the biomedical researcher typically carries out his activities and which apparently exert a variety of pressures on his ethical standards and practice. We should note, first of all, that modern biomedical research on humans is indeed highly collaborative. Of the 424 studies using humans from our Intensive Two-Institution Study, only 19% have only one investigator. Twenty-seven per cent of the studies have two investigators, 24% have three, and 30% have four or more.

As we might expect from what our socialization data have shown about the lack of attention being paid to research ethics in the medical schools, ethical concern for research subjects is not a highly salient consideration for these collaborating researchers when they select each other. When we asked them, 'What three characteristics do you most want to know about another researcher before entering into a collaborative relationship with him?', 86% say 'scientific ability', 45% say 'motivation to work hard', 43% say 'personality', and only 6% say 'ethical concern for research subjects'.

At a more latent level, however, the influence of ethical similarity does seem to be influencing choice of collaboration-group partners. Our data show that the overall tendency is for researchers with approximately the same ethical standards, as measured by their response to the hypothetical bone-metabolism study, to collaborate with each other more frequently than with researchers expressing different standards on the risk-benefit ratio issue. Our data also show, although the differences are not as large, that like goes with like on the consent issue: researchers who express awareness of consent as an ethical issue tend to collaborate with others who share that awareness.

The fact that like works with like in collaboration groups probably decreases the likelihood that one collaborator will disagree ethically with any of his peers. That is fine where collaborators have strict standards. But where collaborators share permissive standards, they are not likely to enforce the ethical standards of the wider biomedical research community on one another.

Fortunately, there seems to be a possible corrective for the ethical standards and behavior that permissive collaborators may allow one another in the social control exerted by another informal social network. We also asked our respondents to whom they went in the past year to discuss ethical questions arising in their own research. The answers show a tendency for investigators to discuss their ethical problems with those who have different ethical standards from their own. Thus, some researchers at least seem to be trying to insure that they will not be too permissive, nor too strict of course.

So far we have seen the effects of collaboration groups on expressed standards with regard to the risk-benefit ratio issue and the consent issue. Do they have any effects as well on actual behavior? We tried to see if permissive collaboration groups are more likely to be engaged in studies where the risks exceed the therapeutic benefits for the subjects, as reported by the researchers themselves. The answer is 'no' for the more innocuous studies where risks are only slightly in excess of benefits. However, for the small group of studies with the worst risk-benefit ratios, there is a tendency for the permissive groups to be doing them. Colleague interaction, thus, through the processes of collaboration and ethical consultation, has definite though complex effects on both expressed standards and actual behavior with regard to the use of human subjects in biomedical research.

Social control: the effects of peer-group review

The last set of social control structures and processes we have investigated are the peer-review committees that have the power to approve, modify, or reject on ethical grounds, and before they may be carried out, all research proposals involving the use of human subjects. The peer-review committee is an important social invention, but a very recent one, and one that has not yet had time to take more than rough shape and to give more than merely satisfactory performance, as our data show.

The need for peer-review committees, according to CURRAN, a medico-legal specialist who has been a pioneer in this field, 'began to receive limited but respectable support in the clinical research community' only in the late 1950's and the 1960's[13]. Two surveys of university medical departments done in the early 1950's show that 'there was a general skepticism toward the development of ethical guidelines, codes, or sets of procedures' in the research community at this time[14]. As a result of the thalidomide disaster in Germany and the Drug Amendment Acts of 1962 (Kefauver-Harris Bill), however, the whole environment for controls on the use of human subjects changed. The Food and Drug Administration issued a regulation requiring that all human subjects be asked by researchers to sign a voluntary consent form. And, even more important, in 1966, the Public Health Service, which has provided about one third of all the funds used in the United States for biomedical research and which has given these funds to just about every biomedical research institution, issued its regulation, 'Protection of the Individual as a Research Subject', mandating therein that all research applications involving the use of human subjects be screened by local-institutional peer-review committees. Such screening was directed to look especially to the two key issues of voluntary consent and the risk-benefit ratio for the subject.

The P.H.S. regulation has had a large and immediate effect on the scope of peer review. Whereas all 293 of the responding institutions in our National Survey had given assurances by 1969 to the P.H.S. that they had peer-review committees, only 68 % of them tell us that they had had such committees before 1966 and a considerable minority of these tell us that they had had to make either major or minor changes in the existing committees to bring them up to the

P.H.S. standards.Despite the present universal existence of these committees, however, all research using humans is still not being screened. While 86% of our respondents tell us 'all clinical research' is now reviewed in their institutions, 9% say they review only research involving a formal proposal for funds and another 4% say only formal proposals to the National Institutes of Health are reviewed. Moreover, when we interviewed the researchers in our Intensive Two-Institution Study, where it was officially reported that all clinical research was reviewed, 9% of our respondents *volunteer* the information that one or more of their investigations using human subjects had not been reviewed. Clearly, a small but perhaps important minority of research proposals are still not being reviewed at all.

How efficacious is the review process when it is carried out? Efficacy is, of course, a hard concept to define and measure in any field of human action. We have used two rough measures: what the committees have done with research protocols and how researchers feel about the efficacy of their committees.

As to results of their action, our respondents tell us that in 36% of the institutions, the committees have never required any revisions or made any rejections; another 38% tell us that some revisions were required, but that after revision the protocols were all approved; another 26% report one or more outright rejections; and, finally, 18% told us that there have been one or more instances where an investigator withdrew his proposal when he sensed that revision or rejection was likely. As to how researchers feel about the committees, some 76% of our individual respondents say they felt the committees were very effective. Thus, on both these rough measures, the review committees have a considerable degree of social control efficacy, yet it is also clear that there is room for improvement. For example, our data on one of these measures, what people say about effectiveness, show that the committees are more likely to be effective when the institution has additional controls over research using human subjects; when the committee reviews *all* research, not just that using P.H.S. funds; and when there is continuing review. These are all social control structures and processes which could be set up, where they do not now exist, to increase the efficacy of peer-group review.

Policy recommendations

In this exceedingly condensed synopsis of our work, we have had to leave out many of our findings and a great deal of the detail on even what we have reported here. In the complete monograph which will report all our findings in detail, we intend also to make certain policy recommendations which can best be supported by our comprehensive and detailed report. Here we can only suggest two broad areas for policy changes. First is the area of socialization. In the light of its high moral aspirations and claims, the biomedical research community is not taking its obligation to train its prospective members in the

medical schools in research ethics as seriously as it ought to, as seriously, for
example, as it takes its obligation to train them in scientific knowledge and research techniques. We recommend that more such teaching programs be set up.
Such programs could easily be set up to use the casebook on readings and cases in
research ethics that has been compiled by Dr JAY KATZ of Yale University [15].

Second, in the area of peer review, it is clear that better policy requires that
absolutely all research be screened and that such procedures as continuing
review and formal appeal be used everywhere. Many of the structural devices
that guarantee efficacy in other types of private and public law could well be
applied in the area of peer review.

In conclusion, we want to emphasize that we feel that biomedical research
is in considerable measure so esoteric an activity that a great deal of the social
control that guides it must be in the hands of the biomedical research community
itself. Yet, like all other specialized and esoteric social activities, biomedical
research is too important to the larger society to be left entirely to its experts.
In part it needs to be effectively and continuously scrutinized and controlled by
outsiders. An effective system of control, including both insiders and outsiders,
will protect all the parties at interest, all the values, both science and humane
therapy. We need to move toward this system of more effective social control
as soon as possible.

References

1. For a historical anthology of expressions of this concern, see LADIMER, I., NEWMAN, R.
W. (Ed.): *Clinical Investigation in Medicine*. Boston: Boston University Law-Medicine Research Institute, 1963.

2. See BEECHER, H.K.: *Experimentation in Man*. Springfield, Ill.: Charles C Thomas,
1959; BEECHER, H.K.: *Research and the Individual: Human Studies*. Boston: Little, Brown
& Co., 1970; and PAPPWORTH, M. H.: *Human Guinea-Pigs*. Boston: Beacon Press, 1967.

3. See the results of these symposia in *Daedalus 98*, No. 2 (1969); and *Ann. N.Y. Acad.
Sci. 169* (1970). For the sociological analysis which has been the source of our work, see
BARBER, B.: Experimenting with Humans. *Publ. Interest 1967*, 91–102.

4. For an account of the development of these regulations, see CURRAN, W.J.: The Approach of Two Federal Agencies. *Daedalus 98*, 542–594 (1969).

5. See U.S. Department of Health, Education, and Welfare – Public Health Service: *Protection of the Individual as a Research Subject*. Washington, D.C.: Government Printing Office,
1969.

6. For information on the thalidomide birth defects see *United States Senate Report of the
Committee on Government Operations: Interagency Drug Coordination*. Washington, D.C.:
Government Printing Office, 1965. The Southam-Mandel case is documented in *Hyman v. Jew-
ish Chronic Disease Hospital*, 251 N.Y.S. 2d 818 (1964). A publication documenting the facts
in regard to Denton Cooley's heart transplant program will be published soon by the American
Heart Institute.

7. A detailed monograph on our work, to be published by the Russell Sage Foundation,
will be finished in 1971. Presently available in unpublished form are: MAKARUSHKA, J.L.:
Learning to Be Ethical: Patterns of Socialization and Their Variable Consequences for the
Ethical Standards of Bio-Medical Researchers (unpublished Ph.D. dissertation, Columbia
University, 1971); SULLIVAN, D. F.: Some Normative and Social Structural Factors Affecting

Ethical Standards and Practices in Bio-Medical Research Using Human Subjects (unpublished Ph.D. dissertation, Columbia University, 1971); BARBER, B.: The Structure and Processes of Peer Group Review. Paper, 137th Meeting of the American Association for the Advancement of Science, Chicago, December 27, 1970, mimeographed; LALLY, J.J.: Are Medical Schools Ethical Leaders? A Comparison of Medical Schools with Other Bio-Medical Research Institutions. Paper, 137th Meeting of the American Association for the Advancement of Science, Chicago, December 27, 1970, mimeographed; and various working papers.

8. On the centrality of this value for science, see MERTON, R.K.: Priorities in Scientific Discovery. *Amer. sociol. Rev. 22*, 635–659 (1957); and: Resistance to the Systematic Study of Multiple Discoveries in Science. *Europ. J. Sociol. 4* (1963); see also HAGSTROM, W.O.: *The Scientific Community*. New York: Basic Books, 1965; STORER, N.W.: *The Social System of Science*. New York: Holt, Rinehart and Winston, 1966.

9. For some evidence, see BEECHER, *op. cit.*[2], and PAPPWORTH, *op. cit.*[2].

10. For the source of this quantity-quality typology, see COLE, J., COLE, S.: Scientific Output and Recognition. *Amer. sociol. Rev. 32*, 377–390 (1967). For a justification of using citations as a measure of recognition, see COLE, J., COLE, S.: Measuring the Quality of Sociological Research: Problems in the Use of the Science Citation Index. *Amer. Sociologist 6*, 23–29 (1971). For the existence of felt competition in biomedical research as measured by the existence of and concern with anticipation of discoveries by others, see HAGSTROM, *op. cit.*[8].

11. In our forthcoming monograph, some of the sources of under-reward will be fully explored. Ethnic discrimination is apparently one source. A feeling of relative deprivation is also important for the under-rewarded.

12. For some earlier basic studies of medical school socialization, which do not, however, refer to socialization in research ethics, see MERTON, R.K., et al.: *The Student-Physician*. Cambridge, Mass.: Harvard University Press, 1957; and BECKER, H.S., et al.: *Boys in White*. Chicago: The University of Chicago Press, 1962.

13. CURRAN, *op. cit.*[4], p. 545.

14. CURRAN, *op. cit.*[4], p. 548.

15. Russell Sage Foundation, forthcoming.

Summary

Accompanying the large number of discoveries made in biomedical science during the last thirty years and all the enormous benefits to the health and welfare of those who enjoy modern medical care that result from this progress there has been rising concern among researchers and the lay public about the need to achieve the highest standards of care and concern for the human subjects being used in biomedical experimental research.

Our Research Group on Human Experimentation has felt the need to contribute some reliable knowledge to the discussion of the two issues that are at the focus of this rising concern, the issue of informed voluntary consent and the issue of the proper risk-benefit ratio. We have felt that such knowledge would be a good basis for constructive social policy in this area.

Toward this end, we have carried out two studies. One is our National Survey, a mailed questionnaire survey which obtained responses from 293 U.S. biomedical research institutions constituting a nationally representative sample of such institutions. In this study we were primarily concerned with the structure, processes and efficiency of peer-review committees. Our second study is an

Intensive Two-Institution Study in which, by lengthy personal interviews with active researchers in two representative biomedical research institutions, we obtained data on (1) their standards and behavior with respect to the consent and risk-benefit issues, (2) their training into ethical norms, and (3) the small-group or interpersonal social networks that help to determine their behavior in regard to these two issues.

Our findings show that there is a certain problem of ethical standards in this area in the sense that a small but significant minority of the researchers we studied do have relatively permissive standards and behavior with regard to consent and risk-benefit. We have tried to explain this more permissive minority in a variety of ways. Some of them are relative failures in the competition for scientific success and apparently sacrifice the value of humane therapy to the value of scientific achievement. Some of them are the victims of ethnic or other forms of discrimination and seek to overcome the effects of this discrimination by too great an emphasis on scientific striving. Some permissiveness results from inadequate training or 'socialization' into the norms of humane therapy. Some is the consequence of less than fully effective peer-review procedures. And some of it, finally, is the result of the types of interpersonal and collaboration-group networks in which researchers are involved and which definitely influence their behavior on the consent and risk-benefit issues.

Our all-too-synoptic paper concludes with some policy recommendations based on our findings and analysis.

Zusammenfassung

Die in den letzten dreißig Jahren gemachten zahlreichen Entdeckungen auf biomedizinischem Gebiet, die all jenen enormen Nutzen gebracht haben, denen die moderne medizinische Betreuung zugute kommt, haben bei Forschern und bei Laien zugleich wachsende Besorgnis hervorgerufen. Es wurde erkannt, daß Betreuung und Sorgfalt bei biomedizinischen Versuchsstudien am Menschen höchsten Ansprüchen genügen müssen.

Unsere Studiengruppe über Versuche am Menschen hielt es für angezeigt, einige zuverlässige Angaben für die Diskussion jener zwei Probleme beizutragen, denen das Hauptinteresse dieser steigenden Besorgnis gilt: das Problem der informierten freiwilligen Zustimmung und das Problem eines angemessenen Risiko–Nutzen-Verhältnisses. Wir waren der Ansicht, daß derartige Erkenntnisse eine geeignete Grundlage für konstruktive Sozialpolitik auf diesem Gebiet bilden könnten.

Zu diesem Zweck haben wir zwei Studien durchgeführt. Die eine war unsere Nationale Untersuchung. Wir verschickten einen Fragebogen und erhielten Antworten von 293 amerikanischen biomedizinischen Forschungsinstituten, die einen repräsentativen Querschnitt derartiger Institute in unserem Lande darstellen. Uns interessierten vor allem Struktur, Vorgehen und Effektivität der Kontrollkommissionen. In unserer Ausführlichen Zwei-Institute-Studie sammelten wir durch persönliche Befragung aktiver Forscher in zwei repräsentativen biomedizinischen Forschungsinstituten Angaben erstens über Normen und Praktiken hinsichtlich des Problems der informierten Zustimmung und jenes des Risiko–Nutzen-Verhältnisses, zweitens über ihre Ausbildung in ethischen Normen und drittens über die soziale Zusammenarbeit in kleinen Gruppen oder zwischen Einzelpersonen, die dazu beiträgt, ihr Verhalten in bezug auf diese zwei Probleme zu bestimmen.

Unsere Ergebnisse zeigen, daß auf diesem Gebiete tatsächlich gewisse Probleme bei den ethischen Normen bestehen. Eine kleine, jedoch signifikante Minderheit der erfaßten Forscher hatte relativ großzügige Normen und Praktiken hinsichtlich Zustimmung und Risiko–Nutzen. Wir haben versucht, das Vorgehen dieser Minderheit auf verschiedene Weise zu erklären. Einige von ihnen sind relative Versager im Wettkampf um den wissenschaftlichen Erfolg; offensichtlich opfern sie den Wert Heilbehandlung des Menschen dem Wert Wissenschaftliche Errungenschaft. Einige von ihnen sind Opfer ethnischer oder anderer Diskriminierung; sie suchen die Auswirkungen dieser Diskriminierung durch zu ausgeprägte Betonung des wissenschaftlichen Strebens zu überwinden. Ein Teil dieser Großzügigkeit ist die Folge einer ungenügenden Ausbildung oder «Sozialisierung» in den Normen der Humantherapie. Ein weiterer Teil ist die Folge der nicht ganz perfekt funktionierenden Methodik der Kontrollkommissionen. Ein letzter Teil schließlich resultiert aus jenen Arten zwischenmenschlicher Kontakte und Gruppenarbeiten, in die die Forscher verwickelt sind und die ganz eindeutig ihr Verhalten bezüglich der Probleme Zustimmung und Risiko–Nutzen beeinflussen.

Unser allzu synoptischer Beitrag schließt mit einigen politischen Empfehlungen, die auf unseren Ergebnissen und Analysen beruhen.

Résumé

A la suite des nombreuses découvertes effectuées dans le domaine biomédical au cours des trente dernières années et des énormes avantages apportés par ces progrès, sur le plan de la santé et du bien-être, à tous ceux qui peuvent bénéficier des soins médicaux modernes, les chercheurs et le public en général soulignent qu'il est indispensable d'appliquer de rigoureuses normes de prudence de manière à protéger les sujets humains soumis à des expériences de recherche biomédicale.

Notre groupe de recherche sur l'expérimentation chez l'homme a estimé qu'il fallait, pour les besoins du débat, faire part de certaines informations sûres concernant les deux points auxquels s'applique principalement cette préoccupation, à savoir la question du consentement volontaire et conscient et celle du rapport optimal risque/avantage. Il nous a semblé que ces renseignements formeraient une bonne base pour l'élaboration d'une politique sociale constructive dans ce domaine.

A cette fin, nous avons procédé à deux études. La première est une enquête nationale, effectuée au moyen de questionnaires envoyés par la poste et à laquelle ont répondu 293 institutions américaines de recherche biomédicale qui constituent un échantillon représentatif de ces institutions sur le plan national. Nous nous sommes surtout intéressés, dans cette étude, à la structure, au fonctionnement et à l'efficacité des commissions de contrôle. Notre seconde étude est une enquête poussée sur deux institutions, grâce à laquelle, moyennant des entretiens personnels prolongés avec des chercheurs travaillant dans deux institutions représentatives de recherche biomédicale, nous avons obtenu des renseignements 1° sur leurs critères et leur comportement en ce qui concerne le consentement des sujets et le rapport risque/avantage, 2° sur leur formation relative aux normes d'éthique et 3° sur les relations en petits groupes ou entre personnes qui contribuent à déterminer leur comportement sur ces deux points.

Nos constatations montrent qu'il se pose un certain problème à propos des normes d'éthique, en ce sens qu'une minorité peu nombreuse, mais néanmoins significative, des chercheurs interrogés appliquent des critères et ont des comportements relativement tolérants en ce qui concerne le consentement des sujets et le rapport risque/avantage des recherches. Nous avons tenté d'expliquer de diverses façons l'existence de cette petite minorité. Certains des membres qui la composent ont relativement échoué dans la course au succès scientifique et font manifestement passer la valeur du résultat scientifique avant celle de la thérapie humaine. D'autres sont victimes d'une discrimination raciale ou autre et cherchent à vaincre les effets de cette ségrégation en mettant trop l'accent sur la vocation scientifique. Un certain degré de tolérance résulte d'une formation insuffisante quant aux normes de la thérapeutique humaine, ou encore de l'inefficacité relative des procédés de contrôle (peer reviews). Enfin, la tolérance tient aussi pour une part aux types de relations personnelles ou de groupe entre les chercheurs, qui influent incontestablement sur leurs comportements en ce qui concerne les problèmes du consentement des sujets et du rapport risque/avantage des expériences.

Nous concluons notre communication extrêmement brève par quelques recommandations qui reposent sur nos constatations et sur les résultats de notre analyse.

Resumen

Paralelamente a los innumerables descubrimientos biomédicos realizados en los últimos treinta años, de enorme provecho para la salud y el bienestar de cuantos gozan de la asistencia médica moderna, se observa. tanto en el investigador como en el profano, una inquietud creciente sobre la necesidad de adoptar normas que aseguren el máximo grado de prudencia y de cuidados a las personas sobre las que se efectúan experiencias biomédicas.

Nuestro grupo de estudios sobre la experimentación con seres humanos ha estimado necesario contribuir con una información bien fundada a la discusión de los dos puntos en que se centra esta preocupación: el consentimiento voluntario del sujeto informado y la justa relación entre el riesgo y el beneficio. Hemos creído que esta información constituiría una buena base para una política social constructiva en este campo.

Con este fin, hemos llevado a cabo dos estudios. Uno de ellos, a escala nacional, fue efectuado mediante un cuestionario enviado por correo. Este fue contestado por 293 instituciones de investigación biomédica de los Estados Unidos, lo cual constituye un porcentaje representativo de la actividad nacional en dicha especialidad. En este estudio tratamos de averiguar en primer lugar la estructura, los procedimientos y la eficacia de los sistemas de supervisión ejercida por los mismos colegas. El segundo es un extenso estudio sobre dos instituciones representativas de investigación biomédica; prolongadas entrevistas personales con investigadores de ambos centros nos proporcionaron datos sobre 1° sus normas y su comportamiento con respecto al consentimiento de los sujetos y a la relación riesgo/beneficio, 2° su formación ética y 3° el trabajo en equipo, que contribuye a determinar su comportamiento ante estas dos cuestiones.

Los resultados de nuestros estudios demuestran que en este terreno existen ciertos problemas en lo tocante a las normas éticas, en el sentido de que una pequeña pero significativa minoría de los investigadores interrogados aplican normas relativamente elásticas cuando se trata del consentimiento de los sujetos y la relación riesgo/beneficio. Hemos intentado explicar de varios modos la actitud de esta minoría. Algunos de sus miembros han fracasado más o menos en la competencia por el éxito profesional y sacrifican, obviamente, el valor del tratamiento terapéutico del hombre al de los logros de la ciencia. Otros son víctimas de la discriminación racial o de otra índole y tratan de compensar sus efectos poniendo demasiado énfasis en el afán científico. Esta relajación de los criterios es la consecuencia de una inadecuada enseñanza – o «socialización» – de las normas éticas que deben regir la terapéutica humana, y también de una supervisión no del todo eficaz. A veces, depende además del tipo de relación que reine entre las personas y los diversos grupos que trabajan juntos y que influye indudablemente sobre el comportamiento del investigador ante los problemas que suscita el consentimiento de los sujetos y la relación riesgo/beneficio.

Nuestra brevísima comunicación concluye con algunas recomendaciones acerca de la conducta que convendría adoptar, fundadas en nuestros análisis y observaciones.

Shifting targets for our magic bullets

by Arnold Burgen

In his personal journal at a blank space immediately below the entry recording the birth of his first child (T. H.) Huxley made another significant entry:

'September 20th, 1860

And this same child, our first-born, after being for nearly four years our delight and joy, was carried off by scarlet fever in forty-eight hours. This day week he and I had a great romp together. On Friday his restless head with its bright blue eyes and tangled hair tossed all day upon his pillow. On Saturday night I carried him here to my study and laid his cold still body here, where I write. Here too on Sunday came his mother, broken by grief.' (From: IRVINE, W.: *Apes, Angels and Victorians.*)

The sorrow and grief at the loss of a child was a common experience of families until so very recently. In England in 1860 one out of every seven children born alive failed to survive his first birthday. Even by 1920 this figure was not much better, but by 1960 it had fallen to less than one in fifty. Scarlatina, which in 1860 was killing two out of every thousand in the population each year, has ceased altogether after 1950 to contribute to the causes of death according to the records of the Registrar General. There is no difficulty in producing statistics attesting to the quite extraordinary degree of control we have achieved over the major causes of early death. Typhus, typhoid and diphtheria have become rarities and even deaths from that tough old enemy of mankind, tuberculosis, have declined at least one hundredfold in the past one hundred years.

Causality in processes involving so many changes is always open to some question, but there can be no serious doubt that the very steep downturn in both morbidity and mortality has followed new developments in treatment. Indeed the improvement has been the direct result of the new concepts of infectious disease developed by Pasteur, Koch, Lister and others, put into positive therapeutic practice by the development of vaccines and chemotherapeutic drugs.

Statistics are cold companions, but the change has been so great that it has affected the relationship of each individual to death and has greatly influenced our attitudes. When the dice of the fates no longer rattle so loudly in our ears, the hazards of accident and the environment loom larger in relative importance and grow monstrous, although in absolute terms they probably are no greater than formerly. There has been a general change in our attitude to death. When it was a common occurrence, due to the sudden assault of an infection against which there was no remedy, it was accepted with sorrow. Now death has come to be regarded as an outrage, a reproach to a negligent or indifferent society.

In parallel with the conquest of fatal disease there has been an equally striking reduction in the burden of pain and fear that man must bear. The introduction of anaesthesia in 1846 came as a tremendous boon. Who can imagine now the appalling experience of surgical treatment before this day? Indeed anaesthesia and antiseptics between them turned surgery from crude butchery to the delicate art of reconstruction it has become today. Think of toothache or a headache before aspirin, the short misery of diabetes before insulin, the miracle of restoring a gibbering cretin to sanity with thyroxin, the control of epilepsy and parkinsonian tremors and one has mentioned only the fringe of what has been achieved in such a short space of time. Medical scientists can be mightily proud of these achievements and the pharmaceutical industry which has brought us together here can be very satisfied with their part in all this. It is curious that our current society should take so perverse a view that these great benefits are taken at best as a right and the residual shortcomings of therapy as due to incompetence, or downright knavery.

There is no sign that this type of advance will not continue. Amongst infectious diseases it is those due to viruses that have been most obstinate. Our rapidly growing understanding of the nature of viruses and viral infection has explained some of the difficulties and should eventually point to a successful means of attack. This is especially important as the evidence favouring a viral origin of many cancers has grown. Other aspects of cancer research are also more hopeful than they have been for years. The remaining major cause of death is cardiovascular disease, and while there are few leads at present it is likely that the great success in treating hypertension will be repeated in the control of atheroma and coronary disease in the next twenty years.

The major result of dealing with these problems is a steady improvement in life expectancy, and we can therefore reckon on a considerable proportion of the population to live to the ninth decade or beyond. We are thus faced with a large and increasing population of partly or wholly incapacitated elderly people whose care absorbs a large part of our resources. Others will be concerned with the social problems this entails, I am concerned with remedies. We surely need to understand far more about the nature of ageing. Is it inevitable that vessels should undergo medial or intimal degeneration, that the skin should atrophy, the muscles and bones lose their strength, and the mind suffer defects of memory and reason? The older view was that the body wore out like a machine, a motor-car, but this is very hard to sustain in view of what we know of the ceaseless renewal and repair that is such a fundamental part of the cellular processes. One theory implies the presence of ageing genes that are turned on as soon as genes concerned with cellular differentiation have been turned off. Another that ageing is due to the accumulation of disadvantageous mutations beyond the level at which repair and repressor mechanisms can compensate so that cell mechanisms become progressively impaired. When the pathological features of ageing are recounted it is striking how insistent is the prominence of changes in collagen and connective tissue; this might suggest a focus on a study of ageing in these tissues. Cellular timing is a very striking feature of development and much effort is going on into finding out how a sequence of processes is produced in cells. It is well known, for instance, that if we take disaggregated cells from a developing tissue they will readily reassemble but if the cells are a mixture of cells of two biological ages they will not form a single aggregate, that is they recognize their ages and are unable to adjust. These are just a few aspects of an area that demands far more study; it would have a very high priority on my list of socially important research. Let us be quite clear about the objectives of research in ageing having what I consider the right orientation. It is not to extend the maximal lifespan, especially not in the face of the con- tinuance of the infirmities of age, but rather to modify the ageing process so that instead of a single tissue weakness leading to infirmity, the ageing of the cells is more synchronous. The idea was well expressed in Oliver Wendell Holmes' poem about the 'wonderful one-hoss shay that was built to last a hundred years to the day' and on the dawn of its hundredth year fell into dust because each part had been built to last as long as each other. In so far as we are successful in removing the disabilities of old age so will great benefits accrue to the individual and to society.

The rapid growth of population is also, to some extent, related to our success in improving health. The reduction of mortality in the young together with greater fertility probably attributable to better nutrition favours an in- creased population growth, but at least in developed countries these are opposed by the availability of effective contraceptive measures and of relatively free abortion. The net balance of these factors has led almost universally to a net growth of the population. The balancing factor seems to be the instinctive urge to reproduce, one of the basic survival instincts of living creatures. This is a capricious factor, it seems reasonably well established that in some western countries the rapid growth of population in the nineteenth century was quite unrelated to and indeed preceded the improvements in health. It is also the case that the reproductive rate is affected by wars, by the political system and by social custom. There are also lags and leads in the system that make short-term trends very difficult to forecast. Perhaps the present social pressure to reduce family size will be in time, but the situation is hazardous and much more study is needed on what controls the desire to reproduce. Indeed an understanding of instinctual drives and ways in which they can be modified, might be turned on aggression, the instinct which in wild animals is concerned with the need to hunt for food and for defence against predators. This is largely an atavistic instinct in civilized societies, that becomes expressed as violent behaviour, and the territorial instinct that underlies most racial and religious intolerance and wars between nations. The experience of many centuries has shown that the reward-punishment structure of society cannot regularly contain these instincts; it is not enough to bewail the failure of man's moral development to measure up to his technological achievements. We need more recognition of the different level of nervous activity that is responsible for instinctual and intellectual activities. It is obvious that if methods of controlling instinctual drives were discovered their application would offer the greatest difficulty in the present organization of society.

Another field where interesting possibilities exist is in the improvement of learning capacity. We have seen the dramatic improvement in mental development that occurs in cretinism with the correction of the underlying endocrine defect and in phenylketonuria by dietary control; it would be splendid if similar results could be achieved with the much larger group of subnormals. But, a further one of the problems of modern life is the way in which knowledge has gone beyond our capacity to assimilate it and the grave problems introduced by mechanisation. The latter is leading to a contraction of employment for unskilled workers and a basically unsatisfied demand for the more highly skilled. These problems would be alleviated if ways of producing an increase in intellectual and learning capacity could be found. Some tentative studies of this problem have been made, but a much more determined effort is needed if there is to be a chance of success.

The general burden of this article is that in the past the target of medical research has been the improvement of man's health and well-being. I believe this to have been a wholly good objective that has been outstandingly successful. It has brought in its train unsought and unforeseen problems, but these should be used neither to denigrate the achievement nor to inhibit further development but rather to point to the new problems to which attention should be given. The objectives of medical research should concentrate on the happiness of man in relation to the society in which he lives.

Summary

In the past decades medical advances have led to really outstanding improvements in man's health and well-being; there is every likelihood of continued major advances. The increased lifespan highlights the problems of ageing as the major area in which research is needed.

Zusammenfassung

In den letzten Jahrzehnten hat der medizinische Fortschritt zu außergewöhnlichen Verbesserungen der Gesundheit und des Wohlergehens der Menschen geführt; alle Anzeichen sprechen für weitere umfassende Fortschritte. Die erhöhte Lebenserwartung der Bevölkerung erfordert, daß die Probleme des Alterns zum Hauptanliegen in der Forschung werden.

Résumé

Les progrès médicaux des dernières décennies ont donné lieu à une amélioration véritablement exceptionnelle de la santé et du bien-être de l'homme, et il est tout à fait probable que ces grands progrès vont se poursuivre. La prolongation de la vie humaine fait nettement apparaître que les problèmes du vieillissement doivent constituer le thème principal de la recherche future.

Resumen

Los adelantos de la ciencia médica en las últimas décadas han contribuido a una mejora extraordinaria de la salud y del bienestar del hombre, y todo parece indicar que estos grandes progresos van a continuar. Con la prolongación de la vida humana, parece evidente que los problemas del envejecimiento deberán constituir el tema principal de la investigación futura.

Health as the physician views it,
and the use of space technology to achieve and maintain it

by CHARLES A. BERRY

At the outset it should be manifestly obvious to all that there are many definitions of health, and certainly discussion of these is one of the primary concerns of our gathering. Health is defined in the dictionary as 'a normal condition of body or mind; that is, with all of the parts functioning normally'. Such a definition immediately raises questions in my mind for we are faced with a second definition which may be even more difficult – that of what is normal? In my daily medical activities in support of manned space flight, I deal with 'normal' individuals who are being exposed to a rather hostile environment. Normal in this sense could be defined as 'free from disease', for many of the individuals the average physician deals with in his daily practice are certainly persons who have some variation of normal in mind or body and are therefore seeking assistance and are willing to pay the charge incurred. One of the unseen benefits of the space program is the continuing effort to define more precisely what we mean by 'normal' as regards functioning of body and mind. The range is great and in our program, which depends upon measuring sometimes minute variations in physiological function, we have resorted to using the individual as his own 'normal' or control and thus measuring his variations from that 'normal' baseline.

The physician and, as a matter of fact, the bulk of people in the world today are preoccupied with sickness or illness. In the light of this preoccupation, much of the medical and health manpower is utilized in therapeutic medicine in contrast to preventive medicine which could be of much greater value. The physician tends to think of health very much in terms of the definition above, i.e. he thinks of a state where there is no measurable alteration of function in body or mind. Thus he becomes body- or organ-oriented, for he must think physiologically and pathologically and finally therapeutically to help his patient achieve the state called 'health'. My activity has been principally in the area of preventive medicine. Great effort is expended in trying to anticipate what might happen to our space crewmen and to protect them against any occurrence that might result in altered physiology. This is not always possible, but I view an illness or injury in one of our crewmen as a preventive medicine failure. In such a case much effort is expended in 'failure analysis', much as our engineering counterparts do in analysing the functioning of the spacecraft and its systems.

In the early 1950's, in general practice, my view of health became considerably different from that held previously as a physician. The general practice of medicine cannot help modifying some of the symptom- and organ-oriented thought. After my experience with general practice, I was assigned as a medical officer in Panama. This position required that I spend time in all the Central and South American countries, attempting to establish Aerospace Medical Programs for the care of their military pilots. One day in 1953 I was visiting with the director of the Military Hospital in San Salvador. He was Salvadorian, but of German descent and had been medically trained in Germany. I spent the better part of a day in surgery with him as we repaired wounds caused by machetes which the natives had used upon each other. The hospital was largely open-air with the families living by the bedside of the patients. The wards were stretched up a hillside. As we walked out into the wards to see the results of our day's handiwork, the physician turned to me and said, 'I become completely discouraged when I think that none of these patients we have operated and casted today will be in the hospital tomorrow. They will all return to their villages and many, if not all, will use a machete to remove the cast because it is a hindrance. Deformity will result and our work will have been in vain, for no matter how fine the medicine practised, if the patient does not have the education to use it, he cannot maintain any state of health.' I have never forgotten that day, and since, I have seen many individuals living in poverty, infested by parasites, suffering from nutritional deficiency diseases, etc.

Following the successful flight of Gemini 5, the eight-day mission of Cooper and Conrad in August of 1965, my wife and I travelled with them on a goodwill tour involving Greece, Turkey, and much of Africa. In a village in Nigeria, I was deeply impressed by the amount of medical pathology I could see, just riding or walking through the streets. The most disturbing aspect of the pathology was that much of it would have been amenable to treatment by readily available drugs in our own country. Again, I was reminded of the time twelve years previously when patients in our country were treated and their pathology cleared. How long would it last here, and would they really achieve a state of health? I am convinced, and I think many others are also, that one cannot take the narrow definition of *health*. It is impossible to separate the functioning of the body from education, from economics and from social pressures. As Hecht has said, 'It has become apparent to the ghetto dweller that the definition of health implies a state of physical, mental and social well-being, and not merely the absence of disease and infirmity. His health hazards include faulty plumbing, lead paints, inadequate nutrition, limited education, inability to receive employment, police harrassment, and infestation with rats, among other problems.' Thus, it can be seen that health requires, and is indeed more than, the 'normal' functioning of all our bodily parts.

The right to health is becoming of increasing concern today. Throughout our world, rising economic expectations are causing people to demand more personal and political rights and privileges. Since 1946, the World Health Organization has set forth as one of its basic principles that 'The enjoyment of the highest attainable standard of health is one of the fundamental rights of every human being without distinction of race, religion, political belief, economic or social condition'. A number of international meetings and declarations have re-iterated many of these rights. At Teheran in 1968, the World Health Organiza-tion was asked to study the problems of those human rights that might be al-tered by recent scientific discoveries and technological advances. In our own country, the 89th Congress enacted social legislation in 1965 and 1966 declaring health to be a human right. In the enactment of Medicare and Medicaid (the heart disease, cancer and stroke amendment and the comprehensive health plan-ning act) the concept of health maintenance was changed from being a matter of individual to being a matter of social responsibility. The purpose of the legisla-tion was stated as follows: 'The Congress declares that the fulfilment of our na-tional purpose depends on promoting and assuring the highest level of health at-tainable for every person in an environment which contributes positively to healthful individual and family living.' There are also a number of bills propos-ing means of achieving this state of health, and all speak in forceful tones about the people's right to health. There are also bills requiring studies of the effect of technological advances on health in human personality.

Such medical groups as the American Medical Association have declared that every individual has a right to adequate medical care. One can hear much discussion these days about medical care as a right, for this right does indeed challenge the current system of delivery of such care. One might well ask wheth-er we really are considering man's right to medical care or his right to health. From the above discussion it is obvious that health is a much more encompass-ing state of being and of greater importance to the individual than is merely the right to medical care. I am convinced that without the ancillary activities that go to bring about a state of health, medical care could be in vain. Therefore, we must try to assure individuals the right to health; but this is an awesome under-taking.

Having agreed upon a rather far-reaching definition of health and upon the fact that every person should have a right to it, how can we provide for its achievement and maintenance? Much has been said about the current shortage of medical personnel in our own country and around the world. The population continues to increase and the ratio of physicians to number of the population continues to become worse. The history of any health programs where prepay-ment has been involved or where free care has been made available reveals an immediate clamor for health checkups of various types. If there is a right to health, then the individual must know whether he is indeed healthy or not. This is not always easily apparent to him, nor sometimes to the examiner. The system used so far has been operated in a one-to-one ratio of patients and physicians. It is quite obvious that we cannot possibly begin to face the task of assuring the right to health if we continue to use the current system. There must be some reassessment, for present-day medical care is therapeutically oriented, and the great bulk of our health care professionals are completely absorbed in therapy.

Our efforts to assure man's capability to perform in a weightless environment of space has led to the development of a great deal of technology and techniques both for conducting an extensive preventive medicine program using the information to predict his performance and for allowing us to monitor that performance at distances of 240,000 miles from the earth. These technological advances can extend the capability of our physicians today. While advocates such as myself use machines as a means to extend the eyes, ears, arms, and hands of the physician and thus give him time to do the things he is best trained to do – make decisions that have an effect on the life of the patient – many would feel that the machine represents an unwarranted intrusion into the doctor-patient relationship. Medicine is basically conservative and there will be obvious resistance to change. Still, while the physician urges, 'Do not put a machine between me and my patient', the patient asks, 'How can I have enough time with a physician so that I may understand my state of health and plan my future?' Both of these concerns must be faced squarely, evaluated and handled.

Technology may be utilized not only to allow us to handle the heavy workload engendered by the right to medical care, but also to provide a more scientific basis for our medical care. An example of where care could be improved by a better scientific basis is a coronary patient who, having recovered from a coronary occlusion with infarction, is now ready to assume his place at work. The conservative physician groping for a way to return his patient to a useful occupation may say, 'Try working two or three hours in the morning and we'll gradually increase this if you do not have any symptoms'. Modern technology could put this decision on a much more scientific basis by placing an electrocardiographic sensor on his chest, attaching it to a small tape recorder or telemetering the electrocardiogram to a central station, while the patient went about his work activity. This would allow the physician to judge by physiologic evidence whether the work undertaken was within the cardiac capabilities of the patient.

It should be realized that the provision of poor health care is not always confined to the underprivileged. An example are the hypertensive patients. It has been estimated that there are some twenty-four million hypertensive patients in the United States and this is probably a conservative estimate. One half of these remain undiagnosed and of those who have been recognized, one half have received no treatment and of those who have received treatment, one half have received ineffective or inappropriate therapy. Thus only one eighth of the hypertensives in this country are provided with what could be considered adequate medical care. Again, modern technology could provide a better scientific basis for prognosis and therapy. It is possible with automatic blood pressure measuring systems and the like to determine on a continuing basis who has an elevated blood pressure and thus establish a diagnosis of hypertension. It is also possible to evaluate hypertensive drug therapy by means of the same devices. Thus, much could be done in this one area with the use of modern technology.

Any attempt to utilize current and future technological hardware and other developments in the provision of health care should consider both the development of modules which may be used in the various settings where health care must be rendered and a system to coordinate the function of these modules. The use of bioinstrumentation and data management systems allows better standardization of measurement techniques and can improve quality and speed of data gathered. The systems design approach where total systems are integrated at the design level, as in the aerospace industry, offers great advantages in the early design of any such health care system. Data management techniques utilizing computer systems, both minicomputers and large central storage computers, help to provide a data base and at the same time may be coordinated with an extensive communications network to provide adequate control and minimize travel time for patients, physicians and paramedical personnel.

In our attempts to provide continuing medical assessment of the crew on the ground and at great distances, we have obtained a great deal of experience in the practice of remote medicine, some understanding of the artifacts that can be engendered and a great deal of experience in the use of computer techniques for providing a data base that can be utilized in a real time manner. One of the benefits of such a preventive medicine program is the provision of a 'normal' for each individual in the system. As this data base grows, variations from the 'normal' may then be recognized at the earliest possible time.

It is manifestly simple to automate such static measurements as height and weight as well as much of the visual and hearing examinations, some tests of the cardiovascular system, the musculoskeletal and the nervous system. Automated techniques involved in assessing each of these body systems are growing at a great pace today. The clinical laboratory information lends itself to automation and computer operation, and all of these techniques allow the physician to have information available while the patient is still present so that he may speed up both the diagnostic and the treatment process, saving time for both himself and the patient. There are a number of facilities utilizing automated techniques of various sorts, and it is certainly time that some systematized operation for such facilities be established as a demonstration of the best that could be done in this area. Much learning remains to be done and the proper mix of paramedical and medical personnel as well as the handling of the 'patient' mix will require continued consideration by all involved.

In our own operation we are concerned with crews and their families and are providing a continuing preventive medicine and therapeutic medicine care program. In order to standardize our measurements, we have continued to automate as many of the examination and laboratory techniques as possible and tie these to minicomputers in the laboratory and these to large central core computers for data storage. The data base computer can then be made to produce the data books on each crewman necessary at the time he flies. We have been convinced that the most important measurements are not the static ones but dynamic testing such as bicycle ergometry for exercise tolerance and lower body negative pressure for cardiovascular response. These stress the total system and can produce information of great value in predicting future performance. I am so convinced of the value of preventive medicine and the use of these techniques that we organized a private corporation to demonstrate such an advanced diagnostic clinic concept for a specialized population – airline pilots and support personnel.

Modules of various types must be designed and then connected to help form a total system. One of the areas that have received great emphasis in recent years is multiphasic health testing or screening examinations, as they are frequently called. As it became more widely known that medical care is a right, the demand for health checkups increased at an alarming rate. Multiphasic health testing was initiated as a means of meeting the demand for health checkups at the best possible cost with the most effective use of manpower. Dr Collen at Kaiser Permanente has been a leader in this field in introducing automated and computer techniques for such screening examinations. The best multiphasic testing program should use automation, panel testing and paramedical personnel, reserving physician involvement to only the essential part of completion of the examination. Such an evaluation serves to determine the health status of a person within the limits of present medical knowledge and practicability. As with any well-designed activity, it also produces an impressive group of by-products. These include separating the well from the sick, providing a preliminary workup for the sick, establishing entry priorities for the sick, detecting illness-prone persons, detecting asymptomatic illness, detecting symptomatic illness, assisting in the diagnostic process, establishing a health profile for continuing health care, saving doctor visits, saving patient visits, saving hospital days for routine and diagnostic studies, optimizing the use of paramedical personnel and establishing a computerized medical data base. Multiphasic health testing, however, is of benefit only if it is used principally as a procedure for helping the doctor provide a comprehensive health evaluation. We have discussed medical care as a right and then noted that a second right must accompany it – the right to know whether one needs medical care. The existing health care delivery system can be inundated with relatively healthy people concerned about this second right: to know the state of their health. These 'worried well' will obtain the answer upon symptom complaints through very costly services from physicians if the answer is not provided by means of a system like health screening examination. Therefore, multiphasic health testing is absolutely essential to make the demand manageable. If it is not provided, it will be virtually impossible to grant quality medical care as a right, for free care without the use of a technique of this sort can only depreciate the quality of care for all.

Modern technology, starting with biosensors on the patient and extending to central data handling systems, and in particular involving communication and television systems to aid in diagnosis and therapy, must be designed for use in the individual office, in group clinics, hospitals, the physician's automobile and in vans used in remote areas. They may be set up as a regional or state system as was studied in New Mexico. Here technology was utilized to form remote stationary and mobile units that could maintain contact with medical expertise at a medical center. Thus paramedical personnel operating these fixed and mobile remote units could provide quality diagnosis and indeed therapy through consultation with the experts at the medical center. We have recently given some thought to the use of a sophisticated satellite communication system, which would become a regional medical network providing the required services for very large areas such as the North American continent. Any operation of this sort must start with a basic unit, however, whether it be a specialized airport clinic, a single remote or ambulance unit, or the more demanding unit of a large medical center.

The individual modules outlined above are important foundation stones of any health care system utilizing technology. They cannot, however, produce the desired results unless some further alterations are made in the medical care delivery system. Garfield has proposed a very intriguing design for the use of multiphasic health testing as the heart of a new medical care delivery system. The elimination of personally paid fees markedly changes the input into the delivery system, for it floods the system with large numbers of 'well' and 'worried well' people, in addition to the sick. This altered entry mix is not suited for today's delivery system, as the current system was evolved on a fee-for-service basis, involving the physician not only in the delivery process but at the point of entry and in every other step. In short, the current system requires a one-for-one doctor-patient service scheme. This tends to waste the physician's time and impairs services for both the well and the sick and leads to much of today's maldistribution and unavailability of medical services in critical areas. The new system design must realistically match the new entry mix. As Garfield proposes, multiphasic health testing could separate the entry mix into its three basic components: the well, the asymptomatic sick and the sick. Three services could then be established to receive these components: a new health care service for the well, a preventive maintenance service for the asymptomatic sick, and the true sick care service for the sick. According to Garfield, and I certainly agree, the first two could use essentially automated and paramedical services and could therefore be more easily and inexpensively staffed. This would relieve the sick care of the considerable load of the remainder of the mix and thereby develop increased capacity for care of the sick. This could be further augmented by the ability to transfer much of the follow-up care of highly prevalent chronic illness to the preventive maintenance area. The system also offers the great benefit that paramedical personnel – with limited training and limited but precise skills enabling them to relieve the physician of routine and repetitive tasks – could see these tasks clearly defined and structured. The entry system would assist greatly in achieving this by effectively using such paramedical personnel. Physicians and other health care personnel can do much to help design optimal multiphasic health testing schemes in order that they may bridge the gap between medical care as a right and the health delivery system as having to fulfil that right. The flow model of Garfield's medical care delivery system is shown in Figure 1. This delivery system is amenable to functioning as neighborhood or regional facilities. It is however aimed only at medical care per se, and if we are to provide a true *health* care delivery system, we should also supply access to dental care, legal and economic advice (job placement), etc.

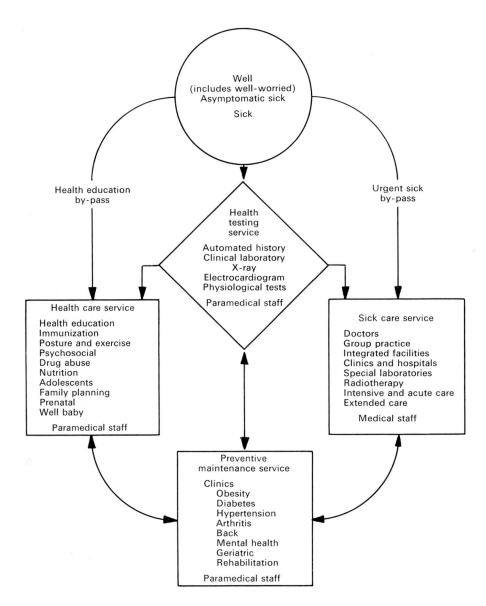

Figure 1. Flow model of medical care delivery system. From GARFIELD, S. R.: Multiphasic Health Testing and Medical Care as a Right. *New Engl. J. Med. 283*, 1087–1089 (1970).

I am sure that many physicians will immediately voice their concern about any such proposed modification of the health or medical care delivery system, on the same grounds that they will object to the utilization of technology, i.e. on the grounds that this would interfere with their relationship with the patient. As a physician deeply concerned about the patient and the doctor-patient relationship, I am also concerned that the physician define his relation to the system of health care delivery that must result from the explosion of interest in health care. At the turn of the century, the delivery system consisted basically of a physician administering to the patient. This evolved to the point where the physician was assisted by secretaries, nurses and even, in some offices, a laboratory staff. The physician of the future must have administrative, diagnostic and therapeutic assistants, and he must have sociological inputs concerning the individual, his family and the community. He must also be supported by a technology that provides him with a machine-patient diagnostic capability, a physician-machine interrogative capability and a patient-machine therapeutic capability. In short, the physician of the future must become a health director of a given area. It is obvious that the population is increasing at least at twice the rate at which we can produce physicians, even if we could secure additional funds to produce more. If, as Hecht has noted, we are to prevent medical bankruptcy, we must concern ourselves with the increasing and new responsibilities of the physician in any health care delivery system. Because of these increasing and different responsibilities, he must rely on a large staff of associates and assistants, who can help him in the day-to-day diagnostic and therapeutic 'tricks of the trade'. He must work in close relations with a sociologist, the family adviser, the urban planner and other leaders in the community health service system. He must be substantially aided by modern data processing techniques connected with modern sensing techniques, so that the patient's history, the results of various physical examination procedures and tests, laboratory procedures, data on the proper titration of medication and lists of differential diagnoses may be presented by a machine for his consideration and discussion with the patient. He will thus become the ultimate decision maker for the health care not only of his individual patient but of his area. He could thus achieve that level of thoughtfulness and logic which is difficult to come by in the present system. Most importantly, these changes will not take from the physician his humanitarian role as confidant and adviser to the sick. On the contrary, they will provide more time for him to devote to his primary patient concern. He will be able to do this with a great deal of scientific knowledge, and will in the end render more humanitarian and better scientific medical care to his patient. If we are able to achieve this, the patient-physician ratio by itself may become an irrelevant figure.

There are a number of questions that are automatically raised in connection with any comprehensive health plan, particularly if the barrier of economics is removed and health is considered a right. Critics have focused on the absence of long-term proof that early detection of illness can materially influence the natural course of disease. I would certainly agree that at the moment there is considerable controversy as to whether we can influence the natural course of disease, but neither is there any long-term proof that we do not influence it. Anything we can do toward initiating treatment at an early time increases the likelihood of recovery of the individual patient. This, after all, is what medical care is all about.

Concerning plans utilizing screening as we have proposed it, critics have questioned the low yield of illness and the high cost of each detected illness. This again is related to our preoccupation with sickness, which understandably has long prevailed in medicine. If the positive approach were taken, we could point with pride to the large number of people who have received assurance at very low cost that they have no evidence of a particular type of cancer, whereas the low number who were found to have the disease may have a better prognosis because it was detected at an early date. There can be no doubt that there is a positive value in detecting health, for anyone who is pronounced healthy gains a certain security that can be transmitted to his life plans. Obviously, the segregation of the healthy also allows a more rational allocation of medical resources.

Another criticism that has been levelled against our proposals is the fact that any system in which health is regarded as a right will be overloaded with minor complaints. We have considered this problem in outlining a system that would utilize paramedical personnel and screening examinations in an effective manner. The problem cannot be solved with technology, other than to help assure the individual that his minor complaint is not of dire significance. Associated with this could be the detection of false positives. False positive information, whether in the laboratory or in a physiologic test, can throw additional loads on any health care system and is always a risk. Effort and experience will help to reduce false positives to the minimum but they will always be part of any system devised.

A related question frequently raised is whether comprehensive health care systems as those discussed here really do maintain health. There are obviously advocates for them, just as there are critics. As noted, I am a firm believer in the value of preventive medicine and its application to individuals and groups. Certainly, there is a lack of solid statistical evidence to prove that you can measure the health maintenance produced by any one of these systems. Changes in the delivery systems for health care will probably be evaluated first from a financial viewpoint, but it is hoped that we may be able to develop statistics which will shed light on the question whether such services maintain health. I believe that the evidence will prove they do.

This leads to the question of whether a so-called detailed or super-system, as the one we now provide for our astronauts, has general applicability to the population at large. It would certainly be costly, at the present time, to apply this system in its entirety to the general population. Moreover, some items are aimed at establishing firm baselines allowing us to measure minute changes as effects of the space flight environment, rather than at maintaining a general state of health. Obviously much remains to be done to define the individual state of health or the 'normal', and much of what we do can gradually be brought to bear in medical systems such as the one outlined.

The proposed advances and changes in health care systems raise obvious social questions. There is the fear that the use of technology is dehumanizing, and there is great impetus today, particularly among the young, to get back to basic human relationships and to personality confrontation. It is interesting that despite this trend I have heard no one attack the use of technology in medicine on this basis. As I said before I firmly believe that we can maintain the humaneness in medicine and in fact improve it by the use of technology. It is a problem, however, to be confronted.

The use of computer techniques and data storage always raises the problem of privacy, and in no area is this of more particular concern to the individual, than when it involves the state of his health. This concern must be kept in mind as we plan computer programs and develop the techniques for data handling. We have considered it at length in our current operations and there are techniques that will allow the shielding of such information in computers. One of the obvious advantages of widespread use of medical data storage would be the availability of medical records on an individual wherever he might travel in our mobile society. This very availability does however raise the spectre of loss of privacy, and it must be seriously confronted.

Any physician interested in preventive medicine and public health will face another very serious social conflict, for if we are successful in maintaining everyone healthy and stopping or markedly reducing disability and death, and in preserving what could be called the 'unfit', we produce problems that have great social implications. There must be food enough to feed increased population and we must find acceptable and effective means of population control, or we will only have shifted mankind's concern from concern about death due to disease to concern about life in an over-populated world. I believe thinking human beings are capable of tackling these problems and seeking wise solutions, though they may not now be evident, and that after all is the purpose of our coming together in Basel.

Summary

There emerges a new concept of health in our society with an increasing world-wide trend to define health in terms of physical, mental and social well-being, rather than merely in terms of an absence of identifiable disease and infirmity. The growing demand for health recognized to be a basic human right implies that existing systems for health care delivery will have to change and that this change will take the form of more wide-spread utilization of modern technology, with paramedical personnel, automated measurements, and electronic data processing and transfer methods serving to extend the capabilities of individual physicians to serve larger segments of the population. Screening and classification of patients need to be established in a manner that will permit appropriately trained physicians to bring their skills to bear on the problems of a larger number of people, with greater efficiency than is now possible. Greater emphasis must be placed on preventive medicine and preventive health maintenance as demands for comprehensive health care increase, and systematic record keeping, again facilitated by modern technology, is essential to establish techniques of real value in health maintenance programs. The physician will face new social challenges as the overall level of available health care improves.

Zusammenfassung

In diesem Beitrag wird der sich wandelnde Gesundheitsbegriff in unserer Gesellschaft besprochen. Es besteht eine wachsende weltweite Tendenz, Gesundheit eher als physisches, psychisches und soziales Wohlbefinden zu definieren denn als das bloße Nichtbestehen einer identifizierbaren Erkrankung oder Invalidität. Die Implikationen der zunehmenden Forderung nach Gesundheit, als einem menschlichen Grundrecht, werden untersucht. Es ist anzustreben, existierende Einrichtungen der Gesundheitspflege zu reorganisieren, wobei die Möglichkeiten der modernen Technik besser genutzt werden sollten (mit medizinischem Hilfspersonal, automatisierten Messungen und elektronischer Datenverarbeitung und elektronischen Übermittlungsverfahren) und damit die Fachkenntnisse der einzelnen Ärzte einem größeren Teil der Bevölkerung zugute kommen. Routineuntersuchungen und Klassifizierungen der Patienten sollten eingerichtet werden, die es den entsprechend geschulten Ärzten ermöglichen, ihr Können bei einer größeren Anzahl von Kranken wirksamer einzusetzen als bisher möglich. Der Präventivmedizin und der Gesundheitsvorsorge müssen größere Aufmerksamkeit geschenkt werden, da der Wunsch nach einer umfassenderen Gesundheitspflege immer stärker wird. Wesentlich ist auch eine systematische Karteiführung, die ebenfalls durch die moderne Technik vereinfacht wird, um Methoden erarbeiten zu können, die für die Aufstellung von Programmen zur Gesunderhaltung von wirklichem Wert sind. Der Arzt wird sich angesichts des verbesserten Gesamtniveaus der verfügbaren Gesundheitspflege mit neuen sozialen Momenten auseinandersetzen müssen.

Résumé

Cet exposé traite de l'évolution du concept de santé dans notre société et met en lumière divers signes révélateurs d'une tendance générale de plus en plus marquée à définir la santé en termes de bien-être physique, psychique et social plutôt que comme l'absence d'affection et de maladie identifiables. L'auteur y étudie les conséquences de cette tendance de plus en plus nette à considérer la santé comme un droit fondamental de l'homme. Il estime que les systèmes actuels d'assistance sanitaire doivent être modifiés et que ce changement prendra la forme d'une utilisation plus généralisée de la technologie moderne – ce qui implique un personnel paramédical qualifié, l'automatisation des méthodes de mesure, le traitement des données ainsi que des méthodes de transmission électroniques afin que les médecins exerçant seuls soient au service d'une plus grande partie de la population. L'auteur souligne ensuite la nécessité d'établir un système de dépistage et une classification des malades qui permettraient aux médecins experts en ces méthodes d'utiliser leur savoir pour résoudre les problèmes d'un plus grand nombre de malades et avec une efficacité plus grande qu'il n'est possible actuellement. L'auteur pense qu'il faut accorder plus d'importance à la médecine préventive et à la sauvegarde de la santé étant donné que l'opinion publique réclame de plus en plus fréquemment une assistance sanitaire le plus complète possible, et il croit qu'un système d'enregistrement systématique, également facilité par la technologie moderne, est essentiel pour établir des méthodes vraiment efficaces dans le cadre de programmes de sauvegarde sanitaire. En conclusion, l'auteur aborde les nouveaux défis sociaux auxquels le médecin devra faire face au fur et à mesure que le niveau général de l'assistance sanitaire s'améliorera.

Resumen

Nuestra sociedad se está formando un nuevo concepto de la salud, y es universal la tendencia a definirla no ya como una mera ausencia de defecto físico o de enfermedad específica, sino como un estado de bienestar a la vez físico, mental y social.

Para satisfacer el creciente deseo de salud, que se ha convenido en reconocer como uno de los derechos inherentes al hombre como tal, los actuales sistemas de administración sanitaria tendrán que transformarse y hacer más amplio uso de la tecnología moderna, personal paramédico idóneo, mediciones automáticas así como del proceso e intercambio electrónico de datos con el fin de aumentar la capacidad individual de cada médico y permitirle así atender a un mayor sector de la población.

La selección y clasificación de los pacientes deberá efectuarse de modo que los médicos, debidamente formados, puedan poner a contribución toda su ciencia y pericia para resolver los problemas de un mayor número de personas, y esto con más eficacia de lo que ha sido posible hasta el presente.

Deberá concederse más importancia a la medicina preventiva y a la conservación de la salud, si se quiere hacer frente al aumento de las demandas sanitarias de la población. El registro sistemático de datos, igualmente facilitado por la tecnología moderna, es esencial en la elaboración de las técnicas que serán necesarias para realizar los programas de mantenimiento de la salud.

El médico tiene que prepararse a desafiar las nuevas exigencias que le presentará la sociedad a medida que mejore el nivel general de prestaciones sanitarias.

Problems of resource allocation in United States medical care

by Kenneth J. Arrow

Medical care in the United States has been and in many ways still is directed by the free play of the market. Individual patients use their incomes as they choose to buy medical services; physicians derive their incomes from these fees and freely decide how much medical services to offer, how to specialize, and where to locate. These decisions may be made for all sorts of reasons, but certainly income is not irrelevant. Such a system for the allocation of medical resources has been largely abandoned in most other leading countries and is undergoing progressive modification in the United States. The state and local governments have always intervened to some extent in providing medical services to the poor; the spread of medical insurance, even though nominally private, has sensibly modified the earlier financial arrangements and motivations; and more recently the Federal government has intervened massively to finance medical services to the aged and to greatly increase those for the poor. Now it is clear that the country is on the way to some form of national health insurance. The only question is what form it will take. We may expect several years of vigorous debate among the contesting proposals emanating from all sides. But when a Republican administration comes forth to urge a definite permanent role for the Federal government in the provision of medical care to the entire population, the issue of principle has been resolved.

At this turning point, a review of the theoretical and practical problems in the allocation of medical resources may be useful. It is convenient to start with the price system as a point of departure, and this for three reasons: first, because it is the system from which the United States is moving; second, because in fact the bulk of economic decisions, both in the United States and in Western Europe are governed by prices, and therefore an explanation for the special treatment of medical care is in order; and third, because there are strong general arguments on theoretical and empirical grounds that the price system is usually an efficient means of providing for mankind's needs for goods and services. I shall therefore start with a discussion of the logic of the price system in general: what it means, how it works, what are the arguments for considering that it leads to an efficient allocation of the resources available. Section 2 deals with the special features of medical care as a commodity which limit the application of the general principles of section 1, specifically, the great importance of several uncertainties in this market. In section 3, a generalized description of the actual workings of the medical care market in the United States is given, with indications how the departures in practice from more usual markets are related to the special features of medical care discussed in section 2. In section 4, some more specific empirical features of recent history of the medical care market are discussed. In section 5, the two leading proposals for changes in the organization of the United States medical care industry are summarized. Finally, in section 6, some implications of these proposals are analysed, and a possible alternative canvassed.

1. The logic of the price system

It may be as well to define what is meant by a price system for allocating resources. There is a category of actual or at least possible goods and services. There is also a set of economic agents, the individuals and organizations who constitute the economy and who make individual decisions to consume or supply goods and services or to convert some goods and services into others (i. e. engage in the act of production). We will use the term *commodity* to cover both goods and services. The goods are commodities embodied in some physical form, as bread; services are commodities which are immaterial in form, as medical in advice or labor in general. From the general economic point of view, the principles underlying the production and distributions of goods are identical with those for services, and no further distinction need be made. Some commodities are useful to economic agents directly and desired by them; others are useful only indirectly because they assist in the production of directly desired goods. Medical advice and automobiles are desired directly; the physician's secretary or her typewriter or laboratory equipment are desired only instrumentally, because they assist the physician in the production of better advice, just as the automobile worker or the assembly have also instrumental or derived value.

Commodities may also be classified in another way, as either available immediately, in which case they are called *primary factors*, or else they are *produced goods*. Typically, land and labor are thought of as primary factors. The classification, however, is not absolute but relative to the time period being considered. Thus, at any moment of time, the stock of capital goods, such as buildings and machinery, is given and can be regarded as a primary factor; but over a longer period of time the stock can be altered by production and by depreciation. A more subtle kind of capital good is skill derived from education or experience. Thus, the stock of knowledge acquired by a medical student in the course of his training is an intangible but nonetheless economically and productively real commodity which is used in the production of medical care.

The problem of allocating resources can be stated in general terms as follows: Each productive organization is to have assigned to it a certain amount of output to be produced by it and an amount of each of the different kinds of inputs needed to produce that output. Each consumer is to receive a certain amount of each good and to supply some of such factors as are under its direct control (e.g. labor services of appropriate skill levels). The allocation as a whole must be *feasible*, that is, there must be a balance between commodities used and commodities available. In the case of a primary factor, the amount used by all productive organizations must not exceed the amount available initially; for each produced commodity, the amount used by consumers and by productive organizations as inputs must not exceed the total output by other productive organizations.

There are in general many possible feasible allocations of resources. Labor and capital can be devoted directly and indirectly to different final uses in varying proportions. Allocations of resources to different uses may be inefficient; that is, it may be that by shifting resources among different uses, more of every commodity can be produced. Thus, the proposals to increase medical care by increased use of paraprofessional personnel can be understood in this way: the heavy material resources needed to train additional physicians could instead be used to increase the productivity of the rest of the economy sufficiently to compensate for the loss of product elsewhere by withdrawing workers and making paraprofessionals out of them.

There is a more subtle meaning of efficiency, that of efficiency in the satisfaction of wants, usually called by economists Pareto efficiency. Assume each individual to be a competent judge of his needs and wants; then he wants to achieve as high a level of satisfaction as possible. An allocation is said to be *dominated* in the sense of Pareto if there is another feasible allocation which will make everybody better off. An allocation then is said to be Pareto efficient if it is not dominated by any feasible allocation. To be Pareto efficient, an allocation must clearly be efficient in the production of commodities, but it must also be true that among the commodities that are produced there can be no further exchange among the individuals in the economy which will make them all better off.

It is clearly desirable to achieve a Pareto-efficient allocation. Efficiency in this sense is not the only possible desideratum, however. For one thing, an allocation which is Pareto efficient need not be equitable; it may give a large proportion of the final commodities to relatively few individuals and yet be efficient according to the definition if there is no way of increasing the welfare of the many without hurting the few. Considerations of equity have come to play an increasingly large role in modern government policy.

A second qualification sometimes advanced, and especially for medical care, is that individuals are not necessarily the best judges of their own interests in deciding how much of certain commodities to acquire. Hence, efficiency in satisfying their expressed wishes is not the ultimate criterion.

However strong these objections are, it is clear that Pareto efficiency remains an important criterion, though not the sole one.

The price system is a particular means of deciding upon the allocation of resources; historically, it has been the dominant mode of allocation in the United States and Western Europe, though decreasingly so. The essential features are that all purchases are made by exchanging money for commodities, where for each commodity the price per unit is more or less the same for all economic agents, that the incomes for paying for the purchases of commodities are derived from the sale of other commodities, and that all commodities, including primary factors, are owned by someone, so that all payments made for purchasing commodities are income to someone and are used to purchase other commodities in an endless circular flow.

Assume that individuals act so as to maximize their level of satisfaction as they see it, in the sense that given the income available to them by sale of the factors they own, they choose among the combinations of commodities they can afford at the market prices that one which yields them the highest satisfaction. (Included in the decisions which yield satisfaction may be decisions to withhold some of their primary factors for their own use; for example, a physician or other laborer may choose to work fewer hours, reserving therefore his primary factor, labor time, for his own leisure-time purposes.) Assume further that productive organizations are in fact firms who seek, at the going market prices, to choose their outputs and corresponding inputs needed to achieve these outputs so as to maximize their profits. From these assumptions plus some further more technical ones certain very important conclusions follow:

(a) There exist a set of prices which clear the markets. That is equilibrium prices can be found such that the aggregate of individual decisions to buy and sell commodities in fact balance. Hence, the quantities determined by the price system in fact constitute a feasible allocation of resources when the prices are equilibrium prices.

(b) The equilibrium allocation is in fact Pareto efficient. The intuitive reasoning behind the last statement is simple enough. If everyone is buying or selling at the same price, then all individuals must value an additional unit of the commodity equally (as measured in terms of money, which means in terms of other commodities that might be purchased). Hence, there can be no gain in transferring some commodities from one individual to another. Also, since the same prices govern the determination of production, prices represent in effect the costs of production, and costs of production, in turn, represents the value of other goods that might have been produced with the same resources. Hence, the price system also insures that there can be no gain to a shift in production from one output to another nor indeed to a shift in the method of producing any one commodity.

If the price system were in fact working properly, there could be little justification for saying that a given commodity, such as medical care, is 'too expensive' or that its financing requires special provision. The production of medical care would be efficient; each physician, for example, would have a strong incentive to minimize the costs of providing medical services by having himself assisted by an appropriate number of paraprofessionals. If it were felt that medical care, even when efficiently provided, was too costly for the poorer members of society, then the proper remedy is to redistribute income to the poor and thereby increase their general purchasing power. They are free to spend it as appropriate to increase their satisfaction, and this may be better achieved by spending on other commodities than medical care, if its high price reflects its true scarcity. A slightly better case can be made for special financial provision if the objection is that individuals habitually undervalue medical care; then it can be argued that paternalistic government should deliberately subsidize medical care, so that individuals will get more of it than they themselves judge proper. Such is indeed the attitude of governments towards education. But it is not usually thought to be the major issue in medical care; typically, individuals have, if anything, an exaggerated idea of its value. The special economic problems of medical care stem rather from the fact that the price system does not work fully in accordance with its ideal form in this area.

2. Uncertainty as a characteristic of medical care

In the preceding discussion of the price system, it has been implicitly assumed that economic agents are not uncertain about the productive and satisfaction-generating implications of their decisions. Thus, in deciding upon a consumption plan over time, the individual is in the simplest model assumed to predict correctly the satisfaction he will get from consumption in the future. Now an essential characteristic of medical care as a commodity is that such certainty is absent.

In fact, there are two types of uncertainty in medical care. The first type is that most usually thought of in connection with health insurance: the occurrence of illness and the cost of medical treatment. The second type is that concerning the possibility of partial or total recovery from an illness. The first has been the object of policy for only some twenty-five years, but the second is basic to the shaping of medical institutions in general and to the peculiar workings of the medical economy in particular.

Let us take up the implications of the second kind of uncertainty first. Where there is uncertainty, there is the opportunity for information, which is the reduction of uncertainty; and the commodity sold by the medical profession is, first and foremost, information. Not merely is there uncertainty, but there is a difference between the uncertainty of the patient and the lesser uncertainty of the physician; and both parties to the transaction know this. This means that the physician is the agent of the patient. The relation between them is one involving trust, not merely the arm's length relation characteristic of the commercial market. The patient cannot, for example, enforce completely standards of care; he has instead a generalized belief in the ability of the physician and in his conscientiousness.

This trust is in part supplemented by social institutions such as licensing and medical school standards. These are ways by which the patient is given some sort of guarantee of effectiveness. The relation of trust must also be given concrete symbolization in certain aspects of the physician's economic behavior; he must not act, or at least he must not appear to act, as if he is maximizing his income at every moment of time. He cannot advertise; in the preinsurance days, he was expected to lower prices or even give free care, as an earnest that he places the welfare of the client above his income.

The control of entry through licensing and medical school standard also means that the supply of physicians is relatively little affected by their income prospects. That is since more want to become physicians than there are places in the medical schools, a moderate reduction in physicians' incomes would have little effect on the supply. It would, however, have some effect on quality; there will be some potential physicians who will go into some other field, perhaps biological research, at somewhat lower income prospects, and their places in the medical schools will be taken by those now rejected. But it seems unlikely that the deterioration of quality would be very large.

The licensing has also had the effect of restricting the use of less well-trained personnel for minor medical tasks. There seems, however, to be increasing possibility in the United States for the use of so-called paraprofessionals to supplement physicians and therefore increase the effective supply of medical services.

The other major component of medical services is the hospital system; the number of hospitals is also not controlled by the usual forces of supply and demand but is determined primarily by the willingness of governments and private philanthropists to finance them. Again this fact is a consequence of the primary need for trust: ostensibly profit-making hospitals are clearly not congruent with this need.

The informational inequality between physician and patient also means that the patient's freedom of choice must in practice be delegated in great part to the physician. He must determine the treatment and the referral to specialists or to hospitals. But this responsibility imposes rigidities upon the physician; there is an obligation to engage in 'best practice'; to compromise on quality, even to save the patient money, is to risk an imputation of failure to live up to the social bond (this imputation may be made concrete in the form of malpractice suits). 'Best practice' in turn is socially conditioned, in particular, conditioned by resource availability, so that patients in those areas which are better equipped medically will get more medical attention.

Let me return to the first type of uncertainty in medical care, that of occurrence and medical cost of illness. For this kind of uncertainty, the market can do somewhat better than the first. It can provide insurance and does so for a considerable variety of risks. Individuals on the average derive satisfaction from the avoidance of risks, particularly large risks. This tendency can be put in a precise way: they prefer a certain cost to an uncertain one, even if the expected value (in the sense of probability theory) of the uncertain costs is less. It is this preference which explains why insurance can be mutually beneficial to insurer and insured.

Insurance increases welfare by reducing risks; but it also has effects on the allocation of medical resources. Insurance reduces the cost of medical care to the patient. The effect is that more medical care will be demanded for given prices for medical services. Since the aggregate supply of medical services is, as has been seen, essentially unresponsive to price, the increased demand is controlled by a combination of two responses: (a) an increase in prices charged for medical services, and (b) a rationing of the medical care available by a series of decisions made at different points in the medical system.

One of the results of insurance is apt to be a shift in the allocation of resources within the medical field, a shift that may well lead to inefficiencies. The most obvious point is that the pressure for efficiency of each individual physician, hospital, or other medical service unit is reduced, since they can charge higher prices with less resistance. A second point is that more expensive kinds of medical care will be sought after by patients, since the difference in cost is greatly reduced by insurance. If the total supply of medical resources is fixed, this increase in specialization can only happen at the expense of the less well-paid parts of the medical profession, in particular, general practice. Such a shift is almost surely adverse to efficiency of provision of medical care. Part of the same point is a shift to desired use of hospitals, a tendency which has been reinforced in the United States by the fact that insurance coverage has been better for hospitalization than for other branches of medical care. To the extent that hospitals are expanded by public policy, there is a use of resources which could have been employed elsewhere; to the extent that hospitals become overcrowded by being used for minor purposes, there is a risk of their being unavailable in more serious cases.

To sum up this section, there are two kinds of uncertainty associated with the provision of medical care: uncertainty about the incidence of illness and the costs of medical care, and uncertainty about the effectiveness of medical care. With respect to the first, insurance, particularly against large and unpredictable costs, provides a significant gain in satisfaction, but it also gives rise to two major problems, a loss of market control over rising prices, and a reduction in the pressures for efficiency in the medical care system, both as a whole and in each of its parts. The second kind of uncertainty and in particular the fact that the uncertainty differs so much as between patient and physician create a social pressure for controls over entry into the profession and for an orientation of the medical-care system away from narrow profit maximization.

3. The medical care market in the United States: an overview

In the analysis of any market it is useful to distinguish short-run and long-run characteristics. As these terms are used in economics, the distinction is based on the fact that some of the factors used in production are stocks rather than flows and can be changed only incrementally, for example, capital goods such as buildings and machines, while others can be substantially altered in short periods of time. Short-run analysis then refers to the allocation of resources in the industry, taking the volume of the relatively fixed factors as given, while long-run analysis is concerned with the forces determining the volume of the fixed factors.

In medical care the physician is the most important fixed factor. The production of physicians is a very slow process indeed, much longer than the production of any physical capital good. The stock of physicians at any moment is determined by their production in the past and can be altered only very slowly. Hospitals constitute the second most important fixed factor; and, of course, technical equipment of various kinds is playing an increasingly important role, though frequently as part of the hospital.

In the short run, the medical-care market consists of the physicians and hospitals, whose number we take as given, the population subject to illness, and the private and public agencies which affect the financing of medical care. The system as a whole and particularly the financing provisions are in a state of flux in the United States. Broadly speaking, physicians, particularly in general practice, operate under a modified *laissez-faire* system. They can locate where they will and determine their own hours of work. They can engage in solo or group practice. The former and some of the latter are paid on a fee-for-service basis; but many groups operate on a prepayment basis, which is a form of medical insurance. The former intense hostility of organized medicine (represented by the American Medical Association) to prepayment plans has abated, and the two types of payment now coexist peacefully enough. The expectation that prepaid group plans would be more efficient in providing medical care both because of economies of scale and because of greater emphasis on preventive medicine does not seem to have been borne out very strongly in practice. At least the superiority of group care has not been so manifest to the public that it has driven out solo practice in competition; and research has suggested only a slight superiority in handling of patients per physician-hour, compensated for by a decrease in the average number of hours worked by physicians in group practice as compared with solo.

The freedom of physicians to choose specialties is less complete than that to choose location. While there are virtually no legal barriers, various unofficial but potent accrediting agencies afford some limitation, and the need for affiliation with a hospital offers a considerably greater restriction. Nevertheless, the increasing trend to specialization is very strong.

Fees are set by physicians, though perhaps more than with other industries, there are strong social pressures for 'fairness' and adherence to 'customary schedules'. These social restrictions have not, however, prevented a rise in physicians' fees considerably more rapid than that in other prices. Hence, it appears that the economist's usual explanation of prices in terms of supply and demand is applicable to physicians.

It was formerly true that physicians' fees varied very considerably with the income of the patient, and a considerable amount of free care was provided to the indigent. As insurance has become more common, the income of the patient has become less relevant to the burden of medical care costs, and physicians have correspondingly been less inclined to adjust fees to income.

Hospitals are overwhelmingly non-profit organizations; they therefore tend to fix prices to cover costs rather than to clear the market. Their cost rise has been even more spectacular than that of physicians; part of the explanation is undoubtedly the lack of incentive for efficiency in such an arrangement.

With respect to the users of medical care, the decision to undertake medical treatment is in the first instance made by the patient. However, as in all medical systems, the ultimate degree of utilization of medical resources is determined in good part by the medical profession itself. The physician advises the patient on further treatments, including the use of specialists and hospitals. Neither the initial decision to seek medical care nor further treatment on the advice of the physician can be independent of the burden on the patient; the presence of insurance therefore increases the utilization of medical resources.

It is the system of financing payments for medical care that is changing most rapidly. Before World War II, medical service was available for the most part on a pure price basis. This was modified by the tendency to adjust prices to income, including at the extreme free medical care for indigents, partly supplied by physicians, partly paid for by charitable organizations and the government. There were also scattered groups offering prepaid medical care. Finally, the deductibility of medical expenses from income for the purpose of calculating income taxes amounted to a partial medical insurance. Because of the progressivity of the income tax, it was much more effective for the rich than for the poor.

After World War II, organized medicine concerned itself with the creation of medical insurance plans, the Blue Cross plans for hospitalization and later the Blue Shield plans for other medical services. In part, the motivation was to avoid national health insurance. In the 1950's, some of the larger insurance companies began also to offer so-called major medical insurance. The bulk of all these forms of insurance is placed in the form of contracts between the insurer and some group, usually an employer on behalf of his employees. The administrative costs per dollar of insurance are so much lower for group contracts than for individual contracts that the latter are virtually infeasible. Medical insurance is now usually a 'fringe benefit' to workers; the employer offers the existence of the contract and usually an obligation to pay part or all the premium as part of the employment agreement. One result of this tendency is that the coverage is much better in well-organized large-scale industry than in more casual and ill-organized occupations. The very poorest workers and those not in the labor force are hardly covered at all by current private insurance plans.

The Blue Cross and Blue Shield plans have usually been categorical in their coverage. That is, they have separate benefits for hospitalization, surgery, and general practice. For each category, there has usually been a deductible (a lower limit of costs which are not reimbursed) and also a ceiling. The first is designed to minimize administrative costs associated with reimbursing a large number of small claims, the second to protect the insurer against unexpected losses. The major medical policies instead protect against the total medical costs to an individual or family; again there are deductibles against the total, ceilings (either for a given time period or for a given illness), and usually co-insurance (that is the insured pays some fraction, in the neighborhood of 20 percent, of the costs that are covered by insurance). It should be added that the Blue Cross-Blue Shield groups now offer major medical protection as one option.

There are two special aspects of these plans that should be specially noticed. One is that the ceilings run counter to the basic values of insurance. The larger the risk, the more satisfaction is derived from insurance; therefore, the individual would be willing to pay more in relation to actuarial expectation for protection against the bigger risks. In the last few years, this defect has begun to be recognized. A number of firms have arranged with insurance companies for policies with so-called deep coverage, that is with virtually no ceiling on expenditures. Deep coverage is possible and apparently with surprisingly small additional insurance premiums because exceedingly expensive illnesses (costing more than, say, $15,000 for treatment) are in fact extremely rare. Thus, the risks of the insurer are very small when pooled over a large population, though such protection is of the greatest value to the individual.

The second major point is that the insurance companies, even the Blue Cross and Blue Shield plans, are in no position to control costs. They must essentially accept the charges made by physicians and hospitals and can guard themselves only against obvious fraud. They have found no practical way of asserting that a given course of treatment is unnecessarily expensive or that a particular hospital is incurring expenses that reflect comfort rather than necessary medical care. Except in extreme cases, they cannot even make judgments that some fee is excessive.

The local governments have always paid some role in medical care, by providing hospital services and some associated outpatient care for the very poor. In the last five or six years, however, there has been a much more massive intervention by the Federal government, in the form of two programs, known as Medicaid and Medicare, respectively. The Medicaid program is a Federal subsidy to the state governments to maintain and expand their programs for the indigent; in particular, the relevant concept of poverty is changed to that of 'medical indigence', defined as a state in which income is low relative to medical expenses. An individual with a moderate income (even $10,000 a year, for example) might be regarded as medically indigent if he needs treatment which would require a substantial portion of that income.

The Medicare program represents a more radical break with American tradition. It is a national health insurance program for all those over 65. Specifically, it consists of free hospitalization insurance plus heavily subsidized insurance for all other forms of medical care. Its effects on the allocation of medical care have been dramatic; there has been a clear reallocation of medical services, both physicians' time and hospital usage, towards the older, less affluent members of the society.

At the beginning of this section, we sharply differentiated between short- and long-run analysis of the medical care market. Up to this point, discussion has been confined to the short run. In the long run, the basic issues are the determination of the numbers of physicians and of hospital capacity. The long-run determinants are probably more similar to those in other countries than are the short-run workings of the system. Only a small percentage of hospital beds are to be found in profit-making hospitals. The majority are in government-run hospitals, with the voluntary hospitals (organized by private philanthropy) an important but decreasing fraction of the total. The basic limit on the supply of physicians is the capacity of the medical school system, which is in turn restrained by a combination of high standards and limited capacity to finance them. There have been recurrent complaints about 'doctor shortages' and demands for increase in the medical school capacity. But although nothing very much has been done, the estimates of the amount of 'shortage' do not seem to be increasing over time. When one considers that the number of physicians per capita in the United States is about double that anywhere else without any corresponding improvement in health, one has a somewhat skeptical feeling about the urgency of very expensive expansion of medical schools. This skepticism is reinforced by observing that within the United States variations in the number of physicians per capita seem to have no relation to such criteria of health as longevity and infant mortality.

The supply of medical schools is determined by the willingness of the government and private philanthropists to finance them; tuition pays probably no more than 20 percent of the cost. If indeed there is to be expansion of medical school capacity, it should be paid for by the physicians receiving the training. This is best done by lending medical students the necessary educational costs, to be repaid out of their future very high incomes (the median annual income of physicians in the United States is about $50,000). The amount repaid could be allowed to vary with the amount of income earned, to provide some insurance to medical students against their uncertainty of future income and to avoid disincentives to enter socially useful, less well-paid medical work such as public health.

The main aspect of long-run provision of medical care under active political discussion in the United States is the further use of paraprofessionals. The trend has been upward. At some stage, though, there will have to be rethinking of present laws and practices for medical care to permit medical technicians to undertake some minor medical tasks. The Russians have had since the eighteenth century what is apparently a very successful use of less well-trained medical workers (called, 'feldshers') permitted to carry out a limited range of medical tasks.

4. Some empirical features of the United States medical care market

There have been a number of careful quantitative studies of the medical care market, in particular of the supply and demand for physicians' services. I draw here on the studies of Martin Feldstein, of Harvard University, and Victor Fuchs, City University of New York.

The most striking empirical fact has been the rise in physicians' fees. Of course, prices in general have been rising through most of the post-war period, but physicians' fees have risen 2.4 percent per annum more rapidly on the average over the period 1948–68. This differential was fairly steady over most of the period but accelerated sharply in 1966–8, to an annual average of 4.1 percent, undoubtedly a reflection of the increased demand due to Medicaid and Medicare programs. Indeed, much of the Federal expenditure for the support of these programs has in effect ended up as increased income to physicians. The rising fees of physicians and the even more rapidly rising costs of hospitals have contributed greatly to the increased pressure for comprehensive medical insurance.

The quantity of physicians' services has on the whole risen over the same period more rapidly than population. (The term *quantity* here refers to a weighted total of physician-hours, the weights being related to fees charged, so that the shift to specialization is considered to be an increase in quantity, even if the total number of physicians did not change.) However, the trends have been most uneven; the quantity of physicians' services per capita actually fell by 1 percent per annum from 1948 to 1956 but rose by 2.9 percent thereafter. It is to be noted that while there were distinct improvements in longevity in the earlier period, there have been none since.

More detailed comparisons over time and among regions of the country permit some further tentative generalizations. In general, price and income have only moderate effects on the demand for physicians' services. An increase of 10 percent in price would reduce demand by only about 2 percent. An increase of 10 percent in income increases demand by 5 to 6 percent. Perhaps less expected is the result that the demand for medical care increases with the amount available for a given price and income. Evidently, physicians make more frequent referrals and have their own patients call back more often if there is an ample supply of physicians and hospitals than otherwise. This suggests strongly that physicians perform part of the rationing function which is performed by prices alone in more usual markets.

While the total supply of physicians is determined by medical school capacity, the allocation of physicians among different regions of the country and the number of hours worked per physician are subject to the choice of the individual physicians. The geographical allocation is very sensitive to prices; but it is also true that at given fee levels, physicians tend to gravitate to high-income areas, presumably because they prefer the life-style to be found there. The net result of these factors is to create an increasing problem of inadequate medical supply in rural and low-income urban areas. The amount of time supplied by each physician seems to be insensitive to prices. It is less in areas where there are more other physicians and higher where there are more hospital beds per capita. The first effect is quite strong, so much so that it has been estimated that if the number of physicians were increased, half or more of the effect would be dissipated by causing a reduction in the amount of time worked per physician.

5. Current proposals for medical insurance

As stated in the beginning of this paper, a great national debate is now developing on a future national health insurance system. The present administration has made some proposals in a message to Congress by the President. An alternative proposal has been drawn by a liberal-labor group and introduced as a bill in Congress by several senators, including Edward Kennedy.

As might be expected, the Nixon Administration plan relies heavily on using the private sector both with regard to medical care and with regard to insurance. The central part of the plan would be a requirement that employers (with some exceptions) must provide a health insurance plan meeting some minimum conditions for their employees. This is to be supplemented by a Federal program for low-income families not covered by the employment-related plan. The employment-related plan must be of the major medical type, with a deductible of $100 per person (slightly more if hospitalization is involved) and coinsurance up to $5,000 (the insured pays 25 percent). The coverage is deep, with a requirement of protection up to $50,000 per person over his lifetime. The employer arranges the contract with a private insurance carrier. The employer pays from 65 to 75 percent of the premiums, the rest being paid by the employees. The supplementary Federal program gives a more basic protection, without deep coverage. Premiums, deductibles, and coinsurance depend on income; all costs are paid for if family income is below $3,000 per annum. The supplementary program is financed from general revenues of the Federal government beyond the amount received in premiums.

The bill introduced by Senator Kennedy, the so-called Health Security plan, proposes a much sharper break with past methods. It is a completely universal compulsory health insurance, with no deductibles, no coinsurance, and no ceilings. The program will be financed half from general revenues and half from special taxes on employers' payrolls and on income.

In the Administration's plan, it is assumed that pricing of medical services will continue to be set by the market. In the Health Security plan, an alternative is needed, since prices no longer have any effect on demand. Instead, it is proposed that each year advance estimates be made of medical costs (separately for physicians and for hospitals), and the actual expenditures in the following year be confined to these advanced budgets. Hospitals are simply paid their budgets. Individual physicians can choose whether to be paid on a fee-for-service, capitation, or retainer basis; but the levels of these payments are so set that the budget will be met. Comprehensive medical organizations (group practice) will be paid, at their choice, on either a capitation basis or a combination of capitation and advance budget. These proposals still dodge the question of determining the level of physicians' fees, since the problem is transferred to that of determining the level of advance budgets. It is simply stated that these will be determined by a Health Security Board after consulting with all parties. Obviously, this will lead to some form of collective bargaining between the physicians and the Government.

Both the Administration and the Health Security proposals have other provisions, for the encouragement of comprehensive medical organizations, for encouraging, by subsidy, the geographical dispersion of physicians to areas presently underprovided, and for subsidies to medical education. None of these proposals are very definite in nature, and presumably they will develop with experience. As I have suggested above, the subsidy to medical education could easily be replaced by a loan program to medical students.

Other proposals for forms of health insurance have been made by the Health Insurance Association of America, the American Medical Association, and the American Hospital Association. These call for voluntary health insurance with incentives and subsidies provided through the income tax. They do not appear politically viable at the present time.

6. Implications and alternatives

Both proposals would go far to meet the primary desideratum of health insurance, that of reducing uncertainty about the costs of medical care. The Health Security bill, of course, is complete in this respect. The Administration bill goes far; only the failure to provide deep coverage for supplementary program for low-income families can be regarded as a serious defect.

However, there are three basic issues that are raised by one or another of these plans: (1) the control over prices; (2) pressures for efficiency in the provision of medical care; (3) the effect on taxes. The desirability of (2) is obvious. With regard to (1), in view of the relatively fixed supply of physicians, a rise in their prices as a result of more comprehensive insurance is hardly an intended or desirable outcome. With regard to (3), it is clear that, other things being equal, taxes tend to injure the efficiency of the general economy. Thus, high income taxes give an undue encouragement to leisure, high payroll taxes an undue encouragement to substituting machinery for labor. The inefficiencies due to taxes are not so great that they constitute a decisive argument against desirable government expenditures; but if they can be reduced or kept from rising while the same ends are achieved another way, this alternative should be pursued. Let us examine the two plans according to these criteria.

(a) The Health Security plan requires government control over prices. There is no market left to do any regulating. In effect, the physicians are employees of the Government, and the problem becomes one of collective bargaining. The United States have been experiencing unionization of many types of government employees, such as teachers and even policemen. The system has built into it the opportunity and indeed the virtual necessity of repeated crises, but over the long run it will work after a fashion. Perhaps the biggest problem is that of determining the relative fees of different types of physicians. For a period of time to come, the fees of specialists may bear the same relation to that of general practitioners as they do now, but over a time the relative scarcities of different types of physicians will change with changing medical knowledge.

Hospitals offer less of a problem; essentially their prices are their costs under any system.

The Administration plan seems to offer less difficulty, since the market remains. But in fact the very wide-spread coverage means that demands will be relatively little checked by price. We will experience a repetition of the price rise which accompanied the introduction of Medicare and Medicaid. Since employers will have no choice but to adopt health insurance plans, neither they nor the insurance carriers can individually provide any effective limit on price rises. I would guess that eventually the Government will have to intervene in some way. Because of the mixed nature of the system, however, any intervention is bound to be less effective than it would under the Health Security bill.

(b) Any spread of insurance weakens the pressures for efficiency, as we have seen. The Health Security bill, by putting the Government in such a strong position, permits it to exert power for efficiency. But the Government is not usually in a position to know how to require efficiency in autonomous organizations; the result is more likely to be a maze of regulations designed to prevent inefficiencies but in the end creating worse ones by their inflexibility.

(c) The Health Security bill would require a large increase in taxation, perhaps $40 billion a year. The Administration plan would not, on the face of it, seem to require a great amount of taxation. But in fact the requirement that employers pay insurance premiums is effectively the same as a tax on payrolls. Hence, both proposals involve a considerable tax burden, not an insupportable one by any means but nevertheless one that would be better to avoid.

These difficulties are to a considerable extent inescapable. However, an interesting proposal has been made by Martin Feldstein that is thoroughly compatible with the general principles of insurance. The aim of insurance is to avoid large risks, more precisely, risks that are large relative to the income of the individual. The gain in satisfaction achieved by covering small amounts is small. On the other hand, in the aggregate, most payments are relatively small. A system which leaves such payments uninsured will cover the important risks and yet involve much smaller sums of money.

The proposal is for a policy of the major medical type, which applies to total annual expenditures on medical care. The deductible would be relatively high compared with present and proposed levels, perhaps $500 a year per person. It could be adjusted to family income, so that it might be zero for very low-income families and rise to $800 for incomes above $8,000. To mitigate still further the hardships, it could be arranged that some part of the costs could be covered by credit, guaranteed by the Government and repaid over a subsequent period of two or three years. Then no family would ever have expenses beyond its ability to pay; nevertheless, insurance would end up covering only about one-third of all medical expenses, though they would be the financially crippling ones.

This proposal has the attractive feature of giving much greater play to the market in allocating medical resources. It would therefore offer more control over costs, since patients would be more careful with their uninsured dollars. The market control would in turn create pressures for efficiency in the utilization of medical resources. On the other hand, very expensive types of care (intensive cardiac care, renal dialysis) would have little control either as to cost or as to use; but after all, spectacular as these are, they utilize only a small proportion of total medical resources.

It is not suggested that this proposal for coverage of major risks meets all objections perfectly. It does leave a considerable total volume of individually small risks uncovered. Further, like any reasonably comprehensive insurance, the coverage of major risks will still weaken the price incentives to economize on demand, so that cost control will not be adequate. Major risk insurance still appears superior to any alternative, but it is my view that it will have to be supplemented by government control over the prices of medical services.

Summary

The financing and allocation of resources in the field of medical care is undergoing rapid modification in the United States, with a weakening of the traditional market controls.

The competitive price system has in its favor a steady pressure for efficiency, not merely efficiency in the production of given outputs, such as medical care, but also efficiency in the allocation of the national productive potential among different end uses. However, in the field of medical care, these arguments are weakened by the presence of uncertainty about both the outcome of medical care and the incidence of the need for it. The first creates the need for a relation of trust between patient and physician, a relation which is partly incompatible with the arm's-length buyer-and-seller relation of competitive markets. A particular outcome of this special relation is that the supply of medical services is largely determined by non-market forces.

The second form of uncertainty, the uncertainty of illness, creates a demand for medical insurance, but this in turn weakens the incentives by patients and physicians for efficiency. The increased demand due to spreading insurance has led partly to higher fees, partly to rationing devices within the medical profession. The insurance carriers have proved to be incapable of controlling costs.

Various proposals for extensions of medical insurance are now being considered. Some offer inadequate extensions of insurance coverage, particularly with regard to coverage of very expensive illnesses. The more thorough plans raise the possibility of major increases in medical fees and the possibilities of inefficiency through excessive medical care. The possibilities of price control and of some limited uses of market mechanisms to check price inflation need further exploration.

Zusammenfassung

Die Finanzierung und die Zuteilung der Mittel auf dem Gebiet des Gesundheitsdienstes in den USA unterliegen einem raschen Wandel, insbesondere angesichts der nun sicheren Abschwächung der traditionellen Marktkontrollen. Für das wettbewerbsfördernde Preissystem spricht eine anhaltende Forderung nach Leistung – nicht nur Leistungsfähigkeit in der Produktion bestimmter *Outputs*, wie zum Beispiel medizinische Betreuung, sondern auch Leistungsfähigkeit bei der Zuteilung des nationalen Sozialproduktes an verschiedene mögliche Endverbraucher. Für das Gesundheitswesen jedoch werden diese Argumente geschwächt durch eine bestehende Unsicherheit in bezug auf den Ausgang medizinischer Behandlung und auf deren Bedarfsbereich. Ersteres erfordert ein Vertrauensverhältnis zwischen Patient und Arzt, ein Verhältnis, das teilweise inkompatibel ist mit der kurzsichtigen Käufer-Verkäufer-Beziehung wettbewerbsorientierter Märkte. Aus diesem besonderen Verhältnis folgt das Angebot medizinischer Dienste, welches weitgehend durch marktunabhängige Kräfte bestimmt wird.

Die zweite Form der Unsicherheit, die der Erkrankung, schafft das Bedürfnis nach einer Krankenversicherung; diese wiederum schwächt den Antrieb zur Leistung beim Patienten und beim Arzt. Die gestiegene Nachfrage als Folge immer ausgedehnterer Versicherungen hat teilweise zu höheren Honoraren, teilweise aber auch zu einschränkenden Regelungen innerhalb des Ärztestandes geführt. Die Versicherungsträger sehen sich außer stande, die Kosten zu kontrollieren.

Man prüft zurzeit verschiedene Vorschläge für eine Ausweitung der Krankenversicherung. Einige bieten ungenügende Versicherungsdeckung, insbesondere hinsichtlich sehr kostenintensiver Erkrankungen. Die umfassenderen Pläne erhöhen die Wahrscheinlichkeit eines stärkeren Anstieges der Arzthonorare und die Gefahr eines Leistungsabbaues durch zu weitgehende ärztliche Betreuung. Die Möglichkeiten, die Preise zu kontrollieren und einige Marktkontrollmechanismen zur Verhütung einer Preisinflation gezielt einzusetzen, bedürfen weiterer Überprüfung.

Résumé

Le financement et la répartition des ressources dans le domaine des soins médicaux sont en train de se modifier rapidement aux Etats-Unis, avec un affaiblissement certain des traditionnels mécanismes de contrôle du marché.

Le système des prix fondé sur la libre concurrence présente l'avantage de pousser constamment à l'efficacité, non seulement dans la production de biens donnés – tels les soins médicaux – mais aussi dans la répartition du potentiel national de production entre les différentes utilisations finales. Toutefois, quand il s'agit de services médicaux, ces arguments sont affaiblis par l'existence d'une incertitude touchant, d'une part, le résultat et, d'autre part, la fréquence du besoin de ces mêmes services. En effet, pour que le résultat soit satisfaisant, il faut qu'un rapport de confiance existe entre le malade et son médecin, rapport qui est cependant en partie incompatible avec la relation acheteur-vendeur des marchés fondés sur la concurrence. Une conséquence de cette situation particulière est que l'offre de soins médicaux est déterminée dans une large mesure par des considérations qui n'ont rien à voir avec le marché.

Le second facteur d'incertitude – l'aléa de la maladie – crée le besoin d'assurances médicales, mais en retour celles-ci émoussent, chez le malade et le médecin, le stimulant qui pousse à l'efficacité. L'augmentation de la demande découlant de l'extension des assurances a entraîné et des tarifs plus élevés et des mesures de restriction au sein de la profession médicale. Les compagnies d'assurances se sont révélées incapables d'endiguer les frais.

Différentes propositions visant à étendre les assurances médicales sont actuellement à l'étude. Certaines prévoient une extension inadéquate des risques couverts, en particulier en ce qui concerne la couverture de maladies très onéreuses.

Les projets plus complets, qui envisagent la possibilité d'élever considérablement les honoraires médicaux, comportent des dangers d'inefficacité découlant d'un excès de soins. Il serait utile d'étudier plus avant la possibilité d'exercer une pression sur les prix en faisant un emploi limité de certains mécanismes du marché pour juguler la hausse des prix.

Resumen

La financiación y el reparto de los medios destinados a la asistencia médica están experimentando un cambio rápido en los Estados Unidos, lo cual lleva consigo un menoscabo seguro de los factores que tradicionalmente rigen el mercado.

El sistema de la competencia en precios ofrece la ventaja de obligar constantemente a una máxima eficacia, no únicamente en la producción de un volumen determinado, en este caso de servicios médicos, sino también en la distribución, entre varios objetivos, del potencial nacional de producción. No obstante, en el sector de las prestaciones médicas, estos argumentos pierden fuerza por la incertidumbre que pesa tanto sobre el resultado de la asistencia médica como sobre la incidencia de enfermedades. La primera de estas dudas crea la necesidad de establecer entre el paciente y el médico una relación basada en la confianza, bastante diferente del antagonismo que existe entre el comprador y el vendedor, característico del mercado sometido a las leyes de la competencia. Una de las consecuencias de esta relación peculiar es el hecho de que la prestación de servicios médicos está determinada predominantemente por factores ajenos a las leyes del mercado.

La segunda incertidumbre, la de la incidencia de enfermedades, crea la exigencia de asegurarse contra ellas. Pero tal seguro disminuye el incentivo que mueve al paciente y al médico a tender a una mayor eficacia. La creciente demanda de servicios médicos que resulta de la extensión del seguro ha traido consigo, por una parte, un aumento de los honorarios, y por otra, un racionamiento de la capacidad médica. Ningún sistema de seguro se ha mostrado capaz de controlar el costo.

Actualmente se consideran varias propuestas tendentes a ampliar el seguro contra la enfermedad. Algunas prevén una extensión insuficiente de los riesgos cubiertos por el seguro, especialmente en el caso de enfermedades cuyo tratamiento es muy costoso. Los planes más completos, aparte de entrañar el peligro de aumentar aún más los honorarios médicos, pueden ser fuente de ineficacia debida a una asistencia excesiva. Es preciso seguir estudiando la forma de regular los precios y de permitir, en cierta medida, el funcionamiento de mecanismos de mercado capaces de contener la inflación de los mismos.

The problem of relieving the physician of unnecessary burdens

by Axel Strøm

The problem of relieving the physician of unnecessary burdens might seem a trivial one, compared with the serious problems that have been discussed by the other authors of this Symposium. However, from a practical point of view, it is an important topic, as the right to health implies the most effective use of the doctor's time.

A shortage of doctors is at present an almost universal phenomenon. In the developing countries this shortage is merely another manifestation of their general shortage of skilled personnel. In the economically and technically advanced part of the world the doctor shortage is due to an imbalance between the demand for health services and the availability of medical personnel. Despite the greatly increased number of medical school graduates the number of doctors has not kept pace with the increasing demand for health services. Even in those countries with the highest doctor/population ratio the demand is far from being satisfied.

This 'explosion of demand' is a rather recent development in most countries. When I was a young doctor some forty years ago, the doctor/population ratio in Norway was about 1:1500, and it was hard for a doctor to make a living. Today the ratio is 1:650 and there is a severe shortage of doctors both in hospitals and in general practice.

There are a number of causes for this growing demand. By mass media the population is continuously told that health is the most precious possession which can and must be protected. 'Consult your doctor as early as possible if there is a disorder. But consult him also if you have no complaints, to have your state of health confirmed.' National health services and social insurance systems have made health care available to all segments of the population and have removed most of the economic barriers to consultation with a doctor. The ageing of the population with the attendant higher incidence of chronic diseases has greatly increased the demand for medical service. The highly complex diagnostic and therapeutic procedures of modern medicine have also added to the demands upon the doctor's time. The mental and physical stress in urbanized, industrialized society leads to mental and emotional disturbances and social maladjustments, the therapy of which requires the assistance of the medical profession. There is a clear tendency in modern society to label more and more problems as 'medical' rather than 'social', as this is more acceptable as a designation. The WHO definition of health, which includes 'social well-being' in the concept of health, has without doubt strengthened this tendency. But in labelling a problem 'medical' it is assumed that it is the duty of the medical profession to deal with it.

There is no reason to believe that the demand for health services will decrease in the years to come. On the contrary, with the development of the welfare state we must expect a further increase. Advances in medicine will tend to augment this trend. If doctors should adopt reasonable working hours like the other members of society, the imbalance between demand and available care would be even greater.

One solution to this problem is to increase the output from medical schools. So far this is the solution that most governments have resorted to. However, medical schools are expensive to run, and even in the prosperous countries there is a limit to how much of the national revenue can be allocated to the training of doctors. In addition, it takes years to produce a doctor, and in the meantime the demands for medical services will have risen to new heights. Of course we must train more doctors. But we must seek other solutions too. And we must bear in mind that if we get more doctors, we will also need increasing numbers of ancillary medical personnel. An editorial in the *World Medical Journal* points out that whereas in 1900 one doctor in the USA needed only one ancillary, the number had risen to 13 in 1968.

The problem of relieving the doctor of unnecessary burdens must therefore be seen in a broader context. The time has passed when practically all health work was done by doctors. A constantly increasing part is now done by other categories of health personnel, and paramedical institutions and social agencies play a more and more important role. We are all familiar with this development. But are the services organized in such a way that the best use is made of the various categories of health personnel and institutions, according to their skills and qualifications?

Surveys of how doctors use their time have shown that most of them spend a considerable part of it on non-professional duties or tasks which could be performed by others. An example of such duties that consume much of the doctor's time, thus reducing his productivity, is the clerical work that social insurance systems and other kinds of social legislation impose upon the doctors: filling out numerous forms, writing medical certificates and so forth. The regulations may vary from one country to another. But in some countries at least, such as mine, these chores represent a considerable load upon the doctors, and most of them feel that it is a waste of their time. Of course, the social insurance bodies and other official bodies must control that their resources are properly used and it is the duty of the medical profession to assist them in this. However, the control may be carried out in ways other than requiring that all benefits be certified by a doctor. It is almost incredible what officials expect doctors to certify. Our Director of Public Health, Karl Evang, M.D., has expressed this by stating that a real addiction to medical certificates has developed in modern society, particularly among lawyers and politicians. I am afraid that it will be as difficult to treat this kind of addiction as the addiction to drugs. It is, without doubt, an honour to the medical profession that official bodies and the public as a whole have such respect for papers signed by a doctor. It does however represent an increasing and often unnecessary load upon the doctor's time. It will be a task first and foremost for the national medical associations to have these duties of the doctors reduced to a reasonable level.

Many more examples could be found if we examined how other categories of health personnel spend their time. It is very easy too, to find examples of a lack of cooperation between the various categories of health workers and institutions: how patients are referred from one institution to another, and how different medical and social agencies may work with problems of the same family, almost without knowing about each other.

The main reason for this situation is in my view that the organization of the health services has not kept pace with the rapid progress of medicine. The advance in the biomedical field has been immense, the spectrum of disease is another than it was some decades ago, the mental and social problems are of far greater importance than before, and the societies are undergoing rapid changes. In most countries, however, the impact of all these changes upon the organization of the health services has not been thoroughly studied.

My feeling is that the time has now come to analyse and evaluate the total situation. How shall we today organize the health services in our societies? How much of our resources shall be allocated to preventive health work and how much to therapeutic medicine? What categories of health personnel do we need? What type of work shall each of them do, and how shall their work be organized? How shall we train them adequately for their jobs and how shall we secure the best cooperation between them? The answer to these questions will, of course, vary from one country to another, depending upon the political system, traditions, economy, population density, etc. Nevertheless, the questions should be considered.

A very important question is how health teams shall be organized and used. We are all familiar with health teams in hospitals, in public health, in mental health work, in rehabilitation, as well as in group practice. But are these teams well organized and do they function in the most effective way? In forming them, have we considered the great change in the disease patterns that has taken place in recent years with mounting mental, emotional and social problems? Are the teams organized in such a way that the skills and qualifications of the various members of the team are used effectively? We know little about these questions, as few thorough analyses have been made. We do know, however, that the impact upon the education of medical personnel has been small. We continue to educate separately physicians, nurses, physiotherapists, social workers, technicians, etc. without giving much thought to the fact that they will be working together in practice. Much more attention should be paid to these questions. The formation of adequate health teams is the best way of securing that the skills and qualifications of the various categories of health personnel are used most effectively. For the doctors this implies that they will be relieved of some of their present duties and be allowed to concentrate upon the services that they alone are competent to provide.

In Norway the question of health teams is a live issue at present as we plan to reorganize our system of medical care in the rural parts of the country. Instead of the offices of the district health officer and the public health nurse, we plan to set up so-called 'health centres' which will serve greater areas and take care of all medical work outside the hospitals, preventive and public health work included. The centres will be staffed with doctors, nurses, physiotherapists, social workers, psychologists and technicians who will work in close cooperation with the hospitals and with the local social agencies. One such centre has been established and more centres will come. They differ in several respects from the group practices which have gained great popularity in many countries in recent years, including Norway. The main difference is that the health centre will be responsible for public health and preventive medicine in the area, in addition to providing medical care for the population. The health centres will first and foremost be organized in the sparsely populated areas and be financed partly by the state, while group practices are private enterprises which need a concentrated population, for example a modern suburb. We are still at the stage of experimentation, and further developments will depend upon the experiences gained. Whatever the results of these experiments may be, however, I feel that the organization of good health teams is one of the best ways of ensuring the most effective use of the doctor's skills and time.

There is, however, one great obstacle to the effect of any reorganization of the health services. Some of the other categories of health personnel are in as short supply as doctors. In Norway shortage of nurses is a more important obstacle to an effective use of our health resources than the shortage of doctors, although we are in short supply of them too. If we cannot solve this personnel shortage problem, it will be very difficult to carry through any plan for a better health service.

In the Soviet Union much health work is done by feldshers, a type of medical personnel requiring a shorter period of training than a doctor. According to the reports from the USSR, experiences with the feldshers are very good. Despite the high doctor/population ratio in the USSR, which is the highest in Europe, feldshers are regarded as indispensable and are trained in increasing numbers.

In the countries of the West we have been reluctant to introduce this type of health personnel, mostly because we have been afraid of a decline in the quality of medical care. It is possible that we have been too reluctant. But do we really need this category of health personnel, and where are we going to find them? We are compelled to draw them from the same manpower pool as the other medical ancillaries, and this will increase the shortage of these categories.

I am therefore of the opinion that it will be better, if possible, to train larger numbers of the existing categories of ancillary personnel instead of introducing a new one.

A much debated question is the role of the doctor in the fight against the many social problems in modern society, whether they are labelled medical or not. Shall the medical profession accept that it is the duty of the doctor to handle such problems in spite of the great expansion of the doctors' duties that this will entail? Would it not be better to leave problems of this kind to other professions and to let the doctors concentrate upon the more specific medical problems? I know that many of my colleagues are of this opinion, and in view of the shortage of doctors it is easy to understand their point of view. However, in modern society medical and social problems are so closely knitted together that they cannot be separated. Many patients cannot be given adequate medical care unless the social and environmental factors are taken into consideration that have contributed to the development of the disease or have even been the main etiological factor. Alcoholics, drug addicts and maladjusted children are well-known examples. In the same way, prevention of disease very often requires a change in the social milieu. I feel therefore that doctors must accept the responsibility for such problems as well. Naturally, this does not mean that the doctor shall work as an almoner or a social worker. The role of the doctor will mainly be to organize the work and to evaluate the results. This will, however, require a reform of medical education. In most medical schools with which I am familiar, medical students are not trained adequately in the social and behavioural sciences, nor are they trained in teamwork. General practitioners who were interviewed in my department expressed it in this way: 'We are well trained in diseases that we do not see in our practice. But we are not trained in the many trivial disorders that take most of our time and have their origin in family conflicts, in economic problems, in difficulties at work, and so forth.' This may be the case also in other countries.

In my department we have in the last few years allowed students of sociology and psychology to take the course in social medicine for medical students. An associate professor of sociology has been on the staff of the department of social medicine, and has been responsible for part of the course. Our experience with this kind of interdisciplinary education is good. There is no doubt that the discussions in the class with the students from the other faculties have broadened the views of the medical students, apart from giving the other students some insight into socio-medical problems. We are therefore interested in extending this kind of teaching. Further steps will be taken in the new medical school in Tromsø. A complete revision of the medical curriculum is planned with much more emphasis upon the social and behavioural sciences and upon interdisciplinary education.

The successful combat in the first half of this century of infectious diseases might create the hope that in the future we shall be as successful in preventing the non-infectious diseases, and that the demand for medical services might thus be reduced. I do not share this hope. It is true that prevention is better than cure and that the medical profession should pay more attention to preventive work than has been the case. But will this reduce the total burden of disease and ill-health? I am afraid the answer is no. Although I am in favour of preventive medicine, I do not believe that it will solve our problem. The character of the doctor's work may be altered, but not the amount of his work.

It is not possible today to envisage the labour-saving effect of automation and its impact upon the practice of medicine. It is conceivable that it will be a means to lessen the burden of the doctor and to augment his productivity. We do not know. But we do know that automation might carry the risk of depersonalization and dehumanization of medical care. We must bear this in mind and try to avoid it.

What then about self-medication? Would it be possible to educate people to treat themselves for commonplace diseases and thus to reduce the number of visits to the doctor's office? This would create a completely new situation as it would mean a total reversal of the teaching of the public that we have practised up to now. Of course, a busy doctor may be annoyed by being consulted for a mere triviality. But does the patient regard the disorder as trivial? Might he not be anxious about it although there may be no reason for his anxiety? It is important to remember that we must look at the situation from the patient's point of view and not from the doctor's. How can we achieve a reduction in the number of consultations for commonplace diseases without running the risk of delaying consultations for serious diseases? Also, we must be aware of the great change that has taken place in our pharmaceutical armamentarium in the last decades. Forty to fifty years ago the number of effective drugs at our disposal was small, and most of them were rather harmless. Today the number of drugs is overwhelming; many of them are very potent, and they are on the whole not suited for self-medication. For these reasons it would mean a serious step backward if we were to rely upon self-medication to a greater extent than is now the case. Of course not all medication can be carried out through a doctor; many preparations must be available to individuals for their own treatment. But in view of the hazard of abuse we should not encourage an extension of self-medication. This does not mean, however, that I am enthusiastic about the type of health education that our mass media offer today. They have a tendency to concentrate upon disease much more than upon health, and more upon sensational news than upon commonplace problems. Many improvements in this area are desirable.

I am fully aware that the suggestions I have made represent no real solution to the problem of how to fill the gap between the demand for medical service and our ability to render such service. I am afraid that this gap will increase rather than decrease in the years to come. But a very serious question arises. Do we use our medical manpower for the benefit of the greatest number of patients? Is it justified from an ethical point of view to continue activities requiring so much time and personnel as heart transplantation, kidney transplantation, use of artificial kidneys and so forth, when there is a severe shortage of doctors in many areas of the country? This question has been raised many times before. The answer has always been that we cannot stop the progress of medical science and that a diagnostic and therapeutic procedure, which today is a medical luxury, might in the future be of benefit to a great number of patients. Many examples of this can be given. I admit this, and certainly agree that the progress of medicine must continue. Nevertheless, the question remains, and it is a serious one for those who must decide upon priorities.

In conclusion: The problem of relieving the physician of unnecessary burdens must be seen in a broader context: What changes are necessary in the organization of the health services in the societies of today? This is a very great problem which will be very difficult to solve. But even if it was solved, I am rather pessimistic as to the possiblities of attaining a significant reduction in the burdens of the doctors. In teaching the public what medicine can do, and in educating them to seek medical service whenever they feel a need for it, we have, like the *Zauberlehrling*, let loose forces we now are unable to control.

Summary

In the last decades the demand for medical service has increased much more rapidly than the number of medical school graduates. As a consequence a gap has developed between the demand for medical services and the availability of medical personnel.

One solution to this world-wide problem is to train more doctors. It is, however, equally important to increase the productivity of the doctors by relieving them of some of the non-professional duties which consume much of their time, and of tasks which could be performed by others.

The clerical work which the social insurance system and other kinds of social legislation impose upon the doctors is an example of non-professional duties which should be reduced to a reasonable level.

Formation of adequate health teams may allow the doctors to concentrate upon the services that they alone are competent to provide. The marked change in disease patterns which has taken place in recent years with the mounting mental, emotional and social problems has confronted the medical profession with problems that the doctors cannot solve alone and that require the cooperation between various categories of health personnel. The role of the doctor has changed from being the main deliverer of health services to becoming a member of a health team. However, more knowledge is needed on how such teams must be organized to function in the most effective way, how the members should be trained and how the best cooperation between the members can be attained.

It will, however, be very difficult to fill the gap between the demand for health service and our ability to render such service. In educating the public to seek medical help whenever they feel a need for it, and in removing the economic barriers to medical care, we have created a demand which will be hard to satisfy.

Zusammenfassung

In den letzten Jahrzehnten ist die Nachfrage nach ärztlicher Behandlung viel stärker angestiegen als die Anzahl Absolventen medizinischer Fakultäten. Als Folge davon hat sich ein Missverhältnis zwischen der Nachfrage nach medizinischer Betreuung einerseits und der Verfügbarkeit ärztlichen Personals anderseits ergeben.

Eine Lösung dieses weltweiten Problems liegt wohl in der Ausbildung von mehr Ärzten. Es ist jedoch genauso wichtig, die Produktivität des Arztes zu steigern, indem man ihn von einigen nichtberuflichen Verpflichtungen befreit, die seine Zeit zu sehr beanspruchen und die von anderen Personen übernommen werden könnten.

Die administrative Arbeit, die die Sozialversicherung und andere soziale Gesetzgebungen den Ärzten auferlegen, ist ein Beispiel für die nichtberuflichen Pflichten, die auf ein vernünftiges Maß reduziert werden sollten.

Die Errichtung funktionstüchtiger Gesundheitsteams würde es den Ärzten erlauben, sich mehr auf Dienstleistungen zu konzentrieren, die nur sie allein erbringen können. Die deutliche Umschichtung der Krankheitsbilder in den letzten Jahren als Folge der Zunahme geistiger, emotioneller und sozialer Schwierigkeiten hat den Arzt mit Problemen konfrontiert, die er nicht alleine zu lösen vermag. Eine Zusammenarbeit zwischen den verschiedenen Kategorien medizinischer Hilfsberufe ist nötig geworden. Die Rolle des Arztes hat sich verändert, denn vom hauptsächlichen Ausübenden ärztlicher Kunst ist er zum Mitglied eines ganzen Teams geworden. Es bedarf jedoch vermehrter Erfahrung und größeren Wissens, um solche Gesundheitsteams funktionstüchtig zu organisieren, ihre Mitglieder auszubilden und die bestmögliche Zusammenarbeit zwischen ihnen zu erzielen.

Das Mißverhältnis zwischen der Nachfrage nach ärztlichen Diensten und unseren Möglichkeiten, diese zu befriedigen, wird schwer zu beseitigen sein. Das Publikum ist dazu erzogen worden, ärztliche Hilfe zu beanspruchen, wann immer es diese für nötig hält. Erwägungen finanzieller Natur vor der Beanspruchung des Arztes wurden weitgehend ausgeschaltet, und wir haben eine Nachfrage geschaffen, die schwer zu befriedigen sein wird.

Résumé

Au cours des dernières décennies, la demande de services médicaux a augmenté bien plus rapidement que le nombre de médecins diplômés sortant des écoles de médecine. Il en est résulté une lacune entre la demande de prestations médicales et le nombre de médecins disponibles.

La formation d'un plus grand nombre de praticiens apporterait une solution à ce problème mondial. Néanmoins, il est tout aussi important d'augmenter la productivité des médecins, en les déchargeant de certaines obligations non professionnelles qui leur prennent beaucoup de temps et des tâches pouvant être accomplies par d'autres.

Le travail administratif que le système des assurances sociales et d'autres institutions sociales imposent aux médecins est un exemple d'obligations non professionnelles devant être réduites à un niveau raisonnable.

La formation d'équipes soignantes adéquates pourrait permettre aux médecins de se concentrer sur les tâches relevant de leur seule compétence. Le net changement survenu au cours des dernières années dans les catégories des maladies fréquentes, changement résultant de l'accroissement des problèmes mentaux, émotionnels et sociaux, place le corps médical devant des problèmes que les médecins ne peuvent pas résoudre seuls et qui exigent la collaboration de différentes catégories de personnel soignant. Le rôle du médecin a changé, en ce sens qu'au lieu d'être le principal dispensateur de soins, il devient un membre d'une équipe soignante. Cependant, il faudrait étudier plus avant la manière dont de telles équipes devraient être organisées pour fonctionner avec le maximum d'efficacité, quelle formation leurs membres devraient recevoir et comment obtenir la meilleure collaboration possible au sein de l'équipe.

Il sera pourtant très difficile de combler la lacune existant entre la demande de prestations médicales et notre capacité de les assurer. En informant le public, par la vulgarisation médicale, en lui conseillant de consulter un médecin chaque fois qu'il le juge nécessaire, et en supprimant les barrières économiques qui l'empêchaient de consulter un médecin sans nécessité, nous avons créé une demande difficile à satisfaire.

Resumen

En los últimos decenios, la demanda de servicios médicos ha crecido con mucha mayor rapidez que el número de médicos graduados que salen de las universidades. El resultado es un desequilibrio entre las prestaciones médicas solicitadas y la cantidad de médicos disponibles.

La formación de un mas elevado número de médicos aportaría la solución a este problema mundial. Pero, al mismo tiempo habría de aumentarse la productividad de los médicos, exonerándolos de ciertas obligaciones ajenas a su profesión, que absorben mucho tiempo y que podrían encomendarse a otras personas.

El trabajo administrativo que el sistema de seguridad social y otras instituciones de la misma índole imponen al médico, es un ejemplo de las obligaciones ajenas a su profesión, que deberían ser reducidas a un nivel razonable.

La formación de equipos de auxiliares capacitados, permitiría a los médicos concentrarse en tareas de su exclusiva competencia. El cambio considerable verificado en los últimos años en la frecuencia de las enfermedades más corrientes, imputable a los crecientes problemas mentales, emocionales y sociales, ha enfrentado al médico con dificultades que él no puede resolver solo.

Se ha hecho necesaria la cooperación de varias categorías de personal auxiliar. El papel del facultativo se ha modificado, en el sentido de que, en lugar de ser el principal dispensador de asistencia médica, se ha convertido en miembro de un equipo. Sin embargo, se necesitan más experiencia y mejores conocimientos sobre la manera de organizar tales equipos, para que funcionen con la máxima eficiencia, y sobre la formación de sus miembros, a fin de lograr la mejor cooperación posible entre ellos.

Con todo, tendremos gran dificultad en colmar la desproporción que existe entre la demanda de prestaciones médicas y nuestra capacidad de asegurar ese servicio. Al enseñar al público, por medio de la vulgarización, a consultar al médico cada vez que lo juzgue necesario y al suprimir las barreras económicas que antes se lo impedían, hemos desatado una demanda que será difícil de satisfacer.

The doctor's dilemma

The right to health. Choices and priorities in research and development in the biomedical field

by Lord ZUCKERMAN

The Doctor's Dilemma, one of GEORGE BERNARD SHAW's most famous plays, was produced in 1906[8]. It dealt not with one, but with several dilemmas. SHAW was writing well before socialized medicine had been introduced to any country. He saw doctors as a body of men with an 'anti-social' interest in health and pleaded for what we would call today the nationalization of the profession. As he put it, 'until the medical profession becomes a body of men trained and paid by the country to keep the country in health, it will remain what it is at present: a conspiracy to exploit popular credulity and human suffering'.

SHAW was clearly deriding the popular conception that the medical man's professional life is governed by an ethical code which could be traced back to the Hippocratic oath which doctors, before entering practice, swore in days gone by. Another of his points was that medical practice is governed not by science, but by supply and demand. 'However scientific a treatment may be, it cannot hold its place in the market, if there is no demand for it; nor can the grossest quackery be kept off the market if there is a demand for it.' Moreover, as SHAW saw it, medical treatment is governed by fashion in the same way as are clothes. And he was quite clear about another central issue – that the belief that 'every individual life is of infinite value is legislatively impracticable'. 'Invalids.., cannot, beyond reason, expect to be kept alive by the activity of others.'

World population, when SHAW wrote, was about 1700 million, of whom probably fewer than a quarter were literate. The corresponding population figure of today is about 3700 million, of whom the vast majority are now exposed, if not to the printed word, then to the message, which is constantly blared out by radio and television, that there will be a better tomorrow. SHAW wrote in the days when a high proportion of children born into the world died before they were a year old – when hardship and starvation, malaria and diphtheria, cholera and tuberculosis were tolerated as the lot of mankind.

Today the doctor's dilemma has become far more acute, far more intractable, and far more pervasive than it was when SHAW wrote. The message he spelt out was addressed mainly to the medical profession of the United Kingdom, and to some extent, one may suppose, to that of Western Europe and North America. Today it is one which human beings the world over, as well as their doctors, face, either consciously or unconsciously. When SHAW's play was first produced, the average expectation of life in the United Kingdom for a child who survived up to the end of its first year was under 60. In countries like India, it was about 30. Today it is between 70 and 75 in England and other advanced countries, and about 50 in a developing country like India. These critical changes in human longevity have been associated with an enormous growth of world population and of education. If the doctor once upon a time had to ask himself 'who shall be saved?', today the answer is shouted by millions and millions of potential patients. The mass media have encouraged people to believe that all can be saved. And seldom does one see the cost of medical salvation being counted, or the consequences spelt out.

I have been asked to address my remarks to the theme 'Choices and Priorities in Research and Development in the Biomedical Field'. This issue had little meaning until recent years. Whatever SHAW may have written, health was usually assumed to be an unquestioned right, however meagerly or however lavishly it could be satisfied within whatever circumstances prevailed. Until very recent years, too, no one regarded the question of research and development in the biomedical field as a matter which necessitated any conscious agreement on priorities. Biomedical knowledge grew under its own momentum, and its fruits became applied automatically. There was little or no point in any authority attempting to dictate which way either medical knowledge or medical practice should develop. The only question that governments had to face was whether the resources which countries made available in order to further the health of the community could be better deployed than they were, so that not just the wealthy, but all citizens could benefit from what was or should have been a social service.

The situation has been totally transformed by the changes that recent years have brought about in the size and age structure of populations, and in the expectation of life in almost all age-groups of society. These changes are not primarily due to better or to significantly improved health services directed at the individual. Equally they are not peculiar to advanced countries. They are also occurring in countries like Nigeria, which has a population of something like 60 million people, served by no more than about a thousand professional medical men. They are occurring in Ceylon, in India – they are occurring almost everywhere we look – basically because of the elimination of such killing diseases as malaria, due to the eradication of the mosquito, and to a lesser extent because of better nutrition and of improved measures of public sanitation. All these changes can obviously be associated with the growth of medical knowledge. But we are also clearly living in an age of paradox, an age in which we can all expect to live longer and to enjoy better health than did our forebears – in spite of the fact that some of us at the same time fear that we are rapidly destroying our physical environment, a destruction which is exacerbated in some countries by the way their populations grow.

This is the general picture of the changes that have occurred in the biomedical field since the first appearance of BERNARD SHAW's play in 1906 and, indeed, since he wrote an addendum to its preface in 1933. The specific picture, as it relates to a developed country such as the United Kingdom[2], is also worth being outlined as a background against which to view the question of choices in the biomedical research and development field in perspective.

Some twenty years ago, at the mid-point of this century, the United Kingdom was at a turning point in the control of some of the worst communicable infections. At that time, its birth rate was 16.2 per thousand and the crude death rate 11.7; the infantile death rate was 31.2 and the stillbirth rate 24. These figures were an enormous improvement on those which characterized the earlier part of Britain's industrial age – the age before the country enjoyed any effective public system of sanitation, or any form of public health service. Since 1950, however, there have been further remarkable changes. The birth rate in 1970 was back to 16.2, after having risen much higher – to 18.7 – while the general crude death rate was more or less as it was, about 11.8. But – and this is the most conspicuous change – the infant death rate, and the stillbirth rate are down by nearly a half, and the maternal death rate by nearly four fifths. As a result of these various factors, the United Kingdom population, now standing at 56 millions, is nearly thirteen percent greater than it was at the end of the Second World War.

The improvement in the health of the British population over more recent years, over say the past twenty years, has been due not to further developments in public sanitation and nutrition – to which we can attribute the major improvement in the United Kingdom's health over the past two hundred years – but to the widespread introduction of antibacterial drugs and of methods of immunization against infectious disease. Scarlet fever, diphtheria and poliomyelitis have all but been wiped out since the Second World War. Whooping cough and measles have declined both in frequency and severity. The death rate from tuberculosis is one eighth what it was twenty years ago. While no one would claim that the battle against infectious disease has been finally won, there can be no doubt that, short of an absolute reversal of current trends, the enemy of infectious disease has been significantly routed – or at least isolated – in the United Kingdom.

As in other advanced countries, the increase in Britain in the size of the population has been associated with startling changes in its age structure. Sixty years ago, children aged ten had an average further expectation of life of less than fifty-five years. Today the figure is nearer sixty-three. Those who reach maturity can also expect to live, on average, to seventy-five years, as opposed to an average expectation of no more than sixty-five some sixty years ago. This does not mean that the more elderly are living significantly longer than did their forebears. What is happening is that more are reaching old age. And the population is growing older as a result. In the United Kingdom 1931 census, there were only 4.4 million people in the country past the age of retirement. By 1975, the figure will be nearly 9.5 million – over 16% of the whole population.

Quite apart from the elimination of infectious diseases, which mostly took their toll of the young, the change in the age structure of the British population has not surprisingly been associated with other significant shifts in the spectrum of disease. A population whose members can expect to survive into old age – and it already contains nearly half a million aged 85 or more – is more subject to degenerative diseases than one whose average expectation of life was, say, no more than fifty years. Mortality rates for cancer have gone up over the past few decades, and cardiovascular disease takes a greater toll than it did before. A higher incidence of degenerative diseases in an ageing population is only to be expected.

The changes that have been occurring in the age structure of the British population pose a basic biological question. Leaving aside for the moment of such deleterious changes as may be taking place in our physical environment, is it conceivable that man's average natural span – as we have known it over the ages – can be raised from, say, seventy-five years to ninety years? My own answer to this question has always been 'no'. Earlier this year, the issue was discussed at the Third European Conference of the International Association of Gerontology. As I understand it, the majority opinion supported my view of the question. On the other hand, some of the gerontologists who were present at the conference did express the belief that in the not-too-distant future the normal life span of human beings might increase to as much as 120 years.

Is this really possible? We sometimes hear about the extraordinary longevity of certain closed communities, such as the famous one in southern Russia where, according to newspaper accounts, a centenarian can regard himself as a relatively young man. There may be a genetic explanation for the claimed longevity of such closed communities, as there may also be for the fact that one finds families in all countries whose members are usually long lived. It is also conceivable that some process of selection might help spread the genes of longevity possessed by such families through a whole community, and so raise the natural span of all people well beyond its apparent potential. My own hunch, however, is that this is unlikely to happen. As I see it, man's potential life span is as much one of his inbuilt genetically determined characteristics as are all those other anatomical and physiological features by which the nature of our species became defined through the processes of evolution.

It is, however, useful to pause a moment here and to consider certain secular changes that have been taking place in the pattern of human growth over the years. In all phases of history, a given population has had its tall people and its short – its Goliaths and its Davids. Henry VIII was a much bigger man than was his average subject, and I have heard it said that so too were most early and mediaeval leaders. There have also always been inbred races, such as the pygmies of the Congo, who have been very small, and others such as the Masai of northern Kenya and Somaliland, who are very tall. The pygmies of New Guinea contrast startlingly with the taller indigenous Australian aborigines. And a common impression is that the Japanese are on average shorter than Europeans. Within a given country there may also be geographical differences in average height. Outlying groups of Highlanders are taller on average than their fellow Scots who live in, say, Glasgow, and outlying groups of Scandinavians are also renowned for their tall stature.

Today many of these differences are being wiped out at the same time as a secular change appears to be taking place in the rate at which children reach their maximum height and weight. These changes have been the subject of considerable study. In Britain, as in Norway and some other countries, it is apparent that they began well over a hundred years ago. TANNER[9] quotes ROBERTS, who in 1876 wrote that 'a factory child of the present day at the age of 9 years weighs as much as one of 10 did in 1833... each age has gained one year in 40 years'.

This secular acceleration in the rate of physical maturation has been occurring in all classes of society and is tending to wipe out the differences in stature which characterized socio-economic groups in the United Kingdom in the earlier part of this century – and, since it appears to be occurring in many countries, the differences which once characterized national groups. Moreover, children are not only achieving their maximum height earlier than did their fathers and grandfathers; the trend to earlier maturation also affects other features of growth, such as the time of eruption of the teeth, and the age at which puberty occurs.

From the point of view of the question of a possible secular increase in the natural life span of man, it is of interest that the average height of fully grown adults in the United Kingdom has also been increasing slightly over recent years, even if not to the same extent as has the average height of children of similar age groups. What, however, is not known is whether a secular change is occurring in the potential maximum height which individuals can attain, that is to say whether the increase in adult height is due to some real change in the genetic make-up of the United Kingdom population, or whether it is a consequence of a greater mixing of the human gene pool, due to more frequent intermarriages between different classes and groups of people – following the breakdown of social barriers as a result of the general improvement that has occurred in standards of living and education on the one hand and the greater mobility of populations on the other.

There is, in fact, no way yet of deciding what lies behind the increase in the average height of adults or indeed in deciding how real it is. Some have speculated that it may be due to some global environmental change, such as a rise in world temperature. But if this were the explanation, we should be justified in expecting that the average height of the world's population went up and down during the ice ages which marked the opening of the geological era in which we live – and there is little or no evidence of that. But whatever the cause of the secular changes that are now definitely occurring in the rate at which children mature, my own hunch is that man's potential ceiling of height is as fixed and

determined by the genetic make-up of the human species, as the latter has determined the average potential span of man's life.

The changes in the vital statistics of the British population represent a
pattern which applies to every developed country and which one can expect to
impose itself on all countries as they develop. They are the consequences of the
practical application of new knowledge in general and of biomedical advances
over the past 30 to 40 years in particular. As I have said, the essential reason
underlying the continuing improvement in the average expectation of life is the
reduction of mortality rates in every age group, but particularly the younger
ones, due primarily to the development of public health measures. In certain
parts of the world the main factor has been the elimination by DDT of the
anopheles mosquito, the carrier of the malaria plasmodium. In industrialized
countries, a decline in a wide category of infectious diseases has, in recent years,
offset an increase in death rates due to diseases such as coronary infarction and
cancer of the lung on the one hand and motor accidents on the other. But in
spite of unprecedented improvements in the facilities available to departments
of academic medicine, and in spite of the numbers of people who have gone
into clinical research, hospital scientists have not been responsible for the major
changes that have transformed man's health over recent years. Here let me
repeat the balanced views of a distinguished British physician, Lord PLATT[6], on
this subject. As he put it in an address he gave in 1967 to the British Royal College
of Physicians: 'The phenomenal success of modern medical treatment seems to
have depended almost wholly on non-clinical, often non-medical scientists frequently working in, or in close collaboration with, the pharmaceutical industry.'
To illustrate his point, he referred to the emergence of antibiotics, modern
anaesthetics, tranquillizers, vitamins, anti-malarials, anti-histamines, hypoten-
sives, sex hormones and oral contraceptives. Not one of these developments, he
pointed out, originated in a department of academic medicine or therapeutics.
Another British authority, Professor HENRY MILLER[4], at the time the Chairman of the British Medical Association's Planning Unit and now the Vice-
Chancellor of the University of Newcastle-upon-Tyne, not so long ago declared
that 'the new drugs for serious mental illness represent the greatest medical
advance since penicillin'. Again these drugs were not the fruits of work done in
some laboratory of clinical research. Both Lord PLATT's and Professor MIL-
LER's observations have, of course, to be seen in perspective. Had there not
been enquiring clinicians to point the way, the chemist or physiologist, not
knowing where to look, could hardly have succeeded in the way he has.

In the light of the transformations that the pharmaceutical industry has
helped bring about in the treatment of disease and in improving public health
services, we can obviously expect it to do even more in the remaining years of
our century. Even if new developments do not change the limits of man's natural span, the treatment of illness should certainly continue to improve, with
more people surviving into old age.

But this kind of medical advance is not what attracts the headlines when people talk about possible future developments in medical practice. Over the past few years public attention has been much more fixed on such dramatic issues as heart transplants and artificial dialysis machines, and on the belief that someone like Dr Issels may hold the key to a cure for cancer. Even faith healers now hit the headlines.

The kind of biomedical advance that more serious people talk about has been outlined in the last number of *Impact*[10], a Unesco publication whose purpose is to consider the interaction of science and society. It talks of the control of human reproductive processes, of the treatment of sterility, of the pre-selection of the sex of unborn babies, of the *in-vitro* fertilization and cultivation of the human ovum – a matter which has been much publicized through the work of R. G. Edwards of Cambridge University – and of the possibility of 'cloning' of human beings. It writes about 'genetic engineering', in which the claim is made that eventually we (who the 'we' may be is not stated) will be able to pre-design the genetic make-up of unborn children... 'to modify hereditary human characteristics, to create humans matching some pre-conceived pattern or model'. It also elaborates the possibilities which lie in organ transplantation, and leaves the impression that here everything is possible bar the transplantation of the human brain. Even the view which I have given about the likelihood that in advanced communities longevity will reach an asymptotic level is challenged by a writer who feels it safe to declare that indefinite postponement of old age is conceivable, even 'if unlikely to be total'.

Before I make my own general comment on these observations, I think it is necessary that they be set into a realistic framework of cost. Health constitutes only one of many social demands. In addition to freedom from pain, people cry for better houses, for a higher standard of living, for better schools, for freedom of individual movement, for leisure. In advanced societies, and even more so in developing countries, all these categories of social demand have to be placed in an order of priority. In some cases, social demand generates a need to develop the technology by which it can be satisfied. The emergence of the technical apparatus for providing clean water and public sewage is a reflection of this interaction, in the same way as public concern today about the spoliation of our physical environment is calling for new technologies to deal with the pollution of the air we breathe, the land on which we live, and the seas around us.

But in many cases, possibly in the majority of cases, social demand emerges as a reflection of new knowledge and of new technology. This is particularly true in the field of health. When it does, problems are posed immediately for the governments which have to see whether the new social demand can be met. This point can again be illustrated by reference to Great Britain.

Health and Welfare services cost the British Exchequer roughly 5% of the country's gross national product. No figures are available for the amount that is now spent in the private medical sector – it can hardly be more than a fraction of the public figure; nor do we know how much was spent on medical care in the 1930's, before the institution of the British National Health Service. Needless to say, the institution of the service has meant a more equitable distribution within the population of the resources that are available for medical care. But it is immediately necessary to ask why these resources should not be double what they are, or half their present volume.

For quite different reasons they could be neither. The level at which the British health budget now stands has been determined by the countervailing demands on the public purse of all forms of public expenditure – roads, schools, the armed services, social security, as well as health. It is hardly likely, therefore, that the health services would be provided in any one year with a significantly higher proportion of national resources than they have been receiving – there are too many other claims, many unfulfilled, on the public purse. Correspondingly, the British Government is not going to be able to say to the public that the medical services are getting too much of the United Kingdom's total resources, or that the state of health of the nation has improved so greatly over recent years that the government can reduce the amount going to the National Health Service to, say, three quarters of its present level. Public demand for medical care will continue, however many diseases are eliminated, and whatever improvements occur in medical practice. While man remains mortal, and so long as pain and distress remain his lot, he will continue to demand that there be doctors and hospitals – as well as improvements in both – in numbers and quality.

A former British Minister of Health, ENOCH POWELL[7], has put the case very clearly. Demand for medical care is for all practical purposes unlimited. 'Every advance in medical science creates new needs that did not exist until the means of meeting them came into existence, or at least into the realm of the possible. For every heart-lung machine or artificial kidney in operation, there must be many times that number of cases to which the treatment would be applicable.' Moreover, the individual is capable of absorbing any amount of medical care, as he cannot, let us say, absorb food and drink, in the same way as there are no limits to improvements in the potential quality of medical care – a feature in which medicine differs in its impact on the public purse from, for example, education, where it is possible to lay down criteria on such matters as the curriculum, school-leaving age, size of class, and so on.

Demand for health being in theory limitless, it is only by rationing supply that governments can prevent the Health Services, through their own growth, from denying resources to other forms of national enterprise. And whatever the resources devoted to health, medical care has to be rationed. If the annual rate of growth of the resources going to the U.K. National Health Service were doubled or trebled, the waiting lists of British hospitals, which stand at the same figure year after year, would probably remain unchanged. The queue at the general practitioner's surgery would also be as long as it is now. Its length is determined not so much by the numbers of doctors inside as by the amount of time each doctor can give a patient.

In the final analysis no community can enjoy more medical service than it can afford. This, of course, is not to say that the more favoured citizen cannot go to the private practitioner or consultant to buy what care and treatment he can pay for – as was the case in BERNARD SHAW's day. But with demand for medical attention in effect limitless, one could in theory visualize the market mechanism stimulating a growth of medical resources out of all proportion to the total volume of resources available to a community, with the latter declining as less went into more productive channels of national enterprise, such as manufacturing industry, until chaos – if that is the right word – once again supervened on the medical scene. In brief, to quote another former British Minister of Health[1], 'it is not the demand that creates the service but the service the demand'. It is the pressure of science and technology and medical skill which results 'in new and evermore expensive services which themselves then generate automatically an even more expensive demand'.

This law of demand seems to apply regardless of the stage of development of a particular society. The United Kingdom is short of doctors and of new hospitals; the demand for drugs seems insatiable, and people cry out for better equipment. But, as I have said, if the resources put into medical services doubled, experience shows that public demand would still not be satisfied. Poor countries with far less favourable medical services than the British face the same dilemma. And so do countries far richer than Britain. It is a cynical thought, no doubt, but only the few sovereign states which for all practical purposes have no modern medical services, and whose citizens expect none, are saved from the dilemma of modern medicine.

It seems indisputable that priorities have to be set in the provision of medical services and in the application of medical knowledge. The key question is who is to set these priorities? There are only three possible answers. We have to look either to the medical profession, or to the people, or to governments.

The dilemma which BERNARD SHAW's play was concerned to expound related essentially to the traditional Hippocratic oath. At least in theory this oath impelled the medical practitioner to do the utmost he could in order to help his patient; and in accordance with his judgment he had to try treatment after treatment in the hope of succeeding. In extreme cases – as some still interpret the relationship between doctor and patient – the doctor has to try to prolong the life of his patient even when all reason shows that he should be allowed to die.

But most of the advances in medicine have in fact occurred not because of any desire of a practitioner to help either the patient or the society of which he is part but, as Professor HENRY MILLER[5] has pointed out, by accident, as in the case of DDT, or as a result of the curiosity that impels a medical research worker to advance his particular branch of knowledge. As a contributor[3] to a recent number of the British medical weekly *The Lancet* has pointed out, a doctor of even average ability every week saves the lives of an appreciable number of people as a consequence not of his particular genius, but of the various new drugs non-medical hands have made available in recent years.

Yet no one in his senses could suppose that with the world as it is, with most countries contending with a rate of population growth that threatens their economic and social development, matters like the *in-vitro* cultivation of new human beings are a social necessity, or that the resources which they demand justify those extremes of surgical practice represented by techniques such as heart transplantation. These developments are the vested interests of medical or scientific enthusiasts, not of the people at large or of social scientists or of governments.

But if matters are left to the discretion of the medical scientist and medical practitioner, then there will be more extreme developments of this kind. Should they be allowed to happen? Who is to say? And who is to cry stop if the answer is 'no'? The medical profession as a whole? Is it organized to do this?

If new techniques do emerge, we can be certain that at least a few people will demand that they be used. In the medical world, I repeat, it is usually the new technology which generates the demand – not the need which calls for a new technology. It follows that the people at large can no more be trusted to set medical priorities in the right social framework than it would seem the doctors can if left to themselves. Each generation of human beings is conditioned to the circumstances into which it is born and rejects the idea of putting up with something more primitive. It is inconceivable that people of today would turn their backs on the anti-malarials, antibiotics and anaesthetics which the science of yesterday produced, any more than present-day doctors will cease using them.

So we are left with the third possibility. Can governments, and particularly democratic governments, undertake the task of setting medical priorities? Governments consist of men who from the point of view of medical practice can be expected to behave in the same way as the people they govern – within the limits of the resources which they can command. They themselves want to be cured and saved. And they are also under the pressure of popular demand. If the public demand that governments should take command of the search, now being pursued mainly through what could be called private enterprise, for a cure of cancer – given that we were dealing with only one cure – how could they resist? But whatever truth there be in the common belief that higher education has always been steered in the interests of the ruling elite, one has to ask whether central government is the authority which should be charged with the responsibility of determining the future direction of medical service, by setting priorities for today's biomedical research and development?

This is an extremely difficult question to answer. And yet insofar as the general public, as the potential beneficiaries for new and better medical practice, cannot be expected to do more than welcome any advances in biomedical science, it is difficult to avoid the conclusion that to some extent governments must become involved in the task. Indeed they already are. In the United States, President Nixon has taken charge of a national campaign to find a cure for cancer. The World Health Organization, acting through governments, tries to stem the spread of pandemics like cholera and supervises the world programme to eliminate the last reservoirs of malaria. The Indian Government encourages sterilization of the human male, and in Great Britain abortion can be called for on the National Health Service. Therefore, to whatever extent medical practitioners now dance to the tune played by governments, they have already given up part of their freedom to deal with patients in accordance with their own individual judgment. Equally, in those countries which have abandoned free market medicine of the kind against which BERNARD SHAW campaigned, medical practitioners are to some extent direct servants of the State, and as much in the queue for higher levels of remuneration from the public purse as are members of other public professions, such as postmen and railway workers.

And yet it is unthinkable that governments, either through advisory or executive boards they might appoint, should decree that medical knowledge should progress along these rather than those lines. If a cure for cancer or a cure for coronary thrombosis were ever to be discovered, it would not be because governments had ordered that they should be. They would have emerged as the acts of creation of individual geniuses, either working alone, or possibly as members of teams of research workers.

We seem trapped in a vicious circle. I have already said that medical research workers have a vested interest in their own fields of enquiry. They hardly ever, if indeed ever, stop to consider what the full social consequences would be of the application of their work, given it were successful. 'The specialist in isolation is a dangerous animal', as Professor HENRY MILLER has put it. Worse than that, the specialist, if successful, is as much a leader of medical fashion today as he was when he was derided by BERNARD SHAW. There never will be enough resources to permit the exploitation of all medical fashions or to cater for the demand an uninformed public makes for both old and new medical service. The more rapidly new medical fashions and technologies emerge, the worse the position will become.

Medical ethics today have become the issue of medical priorities. Priorities have to be set. In my own view they should be set by the medical profession itself, but within a sophisticated framework of governmental information which takes into account not just the amount of money that can be made available either from public or private sources for the direct application of the fruits of new medical knowledge, but also the consequential social costs that may have to be borne given a successful 'break-through' in the control of some particular disease. For example, while no rational person could have wished to see the scourge of malaria continue a moment longer than was necessary, political/economic planning would have been easier in some developing countries if it had been realized at the start that the eradication of the disease would result in so rapid a growth of population that the economic development of the country would be threatened. Equally, if a 'cure' for cancer were found, the net social effect might mainly be an average delay of, it has been calculated, less than seven years in the deaths of a proportion of aged people; an increase in the size of an age group well past working age; and an increased demand for the resources necessary to keep them happy and alive. Moreover, if a cure for cancer were ever discovered and governments found themselves incapable of meeting the social cost of the discovery, a situation might be generated in which inequality in the availability of a particular medical service for which the rich but not the poor could pay, would once again appear as a symptom of social injustice. Then we would again hear the cry – who should be saved? In the case of something that already exists, who, indeed, should be allowed to use the kidney machine?

I do not suppose that any easy way will ever be found for the determination of priorities in biomedical research and biomedical development. But I should certainly like to see priorities set by a body of men who, while not taking any active steps to suppress new work, made it plain which lines of research counted most from society's point of view. The main criterion which I should like to see guide the decisions of such a body would be the old-fashioned one of the greatest good for the greatest number. I should like further emphasis being placed on research such as enquiries into the control of reproduction; further research on the safety of new drugs; further work on the crippling ailments of old age – and not such advanced old age – such as the different forms of arthritis and even backache; further research into the alleviation of pain; further research on the common cold. And I should like to see such work urged forward, even if at the expense of enquiries into those rare ailments whose cure, or presumed cure, is not only easier but becomes so easily dramatized by the mass media. In a rational world, I would give priority to such work even at the expense of further research into such heart-rending conditions as mental defect in the young or the treatment of drug addiction in society's 'drop-outs'. I would do so because by and large more would be made happy if more mundane medical problems were solved first, and equally society would become healthier were we able to deal successfully with the simpler matters that I have picked out. Indeed, if all new medical research were to stop now and the resources it uses put into the further application of the knowledge we already have, enormous gains could still be achieved in the public health of the world.

But I realize all too well that in medical matters we are not dealing with a rational world. The media of mass communication, as well as those specialists whom Professor MILLER has dubbed 'dangerous animals' and who only too easily make the headlines, make sure that it will never become such. A young patient suffering from an incurable cancer commands as much space in the papers and as much TV or radio time as do all the horrors of Vietnam or all the atrocities of East Pakistan. We approach the problem of medical priorities hamstrung by the knife of human sentiment. We need another BERNARD SHAW to help tear away from the medical scene of today what has become a new veil of hypocrisy before we can be certain that it would not be a sheer waste of time to try to set priorities for biomedical research and development. Until this is done, the power of new knowledge, the force of consumer or patient demand, the imperatives of humanitarianism, and the desire of governments to improve the public health will never be allowed to combine into a coherent plan of action for the medical practice of tomorrow.

References

1. CROSSMAN, R.H.S.: *Paying for the Social Services*. Herbert Morrison Memorial Lecture. London: Fabian Society, 1969.
2. GODBER, Sir GEORGE: *Medical Care. The Changing Needs and Pattern*. London: J. and A. Churchill, 1970.
3. LAWLESS, J.: The Role of the Medical Profession as an Elite. *Lancet 1971/I*, 543.
4. MILLER, H.: Psychiatry and the Health Service. *The Listener 80*, 257–258 (1968).
5. MILLER, H.: Medical Education and Medical Research. *Lancet 1971/I*, 1–6.
6. Lord PLATT: *Medical Science: Master or Servant?* The Harveian Oration of 1967. London: British Medical Association, 1967.
7. POWELL, J.E.: *A New Look at Medicine and Politics*. London: Pitman Medical Publishing Company Ltd, 1966.
8. SHAW, G.B.: *The Doctor's Dilemma*. Penguin Plays Edition. London: Penguin Books, 1906.
9. TANNER, J.M.: *Growth at Adolescence*, second Edition. Oxford: Blackwell Scientific Publications, 1962.
10. United Nations Educational, Scientific and Cultural Organization. *Impact of Science on Society XX*, No. 4 (1970).

Summary

In the context of the present Symposium, the basic dilemma is whether priorities should or can be consciously determined by the relative weight either of demonstrable or of manifestly imminent social needs, rather than emerge unpredictably as new knowledge reveals new practical possibilities of diagnosis or therapy – in the way it has mainly done up to now. The dilemma is made all the more acute by the fact that we do not have a free run of options. Some biomedical problems are more easily solved than others. Some are probably insoluble. Whether they are one thing or the other, it is also all but impossible to direct some genius to solve this or that problem. One might hope for a 'break-through' at some particular point on the frontiers of knowledge; one could never rely on it being made.

None of this would matter if there were no limit to the economic and human resources which could be directed to the care of the sick and aged. The man of genius could be left to his own inspiration, at the same time as resources were provided to encourage others to try to find solutions for problems that were defined on the basis of social need. But there are limits to resources, even in the richest countries, and there are enormous disparities in the medical resources which are available to different countries. Moreover in medicine it is the new knowledge, the new technology, which creates the demand for service.

Over the past few decades most of the killing diseases, which previously helped keep population growth in check, have been eliminated as a result of advance in public health measures and in nutrition. The average expectation of life in all age groups has consequently gone up everywhere, and increases in the size of population have been associated with startling changes in its age structure, with increasing numbers reaching old age.

The demographic changes represent a pattern which applies to every developed country and which one can expect to impose itself on all countries as they develop. They are the consequences of the practical application of new knowledge in general and of biomedical advances over the past 30–40 years in particular. But some prominent medical authorities are now openly admitting their doubts of whether further significant advances in the health of the average man or woman can come from laboratory studies. And the major medical schools, previously regarded, and rightly regarded, as the spearhead in the attack on illness, are themselves beginning to come under attack as being the central cause of a growing distortion in the social priorities of medicine. The argument is that the professional people who serve in them are more concerned with esoteric developments in medical knowledge and practice than they are with the social problems of health and disease.

Medical service constitutes only one of many social demands. In some cases, social demand generates a need to develop the technology by which it can be satisfied. The emergence of the technical apparatus for providing clean water and public sewage is a reflection of this interaction.

In medicine it is usually the other way round, with new technology creating new demand. In the final analysis, however, no community, whatever its stage of development, can enjoy more medical services than it can afford. But if the resources put into medical services doubled, experience shows that public demand would still not be satisfied. Poor countries with far less favourable medical services than the British face the same dilemma. And so do countries far richer than Britain.

Some countries which already organize their medical resources in the form of a national health service, and where most expenditure on health is in the public sector, already try to direct at least part of their biomedical research and development on the basis of an agreed set of priorities. Some fields of enquiry are provided with lavish resources, while others are discouraged by the denial of corresponding help.

Medical priorities are in this way obviously becoming influenced by the concept of social justice. But they should none the less be set by the medical profession itself, within a sophisticated framework of governmental information which takes into account not just the amount of money that can be made available either from public or private sources for the direct application of the fruits of new medical knowledge, but also the consequential social costs which may have to be borne, given a successful 'break-through' in the control of some particular diseases. Greater emphasis needs to be placed on research whose results will have the widest impact – such as enquiries into the control of reproduction; into the safety of new drugs; into simpler ailments like the common cold and the crippling troubles of old age, such as arthritis and back-ache, into the alleviation of pain; and into psychiatric conditions. This might well be at the expense of dramatic new surgical advances, such as heart transplantation, or medical enquiries into those rare ailments whose cure, or presumed cure, is not only easier to achieve than that of many common ailments, but becomes all too easily over-dramatized by the mass-media.

Zusammenfassung

Im Rahmen dieses Symposiums stellt sich die dilemmatische Frage, ob Prioritäten bewußt auf Grund des relativen Gewichtes von nachweisbar oder offenkundig bestehenden sozialen Notwendigkeiten bestimmt werden können und sollen oder aber, ob sie unvorhersehbar auftauchen, wenn neues Wissen neue praktische Möglichkeiten der Diagnose oder der Therapie aufzeigt – so wie es bis heute hauptsächlich der Fall war. Das Dilemma wird noch akuter durch die Tatsache, daß wir keine unbeschränkten Möglichkeiten haben. Einige biomedizinische Probleme sind leichter lösbar als andere. Einige bleiben vermutlich unlösbar. Jedenfalls ist es praktisch unmöglich, einem Genie den Auftrag zur Lösung dieses oder jenes Problems zu erteilen. Wohl darf man auf einen «Durchbruch» irgendwo an der Front unseres Wissens hoffen: damit rechnen darf man nie.

Alles das würde keine Rolle spielen, wären die wirtschaftlichen und menschlichen Mittel für die Behandlung der Kranken und der Alten nicht begrenzt. Man könnte das Genie seinen eigenen Eingebungen überlassen, während Mittel zur Verfügung gestellt würden, andere anzuspornen, nach Lösungen für jene Probleme zu suchen, die sich aus der sozialen Notwendigkeit ergeben. Aber die Mittel sind eben beschränkt, selbst in den reichsten Ländern. Es gibt enorme Unterschiede in den medizinischen Mitteln, die verschiedenen Ländern zur Verfügung stehen. Überdies sind es in der Medizin das neue Wissen und die neue Technologie, welche die Nachfrage erzeugen.

Während der letzten Jahrzehnte wurden die meisten der tödlichen Krankheiten, die früher dazu beitrugen, die Bevölkerungszunahme unter Kontrolle zu halten, durch den Fortschritt im öffentlichen Gesundheitswesen und in der Ernährung ausgeschaltet. In der Folge stieg die durchschnittliche Lebenserwartung überall und in allen Altersstufen, was mit überraschenden Veränderungen in der Altersstruktur der Bevölkerung einherging: immer mehr Menschen erreichen ein hohes Alter.

Die demographischen Änderungen zeigen ein Bild, das für alle entwickelten Länder gilt und das – so darf man annehmen – für jedes sich entwickelnde Land einmal Geltung haben wird. Es sind die Folgen der praktischen Anwendung des neuen Wissens im allgemeinen und der biomedizinischen Fortschritte

während der letzten dreißig bis vierzig Jahre im besonderen. Mehrere aner-
kannte Autoritäten auf dem Gebiet der Medizin zweifeln jedoch heute offen
daran, ob Laboratoriumsstudien zu weiteren signifikanten Verbesserungen
der Gesundheit von Mann oder Frau führen können. Und die bekanntesten
medizinischen Schulen, die früher zu Recht als die Anführer im Kampf gegen
die Krankheit galten, kommen heute unter Beschuß, weil man sie als zentrale
Ursache einer zunehmenden Verzerrung der sozialen Prioritäten der Medizin
betrachtet. Das Argument ist, daß die professionellen Kreise sich mehr für
esoterische Entwicklungen im medizinischen Wissen und in der medizinischen
Praxis interessierten als für die sozialen Probleme von Gesundheit und Erkrankung.

Medizinische Betreuung ist nur eine der vielen sozialen Forderungen. In
einigen Fällen wird durch die soziale Forderung die Notwendigkeit geschaffen,
eine Technologie weiterzuentwickeln, mit welcher die Nachfrage befriedigt
werden kann. Das Auftauchen der technischen Anlage zur Bereitstellung von
Frischwasser und zur Beseitigung des Kehrichts ist ein Beispiel für diese
Wechselwirkung.

In der Medizin ist es üblicherweise umgekehrt: Neue Technologie schafft
neue Nachfrage. Letztlich kann aber keine Gemeinschaft – was auch immer das
Stadium ihrer Entwicklung sein mag – mehr medizinische Leistung in Anspruch
nehmen, als sie sich leisten kann. Selbst wenn die Mittel für den Gesundheitsdienst verdoppelt würden, könnte – wie die Erfahrung zeigt – die öffentliche
Nachfrage nicht befriedigt werden. Arme Länder mit weit weniger günstigen
medizinischen Bedingungen als Großbritannien stehen vor demselben Dilemma.
Das gleiche gilt aber auch für Länder, die weit reicher sind als Großbritannien.

Etliche Länder, die bereits einen nationalen Gesundheitsdienst organisieren und in denen die höchsten Kosten für Gesundheit dem Staat zufallen, versuchen zumindest einen Teil ihrer biomedizinischen Forschung und Entwicklung nach einer abgestimmten Reihe von Prioritäten zu richten. Einige For-
schungsgebiete werden reichlich mit Mitteln ausgestattet, während andere durch
Verweigerung entsprechender Unterstützung entmutigt werden.

Auf diese Weise werden medizinische Prioritäten offensichtlich durch das
Konzept der sozialen Gerechtigkeit beeinflußt. Aber sie sollten dennoch durch
die Ärzteschaft selbst gesetzt werden innerhalb eines hochentwickelten Systems
behördlicher Information. Dieses System hat nicht nur die Summe in Betracht
zu ziehen, die aus öffentlichen oder privaten Quellen für die direkte Anwendung
neuen medizinischen Wissens bereitgestellt werden kann, es muß auch die sich
ergebenden sozialen Kosten erwägen, die bei einem erfolgreichen «Durchbruch»
in der Kontrolle gewisser Erkrankungen getragen werden müssen. Größeres
Gewicht muß jener Forschung zukommen, deren Resultate die größte Auswir-
kung haben. Nämlich die Forschung auf den Gebieten der Geburtenkontrolle,
der Sicherheit neuer Medikamente, der einfacheren Erkrankungen (Schnupfen)
und der invalidisierenden Alterserscheinungen (Arthritis und Rückenschmerzen),
der Schmerzlinderung und schließlich der psychischen Erkrankungen. Dies

könnte sicher auf Kosten dramatischer chirurgischer Fortschritte gehen – wie zum Beispiel der Herztransplantation – oder auf Kosten der medizinischen Erforschung gewisser seltener Erkrankungen, deren Heilung, oder vermeintliche Heilung, vielleicht leichter zu erreichen wäre als jene für viele alltägliche Erkrankungen, deren Erfolge jedoch durch die Massenmedien nur zu häufig unnötig dramatisiert werden.

Résumé

Dans le cadre du présent symposium, le dilemme fondamental est de savoir si l'on doit – ou peut – établir consciemment des priorités déterminées par la pression de besoins sociaux évidents ou prêts à se manifester – ou bien s'il vaut mieux laisser ces priorités se dégager à l'improviste, à mesure que les nouvelles acquisitions offrent de nouvelles possibilités pratiques de diagnostic ou de traitement, comme cela a presque toujours été le cas jusqu'à présent. Le dilemme est rendu plus aigu par le fait que nous ne sommes pas libres de nos options. Certains problèmes biomédicaux sont plus faciles à résoudre que d'autres, probablement insolubles. Quelle que soit leur nature, il est néanmoins impossible de charger quelque homme de génie de résoudre l'un d'entre eux. On peut espérer qu'une «percée» sera faite un jour aux confins du savoir, mais on ne peut y compter avec certitude.

Tout ceci n'aurait aucune importance si l'on disposait de ressources économiques et humaines illimitées pour prendre soin des malades et des personnes âgées. On pourrait alors laisser l'homme de génie à son inspiration et, puisqu'on en aurait les moyens, encourager d'autres personnes à chercher des solutions aux problèmes qui seraient définis sur la base du besoin social. Mais les ressources ont des limites, même dans les pays riches, et il existe d'énormes disparités entre les ressources médicales dont disposent les différents pays. A cela s'ajoute qu'en médecine ce sont les connaissances et les techniques nouvelles qui créent la demande de services.

Au cours des dernières décennies, la plupart des maladies mortelles qui autrefois contribuaient à endiguer l'accroissement de la population ont été vaincues par les progrès réalisés dans les domaines de la santé publique et de l'alimentation. En conséquence, l'espérance de vie s'est, dans tous les pays, allongée pour tous les groupes d'âge; l'augmentation démographique s'est accompagnée de saisissants changements dans la structure par âge des populations, un nombre de plus en plus élevé de personnes atteignant la vieillesse.

Les changements démographiques représentent un modèle qui s'applique à tous les pays développés; on peut s'attendre à ce qu'il s'impose aussi aux pays accédant à l'industrialisation. Ils résultent de l'application pratique des connaissances nouvelles, en général, et des progrès biomédicaux réalisés au cours des 30 à 40 dernières années, en particulier. Mais quelques autorités médicales se demandent à présent ouvertement si les recherches de laboratoire peuvent encore se traduire par une amélioration significative de la santé de l'individu moyen. Quant aux grandes écoles de médecine, autrefois considérées – et à juste titre – comme le fer de lance de la lutte contre la maladie, voici qu'elles commencent à se voir reprocher d'être elles-mêmes la principale cause de la distorsion grandissante que subissent les priorités sociales de la médecine. L'argument avancé est que les professionnels qui travaillent dans ces écoles s'intéressent beaucoup plus à certains progrès de la science et de la pratique médicales, progrès intelligibles aux seuls initiés, qu'aux problèmes sociaux de la santé et de la maladie.

Les services médicaux ne sont que l'une des nombreuses exigences sociales. Dans certains cas, la demande sociale crée le besoin de développer la technique permettant de le satisfaire. L'apparition des dispositifs techniques assurant la distribution d'eau potable et la vidange des eaux usées (égouts publics) est un exemple de cette interaction.

En médecine, c'est habituellement l'inverse qui se produit, la technique nouvelle créant la demande nouvelle. En dernière analyse cependant, il n'est pas de communauté – quel que soit son degré de développement – qui puisse bénéficier de plus de soins médicaux qu'elle n'en a les moyens. Toutefois, même si les ressources allouées aux soins médicaux étaient doublés, l'expérience démontre que la demande publique ne serait toujours pas satisfaite. Des pays pauvres avec des services médicaux beaucoup moins favorables que ceux des Britanniques se trouvent devant le même dilemme. Et il en va de même de pays beaucoup plus riches que la Grande-Bretagne.

Certains pays, dont les ressources médicales ont déjà pris la forme d'un service de santé publique et où la majorité des frais de maladie ressort au secteur public, essaient de guider tout au moins une partie de leur recherche biomédicale sur la base d'un ensemble de priorités consenties. On y encourage certains domaines de la recherche en leur allouant d'abondants crédits, tandis qu'on en décourage d'autres en ne leur fournissant pas l'aide appropriée.

Manifestement, la notion de justice sociale intervient donc de plus en plus dans les priorités médicales. Néanmoins, celles-ci devraient être définies par le corps médical lui-même, dans le cadre d'un système complexe d'information gouvernementale qui ne se contenterait pas de tenir compte simplement de la somme d'argent – de source publique ou privée – qui pourrait être allouée à l'application directe des fruits des nouvelles acquisitions médicales, mais qui considérerait aussi les frais ultérieurs que la société aurait à supporter si l'on arrivait à triompher de telle maladie particulière. Il convient de mettre plus l'accent sur la recherche dont les résultats auront les répercussions les plus étendues – ainsi les recherches sur la limitation des naissances, sur la sécurité des médicaments nouveaux, sur les maladies courantes, comme le rhume banal et les maux estropiants de la vieillesse – l'arthrite et les douleurs dorsales –, sur le soulagement de la douleur et enfin sur les troubles psychiatriques. Ceci pourrait bien s'inscrire aux dépens de spectaculaires progrès en chirurgie – la greffe du cœur par exemple – ou de recherches médicales sur ces affections rares dont la guérison – ou prétendue guérison – est non seulement plus facile à obtenir que celle de nombreuses maladies banales, mais n'est que trop facilement montée en épingle par les *mass media*.

Resumen

En este simposio se ha planteado el dilema fundamental de saber si deben o pueden determinarse prioridades conscientemente, según la mayor o menor importancia de las necesidades sociales, demostrables o de inminencia manifiesta, en vez de esperar a que se impongan de manera imprevisible tan pronto se descubran nuevas posibilidades prácticas de diagnóstico o de terapéutica, como generalmente ha sucedido hasta ahora. El dilema es tanto más agudo cuanto que no tenemos libertad de opción. Hay problemas biomédicos que se resuelven con más facilidad. Otros, probablemente, queden sin solución. Sea como fuere, no es sino imposible pedir a un genio que resuelva tal o cual problema. Sólo resta esperar que en algún punto se abran las fronteras del conocimiento, sin embargo no existe seguridad de que ello suceda así.

Nada de ésto tendría importancia, si los medios económicos y humanos que se pudiesen dedicar al cuidado de los enfermos y ancianos fuesen ilimitados. El genio podría confiarse entonces a su propia inspiración, mientras se al mismo tiempo a otros investigadores suministrarían los fondos que les permitiesen buscar soluciones a problemas definidos en función de los imperativos sociales. Pero los fondos son limitados, incluso en los países prósperos, y enormes las desigualdades entre los recursos médicos de que disponen ciertos países. Es de notar, además, que en medicina son los nuevos conocimientos y tecnologías los que engendran la demanda de prestaciones.

En las últimas décadas, el progreso realizado en el ámbito de la salud pública y de la nutrición ha eliminado la mayoría de las enfermedades mortales que antes ponían un freno al crecimiento demográfico. Así, la esperanza de vida media para qualquier grupo de edad ha aumentado en todos los países. Y la expansion demográfica ha modificado de modo alarmante la estructura de la pirámide de población, con un número cada vez mayor de personas que alcanzan una edad avanzada.

Los cambios demográficos presentan en todos los países adelantados las mismas características, y nada indica que éstas puedan ser distintas en los demás países cuando éstos se desarrollen a su vez. Dichas características son consecuencia de la aplicación práctica de los nuevos conocimientos y, especialmente, de los avances realizados por la labor médica en los últimos 30 a 40 años. Sin embargo, eminentes personalidades del mundo médico confiesan hoy abiertamente sus dudas sobre el beneficio que los trabajos de laboratorio puedan aportar a la salud del hombre. Y hasta las más renombradas Facultades de Medicina, antes estimadas justamente por estar a la cabeza de la lucha contra la enfermedad, empiezan a ser blanco de acusaciones que las hacen responsables de la distorsión cada vez mayor de las prioridades sociales de la medicina. Así, se arguye que los especialistas empleados en ellos se interesan más por los progresos esotéricos de la ciencia y de la práctica médica que por los problemas sociales relacionados con la salud y la enfermedad.

Las prestaciones médicas no constituyen sino una necesidad social entre muchas otras. Ocurre, a veces, que una tal necesidad social conduce al desarrollo de la tecnología que permite satisfacerla. Baste citar como ejemplo las instalaciones que suministran agua limpia, y el alcantarillado público.

En medicina, generalmente, es al revés, ya que la demanda nace de las nuevas técnicas. Sin embargo, ninguna comunidad, en ningún momento de su desarrollo, puede obtener más prestaciones médicas de las que sus medios le permiten. La experiencia enseña que, ni aun duplicando los fondos asignados a los servicios médicos, no se conseguirá satisfacer la demanda del público. Y con este mismo problema se enfrentan tanto los países pobres, con servicios médicos bastante más deficientes que los de Gran Bretaña, como otros muchísimo más ricos.

Algunas naciones que organizan sus recursos médicos en forma de servicios estatales de sanidad, sufragados principalmente por el sector público, tratan ya de someter a un orden determinado de prioridades por lo menos parte de su investigación y desarrollo sanitario. Asi, ciertas ramas reciben créditos casi ilimitados, en tanto que otras son desalentadas, negándoseles la ayuda correspondiente. Es indudable que, en este sentido, el concepto de justicia social se está imponiendo en las prioridades médicas. Estas, no obstante, son decisiones que deben ser tomadas por el mismo cuerpo médico en el marco de una política oficial bien asesorada, que no sólo tenga en cuenta los fondos que el sector público o privado estén dispuestos a gastar para la aplicación directa de los nuevos conocimientos médicos, sino también lo que podrían costar las consecuencias sociales de un descubrimiento que permitiese combatir con éxito ciertas enfermedades. Por ello, deben apoyarse aquellas investigaciones de cuyos resultados cabe esperar el mayor impacto, por ejemplo, el estudio del control de la natalidad, la seguridad de los nuevos medicamentos, el tratamiento de afecciones benignas, como el resfriado común, y los males invalidantes de la vejez, como la artritis y los dolores dorsolumbares, así como el alivio del dolor y el estudio de las enfermedades mentales. Todo ésto podría realizarse a expensas de avances espectaculares en el campo de la cirugía, como los trasplantes de corazón, o de investigaciones sobre enfermedades raras, cuya curación, real o presunta, es no sólo más fácil de lograr que la de muchas afecciones comunes, sino que se presta, en cambio, a una publicidad exagerada por parte de los grandes medios de información.

Curricula of the active participants

KENNETH J. ARROW, Ph. D., Professor of Economics, Harvard University, Cambridge, Mass., USA. Born 1926, New York. B.S. in Social Science, The City College, New York; M.A., Ph.D., Columbia University, 1951.

1947–9 Research Associate, Cowles Commission for Research in Economics, The University of Chicago – 1949–68 Assistant, Associate and Full Professor of Economics, Statistics, and Operation Research, Stanford University – since 1968 Professor of Economics, Harvard University – Staff Member, US Council of Economic Advisers, 1962 – Former President, Econometric Society, The Institute of Management Sciences.

Honours: John Bates Clark Medal, American Economic Association – LL.D., The University of Chicago.

Publications: *Social Choice and Individual Values* (1951, 1963) – *Studies in the Mathematical Theory of Inventory and Production* (with S. Karlin and H. Scarf) (1958) – *Studies in Linear and Nonlinear Programming* (with L. Hurwicz and H. Uzawa) (1959) – *A Time Series Analysis of Interindustry Demands* (with M. Hoffenberg) (1959) – *Public Investment, the Rate of Return, and Optimal Fiscal Policy* (with M. Kurz) (1970) – *Essays in the Theory of Risk-Bearing* (1970).

BERNARD BARBER, Ph.D., Professor of Sociology, Barnard College, Columbia University, New York, N.Y., USA. Born 1918, Boston, USA. A.B., A.M., Ph.D., Harvard, 1949.

1946–8 Tutor and Teaching Fellow at Harvard – 1948–52 Instructor to Assistant Professor at Smith College – since 1952 Assistant to Full Professor of Sociology at Barnard College, Columbia University (Chairman of the Sociology Department, 1962–5).

Advisory Editor *Technology and Culture* – Associate Editor *Social Problems* – Consultant, National Science Foundation – Chairman, History of Science Committee – Fulbright Awards Commission – Member of Drug Research Board, National Academy of Sciences.

Publications: *Science and the Social Order* (1952) – *Social Stratification* (1957) – *Drugs and Society* (1967) – *L.J. Henderson on the Social System* (1970).

CHARLES A. BERRY, M.D., Director of Medical Research and Operations, NASA, Houston, Texas 77058, USA. Born 1923, Rogers, Ark., USA. B.A., California, Berkeley; M.D., California Medical School, San Francisco; M.P.H., Harvard School of Public Health, Boston.

1947–8 Rotating Intern, City and County Hospital, San Francisco – 1948–51 Self-employed Physician, California – 1951–2 US Air Force School of Aerospace Medicine, Randolph AFB, Texas (Aviation Medicine Residency Training Program) – 1952–5 Base Flight Surgeon – 1955–6 Harvard School of Public Health, Boston – 1956–9 Assistant Chief and Chief of Department of Aviation Medicine, USAF School of Aerospace Medicine, Randolph AFB, Texas – 1959–62 Chief of Flight

Medicine, USAF – 1962–6 Chief of Manned Spacecraft Center Medical Operations Office, NASA, Houston, Texas – since 1966 Director of Medical Research and Operations, NASA.

Visiting Lecturer on Aerospace Medicine in the Harvard School of Public Health, Boston – Professor and Chairman of the Department of Aerospace Medicine at the University of Texas Medical Branch – Clinical Professor of Aerospace Medicine, University of Texas School of Public Health – Clinical Associate Professor, Department of Preventive Medicine, The Ohio State University.

Editorial Boards: *Aerospace Medicine, Space Life Sciences.*

Honours: Various military medals and awards for contributions to aerospace medicine.

Publications: More than 50 aerospace medical papers.

FRANZ BÖCKLE, Dr. theol., Professor für Moraltheologie an der Universität Bonn. Geboren 1921 in Glarus (Schweiz). Philosophisch-theologisches Studium in Chur, Rom und München.

Assistent in München – Dozent an der Theologisch-philosophischen Hochschule Chur – Professor und Direktor des moraltheologischen Seminars an der Universität Bonn.

Direktor der moraltheologischen Sektion der internationalen Zeitschrift für Theologie *Concilium.*

Publikationen: Viele philosophisch-theologische Veröffentlichungen.

ERNEST BOESIGER, D^r phil., D^r ès sc., professeur; Directeur de recherche, Centre national de la recherche scientifique (C. N. R. S.), Gif-sur-Yvette, France. Né 1914 à Bâle. Dr. phil., Universität Basel; D^r ès sc., Université de Paris.

1933–52 instituteur à Bâle – depuis 1952 attaché de recherche, chargé de recherche, maître de recherche, directeur de recherche au Centre national de la recherche scientifique – depuis 1966 lecteur de population genetics et de behavioural genetics aux Universités de Paris, Rennes et Notre Dame (USA) – Research Associate at the Rockefeller University.

Publications: *Un oiseau est né* (1955) – *Les oiseaux de la nuit* (1958) – *Essais sur l'évolution* (1968).

ARNOLD STANLEY VINCENT BURGEN, F. R. S., M. D., Professor of Pharmacology, Director, National Institute for Medical Research, Mill Hill, London. Born 1922 in England. Middlesex Hospital Medical School; Hospital Physician, Middlesex Hospital, London.

1945–8 Demonstrator – 1948–9 Assistant Lecturer in Pharmacology – 1949–62 Professor of Physiology, McGill University, Montreal – 1957–62 Deputy Director, University Clinic, Montreal General Hospital – 1962–1971 Professor of Pharmacology at Cambridge University, England.

Member of the Medical Research
Council.

Publication: *Physiology of Salivary
Glands* (1961).

AURELIO CERLETTI, Dr. med., Professor für Pharmakologie an der Universität Basel; Leiter des Departe-
ments für Grundlagenforschung der
Sandoz A.G., Basel. Geboren 1918
in Ilanz, Schweiz. 1943 Staatsexamen
in Medizin, Universität Bern; 1945
Dr. med., Universität Basel.

1945 Forschungslaboratorien der
Sandoz A.G., Basel – 1950–51 Assistent von Prof. C. F. Schmidt, Department of Pharmacology, University of Pennsylvania, Philadelphia,
Pa. – 1951–56 Pharmakologische
Forschungslaboratorien der Sandoz
A.G., Basel – 1956 Mitglied des Di-
rektoriums – 1956–69 Leiter der Abteilung für Medizin und Biologie und
seit 1969 Leiter des Medizinischen
Forschungsdepartements der Sandoz
A.G., Basel.

1966 Habilitation an der Medizinischen Fakultät der Universität Basel
– seit 1969 a.o. Professor für Pharmakologie, Universität Basel – 1966
Mitglied der Eidg. Kommission zur
Förderung der angewandten Forschung – 1970 Vizepräsident des
Schweizerischen Wissenschaftsrates.

FRANK CLARKE FRASER, Ph.D.,
M.D., Professor of Genetics, McGill
University, Department of Biology,
Montreal; The Montreal Children's
Hospital Department of Medical
Genetics. Born 1920, Norwich, Conn.,
USA (Canadian citizen). B. Sc. (Hon.

Biology), Acadia University; M. Sc.,
Ph.D., M.D., C.M., McGill University.

McGill University: Lecturer, Assistant and Associate Professor, Professor in Genetics, Department of
Genetics – since 1969 Associate Professor, Department of Pediatrics, and
since 1970 Professor, Department of
Biology.

Chairman, Permanent Committee
for International Conferences of
Human Genetics – Member, WHO
Expert Advisory Committee on Hu-
man Genetics, Geneva – Member,
Expert Committee on Occurrence of
Congenital Anomalies, Department
of National Health and Welfare,
Canada – Member, Genetics Training
Committee, National Institute of
General Medical Sciences, USA,
1966–9 – Member, US National
Institutes of Health Genetics Study
Section, 1961–5 – Member, Advisory
Committee to the National Center
for Primate Biology, University of
California, 1967–9 – Member, Medi-
cal Research Council of Canada
Grants Committee for Cancer,
Growth and Differentiation, since
1967.

Honours: D. Sc., Acadia University,
1967.

Publications: Recent Advances in
Genetics in Relation to Pediatrics.
J. Pediat. 52, 734–757 (1958) – Genet-
ics and Congenital Malformations;
in: *Progress in Medical Genetics*, pp.
38–80. Ed. A. G. Steinberg. New
York: Grune and Stratton, 1961 –
Experimental Teratogenesis in Rela-

tion to Congenital Malformations in Man; in: *Proc. 2nd Intern. Conf. Congenital Malformations*, pp. 277 to 287. Ed. M. Fishbein. Philadelphia: Lippincott, 1964 – Genetic Counselling and the Physician (The Blackader Lecture 1968). *Canad. med. Ass. J. 99*, 927–934 (1968) – The Genetics of Cleft Lip and Cleft Palate. *Amer. J. hum. Genet. 22*, 336–352 (1970).

COUNT D. GIBSON, Jr., M.D., Professor of Community and Preventive Medicine, Stanford University School of Medicine, Stanford, Cal., USA. Born 1921, Covington, Ga., USA. B.S., M.D., Emory University, Atlanta, Ga.

1944–51 Medical Internship, Assistant Resident, and Chief Resident, Columbia-Presbyterian Medical Center, New York – 1945–7 US Army Medical Corps – 1946–7 Chief of Laboratory Service, 110th Station Hospital, Vienna, Austria – 1951–7 Assistant Professor, Medical College of Virginia – 1958–69 Professor and Chairman, Department of Preventive Medicine, Tufts University School of Medicine, Boston, Mass. – since 1969 Professor and Chairman, Department of Community and Preventive Medicine, Stanford University Medical Center – 1958–69 Physician-in-Chief, Home Medical Service, Boston Dispensary – General Director of the Columbia Point Health Center, Boston.

Honours: Phi Beta Kappa; Alpha Omega Alpha; Member, Medical Committee for Human Rights; Diplomate of the American Board of Internal Medicine.

Publications: Papers on medical care and preventive medicine.

ALFRED GILMAN, Ph.D., Professor of Pharmacology, Albert Einstein College of Medicine of Yeshiva University, Department of Pharmacology, Bronx, N.Y., USA. Born 1908, Bridgeport, Conn., USA. B.S., Ph.D., Yale University.

1931–43 Research Associate and Assistant Professor of Pharmacology, Yale University School of Medicine – 1943–6 Major, US Army, and Chief, Pharmacology Division, Chemical Warfare Service – 1946–55 Associate Professor and Professor of Pharmacology, Columbia University, College of Physicians and Surgeons – since 1956 Professor and Chairman, Department of Pharmacology, Albert Einstein College of Medicine.

1946–60 Pharmacology Study Section of NIH – 1960–3 Pharmacology Training Committee of NIH – since 1962 Member, National Research Council, and since 1963 Member, Drug Research Board of the National Academy of Sciences.

Publications: Co-author with Louis S. Goodman: *The Pharmacological Basis of Therapeutics* (1941, 1955, 1965, 1970) – Approximately 100 publications in the field of pharmacodynamics and electrolyte and renal physiology.

AVRAM GOLDSTEIN, M.D., Professor of Pharmacology, Stanford University School of Medicine, Department of Pharmacology, Stanford, Cal.,

USA. Born 1919, New York. A. B., M. D., Harvard University.

1944 Intern, Mt. Sinai Hospital, New York – 1944-6 Captain, US Army Medical Corps – 1947-9 Instructor in Pharmacology, Harvard University – 1949-50 Moseley Traveling Fellow of Harvard University (University of Edinburgh and Stazione zoologica, Naples) – 1950-1 Associate in Pharmacology, Harvard University – 1951-2 Assistant, Pharmacological Institute, Berne – 1952-5 Assistant Professor of Pharmacology and Tutor in Biochemical Sciences, Harvard University – since 1955 Professor and Chairman (1955-70), Department of Pharmacology, Stanford University School of Medicine – 1970 Director, Santa Clara County (California), Methadone Program – Consultant, Fresno County, Methadone Program.

1948 Labor Fellow, Marine Biological Laboratory, Woods Hole, Mass. – 1962-3 Visiting Professor, University Institute of Microbiology, Copenhagen, Denmark – 1968-9 Visiting Professor, Department of Pharmacology, Cambridge University, England – Visiting Fellow, Fitzwilliam College.
1953-8 Associate Editor, *Journal of Pharmacology and Experimental Therapeutics* – 1958-62 Editor for Biochemical and Cellular Pharmacology, *Journal of Pharmacology and Experimental Therapeutics* – 1956-9 Advisory Committee on Therapy, American Cancer Society – 1956-60 Pharmacology Panel, National Board of Medical Examiners – 1965-8 Founder and Editor, *Molecular*

Pharmacology – 1967-71 Board of Scientific Advisors, Roche Institute of Molecular Biology.

Publications: *Biostatistics* (1964) – *Principles of Drug Action* (1968).

PHILIP HANDLER, Ph.D., Professor of Biochemistry and Nutrition, President of the National Academy of Sciences, Washington, D.C., USA. Born 1917. B. S., City College; M. S., Illinois; Ph. D. (Biochemistry), Illinois.

1937-9 Jr. Chemist, Regional Soybean Laboratories, US Department of Agriculture – 1939-41 Instructor of Physiology and Nutrition, Duke University School of Medicine, Durham, N.C. – 1941-4 Assistant and Associate Professor of Biochemistry and Physiology – 1944-50 Assistant and Associate Professor of Biochemistry and Nutrition – since 1950 Professor and Chairman of Department of Biochemistry and Nutrition – 1955-8 Chairman, Biochemistry Study Section, NIH – 1958-62 Member, National Advisory Health Council, US Public Health Service – since 1959 Member, Biological and Medical Research Facilities Panel, National Science Foundation – since 1962 Member (1966-70, Chairman), National Science Board of National Science Foundation – 1964-8 National Advisory Council on Health Resources and Facilities – President's Science Advisory Committee – 1966-7 President's Commission on Heart Disease, Cancer and Stroke – since 1969 President of the National Academy of Sciences. Trustee: Rockefeller University, Foundation for Advancement of Medical Sciences, Cold Spring Harbor Laboratory.

Board of Directors: Squibb-Beechnut, Inc., 1965–9.

Scientific Advisory Committees: Notre Dame University, Johns Hopkins University, Princeton University, Kettering Institute, Scripps Institute.

Honours: D. Sc., LL. D., Litt. D. mult.; Medal of Distinguished Contribution to Medical Science of American Medical Association; Townsend Harris Medal; North Carolina Medal; Medal of Virginia.

Publications: *Principles of Biochemistry – Biology and the Future of Man – The Life Sciences* – many technical papers.

JEANNE HERSCH, Dʳ phil., Professeur de philosophie, Faculté des lettres, Université de Genève. Née 1910 à Genève. Universités de Genève, Paris, Heidelberg et Freiburg i. Br.

1933–54 professeur de philosophie, latin, littérature française à l'Ecole internationale de Genève – depuis 1956 professeur de philosophie à l'Université de Genève – séjours au Chili et en Thaïlande – Visiting Professor of Philosophy at Pennsylvania State University, University Park, Pa., and at Hunter College, City University, New York, N. Y. – 1966–8 directeur de la Division de la philosophie, Unesco, Paris – depuis 1969 membre du Conseil exécutif de l'Unesco.

Publications: *L'illusion philosophique*

(1936) – *Temps alternés* (1942) – *L'Etre et la forme* (1946) – *Idéologies et réalité* (1956) – Traductions de plusieurs œuvres de Karl Jaspers et de Czeslaw Milosz.

NIELS KAJ JERNE, Dr. med., Professor of Experimental Therapy, Director, Basel Institute for Immunology, Basel. Born 1911, London (Danish citizen). Dr. med., University of Copenhagen.

1943–56 State Serum Institute, Copenhagen – 1954–5 California Institute of Technology, Pasadena – 1956–62 World Health Organization, Geneva – 1962–6 Chairman of Microbiology, University of Pittsburgh – 1966–9 Professor of Experimental Therapy, University of Frankfort, and Director of the Paul-Ehrlich-Institut, Frankfort – since 1969 Director of the Basel Institute for Immunology.

1964–8 Member, WHO Advisory Committee on Medical Research – since 1971 Chairman, Council of the European Molecular Biology Organization.

Honours: Golden Apple, Pittsburgh University.

Publications: *The Natural-Selection Theory of Antibody Formation* (1955) – *The Agar Plaque Technique for Recognizing Antibody-Producing Cells* (1963) – *Waiting for the End* (1967) – *The Somatic Generation of Immune Recognition* (1971).

SEYMOUR S. KETY, M. D., Professor of Psychiatry, Harvard Medical School, Massachusetts General Hospital, Boston, Mass., USA. Born

1915, Philadelphia, USA. B.A., M.D., University of Pennsylvania.

1942–3 National Research Council Fellow, Harvard Medical School and Massachusetts General Hospital – 1943–8 Instructor, Assistant Professor of Pharmacology, School of Medicine, University of Pennsylvania – 1948–51 Professor of Clinical Physiology – 1951–6 Scientific Director, National Institutes of Mental Health and Neurological Diseases, Bethesda, Md. – 1956–7 Chief of the Laboratory of Clinical Science, National Institute of Mental Health – since 1967 Professor of Psychiatry, Harvard Medical School – since 1967 Director of Psychiatric Research Laboratories, Massachusetts General Hospital.

Honours: Theobald Smith Award for Contributions to Medical Science: Max Weinstein Award for Basic Research on Cerebral Palsy; Stanley Dean Award for Research on Schizophrenia; Distinguished Service Award, Department of Health, Education and Welfare, USA; Sc. D., University of Pennsylvania and Loyola University.

Publications: Numerous research publications in the fields of: cerebral circulation and energy metabolism, neurochemical aspects of behavior – biochemical studies in schizophrenia and genetic-environmental interactions in schizophrenia.

RENÉ KÖNIG, Dr. phil., Professor für Soziologie an der Universität Köln. Geboren 1906 in Magdeburg. Universitäten Wien, Berlin, Paris; Dr. phil., Berlin.

1938–47 Privatdozent an der Universität Zürich – 1947–49 Titularprofessor an der Universität Zürich – seit 1949 Ordinarius für Soziologie an der Universität Köln und seit 1953 Direktor des Forschungsinstituts für Soziologie der Universität Köln.

Herausgeber der *Kölner Zeitschrift für Soziologie und Sozialpsychologie*.

Ehrungen: Commendatore all'Ordine di Merito della Repubblica Italiana, 1964; Beccaria-Medaille in Gold, 1966; Goldmedaille des Vereins Deutscher Ingenieure, 1968; Hohe Kulturmedaille des Königreichs Afghanistan, 1970; Mitglied der Königlich-Niederländischen Akademie der Wissenschaften, 1970.

Publikationen: *Die naturalistische Ästhetik in Frankreich* (1931) – *Vom Wesen der deutschen Universität* (1935, 1970) – *Zur Kritik der historisch-existenzialistischen Soziologie* (1938) – *Niccolò Machiavelli* (1941) – *Sizilien* (1943, 1954, 1957) – *Materialien zur Soziologie der Familie* (1946) – *Soziologie heute* (1949) – *Grundformen der Gesellschaft – Die Gemeinde* (1958) – *Soziologie* (1958, 1968, 1970) – *Die Mode in der menschlichen Gesellschaft* (in coll.) (1958) – *Der unversorgte selbständige Künstler* (in coll.) (1964) – *Handbuch der empirischen Sozialforschung*, 2 Bände (1968, 1969) – *Families in East and West* (in coll.) (1970).

JOSHUA LEDERBERG, Ph. D., Professor, Department of Genetics, Stanford University School of Medicine, Stanford, Cal., USA. Born 1925. B.A., Columbia University; Ph. D. (Microbiology), Yale University.

1947–59 Assistant, Associate and Full Professor of Genetics, Madison, Wis. – since 1959 Professor of Genetics and Biology and Executive Head of Department of Genetics, Medical School, Stanford.

1961–2 President (Kennedy)'s Panel on Mental Retardation – since 1950 President's Science Advisory Committee Panels: National Institutes of Health, National Science Foundation Study Sections (genetics) – since 1958 National Academy of Sciences: committees on space biology – since 1960 NASA committees: Lunar and Planetary Missions Board – since 1967 NIMH: National Mental Health Advisory Council – since 1970 Consultant, Arms Control and Disarmament Agency.

Since 1966 Columnist (*Washington Post* Syndicate): *Science and Man.*

Honours: Nobel Prize in Medicine, 1958; Sc. D., Yale University, 1960, also Wisconsin, 1967, Columbia, 1967, Yeshiva, 1970; M. D., Turin, 1969.

Publications: Numerous papers in *Genetics, Nature* and *Proceedings of the National Academy of Sciences,* and in other scientific journals.

SALVADOR EDWARD LURIA, M. D., Institute Professor and Sedgwick Professor of Biology, Massachusetts Institute of Technology, Department of Biology, Cambridge, Mass., USA. Born 1912, Torino (Italy). Medical School, University of Torino; M. D., Torino.

1938 Specialist in Radiology and Medical Physics, University of Rome – 1938–40 Research Fellow, Institute of Radium, Paris – 1940–2 Research Assistant in Surgical Bacteriology, Columbia University – 1943–5 Instructor in Bacteriology, Indiana University – 1945–50 Assistant and Associate Professor of Bacteriology, Indiana University – 1950–9 Professor of Bacteriology, University of Illinois – 1959–64 Professor of Microbiology and Chairman, Committee on Microbiology, Massachusetts Institute of Technology – since 1964 Sedgwick Professor of Biology, Massachusetts Institute of Technology – since 1970 Institute Professor, Massachusetts Institute of Technology.

1942–3 Guggenheim Fellow, Vanderbilt and Princeton – 1945–6 With OSRD, Carnegie Institution of Washington – 1950 Lecturer in Biophysics, University of Colorado – 1950 Jesup Lecturer in Zoology, Columbia University – 1959 Nieuwland Lecturer in Biology, Notre Dame University – 1963–4 Guggenheim Fellow, Institut Pasteur, Paris – 1965 Non-resident Fellow, Salk Institute for Biological Studies.

1950–5 Associate Editor, *Journal of Bacteriology* – since 1955 Editor, *Virology* – 1958–62 Section Editor, *Biological Abstracts* – since 1948 Editorial Board, *Experimental Cell Research* – 1958–64 Advisory Board, *Journal of Molecular Biology* – 1960 Advisory Board, *Photochemistry and Photobiology* – 1959–62 Editorial Board, *American Naturalist* – since 1966 Editorial Board, *Proceedings of the National Academy of Sciences,* and since 1966 Editorial Board, *Annual Review of Genetics.*

1965–8 Scientific Advisory Committee, Massachusetts General Hospital – since 1960 Scientific Advisory Committee, Institute for Cancer Research, Philadelphia.

Honours: Lepetit Prize, 1935; Lenghi Prize, Accademia dei Lincei, 1965; D. Sc., University of Chicago, 1967, Indiana University and Rutgers University, 1970; Nobel Prize in Medicine, 1969.

MICHAEL F. J. MARLET, Dr. phil., lic. theol., Professor für neuzeitliche Philosophie an der Theologischen Fakultät der Universität Innsbruck und der Theologischen Fakultät der Freien Universität Amsterdam. Geboren 1921, Rijswijk, Holland.

Studium der Philosophie und der Theologie in Nijmegen und Maastricht (Holland) sowie in München, Münster und Rom. Lic. theol., Theologische Hochschule Canisianum, Maastricht – Dr. phil., Pontificia Università Gregoriana, Rom.

1952–67 Dozent, a. o. Professor, ab 1954 o. Professor für Metaphysik an der Philosophischen Hochschule Berchmanianum, Nijmegen – seit 1961 apl. und a. o. Professor (1970) für neuzeitliche Philosophie an der Universität Innsbruck – seit 1967 a. o. Professor für neuzeitliche Philosophie an der Theologischen Hochschule Amsterdam und seit 1971 auch an der Freien Universität Amsterdam – Vizeobmann des Internationalen Medical Students Center in Österreich – Mitglied des Wissenschaftlichen Beirates der Internationalen Paulusgesellschaft und der Teilhard-de-Chardin-Gesellschaft.

Publikationen: *Grundlinien der calvinistischen Philosophie der Gesetzesidee als christlicher Transzendentalphilosophie* (1954) – *Schuld en verontschuldiging in de medische praktijk* (1966) – *Ethik genetischer Beratung und Massnahmen* (1967).

MARGARET MEAD, Ph. D., D. Sc., LL. D., Professor of Anthropology, The American Museum of Natural History, New York, N. Y., USA. Born 1901, Philadelphia, Pa., USA. Barnard College, Columbia University.

1925–6 National Research Council Fellow (Study of Adolescent Girl in Samoa) – since 1926 Assistant, Associate and Full Curator of Ethnology, American Museum of Natural History – 1928–9 Social Science Research Fellow (Study of Young Children in Admiralty Islands) – 1931–58 four expeditions to New Guinea, Bali, and the Admiralty Islands – 1940–1 Visiting Lecturer in Child Study, Vassar College – 1942–5 Executive Secretary Committee on Food Habits, National Research Council – 1948–50 Director, Columbia University, Research in Contemporary Cultures – since 1954 Adjunct Professor, Columbia University, and since 1957 Visiting Professor, Department of Psychiatry, Medical College, University of Cincinnati – 1959–63 Visiting Professor, Menninger Foundation, and since 1969 Chairman of the Social Sciences Division and Professor of Anthropology at Fordham

University's New Liberal Arts College at Lincoln Center.

Honours: Viking Medalist in General Anthropology, Wenner-Gren Foundation for Anthropological Research, 1957–8; Rice University Medal of Honor, 1962; Award for Distinguished Achievement in Science, American Museum of Natural History, 1969; Proctor Prize, Research Society of America, 1969; Arches of Science Award, Pacific Science Center, 1970; Joseph Priestly Award, Dickinson College, Carlisle, Pa., 1971.

Publications: *Coming of Age in Samoa* (1928) – *Growing Up in New Guinea* (1930) – *The Changing Culture of an Indian Tribe* (1932) – *Sex and Temperament in Three Primitive Societies* (1935) – *Balinese Character: A Photographic Analysis* (in coll.) (1942) – *And Keep Your Powder Dry* (1942) – *Male and Female* (1949) – *Soviet Attitudes Towards Authority* (1951) – *Growth and Culture* (in coll.) (1951) – *The Study of Culture at a Distance* (in coll.) (1953) – *Themes in French Culture* (in coll.) (1954) – *Childhood in Contemporary Cultures* (in coll.) (1955) – *New Lives for Old* (1959) – *An Anthropologist at Work: Writings of Ruth Benedict* (1960) – *Culture and Commitment* (1970) – *A Way of Seeing* (in coll.) (1970) – *Kinship in the Admiralty Islands* (1934) – *Cultural Patterns and Technical Change* (ed. 1953) – *Cultural Determinants of Sex Behavior in Sex and Internal Secretions* (Ed. Young) – Psychiatry and Ethnology; in: *Psychiatrie der Gegenwart. Forschung und Praxis* (1961) – Participant in: *World Health Organization Discussions on Child Development* (Ed. J.M. Tanner and Barbel Inhelder) (1950, 1960) – Research on Primitive Children; in: *Manual of Child Psychology* (Ed. Charmichael) (1946) – The Anthropology of Human Conflict; in: *The Nature of Human Conflict* (Ed. McNeil) (1965) – Research with Human Beings; in: *Daedalus* (1969).

JÜRGEN MOLTMANN, Dr. theol., Professor für systematische Theologie im Evangelisch-Theologischen Fachbereich der Universität Tübingen, Deutschland. Geboren 1926 in Hamburg. Studium der Evangelischen Theologie in England und an den Universitäten Hamburg und Göttingen; Dr. theol., 1952; Dr. theol. habil., 1957.

1958–63 Professor für systematische Theologie an der Kirchlichen Hochschule Wuppertal – 1963–67 o. Professor für systematische Theologie und Sozialethik an der Universität Bonn – 1967–68 Guest Professor der Divinity School, Duke University, N.C. – seit 1967 o. Professor für systematische Theologie an der Universität Tübingen.

Publikationen: *Theologie der Hoffnung* (1964) – *Perspektiven der Theologie* (1967) – *Religion, Revolution and the Future* (1968) – *Umkehr zur Zukunft* (1970) – *Hoping and Planning* (1971).

The Hon. Sir ROGER ORMROD, B.M., LL.D., Royal High Court of Justice, London. Born 1911, Cumberland, England. The Queen's College, Oxford; B.A. (jurisprudence), B.M., B.Ch.

1936 called to Bar, Inner Temple – 1941–2 House Physician, Radcliffe Infirmary, Oxford – 1950–9 Lecturer in Forensic Medicine, Oxford Medical School – 1936–40 and 1945–61 in practice as a barrister-at-law – since 1961 Judge of the Royal High Court of Justice, Probate, Divorce and Admiralty Division – Vice-Chairman of the Institute of Psychiatry – Chairman, The London Marriage Guidance Council – Vice-Chairman of the Board of Governors of St. Bartholomew's Hospital.

TALCOTT PARSONS, Dr. phil., Professor of Sociology, Harvard University, Department of Social Relations and Sociology, Cambridge, Mass., USA. Born 1902, Colorado Springs, Colo., USA. B.A., Amherst College, London School of Economics; Dr. phil., University of Heidelberg.

1924–5 Instructor, Department of Economics, Amherst College – 1931–44 Instructor, Assistant and Associate Professor, Department of Sociology, Harvard – since 1944 Professor and Chairman, Department of Social Relations/Sociology, Harvard.

Publications: *The Structure of Social Action – Toward a General Theory of Action – The Social System – Essays in Sociological Theory – Structure and Process in Modern Societies – Social Structure and Personality – Sociological Theory and Modern Society – Politics and Social Structure – The System of Modern Societies –*

Translation of Max Weber: *Die protestantische Ethik und der Geist des Kapitalismus.*

PIERRE PICHOT, Dr méd., Professeur de psychologie médicale, Centre psychiatrique Sainte-Anne, Paris. Né 1918 à La Roche-sur-Yon (Vendée). Faculté de médecine, Paris, et Sorbonne, Paris.

1955–63 professeur agrégé de psychiatrie, Faculté de médecine de Paris – depuis 1964 chaire de psychologie médicale, Faculté de médecine de Paris.

Publications: Essais mentaux en psychiatrie et en psychologie médicale – articles sur la psychologie médicale, récemment surtout sur la méthodologie d'évaluation de la symptomatologie psychiatrique.

ALFRED PLETSCHER, Dr. med., Dr. phil., Professor für Pathophysiologie an der Universität Basel; Leiter des Forschungsdepartements der F. Hoffmann-La Roche & Co. A.G., Basel. Geboren 1917 in Altstätten SG, Schweiz. 1935–42 medizinische Fakultäten der Universitäten Genf, Rom und Zürich – 1942 Staatsexamen und Dr. med., Universität Zürich – 1949 Dr. phil. (Chemie), Universität Zürich.

1942–54 Assistenzarzt für Chirurgie, Geburtshilfe und Innere Medizin – 1953/54 Leiter der wissenschaftlichen Laboratorien der Medizinischen Universitätsklinik, Basel – 1955 Guest worker am National Heart Institute, NIH, Bethesda, USA – 1955–58 Leiter der Abteilung für experimentelle

Medizin, F. Hoffmann-La Roche & Co. A.G., Basel – 1958–68 Leiter der gesamten Medizinischen Forschung und seit 1968 Leiter des Forschungsdepartements.

1952 Habilitation an der Medizinischen Fakultät der Universität Basel – seit 1960 a.o. Professor für Pathophysiologie, Universität Basel.

ROBERT REICHARDT, Dr. phil., Professor für Soziologie an der Universität Wien. Geboren 1927 in Basel. Soziologische, sozialanthropologische und nationalökonomische Studien an der Universität Basel.

1960–61 Research Associate at the Econometric Research Program of the University of Princeton, N.J., USA – 1961–64 Assistent, Universität Basel – 1965 Habilitation in Soziologie, Universität Basel – 1964–66 Leiter der soziologischen Abteilung des Instituts für Höhere Studien und Wissenschaftliche Forschung, Wien (Ford-Institut) – seit 1966 o. Professor für Soziologie und Sozialphilosophie an der Universität Wien.

Mitglied des Exekutivkomitees des International Social Science Council, Paris – Mitglied des Exekutivkomitees der österreichischen Unesco-Kommission.

Preise: Genossenschaftspreis, Universität Basel, 1961.

Publikationen: *Competition Through the Introduction of New Products* (1962) – *Möglichkeiten einer Soziologie des Kraftfahrverkehrs* (1969) – *Kompromiss-Schemata in kollektiven Wertentscheidungen* (1969) – *Ap-* *proaches to the Measurement of Environment* (1970) – *Dilemmas of Economic Behaviour vis-à-vis Environmental Pollution* (1970).

MAX Lord ROSENHEIM, K.B.E., M.D., P.R.C.P., Professor of Medicine, University College Hospital Medical School, London. Born 1908, London. St. John's College, Cambridge; University College Hospital Medical School.

1932–8 University College and Westminster Hospitals – Massachusetts General Hospital, Boston, USA – 1939 First Assistant, Medical Unit, University College Hospital, London – 1941–6 Royal Army Medical Corps – since 1947 Physician, University College Hospital, London – since 1950 Director of Medical Unit and Professor of Medicine at University of London.

1961–5 Member of Medical Research Council – 1968 Chairman, Advisory Committee on Medical Research, WHO – President, Royal College of Physicians of London.

Publications on hypertension and renal disease.

JOAQUÍN RUIZ-GIMÉNEZ CORTÉS, docteur en droit, Professeur d'éthique sociale et de sociologie et philosophie du droit, Faculté de droit, Université de Madrid, et Faculté des sciences sociales, Université pontificale de Salamanca. Né 1913 à Madrid. Faculté de droit, Madrid.

1935 professeur-assistant de droit international, Université de Madrid – 1940 professeur-assistant de philoso-

phie du droit, Madrid – professeur
d'éthique sociale et de philosophie
du droit: 1945 Sevilla, 1956 Salamanca, 1960 Madrid.

Editeur de *Cuadernos para el dialogo*
(journal mensuel traitant des problèmes sociaux, politiques et culturels).

1948–51 ambassadeur d'Espagne auprès du Vatican – 1951–56 ministre
de l'Education – Président de Pax
Romana – membre de l'Institut international pour les droits de l'homme, Strasbourg – membre du Consi-
lium de Laicis, Rome, et du Comité
pour la promotion humaine et la paix
de la Commission Justitia et Pax,
Rome.

Publications: *La Concepción, Insti-
tucional del Derecho* (1944) – *Introducción a la Filosofia Jurídica* (1945,
1960) – *Derecho y Vida Humana*
(1946) – *La Propiedad – Historia y
Problemas* (1966) – *Los Derechos
Humanos y el Concilio Vaticano II*
(1968).

ALFRED SAUVY, Dʳ phil., Professeur
honoraire au Collège de France, Institut national d'études démographiques, Paris. Né 1898 à Villeneuve de
la Raho (Pyrénées orientales). Ecole
polytechnique, Paris.

1937–45 directeur, Institut de con-
joncture – 1945 secrétaire-général à
la Famille et à la Population –
1945–62 directeur de l'Institut
national d'études démographiques,
Paris – 1959–69 professeur de démographie sociale: La vie des populations, Collège de France – 1950–53

président, Commission de la population des Nations Unies.

Honneurs: Dr. h.c., Universités de
Genève, Bruxelles, Liège, Utrecht;
Commandeur de la Légion d'honneur; Commandeur de la Santé publique; Commandeur d'Académie.

Publications: *Théorie générale de la
population – L'opinion publique* (1956)
– *La bureaucratie* (1956) – *La nature
sociale* (1957) – *La montée des jeunes*
(1959) – *Le plan Sauvy* (1960) – *Les
limites de la vie humaine* (1961) –
Fertility and Survival (1961) – *Population Explosion* (1961) – *La prévention
des naissances* (1962, 1966) – *Malthus
et les deux Marx* (1963, 1966) – *My-
thologie de notre temps* (1965) – *Histoire économique de la France entre
les deux guerres* (1965, 1967) –
Théorie générale de la population
(1954 à 1966) – *Les quatre roues de
la fortune* (1968) – *Le socialisme en
liberté* (1970) – *La révolte des jeunes*
(1970).

AXEL STRØM, Dr. med., Professor of
Social Medicine, University of Oslo.
Born 1901, Oslo, Norway. Dr. med.
University of Oslo; School of Hy-
giene and Public Health, Johns
Hopkins University, Baltimore,
USA.

1927–8 Internist, Oslo Municipal
Hospital – 1928–9 District Health
Officer – 1930–4 Assistant State Epi-
demiologist – 1934–40 Assistant
Commissioner of Health, Oslo Board
of Health – 1940–51 Professor of
Hygiene, University of Oslo – since
1951 Professor of Social Medicine,
University of Oslo – 1956–63 Dean of

the Medical Faculty – 1964–7 Vice-Rector of the University of Oslo.

Publications: Textbooks in hygiene, social medicine and rehabilitation.

ALEXANDER Lord TODD, D. Sc., Dr. phil. nat., D.Ph., F.R.S., F.R.I.C., Professor of Organic Chemistry, University of Cambridge, England. Born 1907, Glasgow, Scotland. Universities of Glasgow, Frankfort on the Main and Oxford.

1938–44 Professor of Chemistry and Director of Chemical Laboratories, University of Manchester – since 1944 Professor of Chemistry in the University of Cambridge – since 1963 Master of Christ's College.

1952–64 Chairman, Advisory Council on Scientific Policy – 1965–8 Chairman, Royal Commission on Medical Education – Chancellor, University of Strathclyde – Managing Trustee, Nuffield Foundation.

Honours: Nobel Prize in Chemistry, 1957; LL.D., Dr. rer. nat., D.Sc.

JAN WALDENSTRÖM, Dr. med., Professor der inneren Medizin, Universität Lund; Allmänna Sjukhus, Medizinische Universitätsklinik, Malmö, Schweden. Geboren 1906 in Stockholm. Universität von Uppsala.

1935–36 Fellow der Rockefeller Foundation in München (Laboratorium Hans Fischer) – 1944–45 USA-Aufenthalt im Auftrag der schwedischen Regierung – 1947 Professor für theoretische Medizin an der Universität von Uppsala – seit 1950 Leiter der Medizinischen Abteilung des Krankenhauses von Malmö und Professor der Medizin an der Universität Lund.

Auszeichnungen: Dr. h.c., Oslo, Oxford, Mainz, Paris, Innsbruck, Dublin; Jahre-Scandinavian-Preis für Medizinische Forschung; Gairdner Award, Toronto.

Publikationen auf den Gebieten Hämatologie, Metabolismus, Endokrinologie, Allgemeinmedizin.

ERNST ULRICH VON WEIZSÄCKER, Dr. rer. nat., Forschungsstätte der Evangelischen Studiengemeinschaft (FEST), Heidelberg, Deutschland. Geboren 1939 in Zürich. Diplom für Physik in Hamburg; Dr. rer. nat. (Biologie), Freiburg i. Br.

Seit 1969 Mitarbeiter des Interdisziplinären Instituts FEST, Heidelberg (Friedensforschung, theoretische Biokybernetik) – Mitglied des Zentralkomitees der Südwestdeutschen Sozialdemokratischen Partei – Leiter einer Reformgruppe für Universitäts- und Erwachsenenbildung.

Publikationen: *Verantwortung der Biologie* (1968) – *Baukasten gegen Systemzwänge* – *Der Weizsäcker-Hochschulplan* (1970) – *BC-Waffen und Friedenspolitik* (1970).

SOLLY Lord ZUCKERMAN, O.M., K.C.B., M.D., D.Sc., F.R.C.S., F.R.C.P., F.R.S., Professor of Anatomy. Born 1904, Cape Town. South African College School; Cape Town University; University College Hospital, London.

1923–5 Demonstrator of Anatomy,

Cape Town University – 1925 Union Research Scholar – 1928–32 Research Anatomist to London Zoological Society and Demonstrator of Anatomy, University College, London – 1933–4 Research Associate and Rockefeller Research Fellow, Yale University – 1934–7 Research Fellow, London University – 1937 Hunterian Professor, Royal College of Surgeons – 1934–45 Demonstrator, Human Anatomy Department, Oxford – 1943–68 Sands Cox Professor of Anatomy, Birmingham University – 1948–64 Deputy Chairman, Advisory Council on Scientific Policy – 1960–6 Chief Scientific Adviser to the Secretary of State for Defence – 1964–6 Scientific Adviser, Cabinet Office –

since 1966 Chief Scientific Adviser to H. M. Government and Chairman, Central Advisory Council for Science and Technology.

Honours: D. Sc., LL. D., Universities of Sussex, Jacksonville, Bradford; Medal of Freedom with Silver Palm (US); Chevalier de la Légion d'honneur (France).

Publications: *The Social Life of Monkeys and Apes* (1932) – *Functional Affinities of Man, Monkeys and Apes* (1933) – *A New System of Anatomy* (1961) – *The Ovary* (1962) – *Scientists and War* (1966) – *The Image of Technology* (1968) – *Beyond the Ivory Tower* (1970).

1972 - 212 - 62105